Nigerian Yearbook of International Law

Volume 2018/2019

The NYBIL has as its main aim analysis of, commentaries on, and reporting of developments in international law that are mostly of relevance within the context of Nigeria in particular, Africa, the black diaspora of the world, and the developing world more generally. But, it is stressed that the publication is not exclusive in that regard: contributions from the perspective of the wider world are also strongly encouraged and welcomed.

Analysis of international law within the context of developing countries in general, the black diaspora, Africa and Nigeria in particular is an area of increasing scholarly and professional interest. This interest will only continue to grow in light of current and emerging global issues such as trade and investment, human rights, armed conflict, humanitarian intervention, transitional justice, international and transnational crimes, transnational migration, environment, international terrorism. The NYBIL provides an authoritative platform for focused analysis of these developments to be readily available to students, academics, practitioners, governments, and international bodies.

More information about this series at http://www.springer.com/series/14355

Chile Eboe-Osuji • Engobo Emeseh •
Olabisi D. Akinkugbe
Editors

Nigerian Yearbook of International Law 2018/2019

Springer

Editors
Chile Eboe-Osuji
International Criminal Court
The Hague, The Netherlands

Engobo Emeseh
School of Law, Faculty of Management and Law
University of Bradford
Bradford, United Kingdom

Olabisi D. Akinkugbe
Schulich School of Law
Dalhousie University
Halifax, Nova Scotia, Canada

ISSN 2523-8868 ISSN 2523-8876 (electronic)
Nigerian Yearbook of International Law
ISBN 978-3-030-69593-4 ISBN 978-3-030-69594-1 (eBook)
https://doi.org/10.1007/978-3-030-69594-1

This Springer imprint is published by the registered company Springer Nature Switzerland AG.
The registered company address is: Gewerbestrasse 11, 6330 Cham, Switzerland

Preface

On behalf of the Editorial Board of the *Nigerian Yearbook of International Law* (NYbIL), I am delighted to present the second volume of the NYbIL.

International law and the scholarly spaces created in relation thereto have not always welcomed voices, perspectives, and critical interventions from the periphery. The contest to refine international law to account for and be accountable to these diverse views has been undertaken across generations of scholars from the Global South. In this regard, essential questions that have been at the heart of insightful analysis by these Global South scholars regarding established international legal orders, and the foundations of international law, as well as its practices have been at the heart of many of the insightful analysis that scholars and jurists in historical and contemporary contexts have undertaken. I am glad that the excellent contributions to this second volume of the NYbIL are built on its inaugural issue in providing critical interventions by a diverse group of scholars and jurists from Nigeria and across the world.

On a personal note, I am extremely thankful to have had the opportunity to not only be part of an amazing team of editors but also curate this volume of the NYbIL with excellent contributions from Nigerians and non-Nigerians who are enthusiastic about redressing the failed promises of international law. For this achievement, I wish to thank Professor Olabisi D. Akinkugbe, Professor Engobo Emeseh, and Ms Odo Ogwuma.

The task of completing the rigor that comes with similar initiatives goes beyond the editorial team. The NYbIL fills an important vacuum for hosting critical and analytical contributions from scholars and jurists all around the world on various subject matters under the broad rubric of international law. To be able to do this, we rely on our peer-reviewers who, in addition to many other tasks they are undertaking, agreed to review the submissions. As such, I would like to thank all our peer-reviewers who did a terrific job of ensuring that we bring our readers the best scholarship from the authors. In turn, I would also like to extend my gratitude on behalf of the editors to Springer Publications Ltd and to Dr. Brigitte Reschke for her support.

The incisive and insightful analysis by all the authors who are experts in their fields holds a great promise for our readers. The editors are glad to bring this second volume of the yearbook to our esteemed readers.

The Hague, The Netherlands
Bradford, UK
Halifax, NS, Canada

Chile Eboe-Osuji
Engobo Emeseh
Olabisi D. Akinkugbe

Contents

Part IV International Criminal Law

Part V International Human Rights and Humanitarian Law

Part VI International Economic Law/International Investment Law

Part VII Contemporary Challenges/Emerging Issues

Part VIII Case Comment

Part I
International Law

New Reflections on Humankind as a Subject of International Law

Antônio Augusto Cançado Trindade

Contents

1 Introduction: A Preliminary Precision

I have been devoting particular attention, along many years, to the condition of humankind as subject of international law. For example, in my General Course of Public International Law, delivered at the Hague Academy of International Law in 2005, I dedicated a whole chapter to the matter.[1] Now that we approach the end of the second decade of the twenty-first century, it is proper to retake my reflections on

[1]Cançado Trindade (2005a), pp. 318–333; and, subsequently, Cançado Trindade (2013a), pp. 275–288.

A. A. Cançado Trindade (✉)
International Court of Justice, The Hague, The Netherlands

C. Eboe-Osuji et al. (eds.), *Nigerian Yearbook of International Law 2018/2019*,
Nigerian Yearbook of International Law 2018/2019,
https://doi.org/10.1007/978-3-030-69594-1_1

the issue, in my perception of much relevance to the present and the future of international. May I start with a preliminary precision.

At the present stage of the progressive development of international law, States no longer have the monopoly of the condition of subjects of international law; they share such condition with international organizations and individuals or groups of individuals, and peoples, and humankind is also endowed with the statute of subject of international law. States cannot thus any longer consider international as being at service of their own interests only. In effect, interests or strategies of individual States cannot pretend to overcome the generaux and superior interest of the international community in domains touching it directly (like, for example, those of disarmament, human rights protection and humanitarian law, protection of the environment, and the erradication of poverty).[2]

2 The Central Place of the Human Person and Limits to State Voluntarism

A basic feature, and a remarkable contribution of the joint work of international human rights tribunals can be found, in my perception, in the position they have firmly taken of asserting precisely the *central place* of the human person in the domain of protection of rights inherent to her, and of setting *limits to State voluntarism*, thus safeguarding the integrity of the respective human rights Conventions and the primacy of considerations of *ordre public* over the "will" of individual States.

There is a growing awareness nowadays that the exercise of the international judicial function encompasses, besides settling disputes, *to say what the Law is* (*juris dictio*), thus contributing to the progressive development of international law.[3] In *saying what the Law is*, international tribunals are to take into account law and justice together, as situations of injustice are not sustainable.

In effect, I have singled this out in the ICJ, e.g., in my extensive Dissenting Opinion (paras. 1-316) in the case of *Jurisdictional Immunities of the State* (Germany *versus* Italy, with Greece intervening, merits, Judgment of 03.02.2012), warning that there cannot be State immunity for international crimes perpetrated in execution of a State policy. I sustained that the victims of oppression and atrocities have the *right to the Law* (*droit au Droit/derecho al Derecho*), the right of access to

[2]A. A. Cançado Trindade, *O Direito Internacional em um Mundo em Transformação*, Rio de Janeiro, Ed. Renovar, 2002, pp. 1068, 1083 and 1094–1095.

[3]Cf., in this sense, e.g., Cançado Trindade (2013b), pp. 16–17; Cançado Trindade (2015a), pp. 345–347; [Various Authors,] *International Judicial Lawmaking* (eds. A. von Bogandy and I. Venzke), Heidelberg, Springer, 2012, pp. 9–15 and 35–36; von Bogandy and Venzke (2016) [reed.], pp. 49 and 62.

justice, which cannot be restrained in cases of *delicta imperii*, of crimes of State[4] (cf. *infra*). The central place is that of the human person.

The basic posture is *principiste*, without making undue concessions to State voluntarism. The assertion of an *objective* law, beyond the "will" of individual States, is, in my perception, a revival of jusnaturalist thinking. After all, the basic foundations of international law emanate ultimately from the human conscience, from the universal juridical conscience, and not from the "will" of individual States.[5] The assertion of the *unity* of the law is intertwined with the *rule of law* at national and international levels, as access to justice takes place, and ought to be preserved, at both levels.[6]

3 The Perception and Awareness of Common and Superior Interests of Humankind as Such

In the contemporary law of nations, States are no longer the sole subjects of international law; they nowadays coexist, in that condition, with international organizations and individuals and groups of individuals; and, moreover, humankind as such has also emerged as a subject of international law. As a result, humankind coexists with States, without replacing them; and States can no longer seek the pursuance of their own interests as the sole motivation for the shaping of contemporary international law.

In effect, the pursuance of State interests has an impact on the effectiveness of international law; but the interests of each individual State cannot make abstraction of, or seek to prevail upon, the pursuance of the fulfilment of the general and superior interests of the international community in matters of direct concern to this latter (such as, e.g., disarmament, human rights and environmental protection, eradication of poverty, among others).[7]

Experience shows that it is when such general interests are duly taken into account, and are made to prevail, by States as well as by other subjects of international law, that this latter has advance. It could hardly be denied that the advances of international law along the last decades have been achieved when the general, superior interests of humankind have been properly acknowledged and given expression to (such as, e.g., in International Human Rights Law, in International Environmental Law, in the Law of the Sea, in the Law of Outer Space). States themselves have contributed to those advances, whenever they have placed basic

[4]For a case-study, cf. Cançado Trindade (2013c), pp. 5–305; Cançado Trindade (2017b), pp. 69–77.

[5]Cançado Trindade (2013a), ch. VI, pp. 139–161; Cançado Trindade (2010), pp. 11–26; Brus (1995), pp. 142 and 182–183.

[6]Cançado Trindade (2017c), pp. 53–56.

[7]A.A. Cançado Trindade, *O Direito Internacional em um Mundo em Transformação*, Rio de Janeiro, Ed. Renovar, 2002, pp. 1068, 1083 and 1094–1095.

considerations of humanity and the general interests of the international community as a whole above their own individual interests.

In this connection, the ultimate aim of *jus cogens*, with its gradually expanded material content, is precisely that of securing the prevalence of the interests and most fundamental values of the international community as a whole.[8] There are, in fact, international obligations pertaining to the safeguard of fundamental values of the international community itself, which are distinct from other international obligations; hence the emergence of concepts such as that of obligations *erga omnes*, ensuing from *jus cogens*, in contemporary international law.[9]

The examination of humankind as a subject of international law does not exhaust itself in the identification and assertion of common and superior interests and values. It is to be kept in mind that international crimes and violations of *jus cogens* affect the basic values of the international community as a whole, and given their particular gravity, entail *aggravated* international responsibility, with all legal consequences.[10]

The key point of humankind as subject of international law calls for the consideration of the fundamental principle of humanity and the basic considerations of humanity which nowadays mark presence in the whole *corpus juris* of international law[11] (with a conceptual precision), of the legal consequences of the emergence of humankind as a subject of international law, of the relevance of the human rights framework, and, last but not least, of the question of humankinds capacity to act and its legal representation.

4 The Fundamental Principle of Humanity

The treatment dispensed to human beings, in any circumstances, ought to abide by the *principle of humanity*, which permeates the whole *corpus juris* of International Law in general, and International Humanitarian Law in particular, conventional as well as customary.[12] Acts which,—under certain international treaties or conventions,—were regarded as amounting to genocide, or as grave violations of

[8]Cf. Cançado Trindade (2009a), pp. 3–29; Cançado Trindade (2009b), pp. 65–79; Gaja (2011), pp. 46–50; Lachs (1980), p. 205. On the importance of securing values, cf. Husson-Rochcongar (2012), pp. 1–941.

[9]The classic vision of a sole and undifferentiated regime of international responsibility no longer corresponds to the present stage of evolution of the matter in contemporary international law; Starace (1976), pp. 272–275, and cf. pp. 289, 297 and 308.

[10]Cf. A.A. Cançado Trindade, *El Ejercicio de la Función Judicial Internacional - Memorias de la Corte Interamericana de Derechos Humanos*, 5th. rev. ed., Belo Horizonte/Brazil, Edit. Del Rey, 2018, ch. VII, pp. 59-74; Cançado Trindade (2005b), pp. 253–269; Cançado Trindade (2011a), pp. 27–46.

[11]Cf. A.A. Cançado Trindade, *International Law for Humankind - Towards a New Jus Gentium*, 2nd. rev. ed., *op. cit. supra* n. (5), ch. XVI–XXIII, pp. 393–528.

[12]Cf. Cançado Trindade (2013d), pp. 188–197; Cançado Trindade (2016), pp. 61–74.

International Humanitarian Law, were already prohibited even before the entry into force of such treaties or conventions, by *general* international law.

One may here invoke, in the framework of this latter, e.g., the universal recognition of the aforementioned principle of humanity.[13] In the perennial lesson of a learned jusphilosopher, "if not the laws themselves, at least their content was already in force" before the perpetration of the atrocities of the twentieth century, in distinct latitudes; in other words, added G. Radbruch,

> those laws respond, by their content, to a Law superior to the laws (. . .). Whereby we see how, by the turn of a century of legal positivism, that old idea of a Law superior to the laws is reborn (. . .). The way to reach the settlement of these problems is already implicit in the name that the philosophy of Law used to have in the old Universities and which, after many years of not being used, comes to reemerge today: in the name and in the concept of *natural law*.[14]

It may be recalled that the *ad hoc* International Criminal Tribunal for Rwanda [ICTR] rightly pondered, in the case of *J.-P. Akayesu* (Judgment of 02.09.1998), that the concept of crimes against humanity had already been recognized well before the Nuremberg Tribunal itself (1945–1946). The Martens clause contributed to that effect (cf. *infra*); in fact, expressions similar to that of those crimes, invoking victimized humanity, appeared much earlier in human history.[15] The same ICTR pointed out, in the case *J. Kambanda* (Judgment of 04.09.1998), that in all periods of human history genocide has inflicted great losses to humankind, the victims being not only the persons slaughtered but humanity itself (in acts of genocide as well as in crimes against humanity).[16]

It can hardly be doubted the content of the condemnation of grave violations of human rights, of acts of genocide, of crimes against humanity, and of other atrocities, was already engraved in human conscience, well before their tipification or codification at international level, be it in the 1948 Convention against Genocide, or in other treaties of human rights or of International Humanitarian Law. Nowadays, international crimes are condemned by general as well as conventional international law. This development has been fostered by the universal juridical conscience, which, in my understanding, is the ultimate material source of all Law.[17]

---

[13]In this respect, it has already been pointed out that "it is increasingly believed that the role of international law is to ensure a minimum of guarantees and of humanity for all, whether in time of peace or in time of war"; Pictet (1966), pp. 29–30.

[14]Radbruch (1965), p. 180.

[15]Paras. 565–566 of that Judgment.

[16]Paras. 15–16 of that Judgment. An equal reasoning is found in the Judgments of the same Tribunal in the aforementioned case *J.P. Akayesu*, as well as in the case *O. Serushago* (Judgment of 05.02.1999, para. 15).

[17]Cf., e.g., Inter-American Court of Human Rights [IACtHR], case of the *Massacre of Plan de Sánchez versus Guatemala* (merits, Judgment of 29.04.2004), Separate Opinion of Judge A.A. Cançado Trindade, par. 13; IACtHR, Advisory Opinion n. 18 (of 17.09.2003), on the *Juridical Condition and Rights of Undocumented Migrants*, Concurring Opinion of Judge A.A. Cançado Trindade, paras. 21–30.

Contemporary (conventional and general) international law has been characterized to a large extent by the emergence and evolution of its peremptory norms (the *jus cogens*), and a greater consciousness, in a virtually universal scale, of the principle of humanity.[18] Grave violations of human rights, acts of genocide, crimes against humanity, among other atrocities, are in breach of absolute prohibitions of *jus cogens*.[19] The feeling of *humaneness*—proper of a new *jus gentium*, of the twenty-first century,—comes to permeate the whole *corpus juris* of contemporary international law.

I have called this development,—*inter alia*, in my Concurring Opinion in the Advisory Opinion n. 16 (of 01.10.1999), of the Inter-American Court of Human Rights [IACtHR], on the *Right to Information on Consular Assistance in the Framework of the Guarantees of the Due Process of Law*,—a historical process of a true *humanization* of International Law.[20] I have been developing this understanding also in successive Individual Opinions lately in the International Court of Justice (ICJ) as well (cf. *infra*).

In its historical trajectory, the ICJ's 1951 Advisory Opinion on the *Reservations to the Convention against Genocide* sustained the recognition of the principles underlying that Convention as principles which are "binding on States, even without any conventional obligation".[21] In its *jurisprudence constante*, the IACtHR, in interpreting and applying the American Convention on Human Rights, has consistently invoked the general principles of law.[22] The same has done the European Court of Human Rights [ECtHR], in its interpretation and application of the European Convention on Human Rights.[23]

Among such principles, those endowed with a truly fundamental character form the *substratum* of the legal order itself, disclosing the *right to the Law* of which are *titulaires* all human beings.[24] In the domain of the International Law of Human Rights, the fundamental principles of the *dignity of the human person* and of the *inalienability of the rights which are inherent to her* fall under this category. In its Advisory Opinion n. 18, on the *Juridical Condition of Undocumented Migrants* (2003), the IACtHR expressly referred to both principles.[25]

---

[18]Elias (2002), pp. 11–12.

[19]Cf., as to crimes against humanity, cf. Jurovics (2002), pp. 1–448; and Bassiouni (1999), pp. 210–211. And cf., as to acts of genocide, Cançado Trindade (2015b), pp. 9–265.

[20]Para. 35 of the Concurring Opinion.

[21]ICJ, *ICJ Reports* (1951) p. 23.

[22]Cf., *inter alia*, e.g., IACtHR, case of the *Five Pensioners versus Peru* (Judgment of 28.02.2003), para. 156; IACtHR, Advisory Opinion n. 17, on the *Juridical Condition and Human Rights of the Child* (of 28.08.2002), paras. 66 and 87; IACtHR, Advisory Opinion n. 16, on the *Right to Information on Consular Assistance in the Framework of the Guarantees of the Due Process of Law* (of 01.10.1999), paras. 58, 113 and 128. For a study, cf. Cançado Trindade (2004), pp. 59–71.

[23]Cf. Caflisch and Cançado Trindade (2004), pp. 5–62.

[24]Cançado Trindade (2003), pp. 524–525.

[25]Para. 157 of that Advisory Opinion. In my own Concurring Opinion (paras. 1–89) in that Advisory Opinion, I made a detailed and extensive account of my own conception of the

The prevalence of the principle of respect of the dignity of the human person is identified with the ultimate aim itself of Law, of the legal order, both national and international. By virtue of this fundamental principle, every person ought to be respected (in her honour and in her beliefs) by the simple fact of belonging to humankind, irrespective of any circumstance.[26] The principle of the inalienability of the rights inherent to the human being, in its turn, is identified with a basic assumption of the construction of the whole *corpus juris* of the International Law of Human Rights. As to the principles of International Humanitarian Law, it has been convincingly argued that one should consider Humanitarian Law treaties as a whole as constituting the expression—and the development—of such general principles, applicable in any circumstances, so as to secure a better protection to those victimized.[27]

In the *Mucic et allii* case (Judgment of 20.02.2001), the *ad hoc* International Criminal Tribunal for the Former Yugoslavia [ICTFY] (Appeals Chamber) pondered that both International Humanitarian Law and the International Law of Human Rights take as a "starting point" their common concern to safeguard human dignity, which forms the basis of their minimum standards of humanity.[28] In fact, the principle of humanity can be understood in distinct ways. Firstly, it can be conceived as a principle underlying the prohibition of inhuman treatment, established by Article 3 common to the four Geneva Conventions of 1949. Secondly, the principle referred to can be invoked by reference to humankind as a whole, in relation to matters of common, general and direct interest to it. And thirdly, the same principle can be employed to qualify a given quality of human behaviour (humaneness).

---

fundamental role and central position of the general principles of law in every legal system (national or international); cf. also A.A. Cançado Trindade, *International Law for Humankind - Towards a New Jus Gentium*, 2nd. rev. ed., *op. cit. supra* n. (5), ch. III, pp. 55–86.

[26] Maurer (1999), p. 18.

[27] Abi-Saab (1987), pp. 386 and 389; and cf. A.A. Cançado Trindade, *International Law for Humankind - Towards a New Jus Gentium*, 2nd. rev. ed., *op. cit. supra* n. (5), ch. III, pp. 55–86.

[28] Para. 149 of that Judgment. - Earlier on, in the *Celebici* case (Judgment of 16.11.1998), the aforementioned ICTFY (Trial Chamber) qualified as *inhuman treatment* an intentional or deliberate act or omission which causes serious suffering (or mental or physical damage), or constitutes a serious attack on human dignity; thus, the Tribunal added, "inhuman treatment is intentional treatment which does not conform with the fundamental principle of humanity, and forms the umbrella under which the remainder of the listed 'grave breaches' in the Conventions fall" (para. 543). Shortly afterwards, in the *T. Blaskic* case (Judgment of 03.03.2000), the same Tribunal (Trial Chamber) reiterated this position (para. 154).

5 The Human Factor in International Adjudication: Conscience Above the "Will"

As already indicated, there has been lately a jurisprudential construction attentive to the principle of humanity (*supra*), but there remains a long way to road, so as to overcome persisting obstacles, to the ultimate benefit of humankind.[29] Conscience, in my understanding, stands above the "will" of States, as I have lately had the occasion to reiterate in four recent Dissenting Opinions that I presented in the ICJ, to which I shall now turn.

5.1 *The Absolute Prohibition and Condemnation of Genocide*

It may here be recalled that, in its Judgment (of 03.02.2015) in the case of the *Application of the Convention against Genocide* (Croatia *versus* Serbia), the ICJ held that, while the prohibition of genocide has the character of *jus cogens*, and the Genocide Convention contains obligations *erga omnes*, its own jurisdiction is based on consent, on which it depends even when the dispute submitted to it relates to alleged violation of norms having peremptory character. After its own examination of the facts, it decided to reject the Applicant's claim.

I appended a lengthy and strong Dissenting Opinion to that Judgment of the ICJ, wherein I began by drawing attention to the framework of the settlement of the dispute at issue, ineluctably linked to the imperative of the *realization of justice*, in the light of *fundamental considerations of humanity*. The *principle of humanity*, in my perception, permeates the whole Convention against Genocide, essentially *people-oriented*, as well as the whole *corpus juris* of protection of the rights of the human person, which is essentially *victim-oriented*, encompassing the converging trends of the International Law of Human Rights, International Humanitarian Law and the International Law of Refugees, besides contemporary International Criminal Law (para. 84).[30]

The principle of humanity,—I proceeded,—has a clear incidence in the protection of human beings, in particular in situations of *vulnerability* or *defencelessness* (paras. 58–65). The Genocide Convention is *people-centered* and *victim-oriented* (rather than State-centric) thus showing the need, in the adjudication of the *cas d'espèce*, to go beyond the strict inter-State outlook, focusing attention on the people

[29]For a recent study, cf. Cançado Trindade (2018a), pp. 98–136.

[30]Cf. Cançado Trindade (2000), pp. 1–66.—The rights protected thereunder, in any circumstances, are not reduced to those "granted" by the State: they are *inherent to the human person*, and ought thus to be respected by the State. The protected rights are *superior and anterior to the State*, and must thus be respected by this latter, by all States.—Cf. also, more recently, cf. Cançado Trindade et al. (2017), pp. 1–221.

or population concerned, in pursuance of a humanist outlook, in the light of the principle of humanity.[31]

In interpreting and applying the Genocide Convention,—I added,—attention is to be turned to the victims, human groups in situations of vulnerability or defencelessness, rather than to inter-State susceptibilities (paras. 494–496). The imperative of the *realization of justice*, calls here for a people-centered outlook, focused on the victims (pp. 520–522); it acknowledges that conscience (*recta ratio*) stands above the "will" of States (para. 518).[32]

5.2 The Absolute Prohibition of Nuclear Weapons

There are other recent examples to the same effect. In its Judgments (of 10.05.2016) in the three recent cases of *Obligations Concerning Negotiations Relating to Cessation of the Nuclear Arms Race and to Nuclear Disarmament* (Marshall Islands *versus* United Kingdom, India and Pakistan), e.g., the ICJ decided, by a split-majority, to uphold one of the preliminary objections, grounded on the alleged absence of a dispute between the contending parties. The ICJ then found that it could not proceed to the consideration of the merits of the cases.

In my extensive Dissenting Opinions appended to those three Judgments, I strongly criticized the "formalistic reasoning" of the ICJ for the determination of the existence of a dispute, introducing a higher threshold that went beyond its own *jurisprudence constante* (paras 11–12). As there is no general requirement of prior notice of the applicant State's intention to initiate proceedings before the ICJ (para. 13),[33]—I added—the ICJ has unduly heightened the threshold to establish the existence of a dispute, in laying down the "awareness" requirement, seemingly "undermining its own ability to infer the existence of a dispute from the conflicting courses of conduct of the contending parties" (para. 19).

Moreover, in my three Dissenting Opinions in the present three cases of *Nuclear Disarmament Obligations*, I deemed it necessary to warn that the presence of evil has marked human existence along the centuries. Ever since the eruption of the nuclear age in August 1945, some of the world's great thinkers have been inquiring whether humankind has a future (paras. 93–101), and have been drawing attention to the imperative of respect for life and the relevance of humanist values (paras. 102–114).

Also in international legal doctrine there have been those who have been stressing the needed prevalence of human conscience, the universal juridical conscience (as "the ultimate material source of international law"), over State voluntarism (paras. 115–118). This is the position I have upheld, pondering that

[31]For a recent study, cf. Cançado Trindade (2017d), pp. 223–271.

[32]For a case-study, cf. Cançado Trindade (2015b), pp. 9–265.

[33]Nor of prior "exhaustion" of diplomatic negotiations (para. 14), I added.

> one cannot face the new challenges confronting the whole international community keeping in mind only State susceptibilities; such is the case with the obligation to render the world free of nuclear weapons, an imperative of *recta ratio* and not a derivative of the 'will' of States. In effect, to keep hope alive it is necessary to bear always in mind humankind as a whole (para. 119).

In my next line of considerations, I focused on the attention of the U.N. Charter to peoples (as shown in several of its provisions) and also to the safeguard of values common to humankind, and to respect for life and human dignity. This new vision advanced by the U.N. Charter, and espoused by the Law of the United Nations, has, in my perception,

> an incidence upon judicial settlement of international disputes. Thus, the fact that the ICJ's mechanism for the handling of contentious cases is an inter-State one, does not mean that its reasoning should also pursue a strictly inter-State dimension; that will depend on the nature and substance of the cases lodged with it. And there have been several cases lodged with the Court that required a reasoning going well beyond the inter-State dimension. Such reasoning beyond the inter-State dimension is faithful to the U.N. Charter, the ICJ being 'the principal judicial organ of the United Nations' (para. 125).

The nature of a case before the ICJ,—I proceeded,—may well call for a reasoning going beyond the strictly inter-State outlook, as the *cas d'espèce* concerning the obligation of nuclear disarmament,—a matter of concern to humankind as a whole,—which requires attention to be focused on peoples, in pursuance of a humanist outlook. The distinct series of U.N. General Assembly resolutions,—I proceeded,—give expression to an *opinio juris communis* in condemnation of nuclear weapons (paras. 45 and 150).

And as also sustained by general principles of international law and international legal doctrine,—I added,—nuclear weapons are in breach of international law, of International Humanitarian Law and of the International Law of Human Rights, of the U.N. Charter, and of *jus cogens*, for the devastating effects and sufferings they can inflict upon humankind as a whole (paras. 142–143).

I further warned that the survival of humankind cannot be made to depend on the "will" and the insistence on "national security interests" of a handful of privileged States; the "universal juridical conscience stands well above the 'will' of individual States" (paras. 150 and 224). In the path towards nuclear disarmament,—I went on,—the peoples of the world cannot remain hostage of individual State consent, in the light of the current historical process of *humanization* of international law (paras. 190–193).

This process of *humanization* which stands against the positivist outlook unduly overlooks the *opinio juris communis* as to the illegality of all weapons of mass destruction, including nuclear weapons, and the obligation of nuclear disarmament, under contemporary international law (paras. 194–200). Conventional and customary international law go together,—I added,—in the domain of the protection of the human person, as disclosed by the Martens clause, with an incidence on the prohibition of nuclear weapons (paras. 201–209 and 315). After all, the existence of nuclear weapons is the contemporary tragedy of the nuclear age; today, more than ever, human beings need protection from themselves. Nuclear weapons have no ethics, and ethics cannot be separated from law, as taught by jusnaturalist thinking (para. 213).

The initiatives, *inter alia*, of the establishment of nuclear-weapon-free zones, and of the Conferences on the Humanitarian Impact of Nuclear Weapons (paras. 246–287), "have gone beyond the inter-State outlook"; in my perception, there is great need, in the present domain, "to keep on looking beyond States, so as to behold peoples' and humankind's quest for survival in our times" (para. 299). Furthermore, as nuclear weapons, "as from their conception, have been associated with overwhelming destruction" (para. 300), there is great need of keeping attentive to issues of principle and to fundamental values (para. 316).

In my own understanding,—I added,—*opinio juris communis*—to which U.N. General Assembly resolutions have much contributed—has had a much broader dimension than the subjective element of custom, being a key element in the formation of a law of conscience, so as to rid the world of the inhuman threat of nuclear weapons (paras. 296–308). There is nowadays a vast *corpus juris* on matters of concern to the international community as a whole, overcoming the traditional inter-State paradigm of the international legal order (paras. 309–310).

This can no longer be overlooked in our days: the inter-State mechanism of the *contentieux* before the ICJ "cannot be invoked in justification for an inter-State reasoning" (para. 310). As "the principal judicial organ" of the United Nations,—I proceeded,—"the ICJ has to bear in mind not only States, but also 'we, the peoples', on whose behalf the U.N. Charter was adopted" (para. 314). I then concluded that "[a] world with arsenals of nuclear weapons, like ours, is bound to destroy its past, dangerously threatens the present, and has no future at all. Nuclear weapons pave the way into nothingness" (para. 331).[34]

The disappointing outcome of the aforementioned three cases of *Nuclear Disarmament Obligations*, dismissed by the ICJ's majority, was followed by the reassuring initiative of the U.N. General Assembly to decide, at the end of December 2016, to convene its Conference on the Treaty of Prohibition of Nuclear Weapons. The work of the Conference extended from March to July 2017, culminating with the adoption (on 07.07.2017) of that Treaty,—with full support of Delegations of African and Latin American countries, among others,—keeping alive the hope for the future of humankind.

6 Humankind and Considerations of Humanity: A Conceptual Precision

From the preceding considerations it can be promptly perceived that distinct meanings have been attributed to the term "humanity" in contemporary international law, such as those found in the jurisprudential construction of the former *ad hoc* ICTFY

[34]For a recent case-study, cf. Cançado Trindade (2017e), pp. 41–224.

and the ICTR (*supra*). This construction is clear in associating "humanity" with the universal principle of respect for the dignity of the human person, or the sense of *humaneness*.

The ECtHR and the IACtHR, for their part, have expressed the same concern by extensively resorting to general principles of law in their converging *jurisprudence constante*. The ICJ has likewise resorted to "elementary considerations of humanity", in a similar line of thinking.[35] The sense of humaneness and the concern with the needed respect for human dignity have thus marked their presence in the case-law of contemporary international tribunals.

When one comes, however, to consider the expansion of international legal personality, that is, the emergence of new subjects of today's universal international law, a conceptual precision is here rendered necessary. The expanded international law of our days encompasses, as its subjects, apart from the States, also international organizations, and human beings, either individually or collectively,—disclosing a basic feature of what I see it fit to denominate the historical process of *humanization* of international law.[36] In the framework of this latter and in addition to those subjects, *humankind* has in my view also emerged as a subject of international law.

The term "humankind" appears not as a synonym of "humanity" (*supra*), but endowed with a distinct and very concrete meaning: humankind encompasses all the members of the human species as a whole (including, in a temporal dimension,[37] present as well as future generations). In fact, there is nowadays a growing body of international instruments (treaties, declaratory and other resolutions, among others) containing express references to "mankind" or "humankind", and attributing rights to it. There are nowadays some conceptual constructions in course to give concrete expression, with juridical consequences, to rights attributed to humankind.[38] It is likely that this conceptual development will intensify in the years to come. Up to the present, all this results from the aforementioned growing perception and awareness of common and superior interests, and of fundamental values, shared by the international community as a whole.

[35] Cançado Trindade (1996), pp. 53–71, and cf. pp. 73–88.

[36] Cf. Cançado Trindade (2015c), pp. 3–789; Cançado Trindade (2013e), pp. 1–324; Cançado Trindade (2013f), pp. 7–185; Cançado Trindade (2012), pp. 45–368.

[37] Cf. A.A. Cançado Trindade, *International Law for Humankind - Towards a New Jus Gentium*, 2nd. rev. ed., *op. cit. supra* n. (5), ch. II, pp. 31–51.

[38] Cf. *ibid.*, ch. XII-XV, pp. 291-390. - And cf. [Various Authors,] *Crimes internationaux et juridictions internationales* (eds. A. Cassese and M. Delmas-Marty), Paris, PUF, 2002, pp. 71, 198 and 256, and cf. pp. 24, 26 and 259–261.

7 The Emergence of Humankind as a Subject of International Law

Along the evolution of contemporary international law, the international legal personality, as already pointed out, became no longer the monopoly of the States. These latter, as well as international organizations and human beings (taken individually and collectively) became *titulaires* of rights and bearers of duties emanating directly from international law.[39] And humankind has gradually come also to appear as a subject of contemporary international law, of the new *jus gentium* of the twenty-first century. Although this is a recent development, its roots go back to the legal thinking of the beginning of the second half of the twentieth century, or even earlier.

It may be recalled that the "conscience of mankind" received judicial recognition already in the Advisory Opinion of 1951 of the ICJ on *Reservations to the Convention against Genocide,*[40] reappearing in the Draft Articles on the International Responsibility of States (of 1976) of the U.N. International Law Commission [ILC].[41] In doctrine, some of the first formulations of the common law of mankind were undertaken in the early twentieth century, from the twenties[42] onwards. In the late forties, Alejandro Álvarez stated that the population (as a constitutive element of statehood) had at last entered into international life, and what mattered most was the identification of the common interests of the international community as a whole; to the Chilean jurist, it was the international juridical conscience and the sentiment of justice that were to achieve the reconstruction of International Law.[43]

This line of thinking was to be retaken, in a systematized way, by C.W. Jenks, in 1958,[44] and R.-J. Dupuy, in 1986,[45] among others; and in 1966, D. Evrigenis called for a new "universal law".[46] On his turn, in a visionary article published in 1950, M. Bourquin called for the attribution to the international community of the function of "guardian of objective law", above all in face of the threat of a "massified" civilization. The State itself acted—distinctly from the traditional conception—not

[39]Cf. A.A. Cançado Trindade, *International Law for Humankind - Towards a New Jus Gentium*, 2nd. rev. ed., *op. cit. supra* n. (5), ch. VII-X, pp. 165–273.

[40]*ICJ Reports* (1951) p. 23.

[41]With the inclusion of Article 19, on "international crimes" and "international delicts"; cf. United Nations, *Yearbook of the International Law Commission [YILC]* (1976)-II, part II, pp. 120–122 and 108–110. And cf., subsequently, provisions of the Draft Code of Offences against the Peace and Security of Mankind, of the same Commission; U.N., *YILC* (1986)-II, part I, pp. 56–57, and Draft Articles of 1991.

[42]Cf. Cf. A.A. Cançado Trindade, *International Law for Humankind - Towards a New Jus Gentium*, 2nd. rev. ed., *op. cit. supra* n. (5), ch. I, III and VI, pp. 9–29, 55–86 and 139–161, respectively.

[43]A. Álvarez, "Méthodes de la codification du Droit international public - Rapport", *in Annuaire de l'Institut de Droit International* - Session de Lausanne (1947) pp. 45–47, 50–51, 54, 63–64 and 68–70.

[44]Jenks (1958), pp. 1–442; and cf. Jenks (1973), pp. 330–346.

[45]Dupuy (1986), pp. 11–182.

[46]Evrigenis (1966), Berlin, Deutsche Gesellschaft für die Vereinten Nationen, 1966, pp. 26–34.

solely in the pursuance of its own interest, but also as a member of such international community. The traditional voluntarist conception of international law,

> en faisant de la volonté de l'État la seule force génératrice du droit, (...) déforme le phénomène juridique; (...) elle oublie que le droit est inhérent a toute société, qu'il existe là-même où aucune organisation étatique ne participe à son élaboration.[47]

The human problems which conform the contemporary international agenda have inevitably drawn increasing attention to the conditions of living of human beings everywhere, with a direct bearing in the construction of Law itself. Human beings were again to occupy a central place in the law of nations,—which led M. Bourquin to conclude that

> ni au point de vue de son objet, ni même au point de vue de sa structure, le droit des gens ne peut se définir comme un droit inter-étatique.[48]

Two decades later, in face of the developments in the law of outer space, there was support in expert writing for the view that the *comunitas humani generis* (which reflected the "moral unity of the human kind" in the line of the thinking of Francisco de Vitoria) already presented a juridical profile, rendering "humanity" itself a "subject of Law", because "its existence as a moral and political unity" is an idea which "is progressively becoming reality with all the juridical implications that it entails".[49]

Ever since, this line of thinking has been attracting growing attention, at least on the part of the more lucid doctrine. To S. Sucharitkul, e.g., there is no reason to impede humanity to be subject of International Law, it being possible to that effect to be represented by the international community itself; this is a conception which is to prevail, through the *humanization* of international law, so as "to strengthen the juridical statute of the human being as subject of law" and to save humanity from an "imminent disaster" (the nuclear threat).[50]

In the lucid observation of Nagendra Singh, the fact that, as time went on, concepts and norms of international law have attained universal acknowledgment (in such domains as International Humanitarian Law, the law of treaties, diplomatic and consular law), independently of the multicultural composition of the international community, reveals the evolution of International Law towards universalization.[51] The need to research into the *status conscientiae* of the States was stressed by R. Quadri, who insisted on the international juridical conscience as the material source of the international legal order wherein pluralism prevailed.[52] In Italian

---

[47]Bourquin (1950), pp. 35 and 45, and cf. pp. 21–54.

[48]*Ibid.*, p. 54, and cf. p. 38.

[49]Legaz y Lacambra (1970), p. 554, and cf. pp. 549–559.

[50]Sucharitkul (1984), pp. 419 and 425–427.

[51]Nagendra Singh, "The Basic Concept of Universality and the Development of International Law", *in L'avenir du Droit international dans un monde multiculturel*, *op. cit. supra* n. (50), pp. 240–241, 246 and 256–257.

[52]Quadri (1964), pp. 326, 332, 336–337, 339 and 350–351.

international legal doctrine, addressing the "unity of the juridical world", a warning is found to the effect that

> il faut voir dans la conscience commune des peuples, ou conscience universelle, la source des normes suprêmes du droit international. (. . .) Les principes qui śinscrivent dans la conscience universelle (. . .) sont à considérer comme également présents dans les ordres juridiques internes (. . .).[53]

The rights of humanity transcend, by definition, reciprocity, proper of relations at the purely inter-State level.[54] It has been contended that the international community should guide itself in the sense of restructuring the international system so as to secure the survival and well-being of humankind as a whole.[55] There are other pertinent manifestations to this effect that are to be taken into account and kept in mind.

The U.N. International Law Commission, while elaborating its Draft Code of Offences against the Peace and Security of Mankind, advanced the understanding (in 1986) that it was possible to conceive a crime against humanity "in the threefold sense of cruelty directed against human existence, the degradation of human dignity and the destruction of human culture". The individual being a guardian of basic ethical values and a custodian of human dignity, an attack that he suffered could amount to a crime against humanity to the extent that such attack came to shock "human conscience"; one could thus find,—in the outlook of the ILC,—a "natural link" between the human kind and the individual, one being "the expression of the other", what led to the conclusion that the term "humanity" (in the expression "crime against humanity") meant the human kind as a whole and "in its various individual and collective manifestations".[56]

In fact, already in the beginnings of international law, recourse was made to "fundamental notions of humanity" which governed the conduct of States. What subsequently was denominated "crimes against humanity" emanated, originally, from customary international law,[57] to develop conceptually, later on, in the ambit of International Humanitarian Law,[58] and, more recently, in that of International Criminal Law.[59] Crimes against humanity are today typified in the Rome Statute of the permanent International Criminal Court (Article 7).[60] We are, here, in the domain of *jus cogens*.[61]

---

[53] Sperduti (1989), pp. 884–885.

[54] Dupuy (1991), p. 137.

[55] Allott (1992), pp. 219–252, esp. p. 251; and cf. Allott (1990), pp. 10 and 186.

[56] U.N., *Yearbook of the International Law Commission* (1986)-II, part I, pp. 56–57.

[57] Ratner and Abrams (1997), pp. 45–48.

[58] Cf. Pictet (1983), pp. 107 and 77; Swinarski (1990), p. 20.

[59] Cf. Robinson (1999), pp. 43–57; and, for the historical antecedents, cf., e.g., Fujita (2000), pp. 1–15.

[60] Cf., e.g., Lee (1999), pp. 30–31 and 90–102; Bassiouni (1999), pp. 332 and 363–368.

[61] Bassiouni (1996), pp. 67–74.

In the occurrence of such crimes victimizing human beings, humanity itself is likewise victimized. This has in fact been expressly acknowledged by the former ICTFY in the *Tadic* case (1997), wherein it held that a crime against humanity is perpetrated not only against the victims themselves, but against humanity as a whole. Again in the *Erdemovic* case (1996), the Tribunal sustained that crimes against humanity "shock the collective conscience", harm human beings and transcend them, as humanity itself becomes a victim of them.[62]

Significant indications pointing towards a common law of mankind can be found in several treaties in force, in distinct domains of International Law. The notion of cultural heritage of mankind, for example, can be found, e.g., in the 1972 UNESCO Convention concerning the Protection of the World Cultural and Natural Heritage.[63] In the ambit of International Environmental Law, ever since the 1972 Stockholm Declaration of the U.N. Conference on the Human Environment referred to the "common good of mankind" (Principle 18), examples in this same line have multiplied themselves, in numerous treaties whereby States Parties contracted obligations in the common superior interest of humankind.[64]

It so happens that mankind gradually emerges, and is acknowledged, in contemporary international law, and increasingly so, as a subject of rights in distinct domains (such as, e.g., International Human Rights Law, International Criminal Law, International Environmental Law, international regulation of spaces, among others). A distinct aspect,—the proper treatment of which remaining still to be undertaken,—is that of its capacity to act.

8 Legal Consequences of the Acknowledgement of Humankind as Subject of International Law

8.1 The Relevance of the Human Rights Framework

Recourse to the very notion of humankind as subject of international law promptly brings into the fore, or places the whole discussion within, the human rights framework,—and this should be properly emphasized, it should not be left implicit or neglected as allegedly redundant. Just as law, or the rule of law itself, does not operate in a vacuum, humankind is neither a social nor a legal abstraction: it is

[62]Jones (1999), pp. 111–112.

[63]Preceded by, e.g., the 1954 Hague Convention for the Protection of Cultural Property in the Event of Armed Conflict.

[64]E.g., examples *in*: A.A. Cançado Trindade, *International Law for Humankind - Towards a New Jus Gentium*, 2nd. rev. ed., *op. cit. supra* n. (5), ch. XIII, pp. 327–352. In addition, another example is found implicit in references to "human health" in some treaties of environmental law, such as, e.g., the Vienna Convention for the Protection of the Ozone Layer (of 1985), preamble and Article 2; the Montreal Protocol on Substances that Destroy the Ozone Layer (of 1987), preamble; and Article 1 of the three aforementioned Conventions on marine pollution.

composed of human collectivities, of all human beings of flesh and bone, living in human societies and extended in time. Just as a couple of decades ago there were questions which were "withdrawn" from the domestic jurisdiction of States to become matters of *international* concern (essentially, in cases pertaining to human rights protection and self-determination of peoples),[65] there are nowadays global issues (such as climate change and disarmament) which are being erected as *common* concern of mankind.

Here, again, the contribution of international human rights protection and environmental protection heralds the end of reciprocity and the emergence of *erga omnes* obligations. The human rights framework is ineluctably present in the consideration also of the system of protection of the human environment in all its aspects; we are here ultimately confronted with the crucial question of survival of the humankind, with the assertion—in face of threats to the human environment—of the fundamental human right to live.

8.2 The Question of the Capacity to Act and Legal Representation.

A subject of law is generally regarded as a bearer of rights and duties conferred upon him, also endowed with the capacity to act. While it is clear today that humankind is the addressee of international norms and has emerged as a subject of international law (the law of the *comunitas humani generis*), its capacity to act is still *in statu nascendi*; this raises the issue of its legal representation. In this connection, an advanced form of representation, despite its shortcomings, is that of the 1982 U.N. Convention on the Law of the Sea,[66] given the degree of institutionalization achieved (through the creation of the International Seabed Authority).

We are at the beginning of a conceptual construction which may still take a long time and considerable endeavours. The conception of humankind, in a time framework encompassing present and future generations, presents the double advantage of not neglecting the time factor[67] and not isolating one generation from the others. This would lead to the difficulty, already detected in expert writing, of asserting rights of future generations, which do not yet exist and may be rather remote in time;

[65] Cf. A.A. Cançado Trindade, *International Law for Humankind - Towards a New Jus Gentium*, 2nd. rev. ed., *op. cit. supra* n. (5), ch. VII, pp. 165–179.

[66] Cf. Blanc Altemir (1992), pp. 37–44 and 243–244; Paquerot (2002), pp. 91–92; and cf. Cf. A.A. Cançado Trindade, *International Law for Humankind - Towards a New Jus Gentium*, 2nd. rev. ed., *op. cit. supra* n. (5), ch. XIII, pp. 327–352.

[67] Cf. Cf. A.A. Cançado Trindade, *International Law for Humankind - Towards a New Jus Gentium*, 2nd. rev. ed., *op. cit. supra* n. (5), ch. II, pp. 31–51.

yet, it is quite conceivable to establish, among the living, legal representation on behalf of humankind, comprising its present and future segments.[68]

The overriding principle of human solidarity holds the living, the present generation, accountable to the unborn (future generations, for the stewardship of the common heritage or concern of humankind, so as not to leave to those who are still to come the world in a worse condition than it found it. After all,

> We all live in time. The passing of time affects our juridical condition. The passing of time should strengthen the bonds of solidarity which link the living to their dead, bringing them closer together. The passing of time should strengthen the ties of solidarity which unite all human beings, young and old, who experience a greater or lesser degree of vulnerability in different moments along their existence. (. . .) In a general way, it is at the beginning and the end of the existential time that one experiences greater vulnerability, in face of the proximity of the unknown (. . .).[69]

We are here still in the first steps, and there remains of course a long way to go in order to attain a more perfected and improved system of legal representation of humankind in international law, so that the rights recognized to it thus far can be properly vindicated on a widespread basis. In my understanding, the present limitations of the capacity to act on behalf of humankind itself at international level in no way affect its emerging legal personality, its condition of subject of International Law.

As I deemed it fit to state in my Concurring Opinion in the Advisory Opinion n. 17 of the IACtHR, on the *Juridical Condition and Human Rights of the Child* (2002), the international juridical personality of all human beings remains intact, irrespective of the existential condition[70] or limitations of the juridical capacity to exercise their rights for themselves; what ultimately matters is that they all have the right to a legal order (at domestic as well as international levels) which effectively protects the rights inherent to them (para. 71). And this applies to all human beings as well as to humankind as a whole.[71]

In historical perspective, humankind as such firmly manifests itself in the treatment of persons in situations of vulnerability, or even defencelessness. When *jus gentium* began to correspond to the *droit des gens*, il came to be considered by its "founding fathers" (F. de Vitoria, A. Gentili, F. Suárez, H. Grotius, S. Pufendorf, C. Wolff) as a law regulating the international community composed of human beings organized socially in (emerging) States, coexisting in harmony with human

[68]Cf. discussion and suggestions *in*: [Various Authors,] *Future Generations and International Law* (eds. E. Agius, S. Busuttil *et alii*), London, Earthscan Publs., 1998, pp. 3–165.

[69]IACtHR, Advisory Opinion n. 17 (of 28.08.2002) on the *Juridical Condition and Human Rights of the Child*, Concurring Opinion of Judge A.A. Cançado Trindade, paras. 4–5.

[70]E.g., children, elderly persons, persons with disability, stateless persons, or any other.

[71]Cf. Cançado Trindade (2011b), pp. 1–236; Cançado Trindade (2001a), pp. 9–104; Cançado Trindade (2001b), pp. 31–63; Cançado Trindade (2018b), pp. 13–49; A.A. Cançado Trindade, "Reflexiones sobre la Presencia de la Persona Humana en el Contencioso Interestatal ante la Corte Internacional de Justicia: Desarrollos Recientes", 17 *Anuario..., op. cit. supra* n. (31), pp. 223–271.

kind, thus corresponding to the *jus necessarium* of the *societas gentium.*[72] This latter prevails over the "will" of individual States, in due respect to each human being and to the benefit of the common good.[73]

In any case, the gradual advances so far achieved towards a regime of legal representation of humankind,—which are bound to continue in the years to come,—added to the recognition of its condition as subject of international law, constitute yet another manifestation of the current process of *humanization* of public international law. The original conception of *totus orbis* of Francisco de Vitoria in the sixteenth century has ever since paved the way for the formation and crystallization of the notions of an international community as a whole and of a true universal international law,[74] having humankind as such among its subjects.

That conception can and should continue to be cultivated in our troubled times, in the context of the circumstances of the contemporary international scenario, if we really wish to leave a better world to the next generations. In my understanding, we have already entered into the *terra nova* of the new *jus gentium* of the early twenty-first century, the international law for humankind. The adoption of the 2017 Treaty of Prohibition of Nuclear Weapons[75] constitutes, in my perception, another example of the current historical process of the *humanization* of the law of nations.

This significant recent initiative towards nuclear disarmament is nowadays added to other manifestations of the humanization of contemporary international law,[76] to the ultimate benefit of humankind as a whole. Human conscience stands above the "will". There is great need today to keep on pursuing the humanization of contemporary international law; it is important to remain attentive to the vindication of the rights of humankind.

---

[72]Cf. F. de Vitoria, *Relecciones del Estado, de los Indios, y del Derecho de la Guerra* (with an Introduction by A. Gómez Robledo), Mexico, Ed. Porrúa, 1985, pp. XLV and LXXXIV; and cf. Cançado Trindade (2008a), pp. 197–212; Cançado Trindade (2014a), pp. 40–109; Cançado Trindade (2016b), pp. 19–51; Cançado Trindade (2016c), pp. 17–55; Cançado Trindade (2016d), pp.15–43.

[73]A.A. Cançado Trindade, *A Humanização do Direito Internacional*, 2nd. rev. ed., *op. cit. supra* n. (36), pp. 9–14, 172, 318–319, 393 and 408; and cf. Cançado Trindade (2008b), pp. 1–187.

[74]We have already reached a stage of evolution of our discipline which has surely transcended the fragmented *jus inter gentes* of the not too distant past.

[75]For an account, cf. Cançado Trindade (2016e), pp. 151–284; Cançado Trindade (2017a), pp. 11–49.

[76]On this historical process, cf. A.A. Cançado Trindade, *A Humanização do Direito Internacional*, 2nd. rev. ed., *op. cit. supra* n. (36), pp. 3–789; A.A. Cançado Trindade, *International Law for Humankind - Towards a New Jus Gentium*, 2a. rev. ed., *op cit. supra* n. (5), pp. 1–726; Cançado Trindade (2014b), pp. 1–324; A.A. Cançado Trindade, *Los Tribunales Internacionales Contemporáneos y la Humanización del Derecho Internacional*, *op. cit. supra* n. (36), pp. 7–185; Cançado Trindade (2012), pp. 45–368; A.A. Cançado Trindade, *Os Tribunais Internacionais e a Realização da Justiça*, 2nd. rev. ed., *op. cit. supra* n. (6), pp. 1–467.

References

Abi-Saab R (1987) Les 'principes généraux' du Droit humanitaire selon la Cour Internationale de Justice. Revue internationale de la Croix-Rouge 766:386 and 389

Allott Ph (1990) Eunomia - new order for a new world. Oxford University Press, Oxford, pp 10 and 186

Allott P (1992) Reconstituting humanity - new international law. Eur J Int Law 3:219–252

Bassiouni MC (1996) International Crimes: *Jus Cogens* and *Obligatio Erga* Omnes. Law Contemp Probl Account Int Crimes Ser Violat Fundamental. Human Rights 59:67–74

Bassiouni MC (1999) Crimes against humanity in international criminal law, 2nd ed. rev. Kluwer, The Hague, pp 210–211

Blanc Altemir A (1992) El Patrimonio Común de la Humanidad - Hacia un Régimen Jurídico Internacional para Su Gestión. Barcelona, Bosch, pp 37–44 and 243–244

Bourquin M (1950) L'humanisation du droit des gens. In: La technique et les principes du Droit public - Études en ĺhonneur de Georges Scelle, vol I. LGDJ, Paris, pp 35 and 45

Brus MMTA (1995) Third party dispute settlement in an interdependent world. Nijhoff, Dordrecht, pp 142 and 182–183

Caflisch L, Cançado Trindade AA (2004) Les Conventions Américaine et Européenne des Droits de l´Homme et le droit international général. Revue générale de Droit international public 108:5–62

Cançado Trindade AA (1996) La jurisprudence de la Cour Internationale de Justice sur les droits intangibles. In: Prémont D, Stenersen C, Oseredczuk I (eds) Droits intangibles et états d'exception. Bruxelles, Bruylant, pp 53–71

Cançado Trindade AA (2000) Derecho Internacional de los Derechos Humanos, Derecho Internacional de los Refugiados y Derecho Internacional Humanitario - Aproximaciones y Convergencias. ICRC, Geneva, pp 1–66

Cançado Trindade AA (2001a) El Acceso Directo del Individuo a los Tribunales Internacionales de Derechos Humanos. Universidad de Deusto, Bilbao, pp 9–104

Cançado Trindade AA (2001b) A Personalidade e Capacidade Jurídicas do Indivíduo como Sujeito do Direito Internacional. Revista do Instituto Brasileiro de Direitos Humanos. Fortaleza, IBDH, 2002, 3:31–63

Cançado Trindade AA (2003) Tratado de Direito Internacional dos Direitos Humanos, vol. III. Porto Alegre/Brazil, S.A. Fabris Ed., pp 524–525

Cançado Trindade AA (2004) La Convention Américaine relative aux Droits de ĺHomme et le droit international général. In: Cohen-Jonathan G, Flauss J-F (eds) Droit international, droits de l'homme et juridictions internationales. Bruxelles, Bruylant, pp 59–71

Cançado Trindade AA (2005a) International Law for Humankind: Towards a New *Jus Gentium* - General Course on Public International Law - Part I. Recueil des Cours de ĺAcadémie de Droit International de la Haye [*RCADI*] ch. XI, 316:318–333

Cançado Trindade AA (2005b) Complementarity between State responsibility and individual responsibility for grave violations of human rights: the crime of state revisited. In: Ragazzi M (ed) International responsibility today - essays in Memory of O. Schachter. Leiden, M. Nijhoff, pp 253–269

Cançado Trindade AA (2008a) *Totus Orbis*: A Visão Universalista e Pluralista do *Jus Gentium*: Sentido e Atualidade da Obra de Francisco de Vitoria. Revista da Academia Brasileira de Letras Jurídicas - Rio de Janeiro 24(32):197–212

Cançado Trindade AA (2008b) Évolution du Droit international au droit des gens - Ĺaccès des particuliers à la justice internationale: le regard dún juge. Pédone, Paris, pp 1–187

Cançado Trindade AA (2009a) *Jus Cogens*: The Determination and the Gradual Expansion of Its Material Content in Contemporary International Case-Law. In: XXXV Curso de Derecho Internacional Organizado por el Comité Jurídico Interamericano de la OEA (2008). OAS General Secretariat, Washington D.C., pp 3–29

Cançado Trindade AA (2009b) Some Reflections on the Reassuring Expansion of the Material Content of *Jus Cogens*. In: Diritti Individuali e Giustizia Internazionale - Liber F. Pocar, Milano, Giuffrè Ed., pp 65–79

Cançado Trindade AA (2010) La *Recta Ratio* dans les Fondements du *Jus Gentium* comme Droit International de l'Humanité. Revista do Instituto Brasileiro de Direitos Humanos 10:11–26

Cançado Trindade AA (2011a) The Expansion of the Material Content of *Jus Cogens*: The Contribution of the Inter-American Court of Human Rights. In: Spielmann D et al (eds) La Convention Européenne des Droits de l´Homme, un instrument vivant - Mélanges en l´honneur de Chr.L. Rozakis. Bruxelles, Bruylant, pp 27–46

Cançado Trindade AA (2011b) The access of individuals to international justice. Oxford University Press, Oxford, pp 1–236

Cançado Trindade AA (2012) Le Droit international pour la personne humaine, Paris, Pédone, pp 45–368

Cançado Trindade AA (2013a) International Law for Humankind: Towards a New Jus Gentium, 2nd rev. edn. Nijhoff/The Hague Academy of International Law, The Hague, ch. XI, pp 275–288

Cançado Trindade AA (2013b) A Century of International Justice and Prospects for the Future. In: Cançado Trindade AA, Spielmann D (eds) A century of international justice and prospects for the future/Rétrospective d´un siècle de justice internationale et perspectives d'avenir. Oisterwijk, Wolf Publs., pp 16–17

Cançado Trindade AA (2013c) La Protección de la Persona Humana frente a los Crímenes Internacionales y la Invocación Indebida de Inmunidades Estatales. IBDH/IIDH/SLADI, Fortaleza/Brazil, pp 5–305

Cançado Trindade AA (2013d) Some reflections on the principle of humanity in its wide dimension. In: Kolb R, Gaggioli G (eds) Research handbook on human rights and humanitarian law. E. Elgar, Cheltenham, pp 188–197

Cançado Trindade AA (2013e) La Humanización del Derecho Internacional Contemporáneo. Edit. Porrúa/IMDPC, México, pp 1–324

Cançado Trindade AA (2013f) Los Tribunales Internacionales Contemporáneos y la Humanización del Derecho Internacional, Buenos Aires, Ed. Ad-Hoc, pp 7–185

Cançado Trindade AA (2014a) Prefacio. In: Calafate P, Mandado Gutiérrez RE (eds) Santander, Ed. Escuela Ibérica de la Paz (1511-1694) - La Conciencia Crítica de la Conquista y Colonización de América. Universidad de Cantabria, pp 40–109

Cançado Trindade AA (2014b) La Humanización del Derecho Internacional Contemporáneo. Edit. Porrúa, México, pp 1–324

Cançado Trindade AA (2015a) Quelques réflexions sur les systèmes régionaux dans le cadre de l´ universalité des droits de l´homme. In: Select Proceedings of the European Society of International Law (vol. IV: 2012 Valencia Colloquy). Hart Publication, Oxford/Portland, pp 345–347

Cançado Trindade AA (2015b) A Responsabilidade do Estado sob a Convenção contra o Genocídio: Em Defesa da Dignidade Humana. IBDH/IIDH, Fortaleza/Brazil, pp 9–265

Cançado Trindade AA (2015c) A Humanização do Direito Internacional, 2nd. rev. ed., Belo Horizonte/Brazil, Edit. Del Rey, pp 3–789

Cançado Trindade AA (2016a) Il Principio di Umanità e la Salvaguardia delle Vittime: Considerazioni sull´Esperienza della Corte Interamericana dei Diritti Umani in Materia di Adempimento di Sentenze e Decisioni. In: Cançado Trindade AA, Barros Leal C (eds) Il Principio di Umanità e la Salvaguardia della Persona Umana. IBDH/IIDH, Fortaleza/Brazil, pp 61–74

Cançado Trindade AA (2016b) Prefácio: A Visão Universalista e Humanista do Direito das Gentes: Sentido e Atualidade da Obra de Francisco de Vitoria. In: Francisco de Vitoria, Relectiones - Sobre os Índios e sobre o Poder Civil. Editora Universidade de Brasília/FUNAG, Brasília, pp 19–51

Cançado Trindade AA (2016c) La Perennidad del Legado de los 'Padres Fundadores' del Derecho Internacional". In: Discurso del Acto de Investidura como Doctor Honoris Causa del Profesor Antônio Augusto Cançado Trindade, Madrid, Ed. Universidad Autónoma de Madrid, pp 17–55
Cançado Trindade AA (2016d) La Perennidad del Legado de los 'Padres Fundadores' del Derecho Internacional. Revista Interdisciplinar de Direito da Faculdade de Direito de Valença 13 (2):15–43
Cançado Trindade AA (2016e) A Plea in Support of Prompt Compliance with the Obligations of Cessation of the Nuclear Arms Race and of Nuclear Disarmament. In: XLIII Curso de Derecho Internacional del Comité Jurídico Interamericano (2016), General Secretariat of the OAS, 2016, Washington D.C. pp 151–284
Cançado Trindade AA (2017a) A Conferência da ONU sobre o Tratado de Proibição de Armas Nucleares. In: Curso de Derecho Internacional del Comité Jurídico Interamericano (2017) General Secretariat of the OAS, Washington D.C., 2017, 44:11–49
Cançado Trindade AA (2017b) Réflexions sur la nécessaire primauté du droit d´accès à la justice sur les invocations indues des immunités de l´État face aux crimes internationaux. In: Écrits sur la communauté internationale: enjeux juridiques, politiques et diplomatiques - Liber Amicorum Stelios Perrakis. I. Sideris Publs., Athène/Grèce, pp 69–77
Cançado Trindade AA (2017c) Os Tribunais Internacionais e a Realização da Justiça, 2nd rev edn. Belo Horizonte/Brazil, Edit. Del Rey, pp 53–56
Cançado Trindade AA (2017d) Reflexiones sobre la Presencia de la Persona Humana en el Contencioso Interestatal ante la Corte Internacional de Justicia: Desarrollos Recientes. Anuario de los Cursos de Derechos Humanos de Donostia-San Sebastián - Universidad del País Vasco 17:223–271
Cançado Trindade AA (2017e) The universal obligation of nuclear disarmament. FUNAG, Brasília, pp 41–224
Cançado Trindade AA (2018a) Reflections on the international adjudication of cases of grave violations of rights of the human person. J Int Humanit Legal Stud 9:98–136
Cançado Trindade AA (2018b) Atos de Genocídio e Crimes contra a Humanidade: Reflexões sobre a Complementaridade da Responsabilidade Internacional do Indivíduo e do Estado. Revista del Instituto Interamericano de Derechos Humanos 67:13–49
Cançado Trindade AA, Ortiz Ahlf L, Ruiz de Santiago J (2017) Las Tres Vertientes de la Protección Internacional de los Derechos de la Persona Humana, 2nd rev edn. Ed. Porrúa / Escuela Libre de Derecho, Mexico, pp 1–221
Dupuy P-M (1991) Humanité, communauté, et efficacité du Droit. In: Humanité et Droit international - Mélanges René-Jean Dupuy, Paris, Pédone, p 137
Dupuy R-J (1986) La communauté internationale entre le mythe et l'histoire. Economica/UNESCO, Paris, pp 11–182
Elias TO (2002) New trends in contemporary international law. In: Freestone D, Subedi S, Davidson S (eds) Contemporary issues in international law. Kluwer, The Hague, pp 11–12
Evrigenis D (1966) Institutionnalisation des droits de l'homme et droit universel. In: Internationales Colloquium über Menschenrechte. Oktober, Berlin
Fujita H (2000) Le crime contre ĺhumanité dans les procès de Nuremberg et de Tokyo. Kobe Univ Law Rev 34:1–15
Gaja G (2011) The protection of general interests in the international community. RCADI 364:46–50
Husson-Rochcongar C (2012) Droit international des droits de l´homme et valeurs - Le recours aux valeurs dans la jurisprudence des organes spécialisés, Bruxelles, Bruylant, pp 1–941
Jenks CW (1958) The common law of Mankind. Stevens, London, pp 1–442
Jenks CW (1973) The new science and the law of nations. In: Évolution et perspectives du droit international - Livre du centenaire de ĺInstitut de Droit International 1873-1973. Bâle, Éd. S. Karger, pp 330–346
Jones JRWD (1999) The practice of the international criminal tribunals for the Former Yugoslavia and Rwanda, 2nd edn. Transnational Publs, Ardsley, pp 111–112

Jurovics Y (2002) Réflexions sur la spécificité du crime contre l´humanité. LGDJ, Paris, pp 1–448
Lachs M (1980) The development and general trends of international law in our time. RCADI 169:205
Lee RS (ed) (1999) The international criminal court - the making of the Rome Statute. Kluwer, The Hague, pp 30–31 and 90–102
Legaz y Lacambra L (1970) La Humanidad, Sujeto de Derecho. In: Estudios de Derecho Internacional Público y Privado - Homenaje al Profesor L. Sela Sampil, vol. II. Universidad de Oviedo, Oviedo, p 554
Maurer B (1999) Le principe de respect de la dignité humaine et la Convention Européenne des Droits de l'Homme. CERIC/Univ. d'Aix-Marseille, Paris, p 18
Paquerot S (2002) Le statut des ressources vitales en Droit international - Essai sur le concept de patrimoine commun de l´humanité. Bruxelles, Bruylant, pp 91–92
Pictet J (1966) The principles of international humanitarian law. ICRC, Geneva, pp 29–30
Pictet J (1983) Développement et principes du Droit international humanitaire. Genève/Paris, Inst. H.-Dunant/Pédone, pp 107 and 77
Quadri R (1964) Cours général de Droit international public. RCADI 113:326
Radbruch G (1965) Introducción a la Filosofía del Derecho [Vorschule der Rechtsphilosophie]. 3rd. Spanish edition, Mexico, Fondo de Cultura Económica, p 180
Ratner SR, Abrams JS (1997) Accountability for human rights atrocities in international law. Clarendon Press, Oxford, pp 45–48
Robinson D (1999) Defining 'crimes against humanity' at the Rome Conference. Am J Int Law 93:43–57
Sperduti G (1989) La souveraineté, le droit international et la sauvegarde des droits de la personne. In: International Law at a Time of Perplexity - Essays in Honour of S. Rosenne, Dordrecht, Nijhoff, pp 884–885
Starace V (1976) La responsabilité résultant de la violation des obligations à l´égard de la communauté internationale. RCADI 153:272–275
Sucharitkul S (1984) L'humanité en tant qu'élément contribuant au développement progressif du Droit international contemporain. In: L'avenir du Droit international dans un monde multiculturel (Colloque de La Haye de 1983, ed. R.-J. Dupuy). La Haye, Nijhoff/Académie de Droit International de La Haye, p 419
Swinarski C (1990) Principales Nociones e Institutos del Derecho Internacional Humanitario como Sistema Internacional de Protección de la Persona Humana. San José of Costa Rica, IIDH, p 20
von Bogandy A, Venzke I (2016) In Whose Name? A public law theory of international adjudication. Oxford University Press, Oxford

Antônio Augusto Cançado Trindade is a Judge of the International Court of Justice; Former President of the Inter-American Court of Human Rights; Emeritus Professor of International Law of the University of Brasília, Brazil; Member of the *Curatorium* of the Hague Academy of International Law, and of the *Institut de Droit International.*

Can the Law Respond to Threatened Apocalypse?

David Baragwanath

Contents

1 Can the Law Respond to Threatened Apocalypse?

> A situation, similar to the present, hath not happened since the days of Noah until now.[1]

In *Nigerian Yearbook of International Law 2017* 17[2] I argued that the global affliction of terrorism, which has created agony for the people of Nigeria, requires urgent legal response. As Security Council Resolution 2462 (2019)[3] has recognized, it still does. The present paper begins with a focus on two further and related threats, each aggravated by and contributing to that of terrorism. The first is global warming. The second is the global loss of biodiversity, which on 6 May 2019 was the subject of the most comprehensive assessment of the topic ever undertaken. The linkage

[1]Thomas Paine *Common Sense* Appendix to the Third Edition www.ushistory.org/paine/commonsense/sense6.htm cited by Gray (2007), p. 107.

[2]"Responding to Terrorism: Definition and Other Actions" p. 17.

[3]28 March 2019.

D. Baragwanath (✉)
Special Tribunal for Lebanon, Leidschendam, The Netherlands
e-mail: baragwanath@un.org

C. Eboe-Osuji et al. (eds.), *Nigerian Yearbook of International Law 2018/2019*,
Nigerian Yearbook of International Law 2018/2019,
https://doi.org/10.1007/978-3-030-69594-1_2

among global warming, global loss of biodiversity, and terrorism needs to be faced and responded to with imagination and vigour.

Cass Sunstein in 2007 identified "the stark difference between ... reactions to terrorism-related risks and. . .reactions to the risks associated with climate change."[4] In a forthcoming essay[5] I have contrasted these risks with the two frogs in the fable: the former risk is so obvious it is like a frog put into boiling water, which will jump out; the latter concerns another frog which, put in tepid water which is then slowly brought to a boil, but oblivious to its incremental danger will be cooked to death.

A more insidious risk is global loss of biodiversity, potentially affecting all species; worse still is the combination of all three. It is appropriate to examine them with specific attention to Nigeria, which has already been the subject of climate change as a driver of terrorism; which must also warrant the careful attention of experts in relation to loss of diversity; and whose status regionally and internationally makes the combination of all three risks—terrorism, global warming, and loss of diversity—of momentous importance.

It is convenient for present purposes to leave terrorism to the 2017 discussion; to move immediately to global warming; and to finish with global loss of biodiversity and its combination with the first two.

2 Global Warming

The imminence of disaster resulting from global warming, coupled with an apathetic public response, places international law at a crucial threshold. Those who have the privilege and responsibility of understanding how it can be reformed and given effect within the decade or so that remains available to avoid disaster must act urgently and decisively.

The law can provide bold initiatives, both old and new. The Treaties of Osnabrück and Münster, ending the Thirty and Eighty Years Wars, after some eight million deaths, resulted in the Peace of Westphalia. Lasting since 1648 its principle was endorsed in 1945 by Article 2(7) of the Charter of the United Nations, excluding foreign intervention "in matters which are essentially within the domestic jurisdiction of any State".

That Charter also endorsed the principle of the 1928 Kellogg-Briand Pact—formally "General Treaty for Renunciation of War as an Instrument of National Policy", by its Article 2(4) stating:

> All Members shall refrain in their international relations from the threat or use of force against the territorial integrity or political independence of any State, or in any manner inconsistent with the purposes of the United Nations.

[4] Sunstein (2007), p. 503.

[5] "Environmental Dispute Resolution and Small States: a Story about a Frog" in Petra Butler (ed) *Environmental Dispute Resolution and Small States* (forthcoming).

The purpose of these measures was to abolish the historic right of a nation State to resort to war as a means of achieving policy objectives save in self-defence (Article 51) or with the authority of Security Council resolution (Chapter VII).[6] The policy change was endorsed on 17 July 2018 by ratification of aggression as a crime under the Rome Statute against international law.

That there is overwhelming need for a further Convention responding to the dire current threat presented by global warming is coupled with the acute problem of achieving it, revealing a parallel need to begin by demystifying international law.

Unhappily both reforms, by the Westphalia Treaties and the UN Charter, required not only logic and common sense but gross evidence of sustained and unacceptable physical disaster. So it seems that to deal with ecological disaster we need to satisfy a third element—a motivation for immediate action.

Robert Louis Stevenson's *Kidnapped* recounts Davie Balfour's revelation, by flash of lightning, that the unlit stone stairway to a tower from which his uncle Ebenezer had asked him to retrieve important papers, ended in an abyss five stories below.[7] We have had such revelation about global warming. Another, on loss of biodiversity, emerged on 6 May 2019. Yet our generation, where lies are too often given the same standing as truth and international law, has yawned. Only such horrors as the body of the child Alan Kurdi on the Turkish beach seem to enliven us, but then only for a while.

It would be agreeable if this Yearbook could help activate the Stevensons of our time. It recognizes the importance of Nigeria to international law. By 2050 that State[8] will become the third most populous nation in the world.[9] As at 31 October 2018, according to UNHCR reports, there were 2,421,372 Nigerian internally displaced persons in the Lake Chad Basin.[10] Of 101,404 Nigerian refugees in Cameroon, 99,489 are in the Far North region, displaced by the Boko Haram armed insurgency[11] with its transnational terrorist agenda, targets and links.[12] A local newspaper advises that "Nigeria has been listed among countries most at risk as global warming brings more high temperatures, necessitating the need to keep people cool and preserve food and medicine."[13] The potential of current trends on Nigeria's expected 380m individual lives is daunting; let alone the rest of the world and its other inhabitants, creatures and resources.

---

[6]Hathaway and Shapiro (2017).

[7]Chapter 4 "I run a great danger in the House of Shaws" https://www.gutenberg.org/files/421/421-h/421-h.htm#link2HCH0004.

[8]With a 2017 population of 190 886,000 https://esa.un.org/unpd/wpp/publications/files/wpp2017_keyfindings.pdf.

[9]With an added 189m https://allafrica.com/stories/201805170218.html.

[10]https://data2.unhcr.org/en/situations/nigeriasituation.

[11]*ibid.*

[12]Onapajo et al. (2012), pp. 337–357.

[13]This Day Nigeria: Global Warming - Nigeria Among Countries At Risk As Temperature Soars. I leave comment on Nigerian politics or media to others; my references to such topics concern States in other Continents.

Globally, human displacement has reached a record level—68,5m persons.[14] The figure is contributed to and sustained by many causes. They begin with failure of international decision-makers to:

> . . . reaffirm faith in fundamental human rights, in the dignity and worth of the human person

as the Charter of the United Nations requires. Hence:

- resumption of self-interest and trends to nationalism;
- continued failure, deplored in the 2017 Yearbook,[15] to achieve an international crime and accompanying systems to respond to terrorism:
- resulting failure to achieve the potential available from settled public confidence and stability.

Today all are coupled with and accentuated by the most subtle and immense phenomenon and threat, of global warming with consequences. They were summed up in the front page headline of *Le Monde*[16] in bold capitals, the white words of the second line emphasized by red background:

> COMMENT
>
> LE CHAOS CLIMATIQUE
>
> VA AFFECTER NOS VIES

The four pages of articles and analysis were headed:

Des catastrophes climatiques en cascade
Décès, pénuries, migrations: la vie humaine touchée dans sa totalité
« En réalité, nous sommes tous climatosceptiques »
Les 467 impacts du changement climatique

The headlined conclusions do not require translation. A note records:

> The majority of human loss will take place in developing States. Developed States will suffer more from economic damage.[17]

The text focuses on a disquieting study published in ***Nature Climate Change*** on 19 November 2018. The study's originality is to bring together evidence of events which have been treated as disparate. There are reports on ten categories of climate change, among them warming, flooding, drought, heat waves, fires, rising sea levels, bearing on six crucial aspects of human life—health, food, water, the economy, infrastructures, and security. It reports that in a globalized world all States are too

---

[14]https://www.unhcr.org/figures-at-a-glance.htm.

[15]"Responding to Terrorism: Definition and Other Actions" *Nigerian Yearbook of International Law 2017* 17.

[16]*Le Monde* 21 November 2018, p. 10 "Nature Climate Change" Monday 19 November 2018; www.nature.com – climate.

[17]«La majorité des pertes humaines auraient lieu dans les pays en développement, les états développés pâtiront davantage de dégats économiques.»

interconnected and interdependent to be able to isolate themselves and limit the effects of climate change. The essays link 780 events of deaths from heat-waves between 1980 and 2014, 3000 drownings in China in 1998, 800,000 famine deaths from drought in Ethiopia in the 1980s, traumas from high winds and asphyxiations from fires, Hurricane Katrina in the USA in 2005, flooding in the UK in 2007, heatwave in France in 2003 and in Australia depression and suicides of farmers during the worst drought in its history.

It brings to mind two classical sources from Nigeria's major religions:

- the Old Testament's vision in Revelation 6:8 of the four horsemen of the apocalypse—pestilence, war, famine, and their consequence death, with its description

  And I looked, and behold a pale horse: and his name that sat on him was Death, and Hell followed with him. And power was given unto them over the fourth part of the earth, to kill with sword, and with hunger, and with death, and with the beasts of the earth

  And the kings of the earth, and the great men, and the rich men, and the chief captains, and the mighty men, and every bondman, and every free man, hid themselves in the dens and in the rocks of the mountains;

  For the great day of his wrath is come; and who shall be able to stand?

- the Qur'an's messages of reconciliation—with newly converted enemies, among believers, between denominations, of claimants under a will, between spouses, following divorce , between brothers, by way of forgiveness following an injury, by way of philanthropy and among mankind.[18]

The nuclear threat of my lifetime to humanity and other life has been joined by chemical and cyber weapons as well as the more insidious and potentially more fatal risk of global warming bringing famine, pestilence, war and death. To avoid apocalypse from each of these, and now loss of biodiversity as well, we need reconciliation. What will be the view from 2050? What can the law do about it?

The strength, persistence and propensity for evil of the four horsemen in their various guises is evidenced by the record level of forcibly displaced persons.

Where to begin? I think we lawyers should start by seeking guidance from other members of the community. To consider what the law can and should do about global warming requires us first to clarify the basics, starting with—what is law?

In the absence of a divine lawmaker stating obligations on tablets of stone there can be no single definitive definition. My preference is for what an informed member of the relevant community would regard as law. Such approach leaves obvious room for different of informed opinion. That is especially so in relation to international law which too often has been regarded as something arcane for scholars and specialists.

[18] *The Noble Qur'an* https://quran.com/search?q=reconcile 4/49, 7/49, 10/4919/49, 25/49, 27/49, 32/49, 34/49, 35/49, 39/49, 43/49, 47/49.

The need to demystify international law is indisputable, observed by the celebrated Finnish jurist Martti Koskenniemi[19]:

> I think international law has a wonderful political and intellectual potential (this is why I am interested in its history) but that it has become in the 20th century become – *malgré soi* – a small bureaucratic discipline at law schools. My project is to try to revive a sense of its original mission, its importance. I suspect I am creating a myth (for it probably never was much better) – but myth-creation is an important aspect of political activity and activism.

Whether or not the suggested answer to the need does justice to the breadth and depth of Professor Koskenniemi's thinking about international law, which is based on both deep scholarship and long practical experience in international law and politics, it suggests that international law is something of a (possibly mythical) concept which, currently trapped in an arcane environment, requires restoration of past glory.

To find a simpler approach to demystifying international law one may start with the basics of the less complex sphere of domestic law.

Donald Harris, following HLA Hart and Jeremy Bentham, has shown that a legal concept is not a *Ding an sich*, standing independent of legal rules but is the expression of their result and indeed synonymous with them.[20] That is why in the English common law of contract, after two centuries, the harsh rule in *Stilk v Myrick* (1809) 2 Camp. 317 that an agreed variation of a contract is unenforceable without new consideration has been accepted by the UK Supreme Court as "probably ripe for re-examination": *Rock Advertising Limited v MWB Business Exchange Centres Limited* (2018).[21] The informed member of that relevant community knows that the law lies in or about the range of the old rule and abandonment of the need for consideration where the mark of intention to form legal relations has been made in relation to the original contract and there are no policy reasons to the contrary.[22] The potential for improvement by even significant change is inherent in the oath of many common law judges:

> . . . to do right to all manner of people.

albeit

> . . . after the laws and usages of this Realm[23]

Respect for past wisdom and stability is the starting point; but ultimately injustice must be avoided, whether by legislature or by judges, having been identified in accordance with contemporary standards.

---

[19]Cited by Professor Jouannet of the Sorbonne in an introduction to Koskienniemi's selected essays *The Politics of International Law* (2011): A Critical Introduction (Hart Publishing Oxford and Portland), p. 1.

[20]"The Concept of Possession in English law" in *Oxford Essays in Jurisprudence* (1961), pp. 69–70.

[21][2018] UKSC 24, [2018] 2 WLR 1603 at [18] per Lord Sumption.

[22]See Coote (2004), p. 19.

[23]S4 Promissory Oaths Act 1868 (UK), adopted widely by other jurisdictions.

As to international law, reprinting in 1924 what had been written for the third edition in 1890, William Edward Hall's preface to his *Treatise on International Law*[24] considered that:

> Looking back over the last couple of centuries we see International Law at the close of each fifty years in a more solid position than that which it occupied at the beginning of the period . . . it has more and more dared to grapple in detail with the fundamental facts in the relations of states.

Read in retrospect, the continuing optimism of each of these predictions, containing much wisdom, was tragically followed and grossly overwhelmed, in both 1914 and 1939 by the then greatest human-made calamities of history.

A new edition of *Hall* could look back with satisfaction at the recent assessment of the Court of Appeal of England and Wales, not contested by the decision of the UK Supreme Court on appeal:

> 115 . . . a fundamental change has occurred within public international law. The traditional view of public international law as a system of law merely regulating the conduct of states among themselves on the international plane has long been discarded. In its place has emerged a system which includes the regulation of human rights by international law, a system of which individuals are rightly considered to be subjects.
>
> *Belhaj v Straw* Court of Appeal of England and Wales (2014)[25]

But current threats, global warming at their head, mean that international law cannot be limited to lawyers. On the contrary, the vast need for its practical operation across disciplines and State borders, as in the operation of Conventions affecting international aviation, against slavery, ozone depletion, enforcement of arbitral awards and certain forms of criminality, is intensely practical and requires broad understanding and rigorous application by all concerned with particular activities.

As elsewhere in law, difficulty arises from attempts to over-refine it and make dogmatic statements about what it is and what it can achieve. Attempts to box law into labelled categories—such as the so-called "schools" of jurisprudence—"Realism", "Critical Legal Studies" and the rest—misuse helpful groupings of certain ideas by treating them as definitive and exclusive. International law is a broad and valuable idea embracing an unlimited range of variants. These range from what Article 53 of the Vienna Convention on the Law of Treaties terms "a peremptory norm of international law ", including such clearly defined pieces of law as the international crime defined by the Convention against Torture and Other Cruel, Inhuman or Degrading Treatment or Punishment (1987) and its interpretation by the International Court of Justice in *Belgium v Senegal* I.C.J. Reports 2012, p. 422, through a continuum of hard and soft law defined by treaties, customary State usage, judicial decisions and other means, some described in Article 38(1) of the Statute of the International Court of Justice.

---

[24](Eighth edition ed A Pearce Higgins Oxford), p. xxv.

[25][2014] EWCA Civ 1394, [2015] 2 WLR 1105, appeal dismissed [2017] UKSC 3, [2017] 2 WLR 456.

Very different aspects can be emphasised by masters of international law, depending on context; from a brute reality expressed by the distinguished international jurist Antonio Cassese:

> . . . at the international level . . . there is no judicial system . . .[26]

to the vision of its potential described by Justice Christopher Greenwood of the International Court of Justice:

> International law is not just a series of fragmented specialist and self-contained bodies of law, each of which functions in isolation from the others; it is a single, unified system of law[27]

For a judge charged with adjudicating competing claims at international law there are frequently powerful arguments on both (or all) sides of a case. The UK Supreme Court has recently stated

> To identify a rule of customary international law, it is necessary to establish that there is a widespread, representative and consistent practice of states on the point in question, which is accepted by them on the footing that it is a legal obligation (*opinio juris*) . . .[28]

The principle that international law is made by States is powerful and provides the first three quarters of Article 38(1) of the Statute of the International Court of Justice:

> 1. The Court, whose function is to decide in accordance with international law such disputes as are submitted to it, shall apply:
>
>   a. international conventions, whether general or particular, establishing rules expressly recognized by the contesting states;
>   b. international custom, as evidence of a general practice accepted as law;
>   c. the general principles of law recognized by civilized nations;

But Article 38(1) also recognizes

> d. . . . judicial decisions and the teachings of the most highly qualified publicists of the various nations, as subsidiary means for the determination of rules of law.
>
> . . .

While a court may not decline to adjudicate, the issue before it may be one not covered by any of these criteria. It must then be evaluated according to the justice of the case which may include analogy from existing principle or even devising a novel approach which, if accepted, may later itself be evidence of custom or general principle as well as a useful "judicial decision [. . .]".

---

[26] *Decision on Appeal of Pre-Trial Judge's Order regarding Jurisdiction and Standing* STL Casebook 2009–2010 139 at para 41.

[27] *Ahmadou Sadio Diallo (Republic of Guinea v Democratic Republic of the Congo) (Compensation owed by the Democratic Republic of the Congo to the Republic of Guinea)* ICJ Judgment 19 June 2012, Declaration of Judge Greenwood para 8, cited by Sir Michael Wood Special Rapporteur *First Report on formation and evidence of customary international law* International Law Commission 17 May 2013 A/CN.4/663 at para 19.

[28] See *Benkharbouche v Secretary of State for the Foreign and Commonwealth Office* [2017] UKSC 62, [2017] 3 WLR 957 para 32 at para 31.

International law is a human construct, always open to clarification and indeed correction. The ever-increasing need to grapple in detail with the fundamental problems in the relations of states[29] has been met by wise use of the powers and principles of the Charter of the United Nations, the Human Rights conventions that followed, successive resolutions of the Security Council and the General Assembly, as well as numerous multilateral treaties. There have been courageous contributions by peace-keepers within the military and outside, and imaginative decisions by many others including parties, counsel and judges of many courts and tribunals.

Yet as well as performing invaluable service on many fronts, international law has displayed a strange preparedness to put up with unresolved illogic in its basics and failed to plan in order to identify its potential. For example, whereas the final UK appellate judges sitting in the Judicial Committee of the Privy Council have presumed that domestic law of Commonwealth States must conform to international law,[30] sitting in the UK Supreme Court[31] they considered that the UK is under no such obligation.

The development of English as *lingua franca,* internet publication, and judges' increased recognition that they must write intelligibly for general readers, should remind both writer and reader that the tale of the Emperor's clothes is about requiring from decision-makers sustained practical commonsense.

The Preamble to the Charter of the United Nations, responding to the horrors of two World Wars, and succeeding human rights treaties, signaled change expressed to:

> . . . reaffirm faith in fundamental human rights, in the dignity and worth of the human person

Martti Koskenniemi challenges "idealism" as:

> open to a familiar objection: There has been no theory of values or needs which would have commanded a significant degree of consensus. Any view on them seems to encapsulate controversial political ideas. If the possibility of verifying needs and values by reference to what goes on in society is excluded (and this was the argument's starting point) how can they at all be verified?[32]

More simply, Bentham had rejected "natural rights" as "nonsense upon stilts".

---

[29]A recent example is *The Law Debenture Trust Corporation P.L.C. v Ukraine* [2017] EWHC 655 (Comm), [2017] QB 1247 where at first instance Blair J applied the principle:

> 308 ix) Some matters are . . . better addressed at the international level, rather than in domestic courts. In civil as well as common law, it appears unsurprising under present conditions that domestic courts should treat acts of government consisting of an act of war or of alleged self-defence at the international level as no-justiciable and should refrain from adjudicating upon them.

but the decision was reversed by the Court of Appeal: [2018] EWCA Civ 2026, [2019] 2 WLR 655.

[30]*Boyce v R (Barbados)* [2005] AC 400, [2004] UKPC 32.

[31]*R (Wang Yam) v Central Criminal Court* [2016] AC 771, [2015] UKSC 76.

[32]Martti Koskenniemi (2005), p. 216.

But Bentham's famous phrase must be read against his competing observation:

> ... The legislator, who cannot pass judgment in particular cases, will give directions to the Tribunal in the form of general rules, and leave them with a certain amount of latitude in order that they may adjust their decision to the special circumstances.[33]

The history of the common law is of creation of principles, often devised by legislators but also devised and developed by judges, expressed in general terms which are construed and applied to the facts of particular cases. There the absence of agreement at high levels of specificity, often found in dissenting judgments of appellate courts, does not carry with it a demolition of legal principle.

Civil lawyers may be less enthusiastic than common lawyers about judge made law. But where the global community has endorsed common principles, as by the Charter, it is the responsibility of all those charged with their administration to construe and give effect to them—even (and indeed particularly) when expressed generally. That is what judges are employed and paid to do.

It was in order:

> To maintain international peace and security[34]

and like values including:

> to bring about by peaceful means, and in conformity with the principles of peace and international law, adjustment or settlement of international disputes or situations which might lead to a breach of the peace[35]

> ... promoting and encouraging respect for human rights and for fundamental freedoms for a, without distinction ...[36]

that by the Charter States Members of the United Nations gave the great institution of the Security Council responsibility, by way of legal duty,[37] to exercise:

> ... primary responsibility for the maintenance of international peace and security,[38]

---

[33]In his *Theory of Legislation* (Etienne Dumont edition translated and edited by CM Atkinson, 1914) at 62.

[34]Article 24.

[35]Article 1(1).

[36]Article 1(3).

[37]"FUNCTIONS and POWERS
Article 24

1. In order to ensure prompt and effective action by the United Nations, its Members confer on the Security Council primary responsibility for the maintenance of international peace and security, and agree that in carrying out its duties under this responsibility the Security Council acts on their behalf.
2. In discharging these duties the Security Council shall act in accordance with the Purposes and Principles of the United Nations. The specific powers granted to the Security Council for the discharge of these duties are laid down in Chapters VI, VII [containing Articles 39-42], VIII, and XII."

[38]Article 24.

and power to:

> . . . determine the existence of any threat to the peace . . . and . . . decide what measures shall be taken in accordance with Articles 41 and 42, to maintain or restore international peace and security[39]

Such Articles empower the Council to:

> . . . decide what measures not involving the use of armed force are to be employed to give effect to its decisions, and . . . call upon the Members of the United Nations to apply such measures;[40]

Alternatively, should it:

> . . . consider that [such measures] would be inadequate . . . it may take such action by air, sea, or land forces as may be necessary to maintain or restore international peace and security . . .[41]

Yet despite the concurrent creation of the International Court of Justice as sibling of both Security Council and General Assembly, and the firm and informed advice of the former President of the ICJ the Rt Hon Baroness Rosalyn Higgins QC:

> The Court has . . . emphasiz[ed] . . .that a UN organ needed legal advice in order to know how to conduct its business. . .[42]

> the greatest role for Advisory Opinions is where there are uncertainties about the institutional arrangements within the UN. . .[43]

> If organs are reluctant to seek advice on the development of their own competencies, except when forced to do so by the behaviour of occasional recalcitrant states, the Court's role as the supreme ín-house counsel' to the UN will remain limited[44]

the Council has never invited the Court to spell out the nature of the legal "duties" of the Council twice appearing in Article 24.[45]

3 The Capacity of Law

Grave moral offence properly triggers calls for better criminal law. Certainly as well as good law there are other means that can help avoid the commission of crime.

---

[39]Article 39.

[40]Article 41.

[41]Article 42.

[42]"A Comment on the Current Health of Advisory Opinions" in Higgins (2009), pp. 1043, 1047.

[43]At p. 1050.

[44]At p. 1052.

[45]N 38 above.

A powerful *LSE-Oxford Commission on State Fragility, Growth and Development*[46] has reported[47] that cutting extreme poverty in half is one of the greatest achievements of the last three decades. The UN Sustainable Development Goals set the mission to eradicate extreme poverty by 2030. Yet nearly a third of the way towards that deadline, almost 900 million people are still living on less than two dollars a day. And in many of the world's poorest countries progress is completely stuck.

Many of them are "fragile states" blighted by conflict and corruption, their governments lacking the legitimacy and capacity to deliver the jobs, public services and opportunities their people need. By 2030 half of the world's poor will live in such states.

The LSE-Oxford Commission describes the characteristics of fragility, its wider consequences, and a recommended new approach to state fragility and international aid.

The Report is valuable in identifying the characteristics of fragility, including the lack of basic security, inadequate government capacity, the absence of a properly functioning private sector, and the presence of divided societies. It also looks at the wider consequences. State fragility does not just condemn people to poverty; it impacts upon the world, driving mass migration, providing safe havens for piracy and trafficking, and enabling terrorist training camps to thrive. The Report concludes that what works is:

1. Realism, not idealism
2. Local, not international priorities
3. Reconciliation first, not elections first
4. Working with governments not around governments
5. Institution building and nation building

(numbering added)

But because the law touches on all of them these lessons warrant consideration when one moves to the specificity required for effective law reform.

As to the first, law must be both practical and visionary. Criminal law must be focused on those who may and do commit crime. But regard must also be had to reconciliation.[48] Both are recognized by standard sentencing criteria.

The second rightly emphasizes the importance of locality. But the law must also serve an increasingly globalized world.

The third is useful, viewed locally. But reconciliation is also the ultimate end goal for both domestic and international law.

---

[46]A research centre established under the auspices of the International Growth Centre based at the London School of Economics operated in partnership with the Blavatnik School of Government at the University of Oxford.

[47]*Escaping the fragility trap* https://www.theigc.org/publication/escaping-fragility-trap/ published on 18 April 2018.

[48]Baragwanath (2019).

The fourth rightly emphasizes the importance of local and State governments. International governance also matters. These are the subject of public and international law.

The fifth includes the aspect of public confidence in institutions, including the wide sphere of the legal system, which plays into enthusiasm to participate in society or the rejection of it that breeds crime.

4 The status quo

Much has been done locally and internationally to create and administer law that will help reduce the fragilities described by the LSE-Oxford Commission. Antisocial conduct has always been a concern of every community. Domestic and international law, its administration and enforcement, includes vast tracts of jurisprudence designed to promote and retain the rule of law.

So The Hague, the City of Peace and Justice, has judges of three tiers of the Dutch legal system with the vision to deliver the *Urgenda* decisions[49] ordering reduction of the contribution to global warming, within its power, of the Government of the Netherlands which also contributes so notably to the work of the international courts and tribunals.

Internationally, little imagination is needed to visualize the disaster of a world bereft of the United Nations and its Charter's prohibition of use of force beyond self-defence and discharge of the duty of the Security Council to protect international peace and security.

But to avoid apocalypse requires more of the law, and fast. I have recently written[50] elsewhere about the consequences of what until May 2019 has been seen as the biggest and most urgent problem, of global warming. *Le Monde*[51] has summarized some of what needs to be said about global warming, its threat, and the inexcusable "climatoscepticism" that substitutes unthinking inertia for the combined focused activity needed to avoid disaster for the planet in various forms of famine, pestilence, war and death. There came into effect on 1 January 2019 the Kigali Amendment under the Montreal Protocol which will drastically reduce hydrofluorocarbons,[52] already the subject of unanimous agreement by 197 States to ban the gases damaging the Earth's ozone layer.[53]

Other initiatives include:

---

[49] Of 24 June 2015, 9 October 2018 and 20 December 2019: urgenda.nl

[50] N 5 above.

[51] N 16 above.

[52] https://www.theguardian.com/environment/2018/oct/08/kigali-amendment-little-noticed-treaty-could-help-delay-climate-catastrophe.

[53] https://www.theguardian.com/environment/2019/jan/20/how-to-stop-the-climate-crisis-six-lessons-from-the-campaign-that-saved-the-ozone.

- in the United Kingdom, mandatory orders against the Government to secure compliance in certain zones with the limits for nitrogen dioxide levels set by European law;[54]
- in the USA, "the great case"[55] of *Masschusetts v Environment Protection Agency* (2007)[56] holding that the EPA powers under the Clean Air Act extend to greenhouse emissions including CO2 from motor vehicle;
- in the European Court of Justice,[57] acceptance on 13 August 2018 of a claim against the EU for "climatic inaction";[58]
- in Canada, an order by the Federal Court of Appeal on 30 August 2018 quashing an Order in Council approving proposed expansion of the Trans Mountain pipeline system for transporting diluted bitumen from Alberta to British Columbia;[59]
- in the International Law Commission, a programme which includes protection of the atmosphere;[60]
- in the Security Council, on 27 March 2018 unanimous adoption of Resolution 2408(2018) explicitly underlining

  General Assembly resolution 63/281 of June 3, 2009, which reaffirms that the United Nations Framework Convention on Climate Change is the key instrument for addressing climate change . . ."

  and concluding:

> in matters relating to the maintenance of international peace and security under its consideration, conflict analysis and contextual information on, inter alia, possible security implications of climate change is important, when such issues are drivers of conflict, represent a challenge to the implementation of Council mandates or endanger the process of consolidation of peace. In this regard, the Council requests the Secretary-General to ensure that his reporting to the Council contains such contextual information.[61]

There are other major threats, among them nuclear, chemical, and cyber.

The pressing urgency of the rapidly approaching climate requires each of us with legal competence to do all in our power to:

---

[54]*R(Client Earth) (No3)* [2018] EWHC 315 (Admin), cited by Lord Carnwath "Climate Justice and the Global Pact" 26 February 2018, p. 7 https://www.supremecourt.uk/docs/speech-180226.pdf.

The proposal brings to mind the "bussing schedules" devised by US courts to give effect to *Brown v Board of Education of Topeka* 347 US 483 (1954).

[55]Lord Carnwath *Human Rights and the Environment* https://www.supremecourt.uk/docs/speech-181010.pdf at p. 11.

[56]*Massachusetts v EPA* 549 US 497 (2007).

[57]*Le Monde* 16 August 2018, p. 5.

[58]http://www.lse.ac.uk/GranthamInstitute/news/first-ever-eu-climate-court-invokes-human-rights/.

[59]*Tsleil-Waututh Nation v. Canada (Attorney General)* [2018] FCA 153.

[60]http://legal.un.org/docs/?path=../ilc/reports/2018/english/a_73_10_advance.pdf&lang=E, pp. 157 ff.

[61]https://undocs.org/S/PRST/2011/15.

- educate ourselves and others as to what the law can do about that and other threats;
- get on with doing what is in our power to engage both the law and ourselves to do what can be done—**now**.

5 The Global Loss of Biodiversity, Reported on 6 May 2019

Since the foregoing was prepared, *Le Monde* on 7 May 2019 headlined a topic as grave as and complementary to global warming:[62]

UN MILLION D'ESPÈCES MENACÉES DE DISPARITION
« IL N'EST PAS TROP TARD POUR AGIR »

Its leader concerned «BIODIVERSITÉ : L'HUMANITÉ FACE A SES RESPONSIBILITÉS »

It concerned the previous day's global assessment report of the Intergovernmental Science-Policy Platform on Biodiversity and Ecosystem Services. A Guardian essay by the chairman of the management committee, Sir Robert Watson,[63] was headed:

> **Loss of biodiversity is just as catastrophic as climate change.** Nature is being eroded at rates unprecedented in human history but we still have time to stave off mass extinction.

It recounted:

> Environmentalists, scientists and indigenous people have been sounding the alarm for decades. Our understanding of the overexploitation of the planet has advanced with grim, sharp clarity over that time.
>
> We have entered an era of rapidly accelerating species extinction, and are facing the irreversible loss of plant and animal species, habitats and vital crops, while coming face to face with the horrific impacts of global climate change.
>
> ...
>
> Despite the profound threat of biodiversity loss, it is climate change that has long been considered the most pressing environmental concern. That changed this week in Paris, when representatives from 130 nations approved the most comprehensive assessment of global diversity ever undertaken.
>
> The report, spearheaded by the Intergovernmental Science-Policy Platform on Biodiversity and Ecosystem Services (IPBES), found that nature is being eroded at rates unprecedented in human history.
>
> One million species are currently threatened with extinction and we are undermining the entire natural infrastructure on which our modern world depends. ... our economies, livelihoods, food security, health and quality of life worldwide are under threat. We are exploiting nature faster than it can replenish itself.

[62] N 16 above.

[63] 6 May 2019.

The IPBES assessment has shown the strong interrelationship between climate change, the loss of biodiversity and human well-being. Climate change has been identified as a primary driver of biodiversity los, already altering every part of nature. Likewise, the loss of biodiversity contributes to climate change, for example when we destroy forests we emit carbon dioxide, the major "human-produced" greenhouse gas.

We cannot solve the threats of human-induced climate change and loss of biodiversity in isolation. We either solve both or we solve nothing.

6 The Relationship Among Global Warming, Loss of Biodiversity and Terrorism

There is an increasing literature which argues that climate change is a significant contributor to terrorism.[64] It includes the prediction of Stephan Lewandowsky, et al.[65] that the inevitable mass migrations that will come from unmitigated climate change will rarely be resolved in a conflict-free manner.

I cannot offer any personal view on events in Nigeria. Others must assess whether there is merit in an article in *Peace Review: A Journal of Social Justice*[66] in which the authors claim that climate change has induced terrorism and internal conflict in most African countries, including Nigeria.

7 What Should International Law Be Doing?

Resort to grave crime such as terrorism may occur for many reasons. But it can hardly be doubted that, internationally, as Aribigbola, et al. contend, families must often migrate to find food or employment, which creates ethnic tension, overpopulation, food scarcity, and artificial increases in the cost of living. Hunger and frustration can lead to aggression and unrest in the society, and when there are no jobs at home for the youth, they may turn to crime to obtain what is needed for their families. Such desperation is likely to accentuate incentives to undertake militancy and terrorism.

The incentives for such crime can only be bolstered by the combination of global warming and loss of biodiversity.

It follows that the law must respond with even greater urgently, and across the full spectrum of options, to incentives to terrorism. The arguments of the 2017 paper to that effect are given greater emphasis by the revelations as to global warming and loss of biodiversity.

---

[64]See the essays collected by Natalie Lye in her May 2017 thesis *Climate Change as a Contributor to Terrorism: a Case Study in Nigeria and Pakistan* https://scholarcommons.sc.edu/cgi/viewcontent.cgi?article=1182&context=senior_theses, pp. 11–16.

[65]Lewandowsky et al. (2013), pp. 487–501.

[66]Aribigbola et al. (2013), pp. 518–525.

- The lead should come from leaders of each State and from the Security Council, the former responsible to protect its citizens; the latter with its "primary responsibility for the maintenance of international peace and security" conferred upon it by Member States "[i]n order to ensure prompt and effective action by the United Nations".[67]
- In the event of veto the General Assembly can pass its own Resolutions and secure advice from the International Court of Justice as to the requirements of international law.

Those of us with access to the tools of international law must exert ourselves to visualize how it can do better. The resources of the Peace Palace Library and its librarians; of the scholars, practitioners and judges of The Hague; and of the wider community with its immense range of important knowledge, need to be brought together systematically for this purpose.[68]

References

Aribigbola A et al (2013) Climate change and insecurity are like a chain reaction. Peace Rev 25 (4):518–525. https://doi.org/10.1080/10402659.2013.846169

Coote B (2004) Consideration and variations: a different solution. LQR 120:19

Gray J (2007) Black mass: apocalyptic religion and the death of Utopia. Allen Lane, p 107

Hathaway OA, Shapiro SJ (2017) The internationalists and their plan to outlaw war. Allen Lane

Higgins R (2009) Themes and theories, vol 2. Oxford, pp 1043, 1047

Baragwanath D (2019) 'Reconciliation' as a philosophical foundational concept in international criminal law. In: Bergsmo M, Buis EJ, Song T (eds). Philosophical foundations of international criminal law: legally protected interests. Torkel Opsahl Academic EPublisher, Brussels (forthcoming).

Koskenniemi M (2005) From apology to Utopia the structure of international law arguments. Cambridge, p 216

Lewandowsky S et al (2013) Misinformation, disinformation, and violent conflict. Am Psychol 68 (7):487–501. https://doi.org/10.1037/a003451

Onapajo H, Uzodike UO, Whetho A (2012) Boko Haram terrorism in Nigeria: the international dimension. S Afr J Int Aff 19:337–357

Sunstein C (2007) On the divergent American reactions to terrorism and climate change. Columbia Law Rev 107:503

David Baragwanath is a Judge of the Appeals Chamber of the Special Tribunal for Lebanon and former President of the Special Tribunal for Lebanon, Leidschendam, The Netherlands.

[67]N38 above.

[68]In an essay "Exploration of Other International For a for Legitimacy and Enforceability" published in *Dispute Resolution and Climate Change: The Paris Agreement and Beyond* (International Chamber of Commerce 2017 ed Wendy Miles) 103–110 I set out some options.

The Rule of International Law: Where Are We Going?

Howard Morrison

When I became a barrister in the UK in 1977, after military service and working in international development in Africa, I had no idea where the law was going to lead me. I started practising criminal, civil and family law with excursions into courts martial defence, employment law and construction law, indeed anything to make a living in a highly competitive legal environment.

After working in the UK and then Fiji and the Caribbean [those are stories in themselves] I started doing defence work at both the UN International Criminal Tribunals for the Former Yugoslavia and Rwanda based in The Hague and Tanzania respectively. That was my real initiation into international criminal and humanitarian law and, of course, international human rights. That led in turn to being a Judge in the UK and the Sovereign Base Areas of Cyprus and then briefly at the Special Tribunal for the Lebanon and then the ICTY as a trial judge in the case of Radovan Karadzic and other trial and appellate cases, and latterly and currently, the International Criminal Court where I am now in the Appeals Division.

I had always been a very strong supporter of the ICC having attended some of the preparatory commissions of what was to become the Rome Statute in my private capacity as a practising QC in order to lobby for the defence to be an organic part of the court structure. It had not been so in the early days of the Yugoslav and Rwanda

I start by emphasising that the views I express are mine alone from the standpoint of a concerned jurist and an observant senior citizen. I do not suggest that my views are necessarily those of any other judge or judges of the International Criminal Court nor that they represent any aspect of official policy for or of the ICC. I am not setting out to make any form of political statement. That is not for a judge to do. The hard reality is that throughout all aspects of international law, politics and both conflict and peace are intertwined. It is impossible to deal with one without illustrating another.

H. Morrison (✉)
International Criminal Court, The Hague, The Netherlands
e-mail: howard.morrison@icc-cpi.int

C. Eboe-Osuji et al. (eds.), *Nigerian Yearbook of International Law 2018/2019*,
Nigerian Yearbook of International Law 2018/2019,
https://doi.org/10.1007/978-3-030-69594-1_3

tribunals and that had made for significant difficulties for the defence. They were resolved by forward thinking individuals.

I mention all this simply to illustrate how I personally became so acutely aware of what is in fact self-evident, that international criminal and humanitarian law and the maintenance of the rule of law at both domestic and international levels are absolutely crucial to the building, and furtherance, of peaceful societies and the reduction of corruption at all levels. Moreover, that peace through the rule of law must be recognized as an essential goal for lawyers and judges as part of the fabric of domestic and international society. The rule of law is fragile and requires constant nurturing and care. When it breaks down it usually does so rapidly and with serious consequences. I am not just talking about, for instance, small failing states. Look what happened to civil society in New Orleans after Hurricane Katrina. Robbery, looting, rape and other violence exploded and there were reports of the police abandoning their duties and even committing criminal acts. There are a host of other examples, past and present. Perhaps Syria is the saddest and most potent that we currently have to face.

We all should now be more aware than ever of the problems we face and the unacceptable consequences of not finding solutions. It is certain that we cannot sit back and say that these are problems for the next generation. They are very much our problems, here and now. We need to be aware and active and determined. And we need to be finding solutions now. Some of the truths are uncomfortable.

It is fortunate that, as a species, humans generally have an innate sense of what is fair. That is apparent from a very early age. Walk past any elementary school playground and listen to children at play. Sooner or later some aggrieved participant in a game or joint activity will complain of behaviour and the complaining cry will go up "that's not fair".

Organised sport, a very human activity and one in which we participate unlike other living species, is predicated upon fairness ranging from formalised rules and referees to a ban of drugs giving offending athletes an unfair advantage. Breaches generate sanctions from individual red cards to the banning of offending teams of even nations. Fairness is thus ingrained in our collective and individual psyche. That, for me at least, is the basis of the rule of law.

The world faces a plethora of challenges to any maintained order or fairness amongst nations. Let me outline some, but only some, of those I consider as being the most urgent.

There have been wars ever since man became societal. Historically we have seen territorial wars, dynastic wars, political and theological wars and wars of simple aggression. We still see them worldwide today. Warfare is widespread and the technology of weaponry advances at an alarming rate. My fear is that the list of causation or excuse to wage war is going to expand.

There are, at the very least, two global factors that will generate further conflicts. The first is a rapidly expanding world population and the second, and very closely connected, is climate change and associated environmental damage.

It is estimated that by the year 2050 the global human population will have expanded from the present 7 plus billion to 10 billion. It went from less than 5 billion to our current number since 1975. That means that, in each decade from now to 2050, something approaching the current population of China will have to be absorbed into the global society.

Uncontrolled population growth, and I see no obvious signs of organized and rational control being undertaken on any substantial scale anywhere in the world, is bound to lead to huge social problems, domestically and internationally. It is inevitably, through those social and practical pressures and discords, going to generate grave challenges to the rule of law and universal justice and peace. How might these challenges arise?

More people means more pressure on all resources, particularly finite resources such as oil and minerals in general. The greater the number of consumers, the faster non-renewable resources are depleted, the higher the price and the greater the temptation to use political and/or military means to secure supplies.

The larger the population becomes the more desperate people will become for living space, and the larger urban centres will become, increasing pressure for housing, food, water, electricity and other requirements. Add resultant conflict to the equation, which will reduce the possibility of settling or staying in certain areas, and the growing population and emigration pressures expand rapidly. We see it now in north Africa and the desperate flight to Europe and the growth in criminal people traffickers.

Globally increased population means the greater the need for sustainable water supplies for human use and farming. Water wars are no longer just the province of fiction writers. They are likely come about. We already have examples of international tensions when cross border rivers are dammed in upstream territories for hydroelectric production or irrigation reducing the downstream flow.

Oil wars, living space wars, food wars, fishing limit wars. All and more can be the product of unrestrained population growth and will be fertile ground for exploitation by political and religious extremists.

Population growth and pollution in turn generate climate change and environmental damage and disaster. Take just two examples. Rising sea levels permanently flooding low-lying coastal agricultural land, for instance in Bangladesh. Add rising temperatures affecting plant growth cycles and torrential rain washing away fertile soil. More people, less food, less water and less viable food growing and living space. Add blind nationalism and intolerance and bigotry into the algorithm and what do we have?

The stark answer is an obvious recipe for serious social unrest and conflict domestically and internationally, and a very real threat to the rule of law and peace on the widest scale. States will become more inward looking, nationalism and intolerance will spread and, almost inevitably, human rights, both individual and collective, will be early victims of self-interest and isolationism, political and religious extremism and the erosion of liberal democratic systems.

All of this is readily foreseeable and, without timely restraints, more than likely. We see some of it already. I do not need to name the places or worst offenders. We know where they are.

What can we do? Indeed, can anything be done to resolve or counter these potential and, frankly, largely man-made disasters? Well of course many thousands of intelligent and concerned people, scientists, medical professionals, agronomists and engineers amongst others have already started to construct protocols and solutions in the fields of pollutants, energy, food and disease control.

Can we change the social and legal architecture, which of course involves legal order as an essential ingredient, to run in parallel to the climate and resource solutions? I very firmly believe we can but it is going to take brave political, religious, academic and not least legal leaders to galvanise and coordinate resolutions and create fair and sustainable peace preserving social and legal architecture. It is on any analysis a massive task. More than that it is a very urgent one.

How do we start? Well of course many have started already. None of us as individuals can change the world. Take for instance Martin Luther King. He did not set out to change the world or create a perfect one. Indeed, it would probably be impossible to agree upon what a perfect world should look like. Instead Martin Luther King set out to publicise and eradicate institutionalised racism in the United States of America by raising awareness and mobilising those who recognised the evil and wanted to do something about it. So what did he do, how did he start? Well, simply by using his talents to do the very best he could. That is surely the key to successful human endeavour; doing the very best that is possible and, vitally, motivating others to do the same. And that is the answer to my reflective question; how do we start? We start and we continue by doing the very best we can as individuals with the abilities we possess and by perusing or goals with courage and tenacity. Vitally we also motivate and encourage others to do the same, at the very least by example. That brings results both individually and collectively. It empowers those who do not yet have power and it gives duty and direction to those already fortunate enough to have positions of influence in whatever sphere they operate. But it is actions and not aspirations that count.

So now I turn more specifically to the challenges that brings for universal justice and peace in a globalised world. Inevitably, as an international law judge, I look specifically at the role of international law and, in particular, international criminal and humanitarian law and, not least, the International Criminal Court.

Globalisation is a process that has radically changed the way in which States and international institutions interact with one another. Economies are more than ever before interdependent and damage to the environment caused by the activities of one State can have profound effects on others. Technology has made information available to a mass of people who 20 or 30 years ago would have been struggling to find access to it, and it now travels virtually instantly around the globe and via television and the internet to millions if not billions of people. The value of that information is measured by its accuracy and quality. Misleading or dishonest information, more accurately described as propaganda, can be particularly damaging as it is often the first information that arrives concerning a particular issue or event that shapes the views and reactions of the recipient thereafter. It also feeds conspiracy theories that often damage real and effective resolutions.

States, which mostly evolved to consolidate dynastic control and common cultures with degrees of individual and collective wealth, at the same time had to provide basic protections to citizens via some species of social contract. This balance was necessary to maintain social order and political stability. Those same States are now being forced to confront newer and more effective ways to maintain power structures and peace. At the international level, until the twentieth century, international relations operated for the most part in the classic Westphalian scheme. After the establishment of the League of Nations and the dramatic effects of two world wars leading to the creation of the United Nations, structures had to be established to both maintain and institutionalise the classic balance of power amongst States as well as between States and their citizens.

Individual States inevitably seek to maintain national, sovereign and cultural characteristics and ambitions. There is no doubt that globalization presents significant challenges to those existing power structures, and the authority of the state itself. As a result the defects inherent in them become more obvious and the tensions greater. As populations grow and information spreads faster and wider the tensions can only increase. Old structures based upon increasingly archaic power dynamics and Realpolitik feel threatened and insecure. One classic diversion is a military excursion to divert attention from economic failure or corruption within a given system. Often that gives rise to breaches, or at least allegations of breaches, of international law, specifically international humanitarian law and the tensions spread from the domestic to the international scene.

Globalization, although often viewed through the lens of the economist, is actually far more than economic cooperation or control. It embraces the extension of social relationships through the transmission of ideas, meanings and values into what might be termed a 'common consumption' of values more recently fuelled by the internet and relative ease of international travel.

Cultural globalization encompasses the transmission of ideas and values around the world in such a way as to extend and intensify intercultural and international social relations including inter-faith dialogue. In a world marked by savage and apparently irrational religious intolerance and extreme violence, the latter may prove to be of exceptional value and necessity in the maintenance of the rule of law. Religious movements and faiths were amongst the earliest cultural elements to globalize, being spread by evangelism, migration and sometimes the force of military occupation. Christianity, Islam and Buddhism are amongst those faiths which have influenced endemic cultures in places far from their origins. The convergence and interaction between belief systems and law is obvious.

We can see globalization in the movement of musical tastes. Young people especially worldwide find commonality in genres spread far from their roots such as reggae and blues. Cuisine now crosses boundaries more than ever, whether it be a result of migration or travel or publicity. Chinese and Indian restaurants abound worldwide. It is almost as easy to find sushi in Germany as it is in Japan.

The creation and expansion of social relations is thus not observed on solely a material level. It is more than some vague notion of multi-culturalism. It involves sharing norms and knowledge with which peoples associate their individual and collective cultural identities. Of course that may dilute the uniqueness of once isolated communities, but the alienation of individuals from their traditions is likely to be of modest effect compared to the overall impact of modernity itself.

In general globalization tends to reduce the importance of individual nation states. Supranational institutions such as the United Nations, the European Union, the World Trade Organisation, the World Bank the G8 or the International Criminal Court replace or extend national functions to facilitate international agreement.

Increasingly non-governmental organisations influence public opinion and policy across national boundaries including humanitarian aid and development efforts. This extends to the protection of environments especially flora and fauna. Private philanthropy is of increasing moment through charities such as the Bill and Melinda Gates Foundation which contributes, for example, multi-billion dollar commitments to immunizations programmes. Associations such as the Global Philanthropy Forum provide multi-million dollar aid to poorer communities that would otherwise be reliant upon scarce national aid programmes.

The hard truth, however, is that the international or global community has, more often than not, been unable to effectively respond to threats to peace and security, violations of human rights, grinding poverty and health issues or even natural disasters. One of the more obvious reasons is that the mechanisms established to react to those disorders are politically-based bureaucratic entities that are slow to implement, or even reluctant to pursue, what may be the most effective remedial policies. Recent illustrations, and there are many, include Syria and Libya and, more historically but with continuing effects, Rwanda and Cambodia.

Power and self-interest struggles between major States only add to the delay and confusion and create opportunities for extreme groups to exploit and extend the violence.

On a narrower, but nonetheless worrying scale, are the tensions that exist between States seeking to preserve their sovereignty [or naked self- interest and often quasi-xenophobic policies under the emotive cloak of sovereignty] and those individuals and NGOs seeking to protect human rights in particular, and democratic freedoms in general. The rise of populist political movements, not least in Europe, is all too obvious.

Another hard but self-evident truth is that focus has been dominant on punishment of perpetrators after the fact, where breaches of human rights treaties and mechanisms by high ranking state officers have occurred, rather than the diligent prevention of such abuses at a very early stage. Criminal law has some proactive deterrent value as well as a regulatory one, but for the most part it is reactive. It operates at its most obvious level to address questions of culpability and sanction after a criminal event. That is especially true in the international sphere.

That may be inevitable as most States have been hesitant to risk violating the actual or purported sovereignty of another State, absent some political or economic interest or benefit for itself. In that regard, and as but one of many examples, I recommend reading "Shake Hands with the Devil" by General Romeo Dallaire, a book that provides valuable and powerful insight into the manifest and avoidable failings that surrounded the horrors in Rwanda.

Even basic study illustrates that almost every human rights mechanism that exists is contingent upon the political will of States rather than solely a commitment to justice and the peace that engenders. At present we need look no further than Syria, Libya, the Yemen or Darfur.

Although the doctrine of the "responsibility to protect" has gained traction it is still widely agreed between States that only the UN Security Council may authorize the use of force, even in obvious cases of crimes against humanity and war crimes. The widely accepted reality is the UNSC is primarily and inevitably a highly political body with the real power being vested in the permanent membership and the end-game power of veto.

Cynics would argue that it is naïve to accept that the inefficiencies embedded in the system are simply inadvertent.

If human rights enforcement mechanisms are to regulate the potentially hostile acts of States, or state officials, against individuals or selected groups then it appears foundationally irreconcilable that the mechanisms should also be controlled solely by States.

Some greater cynics are also likely to be of the view that those bureaucracies that have been established by States to apparently protect the interests of individuals under the rule of law, contain within their structures a regulatory matrix designed, not to prevent, but to slow down and curtail the ability of human rights organisations, and international criminal justice systems, to develop to a level which could seriously undermine the ability of states to pursue their interests both domestically and internationally.

That view would maintain that ineffective, or at least inefficient, mechanisms provide a jurisprudential gloss that reflects well whilst, in reality, being a relatively cost-effective course which is less restrictive of power and the pursuit of national political interests.

In parallel, technology now makes it easier for individuals and pressure groups to communicate, share information and mobilize. In consequence inefficient mechanisms are easier to expose.

Traditionally democracies of all shades of liberalism, and some virtual dictatorships, must to a greater or lesser extent incorporate the will of the masses at a domestic level. History shows us that those that have not have fallen, or will eventually fall.

The rapidity of mass communication has raised the potential platform of the individual, and elements of concerned civil society, up to the international and even global level. That is seen in some circles as a huge advance, but by others, and particularly the more insecure narrow state actors, as a threat. Hence the call in some areas to monitor or control the internet and/or social media, or even reduce popular access to only that information supplied, and therefore controlled, by the state. Of course there may be valid security concerns that necessitate some monitoring or control where the internet or social media is abused for violent purposes. That needs to be taken with the caveat that fake news is destructive and the rapidity of communication only holds its benefits if the information is true.

In addition, as corporations have expanded their reach and spheres of influence beyond the domestic and into the global arena, they have acquired the power to affect the course of international programs to address economic, and environmental issues which gives considerable 'political' power. Some of the larger corporations rival small states in their net financial worth and the scope and amount of services they can control and provide to individuals, and smaller corporations, in the varied national jurisdictions in which they operate. This can easily translate into both overt and covert political influence.

Although not a very recent phenomenon it is one that has expanded hugely over the past three or four decades, perhaps not even two human generations.

This recent paradigm has yet to be fully understood or even defined as it is still in rapid development, but one thing is abundantly clear: the international and global scene is no longer solely the domain of States. As these actors continue to gain influence serious questions need to be asked as to their responsibilities and limitations, their rights, roles and, perhaps above all, their accountability.

We can reasonably expect the process, or at least the pursuit, of globalization to continue, at least on the cultural, economic and commercial levels. However, it is necessary to be aware of reactive nationalism and the limitation that imposes on unbridled globalization or ever expanding internationalism. Another consideration are the developing anti-globalization movements often from the opposite political spectrum to populist national movements, whose proponents support global cooperation and interaction in principle but oppose, sometimes violently, the spread of economic globalization. They usually take the, perhaps not unreasonable, view that such widening of globalization does not adequately promote or protect human values, environmental protection and economic justice amongst other failings.

These dynamics are yet another threat to the pure rule of law and illustrate the conflicts that globalisation, at every level, is capable of generating.

International criminal and humanitarian law are of course two distinct disciplines, but the practical reality is that the two usually both come into complementary play in any given situation, and particularly one that has descended into actual conflict. Indeed it is frequently a breach of international humanitarian law, a very global legal structure, that give rise to criminal charges in international courts or tribunals.

Both those branches of law are very dynamic and globalization gives rise to the real possibility of significant jurisprudential expansion. We now have the crime of aggression coming into the prosecutorial armoury of the Rome statute of the ICC. There may be issues as the ICC is mandated to try individuals and aggression is sometimes more attached to state policy, but those will have to be met on a case-by-case basis.

Looking more into the future I see other areas where the international community may look for control and relief. Those include environment crimes and, in addition and often related, transnational corporate crimes. Looking more broadly we need to ask whether or not it is time to expand international criminal law, or at least the study of it, away from the traditional core crimes into transnational crimes which include corruption, drugs, human trafficking and slavery, illegal arms trading, terrorism [in some better defined terms] and the wider protection of flora and fauna amongst many others.

If any environmental crime causes widespread and serious human suffering, might it be possible for that crime to reach the level of adverse consequence that puts it into the category of a crime against humanity? My answer is to ask 'why not?' If attacks on cultural monuments are comfortably contained within international criminal law then it is difficult to see that avoidable environmental damage that affects the lives and health of communities should not be, at least, equally culpable and worthy of sanction beyond economic reparation.

One very foreseeable consequence of environmental damage is a localised threat to order and peace and thus the rule of law. We have already seen such conflicts arising out of oil pollution and deforestation.

It is sometimes the case that the generators of such [or alleged] environmental damage will be globally operational transnational corporations. Inevitably such entities wield enormous economic and political power, sometimes more than smaller states. However, if we accept that even the highest political and military leaders have no immunity, and therefore no impunity, for genocide, crimes against humanity and war crimes, it is valid to ask where is the logic in legal terms for those responsible for the activities of such corporate entities to avoid individual criminal responsibility for their acts or omissions.

These are questions now being asked in the community of international jurists and, as time passes and the populations and associated conflicts expand, advocates of domestic and international peace and justice are going to demand answers and actions.

Big international peace settlements and military actions initiate all manner of interventions with varying degrees of success. The reality is that people on the ground in conflict zones cannot always relate to interventions or the mechanisms of governance in the same way that the big primary drivers anticipate. For example, many argue that the dissolution of the Iraqi army and police post-2003 in Iraq and the apparent failure to comprehend that it was necessary for Iraqi citizens to be members of the newly proscribed Baath party, as it was in East Germany to be members of the Communist Party, for access to jobs and education, generated a predictable and fundamental power shift with the current horribly complex and violent consequences.

There is a real distinction between positive peace, which requires post-conflict good governance and the rule of law to be put in place, as against negative peace which is relatively easy but short term, and only requires that people stop shooting at each other. If military intervention does not result in good governance and the rule of law it is likely to be rightly viewed as a failure and perhaps worse that no intervention at all.

The relationship between international and national law tends to change according to the vantage point from which the relationship is viewed. From the perspective of national law and constitutionalism it is national law and the constitution that defines the framework. For instance, the requirements to be satisfied before a government can assume international treaty agreements, the place of such treaties in the national legal system, the reception of international customary law, the deference or otherwise that national courts should give to international law and so on.

From the perception of international law the picture changes. The application of international law hinges on the consent of States, whether express or implied. Once a State assumes a treaty commitment, it is bound by the terms of that commitment and the uncontroversial principle reflected in Article 27 of the Vienna Convention on the Law of Treaties provides that a State may not invoke the provisions of its internal law as justification for its failure to perform treaty obligations.

As for customary international law which arises from the conduct of states undertaken out of a sense and appreciation of legal obligation, in Hans Kelsen's conception of the unity of international and national law, this is the font of the sovereign authority of States. Sovereignty must accordingly be exercised, including internally, in accordance with the dictates of international law from whence it was born. On this view, therefore, the supremacy of international law follows from the appreciation that international law is the ultimate source of a State's sovereign authority to exercise jurisdiction.

The jurist Gerald Fitzmaurice took the view that the supremacy of international law was not, on his conception, an issue of content but rather of field of operation. The systems of international and national law did not, and could not, come into conflict because they occupied different realms. The more prosaic question of how to resolve any conflict of obligations that arose would be addressed by reference to the rules applicable in the forum in which the conflict fell to be resolved. The acknowledged consequence was that a State that failed, for reasons of the supremacy of its national law to comply with its international obligations, would therefore have committed a breach of those obligations.

Herch Lauterpachts's conception of the unity of law was more purpose driven, being born of a sense of the ultimate focus of all law, and the need to restrain the unbridled exercise of national sovereignty. The supremacy of international law is required to guard against the abuse of human rights. International law thus becomes the touchstone of principle, establishing a standard with which States are required to comply. For me that is the better and more persuasive view.

After the Nuremberg and Tokyo tribunals and military commissions came the Geneva Conventions and Protocols and the Genocide Convention, the Declaration of Human Rights and numerous vital international treaties and conventions, not least the International Covenant on Civil and Political Rights, but the international community was very light on international court sanctions or decisions. The International Court of Justice did and does fine and demanding work on inter-state disputes as does the tribunal for the Law of the Sea. There are the European and Inter-American Courts of Human Rights, the African Court of Human Rights and many other fine institutions and highly regarded non-governmental organisations. However the concept of individual criminal responsibility and sanction for egregious breaches of international criminal and humanitarian law had taken a back seat.

The last two decades has seen a momentous change in that regard.

There have been notable cases in national courts dealing with allegations of individual criminal responsibility for international crimes, and some attempts in some States to exercise universal jurisdiction.

But more radically from an international legal perspective we have seen the emergence of the UN International Criminal Tribunals for the Former Yugoslavia and Rwanda, the Special Court for Sierra Leone, the Extraordinary Chamber for Cambodia, the court in East Timor, the Special Tribunal for Lebanon and now the International Criminal Court in The Hague.

Of course both Nuremberg and Tokyo endured the criticism of 'victor's justice', and the fact that there was the death penalty and a less than comprehensive appellate procedure made for more refined criticism. The reality was that the most egregious crimes had been deliberately and obviously committed and it was necessary to make sure they were widely publicised and dealt with by a multi-national legal entity.

It is beyond doubt that both the UN tribunals for the former Yugoslavia and Rwanda have breathed new life into international criminal justice. Both were arguably created out, and as a result of, institutionalised United Nations failures in Sbrenica and Rwanda. The choice of Prof Antonio Cassese as the first President of the ICTY was critical. Professor Cassese ranks along with Professor Cherif Bassiouni and Judge Theodore Meron as a founding father and inspirational figure in international criminal law.

If the ICTY had not succeeded then it is doubtful whether or not the International Criminal Court could have been created. The Rome Statute of the ICC, a comprehensive enabling legal treaty, owes much of its final content and acceptance to the care and oversight of Prof Bassiouni.

The ICC is not a UN court although it has a special relationship with the UN and the UNSC can refer cases to the court. It is administered by the Assembly of State Parties to the Rome Statute. Many big players on the world scene are missing, most notably the USA, Russia, China, India and Israel, but they recognise both *de facto* and *de jure* the existence of the court. Whilst the permanent members of the UNSC have only two ASP members, the UK and France, nevertheless in two cases, Libya and Darfur, the UNSC's five permanent members voted in favour of a referral to the ICC.

That a court without inherent UN chapter 7 backing, as both the ICTY and ICTR had, and dealing with issues of immunity and impunity in respect of national leaders accused of egregious international crimes, and relying solely upon mature and responsible State cooperation, was always bound to face great difficulties. It has to be remembered that every party to the Rome Statute knew exactly what they were signing up to in terms of the nature and application of the law, especially with regard to issues of immunity for Heads of State, and the nature of international legal obligation. I do not intend to go into the well-publicised difficulties the court has faced and is facing. That is work in progress. What I can do is to say without reserve that we are doing the best we can with the relatively limited resources we have and sometimes partial cooperation we do receive.

It has to be remembered by all that the ICC is a court of last resort. Not only does it respect national sovereignty but national courts have primacy under the doctrine of complementarity. If a national court is willing and able to properly and fairly try its own citizens accused of genocide, crimes against humanity and war crimes then the ICC has no jurisdiction.

Those who raise narrow issues of sovereignty as a basis for not joining, or not cooperating with, the court apparently either do not understand that doctrine or choose to ignore it. It has to be realised that, in effect, each new case at the ICC is equivalent to an ad hoc tribunal. Each case, even if from the same continent, brings very different issues of language, culture, expectations and levels of investigative cooperation. The ICC has no police force. Mature State party and international cooperation is vital, and thus becomes crucial to the maintenance of the rule of law. Most crucially, in my view that fact that the ICC has no Chapter 7 powers, is a severe handicap. It would assist the court if some states who are members of the Assembly of States Parties took a closer look at Article 27 of the Vienna Convention on Treaties.

The idea that any State had a Golden Age which a re-emergence of narrow nationalism can provide a route back to is simply a myth and any attempt to re-write history to promote some current political or philosophical surge is no more than dishonest narcissism. One does not have to look back further than the rise and destruction of Nazi Germany to see that in sharp focus.

With massive population growth, diminishing resources and the widespread and not fully predictable effects of global climate change, we face huge challenges. I suspect our children and grand-children face even greater ones.

Those challenges have to be met and resolved in a mature legal framework, by national and international efforts and mutually beneficial and globally beneficial treaties and standards.

As we embark upon that, doing the best we can, then all is possible and progress, resolution and, not least, peace, always elusive, may be found. The choice may be as stark as law or war.

If the manifest challenges in our present and future are global, and they are, then so are the solutions.

As has often been said, if we do not learn from the mistakes of the past we are bound to repeat them. Mark Twain wryly observed that the two most important days in your life are, firstly, the day you are born and the second is the day you realise why. As a jurist, with substantial experience of dealing with some of the most violent episodes in recent human history, I have a great deal of faith that we have learnt about most of the mistakes made in the past and that we can find a way forward, all 7 billion of us. Like Martin Luther King and other truly inspirational people, we do the best we can. We need to.

Howard Morrison is a Judge of the Appeals Division of the International Criminal Court, The Hague, The Netherlands.

Part II
Environmental Law and Natural Resources Law

Coastal State Regulation of the Use of Arms in the Private Protection of Commercial Vessels in the Gulf of Guinea: A Nigerian Perspective

Osatohanmwen O. Anastasia Eruaga

Contents

1 Introduction

Increasing vulnerabilities characterise the on-going era of heightened International shipping as a facet of globalised trade. In particular, the International Maritime Organisation (IMO) has identified the waters in and around the Gulf of Guinea as among the particularly dangerous maritime areas due to the prevalence of the threats

O. O. Anastasia Eruaga (✉)
Nigerian Institute of Advanced Legal Studies, Abuja, Nigeria
e-mail: P1405@wmu.se

C. Eboe-Osuji et al. (eds.), *Nigerian Yearbook of International Law 2018/2019*,
Nigerian Yearbook of International Law 2018/2019,
https://doi.org/10.1007/978-3-030-69594-1_4

of piracy and armed robbery against ships.[1] Benin-Nigeria-Togolese axis is identified as the location of most belligerent manifestations.[2] According to statistics from the International Maritime Organisation (IMO), about 573 actual and attempted attacks have occurred around the region from 2010 till date.[3] The attacks persist, despite individual and cooperative efforts of governments within the region.[4] An almost equal amount of attacks occur within the territorial sea, under the national jurisdiction of coastal states while the others take place in international waters. Presently, attacks are described as increasingly persistent and violent.[5]

The prevalence of the maritime security threats created the impetus for shipping companies to seek to involve personnel of private entities commonly known as private maritime security companies (PMSCs) using firearms to protect vulnerable objects at sea. This comes at the heels of their successes in other piracy prone areas especially off the coast of Somalia, where analysts claim that there has been no successful attack on any commercial vessel with armed personnel onboard.[6] The increased use of private entities for vessel protection represents a shift in the once accepted global norm of not arming commercial vessels based on the obligation on states to maintain public order at sea.[7] Nigeria as a coastal state in the region frowns at the presence of armed personnel onboard foreign vessels, as a violation of aspects of her national laws governing the ownership and possession of firearms.[8] and a threat to security within her domain. Consequently, the Nigerian government has, on several occasion, carried out arrests of vessels, due to the perceived presence of privately contracted armed security personnel (PCASPs) on board the foreign vessels.[9]

This article interrogates from a Nigerian perspective, the regulation of the use of armed personnel on board foreign vessels. Understanding coastal state competence in this context is essential since the belief that the use of armed personnel plays a

[1]Piracy is summarily defined as illegal acts 'on the high seas' or 'outside the jurisdiction of any state', from one vessel directed towards another. See UNCLOS (1982), art 101. Armed robbery against ships refers to illegal acts directed against a ship within the jurisdiction of a state. See IMO, Assembly (2010) A 26/Res.1025. While aware of the debates relating to the possibility of disregarding the distinction between the offences, this article maintains the legal distinction between them. See generally Mejia (2003), pp. 153–175.

[2]Joint War Committee (2015), *JWLA/022*; IMB, (2018) 22. See also Eruaga and Mejia (2019), p. 427.

[3]'Till date' means 31 December 2019. Data culled from International Maritime Organisation's Global Integrated Shipping Information System (GISIS) website, https://gisis.imo.org/Public/PAR/Default.aspx.

[4]Hasan and Hassan (2016), pp. 200–215; Eruaga and Mejia (2019), pp. 432–435.

[5]Liwang (2017), p. 401; Eruaga and Mejia (2019), p. 435.

[6]Dutton (2014), p. 109.

[7]Liss (2013), p. 199; Marin et al. (2017), p. 192.

[8]Firearms Act(2004) s.18,19 and 21; Private Guards Act(2004), s.15; Prohibition Order List (other than trade), Items 1 and 16.

[9]Usman (2012) https://www.vanguardngr.com/2012/10/navy-arrests-ship-laden-with-arms-ammunition/; Akomolafe (2015), p. 37.

significant role in the protection of vessels has gained considerable global acceptance. The article argues that the recent phenomenon of the use of force by private personnel to protect vessels stirs up legal controversies concerning the rights of coastal states to adopt and enforce rules prohibiting their presence. These legal controversies exist because the current regime on maritime security, accommodating the protection of merchant ships by private guards presents as an ambiguous and complex framework that creates room for uncertainties and varied interpretation. The article, therefore, suggests clarity and harmonisation, of the interpretations of maritime security law relevant to the use of armed private personnel. This recommendation is especially important, in light of the present realities that the threat of piracy continues to wax and wane, not only in the Gulf of Guinea waters but also in other maritime areas globally and these non-state actors have the potential of contributing to providing respite for commercial ships, from attacks.

The article consisting of five sections, including the introductory and concluding parts, first discusses the trends of the maritime crimes of piracy and armed robbery against ships in the Gulf of Guinea region. This discussion serves as the foundation for exploring in the next section, the emergence of the use of armed personnel onboard foreign merchant vessels. Section 3 also explores the applicable laws concerning and use of firearms and related equipment on board merchant ships. Section 4 examines from a Nigerian outlook, the debates that surround coastal states' capacity to prescribe and enforce laws within the maritime domain, with particular reference to the presence of armed personnel on foreign merchant vessels. This section precedes the closing section of the article. In concluding, the article proffers suggestions that would address the legal quagmire that the new trend of privatisation of security presents which would be relevant both in the GoG and other regions.

2 Nigeria and the Maritime Security Threats of Piracy and Armed Robbery Against Ships in the GoG: A Brief Analysis

This section explores the maritime security trend of the offences of piracy and armed robbery against ships in the Gulf of Guinea briefly, highlighting the significance of Nigeria in the discourse. Through an analysis of the actual occurrence of these threats in the region, the section lays the foundation for the current focus of global attention and the region as a potential new operating field for PMSCs.

2.1 *The Gulf of Guinea and the Rise of Maritime Security Threats*

A contemporary description of the Gulf of Guinea in maritime security discussions depicts the region as an area that includes several countries in West and Central Africa from Senegal to Angola.[10] The geographic location of the region makes it significant in the context of global maritime transportation. The area with its wide shipping lanes, free of chokepoints, serves the transit of international and regional commence in oil and other natural resources.[11] As explained by Hasan and Hassan, the route is integral to the main markets of oil in Europe and America, since the region itself is the location of numerous oil and gas reserves.[12] Furthermore, states in the region rely on these shipping lanes for access to finished goods moved by sea from producing states outside the continent.

The region has in recent years been at the forefront of concerns related to violent maritime crimes, especially since the decline of attacks off the Somali coast in the early 2010s. In 2011, the UN Security Council expressed grave concerns about the threats in the region.[13] This declaration flowed from IMO's prior statement a year earlier that identified the Gulf of Guinea waters as the second most acute piracy area in the African Continent.

The waters within the Nigeria-Beninese-Togolese axis of the region are mainly regarded as high-risk areas and considered by many experts to be as dangerous as the waters off the coast of Somalia.[14] According to the then United Nations Secretary-General,

> The growing incidence of piracy in the Gulf of Guinea constitutes yet another major threat to the peace, security and economic interests of both coastal and hinterland States in the region[15]

Even with the general concerns of underreporting of attacks,[16] a review of the statistics of attacks, as shown in Table 1, reveal that incidents have generally been persistent over the years.

---

[10]Hasan and Hassan (2016), p. 173; Eruaga and Mejia (2019), p. This contemporary description, though contrary to navigational definition reflecting a strict view of the area as being between Cape Lopez, Gabon to three points in Ghana, (0° 38′ S, 8° 42′ E), has gained popularity from its relevance in discussions geared towards combating maritime violence through interregional cooperation. See International Hydrographic Organisation (IHO) (1953), p. 19.

[11]Hasan and Hassan (2016), p. 174.

[12]Hasan and Hassan (2016), p. 174.

[13]UN Security Resolution (2011) S/RES/2018.

[14]Ali-Deen (2015), p. 113.

[15]UN Sec. Gen (2012) S/2012/45, IV par. 60.

[16]MSC (2017) MSC 98/15/1, p. 2; Husted (2019) https://fas.org/sgp/crs/row/IF11117.pdf.

Table 1 Summary of attacks in the Gulf of Guinea (2011–2018)[a]

Year/Source	11	12	13	14	15	16	17	18
IMO	65	68	55	45	35	62	49	81
IMB	53	62	51	41	34	55	45	82

[a]GISIS website, https://gisis.imo.org/Public/PAR/Default.aspx; International Maritime Bureau (IMB) (2015); IMB (2019) https://www.icc-ccs.org/reports/2019_Annual_Piracy_Report.pdf

Attacks till date, occur across the maritime zones and are characterised as extremely violent.[17] The maritime criminals possess highly sophisticated weapons which they willingly use.[18] The primary intent over the years has generally been 'petro-piracy'—oil tanker hijacking for cargo—although the region now witnesses increasingly high cases of kidnapping for ransom.[19]

2.2 *The Significance of Nigeria in the Threat Discourse of the Gulf of Guinea*

Scholarly writings and studies reveal that majority of the incidents of contemporary piracy and armed robbery against ships in the Gulf of Guinea has its roots in Nigeria, particularly in the oil-rich yet impoverished communities of the Niger Delta.[20] Nigeria alone accounts for over 52% of the total incidents recorded in the region since 2010. Experts contend that most of the maritime criminals presently operating in other states in the region are actually of Nigerian descent or have close business connections with the country.[21] For instance, *MT Kerala* hijacked in Angola was subsequently sighted under the control of the attackers off the coast of Nigeria.[22] Similarly, the perpetrators of the criminal attack of the *MT Energy Centurion*, 17 miles to Lomé[23] and MT *Maximus* in the waters of Ivory Coast,[24] were Nigerians.

Notably, in line with accepted international norms and obligations, Nigeria, like other coastal states in the region, bear the responsibility of providing security at sea against the maritime crimes of focus. Sole responsibility exists within the territorial

[17]Otto (2015), p. 21; Hasan and Hassan (2016), p. 179; Liwang (2017), p. 386; Eruaga and Mejia (2019).

[18]Eruaga and Mejia (2019).

[19]Murphy (2013), p. 432; Husted (2019) https://fas.org/sgp/crs/row/IF11117.pdf; Eruaga and Mejia (2019), p. 429.

[20]Hasan and Hassan (2016), p. 171; Husted (2019) https://fas.org/sgp/crs/row/IF11117.pdf.

[21]Hasan and Hassan (2016), p. 171; 427.

[22]IMO (2014) MSC.4/Circ.206, annex 1, p. 3.

[23]Megbolu and Onwubu (2012) http://maritime-executive.com/editorials/maritime-security-in-the-gulf-of-guinea-in-2016.

[24]IMO (2014) MSC.4/Circ.234, annex 1, p. 3.

sea and internal waters for acts of armed robbery against ships.[25] As areas under state jurisdiction, a coastal state obligation stems from the notions of sovereignty and internal competence of domestic jurisdiction. These notions forming the principle of *par in parem non habet iudicium,* prohibit incursion by a foreign government without consent.[26] Furthermore, the State partakes in the universal jurisdiction to suppress the acts of piracy.[27] This obligation is in corporation with other states to the fullest possible extent in other maritime zones that constitute the high sea.[28] As such, states in the Gulf of Guinea, including Nigeria, have individually and collectively undertaken several measures in efforts to suppress the prevalence and persistence of attacks within the region.[29]

Given the persistence of the insecurities within the maritime domain, shipping companies explored several hardening measures to mitigate the effect.[30] One of such measures is the used of armed personnel for the protection of vessels.

3 The Use of Privately Armed Personnel for the Protection of Vessels Against Maritime Crimes

This section provides a brief overview of the emergence of the use of PMSCs in the protection of foreign merchant vessels in the Gulf of Guinea, linking it to the historical trajectory of the normative shift that marked their global acceptance as part of the ocean security governance structure. The section further identifies the current legal framework governing the use of armed personnel.

3.1 The Emergence of Privately Contracted Personnel

The persistent and increasingly rampant incidents piracy and armed robbery against ships in the Gulf of Guinea, especially within and off the coast of Nigeria, created

[25]UNCLOS (1982) art.3.

[26]Korowicz (1959), p. 157; ICJ, *Military and Paramilitary Activities in and Against Nicaragua (Nicaragua v. US)*, Judgment, (1986) ICJ 14, para. 202.

[27]UNCLOS (1982), art 100–107.

[28]UNCLOS (1982) art 100. Debates as to whether the incidents in the EEZ are classified as piracy to determine state jurisdiction are outside the scope of this article. However, it suffices to state that this paper aligns with the position that attacks that occur in the EEZ (except they have a direct bearing on the explorative and exploitative rights of the State) and fulfil other legal requirements as contained in UNCLOS, art 100, are acts of piracy under international law. See generally UNCLOS arts. 56, 58, 86 and 87; Djalal (2005), p. 144; Dubner (2011), p. 93; Eruaga and Mejia (2019).

[29]For an in-depth discussion of the several individual and collective measures, see generally Hasan and Hassan (2016), pp. 200–215; Eruaga and Mejia (2019), p. 430.

[30]BIMCO (2014) Cir.3/14.

room for multidimensional response approach to tackling the threats.[31] Armed personnel involvement provided by PMSCs emerged as one of such additional response which shipowners were willing to explore.[32] Before the possibility of their potential use in the Gulf of Guinea region, PMSCs had gain popularity for similar services in other piracy hot spots such as around the strait of Malacca and off the coast of Somalia.[33] Petrig explains that the strategy employed by these private entities' is primarily to deter attacks, an effect offered by the mere presence of armed guards, prompting the alleged pirates to refrain from an attack and to seek softer targets.'[34]

The utilisation of privately armed personnel in other maritime areas, such as around Southeast Asia and off the Gulf of Aden, was not without legal and operational controversies. Principal among the controversies was the general perception that their presence, based on private contractual arrangements, challenged this conventional view of security at sea as responsibility reserved for states.[35] A traditional view of non-arming of vessels founded on the concept of state responsibility for security at sea based on the use of force had always existed within the maritime domain.[36] The idea of security at sea developed around this common understanding caused the considerable scepticism expressed by varied stakeholders on PMSCs engaging private personnel utilising firearms to protect vessels. In line with this, the IMO had enjoined flag states to 'strongly discourage the carrying and use of firearms by seafarers for personal protection or the protection of a ship'[37] The scepticism has over the years gradually transformed to considerable positive endorsement or at least tacit acceptance among maritime stakeholders, including the IMO.[38] The inability of states in areas recording frequent attacks to provide the much desired security promoted the industry practice of using PCASPs. The practice was backed by flag states adversely affected by the insecurities. There remain however, some stakeholder, including a majority of states in the Gulf of Guinea that adhere tenaciously to the traditional view of the direct state monopoly of violence at sea.

As evidence of considerable global acceptance, several legal reforms occurred at a national and global scale to ensure that states re-established control over security in the maritime domain. These legal reforms forming important aspects of the

[31]UN Sec. Gen (2012) S/2012/45, IV par. 61.

[32]Eruaga (2016), p. 316.

[33]For an in-depth discussion on the use of armed personnel to suppress maritime crimes in other maritime areas such as off the coast of Somalia and Southeast Asia, see generally Parsons (2010), p. 156; Liss (2015), pp. 193–213; Liss (2015), pp. 87–88.

[34]Petrig (2016), p. 675.

[35]Liss (2015), p. 200; Liss (2017)

[36]Marin et al. (2017), p. 193.

[37]IMO (2009) MSC.1/Circ.1333 annex, paragraph 5 (Updated and revoked by MSC.1-Circ.1333-Rev.1 in June 2015).

[38]Eruaga (2016), p. 318.

framework for maritime security target how PMSCs provide their services involving the use of firearms. The subsequent section addresses the legal framework. However, it suffices to state at this point that the IMO through its recommendations meant to guide the use of PCASPs, indicates the absence of an intention to positively endorse or institutionalise their use, although it recognised the need to regulate their involvement, flowing from shipping industry acceptance and flag state practice.[39]

3.2 *The Legal Regime Governing the of Armed Personnel for the Protection of Vessels*

The advent of the use of armed personnel, as explained in the preceding sub-section, triggered legal reforms to accommodate the presence of the 'new' entrants within the law of the sea and ocean security governance. With the level of global acceptance, the focus of the stakeholders of international shipping has moved from whether PMSCs should be engaged in the fight against maritime crime to working out ways to safely engage them.[40] Currently, their presence at sea is governed by what Petrig describes as a 'plethora of applicable legal framework.'[41] The plethora of applicable legal framework can be x-rayed from the perspective of international, national and self-regulatory frameworks.

As a rather recent phenomenon, the significant conventions on international maritime security law make no mention of private protection of vessels or what laws should be applied.[42] However, these conventions remain relevant to the extent that they explore issues of state jurisdiction and responsibilities within the various maritime zones. For instance, in the general discussion of state jurisdiction, merchant vessels under customary international law, have the nationality of the State whose flag they are entitled to fly. According to UNCLOS, art 92, '(s)hip shall sail under the flag of one State only and. . .shall be subject to its exclusive jurisdiction on the high seas.'[43] The presence of arms and armed guards onboard ships are primarily governed by flag state flowing from the duty of such a state to 'effectively exercise its jurisdiction and control in administrative, technical and social matters over ships flying its flag.'[44] This effective control extends to 'assuming jurisdiction under its internal law over the master, officers and crew as well as the general happenings within the vessel.[45] Similarly, the need for port and coastal states to secure their respective maritime interests as recognised by the law of the sea accords them some

---

[39] IMO (2012a) Annex1 par.1.

[40] Hespen (2014), p. 361.

[41] Petrig (2016), p. 675.

[42] Kraska (2015), p. 179.

[43] UNCLOS (1982), art 92(1).

[44] UNCLOS (1982), art 94 (1).

[45] UNCLOS (1982), art 94(2) and(3).

control of vessels under a particular flag state.[46] While the principle of coastal state protection of maritime interest exists, it requires further scrutiny as to whether this protection applies to the use and presence of armed personnel onboard a foreign vessel, and if it does, to what extent.

Following the extensive and heightened use of PMSCs off the coast of Somalia as discussed earlier, the IMO in collaboration with key stakeholders in the maritime established several guidelines consisting of recommendations specifically with regards the use of armed personnel by commercial vessels.[47] The guidelines directed at shipowners and operators, flag states, coastal states as well as PMSC companies are to be read in conjunction with each other as well as the other recommendations and guidance developed by the organisation for preventing and suppressing piracy and armed robbery against ships.[48] These guidelines are considered subject to change as a better understanding of the regulation of PMSC armed personnel emerges. However, the provisions of the IMO guidelines generally reflect the position under the customary law of the sea as it relates to flag and coastal state jurisdiction over vessels.[49] The interim guidelines directed to PMSCs providing PSCAP services (Cir.1443) requires the company to acquire knowledge of the regulation and policies of the flag state, port as well as coastal states.[50] The IMO guidelines provide the first directly relevant consideration of several complexities that surround the use of armed personnel service within the maritime domain. The recommendations are therefore of importance, even though parties that the guidelines address do not incur any liability for failing to adhere to them.

National laws also contribute to the legal regime regulating the use of PMSCs. The transnational nature of global shipping, occurring across maritime zones, makes national laws of both flag and coastal State relevant to the legal regime.[51] Interestingly, Liss opines that 'because no other international institutions offer binding regulations, the task of regulating the employment of PCASP has fallen to flag states'.[52] While there is indeed an absence of a harmonised globally accepted binding regulations, the task of regulating the employment of private armed personnel falls on flag states because the presence of armed PMSC on board vessel forms part of the issues which are covered by the internal law of the State whose nationality the vessel bears. The legal regime at a national level is thus currently shaped by states sculpturing legal norms to suit their specific interests.[53] Hespen asserts that flag states are more willing to create laws that allow the use of armed personnel onboard,

---

[46]UNCLOS (1982) arts 21, 25–28; Hespen (2014), p. 363.

[47]IMO (2012a, b, c, 2014).

[48]MSC.1/Circ.1406/Rev.3, par.6; IMO (2012a) par.5.

[49]Hespen (2014), p. 363; IMO 2015, Annex 1 par.4; IMO (2012b).

[50]IMO (2012c) Annex1, par. 3(3.3).

[51]Notably, the laws of the members of the crew, as well as the law of the place of incorporation of the PMSC company, may also be relevant.

[52]Liss (2015), p. 89.

[53]Bürgin and Schneider (2015), p. 131.

although the laws are not uniform in content.[54] For instance, the type of weapons permitted or the number of armed personnel used on board a vessel varies among states.[55] Following the increasing use of armed personnel especially at the peak of attacks off the coast of Somalia, IMO through a questionnaire, requested states '*to provide information pertaining to their individual requirements regarding the use of PCASP in their territorial waters.*'[56] The responses of states, reflect the diversity of the content of national legislation as well as the interest of flag states. In contrast, coastal states battling with security challenges at sea, show resistance in endorsing the carriage of arms on board vessels.[57] Nigeria's refusal to allow the use of armed personnel on board vessels illustrates a typical response of most states in the Gulf of Guinea. The varied legal responses of states through their national law contributes significantly to the complex legal environment governing the deployment of armed personnel on vessels.[58]

In addition to the variety of relevant regulations both on the international and national level, there also exists a gamut of industry self-regulation.[59] This self-regulation consists of public-private initiatives,[60] Industry initiatives,[61] and individual company codes.[62] They exist as responses to the need to create a more detailed and acceptable operational standard in the use of firearms by PMSCs for vessel protection.[63] Notably, the industry self-regulation is ordinarily not legally binding. Hence, the relevance and capacity of industry self-regulation to generate significant legal consequences hinges on institutional acknowledgement as well as stakeholder's acceptance.[64]

Interrogating the legal framework majorly reveals the practical relevance of soft law norms or instruments with no legal binding force as a residual category to term

[54]Hespen (2014), p. 367.

[55]Petrig (2016), pp. 675–677.

[56]MSC-FAL.1/Circ.2.

[57]Liss (2012), pp. 60–61.

[58]Liss (2015), p. 86.

[59]Industry self-regulation refers to the standard set of understandings among participants in a particular industry or profession regarding specific issues which include norms of conduct, organisation, and limitations on activity. See Richemond-Barak (2014), p. 779.

[60]International Code of Conduct, (2010) https://www.icoca.ch/sites/all/themes/icoca/assets/icoc_english3.pdf; ISO (2015) (ISO/28007-1: 2015). See also Petrig (2016), pp. 1–19; Carreira Da Cruz (2017), pp. 63–81.

[61]--, *Best Management Practices for Protection against Somalia Based Piracy* (Version 4, 2011); BIMCO (2014) Cir.3/14.

[62]Richemond-Barak (2014), p. 779.

[63]Carreira Da Cruz (2017), p. 64.

[64]Williams (2014), pp. 350–351; Carreira Da Cruz (2017). Contrast with Petrig (2016), pp. 1–19; Petrig (2016) Paper delivered at the 5th session of the United Nations Human Rights Council Intergovernmental Working Group on Private Military and Security Companies.

all law-like commitments.[65] From the context of international maritime security law binding agreements currently do not directly address the related subject of armed personnel, creating the vacuum for states to adopt varied approaches. The discussed law-like initiatives thus help to interpret and create a uniform understanding of binding legal rules to cover this new but prominent phenomenon. As Chaisse and Ji explain, soft law '...can accommodate diverse legal systems and cope better with uncertainty...It facilitates innovation and experiment, and it can provide the essential preparatory phase before people are ready for hard law commitments.'[66]

The next section of this article considers the relevant aspects of the legal framework regulating the use of the sea and the legal regime governing the use of PMSCs as discussed in this section, to explore the competence of coastal states and the use of armed personnel on foreign vessels.

4 Coastal State Competence in the Prohibition of the Use of Armed Personnel on Board Foreign Vessel

Global shipping occurs across several maritime zones, connecting several states in one voyage. The laws of the sea provide a broad framework to ensure the peaceful use of the sea. However, the actual location of the ship and specifics of how the vessel interacts with a particular maritime zone are very relevant to determining actual jurisdiction of coastal states over a foreign vessel. Given the established mixed response of states to the regulation of arms onboard vessels, this section of the article considers when and under what conditions, coastal states can regulate the use of armed guards on board a foreign vessel.

4.1 Jurisdiction of Coastal States Over Foreign Vessels

Coastal states possess sovereign rights and jurisdiction in varying degrees over what occurs in the different zones of the sea. A summary of Nigeria's powers within the various maritime zones is necessary to scrutinise the existence of coastal state competence.

4.1.1 Coastal State Powers in the High Seas

The high seas refer to seawater open to all states and excluded from state sovereignty. UNCLOS under art 89 states that 'no state may validly purport to subject any

[65] Guzman and Meyer (2010), p. 173.

[66] Chaisee and Ji (2018), p. 477.

part of the high sea to its sovereignty'. Additionally, as part of the freedom of the seas, freedom of navigation in the high sea restricts other states from interfering in this zone, with foreign flagged vessels, excepted in limited circumstances.[67] In the context of this article, one of such situations in which coastal state interference is permissible is to cooperate to repress acts of piracy. UNCLOS art 105 provides that a state may seize a pirate ship or vessel that is under the control of pirates, and arrest the persons on board. The state may also seize property onboard such vessels.[68] The action of any state in the region with respect to cooperation to repress piracy must be in conformity with the already established principle of freedom of the sea. The presence of armed guards on a vessel is not among the limited circumstances in which a coastal state may interfere with the freedom of navigation. This means that the exclusive jurisdiction and control of a flag state as highlighted in UNCLOS arts 92 and 94 prevails. Hence, Nigeria, as a coastal state lacks the legal competence to proscribe the use of armed personnel on board foreign merchant vessels in this area as one outside her national jurisdiction.

4.1.2 EEZ and Contiguous Zone

The maritime zone next to the high seas is the exclusive economic zone, which is not exceeding 200 nm, beyond and adjacent to the territorial sea.[69] Nigeria claims the prescribed 200 nm.[70] UNCLOS gives coastal states sovereign rights over natural resources within this area.[71] The sovereign rights extend to control of activities related to exploration or exploitation of the natural resources within this maritime zone. In discussing the existence of the threats of piracy and armed robbery against ships and response to improving security generally, dissent exists among scholars as to whether the EEZ qualifies as part of the high seas to fulfil the location requirement of the offence of piracy and consequently trigger the UNCLOS art 100 universal jurisdiction principle.[72] The debates are especially significant in the context of the attacks in the Gulf of Guinea and Nigeria because a significant number of incidents of maritime violence occur within area Nigeria claims as her EEZ. Of the16 incidents recorded by the IMO in the first quarter of 2019 as connected to Nigeria, 12 of them these waters.[73]

---

[67]UNCLOS (1982) arts 99 (prevention of slavery); arts 100(piracy); 108 (traffic in illicit in narcotic drug); 109 (unauthorised broadcasting); Bardin (2002), p. 46; Churchill and Lowe (1988), pp. 208–209.

[68]UNCLOS (1982) art 105.

[69]UNCLOS (1982) art 57.

[70]Exclusive Economic Zone Act (2004) s.1.

[71]UNCLOS(1982) art 56.

[72]Djalal (2005), p. 144; Isanga (2009–2010), p. 1293; Jesus (2003), p. 379; Roach(2010), pp. 397–416; Eruaga and Mejia (2019), p. 433.

[73]Data obtained from IMO GSIS. Date accessed 31 May 2019.

Based on the sovereign rights expressed in UNCLOS, art 56, coastal state jurisdiction may apply to foreign vessels in this area but only to the extent of protecting the exploration and exploitation of resources. Accordingly, Eruaga and Mejia explain that

> A combined reading of Articles 56, 58, 86, and 87 of UNCLOS shows that the EEZ invariably forms part of the high seas for determining rights and obligations under Article 58, including the meaning of the high seas for the definition of piracy, except where the presence of foreign State vessels within the jurisdiction of a State can be interpreted to amount to infringing on expressly provided sovereign rights and jurisdiction.

This means that exclusive flag state jurisdiction ordinarily remains in this area, concerning other matters, including the presence of armed personnel on board a foreign vessel.

Nigeria has several offshore installations within the EEZ for exploration of her oil resources. Section 4 of the Economic Exclusive Zone Act provides that

> Any act or omission which-
>
> (a) takes place on, under or above an installation in a designated area or any waters within 200 meters of such an installation; and
>
> (b) would, if taking place in any part of Nigeria, constitute an offence under the enactment in force in that part,
>
> shall be treated for the purposes of that law as taking place in Nigeria

Nigeria can, for the protection of exploration, and exploitative rights, enforce jurisdiction, especially in light of the provisions of UNCLOS, art 56 and section 4 of the EEZ Act. However, the State cannot arguably claim the application of her national law to prohibit the use of private armed personnel in this zone because of its description as part of the high seas.

The contiguous zone, as a maritime zone, exists under the provisions of UNCLOS, art 33. The entitlement to claim the zone under international law is by proclamation.[74] Notably, a coastal state may fail to claim this zone, making it automatically part of the EEZ.[75] In such instances, the right to apply coastal state laws is determined within this zone, in line with the rights under the EEZ as discussed previously. Although reference is made to the contiguous zone in several local legislation, Nigeria does not expressly lay claim to the zone.[76] Hence, the discussions above on the EEZ is applicable in this instance.

---

[74] Sharama (1987), p. 210.

[75] It is implied that there must be some declaration by the coastal state claiming the right to the Contiguous zone. See UNCLOS (1982), art 77.

[76] Harmful Waste (Special Criminal Provisions etc) Act (1988), s. 12(a).

4.1.3 Territorial Sea and Internal Waters

The territorial sea and internal waters are an extension of the sovereignty of the coastal State.[77] In internal waters, a state enjoys full and exclusive sovereignty. Bardin explains that a foreign vessel, located in internal waters, is subject to the legislative, administrative, judicial and jurisdictional powers of the coastal State concerning any illegal acts committed on board the vessel or on land by crewmembers.[78] Similarly, International law recognises the extension of territorial sovereignty of coastal states over waters adjacent to their landward space, up to 12 nautical miles. Nigeria's municipal law on the extent of her territorial waters conforms with the 12 nautical mile limit under international law.[79] Accordingly, the State exercises full powers in its territorial sea, including the enforcement of its domestic laws. In line with these powers simpliciter, the carriage of arms and the presence of armed guards on board a vessel within the territorial sea arguably constitute a violation of domestic criminal laws in Nigeria. However, to ensure the peaceful use of the seas, the full competence of coastal states is subject to limitations. A major concession of state competence is the right of vessels to innocent passage. This principle found in UNCLOS Article 17 to 23, hinges on the customary law that 'ships of all States, whether coastal or land-locked, enjoy the right of innocent passage through the territorial sea.'[80] According to UNCLOS, coastal states shall not hamper innocent passage, but it may take necessary steps to prevent passage which is not innocent.[81] The movement of vessels in a transit nature or calling at a port facility is deemed to be innocent where such movement is not 'prejudicial to the peace, good order or security of the coastal State.'[82] The Nigerian Territorial Waters Act does not make specific mention of the right to innocent passage but the obligation exists as an application of a rule of customary international law.[83] A significant query flows from this premise to wit- does the presence of arms and armed personnel on a foreign vessel merely traversing the territorial sea or proceeding to or from internal waters constitute an innocent activity?

Article 19 (2) provides a list of activities considered as non-innocent. The provision mentioned above states that:

> 2. Passage of a foreign ship shall be considered to be prejudicial to the peace, good order or security of the coastal State if in the territorial sea it engages in any of the following activities:

---

[77]UNCCLOS (1982), arts.2; Bardin (2002), p. 30.

[78]Bardin (2002), p. 30; ICJ, *Military and Paramilitary Activities in and Against Nicaragua (Nicaragua v United States of America) (Merits)* (1986) ICJ Report 14,111.

[79]Territorial Waters Act (2004) s.1; Egbede (2004), p. 155.

[80]UNCLOS (1982), art.17.

[81]UNCLOS (1982), arts 24 and 25.

[82]UNCLOS (1982), art. 18-19(1).

[83]Egbede (2004), p. 166.

(a) any threat or use of force against the sovereignty, territorial integrity or political independence of the coastal State, or in any other manner in violation of the principles of international law embodied in the Charter of the United Nations;

(b) any exercise or practice with weapons of any kind;

(c) any act aimed at collecting information to the prejudice of the defence or security of the coastal State;

(d) any act of propaganda aimed at affecting the defence or security of the coastal State;

(e) the launching, landing or taking on board of any aircraft;

(f) the launching, landing or taking on board of any military device;

(g) the loading or unloading of any commodity, currency or person contrary to the customs, fiscal, immigration or sanitary laws and regulations of the coastal State;

(h) any act of wilful and serious pollution contrary to this Convention;

(i) any fishing activities;

(j) the carrying out of research or survey activities;

(k) any act aimed at interfering with any systems of communication

or any other facilities or installations of the coastal State;

(l) any other activity not having a direct bearing on passage.

Notably, the wordings of art 19(2) of UNCLOS requires that the vessel 'to engage' in any of the enumerated activities. The mere presence of armed personnel on a vessel without more cannot constitute engaging in any of the activities as envisaged by art 19 (2). In interrogating the catalogue of non-innocent activities, Petrig opines that presence of armed personnel onboard a foreign vessel would constitute innocent activity. In the first instance, the presence of the armed personnel does not amount to a threat against the sovereignty, territorial integrity or political independence as provided for in *litra* a. As Petrig explains, merchant ships fall outside the scope of Art 19(2)(a) which is directed at government-owned vessels.[84]

Secondly, *litra* b as quoted above, like the provisions of Art 19(2)(a) requires some activity or affirmative action by the armed personnel. However, even at that, if the armed personnel uses the weapons as a means of deterring an attack, the principle of the use of force in self-defence still makes the passage an innocent one.[85] The notion of 'exercise with weapons' cannot be interpreted to include actions in defence of self or the vessel against attacks.

[84]Petrig (2016), p. 683.

[85]Anna Petrig (2016), p. 681; Marin et al. (2017), p. 198.

Litra g mentions another activity which is relevant to the presence of armed personnel onboard a foreign commercial ship. Loading or unloading of any commodity or persons contrary to customs, fiscal, and immigration laws and regulations of the coastal State constitutes non-innocent activity. This means that the embarking or disembarking arms and PMSC personnel while in the territorial sea of Nigeria as a third State must be made following her custom laws on such matters. Vijayan asserts that the extent to which carriage of arms on vessels in transit through the territorial waters of a coastal state violate customs restriction is ambiguous.[86] Nigeria's customs law based on the Prohibition List made according to Custom and Excise Management Act, prohibits the importation of specific types of firearms-airguns and pistols[87] Similarly, the Firearms Act also prohibits the importation and movement of weapons without appropriate approval at the seaport.[88] It is unclear whether in a situation where any firearms or those not expressly prohibited under the Prohibition List are left onboard a vessel while within Nigeria's territorial sea, would amount to a violation of *litra* g because the loading or unloading of a commodity (in this case the firearms) did not occur. A literal interpretation of these custom related laws on the movement of arms may be that, where there is appropriate approval for firearms not prohibited, there is no violation, and the arms may be loaded or unloaded from the vessel. Furthermore, the provisions of UNCLOS Art 21 limits the ability of the State to adopt laws regulating innocent passage that affect the design, construction and manning of the foreign vessel unless they are in respect of generally accepted international rules or standards.[89] Restrictions on the competence of a coastal state to affect the issues of manning and equipment ensure that the existence of different coastal laws does not unduly affect global shipping.[90] Petrig notes that the prohibition relates to requirement cannot be altered during a voyage.[91] She argues that because arrangements can be made to disembark both the guards and or their weapons for passage, art 21(2) does not apply to the presence of PMSCs and their security-related equipment per se. An interpretation contrary to that of Petrig on this subject is also tenable. Disembarking security equipment or personnel before entering Nigeria's territorial waters translates to either dumping of weapons at sea or the establishment of floating armouries. Hence, the same logic as it relates to members of the crew of a ship and equipment on the vessel should apply to PMSC personnel and their equipment. Altering the requirements as it relates to flag state provisions on the number of crew, for instance, would mean that members of the crew would be disembarked before entering coastal waters. Where the flag state allows for the use of PMSC sea-based services, such requirements reflecting in the manning and presence of security equipment on the vessel are arguably not alterable.

---

[86]Vijayan (2014), pp. 25–26.

[87]Prohibition List, Schedule 4, Items 1 and 16.

[88]Firearms Act (2004), s. 18, 19 and 20.

[89]UNCLOS (1982) art 21(2).

[90]Petrig (2013), p. 684.

[91]Petrig (2013), p. 684.

Art 19(2)(l) as a general clause is also problematic because it creates further uncertainty as to what amounts to activities not directly having a bearing on passage. The flexible wordings of litra l cause academics such as Tanaka[92] to assert with general reference to what amounts to innocent activity, that Art. 19(2) is not a closed list of what may be considered as prejudicial to the peace, good order and security. Petrig suggests that the specific words should be interpreted to reflect the basic idea entrenched in UNCLOS Art 19(2), irrespective of whether it has a bearing on passage or not.[93]

It is essential to state that an alternative understanding of the provisions of 19 (1) and (2) as independent provisions exist. This interpretation implies that states are allowed to consider issues of security, peace and good order as identified in 19(1) as a standalone provision.[94] The expressions' peace', 'good order' and 'security' as provided for in article 19, are non-determinable terms. If the route of viewing the terms as provided in Art 19(1) as standalone, considerable discretion still exists on the part of states to provide varying interpretations despite the attempt to introduce objectivity in their interpretation by providing a list of activities that render passage non-innocent in Art 19(2).[95] In this regard, it is not an issue of a violation of a law that makes the passage non-innocent but rather, the consideration and interpretation of peace, good order and security.[96] Nigeria appears to treat the presence of armed personnel as a breach of her firearms law and policies and a breach of customs laws. Consequently, the Nigerian government policy on this as voiced by the Nigerian Navy and the Nigerian Maritime Administration and Safety Agency (NIMASA) reflects the stance that armed personnel onboard foreign vessels are prohibited.[97]

Irrespective of how the meaning of innocent activity is interpreted, UNCLOS Art 21 does not envisage the adoption of law and regulation that extend beyond measures aimed at ensuring that arms onboard private ships passing through territorial waters conform with customs laws and regulations. However, as shown under Nigerian law, the effect of the customs law cumulates in an outright prohibition of the carriage of arms for vessel protection. Therefore, the debate remains, at least theoretically, whether a coastal state can exercise its customs law and regulation in a manner that outlaws the presence of armed personnel. The presence of armed personnel on board a foreign vessel as a prerogative of the flag state finds supports in the provisions of UNCLOS and the IMO guidelines earlier discussed in this article. Specifically, the IMO guideline to coastal and port State (Cir. 1408) enjoins coastal states to ensure that

---

[92] Tanaka (2015a), p. 88.

[93] Petrig (2013), p. 683.

[94] Tanaka (2015b), p. 542; Kanehara (1999), p. 105. Japan's interpretation of this provision allows it to view the passage of foreign vessels with nuclear weapons as non-innocent.

[95] UNCLOS art 19(2).

[96] Tanaka (2015a), p. 88.

[97] Usman (2012) https://www.vanguardngr.com/2012/10/navy-arrests-ship-laden-with-arms-ammunition/; Akomolafe (2015), p. 37.

> when developing their policies and procedures on the issue, Governments, aside from ensuring internal coordination and coherence amongst the approaches of the different ministries, departments, authorities or agencies within whose competency the various matters may fall, should not establish policies and procedures which hinder or may hinder the continuation of maritime trade or interfere with the navigation of ships and should ensure that all are consistent with international law.[98]

Since applicable international rules can and are interpreted inconsistently, the extent of coastal state competence remains unsettled in the territorial sea.[99] There is, therefore, a need to coordinate efforts at interpreting existing rules, especially those relating to the principle of innocent passage to avoid the conflicts between jurisdictions and enhance legal certainty. Vijayan suggests that flag states may consider designing laws to meet with global standard recommendations for the regulation of PMSCs.[100] This suggestion is very relevant also for coastal states to ensure that they create new legal norms that reflect the realities of the involvement of armed personnel in providing maritime security.

4.2 *Invoking the Criminal Jurisdiction of the Coastal States for Criminal Violations*

UNCLOS Art. 27 provides that the criminal jurisdiction of a coastal state may not be exercised to arrest or conduct an investigation in connection with a crime onboard a vessel. However, where the consequence of the crime committed on board a vessel extends to the coastal State, or it disturbs the peace or good order of the territorial sea, a coastal state may enforce its criminal jurisdiction against a foreign merchant ship.[101] Arguably, a vessel in the territorial sea not calling at any port with armed personnel onboard, even though in violation of the state law, does not extend the crime to the coastal State. Accordingly, Petrig asserts that;

> it is doubtful that the mere presence of arms as opposed to their use in instances not covered by self- defence or a situation of necessity)-if this is an offence under the coastal State's criminal law does disturb the good order of the coastal State[102]

The Nigerian Territorial Waters Act provides a twist to the issue of criminal jurisdiction within territorial waters. The legislation provides for the arrest and prosecution of any person for an act or omission committed within the Nigerian territorial sea, if such would constitute an offence under any law in force in any part of Nigeria.[103] Section 2 (2) states that the Act covers crimes committed on board a

[98]IMO (2012b) Annex 1, par.6.

[99]Petrig (2016), p. 684.

[100]Vijayan (2014), p. 28.

[101]Egbede (2004), p. 168.

[102]Petrig (2016), p. 698.

[103]Territorial Waters Act (2004). S. 2(1).

vessel. On the premise of this provision, it may be argued that the Nigerian criminal jurisdiction is triggered in this context of a violation of the Firearms Act, prohibiting the carriage of weapons by private security personnel, without proper permits obtained from the government.[104] The provision of the Act seemingly confers unqualified criminal jurisdiction on the Nigerian government contrary to UNCLOS art.27(1). The state's criminal jurisdiction should arguably be interpreted within the confines of international obligation. Egbede argues that the presumption the legislature enacts laws consistent with its international law unless contrary is clearly expressed negates the of an supposition of unqualified criminal jurisdiction.[105] Thus, the violation of the domestic laws of Nigeria flowing from the presence of armed personnel on a transiting vessel does not provide grounds for an arrest.

A different interpretation of state competence to enforce criminal jurisdiction occurs where a vessel with armed person onboard calls at a port in internal waters. This is because, by calling at such a port, a vessel subjects itself to the coastal State's territorial sovereignty where the principle of the innocent passage does not apply.[106] Ordinarily, matters solely concerning the internal economy of a vessel are left to flag authorities.[107] However, a coastal state in such circumstance where the vessel is at port may choose to enforce their laws to protect their interests.[108] The presence of foreign-flagged vessels with arms on board at any Nigerian port constitutes a risk because it may escalate violence in the process of attempting to wade off attacks that do occur within the area. Similarly, their presence may constitute real and possible danger if in violation of import regulations or customs laws, they are taken off the vessel and introduced into the illicit firearms market.

5 Coastal State Jurisdiction and the Use of Private Protection for Commercial Vessels: A Conclusion

Maritime piracy and armed robbery against ship remain a persistent problem in the Gulf of Guinea, especially within and around Nigeria. Because of the inability of the government to adequately tackle these threats, PMSC engagement arises as a response to defend commercial shipping through deterring the commission of these serious criminal offences at sea. In line with the utilisation of their services, there now exists an identifiable body of regulation governing their use. The interrogation of the regulation of the use of armed personnel onboard foreign vessels from a Nigerian perspective reveals the applicability of a scattering of international and domestic laws as well as self-regulatory guidelines. How the provisions of the mesh

[104]Firearms Act (2004) ss.18, 19 and 21.

[105]Egbede (2004), p. 173.

[106]UNCLOS, art 8; Bardin (2002), p. 30; Petrig 698.

[107]Churchill and Lowe (1988), pp. 54–55; Petrig 698, UNCLOS art 25.

[108]Ibid.

framework apply depends on the location of the foreign vessel. This analysis revealed that legal uncertainty pervades coastal state regulation of the use of armed personnel onboard foreign vessels.

In sum, it is clear that Nigeria has no power to regulate in the high sea, EEZ and contiguous maritime zones, the use of armed personnel on foreign-flagged merchant vessels because of the laws of the sea that denies a coastal state general prescriptive jurisdiction within these areas. The same level of clarity is not ascribed to the nature of coastal state competence in the territorial seas, and internal waters due to the varied interpretation of the State's rights and obligations applied under the principle of innocent passage, in the context of the use of armed personnel for vessel protection. Notably, while there is no controversy of the lack of competence of a coastal state to prohibit the use of armed personnel on a foreign merchant vessel in the high sea, the legal uncertainty existing from the territorial sea may have a ripple effect on how states, shipowners and PMSCs conduct their services requiring the use of firearms.

References

--, *Best Management Practices for Protection against Somalia Based Piracy* (Version 4, 2011); BIMCO (2014) Cir.3/14

Akomolafe B (2015) Bad Roads, Weak Naira Cripple Maritime. New Telegraph:36–37

Ali-Deen K (2015) Maritime Security Cooperation in the Gulf of Guinea: prospects and challenges. Brill Njihoff

Bardin A (2002) Coastal State Jurisdiction over Foreign Vessels. Pace Int Law Rev 14(1):27–76

Bürgin A, Schneider P (2015) Regulation of private maritime security companies in Germany and Spain: a comparative study. Ocean Dev Int Law 46(2):123–137

Carreira Da Cruz M (2017) Regulating private maritime security by standards: causes and legal consequences. Maritime Safety Secur Law J 3:63–81

Chaisee J, Ji X (2018) Soft law in international law-making: how soft international taxation law in reshaping international economic governance. Asian J WTO Int Health Law Policy 13 (2):463–509

Churchill RR, Lowe AV (1988) The law of the sea. Manchester University Press, Manchester

Djalal H (2005) Combating piracy: co-operation needs, efforts, and challenges. In: Johnson D, Valencia M (eds) Piracy in Southeast Asia, status, issues and responses. ISEAS Publishers, Singapore

Dubner B (2011) On the on the definition of the crime of sea piracy revisited: customary v treaty law and the jurisdictional implications thereof. J Marit Law Commer 42(1):71–98

Dutton Y (2014) Gunslingers on the high sea: a call for regulation. Duke J Comp Int Law:107–160

Egbede E (2004) The Nigerian territorial waters legislation and the 1982 law of the sea convention. Int J Marine Coast Law 19:2,151–2,176

Eruaga OA (2016) Towards a normative shift in maritime security governance : appraising private maritime security companies in Nigeria's anti-piracy and armed robbery at sea institutional framework. Akungba Law J 4(1):311–327

Eruaga OA, Mejia M (2019) Piracy and armed robbery against ships: revisiting international law definitions and requirements in the context of the Gulf of Guinea. Ocean Yearb 33:421–455

Exclusive economic Zone Act, Cap E17, LFN 2004

Firearms Act, Cap F12, LFN 2004

Guzman AT, Meyer TL (2010) International soft law. J Legal Anal 2(1):171–225

Harmful Waste (Special Criminal Provisions etc) Act, Cap H1, LFN 2004

Hasan S, Hassan D (2016) Current arrangement to combat piracy in the Gulf of Guinea region: an evaluation. J Maritime Law Commer 47:171–218

Hespen I (2014) Protecting merchant ships from maritime piracy by privately contracted armed security personnel: a comparative analysis of flag state legislation and port and coastal state requirements. J Marit Law Commer 45(361–400):361

Husted T (2019) Gulf of Guinea: recent trends in piracy and armed robbery. Congressional Research Services https://fas.org/sgp/crs/row/IF11117.pdf

IMO (2012a) (Revised) Interim Guidance to Ship Owners, Ship Operators and Shipmasters on the Use of Privately Contracted Armed Security Personnel on Board Ships in the High Risk Area, MSC.1/Circ.1405/Rev.2

IMO (2012b) Interim Recommendations for Port and Coastal States Regarding the use of Privately Contracted Armed Security Personnel on Board Ships in the High Risk Area, MSC.1/ Circ. 1408

IMO (2012c) Interim Guidance to Private Maritime Security Companies Providing Contracted Armed Security Personnel on Board Ships in the High Risk Area, MSC.1/Circ. 1443

IMO (2014) Reports on Acts of Piracy and Armed Robbery against Ships: Acts Reported during January 2014, IMO Doc. MSC.4/Circ.206

IMO (2015) (Revised) Interim Recommendations for Flag States Regarding the use of Privately Contracted Armed Security Personnel on Board Ships in the High Risk Area, MSC.1/Circ. 1406/Rev.3

IMO (2016) Reports on Acts of Piracy and Armed Robbery against Ships: Acts Reported during January 2014, IMO Doc. MSC.4/Circ.234

IMO, Global Integrated Shipping Information System (GISIS) website, https://gisis.imo.org/Public/PAR/Default.aspx

IMO Assembly, Code of Practice for the Investigation of Crimes of Armed Robbery against Ships, Resolution A 26/Res.1025 (18 January 2010)

International Hydrographic Organization (IHO) (1953) Limits to Oceans and Seas: Special Publication No. 28, 3rd edn. Monégasque, Monte Carlo

International Maritime Bureau (IMB), Piracy and Armed Robbery Against Ships (1 January-31 December 2015)

International Maritime Bureau (IMB), Piracy and Armed Robbery Against Ships (1 January-31 December 2019). https://www.icc-ccs.org/reports/2019_Annual_Piracy_Report.pdf

Isanga JM (2009–2010) Countering persistent contemporary sea piracy: expanding jurisdictional regimes. Am Univ Law Rev 59(5):1292–1293

Jesus JL (2003) Protection of foreign ships against piracy and terrorism at sea: legal aspects. Int J Marine Coast Law 18:363–400

Kanehara A (1999) The Japanese legal system concerning innocent passage of foreign vessels (1990-1998). Jpn Annu J Int Law 42:90–110

Korowicz MS (1959) Sovereignty in the practice of international law. Domestic Jurisdiction. In: Introduction to International Law. Springer, Dordrecht

Kraska J (2015) Excessive Coastal State Jurisdictional Control: Shipboard Armed Security Personnel. In: Ringbom H (ed) Jurisdiction over ships: post UNCLOS developments in the law of the sea. Brill Njihoff, Boston

Liss C (2012) Commercial anti-piracy escorts in the Malacca Strait. In: Berube CG, Cullen P (eds) Maritime private security: market responses to piracy, terrorism and waterborne security risks in the 21st Century Oxon: United Kingdom, Routledge

Liss C (2013) Private military and security companies in maritime security governance. In: Jakobi AP, Wolf KD (eds) The transnational governance of violence and crime. Palgrave Macmillan, Hampshire

Liss C (2015) (Re)Establishing control? Flag state regulation of antipiracy PMSCs. Ocean Dev Int Law 46:84–97

Liss C (2017) Challenging sovereignty and state control of violence at sea? The operations of private anti-piracy security providers. In: Gertheiss S, & Ors (eds) Resistance and change in world politics: international dissidence. Palgrave Macmillan

Liwang H (2017) Piracy off west Africa from 2010 to 2014: an analysis. WMU J Maritime Affairs 16:385–403

Marin J, Mudric M, Mikac R (2017) Private maritime security contractors and the use of lethal force in maritime domain. In: Andreone G (ed) The future of the law of the sea: bridging gaps between national, individual and common interests, Springer Open

Megbolu C, Onwubu C (2012) Nigeria: NIMASA, Joint Task Force Take Battle to Sea Bandits. This Day

Mejia M (2003) Maritime gerrymandering: Dilemma in defining piracy, terrorism and other acts of maritime violence. J Int Commer Law 2:153–175

Murphy M (2013) Petro-piracy: oil and troubled waters. Orbis 57:424–437

Otto L (2015) Maritime crime in Nigeria and waters beyond: analysing the Period 2009 to 2013. Afr Insight 45:15–29

Parsons DM (2010) Protecting the Booty: creating a regulatory framework to govern increased use of private security companies in the fight against pirates. Tulane Maritime Law J 35:153–182

Petrig A (2013) The use of force and firearms by private maritime security companies against suspected pirates. Int Comp Law Q 62:667–701

Petrig A (2016) Regulating PMSCs at sea: operational and legal specificities. Presentation at the United Nations Human Rights Council Intergovernmental Working Group on Private Military and Security Companies, 5th Session, Geneva, 12-16 December, 2016

Richemond-Barak D (2014) Can self-regulation work? Lessons from the private security and military industry. Mich J Int Law 35(4):773–826

Roach JA (2010) Agora: piracy prosecutions, countering piracy off Somalia: international law and international institutions. Am J Int Law 104:396–416

Sharama S (1987) The single maritime boundary regime and the relationship between the continental shelf and the exclusive economic zone. Int J Estuarine Coastal, 203

Tanaka Y (2015a) The international law of the sea, 2nd edn. Cambridge University Press, Cambridge

Tanaka Y (2015b) Navigational rights and freedoms. In: Rothwell D et al (eds) Oxford handbook on the law of the sea. Oxford University Press, Oxford

Territorial Waters Act, Cap T5 LFN 2004

UN Security Resolution (2011) S/RES/2018

United Nations, *Convention on the Law of the Sea* (Montego Bay,10 December 1982) 1833 UNTS 3/ 21 ILM 1261 (1982) entered into force 16 November 1994)

United Nations Sec. Gen. (2012) Report of the United Nations Assessment Mission on Piracy in the Gulf of Guinea (7 to 24 November 2011) S/2012/45

Usman E (2012) Navy Arrests Ship laden with Arms, Ammunition. The Vanguard (Online). https://www.vanguardngr.com/2012/10/navy-arrests-ship-laden-with-arms-ammunition

Vijayan S (2014) The use of armed forces on merchant vessels without strict rules on the use of force. J Marit Law Commer 45(1):15–26

Williams E (2014) Private armed guards in the fight against piracy. In: Papastavridis E, Trapp KN (eds) La criminalité en me: Crimes at Sea. Brill Nijhoff, Boston, MA

Osatohanmwen O. Anastasia Eruaga PhD, is a Research Fellow at the Nigerian Institute of Advanced Legal Studies, Abuja, Nigeria.

Joint Development of Transboundary Natural Resources: Lessons from the Nigeria-Sao Tome and Principe Joint Development Zone

Adaeze Okoye, Mariam Masini, and Alache Fisho

Contents

A. Okoye (✉)
University of Brighton, Brighton, UK
e-mail: a.okoye@brighton.ac.uk

M. Masini
National Petroleum Agency of Sao Tome and Principe (ANP-STP), Sao Tome, Sao Tome and Principe
e-mail: mariam.masini@anp-stp.st

A. Fisho
Commonwealth Secretariat, London, UK
e-mail: a.fisho@commonwealth.int

C. Eboe-Osuji et al. (eds.), *Nigerian Yearbook of International Law 2018/2019*,
Nigerian Yearbook of International Law 2018/2019,
https://doi.org/10.1007/978-3-030-69594-1_5

1 Introduction

The Treaty between the Federal Republic of Nigeria and the Democratic of Sao Tome and Principe on the Joint Development of Petroleum and other resources, in respect of Areas of the Exclusive Economic Zone of the Two States was signed 19 years ago in 2001.[1] In 2021, the joint development zone (JDZ) celebrates its twentieth anniversary as a provisional arrangement. The Treaty set an initial duration of 45-years with a mandatory review in year 30.[2]

For the past five years, very little interest has been shown by both countries in the zone and activities had been stalled by the apparent reluctance of both states to fund the Joint Authority established under the Treaty.[3] More recently in 2019, there has been renewed activity, including the inauguration of the 8th joint development authority board[4] and a new production sharing contract (PSC) was signed with Total, for the exploration of three key blocks located in the JDZ between Nigeria and Sao Tome and Principe.[5] This has also drawn fresh attention to this joint zone of cooperation across an overlapping Exclusive Economic Zone (EEZ) maritime boundary and so, this is a good time to review the joint development model utilized and compare with other examples. Nevertheless, the joint development has had a chequered history, with the lack of commercial find and allegations of corruption hampering progress.[6] Since its inception, petroleum blocks in the JDZ have been offered in two licensing rounds which were tarnished by a lack of transparency and procedural deficiencies.[7]

The Treaty in reference to 'resources' covers more scope than hydrocarbons, although specific focus is given to petroleum resources of the zone.[8] According to part nine of the treaty, the resources that are covered comprises the joint commercial

[1]Treaty between the Federal Republic of Nigeria and the Democratic of São Tomé e Príncipe on the Joint Development of Petroleum and other resources, in respect of Areas of the Exclusive Economic Zone of the Two States (21 February 2001). Also herein referred to as the Nigeria—STP treaty.

[2]Article 51of the Nigeria—STP treaty. For the sake of certainty to potential investors, despite the expiry or termination of the Treaty itself the provisions related to development contracts remain in full force after the termination date.

[3]The original treaty referred to the joint authority (part 3 of the Nigeria- STP treaty) however in practice it is known as the joint development authority—this terminology is used later in the chapter when the management practice is discussed. The last Joint Ministerial Council (part 2 of the Nigeria-STP Treaty) meeting was in 2014, and between 2015 and 2017 both Governments did not fund the JDA budget. São Tomé e Príncipe 4th EITI Report 2016-2017 (25 of February 2019), pp. 23–24.

[4]See website of Nigeria Sao Tome and Principe Joint development Authority (NSTPJDA) 19 January 2019 https://nstpjda.org/nstpjda-appoints-the-eight-board/.

[5]Goodrich (2019); For a definition of the PSC model, see Sao Tome and Principe (2014) 1st EITI Report 2003–2013 p. 20.

[6]Jeremiah (2018).

[7]Human Rights Watch (2010).

[8]Article 3.5 of the Nigeria-STP treaty. [Part 8 of the treaty].

development of both petroleum and non-petroleum resources.[9] There is specific reference to fishing activity which the treaty defines in reference to 'exploitation of the living natural resources of the zone'.[10] The proportion in which each State shares the benefits and obligations arising from the joint zone is 60% to Nigeria and 40% to Sao Tome and Principe.[11] This chapter examines the Treaty between the Federal Republic of Nigeria and the Democratic of Sao Tome and Principe with a focus on the management structure and other potential lessons. It is viewed as a potential model of international cooperation for African states in the Gulf of Guinea and beyond.[12] This is an area with a number of maritime boundary disputes and it is important that the right lessons are learnt from this zone of cooperation.

As a comparative example, this chapter also examines the Timor Sea Treaty signed in 2002 between Timor Leste and Australia which established a Designated Authority responsible for day-to-day activities in the zone.[13] In this case, The National Petroleum and Mineral Authority (ANPM) of Timor Leste has been appointed the Designated Authority for the zone. The ANPM annual budget is split between the JPDA and the Timor Leste Exclusive Area and varies for each internal department of the organisation.[14]

In 2018, after sixteen years of the Timor Sea Treaty implementation, the Timor Leste and Australia Governments signed a Maritime Boundary Treaty as a result of a compulsory conciliation proceedings initiated by Timor Leste pursuant to the United Nations Convention on the Law of the Sea (UNCLOS).[15] The ANPM record of management and accountability in the joint development zone has been in line with Timor Leste progress in implementing the Extractive Industries Transparency Initiative (EITI) standard,[16] and the new treaty again appoints ANPM as the Designated Authority in the new Sunrise Unitised Area.[17]

The chapter commences with an examination of joint development zones in international law, then looks at the joint development zone between Nigeria and Sao Tome and Principe, the third part, takes a comparative look at the agreement between Democratic Republic of Timor Leste and the Commonwealth of Australia. Finally, the chapter concludes with lessons learnt from the implementation so far and

---

[9] Article 32 Nigeria—STP Treaty.

[10] Article 1(11) Nigeria—STP Treaty.

[11] Article 3.1. Nigeria—STP Treaty.

[12] Tanga Biang (2010).

[13] Article 6 Timor Sea Treaty (2002).

[14] National Petroleum and Mineral Authority of Timor-Leste 2017 Annual Report (10 of July 2018), p. 20.

[15] "Conciliation Between the Democratic Republic of Timor-Leste and the Commonwealth of Australia", Timor-Leste Maritime Boundary Office (6 March 2018 see Article 298(1)(a)(i) and Annex V of the UNCLOS.

[16] In 14 February 2018, Timor-Leste has been assessed to have meaningful progress in implementing the EITI Standard. https://eiti.org/news/timorleste-meets-all-of-requirements-of-eiti-standard.

[17] Article 6 of Annex B to the 2018 treaty (Greater Sunrise Special Regime).

suggests some key principles that will be of relevance to African states seeking to pursue cooperative and joint development of petroleum and non-petroleum marine resources.

2 Joint Development Zones in International Law

International judicial recognition of the joint development concept can be found in the International Court of Justice (ICJ) 1969 *North Sea Continental Shelf Cases.*[18] *The ICJ* in this case, pointed out that methods chosen for delimitation may lead to overlapping claims which could be resolved:

> ...by an agreed, or failing that by an equal division of the overlapping areas, or *by agreements for joint exploitation, the latter solution appearing particularly appropriate when it is a question of preserving the unity of a deposit.* [para. 99][19]

This recognised the necessity for joint development across national boundaries. An earlier practice of joint development can be traced to the United States in the 1930s[20] but this was in the form of unitisation between fields or tracts with separate rights holders in a national jurisdiction, in order to preserve the unity of the deposit and produce more efficiently.[21] Transboundary or cross-border unitisation can also occur, when an identified reservoir extends beyond the delimited countries boundary line to which a company or companies hold rights to exploit.[22] Such unitization may require agreement on two levels: country and company level.[23] The notion of joint exploitation in both these senses (joint development and transboundary unitisation) deals with the notion of mutual benefit to preserve and maximise efficiency in view

---

[18]Miyoshi (1999), p. 1.

[19]*North Sea Continental Shelf Cases* (1969).

[20]Miyoshi (1999).

[21]The practice in the US would have been more akin to unitisation than joint development. See Bastida et al. (2007).

[22]An example can be found in the treaty between the Federal republic of Nigeria and the republic of Equatorial Guinea concerning their maritime boundary (2000).

Article 6.2 "In implementing paragraph 1 of this Article within the area formed by straight lines connecting points (ii), (iii), (iv) and (v) set forth in Article 2, the Contracting Parties shall authorise the relevant government entities in association with the relevant concession holders to establish appropriate unitisation and other arrangements to enable this area to be developed in a commercially feasible manner. Such arrangements shall not be effective until the entry into force of this Treaty". The protocol implementing this article was signed in 2002; See also: Offshore Magazine (2001) which states "The agreed boundary left the Ekanga oilfield on the Nigerian side of the line, and the larger Zafiro oilfield that was already in production on the Equatorial Guinean side. Nigeria stipulated that there must be an agreement, that the two oilfields, which form a single structure straddling the new boundary, be exploited jointly for the benefit of both states and their oil concessionaires in pre-agreed proportions." Other examples include UK/Norway Frigg Agreement 1976 see Fox (1989), p. 30.

[23]See the UK—Norway example (Frigg field, Statjford field and Murchison field) Taylor et al. (1988).

of the nature of petroleum deposits which often do not lie wholly within a delimited region or may exist in a contested area.[24]

Joint development zones (JDZs) can be created in any geographic location but it is often used in offshore maritime zones.[25] Therefore the regime and nature of maritime boundary delimitation has contributed to the development of the concept. Maritime boundary delimitation in international law is governed by the UNCLOS 1982 which came into force in 1994.

The provisions of the UNCLOS on the Continental Shelf and the Exclusive Economic Zones (EEZ), while clarifying the position and distance of the continental shelf and the EEZ, has also led to an increase of boundary delimitation disputes.[26] The two regimes of the continental shelf and the EEZ co-exist but are also independent of each other.[27] The right to a continental shelf is inherent in the coastal state and does not have to be expressly proclaimed.[28] Whereas there appears to be the need for express proclamation of the EEZ.[29] Nevertheless the concept of the EEZ has more relevance to the African countries as it became an essential part of UNCLOS compromise taking into account the interests of developing countries in the management of the living natural resources.[30]

Historically in the early 70s, African states (following Latin American states) sought recognition for exclusive economic and fishing zones.[31] This can be seen in the 1974 Organisation of African Unity (OAU) Declaration on the issues of the Law of the Sea, where part C is titled: *Exclusive economic zone concept including exclusive fishery zone*.[32] The concept of the EEZ is therefore linked to rights to fishing and the rights to explore living and mineral resources. This can be seen in the Nigeria—STP treaty which focuses on joint development in respect of the EEZ covering both petroleum development and fishing.

Under UNCLOS, the territorial sea is given an upper limit of 12 nautical miles from the convention baselines.[33] Furthermore Article 76 of UNCLOS also provides for the continental shelf regime and it states that:

> The continental shelf of a coastal State comprises *the seabed and subsoil of the submarine areas* that extend beyond its territorial sea throughout the natural prolongation of its land

---

[24]Miyoshi (1999).

[25]Bastida et al. (2007).

[26]Mensah (2006), p. 144. Mensah was ITCLOS judge from 1996 to 2005.

[27]GrBec (2014), pp. 69–70; Attard (1987).

[28]Article 77(3) UNCLOS "The rights of the coastal State over the continental shelf do not depend on occupation, effective or notional, or on any express proclamation."

[29]Fox (1989), p. 29.

[30]Nandan (1987).

[31]Ibid, Charles (2019), pp. 22–28.

[32]16th July 1974. This was the result of council of ministers meetings on 17–24 May 1973 (Ethiopia) & 6–11 June 1974 (Somalia). This also followed the 1972 African seminar on the law of the sea. African States.

[33]Article 3 UNCLOS.

> territory to the outer edge of the continental margin, or to a distance of 200 nautical miles from the baselines from which the breadth of the territorial sea is measured where the outer edge of the continental margin does not extend up to that distance.

The right of coastal states to the continental shelf is now seen as a customary international right as well as a convention right.[34] This is coupled with sovereign rights in the exclusive economic zones: "for the purpose of ***exploring and exploiting, conserving and managing the natural resources, whether living or non-living, of the waters superjacent to the seabed and of the seabed and its subsoil,*** and with regard to other activities for the economic exploitation and exploration of the zone, such as the production of energy from the water, currents and winds;"[35] The breadth of the EEZ should not to extend beyond "200 nautical miles from the baselines from which the breadth of the territorial sea is measured."[36] The EEZ regime provides a more extensive scope for control of the marine environment.[37]

Under UNCLOS, the notion of cooperation can also be identified in the preamble, Article 74(3) and Article 83(3). These articles support the argument that these cooperative agreements should be made pending a final delimitation agreement, that is as a temporary cooperative measure. It states that:

> Pending agreement as provided for in paragraph 1, the States concerned, in a spirit of understanding and cooperation, shall make every effort to enter into provisional arrangements of a practical nature and, during this transitional period, not to jeopardize or hamper the reaching of the final agreement. Such arrangements shall be without prejudice to the final delimitation.[38]

This need for cooperation is heightened in African countries because of economic and human development needs as well as the challenging geographical boundaries. These boundaries are the result of the OAU 1964 declaration[39] which preserved the notions of territorial sovereignty based on colonial boundaries. This is somewhat counter-intuitive as these boundaries were established with a lack of sensitivity to the

---

[34]Ong (1999).

[35]Article 56(1)(a) UNCLOS.

[36]Article 57 UNCLOS.

[37]Fox (1989), p. 29 although the BIICL conclude their recommendations for a model on the basis of the continental shelf because of debates about the necessity for national proclamations. For example, US Proclamation of EEZ 1983.

[38]Article 74(3) & Article 83(3) UNCLOS.

[39]"SOLEMNLY DECLARES that all Member States pledge themselves to respect the borders existing on their achievement of national independence." AHG/Res 16(1) see also: Touval (1967), p. 102 where points out quite clearly the irony: "Aversion to the international borders drawn by the colonial powers, if not their complete rejection, has been a consistent theme of anticolonial nationalism in Africa. The borders are blamed for the disappearance of a unity which supposedly existed in Africa in precolonial times; they are regarded as arbitrarily imposed, artificial barriers separating people of the same stock, and they are said to have balkanized Africa. The borders are considered to be one of the humiliating legacies of colonialism which, according to this view, independent Africa ought to abolish."

pre-colonial history, cohesiveness of ethnic groups and cultures or concerns for the geography of the continent[40] and as a result there are significant boundary disputes which can be tedious, costly and detrimental to commercial success. [41]

The African Charter on Maritime Security, Safety and Development (Lomé Charter) signed in 2016 identifies this further impetus in the African context because the scope includes "all measures for the sustainable exploitation of marine resources and optimisation of development opportunities of sectors related to the sea" (Article 4(c). This emphasises a commitment in the African continent to exploring sustainable and efficient ways of developing joint resources. [42] Articles 30–40 stress cooperation in a number of areas including exploitation, fishing, security and legal matters.

In a regional maritime sense this drive for cooperation can be seen in the establishment of the Gulf of Guinea Commission (GGC). The GGC treaty signed on 3 July 2001 points out that: "the Commission shall constitute a framework of consultation among the countries of the Gulf of Guinea for cooperation and development, as well as for the prevention, management and resolution of conflicts that may arise from the delimitation of borders and the economic and commercial exploitation of natural resources within the territorial boundaries, particularly in the overlapping EEZ of our States."[43] This demonstrates the centrality of cooperation to that regions. This Commission has met with limited success although it has been revitalized.[44]

There is increasing state practice of joint development agreements both in the absence of boundary delimitation[45] or across delimited lines,[46] although the new UNCLOS regime, has created heightened interest in maritime boundary delimitation

---

[40]Okafor-Yarwood (2015).

[41]For example land and maritime boundary between Cameroon and Nigeria (Cameroon v Nigeria: Equatorial Guinea intervening) (2002) ICJ Reps p. 303.

[42]Okonkwo (2017).

[43]Article 2 Lomé Charter.

[44]See website: "From July 2015 to February 2017, the Executive Secretariat carried out various activities to revitalize the GGC in order to make the Commission more relevant in regional affairs" https://cggrps.com/en/actividades-do-secretariado-executivo/.

See also Additional Protocol to the Treaty establishing the Gulf of Guinea Commission (2013).

[45]Miyoshi (1999) gives the following list: Kuwait—Saudi Arabia Agreement of 7 July 1965, Iran—Sharjah Memorandum of Understanding of 29 November 1971, Japan—South Korea Agreement of 30 January 1974, Malaysia—Thailand Memorandum of Understanding of 21 February 1979, Australia—Indonesia Treaty of 11 December 1989, Malaysia—Vietnam Memorandum of Understanding of 5 June 1992, Colombia—Jamaica Treaty of 12 November 1993, Argentina—United Kingdom Joint Declaration of 27 September 1995.

One can add the Nigeria—Sao Tome and Principe agreement of 21 February 2001.

[46]Miyoshi (1999) list: Bahrain—Saudi Arabia Agreement of 22 February 1958, Bahrain—Saudi Arabia Agreement of 22 February 1958, Saudi Arabia—Sudan Agreement of 16 May 1974, Iceland—Norway Agreement of 22 October 1981, Libya—Tunisia Agreement of 8 August 1988, Guinea-Bissau—Senegal Agreement of 14 October 1993.

for economic reasons including exploitation of natural resources.[47] It is doubtful whether, there is a customary international rule to cooperate.[48] However Onorato argues in the converse, that there is no 'rule of capture' in international law.[49] He points out that "in no case could any party in interest proceed unilaterally with exploitation procedures based on unrestricted capture to the prejudice of all other interest-holders involved."[50]

Therefore the increase in state practice of joint development may be linked to arguments which push for equitable sharing and effective utilisation of natural resources in opposition to absolute sovereignty and delimitation. In this sense: 'equitable utilization' should create a reconciliation of sovereignty with cooperation or joint transboundary resource management.[51] In the case of Petroleum, its fluid and migratory nature acts as a further justification for the need to maximise exploitation and production in an efficient manner.[52]

Joint development zones typically involve inter-governmental development of petroleum deposits in agreed proportions within a designated zone.[53] The example under examination is Nigeria-STP treaty signed in 2001.[54] It was driven by equitable utilisation and the need to avoid the lengthy dispute such as that which led to the ICJ *Nigeria v Cameroon* decision.[55] It follows the classic pattern of joint development which Onorato identifies:

i. A treaty between the interested States which establishes the accord and legal basis for such joint development.
ii. The establishment thereunder of an international joint commission, of equal representation between the contracting States, which acts as the administrative, supervisory and consultative overseer of the venture.
iii. The grant of exploitation rights to licensees or concessionaires (rights holders)—normally by the interested States but, possibly, also directly by the joint commission; and,
iv. The nomination by the rights-holders, subject to approval by the joint commission, of a single operator to conduct joint operations on their behalf.[56]

[47]Daniel (2005).

[48]Onorato (1977) and Ong (1999).

[49]Onorato (1968).

[50]Ibid.

[51]Schrijver (1997), p. 338.

[52]Bastida et al. (2007).

[53]"An inter-governmental arrangement of a provisional nature, designed for functional purposes of joint exploration for and/or exploitation of hydrocarbon resources of the seabed beyond the territorial sea." Miyoshi (1999); see also Bastida et al. (2007) "The joint petroleum development agreement refers to an arrangement between two states to develop and share jointly in agreed proportions the petroleum found within a designated zone of seabed and subsoil of the continental shelf or EEZ, to which both states are entitled under international law".

[54]See (n1).

[55]Daniel (2005) & Ifesi (2003).

[56]Onorato (1990).

Onorato points out the separation of distinct functions of supervision, administration and consultation by states from operations by the rights-holders and their operator.[57]

The British Institute of International and Comparative Law (BIICL) in its work on a model agreement for states for joint development identifies three main joint development models.[58] Groves condenses these models as follows:[59]

> * Model I: each state retains authority to license its own nationals (or other licensees selected by the state) to operate within the joint development zone, with provision for compulsory joint ventures between these licensees;
>
> * Model II: a joint authority with licensing and regulatory powers manages development of the resources on behalf of both states; and
>
> * Model III: one state manages development of the resources on behalf of both with the other state's participation limited to revenue sharing and monitoring.

Model I: This is described as "a system of compulsory joint ventures between the states and their nationals".[60] The examples given include the 1974 Japan/South Korea Agreement and the Kuwait/Saudi Arabia Agreement 1965 variant.

In the example given (JSKA) the states retain control of development through splitting the wider area into subzones and each state then authorises its own concessionaries to explore under a joint operation with the concessionaires chosen by the other state.[61] Concessionaires of both parties shall be entitled to equal shares of natural resources in the zone and the expenses also equally shared.[62] There is a joint commission which has a limited general supervisory function.[63] This model is also interesting because it has a separate taxation system where each party including local authorities may impose taxation on its own concessionaires.[64]

Model II: This refers to a supra-national authority. The example given here was the Malaysian Thailand Memorandum of Understanding 1979[65] and the negotiations between Australia and Indonesia in respect to Area A of the Timor Gap zone of Co-operation.[66] The Nigeria and Sao Tome and Principe agreement discussed in this chapter, would be a further example of this model.

---

57 Ibid.

58 Fox (1989), pp. 115–153.

59 Groves (2005), p. 81.

60 Fox (1989), p. 116.

61 See the treaty—Agreement between Japan and the Republic of Korea concerning joint development of the southern part of the continental shelf adjacent to both countries—signed at Seoul on 30th January 1974—Article IV & V.

62 Article IX (1 & 2) of the Japan—Korea treaty.

63 Article XXIV of the Japan—Korea treaty.

64 Article XVII (2) of the Japan—Korea treaty.

65 Fox (1989), p. 115 although problems were noted in its implementation see treaty text: https://www.un.org/depts/los/LEGISLATIONANDTREATIES/PDFFILES/TREATIES/jap-kor1974south.pdf.

66 See Fox (1989), p. 115 & Chap 3.

Model III: One state manages development on behalf of another with the other state taking part in monitoring and a share of revenues. There are almost no pure examples of this but some variant examples given include: Qatar/Abu Dhabi 1969[67] but more relevantly the agreement in principle between Indonesia and Australia 1988 in respect of areas B and C of the Timor Gap zone of co-operation.[68] This later became the Timor-Leste—Australia Development Agreements also discussed extensively in this chapter.

3 Joint Development of Petroleum and Other Resources Between Nigeria and Sao Tome and Principe

3.1 Background

In 1998, when Sao Tome and Principe pursuant to Article 75(2) of UNCLOS deposited with the Secretary-General of the United Nations a copy of the geographical coordinates with its official maritime claim at the median line with Nigeria,[69] there was a considerable overlap between the maritime boundaries of the two African states located in the Gulf of Guinea.[70]

The Gulf of Guinea hosts one of the most important regions for oil and gas exploration, production and transportation.[71] The area of dispute between Nigeria and Sao Tome and Principe was perceived to have a high hydrocarbon potential. Therefore, between 1999 and 2000 the countries held talks in order to establish a single maritime boundary, however, without significant developments.

After several negotiations meetings, as the solution of last resort the parties were ready to refer the dispute to an international court in order to obtain a judicial resolution for their maritime boundary dispute and bearing in mind that it would be a lengthy process. In the spirit of African cooperation, during a visit to Sao Tome

[67]For treaty text see: https://www.un.org/Depts/los/LEGISLATIONANDTREATIES/PDFFILES/TREATIES/QAT-ARE1969MB.PDF.

[68]Fox (1989), p. 115.

[69]Nigeria, on the other hand, prefers to delimitate maritime boundaries with other countries based on agreement with neighbouring states. There is some support for this in Sholanke (1993).

[70]According to the United Nations Secretariat database on the deposits of charts or geographical coordinates of points, Sao Tome and Principe (STP) defined its Territorial Sea and the Exclusive Economic Zone by Law no. 1/98 of 23 March 1998. In the case of Nigeria, it was recognised by the Exclusive Economic Zone Decree no. 28 of 5 October 1978 and the Territorial Waters (Amendment) Decree 1998. The amendment of the Exclusive Economic Zone Decree by Decree no. 41 of 1998 removed the reference to median lines and replaced by a claim to a 200 mile exclusive economic zone, subject to agreement with neighbouring states. See For Nigeria see https://www.un.org/Depts/los/LEGISLATIONANDTREATIES/STATEFILES/NGA.htm For STP https://www.un.org/Depts/los/LEGISLATIONANDTREATIES/STATEFILES/STP.htm.

[71]Banchani (2016).

in August 2000 of Nigerian President Olusegun Obasanjo where he met with Sao Tome and Principe President Miguel Trovoada, the two Heads of State decided on the establishment of a Joint Development Zone (JDZ) under Article 74(3) of UNCLOS and mandated a joint technical committee, composed of representatives of each country, to negotiate the JDZ treaty.[72]

Following months of discussions and negotiations, the technical committee arrived at a consensus on a draft proposal for a treaty that would allow both countries to jointly explore petroleum and other resources on a joint development zone in areas of the EEZ of the two countries.

The JDZ represents the departure from the prevalence of boundary disputes and protracted legal disputes in the African continent into a project of cross boundary cooperation between two opposite coastal states. In essence, therefore, the path chosen by the leaders of Nigeria and Sao Tome and Principe was to put economic cooperation above the two countries' maritime boundary claims.

This is a considerable step forward bearing in mind that Sao Tome and Principe has a population of about 211,122, while Nigeria is the most populous country in Africa with a population of 214,028,302.[73] Nigeria is one of the largest economy in sub-Saharan Africa and an established oil exporter, however, in turn Sao Tome and Principe is a small island developing state and considered a country in fragile situation carrying out petroleum exploration activities.[74] In the spirit of the Lomé Charter, establishing the JDZ as a "provisional arrangements of a practical nature" under UNCLOS is seen as an exemplary model of how states can avoid delays for countries with different economic terms and allow both governments to reap immediately the economic benefits of resource exploitation while reserving their sovereign rights over the claimed areas.[75]

3.2 *Zone of Cooperation*

The Nigeria and Sao Tome and Principe joint development Treaty covers an area of approximately 34,500 Km^2, and it is subdivided into an area with a total of 11 delineated blocks and an un-delineated area designated as "Area for Future Development".[76] As opposed to other joint development treaties, the Nigeria and Sao Tome and Principe JDZ establishes a single zone (see Fig. 1).[77]

[72]Okafor (2007).

[73]Central Intelligence Agency (CIA) (2020).

[74]See IMF (2019).

[75]Article 74 (3) UNCLOS.

[76]Nigeria and São Tomé e Príncipe Joint Development Authority website available at http://nstpjda.org.

[77]Article 2 Nigeria—STP Treaty.

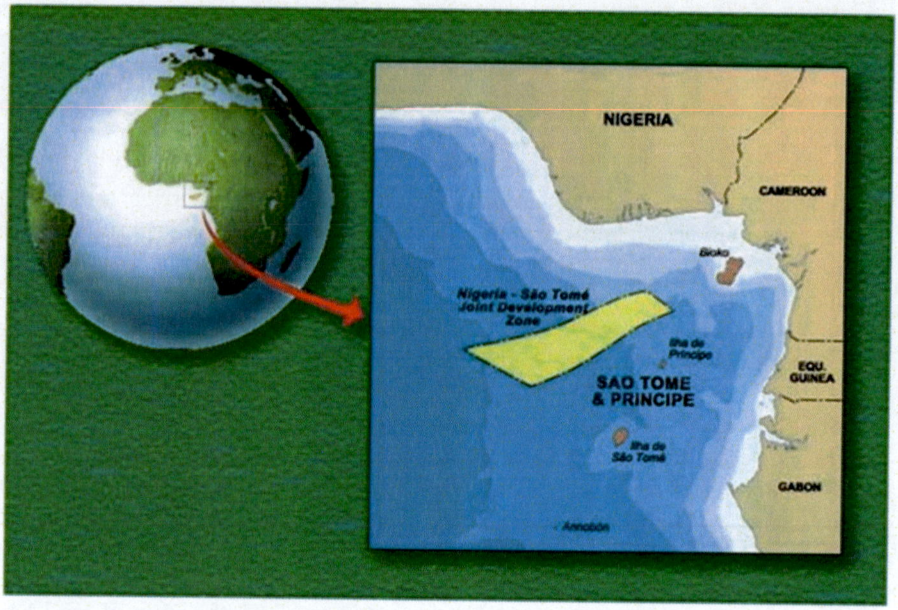

Fig. 1 Map of the Nigeria and Sao Tome and Principe Joint Development Zone. Source: Nigeria Sao-Tome & Principe Joint development Authority (Nigeria and Sao Tome and Principe Joint Development Authority website available at https://nstpjda.org/monitoring/)

A Special Regime Area within the joint development zone has been foreseen under the Treaty.[78] The special area is subject to a particular regime other than the provisions of the Treaty, which resulted in the signing of a Memorandum of Understanding on the Special Regime Area as an Appendix to the Treaty. The Memorandum required Nigeria to provide specific assistance to Sao Tome and Principe in return for assigning managing responsibilities over the Special Regime Area.[79] However, Sao Tome and Principe did not ratify the Memorandum of Understanding and, therefore, it did not enter into force.

The treaty settled in February 2001 between the two states established that all benefits arising from development activities carried out in the zone shall be shared in the proportion Nigeria 60% and Sao Tome and Principe 40%. The signing of the treaty marks an important milestone of the growing resource boom expectation in Sao Tome and Principe from the period 1997 to 2000.[80] The expectation of vast offshore oil resources has brought Sao Tome and Principe to centre stage with

[78]Article 5 and 31.5. Nigeria-STP Treaty.

[79]Memorandum of Understanding Between The Federal Republic of Nigeria and the Democratic Republic of São Tomé and Príncipe on The Special Regime Area (21 of February 2001) see http://www.marineregions.org/documents/STP-NGA2001.pdf.

[80]Frynas and Wood (2017).

sensationalist reports on the huge prospects of the resources contained within the JDZ.[81]

From inception till date, a total of two licensing rounds have been conducted in the JDZ one in 2003 and one in 2004, with a total of six blocks being awarded. In the first licensing round only Block 1 was awarded, while Blocks 2, 3, 4 and 5 resulted from the second licensing round, with negotiations for Block 6 being inconclusive.

In spite of having a maritime area under its exclusive jurisdiction, the vast majority of Sao Tome and Principe oil revenues derives from the JDZ activities.[82] From 2003 to 2013 the JDZ declared approximately $302 million dollars of revenues from activities in the area, from which only signature bonuses have been transferred to the states and other revenues are used as part of the zone budget.[83]

In the same way there were high hopes for the future of Sao Tome and Principe as a future oil producing nation, after the licensing rounds there were mounting fears of resource mismanagement or as known in the academic literature as the "resource curse". In economic terms, the resource curse postulates that mineral intensive economies have a slow growth and, consequently, slow economic development.[84] There is not, however, a commonly shared recommendation to fight the "resource curse".[85] One of the key policy responses advocated by civil society organisations have been enhancing accountability and ensuring transparency.

With the anticipation of revenue windfalls from the JDZ, Sao Tome and Principe received significant attention from international civil society organizations, international donors and other states. Between 2003 and 2007 different projects contributed to building a legal and institutional framework for developing a transparent framework for oil activities, including the country signing up to the EITI in 2008.

For instance, as result of the legal advisory project by the Earth Institute at the Columbia University sponsored by the Open Society Institute, Sao Tome and Principe enacted an Oil Revenue Management Law in 2004.[86] The law requires public publication of payments made by companies, audits of utilization of funds, fundamentals of all awards and imposes disclosure obligations for public entities and third party obligations on petroleum contract holders to declare any benefit or unlawful advantage. Moreover, the transitional provisions of the law subjected those persons or agents and revenues belonging to Sao Tome and Principe from the JDZ to the disclosure requirements prescribed in the law.[87]

The law also established a National Oil Account (*Conta Nacional de Petróleo*) held at the New York Federal Reserve Bank, created a Permanent Fund (*Fundo Permanente*) to ensure that oil proceeds are available for future generations, a

[81]Weszkalnys (2008).

[82]Nigeria São Tome and Principe (2014), JDZ First EITI Report 2003–2013.

[83]Ibid.

[84]Gelb et al. (1988).

[85]Auty (1995).

[86]Law no. 8/2004—Oil Revenue Management Law (Lei-quadro das Receitas Petrolíferas).

[87]Article 29 ibid.

Petroleum Oversight Commission (*Comissão de Fiscalização do Petróleo*) and the Public Registration and Information Office (*Gabinete de Registo e Informação Pública*), an office mandated to keep public archives of all documents and information related to oil and its revenues.

Also, in 2004, under a governance capacity building project supported by the World Bank, a National Petroleum Agency (*Agência Nacional do Petróleo*) separated from the Ministry was established and discussions begun on the legal framework for granting petroleum licenses and conducting petroleum activities that was later adopted in 2009.[88]

On the other hand, Nigeria also seemingly started moving towards greater transparency in the natural resource industry. It voluntarily joined the EITI in 2003 and enacted the Nigeria EITI (NEITI) Act in 2007 which established NEITI as an agency of the federal government to ensure prudent management of revenues from its natural resources.[89]

However, that has not prevented allegations of corruption in the management of the licensing rounds held in the JDZ. Groves in an article examining the problems surrounding the first and second round of the licensing rounds found significant issues with the lack of transparency and the quality of bidders.[90] In fact, in 2005 the Sao Tome and Principe State Prosecutor's General Office launched an official investigation into the JDZ second licensing round which questioned the inclusion of several small Nigerian companies with little apparent expertise or capacity to develop deep water petroleum operations and alleged collusion by Sao Tomean officials.[91]

Nevertheless, the award of blocks following the second licensing round moved forward in spite of the signing of the Abuja Joint Declaration Regarding Transparency and Governance in the JDZ (Abuja Joint Declaration) in June 2004 by the then Presidents Obasanjo and President de Menezes.

This resulted in the delisting of Sao Tome and Principe from the EITI in 2010 for non-compliance mainly due to the failure to disclose information from the JDZ.[92] Human Rights Watch (HRW) reported based on interviews with Sao Tomean officials and international observers that the Nigerian side exercises greater influence over the JDZ, creating power asymmetries between the two states.[93] Thus, the acceptance by the EITI Board of Nigeria shortly after as a compliant country in

[88]Decree-law no. 5/2004 (as amended by Decree-law no. 7/2014) establishing Agência Nacional do Petróleo and Law 16/2009—Framework-Law governing Oil Operations see https://eiti.org/sao-tome-principe.

[89]Nigerian Extractive Industries Transparency Initiative (NEITI) website available at https://www.neiti.gov.ng/index.php.

[90]Groves (2005), p. 87.

[91]Procuradoria Geral da República São Tomé e Príncipe, 2005. Investigação e Avaliação Segundo Leilão Zona de Desenvolvimento Conjunto. December 2005 see: Weszkalnys (2008).

[92]Nigeria São Tome and Principe, JDZ First EITI Report 2003-2013 (n83), p. 14.

[93]HRW (2010), p. 16.

2011 appeared to spur good governance in the zone.[94] Therefore, examining the legal framework and the management structure would seem more sensible to understand the JDZ chequered history.

3.3 *Regulatory Framework and Transparency Status*

The 2001 Treaty between the Federal Republic of Nigeria and the Democratic Republic of Sao Tome and Principe establishes the reference framework for joint exploration and other resources in the JDZ. A Petroleum Regulations regulating the rights and obligations of license and lease holders, and contractors as well as a Model Production Sharing Contract were adopted in 2003. Furthermore, Tax Regulations have been adopted to establish the parameters of the fiscal system.

In the wake of legal and institutional reforms in Sao Tome and Principe's oil and gas sector, the Abuja Joint Declaration Regarding Transparency and Governance in the JDZ was adopted in 2004. The Abuja Joint Declaration provides a set of principles that requires fundamentals of all awards, contracts, company payments, and utilization of funds relating to resources in the zone be made public, including the budget of the Joint Authority and its annual audits.[95] Public means that all information subject to the disclosure requirements of the declaration shall be posted and maintained on the internet page of the Joint Authority.[96] As of this writing neither the Abuja Joint Declaration nor information subject to disclosure have been made public in the website.[97]

Nevertheless, the JDZ established its Joint Authority—EITI Subcommittee in 2014 following the approval of Sao Tome and Principe's application for EITI candidate status in 2012 and produced the first EITI JDZ report that captured a ten year period between 2003 and 2013.[98] Whilst at the same time, Sao Tome and Principe produced its first EITI Report for the same period.[99] In turn, the NEITI published in 2011 the first Nigeria EITI Report covering oil and gas for the period 2006–2008 and in 2015 its 2012 and 2013 reports.[100]

To date, Sao Tome and Principe has published its 2017 EITI report covering the oil and gas sector and Nigeria its 2018 report.[101] The NEITI has been hailed as an

[94]Nigeria São Tome and Principe, JDZ First EITI Report 2003-2013 (n83), p. 14.

[95]Ibid at p. 15.

[96]Ibid.

[97]Nigeria and São Tomé e Príncipe Joint Development Authority website available at http://nstpjda.org/monitoring/.

[98]Nigeria São Tome and Principe, JDZ First EITI Report 2003-2013 (n93).

[99]São Tome and Principe First EITI Report 2003-2013 (2014).

[100]For the reports see https://eiti.org/nigeria.

[101]Ibid.

EITI showcase,[102] however, notwithstanding the progress that has been made in the Nigerian oil and gas sector the JDZ has published a single EITI report.

Due to difficulties in obtaining data from the JDZ, at the request of the Government of Sao Tome and Principe the EITI Board accepted in 2016 the adapted implementation with respect to reconciliation of revenues and disclosure of information related to the Nigeria-Sao Tome and Principe joint development zone concerning the 2015 and 2016 reports.[103] The decision acknowledged that the Government of Sao Tome and Principe and the Sao Tome and Principe EITI National Committee do not have the legal authority to compel the Joint Authority or companies operating in the JDZ to participate in the EITI process. Yet, as seen with the implementation of classic models for joint development of hydrocarbons, no example exists of the right management structure that will ensure transparency. The lesson, then, at least in the abstract appears to be the practical outcomes in the implementation of the different models.

3.4 Management Structure of the JDZ Treaty

The choice of a management structure for a joint zone is not an easy task. According to the BIICL's models, model I is a joint venture model based on a two-state structure, while model II creates a joint authority and, finally, model III a single state structure where one state will be responsible of managing the zone on behalf of both states. In theory, the Nigeria and Sao Tome and Principe JDZ falls within model II.

The Joint Authority or the Joint Development Authority (JDA) established under the Treaty manages the joint zone on behalf of both states. The Board that was initially inaugurated in 2002, is governed by four Executive Directors, two of which appointed by each Head of State.[104]

Each Executive Director heads one department, as follows: (i) Monitoring and Inspections Department which is responsible for regulating the exploration and development of the petroleum resources in the JDZ; (ii) Commercial and Investments Department with the responsibility for commercial issues, planning and management of investments; (iii) Non-Hydrocarbon Resources Department to promote and develop other natural resources in the JDZ, especially fisheries; and, finally, (iv) Finance and Administration Department in charge of finance and accounts, budgets, procurement and human resources.

[102]EITI "Nigeria EITI: Making transparency count, uncovering billions" https://eiti.org/files/documents/2012_case_study_-_eiti_in_nigeria.pdf.

[103]EITI "The EITI Board accepts the São Tomé and Príncipe request for adapted implementation" (2016) https://eiti.org/board-decision/2016-03.

[104]Article 9 and 10 Nigeria—STP Treaty.

The provisions of the treaty grant privileges and immunities entered into between both states to the JDA.[105] For this reason, none of the states has the power to exercise unilateral jurisdiction over the zone.

In practice, the Authority is accountable to the Joint Ministerial Council (JMC), composed of a maximum of four ministers or persons of corresponding rank appointed by the Heads of State of each state, with the overall responsibility for matters relating to exploration and exploitation of the resources in the joint development zone.[106] The Treaty also establishes a Secretariat to assist the Joint Ministerial Council and the Joint Authority in their administrative work.[107]

It is, thus, the case that the JDZ separates the distinct functions of a classical joint development model of international political oversight, management and allocation of resources from the commercial activities.[108] However, the role of the JMC and the JDA can be seen in a certain blurring of the borders between the functions of political oversight and management.

The JMC role with assigned overall responsibilities with respect to the development of the activities within the joint zone includes, for instance, granting prior approval for the JDA to enter into a PSC which may subject the award process to elite pressure as decisions are approved by consensus.[109] Not surprisingly, in spite of a criminal investigation of corruption, the second licensing round in the JDZ went ahead with the award of PSC.

In furtherance of the management powers granted to the JMC under the treaty, are the approval of rules, regulations and procedures for the functioning of the JDZ and the approval of management documents.[110] The administrative oversight functions attributed to the JMC requires at least two annual meetings between the ministers from each state party, and that has not been the case recently. Electoral cycles have had an impact on the frequency of meetings and the JDA has resorted to the practice to request the states for out of council approvals to ensure operation.[111] Thus, from the inception of the JDZ, the regulatory and policy framework did not suffer any changes. The absence of a commercial find has also hampered substantial investment and development activities in the JDZ.

Under BIICL model II, a Joint Authority structure is complex and involves the creation of additional bureaucracy. In contrast, model I is a more simplistic solution for allowing that each state retain control of development, as well as model III by

---

105 Article 12 Nigeria—STP Treaty.

106 Articles 6.2., 8.1 and 11.1 of the Nigeria—STP Treaty.

107 Article 14 Nigeria—STP Treaty.

108 Onorato (1990) at p. 660.

109 Articles 7.4 and 8.2(f) of the Nigeria—STP Treaty.

110 Article 8 of the Nigeria—STP Treaty.

111 Since the last JMC meeting in 2014, Nigeria held Presidential and National Assembly elections in 2015 and 2019, and São Tomé e Príncipe legislative elections in 2014 and 2018. See CIA (n73).

providing that one state manages the zone for both and the other state participates in the revenue sharing and monitoring.[112]

Evidence from the Sao Tome and Principe EITI report 2016–2017, reveals that from 2003 to 2017 the JDZ generated a cumulative revenue of about USD 300 million. However, over USD 150 million out of the USD 300 million was used for the JDZ operational management structure.[113] During this period the total contributions to the budget of the JDA by both Governments has been USD 104.730.085, with Nigeria contributions of USD 62.838.051 equivalent to 60% share and Sao Tome and Principe of USD 41.892.034 equivalent to 40% share.[114]

Due to the high costs of maintaining the JDA structure, the JMC has mandated the JDA to start an administrative restructuring process.[115] Despite the 60:40 split, Nigeria has had a dominant management role in the JDA as the head office is located in Abuja.[116] The recruitment of staff has also been unevenly distributed, with overstaffing pointed as one of the main hurdles of the very high operating cost.

Although a Joint Authority model was selected, the reality of practical implementation is that one state exerts a stronger influence on the JDA, and the results are plain to see. Indeed, Nigeria's industry practice has been used in designing the regulatory framework of the JDZ which has cast doubt on the transparency of procedures within the zone.[117]

In reviewing the BIICL model III, some have argued that the Nigeria and Sao Tome and Principe joint development treaty could have benefited from adopting a model in which Nigeria manages the zone on behalf of both states on the basis of the experience as a matured oil producer.[118] From the existing allegations of mismanagement in the JDZ,[119] it would appear reasonable to surmise that it could have the opposite of the desired effect by driving away from a joint zone of cooperation that is transparent to the fullest degree.

Sao Tome and Principe has a transparency framework governing extractive industries which the country has successfully passed in the intervening years. While the first EITI JDZ report still concludes there is work to do in increasing transparency flows between the JDZ and civil society as well as improving compliance and transparency of flows, the Sao Tome and Principe legal framework could be the reference basis to further enhancement of transparency in the JDZ.

---

[112]Lerer (2003), p. 9.

[113]São Tomé e Príncipe 4th EITI Report 2016-2017 (25 of February 2019), p. 23. (in Portuguese).

[114]Ibid, p. 24. In the case of São Tomé e Príncipe, Nigeria has been paying its 40% commitment until first oil revenue. This situation is particularly problematic since production could be a long time coming and, for instance, as per Article 4 of the total expenditures in São Tomé e Príncipe Law of the General State Budget for 2017 the country's annual budget is about USD 147 million which is less than the cumulative budget of the JDA over the period 2003–2017.

[115]Mac-Leva (2018).

[116]See Groves (2005), p. 86.

[117]Groves ibid p. 87.

[118]Ibid.

[119]The Economist Intelligence Unit (2016).

In this sense the recent signing of Total PSC mentioned earlier[120] is a very welcome development. Nevertheless, in view of the foregoing, the JMC ought to find a more practical mechanism to exercise administrative oversight over the zone. The next part will examine a different development model between a large and smaller country to deduce if lessons could be learnt which may be applicable to future negotiations of the Nigeria Sao Tome and Principe JDZ.

4 Timor Leste and Australia Joint Development Area

4.1 Background

The oil and gas fields in the Timor Gap are estimated to be worth roughly $ US65 billion. The Timor Gap has always posed a problem because of its geological complexity and overlapping seabed claims by different countries.[121]

The maritime boundary between Australia and Timor Leste has long been a matter of contention first with Portugal as the colonizing power, then Indonesia during the occupation and finally with Timor Leste. When Indonesia and Australia negotiated and had their maritime boundaries established in 1972, a gap was left which became known as the Timor Gap. Both countries eventually came to an agreement regarding this area in order to establish a 'stable environment for petroleum exploration and exploitation' without prejudicing either country's maritime boundary claims.[122] The Timor Gap Treaty was an interim measure to allow development of the oil and gas reserves in the area.

The Timor Sea resource potential was legally recognised in the 1989 Timor Gap Treaty between Australia and Indonesia. With the separation of Timor Leste from Indonesia on 25 October 1999, Australia entered into an Agreement with the United Nations Transitional Administration in East Timor (UNTAET) in February 2000[123] to govern the continuation of exploration and exploitation activities in the Timor Sea for the benefit of Australia and the soon to be independent state of Timor Leste.

The February 2000 Agreement with UNTAET was superseded by the Timor Sea Treaty (TST) which was signed in 2002 between Australia and Timor Leste on the day of Timor Leste's restoration of independence.[124] In order to safeguard ongoing seabed resource developments in the Timor Sea, the TST established a Joint Petroleum Development Area (JPDA), which coincides with the central part of the old Australia-Indonesia joint zone (Zone A). Whereas in the past revenues from

[120]See n6.

[121]Schleich (2018), p. 2.

[122]Timor Gap Treaty 1989.

[123]Australia- UNTAET agreement 1999—entered into 10th February 2000 but with effect from 25th October 1999.

[124]Timor Sea Treaty (2002).

Zone A had been shared between Australia and Indonesia on an equal basis, under the TST, revenues from seabed resources exploited within the JPDA are split 90:10 in Timor Leste's favour. In 2003, the Greater Sunrise Unitization agreement was signed and it apportioned the JPDA 20.1% and 79.9% to Australia.[125] The area from the Greater Sunrise falling within the JPDA was to be developed in similar manner. However in 2006, a treaty on Certain Maritime Arrangements in Timor Sea was reached which agreed a 50: 50 split of revenues from the area of the Greater Sunrise falling within the JPDA. This was however the subject of some controversy with allegations of espionage and an arbitration.[126] In January 2017[127] the treaty was unilaterally terminated by Timor Leste and following agreement by Australia, it ceased to be in force April 2017.[128] In 2018 a treaty was agreed between the Democratic Republic of Timor Leste and Australia establishing their maritime boundaries in the Timor Sea. The TST and the Greater Sunrise Unitization Agreement ceased to be in force as a result of the 2018 Treaty.[129] The old JPDA area under the TST now falls within the exclusive boundary of Timor Leste.[130] Rothwell observes that with the delimitation "the eastern lateral boundary comprises a number of segments that extend much further to the east and north east than the 2002 treaty, ultimately giving Timor Leste much greater entitlements over the Greater Sunrise field".[131]

The Timor Sea oil and gas fields are important to the Australian economy and include fields such as Laminaria and Greater Sunrise.[132] Laminaria is one of Australia's biggest oilfield and has provided billions to the Australian economy. The Sunrise and Troubadour ("Greater Sunrise") gas fields in the Timor Sea are estimated to contain 226 million barrels of condensate and 5.1 trillion cubic feet (TCF) of natural gas.[133]

Timor-Leste's economy is heavily dependent on oil and gas. According to the EITI Report for the 2017 financial year which was published in 2019, the oil sector accounted for 36% of the country's GDP, 98% of exports and 41% of total imports in

[125]"Production of Petroleum from the Unit Reservoirs shall be apportioned between the JPDA and Australia according to the Apportionment Ratio 20.1:79.9, with 20.1% apportioned to the JPDA and 79.9% apportioned to Australia." Article 7 The Greater Sunrise IUA.

[126]Anton (2014).

[127]Parliament of Australia (2007) *Consequences of termination of the Treaty between Australia and the Democratic Republic of Timor Leste on Certain Maritime Arrangements in the Timor Sea* https://www.aph.gov.au/Parliamentary_Business/Committees/Joint/Treaties/CMATS/Report_168_-_Certain_Maritime_Arrangements_-_Timor-Leste/section?id=committees%2Freportjnt%2F024051%2F24472.

[128]Ibid.

[129]Article 9(1) the 2018 Treaty.

[130]Strating (2018).

[131]Rothwell (2018).

[132]Mercer (2004).

[133]Wilkinson (2018).

2017.[134] Production is rapidly declining and exploration activities are limited, giving rise to discussions on the need for economic diversification.

4.2 Legal Framework for Regulation of the JPDA[135]

4.2.1 2002 Timor Sea Treaty (TST)

The 2002 treaty which established the JPDA, created a three-tiered joint administrative structure for the governance of the JPDA consisting of (i) Designated Authority, (ii) Joint Commission and (iii) Ministerial Council.[136]

The Designated Authority was the body responsible for the day-to-day regulation and management of petroleum activities within the JPDA. The National Petroleum and Mineral Authority (ANPM) of Timor-Leste was appointed as the Designated Authority for the JPDA.

The Joint Commission consisted of commissioners appointed by Timor Leste and Australia with Timor Leste having the right to appoint one more commissioner than Australia. The Joint Commission was responsible for setting policies and determining regulations relating to petroleum activities in the JPDA and oversight of the Designated Authority.[137]

The Ministerial Council consisted of an equal number of Ministers from East Timor and Australia. Its responsibility was to consider any matter relating to the operation of the Treaty referred to it by either Timor Leste or Australia.[138]

Under the terms of the treaty, Timor Leste and Australia jointly controlled, managed and facilitated the exploration, development and exploitation of the petroleum resources of the JPDA for their mutual benefit.[139]

While the Timor Sea Treaty retained a joint development approach to resource exploitation in the JPDA, it does so on terms that differ significantly from those applicable in Area A of the original Timor Gap Treaty.

4.2.2 Petroleum Mining Code of 2003

Timor Leste and Australia jointly enacted a Petroleum Mining Code (PMC) to govern the exploration, development and exploitation of petroleum within the JPDA, as well as the export of petroleum from the JPDA.

[134] For the report see: https://eiti.org/timorleste.

[135] See reference list. Also see the Timor Leste authority website: http://www.anpm.tl/jpda2/.

[136] Article 6 TST (n125).

[137] Article 6(2) (c) TST.

[138] Article 6 (2) (d) TST.

[139] Article 3(b) TST.

The form and structure of the Petroleum Mining Code follows that of a typical national legislation for regulation of the petroleum sector with necessary adaptations to provide for the joint rights and obligations of the two countries.

The PMC provided for the graticulation of the JPDA,[140] authorisations for activities, appointment of an operator, assignment and change of control, execution of Production Sharing Contracts[141] between the Designated Authority and proposed contractor parties, the rights and obligations of parties under a PSC,[142] unitization,[143] termination off rights etc.

4.2.3 2003 International Unitization Agreement (IUA) for Greater Sunrise

This agreement created the framework to develop the Greater Sunrise fields as a single unit. Australia claimed that 79.9 of the fields were in exclusive Australian seabed jurisdiction with 20.1% located in the JDPA and so the IUA allocated revenues from the field in that proportion.[144] The agreement automatically terminated when the 2018 Treaty between the Democratic Republic of Timor Leste and Australia establishing their maritime boundaries in the Timor Sea entered into force.

4.2.4 2006 Treaty on Certain Maritime Arrangements in the Timor Sea

The Treaty on Certain Maritime Arrangements in the Timor Sea (CMATS) was signed in 2006. The treaty established a further interim resource sharing agreement whose area of application coincided with the 'Unit Area' defined in the previously negotiated unitization agreement and therefore encompassed the Greater Sunrise complex of fields. The agreement provided for the equal sharing of revenues deriving from the upstream exploitation of petroleum resources within this zone. The CMATS was without prejudice to either side's claims to maritime delimitation and included stringent requirements for a moratorium on claims while the treaty was in force. The CMATS was contentious and ceased to be in force in 2017.[145]

---

[140] Section 2 Petroleum Mining Code 2003.

[141] Section 6 Petroleum Mining Code 2003.

[142] Section 7 Petroleum Mining Code 2003.

[143] Section 10 Petroleum Mining Code 2003.

[144] Article 7 Greater Sunrise Unitisation Agreement—Apportionment of Unit Petroleum.

[145] This treaty was contentious see: In 2013 Timor-Leste instituted arbitral proceedings against Australia in which it sought to have CMATS declared invalid or void: https://pcacases.com/web/sendAttach/2107.

In 2017 Australia accepted that CMATS ceased to be in force at the request of Timor Leste: https://cil.nus.edu.sg/databasecil/2006-treaty-between-australia-and-the-democratic-republic-of-timor-leste-on-certain-maritime-arrangements-in-the-timor-sea/.

4.2.5 2018 Treaty Between Australia and Timor Lester Establishing Their Maritime Boundaries

The Treaty establishes permanent maritime boundaries between Australia and Timor Leste in the Timor Sea and establishes the Greater Sunrise Special Regime for the joint development, exploitation and management of the Greater Sunrise gas fields.[146] The settlement of the lingering boundary dispute hopefully establishes a stable legal framework for resource development and thus provides certainty and stability for investors.

Revenue derived from the gas fields is shared in the ratio of: (a) 30% to Australia and 70% to Timor-Leste in the event that the Greater Sunrise Fields are developed by means of a Pipeline to Timor-Leste; or (b) in the ratio of 20% to Australia and 80% to Timor-Leste in the event that the Greater Sunrise Fields are developed by means of a Pipeline to Australia.[147]

A two-tiered regulatory structure for the regulation and administration of the Greater Sunrise Special Regime, consisting of a Designated Authority and a Governance Board is established under the treaty.[148] Similar to the Timor Sea Treaty, the Designated Authority[149] is responsible for carrying out the day-to-day regulation and management of Petroleum Activities in the Special Regime Area on behalf of Australia and Timor-Leste and reports to the Governance Board.

ANPM is also recognised as the Designated Authority under the treaty, while the Governance Board[150] is comprised of one representative appointed by Australia and two representatives appointed by Timor-Leste.

4.3 Petroleum Operations in the Joint Petroleum Development Area

With the 2018 treaty, the JPDA area lies within the Timor-Leste continental shelf (see Fig. 2). Prior to that, there was only one field wholly within the JPDA that was operational—the Bayu Undan gas and condensate field operating as a joint venture between Conoco Phillips, Santos, INPEX, Eni, Tokyo Electric (JERA) and Tokyo Gas.[151]

The 2018 Treaty provides that the security of title and any other rights held by the titleholders previously under the Timor Sea Treaty and the International Unitisation

---

[146] Article 7 of the 2018 Treaty (and Annexe B).

[147] Annexe B of the 2018 Treaty—Article 2.

[148] Annexe B of the 2018 Treaty—Article 5.

[149] Annexe B of the 2018 Treaty—Article 6.

[150] Annexe B of the 2018 Treaty—Article 7.

[151] Santos website information 14 October 2019 https://www.santos.com/news/acquisition-of-conocophillips-northern-australia-interests/.

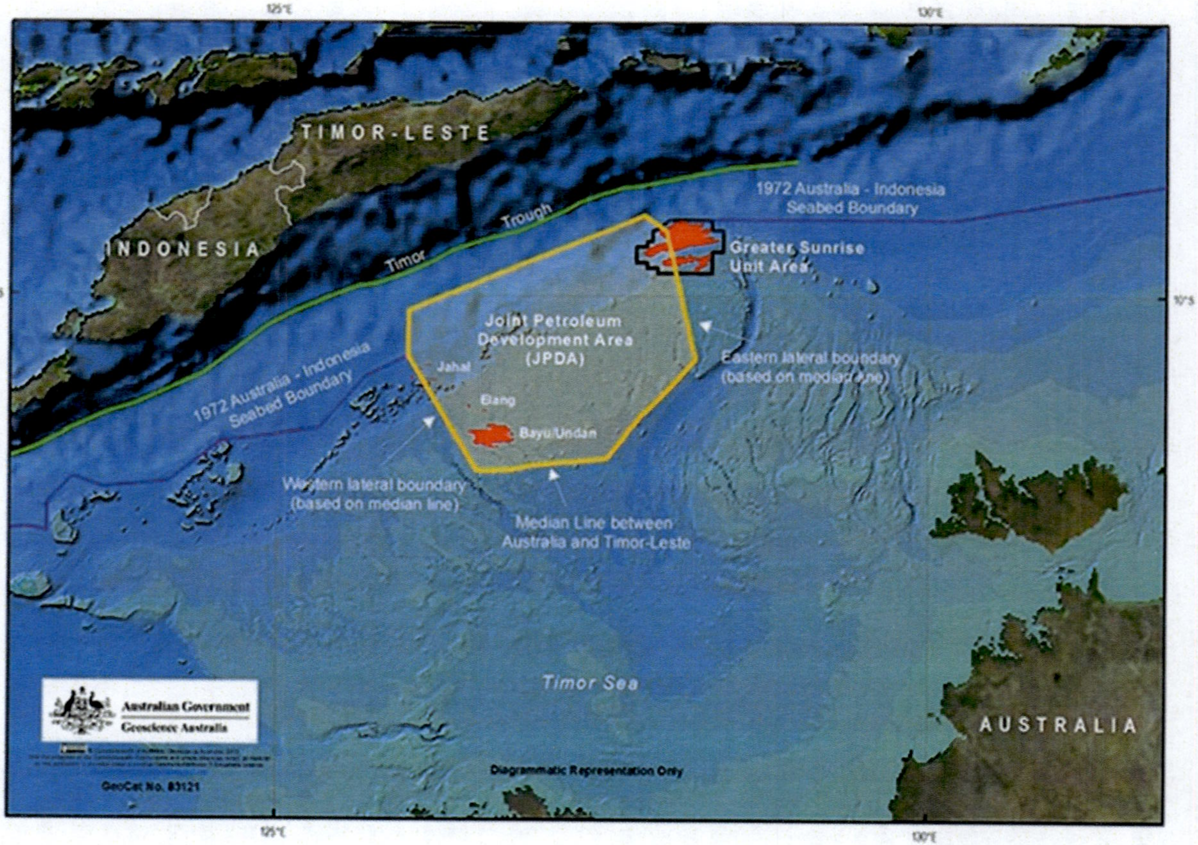

Fig. 2 Map of the Joint Petroleum Development Area. Source: Australian Government, Department of Foreign Affairs and Trade (https://www.dfat.gov.au/geo/timor-leste/Pages/australias-maritime-arrangements-with-timor-leste)

Agreement will be preserved through ensuring conditions and terms equivalent.[152] This provision secured the regime agreed with the joint venture partners under the TST and IUA and ensured the stability of operations within the affected assets.

The 2018 treaty also includes local content provisions in favour of Timor Leste.[153] This appears to consolidate on local content provisions issued under the regulations made pursuant to Timor Leste's Petroleum Activities Law which incorporates specific provisions on local content including the submission of a local content plan. It appears that this drive for increased local content influenced the position of Timor Leste's negotiators who made clear that they favoured the development of a pipeline and an onshore facility in Timor Leste to help develop the country's industrialisation and create urgently needed employment.[154]

4.4 Analysis of the Timor Leste-Australia Model of Joint Development

The development model adopted by Timor Leste and Australia is a hybrid model combining elements of model II and model II of the BIICL development models.

While model II describes a regime where *a joint authority with licensing and regulatory powers manages development of the resources on behalf of both states,* under a model III approach, *one state manages development of the resource on behalf of both with the other state's participation limited to revenue sharing and monitoring.*

The tiered administrative structure adopted both under the TST and the 2018 Treaty recognizes the ANPM as the Designated Authority responsible for managing the day to day activities in the JDPA. Seeing as it is a statutory organ of the Timor Leste Government, ANPM's regulatory role carried out on behalf of both states aligns with model III of the BCIIL models. However, the establishment of a Joint Commission under the TST and a Governance Board under the 2018 treaty, both comprised of representatives from the two states with powers of oversight over the Designated Authority is more aligned with model II. Additionally, both states have enacted a special legislative regime for regulating activities within the JDPA

The adoption of this hybrid model may have been influenced by the historic issues arising from legacy arrangements in place prior to Timor Leste's restoration of independence and on-going negotiations for a definitive delineation which culminated in a decision largely in favour of Timor Leste under the 2018 treaty. In the light of Timor Leste's significant claim over the resources in the JPDA, an argument could be made for the adoption of model III, however this may have been

[152] Article 4 of Annex B, Treaty of 2018.

[153] See Article 15 of ANNEX B: Greater Sunrise Special Regime.

[154] Schleich (2018), p. 5.

counterbalanced by Australia's position as an advanced economy with significant experience in the technical and commercial regulation of petroleum operations.

5 Conclusion

The joint development zone created by the Treaty between the Federal Republic of Nigeria and the Democratic of Sao Tome and Principe, remains one of the models for cooperation in the Gulf of Guinea.

There have been significant implementation and institutional issues which cannot be separated from the political issues faced by each of the countries involved. Practical outcomes of the implementation have resulted in a more complex picture than the basic model I would suggest. The current practice between the JMC and the JDA blurs the borders between the functions of supervision and oversight. There is some evidence that Nigeria exerts more control over the JDA because of the dominant management role and the location of the head office in Abuja, nevertheless under the terms of the treaty no state is able to exercise unilateral control over the zone. The lack of a commercial find has also meant that there has been some reluctance to continue to invest in the zone.

The experience of the Timor Leste—Australia may mean that future negotiations may take on a different model of management. However the peculiar circumstances which gave rise to the Timor Leste Australia 2018 treaty, may not make this model fully attractive to Nigeria. Nigeria is still a developing country with significantly developmental needs and in this sense differs significantly from Australia. It also does not have the legacy of inherited agreements, in the manner that Australia had negotiated initial agreements with occupying countries such as Indonesia. However a modified version of model III such as that currently used in Timor-Leste—Australia may counter allegations of the dominance of the Nigerian authorities in licensing arrangements. The question of new funding arrangements may need to be dealt with when a commercial find is made, as the Timor Leste—Australia arrangements works well in view of very productive oil fields and gas reserves.

There could be better arrangements for information sharing and use of websites. Both states are members of EITI and could utilize that global platform better to publicise information about the joint development efforts. This would mean that, if oil is found, Sao Tome and Principe has the opportunity to create an oil legacy which is different from the well documented problematic legacy in Nigeria. The renewed emphasis on transparency may also pay dividends for Nigeria as this presents a novel platform to demonstrate greater transparency and anti-corruption practice.

Nevertheless there should also be an equal focus on living natural resources such as fishing because this could present a unique feature within this EEZ for two reasons. Firstly, Nigeria relies heavily on multinational companies for exploration and production although it is a major oil producer. This is demonstrated by the recent Total PSC. This would mean that when it comes to the commercial measure of any future find, corporate interests will be paramount. Secondly, there is a renewed focus in African states on reduction on resource dependency especially oil. Therefore building up indigenous capacity and markets in the fishing industry should be an attractive prospect for the JDA.

Finally both states still reserve the right to pursue maritime boundary delimitation and then follow a programme of transboundary or cross-border unitization for any overlapping fields but it is clear that the joint development has created the capacity and funding for significant exploration currently taking place. Overwhelmingly the issue of transparency and technical expertise will also be vital to the ability to make the JDZ a success however, for long term sustainability and technical knowledge transfer, a transparent scheme of local content activity in the joint development area, should be encouraged. This must however be done with full consent of the JMC and JDA. This need for local content provisions is indicated in the 2018 Timor-Leste—Australia Treaty.

In the wider African context, the continued presence of maritime boundary disputes is viewed as an impediment to holistic sustainable development and security, the joint development zone mechanism still presents a viable alternative which privileges sustainable and efficient development over the continued insistence on delimitation and delineation. This will also tie in with regional progress towards joint activities in trade. The Agenda 2063 blueprint for Africa by the African Union points to the goal of an integrated, prosperous and peaceful Africa and this will involve cooperation and successful engagement between states such as that demonstrated by the spirit of the original treaty.

References

Additional Protocol to the Treaty establishing the Gulf of Guinea Commission, relating to the ad hoc Arbitration Mechanism (with provisions for mediation, conciliation and arbitration). https://cggrps.com/wp-content/uploads/Protocolo_adicional-EN.pdf

African Seminar on the Law of the Sea (1972) African States: conclusions of the regional seminar on the law of the sea (1973). Int Legal Mater 12(3):210–213

Agreement between Abu Dhabi and Qatar on the settlement of maritime boundaries and ownership of islands 1969. https://www.un.org/Depts/los/LEGISLATIONANDTREATIES/PDFFILES/TREATIES/QAT-ARE1969MB.PDF

Agreement between Australia and the Democratic Republic of Timor-Leste relating to the Unitization of the Sunrise and Troubadour fields (collectively known as the greater sunrise) (6 March 2003). https://www.un.org/Depts/los/LEGISLATIONANDTREATIES/PDFFILES/TREATIES/AUS-TLS2003UNI.PDF

Agreement between Japan and the Republic of Korea concerning joint development of the southern part of the continental shelf adjacent to both countries – signed at Seoul on 30th January 1974. https://www.un.org/depts/los/LEGISLATIONANDTREATIES/PDFFILES/TREATIES/jap-kor1974south.pdf

Australia – UNTAET agreement (1999) Exchange of Notes constituting an Agreement between the Government of Australia and the United Nations Transitional Administration in East Timor (UNTAET) concerning the continued Operation of the Treaty between Australia and the Republic of Indonesia on the Zone of Cooperation in an Area between the Indonesian Province of East Timor and Northern Australia of 11 December 1989 http://www.austlii.edu.au/au/other/dfat/treaties/2000/9.html

Anton DK (2014) 'The Timor Sea Arbitration: Timor Leste Challenges Australian Espionage and Seizure of Documents 18 (3) The American Society of International Law Insights Feb 24 2014 https://www.asil.org/insights/volume/18/issue/6/timor-sea-treaty-arbitration-timor-leste-challenges-australian-espionage

Attard D (1987) Exclusive economic zone in international law. Clarendon Press, Oxford

Auty RM (1995) Economic development and the resource curse thesis. In: Morrissey O, Stewart F (eds) Economic and political reform in developing countries. Palgrave Macmillan, London

Banchani JS (2016) The relevance of the Gulf of Guinea in global energy politics. Afr Secur Rev 25 (4):420–426

Bastida AE, Ifesi-Okoye A, Mahmud S, Ross J, Walde T (2007) Cross-border unitization and joint development agreements: an international law perspective. Houst J Int Law 29(2):355–425

Charles Q (2019) The exclusive economic zone. Vernon Press

Central Intelligence Agency (CIA) (2020) The World Facebook https://www.cia.gov/library/publications/the-world-factbook/

Certain Maritime Arrangements in the Timor Sea(CMATS) 2006 Treaty 2006 Treaty between Australia and the Democratic Republic of Timor-Leste on Certain Maritime Arrangements in the Timor Sea. https://cil.nus.edu.sg/databasecil/2006-treaty-between-australia-and-the-democratic-republic-of-timor-leste-on-certain-maritime-arrangements-in-the-timor-sea/

Conciliation Between the Democratic Republic of Timor-Leste and the Commonwealth of Australia", Timor-Leste Maritime Boundary Office (6 March 2018). http://www.gfm.tl/wp-content/uploads/2018/03/PCA-6-march-2018-signing-ceremony-.pdf

Daniel T (2005) Africa maritime boundaries. In: Coulson DA, Smith RW (eds) International maritime boundaries. ASIL/Martinus Njihoff, pp 3429–3437, 3429

Fox H (ed) (1989) Joint Development of Offshore Oil and Gas I, Chapter 4, "Development Models". The British Institute of International and Comparative Law, London

Frynas JG, Wood G (2017) The resource curse without natural resources: expectations of resource booms and their impact. Afr Aff 116(463):233–260

Ifesi A (2003) Offshore delimitation of resource deposits situated across maritime boundaries: the ICJ decision in Cameroon v Nigeria – Lending clarity or compromise. J World Invest Trade 4 (1):62–72

Gelb A et al (1988) Oil windfalls – Blessing or curse?, World Bank. Available at http://documents.worldbank.org/curated/en/536401468771314677/Oil-windfalls-Blessing-or-curse

Goodrich G Africa Oil and Power, Total to begin exploration in Nigeria-São Tomé and Príncipe Joint Development Zone, 18 March 2019. available at https://africaoilandpower.com/2019/03/18/total-to-begin-exploration-in-nigeria-sao-tome-and-principe-joint-development-zone/

Groves H (2005) Offshore oil and gas resources: economics, politics and the rule of law in the Nigeria-São Tomé E Príncipe Joint Development ZONE. J Int Affairs 59(1):81–96

GrBec M (2014) Extension of Coastal State Jurisdiction in enclosed or semi-enclosed seas – a Mediterranean and Adriatic perspective. Routledge

Human Rights Watch (2010) An Uncertain Future: Oil Contracts and Stalled Reform in São Tomé e Príncipe available at https://www.hrw.org/sites/default/files/reports/saotome0810webwcover.pdf

International Monetary Fund (2019) Sub-Saharan Africa Regional Economic Outlook: Recovery Amid Elevated Uncertainty, available at https://www.imf.org/en/Publications/REO/SSA/Issues/2019/04/01/sreo0419#TOC

Jeremiah K (2018) The Guardian, São Tomé and Príncipe: 17 Years After, Nigeria-Sao Tome's JDZ Remains Unproductive 9 September 2018 available at https://allafrica.com/stories/201809100021.html

Law no. 8/2004 – Oil Revenue Management Law (Lei-quadro das Receitas Petrolíferas) https://resourcegovernance.org/sites/default/files/STP%20Oil%20Revenue%20Law.pdf

Lerer D (2003) Joint Development Zones: Negotiating and Structuring a Joint Development Agreement. Oil Gas & Energy Law online https://www.ogel.org/article.asp?key=776#citation

Mac-Leva F (2018) Nigeria: lack of funding Cripples Nigeria, Sao Tome Agency'. Daily Trust, Available at https://allafrica.com/stories/201808220033.html

Mensah TA (2006) Joint development zones as an alternative approach in maritime boundary delimitation. In: Lagoni R, Vignes D (eds) Maritime Delimitation (Publications on Ocean development), vol 53. Brill/Nijhoff, pp 143–151

Mercer D (2004) Dividing up the spoils: Australia, east Timor and the Timor sea. Space Polity 8 (3):289–308

Miyoshi M (1999) The Offshore development of oil and gas in relation to maritime boundary delimitation Volume 2 Number 5 Maritime briefing (ed. C Schofield) International Boundaries Research Unit (IBRU) Durham 1999

Nandan SN (1987) The Exclusive Economic Zone: A historical Perspective" *Under Secretary-General, Special Representative of the Secretary-General for the Law of the Sea* in The Law and the Sea Essays in honour of Jean Carroz Food and Agricultural organization of the UN (Rome) available at http://www.fao.org/3/s5280t/s5280t0p.htm

National Petroleum and Mineral Authority of Timor-Leste 2017 Annual Report (10 of July 2018). http://www.anpm.tl/wp-content/uploads/2018/07/Annual-Report-2017-ENGLISH.pdf

Nigeria – Sao Tome 1st EITI Report 2003-2013. http://cipstp.st/wp-content/uploads/2014/12/First-Report-2003-2013-Nigeria-Sao-Tome-and-Principe.pdf

North Sea Continental Shelf Cases (1969). https://www.icj-cij.org/files/case-related/51/051-19690220-JUD-01-00-EN.pdf

Offshore Magazine (2001) Cross –Boundary Unitisation makes some Gulf of Guinea fields more economic. Oct 1st 2001 https://www.offshore-mag.com/home/article/16758865/crossboundary-unitization-makes-some-gulf-of-guinea-fields-economic

Okafor CB (2007) Model agreements for joint development: a case study. J Energy Nat Resour Law 25:58–102

Okafor-Yarwood I (2015) The Guinea-Bissau –Senegal Maritime Boundary Dispute. Marine Policy 61:284–290

Okonkwo T (2017) Maritime boundaries delimitation and dispute resolution in Africa. Beijing Law Rev 8:55–78

Ong DM (1999) Joint development of common offshore oil and gas deposits: "mere" state practice or customary international law. Am J Int Law 93(4):771–804

Onorato WT (1977) Apportionment of an international common petroleum deposit. Int Comp Law Q 26:324–337

Onorato WT (1968) Apportionment of an international common petroleum deposit. Int Comp Law Q 17:85–102

Onorato WT (1990) Joint development in the international petroleum sector: the Yemeni variant. Int Comp Law Q 39(3):653–662

Organisation of African Unity (OAU) 1974 Declaration on the issues of the Law of the Sea 16th July 1974 UN Doc A/CONF.62/33 UNCLOS volume III documents https://legal.un.org/diplomaticconferences/1973_los/vol3.shtml

Petroleum Mining Code (2003) of the Joint Petroleum Development Are a http://web01.anpm.tl/webs/anptlweb.nsf/vwAll/Resource-Petroleum%20Mining%20Code/$File/PMCtoCoM0602.pdf?openelement

Rothwell DR (2018) 'Australia and Timor Leste settle maritime boundary after 45 years of bickering' March 7 2018 The Conversation. https://theconversation.com/australia-and-timor-leste-settle-maritime-boundary-after-45-years-of-bickering-92834

São Tomé e Príncipe 4th EITI Report 2016-2017 (25 of February 2019a) (in portuguese) https://eiti.org/document/sao-tome-principe-2016-2017-eiti-report

São Tomé e Príncipe 4th EITI Report 2016-2017 (25 of February 2019b), https://eiti.org/document/sao-tome-principe-2016-2017-eiti-report

Schleich A (2018) ISPSW Strategy Series: Focus on Defense and International Security; Issue no. 573 September 2018 The Historic 2018 Maritime Boundary Treaty between Timor-Leste and Australia https://css.ethz.ch/content/dam/ethz/special-interest/gess/cis/center-for-securities-studies/resources/docs/ISPSW-573%20Schleich.pdf

Schrijver N (1997) Sovereignty over natural resources: balancing rights and duties. Cambridge University Press

Sholanke OO (1993) Delimiting the territorial sea between Nigeria and Cameroun: a rational approach. Int Comp Law Q 42(2):398–411

Strating B (2018) 'Agreement on the Timor Sea Boundary – An incomplete victory April 18 2018 Asia Maritime Transparency Initiative Update https://amti.csis.org/timor-sea-boundary-agreement-incomplete-victory/

Tanga Biang J (2010) The Joint development zone between Nigeria and São Tomé and Príncipe: A case of provisional arrangements in the Gulf of Guinea, International law, state practice and prospects for regional integration, UN Fellows Papers Division of Ocean Affairs and Law of the Sea. https://www.un.org/depts/los/nippon/unnff_programme_home/fellows_pages/fellows_papers/tanga_0910_cameroon.pdf

Taylor PG, Winsor TP, Tyne SM (1988) The joint operating agreement: oil and gas law. Longmann

Timor Sea Treaty 2002 20 May 2002. https://www.un.org/Depts/los/LEGISLATIONANDTREATIES/STATEFILES/TLS.htm

Touval S (1967) The organisation of African Unity and African Borders. Int Organ 21(1):102–127

The African Charter on Maritime Security, Safety and Development (Lomé Charter) (2016). https://au.int/en/treaties/african-charter-maritime-security-and-safety-and-development-africa-lome-charter

The Economist Intelligence Unit (2016) "Sao Tome –Nigeria Joint Development Authority under scrutiny" May 4th 2016. http://country.eiu.com/article.aspx?articleid=244189408&Country=Nigeria&topic=Economy&subtopic=Fo_9

The OAU 1964 declaration "Border disputes among Africans" AHG/Res 16(1). https://au.int/sites/default/files/decisions/9514-1964_ahg_res_1-24_i_e.pdf

The treaty – Agreement between Japan and the Republic of Korea concerning joint development of the southern part of the continental shelf adjacent to both countries – signed at Seoul on 30th January 1974-Article IV & V https://www.un.org/depts/los/LEGISLATIONANDTREATIES/PDFFILES/TREATIES/jap-kor1974south.pdf

The treaty between the Federal republic of Nigeria and the republic of Equatorial Guinea concerning their maritime boundary 23 September 2000. https://www.un.org/Depts/los/LEGISLATIONANDTREATIES/PDFFILES/TREATIES/NGA-GNQ2000MB.PDF

Treaty between Australia and the Democratic Republic of Timor-Leste Establishing their Maritime Boundaries in the Timor Sea (6 March 2018). https://www.dfat.gov.au/sites/default/files/treaty-maritime-arrangements-australia-timor-leste.pdf (The 2018 Treaty)

Treaty between the Federal Republic of Nigeria and the Democratic of São Tomé e Príncipe on the Joint Development of Petroleum and other resources, in respect of Areas of the Exclusive Economic Zone of the Two States (21 February 2001). http://nstpjda.org/wp-content/uploads/2017/10/TREATY-english.pdf https://www.un.org/Depts/los/LEGISLATIONANDTREATIES/PDFFILES/TREATIES/STP-NGA2001.PDF

United Nations Convention on the Law of the Sea (UNCLOS) 1982 1834 UNTS 397

United States (1983) Proclamation on an EEZ. Int Legal Mater *22*(2):461–465

Weszkalnys G (2008) Hope & Oil: expectations in São Tomé e Príncipe. Rev Afr Polit Econ 35 (3):473–482

Wilkinson (2018) 'East Timor moves to major stake in sunrise gas field' Nov 27th 2018 Oil and gas Journal https://www.ogj.com/general-interest/companies/article/17296185/east-timor-moves-to-majority-stake-in-sunrise-gas-field

Adaeze Okoye Senior Lecturer (Law), University of Brighton, United Kingdom.

Mariam Masini Legal Director, National Petroleum Agency of Sao Tome and Principe (ANP-STP), Sao Tome, Sao Tome and Principe.

Alache Fisho Legal Adviser, Natural Resources at the Commonwealth Secretariat, London, United Kingdom.

Implementing Extended Producer Responsibility (EPR)-based Electronic Waste Institutions in Nigeria: Lessons from the Global North

Irekpitan Okukpon

Contents

Parts of this paper are excerpts from my unpublished PhD Thesis 'Towards the Sustainable Management of Electronic Waste: South Africa as a Model' (2015).

I. Okukpon (✉)
Nigerian Institute of Advanced Legal Studies (NIALS), Lagos, Nigeria

C. Eboe-Osuji et al. (eds.), *Nigerian Yearbook of International Law 2018/2019*, Nigerian Yearbook of International Law 2018/2019,
https://doi.org/10.1007/978-3-030-69594-1_6

1 Introduction

The advent of information technology (IT), internet systems, and the reliance by various industries on electrical and electronic equipment (EEE) to run efficient day-to-day activities has led to huge demands and consumption of EEE. Whilst this has led to a simpler, technologically advanced way of life, it translates into increased human dependence on electrical and electronic equipment ranging from computers, televisions, mobile phones, air-conditioners, washing machines, etc. in businesses and households of many developed countries. With disparities in the economic situations of individuals in developing and least developed countries (LDCs), the increased demand for EEE at affordable rates has fuelled the trade in Used Electrical and Electronic Equipment (UEEE). The imports of UEEE into developing countries has been primarily economic: disposal costs in developing countries are often a fraction of the costs in the developed world. This is due to the lower cost of living in developing countries and lack of environmental regulation.[1] These countries also lack the trained personnel and financial resources to implement and enforce them. Thus, the demand for used electronics by developing countries such as Nigeria facilitated the illegal trade in electronic waste (hereafter "e-waste") which has plagued the international community for the past few decades.

E-waste is the fastest growing waste stream in the world,[2] reaching 50 million tonnes in 2018. The United States and the United Kingdom have been touted as being directly responsible for roughly half (25 million tonnes) of annual e-waste produced[3] worldwide and it contains a mixture of toxic substances which has fatal consequence for human health and the environment when ineffectively disposed. E-waste can be toxic, is not bio-degradable and accumulates in the environment, in the soil, air water and living things.[4] When such waste is disposed in developing countries in unregulated, open dumpsites rather than in registered landfills, incinerators or through proper recycling methods, it becomes a cause for global concern.

Whilst various international efforts towards halting the trade in e-waste have been applied from 1989 till date via the Basel Convention 1989, Bamako Convention 1991, soft law instruments originating from Conference of Parties (CoP) meetings of the Basel Convention and the Basel Ban, it appears that efforts at the national level are more fundamental in the search for effective management of e-waste.

[1]Donald (1999), p. 425.

[2]An estimated 50 million tonnes of e-waste is produced each year. The USA discards 30 million computers each year and 100 million phones are disposed of in Europe each year. SUNEP Backs Action for E-Waste Regulation in Africa' http://www.africaninstitute.info/UNEP_EA; E-Waste Guidelines for Kenya. http://www.gesci.org/e-waste-guidelines-for-Kenya.html; Elisha (2010–2011), p. 199. PACE/WEF A New Circular Vision for Electronics – Time for a Global Reboot http://www3.weforum.org/docs/WEF_A_New_Circular_Vision_for_Electronics.pdf.

[3]At 50 Million Tons, E-Waste is the "Fastest-Growing Waste Stream" Word & Way, February 14, 2019, https://wordandway.org/2019/02/14/at-50-million-tons-e-waste-fastest-growing-waste-stream/.

[4]PACE-WEF (n 2).

Consequently, while domestic legislation presents a blueprint for action for the management of e-waste in any jurisdiction, it appears that the goal of any effective waste management program in any jurisdiction should be an alteration in the behaviour of the organisations that manage such waste.[5] Probst and Beierle put forward the argument that the key components of building such a goal should be firstly, building an effective regulatory program, and secondly, developing adequate treatment, storage and disposal facilities. These authors further emphasize that both components present challenges to a country seeking to move from a situation in which there is little or no regulation of hazardous waste, to one in which the majority of generators treat, store and dispose of hazardous waste in an environmentally safe way.[6]

Since the 1988 Koko Toxic Dump in Warri Nigeria,[7] efforts have been made by the government to manage general waste trade import into Nigeria through general hazardous waste legislation. Whilst this has not deterred the importation of same, the management and disposal of e-waste in Nigeria has become a source of concern over the past few years because the environmental and health implications of improper disposal of components of EEE.

Relying on this argument, this paper provides an analytical expose of the effective management of e-waste in Nigeria. It examines global and regional initiatives on e-waste in order to situate the roles which countries are expected to play at the national level in ensuring effective management of this waste stream. The paper discusses the need for utilization of an extended producer responsibility (EPR) principle which seeks to shift responsibility of EEE management on producers and other parties along the chain of an EEE life span. The jurisdictions of Japan and Netherlands are discussed in this paper to emphasize the 'Global North'—representative of economically developed countries. The utilisation of both jurisdictions in this paper emphasize the importance of establishing key EPR-based e-waste institutions at various levels of government, to ensure proper disposals and protection of citizens from the effect of improper disposals. The paper analyses e-waste legislation in Nigeria to determine the reality of establishing e-waste institutions in Nigeria, in view of the examples set out in the jurisdictions earlier analysed. The paper concludes with proposals for ensuring effective implementation of EPR-based e-waste institutions in Nigeria.

[5]Probst and Beierle (1999), p. vii.

[6]Probst and Beierle (1999).

[7]Koko is a little port town located in the South-West of Bendel State (now Edo and Delta States), approximately 40 km from Benin City, the capital of Edo State. In 1988, an Italian ship carrying toxic wastes from Italy dumped over 6000 drums of toxic waste in Koko leading to the deaths and ill-health of various residents of Koko. Lipman (1999), p. 267; Ikhariale (1989), pp. 73–74.

2 Contextual Definitions

The term 'waste', described as one of the less charismatic areas of global environmental regulation,[8] has been defined as 'an unwanted matter or material of any type, often that which is left after useful substances or parts have been removed,'[9] 'no longer useful and to be thrown away.'[10] Waste may also refer to unwanted materials or substances[11] produced by human activity, which has the potential to cause pollution when released into the environment, if causing a risk to human health, or exceeding the environmental carrying capacity.[12] Waste is regarded as hazardous if by circumstances of use, quantity, concentration or inherent physical, chemical or infectious characteristics, may cause ill-health or increase mortality in humans, fauna and flora, or adversely affect the environment when improperly treated, stored, transported or disposed of.'[13] The potential for hazardous waste to pose a direct or indirect threat to human health or the environment, due to the variety of risks it introduces,[14] brings e-waste under the specific umbrella of a hazardous waste.

There is no international definition of the term e-waste, and more often than not, it appears that each jurisdiction adopts a working definition of the term in line with prevailing circumstances surrounding the production, importation and handling of electrical and electronic equipment. (EEE). The United Nations Environmental Programme (UNEP) defines e-waste as 'any electrically powered appliance that fails to satisfy the current owner for its originally intended purpose.'[15] This paper adopts a 2019 definition proffered by the World Economic Forum, which regards e-waste as 'anything with a plug, electric cord or battery (including electrical and electronic equipment) from toasters to toothbrushes smartphones, fridges, laptops and LED televisions that has reached the end of its life, as well as the components that make up these end-of-life products.'[16] Such waste is also referred to as Waste Electrical and Electronic Equipment (WEEE). The terms 'e-waste' and 'WEEE' will be used interchangeably in this paper. Hence, 'e-waste institutions' is described in

[8]Lee (2005), p. 297.

[9]Cambridge Advanced Learners Dictionary 2ed (2005), p. 1459.

[10]Oxford Advanced Learners Dictionary, 4ed; Atsegbua et al. (2004), p. 101.

[11]Asante-Duah (1993), p. 1.

[12]Section 2 (4) (a) of the South African National Environmental Management Act, No. 62 of 2008. http://www.capegateway.gov.za/Text/2009/2/national_environmental_management_amendment_act_(62_of_2008)_9jan2009.pdf.

[13]Noble (1992), p. 162.

[14]Noble (1992). It should be noted that wastes are of different types and can be solid, liquid, gaseous or radioactive and are often categorized according to their source. Waste Management http://www.libraryindex.com/pages/3430/Waste-Management.html; Bosman (2008), p. 700.

[15]United Nations Environment Programme, Division of Technology, Industry, and Economics, Sustainable Consumption & Production Branch ('UNEP DTIE SCP Branch') E-Waste Management. http://www.unep.fr/scp/waste/ewm/faq.htm.

[16]PACE-WEF Document, p. 7.

this paper as governmental practice and implementation of e-waste governance structures set out by legislation.

2.1 E-waste Disposal Methods

E-waste constitutes a complex mixture of materials and components, often containing several hundreds of different substances, many of which are toxic and create serious pollution upon improper disposal.[17] These include heavy metals such as cadmium, lead, chromium, nickel and mercury and which are harmful to human health and the environment on improper long-term exposure to these metals. The impact of e-waste on human health and environment can be better understood from the point of disposal. The four common methods of e-waste disposal are incineration, land-filling, open dumping and re-use/recycling. However, the best practicable option for e-waste disposal appears to be re-use and recycling.

E-waste can be incinerated if it cannot be re-used or recycled or disposed safely in a landfill because of excessive toxicity or risk of infectious transmission.[18] Landfilling,[19] on the other hand, involves the open dumping of e-waste.[20] Before any form of hazardous waste or e-waste can be placed in a landfill, they must undergo treatment, or the properties of the hazardous waste will remain and cause damage to the lining of the landfills.[21] E-waste is commonly disposed of in landfills where no separate collection and recycling systems have been established.[22] The use of a landfill is a conventional method for the disposal of all types of waste, but in the case of e-waste, it needs to be regarded as environmentally unsuitable.[23] This is because landfills do not provide a fool-proof solution to effective disposal of e-waste as majority of landfills are expected to eventually leak because they were either built prior to the introduction of modern day designs, or because of errors in the construction or management of modern-day sites.[24] This leaking contributes to the

---

[17]UNEP Environmental Alert Bulletin, E-Waste, The Hidden Side of IT equipment's Manufacturing and Use. http://www.grid.unep.ch/product/publication/download/ew_ewaste.en.pdf.

[18]Rosenfeld and Feng (2011), p. 158.

[19]A landfill is a natural or man-made depression on a large expanse of land with a soil foundation, and are usually equipped with a double liner and a leak detection system, at least two leachate collection and removal systems, storm-water run-off and run-off controls to withstand years of storms, and a cover to prevent wind dispersal. Rosenfeld and Feng (2011).

[20]A dump is an area allocated for the public to dispose of unwanted waste. Wastes disposed of at these landfill sites are often not closely monitored. See Finlay A, E-Waste Challenges in Developing Countries: South Africa as a Case Study. http://www.apc.org/en/system/files/e-waste_EN.pdf.

[21]Naude (2010), p. 138.

[22]UNEP E-Waste Management. (n 15); Hoeveler (2009), p. 118.

[23]Lin et al. (2001–2002), p. 532.

[24]Rosenfeld and Feng (2011), p. 160. Hoeveler (2009), p. 124.

environmental and health risks of people living in neighbourhoods where the landfills are located.

Conversely, open dumpsites—which are usually large expanse of land designated for dumping of municipal and other types of waste—are usually resorted to in developing countries which do not have the landfill/incineration infrastructure in place, and for specific countries which may have them in place, the institutional, legal and financial challenges cannot be faced and the weak administrative structures result in open dumpsites.[25]

Recycling of e-waste, which is an attractive, yet viable option for the proper management of e-waste, involves the collection, sorting/dismantling and pre-processing (including sorting, dismantling and mechanical treatment) and end-processing, and is an integral part of the EPR concept which will be discussed in a later part of this paper.[26] This disposal practice is typical in most developing countries in sub-Saharan Africa, but is not formalized. As most developing countries lack the capacity and financial means to set up adequate recycling facilities, common recourse is made to disposal of e-waste in open dumpsites, rather than being incinerated or landfilled.

2.2 *Impacts of E-waste on Human Health and the Environment*

The impacts of improper disposal of e-waste on human health and the environment cannot be quantified. The unsupervised burning (incineration) of e-wastes, are most often carried out near agricultural land or dwelling houses of individuals. The fumes emanating from these wastes can constitute some form of discomfort for the dwellers who are situated directly near places where these wastes are dumped. E-waste disposals impact human health in two ways which include: (a) food chain issues: contamination by toxic substances from disposal and primitive recycling processes that result in by-products entering the food chain and thus transferring to humans; and (b) direct impact on workers who labour in primitive recycling areas from their occupational exposure to toxic substances.[27] Along with this, numerous researchers have demonstrated a direct impact of backyard recycling on workers.[28] The danger

[25]Mavropoulou (2015), p. 39.

[26]UNEP Recycling- From E-Waste to Resources July 2009. http://www.unep.org/pdf/.../E-waste_publication_screen_finalversion-sml.pdf.

[27]Kiddee et al. (2013), p. 1238.

[28]Researchers have now linked dismantling of e-waste components by workers to resultant adverse effects on human health, such as inflammation and oxidative stress—precursors to cardiovascular disease, DNA damage and possibly cancer. E-waste pollution: Threat to human health. 31 May 2011. http://www.iop.org/news/11/may/page_51103.html.

of e-waste toxicity to human health, both in terms of chronic and acute conditions, has become a serious societal problem.[29]

The generation of waste is acknowledged to be an environmental problem worthy of legal regulation because it presents a risk of causing environmental harm.[30] Waste can cause environmental harm through pollution (harmful interaction of contamination with living organisms and by other mechanisms.[31] Direct pollution occurs when waste becomes a contaminant which inflicts environmental harm. For example, landfilling creates a risk of direct environmental harm through leaching of pesticides, organic compounds and heavy metals into substrata which can infiltrate and contaminate groundwater.[32] Incineration creates air pollution in the form of sulphur dioxide and nitrous oxides which may create public health risks and "fall out" onto nearby land or water.[33] Additionally, the dumping of e-waste on land surfaces leaches toxins into the soil, air and groundwater which later enter into crops, animals and human body systems causing contamination and pollution.[34]

These increasing impacts provided sufficient concern and impetus for the international community to call for the adoption of an international regime on the trade in and management of hazardous waste via the Basel Convention 1989 and the Bamako Convention 1991.

3 Electronic Waste: A Global Concern

The United Nations Basel Convention on the Control of Transboundary Movements of Hazardous Wastes and Their Disposal represents global leadership to address the problem of hazardous waste.[35] It entered into force on 5 May 1992 upon deposit of the twentieth instrument of accession in accordance with its Article 25,[36] and is kept under review by a Conference of Parties and a secretariat.[37] The scope of the

---

[29] Ibid.

[30] Alder and Wilkinson (1999), p. 282.

[31] Ibid.

[32] Ibid.

[33] Ibid.

[34] Osuagwu and Ikerionwu (2010), p. 143.

[35] Ogunseitan (2013), p. e313.

[36] History of the negotiations of the Basel Convention. http://www.basel.int/TheConvention/Overview/History/Overview/tabid/3405/Default.aspx.

[37] Arts. 15 and 16 of the Basel Convention. The Conference of the Parties is the governing body of the Basel Convention and is composed of governments of countries that have accepted ratified or aced to it. The implementation of the Basel Convention is advanced through the decisions it takes at its meetings. It also promotes the harmonization of appropriate policies, strategies and measures for minimizing harm to human health and the environment by hazardous wastes and other wastes. It also adopts the programme of work and budget of the Convention for each biennium. The Secretariat of the Basel Convention is administered by UNEP and it is located in Geneva,

Convention is limited to transboundary movements of hazardous wastes i.e. wastes that belong to any category contained in Annex I, unless they do not possess any of the characteristics contained in Annex III;[38] and wastes that are not covered under Annex I or III, but are defined as, or are considered to be hazardous wastes by the domestic legislation of the part of export, import or transit.[39] The Convention also covers 'other wastes' that belong to any category contained in Annex II[40] that are subject to transboundary movement.[41] However, since the initial adoption of the Convention with Annexes I–VI,[42] the Convention has evolved in terms of its definition of what constitutes hazardous and non-hazardous wastes.[43] Two new annexes, Annex VIII (comprising wastes likely to be hazardous under the Convention),[44] and Annex IX (wastes not likely to be hazardous under the Convention),[45] were adopted at the fourth COP in Malaysia in February 1998.[46]

These Annexes are noteworthy because of their recognition of certain hazardous properties contained in various electrical and electronic equipment (EEE). Thus, the Basel Convention regulates e-waste by virtue of the following. Mobile phones contain Annex I constituents including beryllium (Y20), copper compounds (Y22), zinc compounds (Y23), arsenic (Y24), cadmium (Y26), antimony (Y27), mercury (Y29), lead (Y31) and brominated flame retardants- BRTs (Y45), and as such, they are hazardous wastes which are required to be controlled under the Convention. List A of Annex VIII also regulates certain hazardous constituents used in the production of EEE or found in EEE when disassembled for

---

Switzerland. Overview – Conference of the Parties (COP). http://www.basel.int/TheConvention/ConferenceoftheParties/OverviewandMandate/tabid/1316/Default.aspx. Text of the Basel Convention. http://www.env.go.jp/recycle/yugai/law/conv_e.pdf. Sands (2003), pp. 1–1074.
694.

[38]Article 1 (a) of the Basel Convention.

[39]Article 1 (b) of the Convention.

[40]Annex II covers wastes collected from households and residues arising from the incineration of household wastes.

[41]Article 1 (2) of the Basel Convention.

[42]Annex I lists the various wastes streams to be controlled; Annex II deals with categories of wastes requiring special consideration i.e. household wastes and residues arising from the incineration of household wastes); Annex III lists hazardous characteristics of waste; Annex IV lists disposal operations of waste; Annex VA specifies information to be provided on notification by state of export to state of import; Annex VB specifies particular information to be provided on the movement document and Annex VI deals with Arbitration in case of a dispute between Parties to the Convention.

[43]Salehabadi (2013), p. 10.

[44]As amended by Decision VI/35 adopted by the Conference of the Parties at its Sixth Meeting held from 9 to 13 December 2002. The amendments under Decision VI/35 entered into force on 20 November 2003. Basel Convention (n 36).

[45]As amended by Decision VI/35 adopted by the Conference of the Parties at its Sixth Meeting held from 9 to 13 December 2002. The amendments under Decision VI/35 entered into force on 20 November 2003. Basel Convention (n 36).

[46]Kreuger (2001), p. 45.

refurbishment. These hazardous wastes include: A1010—metal wastes and wastes consisting of alloys of any of the following (antimony, arsenic, beryllium, cadmium, lead, mercury. Selenium, tellurium and thallium); A1090—ashes from the incineration of insulated copper wire; A1150—precious metal ash from incineration of printed circuit boards; A1170—unsorted waste batteries; A1180—waste electrical and electronic assemblies or scrap containing components such as accumulators and other batteries included on List A, mercury-switches, glass from cathode-ray tubes and other activated glass and PCB-capacitors, or contaminated with Annex I constituents (e.g., cadmium, mercury, lead, polychlorinated biphenyl); A1190—waste metal cables; and A2010—glass waste from cathode-ray tubes and other activated glasses.[47] However, List B (B1110) of Annex IX doesn't regulate electrical and electronic assemblies or electronic scrap including printed circuit boards and electronic components and wires destined for direct re-use[48] and recycling or final disposal. These electronic assemblies or scrap can also be referred to as 'second-hand' EEE.

The Convention has three key control systems to the transboundary movement of hazardous wastes. They are: first, the minimisation of generation of hazardous waste and the proximity principle, which requires parties to cooperate in the development and implementation of new environmentally environmentally-sound technologies and the improvement of existing technologies to eliminate the generation of hazardous wastes and achieve more effective management methods.[49] Second, the obligation that Parties are to ensure that the transboundary movement of hazardous wastes and other wastes is reduced in such a manner that is consistent with the environmentally sound and efficient management of such wastes, and is conducted in a manner which will protect human health and the environment against the adverse effects which may result from such movement.[50] Although the Convention fails to elaborate on what 'efficient management of such wastes' require, it defines ESM as 'taking all practicable steps to ensure that hazardous wastes or other wastes are managed in a manner that will protect human health and the environment against the adverse effects which may result from such wastes.'[51] Third, the Convention expressly requires Parties to prohibit the export of hazardous wastes and other wastes if the State of import does not consent in writing to the specific importation, especially in a case where the State of import has not prohibited the import of such wastes i.e. the prior informed consent (PIC) procedure[52] The Convention

[47]Basel Convention (n 36).

[48]Re-use in this context can include repair, refurbishment or upgrading but not major assembly. In some countries, materials destined for direct re-use are not considered wastes. Basel Action Network Wireless Waste: Basel Convention's Next Hazardous Waste Challenge. 1–9 http://www.ban.org/basel-convention-meetings./.

[49]Article 10 (2) (c), Basel Convention. Lipman (1999), p. 273.

[50]Article 4 (2) (d), Basel Convention.

[51]Article 2 (8), ibid.

[52]Article 4 (1) (c).

defines an 'exporter' as any person under the jurisdiction of the State of export who arranges for hazardous wastes or other wastes to be exported. The definition of an importer is presented in similar form and content,[53] while a 'generator' refers to any person whose activity produces hazardous wastes or other wastes, or if that person is not known, the person who is in possession and/or control of those wastes.[54] The PIC is encapsulated in Articles 6 and 7 and in Annex V (A) of the Convention.

The Basel Convention has been severely criticised over the years as being insufficient to tackle the trade in used EEE and ineffective disposal of e-waste in developing countries, with various CoPs adopting amendments to the Convention to encompass changing trends in the various waste streams covered under the Convention. By 1997, at the Second CoP meeting, parties agreed to immediately ban the export from developed to developing countries all hazardous wastes intended for final disposal or the export of wastes intended for recovery and recycling—a category in which e-waste falls into.[55] This decision, referred to as the Basel Ban Amendment, was adopted to further strengthen the Basel Convention and legalise the ban on such specific waste. As at the time of writing this paper, 66 countries had ratified the Basel Ban Amendment but it is yet to enter into force,[56] as there is the expectation that the Basel Ban would be legalised on the receipt of the 66th instrument of ratification.[57]

The adoption of the Bamako Convention in 1991 sought to provide more regional clarity and guidance to Parties in the African region, particularly with regards to the management and transboundary movement of hazardous waste, and e-waste in general. Unfortunately, this Convention has failed to garner the number of ratifications required to bring it into force,[58] showing the lack of political will of African states (including Nigeria) to apply concerted efforts in the effective management of electronic waste.

---

[53] Article 2. 15 and 2. 16.

[54] Article 2.18.

[55] UNEP/CHW.2/30, Report of the Second Meeting of the Conference of the Parties to the Basel Convention on the Control of Transboundary Movement of Hazardous Wastes and Their Disposal. 25 March 1994. Kiss and Shelton (2007), p. 213.

Decision II/12, Para. No. 1, at in Report of the Second Meeting, ibid. Kiss and Shelton (2007), p. 230.

Para. No. 2, ibid. Kiss and Shelton (2007).

[56] Status of Ratifications – Amendment to the Basel Convention on the Control of Transboundary Movements of Hazardous Waste. http://www.basel.int/Countries/StatusofRatifications/BanAmendment/tabid/1344/Default.aspx.

[57] BAN Just Two More Ratifications Needed to Ensure a COP14 Ban Amendment Celebration. March 28 2019. https://myemail.constantcontact.com/BAN-s-COP14-Action-Alert%2D%2D1%2D%2DRatify-and-Celebrate-the-Ban-Amendment-.html?soid=1114999858498&aid=byC9DL1rcJU.

[58] The Bamako Convention has 29 ratifications and is yet to enter into force. Ratify, implement Bamako Convention, SRADev tells FG. The Punch, January 15, 2018. https://punchng.com/ratify-implement-bamako-convention-sradev-tells-fg/.

Consequently, the failure of international and regional instruments to provide a holistic approach to the effective management of hazardous waste warranted recourse to national governments to establish e-waste legislation and policies and attendant institutions for the governance of same. One of such governance procedures is exemplified in the extended producer responsibility (EPR) principle.

4 The Extended Producer Responsibility (EPR) Principle

Most legislation and policies currently refer to the principle of "Extended Producer Responsibility", which emerged in academic circles in the early 1990s.[59] It is generally seen as a policy principle that requires manufacturers to accept responsibility for all stages in a product's lifecycle, including end-of-life management.[60] Lindhqvist aptly defines the concept as:

> an environmental protection strategy to reach an environmental objective of a decreased total environmental impact from a product, by making the manufacturer of the product responsible for the entire life-cycle of the product and especially for the take-back, recycling and final disposal of the product. The Extended Producer Responsibility is implemented through administrative, economic and informative instruments. The composition of these instruments determines the precise form of the Extended Producer Responsibility.[61]

There are four key responsibilities under the EPR principle: These responsibilities include legal liability, economic responsibility, physical responsibility and informative responsibility.[62] Liability refers to the legal responsibility for proven environmental damages caused by the product in question, and the extent of this liability is determined by legislation, which may encompass different life cycles of the product, including usage and final disposal.[63] Economic responsibility, on the other hand, means that the producer covers all or part of the expenses for the collection, recycling or final disposal of the products he manufactures. These expenses could be paid for or directly by him or by a special fee.[64] Physical responsibility alludes to a characterisation of the systems in which the manufacturer is involved in the physical management of the products and/or their effects. This means that the manufacturer retains ownership of the products all through their life cycle and is consequently linked to any environmental problem of the product, if any.[65] Informative responsibility envisages the extension of responsibility for the products by

---

[59] Lindhqvist and Lidgren (1990), fn 1, p. ii.

[60] Balde et al. (2017), p. 49.

[61] Lindhqvist Thesis (n 60), p. 8.

[62] Lindhqvist Thesis, ibid, p. 9.

[63] Ibid.

[64] Ibid.

[65] Ibid.

requiring the producers to supply information on the environmental properties of the products they are manufacturing.[66]

The key principle behind the reasoning that producers or manufacturers should be primarily responsible for this post-consumer phase is that most of the environmental impacts are predetermined in the design phase.[67]

4.1 *Methodologies and Approaches to Implementation of EPR to E-Waste*

There are three main methodologies to be utilised in the management of e-waste in a sustainable manner. The first is the EPR approach as analysed above. The 'purest' form of EPR is reflected through the 'take-backs' of products by the producer.[68] Take-backs refer to an inter-related system geared towards collection and processing of e-waste through direct regulation or necessary incentives.[69] Such a system has four key components: (a) the rules that govern the system; (b) the operational areas of collection and processing; (c) financing of the system; and (d) how to control the flow of e-waste in and out of a jurisdiction.[70]

The second is a referred to as 'product stewardship (PS).' Elisha refers to it as a 'diluted version' of 'pure EPR initiatives,' as pure EPR places the full responsibility on producers for end-of life EEE recycling and disposal[71] PS is an 'umbrella term adopted in the United States of America for a 'shared responsibility approach for managing products at end-of-life,'[72] and therefore, an extended form of the EPR principle. This principle of shared responsibility[73] is one where producers, retailers, consumers, waste operators, and state and local governments voluntarily share the responsibility for e-waste management.[74] It involves dialogues between state governments, industry, and consumer and environmental groups to arrive at better management practices for particular products.[75] Product stewardship schemes are basically a 'cradle to grave' tool and at any of the stages, commonly uses methods such as product redesign, consumer information, collection and recycling schemes, special financing mechanisms, deposit refund, or advance disposal fee schemes can

[66]Ibid.

[67]Balde et al. (2017), p. 49.

[68]Coopman (2015), 27.

[69]McCann and Wittmann (2019), p. 13.

[70]Ibid.

[71]Elisha (2010–2011), fn 116, p. 210.

[72]Lewis (2005), p. 48.

[73]Hoeveler (2009), p. 140.

[74]Product Stewardship: Basic Information. US Environmental Protection Agency. http://www.epa.gov/waste/partnerships/stewardship/basic.htm.

[75]Sachs (2006), p. 90.

be utilised to reduce environmental impact of e-waste.[76] The product stewardship scheme could also be mandatory. As an environmental policy tool, it is similar to the EPR principle but the latter is broader in scope and confined to the 'producer.' However, it appears that product stewardship schemes may be most effective if the environmental responsibility of all participants outweighs their economic interests.[77]

The third system is referred to as Advanced Recycling Fee (hereafter 'ARF'). This system places the financial burden of e-waste disposal on consumers and puts the physical burden of disposing, and recycling used electronic goods on the government.[78] Under ARF systems, consumers pay an advance collection deposit fee when they purchase electronic products. Retailers collect these fees for the government, and the government then redistributes the funds to public and private entities that manage disposal and recycling.[79] An ARF has an additional benefit, nor present in a producer-funded take-back system; it would help consumers understand that there is a real environmental and disposal cost for [EEE] products that they purchase that contain hazardous substances.[80] It also would help consumers understand that pollution is not caused only by industrial firms, but also by individual consumption decisions.[81] As stated above, a Disposal Fee, rather than an ARF can be utilised separate from the ARF, or in conjunction with the ARF. The difference between both approaches is the timing of fee charge. With ARF, the fee is charged at the moment of purchase of EEE, and with the Disposal Fee, the fee is charged at the point of depositing the end-of-life EEE at the collection centre or recycling facility. Therefore, both product stewardship and ARF together form part of the concept of EPR.

These schemes exist independently of each other but are structured in such a manner that they are meant to assist each other in any jurisdictional framework regulating e-waste. They are all policy measures, and the difference between all three schemes lies in the onus of responsibility, with EPR placing sole responsibility on manufacturers; product stewardship ensuring that there is shared responsibility between various stakeholders and the ARF placing responsibility for payment for e-waste disposal on the consumers. The ARF system, Disposal Fee or applicable financial instrument is particularly attractive because its aim is to place financial responsibility on consumers who use and enjoy these EEE.

Accordingly, whilst the EPR principle is promoted as the key policy tool for sustainable environmental management of e-waste, the strict application of the 'pure EPR' principle to a producer only may not be practicable. This is because most new EEE are produced in developed countries, and not in developing countries. As such, a pure form of EPR envisages the application of the responsibilities under EPR to be

[76]Hoeveler (2009), p. 140.

[77]Ibid.

[78]Elisha (2010–2011), p. 213.

[79]Elisha (2010–2011). Kutz (2006), p. 323.

[80]Sachs (2006), p. 96.

[81]Sachs (2006).

placed solely on the producer. However, this paper argues that in order to achieve the stated objective of sustainable management of e-waste in a developing country like Nigeria where e-waste is imported under the guise of used EEE, it is imperative that the EPR principle be extended to include a mix of product stewardship and ARF i.e. EPR/PS/ARF. The reason for this is because policy measures produce the best results when they are applied in a mix.[82] The notion of 'shared responsibility' will find better expression in a country like Nigeria, where there are no existing recyclers or e-waste collection facilities, rather than waiting on a producer of EEE from e.g. Germany to take up the legal, economic, physical and informative responsibility for EEE utilised in Nigeria. Rather, if there is a mix of EPR/PS/ARF systems, it imposes responsibility on the *importer* of new and used EEE in a developing country context. Accordingly, the kind of economic instrument which would be applicable therein would be an import levy on the importer, to be collected and utilised towards the development of e-waste collection centres by the government, and/or recycling facilities, in the absence of private e-waste recycling facilities. The peculiarity of the Nigerian situation is such that poverty underpins all sectors of its society. Directing consumers to pay a 'tax' as they purchase EEE will only encourage them to purchase electronics in states or countries which have no ARFs in order to avoid the fee.[83] Consumers will also resort to 'back-door' tactics of buying EEE whenever they travel overseas and which can be smuggled in through their luggage entering the country. Consequently, it would appear that the best approach with the possibility of implementation would be a combined application of pure EPR initiatives, product stewardship (which also places responsibility on government and retailers); and the ARF. This combined approach of policy tools further encapsulates and promotes the notion of sustainable e-waste management. However, in order for this inter-linkage of EPR schemes to work, there has to be a clear expression and definition of a producer, as differentiated from an importer/waste broker, retailer and consumer. There also has to be a dedicated focus on enforcement and compliance. This can best be done by mandatory WEEE policy instruments or WEEE specific legislation to that effect.

Taken independently, it can be argued that EPR has become a more conventional system because it not only independently lifts the burden off consumers and taxpayers, it also encourages manufacturers to evaluate and internalize the end-of-life costs of their products.[84] This manner of evaluation means that in recent times, with emphasis on environmental protection and development, most producers have become aware of the need to create new EEE in such a manner as to reduce the

---

[82]Coopman (2015), p. 27.

[83]Natural Resources Defense Council, Statement of the Natural Resources Defense Council before the New York City Council's Committee on Sanitation and Solid Waste Management Regarding Intro. 643, The Electronic Equipment Recycling and Reuse Act of 2005, October 24, 2005. In: Elisha (2010–2011), p. 227.

[84]Kutz (2006), pp. 324–325. Key Elements of EPR Plan, Clean Production Action. http://www.cleanproduction.org[Producer.Key.Examples.php.

effects on the environment. This new 'eco-design' is then 'internalized' and applied by virtue of the producer responsibility organisations (PROs). This is detailed below.

Accordingly, the EPR mechanism is a central one because it implements the PPP in effect by acknowledging that the manufacturers are the polluters themselves. These manufacturers are referred to as polluters because the components used for the creation and packaging of the EEE are 'eco-toxic i.e. the components, contain certain toxic substances which pollute the environment when improperly handled or disposed. Accordingly, manufacturers who know they will ultimately be responsible for disassembling and recycling the electronic goods they produce are more likely to use less toxic materials in the production process. The EPR therefore, compels the producer to design products with longer life spans that are easier to disassemble and recycle.[85] This systemic approach to manufacturing EEE while ensuring minimal environmental impact is integration under the concept of sustainable development.

However, in order to ensure that producers of EEE are held accountable for their actions in the manufacture of EEE and other products, a central organization called Producer Responsibility Organisations (PROs) exists. It is a co-operative industry initiative which requires producers to collectively handle collection and arrange for recycling on behalf of industry to ensure that member companies are able to meet their obligations.[86] PROs have no universally accepted global definition. In some states and countries, PROs are consortia of companies obligated to meet collection or recycling requirements. In others, the PROs are commercial contractors servicing the obligated companies.[87] The two types of producer responsibility are discussed below.

4.2 *Producer Responsibility Organisations: Individual Producer Responsibility (IPR) and Collective Producer Responsibility (CPR)*

The EPR principle is implemented in a variety of legislations and policies. Under an EPR principle, responsibility can be assigned either individually, where producers are responsible for their own products, or collectively, where producers in the same product type or category fulfil the responsibility for end of life (EoL) management together. A system as close as possible to Individual Producer Responsibility (IPR) can more easily stimulate the improvements in the design phase because the producer is interested in the benefits obtained by the improved design. However, the complexity of such a system has so far prevented its development, resulting in

---

[85] About Producer Responsibility, Electronic Take back Coalition. http://www.electronicstakeback.com/promote-good-laws/about-producer-responsibility/. Elisha (2010–2011), p. 34.

[86] Nahman (2010), p. 165.

[87] Lifset et al. (2013). Mayers and Butler (2013).

policies and legislation that refer to collective responsibility rather than individual.[88]

However, in developing countries, a major hurdle to the producer adopting responsibility results from the lack of treatment facilities (TF) that are compliant with international standards and a lack of collection infrastructure that channels e-waste to these sites. These challenges are discussed in Part 4 of this paper.

4.3 EPR Approaches to E-waste Management

The purest form of EPR is undoubtedly the take-back of products by the producer.[89] EPR can be implemented through either mandatory or voluntary EPR schemes. The reason behind *take-backs* is mainly ecological i.e. ensuring that EEE is no longer being disposed of crudely by way of landfill sites and incineration which release heavy metals such as chromium, lead, mercury and other brominated flame retardants,[90] becoming toxic if improperly disposed. These take-back schemes are achieved by introducing tax incentives (as envisaged by the ARF system above) which will in turn be passed on to manufacturers to enable them dispose, recycle or eliminate/reduce the amounts of toxic materials in the EEE at the design and manufacturing stages,[91] or where applicable, the consumer and government.

Voluntary EPR approaches may be created by agreements arising out of a memorandum of understanding between the industry and government, often stemming from a desire by the industry to avoid the imposition of potentially harmful regulations.[92] Government must set a framework within which industry must act, but producers should be given the financial and physical responsibility to ensure that they fulfil their obligations, and the freedom to find the most cost-effective way of doing so.[93] Under this approach, there are no laws or government regulations mandating compliance, and no penalties for not meeting the goals.[94] The advantage of the voluntary take-back approaches lies in industry's willingness to recycle EEE to avoid debilitating effects of disposal. It signifies a recognition of the need to apply mechanisms to avoid environmental pollution at all costs and the need to manage EEE in a more sustainable manner. The disadvantage of this approach is that since more often than not, they are voluntary initiatives by industry, there is no binding

---

[88] Balde et al. (2017), p. 49.

[89] Coopman (2015), pp. 27–28.

[90] Hoeveler (2009), p. 124.

[91] Nnorom and Osibanjo (2008), p. 847.

[92] Widmer et al. (2005), p. 845.

[93] Wilson (1996).

[94] Walls M Extended Producer Responsibility and Product Design: Economic Theory and Selected Case Studies. March 2006, Discussion Paper. RFF DP 06-08, Resources for the Future, Washington. http://www.rff.org/Documents/RFF-DP-06-08.pdf.

obligation on voluntary recycling companies to adhere to certain standards or rules, apart from that which the company has set for themselves.

Mandatory EPR approaches allude to a situation where the government mandates manufacturers, importers, distributors and/or retailers to take products back at the end of their useful life, usually in combination with a recovery or recycling target. Mandatory recycling requirements are important components of EPR (e-waste) programmes, as there would be no point in separately collecting products under an EPR programme if producers or their contractors were permitted to landfill or incinerate the products once collected.[95] These mandatory obligations are usually in form of legislation on recovery laws or general regulatory framework relating to waste. Mandatory product take-back laws are important, not only because they reduce the environmental impacts of end-of-life products by avoiding the release of hazardous materials into discharge streams, but also with the rationale of providing incentives for manufacturers to design products that are easier to recover so as to effectively reduce the costs of product recovery.[96] The problem associated with mandatory take-back regulation lies in its enforcement and ensuring that manufacturers are in compliance with the relevant regulation. As is typical with waste management, there will also be the problem of collating accurate data of number of products manufactured and particular products which have been re-designed, if there is ineffective monitoring and control by the relevant departments in charge.

Both voluntary and mandatory take-back approaches can work together embedded in regulatory framework on e-waste in any jurisdiction. As such, part 3 of this paper provides an analytical foray into the success of EPR schemes and take-back approaches in Japan and Netherlands.

5 EPR-based Approaches to WEEE and Implementation of E-waste Institutions in Japan and Netherlands

This part of the paper analyses the success of the combination of both EPR voluntary and mandatory take-back schemes in Japan and the Netherlands. In view of Redclift's warning of the need to exercise caution before embarking on cross-cultural exercises in environmental policy,[97] exemplifying the take-back schemes in this jurisdiction is necessary because they both have the potential of application in a developing Nigeria. The purpose of utilising these two jurisdictions here is not to show a comparison between what obtains in Asia, Europe and Africa. The two countries are utilised to demonstrate the ways in which take-backs, and the combination of pure EPR, product stewardship and ARF schemes are applied in conjunction with government as an as 'e-waste institution'.

---

[95] Sachs (2006), p. 80.

[96] Lifset and Lindhqvist (2008), p. 1042.

[97] Redclift (1993).

5.1 Netherlands

The Netherlands was the first country in Europe to adopt and fully implement take-back legislation prior to the WEEE Directive 2002/96/EC.[98] Its "system approach" or take-back approach is geared towards a scheme for assigning costs, relies on national system of collection points, and employs profit-oriented establishments to disassemble and process EOL products.[99]

Between 1994 and 1996, as part of the goals of the Dutch government to make producers responsible for white and brown goods,[100] it drafted the so-called White and Brown Goods disposal Decree.[101] The Decree obliged producers to take back free-of-charge all discarded white and brown goods (electronics) and process them in an environmentally-sound way.[102] It also required producers, when supplying a new product, to take-back a similar product that had been discarded, at least, free of charge.[103] Following this Decree, in 1999 the representative bodies[104] of the white and brown goods sector formed two voluntary organisations—the NVMP and ICT Milieu. These voluntary programmes have since become the framework for the operation of the WEEE in the Netherlands.[105]

The ICT Milieu was directly responsible for the disposal and processing of all Information and Communications Technology (ICT) waste stream,[106] including IT equipment, printers, fax machines, photocopiers and telecommunication equipment (all WEEE).[107] It charged producers for the handling of these specific brands of EEE and the individual producers received monthly invoices from the ICT milieu based

[98]Elisha (2010–2011), fn 183 at p. 220.

[99]Gutowski et al. (2005).

[100]The white goods sector is composed of all companies that manufacture domestic equipment and appliances from the following product lines of consumer goods like washing machines, cookers, refrigerators. It is differentiated from the brown goods sector which encompasses electronic consumer products as mobile phones, television, CD/DVD player, and personal computer etc. Trends and Developments in the White Goods Sector in Europe – A working paper of the EMF. http://www.emf-fem.org/content/download/.../Focus+no.+4+White+Goods.pdf. White Goods v Brown Goods. http://www.interioguru.com/article/home_appliances_ideas/3104-brown_vs_white.html.

[101]It entered into force on 1st June 1998. Jan Jans Producer Responsibility in Dutch Waste Law. January 2004, Avosetta Group. http://www-user.uni-bremen.de/~avosetta/netherlands.pdf.

[102]Kristensen et al. (2011), p. 35.

[103]Kristensen et al. (2011).

[104]The Association of Suppliers of Domestic Equipment in the Netherlands (VLEHAN) was the representative body for the white goods sector. At the time of the Order, the Association's members accounted for about 60% of all producers and distributors of white goods in the Netherlands. Similarly the Union of Manufacturers, Importer and Agents in the Electronics Area (FIAR) with members such as JVC, Phillips and Sony was the representative body for the brown goods sector. Bressers et al. (2002).

[105]INSEAD Faculty & Research Working Paper (2010), p. 30.

[106]Kristensen et al. (2011), p. 37.

[107]INSEAD Working Paper (2010), p. 30.

on the weight of their brand portions for the recycled WEEE.[108] To achieve this, every container of WEEE delivered to ICT Milieu is hand-sorted, and all WEEE logged according to weight and brand, so that costs of treating them were charged to appropriate producers. However, brands not belonging to any of the ICT Milieu partners were registered as 'free riders.[109]

The WEEE Directive 2002/EC/96 was transposed into Dutch national law in 2004 via the WEEE Management Decree and the WEEE Management Regulations.[110] These laws reiterated the prior voluntary obligation in the White and Brown Goods Decree for producers to take back at least free of charge, any product which consumers bring in when buying new products.[111] The 2004 WEEE Management Regulation included the EPR concept[112] and established common collection from municipal points, transport and treatment for WEEE[113] in order to live up to standards set by the WEEE.[114] It achieved this via a two-tier collection system through 540 municipal collection sites and 65 regional collection and sorting depots.[115] One major change created by the legislation was that from the beginning of 2003, ICT manufacturers/producers switched from a take-back system of individual producer responsibility (IPR) for their own brands to a collective system with costs allocated based on market-share.[116] This is principally because of the logistics

[108]Dempsey and McIntyrre (2009), p. 213.

[109]"Free-rider" is a general term used for businesses (in this context, producers that do not actively participate in a programme but nevertheless benefit from it and thus threaten the scheme's successful development. Hoeveler (2009). MfE, Product Stewardship and Water Efficiency Labeling - New Tools to Reduce Waste (August 2006). http://www.mfe.govt.nz/publications/waste/product-stewardship-waterlabelling-aug06/product-stewardship-labelling-aug06.pdf. Kristensen et al. (2011), p. 37.

[110]The WEEE Management Decree repealed the Management of White and Brown Goods Decree from 1999, which up until the adoption of the WEEE Directive, had been the legal basis for the handling of WEEE in the Netherlands. Article 7 of the WEEE Management Decree of July 6, 2004. http://www.cfsd.org.uk/seeba/countries/netherlands/reports/200409_engelsevertaling_besluit_elektrapp%5B1%5D.pdf. Kristensen et al. (2011).

[111]WEEE Management Decree 2004. http://www.epeat.org/weee-registration/Netherlands_WEEE-management-decree_200409_engelsevertaling_besluit_elektrapp.pdf. WEEE Management Regulations. http://www.epeat.org/weee-registration/Netherlands_WEEE-management-regulations_200409_engelsevertaling_regeling_elektrapp.pdf.

[112]Section 1 and 7 of the Regulations.

[113]Section 3 of the Regulations.

[114]Kristensen et al. (2011), pp. 38–39.

[115]INSEAD Working Paper (2010), p. 79, p. 31.

[116]Sachs (2006), p. 30.

of implementing individual responsibility[117] and associated problems of 'free riders,' and orphan products (products from defunct producers).[118]

The uniqueness of the Netherland system, apart from it being EPR based, lies in its adherence to Article 5 (4) of the WEEE Directive 2002 which requires that member States of the EU who have domesticated the Directive are to ensure that on average, per inhabitant per year, a collection rate of 4 kg of WEEE from private households be achieved by 31 December 2006. With the transposition of the WEEE Directive into its laws incorporating the EPR approach to WEEE, and with joint co-operation of the voluntary take-back scheme of ICT Milieu and NVMP, the Netherlands has been able to achieve a collection rate exceeding 7.8 kg per inhabitant.[119] Currently, the WEEE regulations are enforced by way of penalties and where necessary, criminal sanctions,[120] but enforcement within the ICT Milieu and MVP largely depends on a degree of operational trust, as data supplied by recyclers and producers are self-certified.[121] The ICT Milieu and NVMP are still the only two collective PROs in the Netherlands responsible for handling WEEE, and they report directly to the Dutch Environmental Assessment Agency.[122]

The Netherlands has been successful in incorporating a mandatory EPR take-back approach in its 2004 legislation and establishing a n e-waste based institution via the working synergy between the Dutch government, the ICT milieu, the NVMP and consumers. This mandatory EPR approach set out in attendant regulations work in tandem with voluntary organisations involved in the recycling of EEE. Their system is a laudable one particularly because in accordance with the WEEE Directive 2002, it has been able to achieve a commendable EEE collection rate via its laws which domesticate the WEEE Directive. The inclusion of penalties and sanctions in the Dutch WEEE Regulations are a familiar phenomenon atypical of few environmental legislation. Additionally, the change from an individual to collective producer responsibility to ensure effective take-back system is also noteworthy as the

[117]These logistics included changing role of market shares or members. For example, a large PC manufacturer with a considerable market share in the past had seen a reduction in sales at the end of the 1990s. Given its historical presence in the market a large proportion of the total product returns at this time were from its own brand. Coupled with more recent reduced sales, this meant that this particular PC manufacturer had—in comparison with its competitors—much higher costs when proportioned to per unit placed on the market. In view of these circumstances, the manufacturer would threaten to leave the system unless the financing model was changed. INSEAD Working Paper (2010), p. 31.

[118]INSEAD Working Paper (2010).

[119]This figure signifies the average WEEE collection rate per EU inhabitant in 2010. Netherlands had collected about 8 kg of WEEE by 2010. WEEE Forum Annual Report 2010. http://www.weee-forum.org/system/files/various/2010_annual_report_final.pdf. Kristensen et al. (2011).

[120]Paragraph 5 of the Explanatory Memorandum to the WEEE Regulations provides that the scope provided for enforcement exists under both administrative and criminal law and infringement of the regulations is punishable under the Economic Offences Act. Text of the WEEE Regulations (n 110). Pak (2008), pp. 271–272; Elisha (2010–2011), p. 223.

[121]INSEAD Working Paper (2010), p. 32.

[122]Kristensen et al. (2011), p. 38.

producers can also jointly acquire gains if the market share of the re-designed EEE products is productive. The Dutch system therefore correctly recognises and accepts economic and physical responsibility for EEE, as envisaged under the classification system set out above on what an effective EPR system should encompass.

5.2 *Japan*

Japan may be considered one of the world's leading countries in the development and manufacturing of electronic equipment.[123] It is assumed to be the most advanced and experienced country in respect of recycling measures for such equipment.[124] Due to the severely short lifespan of Japanese municipal disposal sites and a densely populated urban environment, the government has taken steps to promote recycling and resource conservation.[125] It enacted WEEE legislation based on the concept of EPR—i.e. the Shared Home Appliances Recycling Law ('SHARL') and the Revised Law for Promotion of Effective Utilisation of Resources ('Recycling Promotion Law'), which both went into effect in 2001.[126] However, rather than placing full end-of-life (EOL) responsibility on producers as the EU's WEEE Directive and the Netherlands does, Japan's system distributes e-waste recycling responsibility between four different stakeholders: producers, consumers, retailers and the government[127] i.e. (product stewardship).

5.2.1 Shared Home Appliances Recycling (SHAR) Law

The scarcity of final disposal sites, increased volumes of EEE in the waste stream and inadequate treatment facilities were the main driving forces for the enactment of this law.[128] It laid down specific recycling targets for four specific types of household EEE i.e. air conditioners (60%), televisions (55%), fridges/freezers (50%) and washing machines (50%).[129] Producers are mandated to accept end-of-life products from consumers for processing when they (producers) sell products similar to the

---

[123]Kutz (2006), p. 322.

[124]McKenna (2007), pp. 116, 122.

[125]INFORM Strategies for a better environment, Electric Appliance Recycling in Japan. http://www.informinc.org/fact_JapanEPR.pdf.

[126]Revised Law for the Promotion of Effective Utilization of Resources, April 2001 (promulgated June 2000, as an amendment to the Resource Recycling Promotion Law, enacted in 1991). Hoeveler (2009), p. 156.

[127]Pak (2008), pp. 271–272. Elisha (2010–2011), p. 224.

[128]Tojo (2004), p. 17. INSEAD Working Paper (2010).

[129]As at 2011, SHAR Law was being reviewed by the national authorities and there was strong indication that two additional product groups—clothes dryers and LCD Display and Plasma-display TV sets would be included in the scope of the law. INSEAD Working Paper (2010), p. 17.

replacement products.[130] They are also charged with developing the infrastructure and facilities needed to transport, treat and recycle discarded electronic products in an environmentally-sound manner.[131]

On the other hand, consumers are mandated to discard bulky electronic items at specified collection locations maintained by large appliance retailers and local government agencies.[132] Japanese consumers pay disposal fees to the producer when they drop off their used electronic goods at these collection centres[133] and they are issued a 'recycling ticket,'[134] which is forwarded to the appropriate producer account within the recycling ticket management organisation known as RKC.[135] This recycling ticket is used to track the product from the point of collection through to the regional aggregation centre and recycling plant.[136] It is beneficial to consumers as they are able to track the status of their waste appliance and producers are able to trace how many waste products they have collected fees on and when and where these products have been managed.[137]

In order for Japanese producers to meet up with their operational responsibility under the law, they formed two groups/consortia. The first consortia includes Electrolux, GE, Matsushita, Toshiba[138] and others who contract with existing recycling operators or invest in their own recycling plants.[139] The second group/consortia includes a group of EEE manufacturers such as Daewoo, Hitachi, Sanyo, Sharp, Sony and others who establish their own recycling plants through voluntary joint ventures. Under this group, ownership of each recycling plant appears to be dominated by one key shareholder with financial contributions from other members of the group.[140] Recycling fees charged by all manufacturers in both groups are the same. However, for Group 2 producers who jointly own recycling facilities, any cost

---

[130]INSEAD Working Paper (2010), p. 18. See also Elisha (2010–2011), p. 224.

[131]Elisha (2010–2011).

[132]Lin et al. (2001–2002), pp. 541–542.

[133]Pak (2008), pp. 196, 272.

[134]Japanese consumers pay two fees when they discard e-waste at collection centers: a collection fee which covers the cost of collection, and a recycling fee based on the cost of recycling that particular item. See INSEAD Working Paper (2010). INFORM Appliance (n 125); Elisha (2010–2011), p. 224.

[135]INSEAD Working Paper (2010), p. 20.

[136]The recycling ticket has five copies of which the consumer retains the original. The retailer keeps another copy and the remaining 3 copies accompany the product to the regional aggregation points. One copy is filed at the regional aggregation center and the other 2 are transported with the product to the recycling plant. The recycling plant retains the 4th copy which is then sent back to retailer to complete the cycle. On each copy of the ticket, product details—model number and manufacturer name—and name of the retailer that collected the waste product are recorded. INSEAD Working Paper (2010), p. 20.

[137]INSEAD Working Paper (2010).

[138]Hoeveler (2009), p. 156.

[139]INSEAD Working Paper (2010), p. 20.

[140]DTI (2005), p. 49. INSEAD Working Paper (2010).

savings through efficient processing or product design remain with the producers.[141] This creates incentives for the manufacturers to design recyclable products. This incentive is driven by the competition between the two collective systems since, if manufacturers in one collection system recycle their products cheaper, they would get a cost advantage over the competitors in the other collective system.[142]

Although it allows producers to work within a collaborative network, Japan's SHAR Law enforces IPR by requiring manufacturers to take physical responsibility for the disposal and recycling of their e-waste, allowing them to determine disposal costs for their own products.[143] Tojo[144] also provides empirical evidence that SHAR Law provides tangible incentives for environmentally-conscious design of EEE in Japan. The analysis of her study revealed that all manufacturers that were interviewed considered anticipated regulatory requirements posed by SHAR Law in their EEE product development strategies.[145] Therefore, it appears that the mandatory requirements to producers under legislation, working jointly with voluntary schemes by producers are e-waste institutions vital to the effective regulation and management of e-waste in any jurisdiction.

5.2.2 Revised Law for Promotion of Effective Utilisation of Resources ('Recycling Promotion Law')

This law was enacted in 1991 to promote increased recycling of a variety of products and materials. One of the major goals of the legislation was to promote designs that facilitate waste reduction, recycling and reuse.[146] In 2001, the law was revised to include personal computers,[147] and other electronic accessories such as mice and keyboards.[148]

The Recycling Promotion Law requires discarded computers to be recycled through a governmental system too and is based on the same principles of shared responsibility as SHAR Law.[149] What both laws have in common is the requirement for manufacturers to establish collection and recycling systems, whereas consumers have to pay end-of-life fees to finance the scheme. The main difference is that the consumer is burdened with varied costs depending on the date the discarded PC was

[141] INSEAD Working Paper (2010), p. 21.

[142] INSEAD Working Paper (2010).

[143] INFORM Appliance (n 125), p. 1.

[144] Tojo (2004), pp. ix, 68.

[145] Pak (2008), p. 273; Tojo (2004), p. 171.

[146] INSEAD Working Paper (2010), p. 1.

[147] Ordinance of the Ministry of Economy, Trade and Industry No 62 of 2001 and Ordinance of the Ministry of Economy, Trade and Industry No 77 of 2001.

[148] Copy machines are also regulated under the disposal guidelines. Kutz (2006), p. 322. INFORM. APPLIANCE (n 125). Elisha (2010–2011), p. 224.

[149] Pak (2008), p. 272. Hoeveler (2009), p. 158.

purchased.[150] In October 2003, manufacturers voluntarily started to include a recycling mark on computers entitling consumers to return them free of charge at their EOL but with an additional recycling fee incorporated in the sale of the product.[151] For computers purchased before October 1, 2003, the end-of-life fees are the same, regardless of whether units are brought to a post office or picked up at home. Computers sold after October 1, 2003, bear the PC Recycling Mark and are collected free of charge by the federal postal service—Japan Post.[152] The collection of discarded computers is organised by the Japan Post, which is a unique approach in this context.[153] Japan Post provides 20,000 offices where computers can be dropped off and in addition a service is offered to collect products from private residences.[154]The recycling programme is mainly operated on behalf of manufacturers by the Japan Electronics and Information Technology Industries Association ("JEITA"), an industry trade association that seeks to ensure industry compliance with the legislation.[155]

In addition, to further prevent illegal shipments violating the Basel Convention 1989, the Japanese government requires traders to submit pictures of the contents of containers to customs authorities in addition to other export of the contents of containers to customs authorities in addition to other export application documents.[156] Though this system is not fool proof as exporters could also replace the contents after preparing export application documents and pictures of the contents of containers to Customs,[157] it is a good step in the right direction in a bid to prevent illegal shipments of the WEEE.

Taken together, the above legislation has enabled Japan to reach a collection rate that is close to the EU's target of 4 kg per year. Though the systems are different, this collection rate is emphasized here to highlight the success rate of the Japanese and Netherland system as a result of utilising innovative EPR-oriented approaches to e-waste management.[158] The Japanese idea of sharing responsibility for WEEE between stakeholders (product stewardship), imposing a financial fee on consumers (ARF—see above) and the mandatory take-back requirement provided in both WEEE legislation above is worthy of note. While the Netherlands system wholly incorporates economic and physical responsibilities under the EPR classification

[150]Pak (2008). Hoeveler (2009).

[151]DTI Paper (2005), p. 21.

[152]INFORM APPLIANCE (note 125), p. 2.

[153]Hoeveler (2009), p. 158.

[154]Hoeveler (2009). INSEAD Working Paper (2010), p. 24.

[155]INSEAD Working Paper (2010).

[156]Aoki-Suzuki (2013), p. 174.

[157]*ibid.*

[158]It should be noted however that the Dutch EPR-based legislation has been criticized as not being wholly encompassing in the management of e-waste because of the absence of an EU Clearing House which can facilitate compliance of producers to pay a financial guarantee according to the market share of their products. Kristensen et al. (2011), p. 2.

system set out above, the Japanese system basically incorporates the different responsibilities accordingly. Additionally, the foresight of both legislation placing financial responsibility on consumers while also doing same on producers, accentuates the principle of shared financial responsibility under product stewardship and advanced recycling fee scheme. It is therefore pertinent to reiterate here that as stated above, both schemes can be effectively incorporated jointly to ensure smooth and effective EPR-based relationship between industry and government in any jurisdiction.

6 The Application of the EPR Approach in Nigeria

The pertinent question which arises from the above discourse is: can industry and government-led initiatives on WEEE as exemplified in the above jurisdictions find expression in Nigeria? This paper is inclined to believe that it will. Majority of existing environmental legislation—are either obsolete or still in the process of being amended.[159] However, the government has shown extraordinary effort towards the e-waste trade by enacting the National Environmental (Electrical/Electronics Sector) Regulations 2011. It incorporates the polluter pays principle, recognises the need to set up collection points for EEE rather than improper disposal; and also adopts the EPR approach to EEE management.[160] Unfortunately, this Regulation has not yet been implemented and the e-waste trade continues. This Regulation also fails to define who a "Producer" is and there are no plans in place yet for a synergy between industry and government.

The loopholes inherent in the application of this Regulation necessitates a discourse into the relative success of take-back schemes and the role of Nigerian legislation.

6.1 E-waste Legislation

6.1.1 National Environmental (Sanitation and Wastes Control) Regulations 2009

The 2009 Regulations defines 'end-of-life waste' as 'a post-consumer waste of products, appliances, equipment, machinery that may have physical integrity but have lost its utility value (e.g. tyre, vehicle, television, cooker, refrigerator, mobile

[159]This is exemplified by virtue of the Harmful Waste (Special Criminal Provisions) Decree of 1989, of which a bill for amendment was only passed in 2012, since the adoption of the legislation in 1989.

[160]Sections 7 (1), 11 (1) and 11(4), ibid.

phones, etc.) which the owner has discarded, intends to discard or is required to discard).'[161]

The Regulations also incorporate the Extended Producer Responsibility (EPR) approach, stating that manufacturers and producers shall incorporate 'environmental concerns' in the design, process and disposal of a product.[162] The Regulation does not provide any further explanation of what 'environmental concerns' entail and implies that NESREA, which is responsible for these regulations, is to know what that entails. It can be assumed that it alludes to Lindhqvist's physical classification which requires producers to adopt an 'eco-design' approach to EEE production to minimise further environmental impact arising from the product. While the Regulations do not define who a 'producer' is in this context, it also incorporates the Polluter-Pays Principle, an integral part of the Extended Producer Responsibility (EPR) approach by providing that all generators of wastes, owners or occupiers of premises where wastes are generated shall be legally and financially responsible for the safe and environmentally sound disposal of their wastes.[163] The Regulations also emphasize that all generators and managers of waste shall apply sustainable practices to minimize pollution.[164]

In line with the EPR approach, the Regulations also mandates all manufacturers and importers of EEE to register with NESREA, undertake buy-backs for recycling, and embark on individual or collective Product Stewardship Programme contained in its Schedule 9.[165] This Schedule sets out guidelines for an EPR programme, directing manufacturers and importers of e-waste to, either individually or collectively submit a Product Stewardship Programme (PSP) to NESREA for approval.

The PSP is required to (a) establish a process for the collection, handling, transportation and final treatment of post-consumer products regardless of who the original brand owner of the products or the consumer is; (b) employ various types of processes to reduce, re-use, recycle or recover post-consumer products, including but not limited to details of efforts to incorporate the priorities of a pollution prevention hierarchy by moving progressively from disposal to reduction, reuse, recycling and recovery of post-consumer products.[166]

A report on their consumer PSP for e-waste must be submitted on or before June 30 annually to NESREA, including the following information: (i) total amount of consumer products sold and post-consumer waste collected; (ii) the total amount of post-consumer waste processed or in storage; (iii) the percentage of post-consumer waste that was treated, contained, reused, recycled or recovered; efforts taken

[161]Ibid.

[162]Section 16 of the Regulations.

[163]Section 14 of the Regulations.

[164]See definition in section 15 above.

[165]Section 32.

[166]Section 3 (a) i and ii, of Schedule IX.

through consumer product marketing strategies to reduce post-consumer waste; (iii) Any other information requested by NESREA.[167]

The Regulations also provide that 'failure to participate shall attract penalties.' This provision appears vague, as it is not clear if the intention of the drafters was to penalise non-participation of the manufacturers and importers of e-waste in an individual or collective PSP, or if the penalty is meant for non-inclusion of the appropriate information required in the annual PSP report.

The Sanitation and Wastes Regulations represent an effort by the government to adopt a regulation which incorporates the EPR principle to e-waste management in Nigeria. Unfortunately, it is riddled with loopholes which should have been carefully avoided in the drafting of same. Though the Regulations are laudable in its inclusion of 'buy-backs' for recycling and a collective Product Stewardship Programme, NESREA is yet to publish any information relating the compulsory requirement for annual reports on consumer e-waste submitted by any manufacturer or importer of same. It can be implied from this that NESREA is not properly enforcing the provisions of the Regulations and manufacturers and importers are not complying with same. This lack of compliance and enforcement highlights the weakness of this piece of legislation. Additionally, as at the time of writing this paper, there was no Product Stewardship Plan in place by any manufacturer or importer for the establishment of a process for collection, handling, transport and final treatment of post-consumer product as required by section 32 (c) of the Regulations.

This regulation focused more on municipal solid waste (MSW) and health care waste (HCW) and its generation and management, rather than the e-waste. As such, NESREA began to put appropriate modalities in place for the adoption of additional air-tight regulations to ensure effective environmental governance through compliance monitoring and enforcement for e-waste management.[168] In 2011, an additional e-waste specific regulation referred to as the National Environmental (Electrical/ Electronics Sector) Regulations was adopted in accordance with section 34 of the NESREA Act.

6.1.2 National Environmental (Electrical/Electronics Sector) Regulations 2011

The National Environmental (Electrical/Electronics Sector) Regulations ('EES Regulations') was published in 2011.[169] It covers both new and used electrical/electronic equipment (EEE/UEEE).[170] In view of the fact that majority of the EEE imports entering the country are unusable and non-functional, the EES Regulations

[167]Ibid at Schedule IX.

[168]E-Waste concerns re-echoes at clean environment forum. http://www.vanguardngr.com/2010/08/e-waste-concerns-re-echoes-at-clean-environment-forum/.

[169]S. I. No. 23 in *Government Gazette* Notice No. 137, 25th May 2011.

[170]Regulation 3 (1).

specifically provides that 'all new EEE imported into the country shall be functional…'[171] The implications of this under the Regulations are that non-functional EEE shall be classified as e-waste or waste electrical and electrical equipment (WEEE), the importation or exportation of which are expressly prohibited.

The Regulation defines an 'EEE facility' to mean facilities involved with either manufacturing, processing, installing, deploying or recycling any of the following: (a) Electrical/electronics; (b) refrigerators and air-conditioning appliances; (c) Electric bulbs, lamps, accessories and fittings; (d) electrical power control and distribution equipment (e) electrical wire and cable; and (f) telecommunication equipment and base station.[172]

The EES Regulations prohibits the discarding, throwing or dropping of e-waste by a body corporate or organisation, technician, assemblers or scavengers and directs such person to practice environmentally sound management (ESM) of e-waste. Thus, the burning of e-waste, disposal of e-waste alongside domestic and/or municipal waste; disposal of e-waste at dumpsites, landfill sites, water bodies, etc.; breaking CRTs in an unsound environmental manner; releasing chlorofluorocarbons (CFCs) from fridges and other cooling systems; and leaching of precious metals with acids and other hazardous waste from printed wire boards (PWBs) or Printed Circuit Boards (PCBs) is prohibited.[173]

The activities that require a permit under the EES Regulation are: the export or transit of e-waste;[174] and the importation of used EEE. The EES Regulations also specify that the implementation of cleaner production processes and pollution prevention measures to yield economic, social and environmental benefits as specified in Schedule V to the Regulations.[175] Moreso, it requires all EEE manufacturing, processing, assembling organisation or corporate body to apply new technologies arising from the elimination of hazardous material in many new-model EEE.[176] The inclusion of this requirement in the regulations is indicative of the government's need to apply a sustainable approach to environmental management of e-waste in Nigeria. Unfortunately, Schedule V to the EES Regulations which seeks to guide the implementation of such sustainable cleaner production methods of EEE has not yet been drafted.

The EES Regulations expressly prohibits the importation of end-of-life, unusable or unserviceable EEE into Nigeria, and clearly bans the importation of Cathode Ray

[171]Regulation 69.

[172]Regulation 69.

[173]Reg. 36 (2) (a)–(e).

[174]Such export cannot be carried out without a valid transboundary and movement permit issued from the Federal Ministry of Environment. Such a permit also relates to the specific export transaction and shall not be valid for any subsequent export transaction. See Regulation 41 (1) and (2).

[175]Reg. 8 (1).

[176]Reg. 8(2).

Tubes (CRTs) into the country.[177] Such actions constitute an offence under the Regulations and on conviction, such a person is liable to a fine not exceeding N500, 000 (R30, 000) or 2 year imprisonment or both. In the case of importation of CRTs, a fine not exceeding N200, 000 (R13, 000) or 6 months imprisonment or both such fine and imprisonment, and an additional fine of N5,000 for every day the offence subsists.[178] This ban appears to be in acknowledgement of the fact that the government lacks the capacity to handle disposal of CRTs in registered landfill sites, in contrast to what is being done by voluntary e-waste recycling companies in other developed countries.

6.2 *Extended Producer Responsibility (EPR) Principle Under the EES Regulations*

The EPR principle is an integral part of the EES Regulations. It requires every importer, exporter, manufacturer, assembler, distributor and retailer of various brands of EEE products to subscribe to an EPR Program including the Buy Back Program specified in its Schedule VIII.[179] Manufacturers and Importers of EEE must also partner with NESREA on the EPR Program within two years of the commencement of the Regulations in order to achieve the Buy Back Program within a two year period.[180]

Thus, in order to ensure effective implementation of the EPR program, the EES Regulations imposes responsibilities on—(a) manufacturers, importers, distributors or retailers to take back the end-of-life EEE and setup collection points/centres; (b) manufacturers and producers of EEE to ensure environmentally sound management of e-waste from collection points or centres to NESREA accredited recyclers;[181] and (c) consumers to return end-of-life EEE to the collection points or centres.

These appear to be mandatory 'take-back' obligations on these identified categories of persons.[182] Such mandatory product take-back laws are important, not only because they reduce the environmental impacts of end-of-life products by avoiding the release of hazardous materials into discharge streams, but also with the rationale of providing incentives for manufacturers to design products that are easier to

[177] Reg. 34 (2) and (3).

[178] Reg. 61 (1) (a) and (c) and Reg. 67 (1) and (2).

[179] Reg. 11 (1). Also, importers/distributors for all EEE equipment traded or donated to individuals, educational institutions, religious organizations, communities or body corporate by whatever means, shall comply with sub-regulation (1). See Reg. 11 (2).

[180] Reg. 11 (3).

[181] Reg. 11 (4) (a)–(c).

[182] Consumers are also to return end of life EEE to collection points and centres. Regulation 11 (4) (a)–(c).

recover so as to effectively reduce the costs of product recovery.[183] However, it must be reiterated that the problem associated with mandatory take-back regulation lies in its enforcement and ensuring that manufacturers are in compliance with the relevant regulation. As is typical with waste management, there will also be the problem of collating accurate data of number of products manufactured and particular products which have been re-designed, if there is ineffective monitoring and control by the relevant departments in charge. Mandatory take-backs work effectively where there are various collection centres set up by government or voluntary recycling companies working in conjunction with government. The analysis below examines the reality of collection centres in Nigeria.

Although Schedule VIII of the Regulation sets out Guidelines for Extended Producer Responsibility in accordance with Regulation 11 (1), it makes no reference to the plan to be submitted by manufacturers and importers under the Product Stewardship Programme in the Sanitation and Waste Regulations 2009 above. It is unclear whether the EES Regulations 2011 is to be read in consonance with the 2009 Regulations to enable producers and importers decide which plan ought to be applied/submitted, or if the EES Regulations supersedes the 2009 one which is still in existence. It can be implied that the provisions of the EES Regulations are more e-waste specific and the proposal to be submitted for an EPR programme should suffice as it includes the participation of producers, importers and other players in the EEE chain, unlike the 2009 regulations which mention only producers and importers.

Thus, though the responsibilities set out under the Regulations appear to be at par with the responsibilities required of a producer in developed countries, they absence of an existing producer responsibility organization in Nigeria is inimical to the attainment to these responsibilities. 'Producer responsibility is one of the means of encouraging the design and production of EEE which take into full account and facilitated their repair, possible upgrading, re-use, disassembly and recycling.'[184] The absence of any such PRO in Nigeria to reinforce cleaner production among such local manufacturers/assemblers in Nigeria contributes to the issues of improper disposal and handling of EEE which leads to degradation of the environment. This is not effective management of e-waste and is in total contrast with what obtains in Japan and Netherlands.

Additionally, the Regulations provide modalities for the establishment and licensing for persons who want to set up EEE facilities or collection centres in Nigeria.[185] Currently, there are only two licensed e-waste recycling and state-of-the-art disposal

[183]Lifset and Lindhqvist (2008). Avasu and Subramanian (2012), p. 1042.

[184]Recital 12 of the EU Directive 2002.

[185]Reg. 61 (3) (n) and 67(2).

Reg. 5 (3); Schedule IV sets out a Guide Template for Emergency Procedures in EEE Facility.

Reg. 61 (2) and (3) (j) and (k).

Reg. 69.

facilities in the country.[186] These two facilities are not enough to handle the volume of e-waste generated daily by users of EEE in Nigeria. As a result, a lot of unusable EEE are being stockpiled in homes and offices, until they are piled so high that they are disposed of crudely by open burning in private homes or dumped among general domestic/business waste. The cost of setting up an efficient e-waste recycling facility is upwards of N85 million naira.

Although the provision of the EES Regulations attests to the palpable commitment of the Nigerian government to fulfil its obligations under the Basel Convention 1989 in the minimization of waste, and highlights its unwavering commitment to the control of imports of e-waste into the country, Nigeria is not ready for the implementation of e-waste institutions and producer responsibility organisation in Nigeria. The thriving informal e-waste sector in Lagos, Nigeria is a constant hurdle to the implementation of the EES Regulations in Nigeria.

Generally, the EPR scheme has good prospects in Africa but may be problematic due to several factors, including the mistrust of the scheme by an apprehensive informal sector, the lack of recycling infrastructure and standards, socio-cultural difficulties with take-back schemes, choice of appropriate EPR models, difficulty with defining who is a 'producer' in the context of a lack of real manufacturers, and generally poor financial support for the scheme.[187]

E-waste management in Africa is dominated by thriving informal sector collectors and recyclers in most countries, as take-back schemes and modern infrastructure for recycling are non-existent or grossly limited. Government control of this sector is at present very minimal and inefficient. Handling of e-waste is thus characterised by manual stripping to remove electronic boards for resale, open burning of wires to recover few major components (copper, aluminium, iron), and the deposition of other bulk components, including CRTs, in open dumpsites. This practice by the informal sector often involves the use of illicit labour of pregnant women and minors, as well as a lack of personal protection equipment for the workers. Resulting from such practices is the severe pollution of the environment, very poor efficiencies in recovery of expensive, trace, and precious components, and the exposure of labourers and the general populace to hazardous chemical emissions and releases.[188] This is the true picture of what obtains in Nigeria. The establishment of proper e-waste institutions will require years of strategic planning and focused implementation of the EES regulations in order to ensure proper enforcement and conformity between the informal sector and the government. Japan and Netherlands have been able to establish successful EPR schemes in e-waste management because of the synergic management between government, consumers, producers and retailers. This may be problematic in Nigeria, firstly because Nigeria is an EEE importing

---

[186]These e-waste recycling companies are E-Terra Technologies Limited and Hinckley E-waste Recycling, located in Lagos Nigeria. As at the time of publication of this paper, the author was yet to conduct a site observation of these facilities to enable an inclusion of the findings in this paper.

[187]Balde (2017), p. 68.

[188]Ibid.

country and it may be difficult to compel the producers of the manufactured or Used EEE to contribute to the EoL of EEE imported into the country. Nevertheless, the provisions of the EES Regulations provide sufficient grounds for there to be a workable EPR-based system between the government, consumers and the informal sector.

7 Challenges in the Implementation of EPR to E-waste Management in Nigeria

The analysis of Netherlands and Japan highlight a fundamental difference in their methods of implementing EPR measures, While Netherlands adopts a 'take-back' approach with a synergy of management for this waste stream between the government, ICT Milieu, consumers and producers, Japan adopts the Advanced Recycling Fee (ARF) method of consumers paying a disposal fee when buying EEE or when dropping off EEE which have reached their end of life in designated centres. Japan is also able to enforce compliance through its producer consortia who may set up their own recycling facilities or work with owners of recycling facilities so they can track the life cycle of the purchased EEE to its end of life and facilitate the effective recycling/management of same.

This is not the case in Nigeria. The provisions of the EES Regulations require manufacturers, retailers and importers of EEE and UEEE to take back end-of-life or used EEE and that consumers are to return end-of-life EEE to collection centres. Sadly, there is no coalition or consortia of manufacturers/producers, retailers and importers of EEE in Nigeria as most EEE is imported into Nigeria. In terms of management of UEEE within Nigeria, there are no established e-waste collection centres in Nigeria. Thus, it is one thing for the legislation to provide for specific scenarios or transplant similar provisions from e-waste legislations in other jurisdictions; it is another for government to facilitate the enforcement of these provisions in the absence of e-waste institutions.

Another challenge with implementation of EPR measures in Nigeria in comparison with Netherlands and Japan is that due to the high level of importation of new and used EEE into Nigeria, it is almost impossible to place the 'take-back' responsibility on the importer of UEEE when the process of importation or trade in new EEE and UEEE is so convoluted that the real identify of the 'importer' becomes distorted.

In addition, the absence of various e-waste recycling facilities by private practitioners and government in Nigeria puts paid to the idea of 'collection centres' as the latter must be present to complement the former. The debilitating cost of setting up an e-waste recycling facility in Nigeria, together with the high interest rates charged by financial institutions with regards to acquisition of personal property or property to be used for business such as recycling facilities in Nigeria is also a source of concern. AS such, while lauding the inclusions of EPR mechanisms in EES

Regulations and the Sanitation and Waste Regulations, the management of e-waste in Nigeria still leaves much to be desired.

8 Recommendations and Conclusion

Since the adoption of the Basel Convention 1989, it appears that the focus of the international community was prevention of the trade in (particularly the exportation) hazardous waste from developed to developing countries. Whilst this challenge has been plugged by the adoption of legislation which punishes perpetrators who are caught importing or exporting toxic or hazardous waste in various jurisdictions, the effective management of e-waste has gained traction over the last decade. Whilst acknowledging that the effective management of electronic waste in any jurisdiction cannot be actualised through a one-size-fits-all approach, it however can be achieved through concerted efforts toward development of workable e-waste institutions which utilise global best practice methodologies in strengthening same. For developing countries like Nigeria, it is important to continuously study the implementation strategies utilised by the Global North in establishing effective e-waste institutions. The adoption of EES regulations and appointment of NESREA to enforce same is not enough to facilitate the proper management of electronic waste. The combination of the EES Regulations 2011 and the Sanitation and Waste Regulations 2009 provide sufficient impetus for the adoption of an EPR-based institution in Nigeria for new and used EEE. Unfortunately, in comparison with established e-waste institutions in Japan and Netherlands which have working producer responsibility organisations, the possibility of establishing such PROs in Nigeria in conjunction with government is very slim, particularly because new and used EEE are being imported in Nigeria, with one or two manufacturing companies in Nigeria which import the components for manufacture from the Global North.[189] The thriving informal sector in Nigeria comprises of scavengers, assemblers, recyclers and refurbishers. As such, a collective responsibility must be established between the informal sector and the government, and existing e-waste legislation in Nigeria must be reviewed to encompass a working relationship between government, the informal sector and established e-waste facility owners (when established) in Nigeria.

In the absence of working e-waste institutions in Nigeria, this paper makes the following proposals. First, NESREA must ensure that it has an e-waste database to facilitate the collection of data to encompass new and used EEE entering the country. With the advent of information and communications technology (ICT) tools within the last few decades, this should not be a herculean task if appropriate synergy can be established between the Nigerian Port Authorities, Nigerian Customs and NESREA. Second, for Nigeria to tackle the challenges of lack of infrastructure, lack of

[189] For example, Zinox Technologies Limited.

collection centres, lack of implementation and enforcement of the EES Regulations by NESREA, regular stakeholder meetings between e-waste industry in Nigeria and government must be set up. In such meetings, modalities towards developing an e-waste responsibility organisation can be discussed to ensure implementation of an EPR-based program for e-waste in Nigeria. Third, the problem of electronic waste management cannot be effectively tackled if e-waste is collected along with municipal solid waste (MSW). State and local governments must take the initiative of facilitating the construction of electronic waste receptacles or bins to differentiate them from MSW, so they can be appropriately sorted. However, sorting of e-waste is more effective where established e-waste recycling plants have been set up. Thus, government should provide financial incentives for foreign investors, companies and private individuals to establish e-waste recycling facilities in Nigeria. Fourth, the government must be willing to invest in research and development particularly with regards to e-waste management. As such, continued investment in training and exchange programs between NESREA and environmental regulatory agencies in the Global North will provide current innovations and workable solutions towards ensuring effective e-waste management in Nigeria.

References

Journal Articles

Avasu A, Subramanian R (2012) Extended producer responsibility for E-waste: individual or collective producer responsibility? Prod Oper Manag Soc 21(6):1042–1059

Coopman P (2015) Extended producer responsibility: getting it right. March–April Waste Management World 27–28

Donald JW (1999) The Bamako Convention as a solution to the problem of hazardous waste exports to less developed countries. Colum J Environ Law 17:419–458

Elisha HH (2010–2011) Addressing the E-waste crisis: the need for comprehensive federal E-waste legislation within the United States. Chap Law Rev 14:195–236

Gutowski T et al (2005) Environmentally benign manufacturing: observations from Japan, Europe and the United States. J Clean Prod 13:1–17

Hoeveler JA (2009) International approaches to dealing with electronic waste. N Z J Environ Law 13:117–160

Kiddee P et al (2013) Electronic waste management approaches: an overview. Waste Manag 33:1237–1250

Kutz J (2006) You've got waste: the exponentially escalating problem of hazardous e-waste. Vill Environ Law J 17:307–330

Lewis H (2005) Defining product stewardship and sustainability in the Australian packaging industry. Environ Sci Policy 8(1):45–55

Lifset R, Lindhqvist T (2008) Producer responsibility at a turning point? J Ind Ecol 12:144–147

Lifset R, Atasu A, Tojo N (2013) Extended producer responsibility – national, international and practical perspectives. J Ind Ecol 17(2):162–166

Lin CK, Yan L, Davis AN (2001–2002) Globalization, extended producer responsibility and the problem of discarded computers in China: an exploratory proposal for environmental protection. Geo Int Environ Law Rev 14:525–576

Lipman Z (1999) Transboundary movement of hazardous waste: environmental justice issues for developing countries. Acta Juridica:266–276
Mayers K, Butler S (2013) Producer responsibility organisations development and operations – a case study. J Ind Ecol 17(2):1–13
McCann D, Wittmann A E-waste prevention, take-back system design and policy approach step Green Paper, 13 February 2019
McKenna A (2007) Computer waste: a forgotten and hidden side to the global information society. Environ Law Rev 9:116
Nahman A (2010) Extended producer responsibility for packaging waste in South Africa: current approaches and lessons learned. Resour Conserv Recycl 54(3):155–162
Nnorom IC, Osibanjo O (2008) Overview of electronic waste (e-waste) management practices and legislations, and their poor applications in the developing countries. Resour Conserv Recycl 52:843–858
Ogunseitan OA (2013) The Basel Convention and e-waste: translation of scientific uncertainty to protective policy. Lancet Global Health 1(6):e313–e314
Osuagwu OE, Ikerionwu E (2010) E-cycling E-waste: the way forward for Nigeria IT and electro mechanical industry. Int J Acad Res 2(1):142–149
Pak P (2008) Note: Haste makes E-waste: a comparative analysis of how the United States should approach the growing E-waste threat. Cardozo J Int Comp Law 16:241–272
Sachs N (2006) Planning the funeral at the birth: extended producer responsibility in the European Union and the United States. Harv Environ Law Rev 30:51–96
Tojo N (2004) Extended producer responsibility as a driver for design change – Utopia or reality. IIIEE Doctoral Thesis, Lund; IIIEE, Lund University
Widmer R et al (2005) Global perspectives on e-waste. Environ Impact Assess Rev 25:436–458
Wilson DC (1996) Stick or Carrot? The use of policy measures to move waste management up the hierarchy. Waste Manag Res 14:385–398

Books

Alder J, Wilkinson D (1999) Environmental law and ethics. Palgrave MacMillan, United Kingdom, pp 1–410
Asante-Duah K (1993) Hazardous waste risk assessment. CRC Press, USA
Atsegbua L, Akpotaire V, Dimowo F (2004) Environmental law in Nigeria: theory and practice. Ababa Press Ltd, Lagos
Balde CP, Forti V, Gray V, Kuehr R, Stegmann P (2017) The Global E-waste Monitor – quantities, flows and resources. United Nations University (UNU), International Telecommunication Union (ITU) & International Solid Waste Association (ISWA), Bonn/Geneva/Vienna, pp 1–108
Bosman C (2008) Integrated waste management. In: Strydom HA, King N (eds) Environmental management in South Africa. Juta & Company Ltd, South Africa, pp 1–1142
Kiss A, Shelton D (2007) Guide to international environmental law. Martinus Nijhoff Publishers, Leiden, pp 1–303
Lee M (2005) EU environmental law – challenges, change and decision making. Hart Publishing, Oxford
Naude A (2010) Conceptualising waste management, 1st edn. Source Corporation, Cape Town
Noble G (ed) (1992) Hazardous waste in South Africa. In: Kidd M (2008) Environmental law. Juta & Company Limited, South Africa
Probst KN, Beierle TC (1999) The evolution of hazardous waste programs: lessons from eight countries resources for the future. Washington DC
Rosenfeld PE, Feng LGH (2011) Risks of hazardous waste. Elsevier Inc, UK, pp 1–454

Sands P (2003) Principles of international environmental law, 2nd edn. Cambridge University Press, UK, pp 1–1074

Chapters in Books

Aoki-Suzuki C (2013) Controlling trade in electronic waste. In: Hieronymi K, Kahhat R, Willliams E (eds) E-waste management: from waste to resource. Routledge, London
Bressers HT et al (2002) The disposal of white and brown goods. In: De Clercq M (ed) Negotiated environmental agreements in Europe: critical factors for success. Edward Elgar, Cheltenham
Dempsey M, McIntyrre K (2009) The role of collective versus individual producer responsibility in e-waste management: key learning from around the world. In: Hester RE, Harrison RM (eds) Electronic waste management. RSC Publishing, Cambridge
Ikhariale M (1989) The Koko Incident, the environment and the law. In: Shyllon F (ed) The law and the environment in Nigeria, pp 73–74
Kreuger J (2001) The Basel Convention and the international trade in hazardous wastes. In: Stokke OS, Thommessen OB (eds) Yearbook of international co-operation on environment and development. Earthscan Publishers, London
Redclift M (1993) Environmental economics, policy consensus and political empowerment. In: Turner RK (ed) Sustainable environmental economics and management – principles and practice. Belhaven Press, London

Online Publications

About Producer Responsibility, Electronic Take back Coalition. http://www.electronicstakeback.com/promote-good-laws/about-producer-responsibility/
BAN Just Two More Ratifications Needed to Ensure a COP14 Ban Amendment Celebration. March 28 2019. https://myemail.constantcontact.com/BAN-s-COP14-Action-Alert%2D%2D1%2D%2DRatify-and-Celebrate-the-Ban-Amendment-.html?soid=1114999858498&aid=byC9DL1rcJU
Basel Action Network Wireless Waste: Basel Convention's Next Hazardous Waste Challenge. 1–9 http://www.ban.org/basel-convention-meetings./
DTI Waste Electrical and Electronic Equipment: Innovating Novel Recovery and Recycling Technologies in Japan. Global Watch Mission Report, September 2005
http://cfsd.org.uk/aede/downloads/JapaneseWEE.PDF. E-Waste concerns re-echoes at clean environment forum. http://www.vanguardngr.com/2010/08/e-waste-concerns-re-echoes-at-clean-environment-forum/
E-waste pollution: Threat to human health. 31 May 2011. http://www.iop.org/news/11/may/page_51103.html
Finlay A E-Waste Challenges in Developing Countries: South Africa as a Case Study. http://www.apc.org/en/system/files/e-waste_EN.pdf
E-Waste Guidelines for Kenya. http://www.gesci.org/e-waste-guidelines-for-Kenya.html
Waste Management. http://www.libraryindex.com/pages/3430/Waste-Management.html
History of the negotiations of the Basel Convention. http://www.basel.int/TheConvention/Overview/History/Overview/tabid/3405/Default.aspx
INFORM Strategies for a better environment, Electric Appliance Recycling in Japan. http://www.informinc.org/fact_JapanEPR.pdf

INSEAD Faculty & Research Working Paper (2010) Individual Producer Responsibility: A Review of Practical Approaches to Implementing Individual Producer Responsibility for the WEEE Directive. 1–87 http://papers.ssrn.com/sol3/papers.cfm?abstract_id=1698695

Jan Jans Producer Responsibility in Dutch Waste Law. January 2004, Avosetta Group. http://www-user.uni-bremen.de/~avosetta/netherlands.pdf

Key Elements of EPR Plan, Clean Production Action. http://www.cleanproduction.org[Producer.Key.Examples.php

Kristensen E, Lindblad B, Mortensen J (2011) The WEEE Directive & Extended Producer Responsibility – Lost in Transposition. Rosklilde University. http://rudar.ruc.dk/bitstream/1800/7209/1/Group%20No.%20764%20project%20-%20The%20WEEE%20Directive%20%26%20Extended%20Producer%20Responsibility.pdf

Lindhqvist T Extended Producer Responsibility in Cleaner Production – Policy Principle to Promote Environmental Improvement of Product Systems. May 2000, Doctoral thesis. http://www.lub.lu.se/luft/diss/tec355.pdf

Lindhqvist T, Lidgren K (1990) Modellerförförlängtproducentansvar [Models for extended producer responsibility]. In Ministry of the Environment, Frånvaggan till graven - sex studier avvarorsmiljöpåverkan [From the Cradle to the Grave – six studies of the environmental impact of products] (Ds 1991:9)

MfE, Product Stewardship and Water Efficiency Labeling - New Tools to Reduce Waste (August 2006). http://www.mfe.govt.nz/publications/waste/product-stewardship-waterlabelling-aug06/product-stewardship-labelling-aug06.pdf

Overview – Conference of the Parties (COP). http://www.basel.int/TheConvention/ConferenceoftheParties/OverviewandMandate/tabid/1316/Default.aspx

Product Stewardship: Basic Information. US Environmental Protection Agency. http://www.epa.gov/waste/partnerships/stewardship/basic.htm

Salehabadi S Transboundary Movements of Discarded Electrical and Electronic Equipment' Solving the E-waste Problem (StEP) Initiative Green Paper Series. 25 March 2013. http://www.step-initiative.org/index.php/Publications.html

Status of Ratifications – Amendment to the Basel Convention on the Control of Transboundary Movements of Hazardous Waste. http://www.basel.int/Countries/StatusofRatifications/BanAmendment/tabid/1344/Default.aspx

Trends and Developments in the White Goods Sector in Europe – A working paper of the EMF. http://www.emf-fem.org/content/download/.../Focus+no.+4+White+Goods.pdf

White Goods v Brown Goods. http://www.interioguru.com/article/home_appliances_ideas/3104-brown_vs_white.html

Text of the Basel Convention. http://www.env.go.jp/recycle/yugai/law/conv_e.pdf

Walls M Extended Producer Responsibility and Product Design: Economic Theory and Selected Case Studies. March 2006, Discussion Paper. RFF DP 06-08, Resources for the Future, Washington. http://www.rff.org/Documents/RFF-DP-06-08.pdf

WEEE Forum Annual Report 2010. http://www.weee-forum.org/system/files/various/2010_annual_report_final.pdf

WEEE Management Decree 2004. http://www.epeat.org/weee-registration/Netherlands_WEEE-management-decree_200409_engelsevertaling_besluit_elektrapp.pdf

WEEE Management Regulations. http://www.epeat.org/weee-registration/Netherlands_WEEE-management-regulations_200409_engelsevertaling_regeling_elektrapp.pdf

WEEE Management Decree of July 6, 2004. http://www.cfsd.org.uk/seeba/countries/netherlands/reports/200409_engelsevertaling_besluit_elektrapp%5B1%5D.pdf

UNEP Environmental Alert Bulletin, E-Waste, The Hidden Side of IT equipment's Manufacturing and Use. http://www.grid.unep.ch/product/publication/download/ew_ewaste.en.pdf

UNEP Recycling- From E-Waste to Resources July 2009. http://www.unep.org/pdf/.../E-waste_publication_screen_finalversion-sml.pdf

News Articles

At 50 Million Tons, E-Waste is the "Fastest-Growing Waste Stream" Word & Way, February 14, 2019., https://wordandway.org/2019/02/14/at-50-million-tons-e-waste-fastest-growing-waste-stream/

Mavropoulou N (2015) Top Trumps for Big Dumps Waste Management World. https://waste-management-world.com/a/top-trumps-for-big-dumps

PACE/WEF A New Circular Vision for Electronics – Time for a Global Reboot. http://www3.weforum.org/docs/WEF_A_New_Circular_Vision_for_Electronics.pdf

The Bamako Convention has only 29 signatories out of the number required. Ratify, implement Bamako Convention, SRADev tells FG. The Punch, January 15, 2018. https://punchng.com/ratify-implement-bamako-convention-sradev-tells-fg/

UNEP Backs Action for E-Waste Regulation in Africa. http://www.africainstitute.info/UNEP_EA

UNEP Environmental Alert Bulletin, E-Waste, The Hidden Side of IT equipment's Manufacturing and Use. http://www.grid.unep.ch/product/publication/download/ew_ewaste.en.pdf

Irekpitan Okukpon PhD (Cape Town), Senior Research Fellow, Nigerian Institute of Advanced Legal Studies (NIALS), Lagos, Nigeria.

Part III
Intellectual Property

The Participation of Pharmaceutical Drug Industry in Patent Governance and Law-Making: A Case Study of India and Nigeria

Amaka Vanni

Contents

1 Introduction

Since the onset of the World Trade Organisation (WTO) Agreement on Trade-Related Aspects of Intellectual Property Rights (TRIPS)[1] in 1995, there has been a substantial evolution in incorporation of the Agreement in many domestic forums—

I would like to thank the anonymous reviewers whose perspective and constructive comments greatly helped improve the article. Needless to add, I alone am responsible for errors and infelicities.

[1]*Marrakesh Agreement Establishing the World Trade Organization*, opened for signature 15 April 1994, 1867 UNTS 3 (entered into force 1 January 1995) annex 1C, *The Agreement on Trade Related Aspects of Intellectual Property Rights* (*'TRIPS Agreement'*).

A. Vanni (✉)
School of Law, University of Leeds, Leeds, UK
e-mail: n.vanni@leeds.ac.uk

C. Eboe-Osuji et al. (eds.), *Nigerian Yearbook of International Law 2018/2019*,
Nigerian Yearbook of International Law 2018/2019,
https://doi.org/10.1007/978-3-030-69594-1_7

including in key emerging economies of Argentina, Brazil, India, Thailand and South Africa. Notably, these emerging countries have sought to incorporate TRIPS standards on patents in a manner aimed at ensuring a fair balance between the public interest and the legitimate interests of rights-holders. For instance, in 2005 India introduced a new section in its domestic patent law, section 3(d), which prevents the patenting of new forms of known substances unless they exhibit enhanced efficacy. Based on this criterion, the Indian Supreme Court rejected the claim of Novartis, the Swiss pharmaceutical company, for exclusive rights for manufacturing the cancer drug, Gleevec.[2] In 2012, Argentina issued, via its National Institute of Industrial Property (INPI) and Ministries of Industry and of Health, a new resolution akin to India's section 3(d). The resolution seeks to make it harder to get a patent for "inventions" that offer little to no real improvement over existing drugs.[3] Brazil, in 2016, amended its "prior consent" ("anuência prévia") mechanism to its industrial property law, which requires the Brazilian National Health Surveillance Agency (Agência Nacional de Vigilância Sanitária—ANVISA) to analyse whether a patent application is a health risk.[4] South Africa is in the process of amending its patent laws after releasing in 2017 draft intellectual property (IP) policy, which identifies public health as an important constitutional measure "to achieve the progressive realisation" of the right to health.[5] Yet in these interactions and reforms ongoing in other developing countries, Nigeria continues to lag behind. That is, these domestic recalibrations of patent law are lacking in the country's domestic space. Nigeria, like the aforementioned emerging economies, has always been an active interlocutor at the international level on issues concerning the TRIPS Agreement and its impact on development, medicines access, knowledge and technology transfer. The country, for example, was vehement, during Uruguay Rounds negotiations in its opposition to the incorporation of IP into the larger framework of global trade, specifically noting, "GATT should confine itself to only trade-related issues."[6] However, while fellow emerging-economy countries have gone ahead to include what many scholars observe as progressive and innovative features that protect public health interests in their domestic patent laws,[7] Nigeria has not taken similar steps. It must be mentioned, however, that there have been recent discussions for the introduction of a

---

[2]*Novartis A.G. vs. Union of India*, 2013. The Indian Patent Office and subsequently the Intellectual Property Appellate Board (IPAB) had earlier rejected the Novartis application for patent protection. See Rangnekar (2013), p. 39.

[3]Joint Resolution 118/2012, 546/2012 and 107/2012 (Ministry of Industry, Ministry of Health and National Industrial Property Institute; Galuchi 2012).

[4]In 2006 when ANVISA was originally created, its role was to approve any pharmaceutical patent application as means to ensure protection of the public health. See Chavez and Reis (2011), p. 25; See also Vanni (2020), pp. 81–82 on controversies concerning ANIVSA's role on patent approval.

[5]Draft Intellectual Property Policy of the Republic of South Africa, Phase I, 2017.

[6]Ukpanah (1990).

[7]Okediji (2014), Dreyfuss (2009), p. 5; Abbott et al. (2013), p. 6.

new progressive bill entitled Industrial Property Commission Bill (IPCOM). However, the IPCOM bill is yet to be passed into law by the Nigerian lawmakers. Thus, the Patents and Designs Act, Cap. P2, Laws of the Federation of Nigeria 2004 (a codification of the 1970 Act) is still in enforce and remains the preeminent law on patents in Nigeria.

Bearing in mind the aforementioned innovative pharmaceutical patent law-making in key emerging economies, several studies have documented the presence and involvement of non-state agents such as multinational corporations (MNCs) and civil society groups in the globalisation of IP, including the introduction the aforementioned progressive policies in local forums.[8] These actors, particularly transnational business groups, have been able to mould the contours of national discourse on IP and as a result, motivated some countries to place demand for IP regulation as not only part of a national strategy but also as part of free trade agreements.[9] These interactions typically take the form of dialogue, democratic bargaining or contestation of ideas.[10] These transnational business groups such as multinational corporations (MNCs) bring a foreknowledge or expertise on a specific issue to their chosen site of interaction either domestic or otherwise in the hope of influencing a policy or legal outcome. This interaction, in turn, leads to a production of knowledge on IP matters, which then circulates within state decision-making (in this case, by influencing the conceptualization of what an appropriate IP policy and agenda looks like). In fact, an analysis of the negotiating history of TRIPS Agreement provides a glimpse into the dynamic nature of MNC participation in international IP standard setting—specifically, the ways in which transnational corporations pushed for the inclusion of IP within the broader framework of global trade regime and public international law.[11] Many scholars have mentioned how the creation of key business organizations such as the intellectual property committee (IPC),[12] the international intellectual property alliance (IIPA)[13] and the business software alliance (BSA)[14]—dedicated exclusively to the cause of globalizing IP

---

[8]Drahos (1995), p. 16; Braithwaite and Drahos (2004); Braithwaite and Drahos (2000), p. 64; Kapczynski and Krikorian (2010), p. 25; Kapstein and Busby (2013).

[9]Drahos (1995) and Weissman (1996).

[10]Drahos and Mayne (2002).

[11]Sell (2003), Drahos (2010), Drahos and Braithwaite (2004) and Weissman (1996).

[12]The IPC was borne out of the Advisory Committee for Trade Negotiations (ACTN)—as a public-private forum to ensure the private sector was represented in negotiation of US trade policies and agreements. Consisting of international business community such as Bristol-Myers, Dupont, FMC Corporation, General Electric, General Motors, Hewlett-Packard, IBM, Johnson & Johnson, Merck, Mosanto, Pfizer, Rockwell International and Warner Communication.

[13]The IIPA is a copyright lobbyist group and consists of the American Film Marketing Association, the Association of American Publishers, the Business Software Alliance, the Computer and Business Equipment Manufacturers Association, the Information Technology Association of America, the Motion Picture Association of America, the National Music Publishers Association and the Recording Industry Association of America.

[14]BSA consists of top US software industry.

standards—helped shape and propel the current IP-trade paradigm.[15] As Braithwaite and Drahos note, the work of these business actors on global IP regime reveals a multiplier effect of business networks on economic power and their role in global IP harmonization.[16]

Bearing the above in minds, this paper therefore, traces the participation of pharmaceutical drug manufacturers in patent governance and law-making India and Nigeria. It also highlights the complex interrelationship between state and private actors involved in IP knowledge governance. Accordingly, this article contributes to advancing our knowledge on how the relationship between a variety of actors shape the framing and responses to national implementation of patent law. This paper is structured in four sections. Section 2 presents an analysis of the role, participation and influence of the Indian pharmaceutical manufacturer (here, focus is on both generic and brand-name manufacturers) in the shaping and evolution of the Indian patent regime to reflects certain choices and orientation. Specifically, it underscores the role the country's pharmaceutical sector actors has played (and continues to play) in influencing pharmaceutical patent regime in India in the wake of country's full transition into the TRIPS Agreement and thereafter. Thus, this section focuses on these series of interventions and influence exerted on state structures ultimately causing shifts on national discourse on patents, development and access to medicines. Of course, the increased involvement of the sector did not happen in vacuum. The sector developed based on a select but specific policy interventions by the Indian government that created an enabling environment, which allowed the country to become known as the "pharmacy of the developing world"[17] and a leading supplier of affordable medicines to many countries. Section 3 spotlights Nigeria and its pharmaceutical sector. Attention is drawn to series of policy interventions by the Nigerian government, which devastated the sector rendering it incapable to participate in patent law-making. Section 4 provides conclusions.

2 The Indian Patent Regime and the Participation of the Domestic Pharmaceutical Sector

Like many other developing countries, India's interaction with patent law came about as a result of colonial rule. The first patent law introduced by the British, Act VI of 1986, granted exclusive privileges to inventors for a period of 7 years.[18] Even

---

[15]Drahos (1995), p. 13.

[16]Braithwaite and Drahos (2000), p. 87. Balakrishnan Rajagopal expressed similar sentiment regarding the role and activism of grassroot social movement, particularly in the reinterpretation of the TRIPS Agreement to allow the sale of generic HIV/AIDS drugs that resulted in the Doha Declaration. See Rajagopal (2003), p. 146.

[17]Médecins Sans Frontières Access Campaign (2004).

[18]Narayanan (2013), p. 6.

though Act VI was amended and changed numerous times,[19] the attendant laws still retained aspects of colonial legacy of exploitation. When India gained its independence from the United Kingdom, one of the first things the newly independent government did was change the colonial patent law to encourage development. To do this, the government set up two committees to review the patent law in India.

The first committee chaired by Dr Bakshi Tek Chand (1948) suggested the introduction and use of compulsory license for food and medicine's related inventions to prevent abuse of the patent system. According to commentators, the fundamental contribution of the Tek Chand Committee was the defence of public interest in food and medicines, hence, the focus on compulsory license.[20] The nascent pharmaceutical sector was equally active in lobbying for an amendment of the colonial-era patent law so as to allow for the development of the sector.[21] For instance, Dhavan et al. note the presence and participation of notable pharmaceutical industrialists as part of the Tek Chand Committee such as G. Bewoor from Tata Industries and S.P Sen from the Bengal Chemical and Pharmaceutical Works.[22] In addition, members of the Indian Chemical Manufacturers and the Indian Pharmaceutical Association also contributed to the Report.[23] The involvement of the pharmaceutical industry groups, Dhaven et al. inferred, contributed to suggestions of changes in the compulsory license made by the Tek Chand Committee. For instance, the Indian Penicillin Committee pressured the government to change the law and "allow compulsory licensing for food, medicines, curative and surgical inventions."[24] As a result, one of the main recommendations of the Tek Chand Committee was a reform of the sections on compulsory license of the existing patent law at that time to curb patent abuse.

The early participation of the pharmaceutical sector in the discourse and reforms surrounding the Indian patent law is not surprising as the colonial patent law existing at that time provided patent-holders, usually foreign companies, with too little responsibility as they were not required to work the patent locally.[25] In addition, these foreign companies included all the known, possible and even old processes in patent application, and because these colonial patent laws did not categorically list what was patentable, the indigenous companies were forbidden by the patent office to use it.[26] This led to high prices for basic drugs in India and also stunted the growth of local drug manufacturing.[27] Thus, it was beneficial and important for the

[19]Vanni (2020), pp. 109–113.

[20]Dhavan et al. (1990), p. 432.

[21]Ibid.

[22]Ibid, p. 431.

[23]Ibid.

[24]Ibid., p. 437.

[25]Vanni (2020), pp. 113–115.

[26]Chaudhuri (2006).

[27]The Ayyangar Report, which facilitated the IPA cited the US Senate Committee Kefauver Committee Report headed by Senator Estes Kefauver, which mentioned that India had one of the

indigenous pharmaceutical actors at that time to participate and cohere around the issue of patent law amendment to ensure a favourable protection and outcome.

The second Committee headed by Shri Justice N. Rajagopal Ayyangar (1959) suggested a radical change of the Indian patent law and for an introduction of new patent system cognizant of the country's economic needs, developmental aspirations and level of technological advancement. According to the Ayyangar Committee, patents taken in foreign countries are not taken in the interests of the economy granting the patents or with a view to manufacture there but with the main objective of protecting an export market from rival manufacturers, particularly those in other parts of the world.[28] Consequently, the Ayyangar Report and attendant proposal argued for a patent system that protects inventions but also strongly safeguarded public interest and national development.

As with the Tek Chand Report, the pharmaceutical industry lobby was also active and busy in pushing for supportive patent law. In preparing the Report, the Ayyanggar Committee attended private meetings with pharmaceutical industry groups such as the Pharmaceutical Development Council, with the Director of the National Physical Laboratory and the Hindustani Antibiotics. The insight gleaned from these meetings, Dhaven et al. note, gave the report produced Ayyangar Committee a sharper edge—an acute understanding of the economic issues at stake, with more reasoned arguments and a greater assimilation of the economics underlying patent law.[29] However, despite its robustness in calling for sweeping reform of the Indian patent law, the counter pressure mounted by foreign chemical and pharmaceutical companies led to a retreat in the original proposal when it was eventually put before the Parliament.[30] According to Dhavan et al, the Bill which was eventually tabled before Indian legislators in following years and resulted in the 1970 Act was much milder due to the powerful lobby mounted by the foreign pharmaceutical companies operating in the country at that time[31] Important deviation from the Ayyanger Report compared to the Bill presented to legislators include change on terms for which a patent is granted, and increase on royalty to be paid to patent owners. In fact, an archival study conducted by Dhaven et al. showed that foreign pharmaceutical companies operating in India at that time mounted a powerful lobby on the Joint Committees of 1965 and 1967 respectively, which not only had a decisive influence on the patent discourse among Indian legislators but also influenced the content of patent legislation that was eventually passed into law.[32]

---

highest prices for drugs at that time. See Justice N. Rajagopala Ayyangar, *Report on the Revision of the Patents Law*, Sept. 1959 (hereinafter referred as the Ayyangar Report).

[28]Ayyangar Report, p. 13.

[29]Dhavan et al. (1990), pp. 444, 450.

[30]Dhavan et al. (1990), p. 453.

[31]Ibid, pp. 455–457.

[32]Ibid., p. 453. Dhaven et al. note several lakhs were spent over the last few months leading to the presentation of the Bill to the parliament on high powered, concentrated campaigned against any form of amendment to the colonial patent law existing at that time. The impact, they note, is a shift from the question of whether India even needs a patent system at that time to how to amend existing

In 1970, the Indian government implemented the Indian Patents Act of 1970 (hereafter "IPA") and came into force in 1972. The IPA allowed for seven-year patents on pharmaceutical *products* but not on *processes*.[33] The process patent regime excluded protection of the end-product, but protected the method or the process of making the product. This clause allowed Indian manufacturers to reverse-engineer generic versions of medicines patented in other countries. The rationale for this section is to encourage and ensure access to foreign technologies (e.g. pharmaceuticals) and cheaper drugs in India that might otherwise be unavailable to its people due to cost and pricing structures.[34] In particular, Indian policymakers believed it was a matter of national security that the country provide medicines and treatment at prices its people could afford for diseases and illnesses prevalent within the subcontinent.[35] Domestic legalisation of reverse engineering allowed the country to develop a robust and efficient generic drugs industry. Commentators note that from a virtually non-existent domestic sector in 1970 (15% of Indian firms as against 85% foreign firms in the local market), the market structure transformed into one where both Indian and foreign firms held a 50% share in 1982, to 61% Indian and 39% foreign shares in 1999.[36] By 2000, eight of the 10 top firms in the Indian domestic sector were Indian firms, and only two were subsidiaries of multinational companies.[37] In the 2003 fiscal year, Indian firms held a local market share of 75%, and the annual value of retail formulations in the domestic market had reached an estimated USD4.3 billion.[38] In recent times, India is the largest provider of generic drugs globally supplying over 50% of global demand for various vaccines, 40% of generic demand in the US and 25% of all medicine in UK.[39] In 2017, the sector was valued at US$ 33 billion while in the 2018 financial year, exports stood at US$ 17.27 billion.[40] The sector is also one of the most innovative pharmaceutical markets in the world. Thus, the Indian Patent Act served as an important instrument to establish and maintain generic manufacturing capacity, which in turn spurred indigenous pharmaceutical industry and ensured that drugs are available at an affordable cost.

---

patent regime to something tolerable to both Indian and foreign pharmaceutical actors. As result, India missed an opportunity to develop an alternative to the patent system.

[33] *See* Patents Act, 1970, 27 India A.I.R. Manual 450, § 84 (1979).

[34] Chaudhuri (2005), pp. 21–22. See also Ministry for Commerce and Industry, Justice Ayyangar Report on the Revision of Patent Law (1959), para 29. After the release of the Ayyangar Committee Report and the implementation of the Indian Patent Act, the number of patents granted per year within India fell by three quarters between the years 1970–71 and 1980–81. See also Padmashree (2005), p. 12.

[35] Palombi (2009), p. 402.

[36] Padmashree (2005), p. 13.

[37] Ibid.

[38] Ibid.

[39] India Brand Equity Foundation (2019).

[40] Ibid.

The Indian Government also implemented other policies to create an enabling environment for an indigenous pharmaceutical advantage. For instance, the Drugs and Cosmetics Act of 1940 was amended to give the central government concurrent powers with states over the manufacture of drugs.[41] A price-control regime was also introduced, which sets the prices of drugs sold within India and puts a ceiling on the overall profits of pharmaceutical companies—thus promoting affordable medicines for the masses. The government established the National Pharmaceutical Pricing Authority (NPPA) to "fix and revise the prices of controlled bulk drugs and formulations and to enforce prices and availability of the medicines in the country."[42] In 1978, the government also implemented a Drug Policy that imposed several restrictions on the operations of foreign companies while providing preferential treatment to Indian companies.[43] The government also invested in local manufacturing firms and education, especially in the areas of chemistry and pharmaceutical research and biotechnology, which spurred the development of sophisticated research institutions.[44] The aim of these investments has been to encourage innovation by developing an extensive scientific infrastructure, and skilled human capital that can be absorbed into the pharmaceutical sector. As a result, Indian firms are able to invest in manufacturing therapeutically innovative drugs discovered elsewhere and launching them on both domestic and foreign markets. An example of Indian drug innovation was the release in 2001 of the HIV drugs, *Triomune*—the world's first fixed-dose antiretroviral drug. Produced by Cipla, *Triomune* was sold at US$600 per year but reduced to US$1 per day for Medicines San Frontiers (MSF)—a price much less than the US$10,000 per year that it cost to acquire a combination of three drugs separately in the US and Europe.[45] The low price of *Triomune* by Cipla encouraged Merck—a US pharmaceutical company—to reduce the price of *Crixivan* (a protease inhibitor) to roughly the same price, which in turn caused Bristol Myers Squibb and Glaxo SmithKline to follow suit.

In 1994, India became a signatory to General Agreement on Tariffs and Trade (GATT), and consequently, India had to implement the TRIPS Agreement. However, because of its developing country status, India had until 2005 to fully phase-into TRIPS. This means country must provide patent protection for all products and processes for a period of 20 years. Of course, the implementation of TRIPS has severe consequences for the generic industry as they will no longer be able to reverse-engineer drug patented elsewhere. Therefore, it is not surprising the sector campaigned heavily during the Uruguay Round of negotiations that led to the creation of the World Trade Organisation as well as the interim years before the country transitions fully to TRIPS to ensure its interests are well safeguarded.

---

[41] *See* Drugs and Cosmetics Act, 1940 (amended, 1995) (India), available at http://cdsco.nic.in.

[42] WHO India (2006); Ragavan (2012), p. 52.

[43] Sengupta (2010).

[44] Padmashree (2005), p. 20.

[45] McNeil Jr (2001).

During the Uruguay Round discussions, the indigenous Indian drug manufacturing companies played a foundational role in generating knowledge and scientific expertise relevant to the Indian Government's patent policy stances in the run-up to TRIPS and beyond. The sector was influential in fuelling India's opposition to the inclusion IP with global trade regime. This involved producing policy documents and organising talks on the negative impact a global IP regime would have on the booming generic drugs sector. The Indian Drug Manufacturers' Association (IDMA), the largest and best-known association representing the generic drug manufacturers, was one of the most outspoken industry bodies on this issue. The IDMA heavily lobbied the government and prepared draft letters to various Members of Parliament urging them to oppose an IP dimension to GATT in order to protect the health rights of its citizens and the pharmaceutical sector.[46] It pushed for public resistance to the 1991 Dunkel Draft treaty at GATT by working with social movements and civil society groups to generate opposition at both grassroot level and within policy circles involved in the Uruguay Rounds of negotiation.

The generic pharmaceutical companies also worked with local civil society groups such as the National Working Group on Patent Laws (NWGPL) in generating a common discourse about the impact of a global patent regime on Indian drug industry. For instance, Ranbaxy financed the work of NWGL to develop research and build public opinion, and even provided office space.[47] The financial assistance from Ranbaxy allowed NWGPL to specifically play an active role in providing studies to fuel debate in Parliament and in the media.[48] The group was influential in expertise production and resistance, organising national and international seminars, conferences and facilitating research on the constitutional dimensions of signing onto TRIPS. These public discourses, organised at various sites and different levels, sensitised policymakers, government officials, the media and the wider citizenry on the potential implications of higher IP standards on availability and affordability of medicines. The influence of Indian generic drug companies in funding the activities of the civil society groups such as NWGPL underscores the ability of big corporations to mobilise leading sources of expertise to elaborate, interpret, and defend their agendas and influence law-making.[49] As a result, NWGPL was able to perform the "boundary work"[50] of educating the public and political authorities on the complex

---

[46]Vanni (2020), p. 127.

[47]Ibid.

[48]Fieldwork interview with Amit Sengupta (Delhi, August 2016) (transcript on file with author).

[49]Ranbanxy was not the only Indian generic working in collaboration with the Indian government and civil society. Other companies such as Cipla and Dr. Reddy's funded research activities on the potential impact of the proposed IP regime on the country's pharmaceutical sector and public health. See Vanni (2020), pp. 127–130.

[50]Gieryn (1983), pp. 782–783. Thomas F. Gieryn explains "boundary work" as a work in public science in which scientists describe science for the public in order to enlarge the material or symbolic resources of scientists or defend political autonomy. It is used this article to explain the ways civil society groups blurs the demarcations, or other divisions between fields "science" and

issue of IP and the impact of the global IP regime on the generic drug sector as well as the autonomy of the government to make development policies.

2.1 Indian Generics and Patent Standard Setting

The pharmaceutical sector continued to play a vocal role in the lead-up to the 2005 amendments to the IPA. As part of its obligation as member of the World Trade Organisation (WTO), India must amend its patent law to bring it into full compliance with the TRIPS Agreement. These amendments include granting a twenty years patent protection in all fields of technology, including pharmaceuticals[51] and were obviously a concern for the generic drug sector, particularly the ability of the sector to reverse-engineer patented medicines. The drug manufacturers sought to ensure protection of their interests via the inclusion of protective clauses in the IPA. Notably, the IDMA provided the language of the important section 3(d) on patentability criteria, which limited patents for pharmaceutical substances to "new chemical entities" or to "new medical entities involving one or more inventive steps."[52] This particular clause protects not only public health interests in ensuring that only genuine patent applications are approved, but also the generic sector by preventing patent "evergreening". The term evergreening refers to the practice by patent owners to extend the patent term beyond the statutory prescription.[53] The IDMA and other civil society groups were also able to push for the inclusion of post- grant opposition to allow innovation in a manner conducive to and balanced with its local realities. Commentators, for instance, note that the inclusion of both pre- and post-grant allows for public scrutiny and for third party contest of a patent application as well as to prevent patents on minor innovations and ensure the genuineness of an application.[54] By successfully including the post grant opposition clauses whilst also pushing for a limiting and clearer language of only new chemical entities to patent application, the IDMA was able to achieve a tempered patent regime for India, thereby eliminating the space for frivolous patenting.

Of course, patent law-making and IP governance in India did not occur in a simple, linear fashion. The politics of patent law-making in particular also saw the involvement of other factions interested in IP and keen to maintain dominance of its network in IP governance. The Organisation of Pharmaceutical Producers in India

"politics", by showing how seemingly disconnected "science" is closely entwined with politics and policies, in order to demand specific policy or legal interventions.

[51]WTO TRIPS Agreement, article 27.

[52]Fieldwork interview with Amit Sengupta (Delhi, August 2016) (transcript on file with author). See also Patents (Amendment) Act, 2005, No. 15, Acts of Parliament, 2005 (India), § 3(d). http://www.wipo.int/wipolex/en/text.jsp?file_id=128116 [hereinafter "Patents (Third) Amendment Act"].

[53]Ragavan (2012), p. 155. See also Ragavan (2006) and Rangnekar (2006).

[54]Ragavan (2012), p. 117; Khader (2009), p. 52.

(OPPI), which is primarily an association of foreign pharmaceutical transnational corporations (TNCs) operating in India, is another private sector actor bent on diluting the influence of the IDMA and amplifying the importance of stronger, higher IP regime for research, investment and innovation. The OPPI wanted a domestic IP regime that made it difficult for domestic generic drug manufacturers to engage in reverse engineering. As such the group lobbied for the adoption of TRIPS on the grounds that it "would encourage genuine scientific and technological research, reverse years of brain drain in the science and technology sector and spur foreign direct investment."[55] The groups also opposed the pre-grant patent opposition clause in the Act, which was part of the final amendment in 2005, as they believed it unduly elongated the patent application process. In so doing, they opposed several of the policy provisions pushed by both the NWGL and the IDMA, couching their argument on the potential economic and innovation benefits for India in having high patent protection thresholds. The interaction between the IDMA and the OPPI indicates how a reform preferred by one sectorial player might be seen as damaging by another as well as the predictable bipolarity among actors with diverged interests.

A third group, the Indian Pharmaceutical Alliance (IPA) was established in 1999. The IPA consists of the biggest generic companies, namely Cipla, Dr. Reddy's, Ranbanxy, Lupin Laboratories, Alembic Limited, Primal India, Sun Pharmaceutical, and Wockhadt Limited. According to current figures, together these companies account for 50% of domestic sales and 80% of exports.[56] Unlike the IDMA, members of the IPA are keen on owning IP because these companies engage in substantial research on new chemical entities and generics, new drug delivery systems and biopharmaceutical research. It is therefore not surprising that the IPA and OPPI took compatible positions on certain matters—including but not limited to the licensing of rights and compulsory licenses—in the lead-up to the 2005 amendments. Consequently, the IPA made a strong push for provisions strengthening compulsory licenses as well as the removal of automatic licensing of rights.[57] The implicit consensus between the IPA and the OPPI on patent reform reveals the changing self-interest of sections of Indian pharmaceutical industry. Key members of the IPA were the original campaigners for the reform of the colonial era patent law to a relaxed IP regime that transformed India's pharmaceutical industry. By swinging in favour of less relaxed patent regime, the IPA provides insight into how internal compulsions rather than altruism fuel sectoral engagement with the government and law-making processes. In fact, Rangnekar contends that this changing self-interest among the local pharmaceutical industrialists might have constrained the opportunities to launch a radical challenge to the proposed amendments of Indian Patent Act.[58] Thus, when the Indian Parliament passed the second amendments to the 1970

[55]Khusrokhan (1999).

[56]Indian Pharmaceutical Alliance, https://www.ipa-india.org/about-ipa/profile.aspx.

[57]Muran (2002).

[58]Rangnekar (2006).

India Patent Act, many of suggestions put forward by both the OPPI and IPA were included, such as the removal of all references to the automatic licences of rights,[59] and the explicit provision of four grounds for the issuance of compulsory license, which many commentators contend makes the IPA the broadest, most comprehensive of all the world's patent systems.[60]

Post 2005 amendment, indigenous Indian drug makers have also been active in employing various sections of the law to engage with patent law-making and governance. Two incidents stand out. First, the *Bayer Corporation* v. *Natco Pharma Ltd* case.[61] In 2011, Natco, an Indian generic drug maker applied for compulsory license to produce a generic version of Bayer's patented medicine *Nexavar* used in the treatment of cancer of the kidney under §84(1) of the Indian Patents Act, 1970. Natco applied for the compulsory license on three grounds—(a) that *Nexavar* has not been made available to the public at a reasonably affordable price, (b) the reasonable requirements of the public had not been met and (c) Bayer has failed to work the patent in India within the specified three years period.[62] Natco also argued it will not only produce the drugs at a fraction of the Bayer exorbitant price but will also donate the tablets to patients that cannot afford even the cheaper generic version. The Controller of Patents granted the license to Natco in 2012 but requested Natco pay Bayer six per cent royalty. The Natco case is so far the only successfully compulsory license application in India. The second incident denoting the pharmaceutical participation in patent law-making is the use of pre- and post- grants opposition by indigenous pharmaceutical companies in India. The use of patent opposition applications India has helped to not only prevent the grants frivolous patent but also reduce incidents of evergreening. For instance, in 2012 Cipla successfully filed post-grant opposition against Pfizer's *Sutent* used in liver and kidney cancer treatment.[63] Similarly, Natco also filed patent opposition against Gilead's *Solvadi* used in hepatitis C treatment though the patent was eventually granted in 2016.[64]

The above analysis show how fragmentation, and contestation as well as cooperation among non-state actors, exert significant complexity in how patent standards are created, governed and determined in domestic policymaking spaces. It shows that patent governance regimes do not emerge in a seamless fashion, as intra-sector resistances and contestations occur. And, most importantly for the purposes of this article, the examples outlined underscores the dynamic influence that Indian drug manufacturers have been able to exert on the Indian patent policy space, through coordinated action in various sites. In the next section, I focus on Nigeria drug manufacturers. In doing so, I find that unlike their Indian counterparts, the Nigerian pharmaceutical sector is absent in matters of IP standard-setting and governance. I

59 Rangnekar (2006).

60 Mueller (2007), p. 580.

61 Bayer Corporation v. Natco Pharma Ltd.

62 Ibid. See also Vanni (2020), pp. 140–142.

63 India revokes Pfizer's patent on Sutent (2012).

64 Silverman (2016).

explain the reason for this absence through a brief examination of series of policy disconnects and discontinuities that eviscerated the pharmaceutical sector thereby weakening its ability to participate in patent law-making.

3 The Nigerian Pharmaceutical Sector

As a former British colony, IP law was first introduced to the Lagos colony and Southern Protectorate in 1900 in the form of the Patent Ordinance[65] and Patent Proclamation.[66] Two years later, the Patent Proclamation of 1902 introduced patent law and protection to the Northern Protectorate.[67] Each of these enactments contained full-scale provisions for the recognition, grant and control of patents in Nigeria and were comparable to the English law on the subject at that time. After the amalgamation of the Southern and Northern protectorates in 1914, the Patent Ordinance (1916), which repealed previous patent ordinances and made the new ordinance applicable throughout the country was promulgated two years later in 1916. In 1925, the United Kingdom Patent Ordinance 1925 was introduced, which replaced the Patent Ordinance 1916. The Ordinance disallowed patents application in Nigeria and provided instead for the registration in Nigeria of patents already granted in the UK provided the application for registration was made within three years from the date of the issue of patent.[68] This created a dependent patent regime by conferring rights and privileges in Nigeria to the extent to which it was granted by the UK law. The Ordinance remained in use for forty years until it was repealed by the military government in 1965.

The repeal of the colonial patent law in Nigeria did not occur in a vacuum. It was precipitated by the first patent case in Nigeria, which tested the applicability of colonial patent laws in the country. In *Rhone- SA Poulenc and May & Baker v. Lodeka Pharmacy* [1965] 9 (LLR) the parties were importers of chemical products as well as other pharmaceutical preparations. The applicants took out a United Kingdom Patent No. 716207 in 1951, which they subsequently registered in Nigeria in 1957 under the 1925 UK Patent Ordinance as Patent No. 367. The Federal Ministry of Health in 1964 placed a supply order for the patented product. The defendant, Lodeka Pharmacey—an indigenous pharmaceutical company—supplied in large quantities the patented product to the Federal Ministry of Health. The defendant acknowledged the patent right of the claimants, but argued that it was

[65]The Southern Protectorate consisted mainly of Lagos and the South West region of Nigeria. The British annexed Lagos in the year 1861.

[66]Patent Ordinance No 17 of 1900.

[67]The Northern Protectorate consisted of the North Central, Northeast, and Northwest of modern Nigeria.

[68]No 6 of 1925; Ezejiofor (1973), p. 40.

no infringement to supply to the Federal Ministry of Health for the use by the public. The defendant relied on s.46 (1) of the United Kingdom Patents Act 1949.[69]

In deciding the case, the judge ruled that the patent regime did not permit Nigerian Government to exercise the prerogative of the British Crown under the 1925 Patent Ordinance and the UK Patents Acts of 1949, which were enforced in Nigeria at that time.[70] Consequently, His Lordship gave judgment in favor of the applicant and issued an injunction against the defendant. The *Poulenc* case prompted the Federal Military Government in 1968 to repeal the Patent Act of 1925 and introduce the Patent (Limitation) Decree 1968. Specifically, the new decree allowed the government to purchase patented pharmaceutical products, if the government is satisfied it is in the public interest to do so.[71] It also exempted the government from infringement of a patent granted or the liability to pay royalties or compensation to the patentee.

The Patent Limitation Decree was a reaction to the *Poulenc case* and was introduced at a time when Nigeria had no robust national technological base. The law was made not to support local industrial base or to address a particular policy need but was enacted instead in response and as a reaction to the *Poulenc* case. At the time the Patent Limitation decree was enacted, Nigeria had a growing pharmaceutical sector comprised mostly of foreign companies with assembling plants in the country.[72] However, indigenous manufacturers were almost none existent while existing foreign pharmaceutical companies did not engage in the research and development of new drugs.[73] This absence of an indigenous manufacturing class to create patent norms and provide IP-related expertise resulted in the adoption of a patent regime that did not prioritize national development especially in a country where poverty remains the main challenge. The absence of indigenous drug makers in shaping appropriate patent regime, as seen in India, meant that national objectives, particularly the development of a domestic pharmaceutical sector with the technological know-how were not taken into consideration in the establishment of the country's first postcolonial patent regime.

As Nigeria became increasingly industrialized, the Patent Ordinance was changed into the Patent and Design Act (PDA) 1970[74] with certain modifications to encourage inventions and enable inventors to reap rewards of their work. Under the Act, a patent may be granted either for a product or for a process, as long as the invention is new, involves an inventive step, is capable of industrial application and is not

[69]Section 46 states that "stated that: notwithstanding anything in this Act, any Government department, and any person authorized in writing by a Government department, may make, use and exercise any patented invention for the service of the Crown in accordance with the provisions of this section.

[70]Ezejiofor (1973), p. 40.

[71]Section 15 Patent (Limitation) Decree, No. 8 1968 (NGN).

[72]Peterson (2016), p. 238.

[73]Vanni (2020), p. 186.

[74]Laws of the Federation of Nigeria, Patents and Designs Act 1990. PDA hereafter.

specifically excluded in the Act (e.g. inventions which may be contrary to public order or morality).[75] This should be contrasted with India, which prohibited patents on pharmaceutical *products* but not on *processes,* which encouraged innovation in the methods of making known products. In the Nigerian case, by allowing patents in both products and process, the Patent Ordinance discouraged the ability to produce patented products, particularly pharmaceuticals, using different processes.[76] Furthermore, unlike the Indian Patent Act, which allowed for 5 years patent protection, the PDA allows for twenty years.[77] Research has shown that patent monopoly by pharmaceutical companies tend to limit indigenous innovation,[78] thus, from the get go, the policy environment was not conducive for the growth of local pharmaceutical industry. The Patent Act of 1970 was also updated in 1990 to bring it up to date with modern times and is still in force till date.

3.1 *The Oil Boom, and the Rise and Fall of Nigerian Drug Sector*

The oil boom of the 1970s, caused by price increases orchestrated by the Organisation of the Petroleum Exporting Countries (OPEC) in 1973–74 and 1979–80 triggered a substantial financial windfall for Nigeria and resulted in large transfers of wealth into state coffers.[79] The boom made the country suddenly wealthy, and completely restructured the economy from agrarian-based to oil-export-based, with a consequential general decline in national production in other sectors.[80] For example, in 1969 the oil sector accounted for less than 3% of GDP and a modest USD370 million in exports, but by 1980, the oil sector had come to account for nearly 30% of GDP and exports totalled USD25 billion.[81] The upsurge in oil-export earnings had a number of structural effects in the drug industry. For instance, it led to an increase in the number of brand-name pharmaceutical companies setting up manufacturing plants in the country, which greatly expanded the manufacturing sector.[82] Brand name foreign companies such as May and Baker, Pfizer, Roche, Bayer, Wellcome, Boots and Glaxo previously had only Nigerian distribution outlets. The oil boom helped them scale their presence to include basic manufacturing plants thanks to the increased number of middle-class aflush with new wealth. However, these

[75]Ezejiofor (1973), p. 45.

[76]According to Ebohon, Pfizer in 1982 held 45 patents in Nigeria and of these, only 12 were being exploited. Ebohon (1985), p. 166.

[77]Ezejiofor (1973), p. 49.

[78]Vaitsos (1972), pp. 71–97.

[79]Okonjo-Iweala (2008).

[80]NCEMA (2004).

[81]NCEMA (2004).

[82]Peterson (2014), p. 41.

manufacturing plants did not engage in any research or development of new chemical entity or transfer of pharmaceutical technology. According to commentators, this middle class was able to afford "luxury goods and [had] sensibilities oriented toward the high symbolic value associated with brand name drugs."[83] Meanwhile, with the growing presence of pharmaceutical companies, Nigeria metamorphosed into a regional hub for export of pharmaceuticals assembled in the country by TNCs into other parts of West Africa.[84] Commentators estimated industry earnings at around USD48 million in 1973, increasing to about USD200 million in 1980, with the industry employing nearly 10,000 Nigerians.[85]

Despite the growth in the pharmaceutical sector, drug makers still did not participate or influence change in patent regime and standards for two reasons. First, while many foreign affiliated pharmaceutical companies were able to set up local manufacturing bases in Nigeria due to the oil boom, these manufacturing bases were involved in minor quality-control activities and mixes, and not in advance reverse-engineering or the development of new pharmaceutical molecule.[86] Citing a 1978 draft report by the Nigerian Institute of Social and Economic Research, Ebohon mentions that most of the companies which "claim to be manufacturing drugs locally still import completed finished products to be packaged by and distributed through their factories."[87] As these companies did not engage in original research and development of drugs, there was no backward integration into local manufacture of basic drugs or even local technological transfer. Moreover, many of the local affiliate of foreign companies were concerned with repatriating profits to the parent company, usually located in Europe or North America.[88] Understandably, in this environment, these foreign subsidiaries were not interested in participating in any form of active engagement in patent discourse, law-making or governance.

Second, unlike India, which had its own home-grown drug industry that proved to be highly competitive, the very few indigenous Nigerian-owned pharmaceutical companies existing at that time were focused on establishing themselves amidst competition from their foreign counterparts.[89] Meanwhile, poor infrastructure, absence of a chemical industry and absence of well-educated citizens versed in pharmacology and pharmaceutical sciences[90] also hampered the ability of indigenous firms to invest and engage in extensive research and development of new drugs.

[83]Peterson (2014), p. 42.

[84]Ibid.

[85]Ibid.

[86]Ebohon (2012), p. 26. Vanni (2020), p. 186.

[87]Ebohon (2012), p. 26.

[88]Baker (2012), p. 59.

[89]Vanni (2017), p. 216.

[90]Though universities in Nigeria had pharmacy programs as early as 1957, the local universities offering pharmaceutical degree was limited. In fact, the first local tertiary institution to offer a course in pharmacy/pharmacology was the School of Pharmacy in Yaba, Lagos. The school was later moved to the Nigerian College of Arts, Science and Technology, Ibadan. By the 1970s and early 80s, there were only 6 universities in Nigeria offering degree programs in pharmacy and most

It can, therefore, be argued that lack of R&D means no innovation within the indigenous pharmaceutical space as well little to no prospect for local technological development. The absence of R&D, innovation and invention of new pharmaceutical entity means there will be no need for reward for such inventive activity—in this case, patent right—to determine the terms of use of such invented product with a view of not only incentivising further innovation/invention, but to also recoup the financial investment involved in the development of an innovative product. Thus, since there was no local technological development going on, there were no need for the few indigenous pharmaceutical firms to participate or influence government policies on patents.

Other policy and market factors compounded to debilitate the Nigeria drug sector, which further worsened the ability of the sector to participate in IP governance. These policies included the Import Substitution Industrialisation (ISI) strategy of the late 1970s, the IMF/World Bank-mandated Structural Adjustment Programme (SAP) implemented in 1986 and the end of the oil boom in the 1980s. These factors compounded to exacerbate the unfavourable fate of the Nigerian pharmaceutical sector as shall be discussed below.

3.2 *Bad Policy Reforms: Import Substitution Industrialization Policy and the Structural Adjustment Programs*

The ISI policy sought to eliminate importation of commodities in order to allow for domestic production and spur local industrialisation.[91] It proved to be a highly ineffective strategy for development as many industries, including the pharmaceutical sector were heavily dependent on importation, particularly imported raw materials, foreign technology, and skilled manpower.[92] Estimates show that 80–90% of raw materials required by foreign companies with manufacturing bases in Nigeria in the 1970s and early 1980s were imported.[93] Thus, the ban on importation—one of the features of the ISI strategy—constituted an impediment to the growth of the sector. The failure of ISI strategy was also due to lack of human capital. Public investments in technological innovation were absent and most of the Nigerian labour force, especially in sectors such as pharmaceuticals had little or no relevant background and knowledge of technology.[94] Meanwhile, balance of payments problems also affected imports and other resources required for industrial

of these degrees were patient focused e.g. drug dispensing and rational use of medication in health care. See Ogaji and Ojabo (2014), p. 48.

[91] Alexander (1967), p. 298; Mendes et al. (2014), p. 121.

[92] Egwaikhide (1997), p. 39; Chete et al. (2014), p. 1.

[93] Ebohon (2012), p. 27.

[94] Mendes et al. (2014), p. 135.

production, thereby imposing additional obstacles to industrial development.[95] Thus by neglecting these important domestic factor endowments, ISI policy instead crippled the sector as the country did not have the raw-materials, money, expertise and the techno-managerial capacity for the ISI policy to be sustainable.

The IMF/World Bank-imposed SAP further crippled the drug sector. The SAP was aimed at readjusting the aggregate domestic expenditure and production patterns so as to significantly reduce dependence on imports, improve non-oil export base and bring the economy on the path of steady and balanced growth.[96] Structural adjustment was introduced in Nigeria after external shocks caused by the sharp drop in oil prices in the 1980s left the country fiscally and economically exposed.[97] This led to a deterioration of public finances, foreign exchange shortage, and debt crisis.[98] Of all the fiscal and monetary policies introduced by the SAP, the devaluation of the Nigerian currency had the most negative impact on the pharmaceutical sector. Devaluation decreased earnings and increased the prices of food and other basic necessities, which in turn caused a sharp deterioration in the living standards of the majority of the people. Per capita income declined from USD949.4 in 1985 to USD280.7 in 1987, and fluctuated between USD240 and USD361 between 1988 and 2000.[99] Consequently, the population living below the poverty line rose from 34.7% (75 million people) in 1985 to 67.1% (102.3 million people) in 1996.[100] A general decline in per capita income meant that most members of the previously relatively affluent middle class could no longer afford luxury goods and brand name drugs.

Additionally, as Peterson points out, multinational drug companies who had previously occupied a major portion of the Nigerian market could no longer operate in the country because the Nigerian currency, the naira, was rapidly losing value, leading to a general decline in sales.[101] Further, devaluation also increased the cost of imports of the active pharmaceutical ingredients needed to make even the simplest of over-the-counter drugs. The situation worsened further when government scaled back on public health financing of medicines and essential health services provision. Due to significant financial and market losses, the few indigenous drugs firms were pushed into bankruptcy while the foreign, brand name companies divested from their Nigerian businesses, generating massive shortages of essential drugs. By 1994,

[95]Chete et al. (2014).

[96]NCEMA (2004), p. 14. See also Olukoshi (1993) and Lubeck and Watts (1994) on the structural adjustment as a response to the 1980s economic crisis.

[97]Bagura (1987), p. 100; Soludo and Mkandawire (2003).

[98]Bagura (1987), p. 100.

[99]NCEMA (2004), p. 20.

[100]NCEMA (2004), p. 35.

[101]Peterson (2014), p. 55.

10 years after the implementation of the SAP, most of the domestic production of pharmaceutical ceased altogether.[102]

In 1999, Nigeria transitioned into democratic government. The end of military rule brought about a new era of regular elections as well as the return of civil liberties. The coming of the democratic government as well as the implementation of healthy economic policies revived the Nigerian manufacturing sector, including pharmaceuticals. According to a 2014 Report by PricewaterhouseCoopers, there are 130 pharmaceutical companies in Nigeria[103] while McKinsey & Co estimates that the value of the Nigerian pharma market could rise by as much as 9% a year over the next ten years to reach $3.6 billion by 2026.[104] Despite the significant growth in the number of pharmaceutical companies in recent years, the sector still not only heavily reliant on importation of key ingredients, but still does not engage in the research and development of new drugs/chemical entity.

A report by the United Nations Industrial Development Organisation (UNIDO) notes that Nigerian drug manufacturers were importing all their active pharmaceutical ingredients and virtually all their inactive pharmaceutical ingredients, such as adhesives and syrups.[105] A recent empirical research conducted by the author in Nigeria in 2015 and 2016 also found that majority of all the ingredient necessary for pharmaceutical drug making are wholly imported.[106] In fact, all the pharmaceutical company executives interviewed confirm the most of ingredients used in their manufacturing of even basic over-the-counter medicines and formulations are still imported. Additionally, most of these firms are not engaged in original research in drug development.[107] An interview with the Nigerian pharmaceutical industry lobby group also noted this. According to a spokesperson of the Pharmaceutical Manufacturers Group of Manufacturers Association of Nigeria (PMG-MAN), because its members are not engaged in innovative R&D and as most of the drugs sold in Nigeria are imported generics, the group is not involved in patent law-making. Rather, they are mostly focused on drug procurement from the government as well as the enforcement of favourable business policies.[108] This, according to the

---

[102]Ibid. A recent study by Forster et al. notes that the SAPs reform instituted by the IMF caused massive health inequity in countries that implemented the program as it led it lower health system access and increase in neonatal mortality. See Foster (1998).

[103]According to a 2014 report by PricewaterhouseCoopers (PWC), there are pharmaceutical companies in Nigeria. See https://www.pwc.com/ng/en/assets/pdf/pakistan-and-nigeria-pharma-relations.pdf.

[104]Holt et al. (2017), p. 3.

[105]Wambebe and Ochekpe (2011), p. 35.

[106]Field work was conducted from November 2015 to February 2016, and July 2016. A total of 21 individuals were interviewed composing of C-suite pharmaceutical company executives including both Nigerian and foreign-affiliated pharmaceutical companies. See Vanni (2017) and Vanni (2020), pp. 180–193 for an analysis of these interviews.

[107]Vanni (2017), p. 221.

[108]Fieldwork interview with interviewee from PMG-MAN (Lagos, July 2016) (transcript on file with author).

spokesperson, is to ensure that the few pharmaceutical companies currently operating in Nigeria are being patronised by the government and also to ensure that the few generic medicines produced in the country are of the highest international quality.

Crucially, the presence of imported cheap generic drugs from India, China and other countries as well as the overwhelming presence of donated medicines from foreign organizations means Nigeria does not really encourage original research and return on investment.[109] Consequently, pharmaceutical drug companies who normally would have championed and participated in patent governance via the production of knowledge on the importance of patent regime for the development of the sector and as a way to attract foreign investment are absent. Since the patent regime is grounded on the development of innovative products, it means that the patent regime will also be absent in contexts where development of innovative drugs does not exist. Conversely, since the country lacks widespread patent infrastructure, industry actors are not interested in challenging and/or influencing the law-making or governance. This scenario should be contrasted with India where the presence of robust generic industry with the technological ability and favourable environment to research and produce innovative pharmaceutical products has led to a development of active pharmaceutical actors. As a result, both indigenous and foreign drug manufacturers—the latter well aware of the country's extensive scientific infrastructure, skilled human capital and the advanced expertise in chemistry-based reverse engineering—have interest in patent law. These factors and conditions explain why the Indian pharmaceutical drug makers are actively involved not only in patent law-making in their country but also in the enforcement of favorable patent standards, while in Nigeria their counterparts are not.

4 Conclusions

This paper traces the participation of pharmaceutical drug manufacturers in patent governance and law-making. It also highlights the complex interrelationship between state and private actors involved in IP knowledge governance. Taking a comparative approach, it contrasts the behaviour of Nigerian pharmaceutical actors with that of their Indian counterparts in the shaping and evolution of their respective patent systems. Unlike India, which has its own homegrown drug industry that has proved to be highly active in standard-setting and legal formative processes, Nigerian counterparts have not had the capacity to participate in any element of local IP standard setting. This is due to a combination of various factors including poor economic policies and policy disconnects that ignored the correlation between the introduction of patents and the different stages of development. Finally, the article has shown that the case of IP is the case multiplier effect of networks. Indian generic drug manufacturers played (and continues to play) key role in the formation and

[109] Ibid.

amendment of the country's patent regime. However, as this paper has shown, regulatory innovations happening in other emerging countries cannot happen in Nigeria if the key actors (in this case drug manufacturers) are not present to perform the analytical work, lobbying and expertise production required to push forward particular patent standards. Still, the sector cannot grow without responsible economic and fiscal policies in place, as well suitable infrastructure. It is hoped that analyses from this paper contribute to our understanding of the importance of local actors and strong institutions in the creation of national patent law, and its relationship with knowledge governance and economic development.

References

Abbott F, Correa C, Drahos P (2013) Emerging markets and the world patent order – the forces of change. Emerging markets and the world patent order, 1st edn. Edward Elgar

Alexander RJ (1967) The import-substitution strategy of economic development. J Econ Issues 1:297–308

Bagura Y (1987) IMF and World Bank conditionality and Nigeria's Structural Adjustment Programme. In: Havnevik KJ (ed) The International Monetary Fund and the World Bank in Africa: conditionality, impact and alternatives - seminar proceedings. Scandinavian Institute of African Studies, Uppsala

Braithwaite J, Drahos P (2000) Global business regulation. Cambridge University Press, Cambridge

Chaudhuri S (2005) The WTO and India's pharmaceuticals industry: patent protection, TRIPS, and developing countries. Oxford University Press, India

Chaudhuri S (2006) The WTO and India's pharmaceuticals industry: patent protection, TRIPS, and developing countries. Oxford University Press, Oxford

Chavez G, Reis R (2011) Health, intellectual property and innovation: a case study of Brazil. South Centre, Geneva

Chete LN, Adeoti JO, Adeyinka FM, Ogundele O (2014) Industrial development and growth in Nigeria: lessons and challenges. Available at http://www.brookings.edu/~/media/Research/Files/Papers/2014/11/learning-to-compete/L2C_WP8_Chete-et-al.pdf?la=en

Dhavan R, Harris L, Jain G (1990) Whose interest? Independent India's patent law and policy. J Indian Law Inst 32:429–477

Drahos P (1995) Global rights in information: the story of TRIPS at the GATT. Prometheus 13:6–19

Drahos P (2010) "IP World"—made by TNC Inc. In: Krikorian G, Kapczynski A (eds) Access to knowledge in the age of intellectual property. Zone Books, New York

Drahos P, Braithwaite J (2004) Who owns the knowledge economy? Political Organising Behind TRIPS. Available at http://www.thecornerhouse.org.uk/resource/who-owns-knowledge-economy

Drahos P, Mayne R (2002) Global intellectual property rights. Palgrave Macmillan, Houndmills, Basingstoke, Hampshir

Dreyfuss R (2009) The role of India, China, Brazil and other emerging economies in establishing access norms for intellectual property and intellectual property lawmaking. SSRN Electron J

Ebohon S (1985) Nigerian policy towards foreign companies: case study of the multinational pharmaceutical formulation plants, 1972–1983. PhD, University of Manchester

Ebohon S (2012) Globalization, technology transfer and the knowledge gap: case study of the global pharmaceutical industry in Nigeria. Global J Soc Sci 11:21–31

Egwaikhide F (1997) Import substitution industrialisation in Nigeria: a selective review. Niger J Econ Soc Stud 39:183–203

Ezejiofor G (1973) The law of patents in Nigeria: a review. Afr Leg Stud 39

Foster G (1998) Opposing forces in a revolution in international patent protection: the U.S. and India in the Uruguay round and its aftermath: comment. UCLA J Int Law Foreign Aff 3

Holt T, Millroy L, Mmopi M (2017) Winning in Nigeria: Pharma's next frontier. McKinsey & Company

India Brand Equity Foundation (2019) Indian Pharmaceutical Industry. Available at https://www.ibef.org/industry/pharmaceutical-india.aspx

Kapczynski A, Krikorian G (2010) Access to knowledge in the age of intellectual property. Zone Books

Kapstein EB, Busby J (2013) AIDS drugs for all. Cambridge University Press, Cambridge

Khader FA (2009) The touchstone effect: the impact of pre-grant opposition on patents. LexisNexis Butterworths, Wadhwa Nagpur

Khusrokhan H (1999) Letter to the Ministry of Science and Technology. Available at https://drive.google.com/file/d/0Bxi2TzVXul5ZcTNRNVdoVGV0XzA/view?pli=1

McNeil D Jr (2001) Indian company offers to supply AIDS drugs at low cost in Africa. Available at https://www.nytimes.com/2001/02/07/world/indian-company-offers-to-supply-aids-drugs-at-low-cost-in-africa.html?module=inline

Mendes APF, Bertella MA, Teixeira RFAP (2014) Industrialization in Sub-Saharan Africa and import substitution policy. Revista de Economia Política 34:120–138

Mueller J (2007) The Tiger awakens: the tumultuous transformation of India's patent system and the rise of Indian pharmaceutical innovation. Univ Pittsbg Law Rev 68

National Centre for Economic Management and Administration (NCEMA), 'Understanding Structural Adjustment Programme in Nigeria' (Global Development Network (GDN) 2004). Available at http://www.gdn.int/html/GDN_funded_papers.php?mode=download&file=Nigeria-first-draft_176.pdf

Narayanan P (2013) Patent law, 4th edn. Eastern Law House

Ogaji J, Ojabo C (2014) Pharmacy education in Nigeria: the journey so far. Arch Pharm Pract 5

Okediji R (2014) Legal innovation in international intellectual property relations: revisiting twenty-one years of the TRIPS agreement. Univ Pa J Int Law 36

Okonjo-Iweala N (2008, December 1) Finance and Development. Available at http://www.imf.org/external/Pubs/FT/fandd/2008/12/okonjo.htm

Padmashree GS (2005) Economic aspects of access to medicine after 2005: product patent protection & emerging firm strategies in the Indian Pharmaceutical Industry. CIPIH/World Health Organization, Geneva

Palombi L (2009) The role of patent law in regulating and restricting access to medicines. Scripted 6:394–410

Patents (amendment) act, 2005, no. 15 of 2005§ (2005)

Peterson K (2014) On the monopoly: speculation, pharmaceutical markets, and intellectual property law in Nigeria. Am Ethnol 41:128–142

Peterson K (2016) Volatility, speculation, and therapeutic revolutions in Nigerian drug markets. In: Therapeutic revolutions: pharmaceuticals and social change in the twentieth century. University of Chicago Press, Chicago

PM Live (2012) India revokes Pfizer's patent on Sutent. Available at http://www.pmlive.com/pharma_news/india_revokes_pfizers_patent_on_sutent_434858

Ragavan S (2006) Of the inequals of Uruguay rounds. Marquette Intellect Prop Law Rev 10:273–304

Ragavan S (2012) Patent and trade disparities in developing countries. Oxford, Oxford University Press

Rajagopal B (2003) International law from below: development, social movements and third world resistance

Rangnekar D (2006) No pills for poor people'? Understanding the disembowelment of India's patent regime. Econ Polit Wkly 41:409–417

Rangnekar D (2013) The Supreme Court Judgment: lawmaking in the South. Econ Polit Wkly 48:39–40

Sell SK (2003) Private power, public law. Cambridge University Press, Cambridge

Sengupta A (2010) Take over of Indian companies. Econ Polit Wkly 45:4

Silverman E (2016) Gilead Gets A Big Win as India Upholds A Sovaldi Patent, After All. Available at https://www.statnews.com/pharmalot/2016/05/10/gilead-hepatitis-patents-drug-pricing/

Soludo C, Mkandawire P (2003) African voices on structural adjustment: a companion to our continent, our future. International Development Research Centre

Ukpanah S (1990) (Minister of Trade and Tourism). Statement at the Ministerial Level Meeting in Brussels. MTN.TNC/MIN (90)/ST/34, Multilateral Trade Negotiations, Uruguay Rounds

Vanni A (2017) Narratives and counter-narratives in pharmaceutical patent law making: experiences from 3 developing countries. PhD Thesis, University of Warwick

Vanni A (2020) Patent games in the global south: pharmaceutical patent law-making in Brazil, India and Nigeria. Hart/Bloomsbury, Oxford

Wambebe C, Ochekpe N (2011) Pharmaceutical Sector Profile: Nigeria. Global UNIDO Project: strengthening the local production of essential generic drugs in least developed and developing countries. Available at https://www.unido.org/fileadmin/user_media/Services/PSD/BEP/Nigeria_Pharma%20Sector%20Profile_032011_Ebook.pdf

Weissman R (1996) A long, strange TRIPS: the pharmaceutical industry drive to harmonize global intellectual property rules, and the remaining WTO legal alternatives available to third world countries. Univ Pa J Int Econ Law 17:1096–1125

Further Reading

Adikibi OT (1988) The multinational corporation and monopoly of patents in Nigeria. World Dev 16:511–526

Agada J et al (2009) Globalization of intellectual property rights: implications of the TRIPs Agreement for access to HIV/AIDS drugs in Africa. Proc Am Soc Inf Sci Technol 46:1–11

Apter A (2005) The Pan-African Nation: oil and the spectacle of culture in Nigeria. University of Chicago Press, Chicago

Bayer Corporation v. Natco Pharma Ltd., Order No. 45/2013. Available at Intellectual Property Appellate Board, Chennai, available at http://www.ipab.tn.nic.in/045-2013.htm

Chakravarthi R (1990) Recolonization: GATT, the Uruguay round and the Third world. Zed Books, London

Chaturvedi K (2005) Policy and technology co-evolution in the Indian Pharmaceutical Industry. Open University DPP Working Paper No 50: Open University

Chibber V (2003) Locked in place: state-building and late industrialization in India. Princeton University Press, New Jersey

Chimni BS (1992) Political economy of the Uruguay round of negotiations: a perspective. Int Stud 29:135–158

Clarke M (2012) New guidelines for patentability examination of patent applications directed to chemical and pharmaceutical inventions. Available at http://www.ipindia.nic.in/writereaddata/Portal/IPOGuidelinesManuals/1_37_1_3-guidelines-for-examination-of-patent-applications-pharmaceutical.pdf

Drahos P (2001) Trade-offs and trade linkages: TRIPs in a negotiating context. Available at from https://www.anu.edu.au/fellows/pdrahos/reports/pdfs/2001tradeoffstradelinkages.pdf

Drahos P (2002) Developing countries and international intellectual property standard-setting. J World Intellect Prop 5:765–789

Drahos P, Braithwaite J (2002) Information feudalism: who owns the knowledge economy? Earthscan, London

Economic Times, Generic Drug Industry to Touch $27.9 bn by 2020: Study. Available at http://articles.economictimes.indiatimes.com/2015-09-09/news/66363370_1_pharma-market-sun-pharma-indian-pharma-firms

Fasan O (2012) Commitment and compliance in international law: a study of the implementation of the WTO TRIPS Agreement in Nigeria and South Africa. Afr J Int Comp Law 20:191–228

Harris G (2014) Medicines made in India set off safety worries. Available at http://www.nytimes.com/2014/02/15/world/asia/medicines-made-in-india-set-off-safety-worries.html

Iwuagwu O (2009) Nigeria and the challenge of industrial development. Afr Econ Hist 37:151–180

Médecins Sans Frontières Access Campaign (2004) Pharmacy of the developing world. Available at https://msfaccess.org/spotlight-pharmacy-developing-world

Mendes A, Bertella M, Teixeira R (2004) Understanding structural adjustment program in Nigeria. Available at http://www.gdn.int/html/GDN_funded_papers.php?mode=download&file=Nigeria-first-draft_176.pdf

Mkandawire T, Soludo CC (eds) (2003) African voices on structural adjustment: a companion to our continent, our future. International Development Research Centre, Ottawa

Ogbuagu C (1983) The Nigerian indigenization policy: nationalism or pragmatism. Afr Aff 82:241–266

Sell SK (1995) Intellectual property protection and antitrust in the developing world: crisis, coercion, and choice. Int Organ 49:315–349

Selvaraj S, Abrol D, Gopakumar KM (eds) (2015) Access to medicines in India. Academic Foundation, Delhi

Amaka Vanni Independent Legal Scholar and Consultant.

Part IV
International Criminal Law

The International Criminal Court: What Has It Accomplished?

Chile Eboe-Osuji

Content

The story of the International Criminal Court so far exemplifies the facility of the rule of law and multilateral cooperation to make the world a little better for humanity.

In the summer of 1998, following three years of preparatory negotiations—and decades of feasibility studies—members of the diplomatic community and of civil society and jurists from around the globe gathered in Rome, to deliver a vision that was both tall and large—to be seen and felt around the world.

It was a moral and jural vision of a world in which atrocities that shock the conscience of humanity would no longer be committed against victims, with the usual assurance of impunity that resulted from inaction—either due to wilful indifference or even impotent outrage. It was no longer seen as good enough for the world to condemn, denounce and protest the latest genocide (or other crimes against humanity)—pounding table with every possible vigour; but then move on—thinking or saying that nothing could really be done.

That new moral and jural vision was to establish an international criminal court—as a permanent institution capable of looming large—as a veritable edifice of the rule of law at the international level. It is meant to loom large in the consciousness of those inclined to commit such crimes. It is meant to be a place of accountability, where they will one day be compelled to answer questions about their conducts, regardless of station. And, yes, it is meant to be a place of justice, where the defendant would be acquitted of the charges against him, if those charges are not proved beyond reasonable doubt, following proper judicial inquiry.

C. Eboe-Osuji (✉)
International Criminal Court, The Hague, The Netherlands
e-mail: Chile.Eboe-Osuji@icc-cpi.int

C. Eboe-Osuji et al. (eds.), *Nigerian Yearbook of International Law 2018/2019*,
Nigerian Yearbook of International Law 2018/2019,
https://doi.org/10.1007/978-3-030-69594-1_8

On 17 July 1998, that vision became reality, with the adoption of the Statute of the International Criminal Court, named the 'Rome Statute'—after the city where its text was agreed upon by 120 States.[1]

Agreement on the text of the treaty was reached at the very last minute, during the last hours of the last day of the five-week diplomatic conference. After all was said and done, it came down to the determination of the majority of States to overcome their differences, in the interest of the greater good. Some events remain in history as defining moments, and this was definitely one of them.

A product of joint action amongst nations, the ICC was meant to be a court of last resort—whose jurisdiction arises only when the State concerned proves unable or unwilling to do justice within the national jurisdiction.[2] In a manner of speaking, it is a rescue mission for justice—ensuring that justice does not become a neglected orphan in the territory of national sovereignty.

The ICC's mandate is to try those who commit some of those 'unimaginable atrocities that deeply shock the conscience of humanity'.[3] For present purposes, let us call these crimes by their names. They are genocide, crimes against humanity, war crimes and the crime of aggression.[4]

These are crimes that had blighted humanity frequently and for long periods of time up until the negotiation and adoption of the Rome Statute.

We can be even more specific in recalling the history of evil in the period leading up to adoption of the Rome Statute in 1998.

And it may be recalled that no less than 7000 Bosnian Muslim men and boys were massacred in Srebrenica in 1995.[5] The International Criminal Tribunal for the former Yugoslavia has pronounced their killing as amounting to genocide.[6]

The year before—in 1994—about 800,000 Tutsis were killed in the Rwandan Genocide.[7]

About 50 years before that, six million innocent human beings were killed in a genocide in Europe, because they were Jews. History books teach us that the world has seen other genocides throughout the ages.

Let us also recall that beginning in 1991, Sierra Leone was engulfed by a brutal civil war. In addition to the killings, the rapes, the sexual slavery, and the conscription of children into military use, that civil war was also marked by a particular brand

[1] A/CONF.183/9.

[2] Rome Statute, article 17.

[3] Rome Statute, second preambular paragraph.

[4] Rome Statute, article 5.

[5] Appeals Chamber Judgement in the case of the *Prosecutor v. Radislav Krstić*, 19 April 2004, paragraph 2.

[6] *Ibid*, paragraph 39.

[7] Scharf (1994).

of cruelty and terror.[8] It involved the heartless amputations of the arms of human beings by their fellow human beings: leaving the victims with disabling physical and mental scars that last a life-time. It was a crime against humanity that left its very visible hallmark on that country and on our collective conscience as human beings—even today.

And, we must recall that it was only in the early 1990s, shortly before the adoption of the Rome Statute that apartheid came to an end in South Africa. Apartheid is a crime against humanity, over which the ICC now has jurisdiction.

Just weeks before the adoption of the Rome Statute in 1998, President Nelson Mandela—a storied victim of the crime of apartheid and a true hero of that experience—reminded the world that there had been enough horrors that human beings had visited unto their fellows. He observed that many of those horrors might have been avoided, or at least minimised, if there had been an effective, functioning International Criminal Court.[9]

We now have in place that ICC that Madiba had wished for—a permanent mechanism to ensure eventual accountability for those who subject others to such cruelty in future.

The Rome Statute entered into force once 60 States had ratified it.[10] That milestone was reached in less than four years—Senegal being the first, and Ghana being the sixth; leading the way for the others.

It is essential that we encourage more States to ratify the Rome Statute, in order to make the dividends of the ICC truly universal. In a speech he delivered at the ICC in July 2018, President Buhari of Nigeria called on all States to make it a matter of national priority to ratify the Rome Statute, if they had not already done so.[11] It is a most welcome call. We must join him in that appeal.

As a treaty-based institution, the ICC will only have true universal jurisdiction when all nations of the world have ratified the Rome Statute. To understand what is meant by 'true universal jurisdiction' we only need to consider that the ICC's strongest footing of competence is engaged when crimes are committed in the territory of one of the 123 States Parties, or are committed by a national of a State Party to the Rome Statute.[12] It is in those circumstances that a State Party or the Prosecutor can motivate the Court's exercise of jurisdiction.

In theory, the Court's jurisdiction can also extend to States who are not parties to the Rome Statute—if the UN Security Council refers the concerned situation to the

[8]See Trial Chamber Sentencing Judgement in the case of the *Prosecutor v. Alex Tamba Brima et al*, 19 July 2007; Appeals Chamber Judgement in the case of the *Prosecutor v. Prosecutor v. Alex Tamba Brima et al,* 22 February 2008.

[9]Opening address by President Nelson Mandela at the 2nd Conference of African National Institutions for the Promotion and Protection of Human Rights, 1 July 1998.

[10]Rome Statute, article 126.

[11]Remarks by his Excellency Muhammadu Buhari President of the Federal Republic of Nigeria at the Occasion of the 20th Anniversary Celebration of the International Criminal Court, 17 July 2018.

[12]Rome Statute, article 12(2).

ICC.[13] But, given the politics that often tend to bog down its processes, it is an open question whether the Security Council can always be depended upon to make such referrals whenever the spirit of humanity cries out for justice.

In practice this means that some of the tragic conflicts that vex the world's attention, conscience, and morality are simply beyond the ICC's reach, when crimes of atrocity are committed within the territories of those States that have not ratified the Rome Statute. That is to say, the victims of such atrocities are left to languish outside the zone of justice. They are thus doubly victimised: by the atrocities that they have endured and by the impunity that the perpetrators apparently enjoy.

Everyone should have access to justice—as the UN's Sustainable Development Goal 16 urges us to ensure.

However, during 16 years of operations, the ICC has done much more than many imagined it could do.

The Office of the Prosecutor of the ICC—currently headed by Ms Fatou Bensouda of The Gambia—has conducted investigations into conflicts in numerous countries. Court cases have been initiated against 45 persons—some of them heads of state. Nine accused have been convicted, and four have been acquitted (some of these convictions and acquittals are still pending on appeal). Crimes charged have included murder of civilians, rape and sexual slavery, conscription of children into military use, forced displacement and deportation, destruction of religious monuments, and election related violence.

More than ten thousand victims have been admitted to participate in the ICC's proceedings and to request reparation for the harm they have suffered. This new focus on reparative justice represents a major shift in paradigms; compared to the *ad hoc* tribunals, which were focused almost exclusively on punitive justice.

The ICC's Trust Fund for Victims[14] is implementing the Court's first judicial orders on reparation. What does this mean in actual terms? Well, we can look for instance at the case of *Al Mahdi*, who pleaded guilty to the war crime of destruction of religious monuments in Timbuktu. The judges ordered a range of reparation measures, tailored to the circumstances of the case. These included individual compensation to those whose livelihoods depended upon the protected heritage sites; symbolic measures to signal public recognition of the moral harm suffered; community measures aimed at restoring lost economic activity; as well as dissemination of Mr Al Mahdi's apology to victims in the main languages spoken in Timbuktu.[15]

In another case, that of *Katanga*, the judges ordered individual monetary compensation as a symbolic measure; but also collective reparation in the form of

[13] Rome Statute, articles 12 and 13(b).

[14] See Rome Statute, article 79.

[15] Public redacted Judgment on the appeal of the victims against the "Reparations Order", 8 March 2018, ICC-01/12-01/15-259-Red2.

psychological support, as well as support for housing, support for an income-generating activities, and support for education.[16]

The overarching idea is that the reparation measures are aimed at addressing in a specific way the harm that the victims have suffered, as a result of the crimes for which the Court finds the defendant guilty. If the defendant has means, these will be garnisheed for the reparation. But if he or she is indigent, the ICC's Trust Fund for Victims can use voluntary donations received from governments as well as private donors.[17]

Furthermore, beyond the four-corners of the cases in the courtroom, several hundred thousand victims in Uganda and the Democratic Republic of the Congo have benefited from the programmes of the ICC's Trust Fund for Victims under its assistance mandate. The 'assistance' mandate of the ICC's Trust Fund for Victims describes the aspect of the Trust Fund's work that seeks to bring some succour to obvious victims of crimes, unrestrained by considerations of proof of guilt (or not) of the perpetrator for the harm that the victims suffered.

These are some of the accomplishments of the Rome Statute system—that underscores the values of the ICC.

Still on the accomplishments of the Court in its short period of existence: the ICC has continued to fine-tune its procedures; in a way that takes into account practice and precedents from the principal legal systems of the world.

And what lends a particular accent to accomplishments in this regard is that this has been done by legal professionals (judges and lawyers), who come from dozens of countries, representing diverse legal systems, and who would often tend to interpret the same legal provision each in their own way. This is challenging, of course, but there is a sense of common purpose that has always helped to propel progress.

So, there has indeed been much to be proud of—though we permit ourselves no celebration at the Court.

We are not free to celebrate achievement, because the ICC has faced significant challenges. These come in the manner of: inadequate cooperation from some States; fugitives that remain at large (in circumstances in which there is very little we can do in that regard, because we have no police force to search for and arrest fugitives); insufficient resources for the scope of work that faces the Court; trenchant political attacks on the Court, precisely because it dares to want to do its work.

But, we (the functionaries of the Court) also have our share of the blame. Chief amongst them is that proceedings sometimes taking too long, causing much frustration amongst victims as well as the Court's supporters and observers. At other times, it appears that we have been our own worst enemies, the officials of the Court, by

---

[16]Order for Reparations pursuant to Article 75 of the Statute, 24 March 2017, ICC-01/04-01/07-3728-tENG.

[17]Assembly of States Parties, Resolution ICC-ASP/4/Res.3, Regulations of the Trust Fund for Victims, Chapters I and II.

taking public support for granted and for not always being careful as to how we comport ourselves.

Yes, indeed, there is much room for improvement. This is so, of course, for any human institution—even the best judicial systems.

It is for that reason that the Court has fully welcomed and embraced the idea of a review of the entire Rome Statute system. That is to say, a review of the Court itself as well as the supporting structure intended for it in the manner of the Assembly of States Parties[18]—in order to see how the entire system can be improved and strengthened to serve its mandate of humanity in a better way.[19]

But, pending that holistic review and its outcome, the Court continues hard at work to address what it can on its own. For instance, the judges collectively agreed to adopt guidelines on time frames for proceedings and judgments—specifically to address concerns about how long the proceedings take to conduct and how long judgments take to render.

We have also now embarked on a conscious project of continuously doing more to foster a more respectful work environment, which stresses civility and collegiality in the work place.

We must improve the Court's efficiencies. And we are doing so.

Still, we must not allow the impressions of these challenges to obscure the big difference that the Court has made in our world since its creation.

Here, it is stressed that even with all the challenges that it has faced, the ICC has fundamentally changed the way the world looks at accountability for atrocities.

On the occasion of the adoption of the Rome Statute, United Nations Secretary-General Kofi Annan said: 'Until now, when powerful men committed crimes against humanity, they knew that as long as they remained powerful no earthly court could judge them'.[20]

That observation captured the essential purpose of the ICC, and its enduring value to humanity.

With a permanent international criminal court in place, even the most powerful people can no longer be certain that they will get away with impunity, if they commit some of the most heinous acts against their fellow human beings. Even if prevailing circumstances seem to make impunity possible for the time being, perpetrators and their accomplices will—now—recognise that their impunity will always be illicit and will not endure.

And with that comes the ICC's correlative value of deterrence. This value cannot be overemphasised.

There are, indeed, many reasons to insist that the mere existence of this permanent judicial mechanism for accountability does truly serve as an inconvenient obstacle to the freewill of those inclined to commit crimes of atrocity.

---

[18] See Rome Statute, article 112.

[19] Assembly of States Parties, Resolution ICC-ASP/18/Res.7, Review of the International Criminal Court and the Rome Statute system.

[20] United Nations Press Release SG/SM/6643L/2891, 20 July 1998.

This is all too evident in the context of elections on the African continent, where politicians and their thugs had no qualms about winning political power through violence. Since the advent of the ICC and its first cases concerning election violence, there has been a noticeable reduction of that deplorable phenomenon that tends to blight the experience of democracy in Africa.

Leaders of States, government ministers and civil society leaders in several countries have reported that the ICC's existence was a very significant factor that prevented bloodshed in the context of elections in their countries. This is because everyone had seen that whoever would commit such violence might end up before the ICC to answer for their actions.

That deterrent value alone is enough of a return on the ICC investment. But the Court's critical value goes beyond that.

The ICC also has palpable value in the order of sustainable economic and human development. Nations desire economic and human development in a sustainable way.

In his address to the 74th session of the United Nations General Assembly, President Akufo-Addo called on the world to join him in recognising that 'poverty anywhere degrades us all'. So, too, it should be added, does injustice—as Martin Luther King Jr observed in his famous quote that also serves us in other respects: 'injustice anywhere is a threat to justice everywhere'.[21]

There cannot be sustainable development, where conflicts, atrocities and fear reign supreme. That is to say, socio-economic development will remain a pipe-dream:

- Where people are being killed, injured and traumatised for life by all the violence
- Where millions of people are unable to work, because of economic slowdown
- Where farmers cannot go to their farms because of active military operations, or landmines
- Where entrepreneurs cannot do business, because of raging wars that always result in the destruction of economic infrastructures
- Where children cannot go to school, because of war
- Where precious resources—already scarce in many cases—are wasted on weapons, rather than education, healthcare and economic sustainability
- Where investors are frightened away by conflict and instability
- Where the best brains of the nation are compelled to flee in droves in search of safer and more prosperous countries
- And, where neighbouring countries—and even those much further away—are required to struggle to cope with refugee flows from countries at war.

The International Monetary Fund and the World Bank have been pointing for a long time to the relationship between armed conflicts and economic development.

[21] Address by the President of the Republic of Ghana at the 74th Session of the United Nations General Assembly, 'Galvanizing Multilateral Efforts for Poverty Eradication, Quality Education, Climate Action and Inclusion', 25 September 2019.

According to an important study published in 2011 by the World Bank, 'the average cost of civil war is equivalent to more than 30 years of GDP growth for a medium-size developing economy [;] [and] [t]rade levels after major episodes of violence take 20 years to recover'.[22]

Moreover, these negative implications do not stop at national borders. The effects of conflict impede growth not only in the countries directly embroiled in war: they also impede regional development.

All of this is to say that preventing conflicts and atrocities, and addressing them forcefully through the rule of law, comprise an objective with far-reaching significance for the most critical aspects of human life, including economic development.

The Rome Statute contributes to this objective: by criminalising wars of aggression; by underscoring the risk of criminal prosecution when war crimes are committed as part of armed conflicts notwithstanding who started the conflict, and when crimes against humanity and genocide are committed (as they often are) under the cover of armed conflict.

These are some of the ways in which the existence of the ICC helps to improve our world—though the Court remains an imperfect human institution.

Reference

Scharf MP (1994) Introductory remarks to Statute of the International Criminal Tribunal for Rwanda, (Security Council resolution 955, 8 November 1994). United Nations Codification Division

Chile Eboe-Osuji President and Appellate Judge of the International Criminal Court, The Hague, The Netherlands.

[22]World Bank, World Development Report 2011, Overview, pages 5–6.

Improving the Efficiency of International Criminal Courts and Tribunals: The Paris Declaration on the Effectiveness of International Criminal Justice

Ivana Hrdličková, Adrian Plevin, and Amanda Fang

Contents

1 Introduction

Decades after the landmark introduction of the Nuremberg and Tokyo tribunals following the end of WWII, the call for international mechanisms as a means of ensuring individual responsibility for grave international crimes remains strong. Initially, however, progress was slow. The bipolarity of global politics in the Cold War era stagnated post-WWII developments. Following the dissolution of the Soviet Union, by contrast, the response of the international community in the United Nations (UN) Security Council was prompt and optimistic: first came an

I. Hrdličková · A. Plevin (✉)
Special Tribunal for Lebanon, Leidschendam, The Netherlands
e-mail: hrdlickova@un.org; plevin@un.org

A. Fang
Special Tribunal for Lebanon, Leidschendam, The Netherlands

New York University, New York, NY, USA
e-mail: amanda.fang@law.nyu.edu

C. Eboe-Osuji et al. (eds.), *Nigerian Yearbook of International Law 2018/2019*,
Nigerian Yearbook of International Law 2018/2019,
https://doi.org/10.1007/978-3-030-69594-1_9

international criminal tribunal to address violations of the laws of war during the dissolution of the former Yugoslavia (the ICTY) in 1993, then the International Criminal Tribunal for Rwanda (ICTR) in response to the genocide in that country in 1994. The adoption of the Rome Statute of the International Criminal Court (ICC) in 1998 heralded a new era for international criminal justice and the establishment of the first permanent international criminal tribunal. *Ad hoc* responses to internationalized criminal justice continued to be embraced as the scope of crimes of international concern exceeded the jurisdiction of the ICC. The international community experimented with different models, creating, the Special Panels for Serious Crimes under the auspices of the UN peacekeeping mission to East Timor, in 2000, and the hybrid international tribunals: the Special Court for Sierra Leone (SCSL) in 2002, Extraordinary Chambers in the Courts of Cambodia (ECCC) in 2005, and the Special Tribunal for Lebanon (STL) in 2007. Despite various crises of donor fatigue in the sector,[1] the international community's general enthusiasm for international criminal courts and tribunals (ICCTs) has not wavered. The ICC, for example, has received upwards of 13,200 requests to open investigations since becoming operational in 2002;[2] the European Union (EU) has supported the establishment of the Kosovo Specialist Chambers (KSC) and Specialist Prosecutors Office in 2015; the UN has created new international mechanisms to support national authorities to prosecute alleged perpetrators of international crimes in Syria,[3] Iraq,[4] and Myanmar,[5] and calls for the establishment of new *ad hoc* tribunals to prosecute war crimes committed in these states.[6] Increased interaction between different actors fuelled by hyper-globalization in the modernizing world, has amplified friction and conflict as well.[7] As a result, ensuring individual responsibility for international crimes of the scale and complexity of those committed on the global stage continues to prove to be a greater challenge than domestic criminal justice institutions alone can address. In this context, the need for international criminal justice institutions as a continuing fixture on the global stage to respond to grave international crimes is clear.

With the great responsibility entrusted to ICCTs, however, come great obstacles. The daunting task of bringing about justice for victims of grave international crimes is compounded by a multitude of ambiguities surrounding how that mission should be carried out. Such ambiguities have spurred criticisms that ICCTs proceed too slowly or indict too few suspects and have resulted in charges of inefficiency and questions concerning the utility of international criminal justice mechanisms as a

[1] See e.g. Ciorciari and Heinde (2013), p. 370; Sperfeldt (2013), p. 1114; Hignonnet (2005), p. 347; Kendall (2011), pp. 599–601; Brinkley (2008), p. 47; Barria and Roper (2005), p. 287; Zacklin (2004), p. 543.

[2] ICC (2018).

[3] UNGA (2016), paras 1, 4.

[4] See e.g., 'UNITAD Submits Biannual Report . . .', UN Iraq (2019).

[5] HRC (2018).

[6] Warrell (2019); Griffiths (2018).

[7] Tidwell and Lerche (2004), p. 50.

whole.[8] Certain issues that can hamper ICCTs find their origins in the general foundations of international criminal law and cannot be attributed as inherently arising from the conduct of individual institutions themselves.[9] Nevertheless, practice has revealed surmountable challenges that, while manifesting themselves differently at individual institutions, are common across the international criminal justice sector.[10] The passage of time and accrual of experience have allowed practitioners and commentators to look back at the internal dynamics of tribunals with a learned, informed and yet analytical eye. An example of such—and the focus of this paper—is the 2017 Paris Conference on the Effectiveness of International Criminal Justice, chaired by former ICC Judge, Bruno Cotte, and attended by Presidents and Judges of ICCTs, and other international criminal law experts, representing various international criminal justice institutions. Their collective experiences resulted in the creation of the Paris Declaration on the Effectiveness of International Criminal Justice,[11] a compilation of thirty-one recommendations on how to ensure the effectiveness, and ultimately, the sustainability of ICCTs, by improving their predictability, expediency, and systems of judicial governance. The nexus between these recommendations is the overarching theme of effectiveness of international criminal justice, and how to attain it through efficient ICCTs.

2 Improved Effectiveness Through Increased Efficiency: A Role for the Paris Declaration

If an institution's effectiveness is the measure of producing the results intended of it, efficiency is the quality of doing those things well and with minimal waste. The two concepts are inexorably linked: the most efficient processes are of little value if they lead to ineffective results. Inherent in any discussion of institutional efficiency, therefore, is an assumption that institutions work towards intended results. But the measurable parameters of both efficiency and effectiveness can be difficult to identify; no less so in the context of ICCTs.

Some commentators consider the pace of proceedings to be a defining factor of efficiency,[12] while others point to what they see unsatisfactorily low numbers of indictments or convictions, and the comparatively high costs of international criminal justice institutions as evidence of inefficiencies.[13] Without wishing to underplay the significance of these quantitative assessments, it is important to acknowledge

[8]See, e.g., Zacklin (2004), p. 545; Higgins (2007).

[9]See Sloan (2007), p. 41.

[10]See Cassese (2006), p. 22.

[11]Herein after 'Paris Declaration'. Two of the authors, Hrdličková and Plevin, were delegates at the Paris Conference.

[12]See e.g., Sokolić (2018), pp. 97–98.

[13]See e.g., Murdoch (2018).

their limitations in assessing whether efficiencies are directed towards effective outcomes.

Numbers of suspects indicted and arrested, convictions entered, cases finalized, and similar performance parameters are often used in the audit and reporting procedures of the ICCTs and are standard measurements in national systems. But not *all* processes or outcomes of international criminal justice can be reliably assessed or quantified. Oftentimes, mere numerical assessment is too simplistic.[14] There are also qualitative outputs, the efficiency of which cannot be measured in discrete units, such as how well international criminal justice mechanisms contribute to cessation of a conflict or the healing of victims, or to deterring the commission of further crimes of an international character, or to retribution against those who have committed crimes, or the quality of an institution's contribution to the development of international criminal law and procedure.

Critics of quantitative assessments of efficiency argue that qualitative factors are often overlooked or disregarded in efficiency analyses as the latter do not fit squarely within traditional cost-benefit metrics. However, the measurement of efficiency is more complex than the aforementioned dichotomy still, because even these qualitative outcomes are affected by the number, length and cost of proceedings. For instance, scholarship has linked problems of cost and time (efficiency) with goals and accomplishments of ICCTs (effectiveness), arguing that "credibility and [...] inability to significantly influence the return of peace, security and reconciliation [...] from a legal perspective, [...] is directly linked to potential infringements on the rights of the accused".[15] In international criminal justice, therefore, these concepts should not be evaluated narrowly.

It is little wonder then, that the issue of goal ambiguity has plagued international criminal law.[16] The more ambiguous and unclear an institutions' goals—the markers by which we assess whether they are effective—the more difficult assessing and attaining efficiency will be. In the context of international criminal law, ambiguity stems from lack of consensus amongst practitioners, scholars, advocates and States over the purpose of international criminal justice, and likewise of the individual institutions themselves.[17] Questions seeking to identify the goals of international criminal justice have resulted in a wide array of answers. These range from the classic purposes of criminal punishment—retribution, deterrence, incapacitation, and rehabilitation—to more international criminal law-specific purposes, such as the intention to produce a reliable historical record of the context of international crimes, to provide a venue for giving voice to victims, to propagate universal human rights values or to halt ongoing conflicts.[18] These multi-layered tensions inherent in the pursuit of justice for international crimes have left international criminal justice

---

[14]Stahn (2012), pp. 257, 262.

[15]Bourgon (2004), p. 527.

[16]Shany (2012), p. 233.

[17]Keenan (2016), p. 422.

[18]Hafetz (2018), p. 8. Damaska (2008), p. 311. See also Keenan (2016), p. 423.

institutions torn between either primarily serving the ephemeral "global community" or "acting as surrogates" for local justice systems unable to cope.[19]

This phenomenon of goal ambiguity is further exacerbated by the complexity of ICCTs' mandates. As Mirjam Damaska wrote, "it does not require much pause to realize that the task of fulfilling all these self-imposed demands is truly gargantuan. Unlike Atlas, international criminal courts are not bodies of titanic strength, capable of carrying on their shoulders the burden of so many tasks."[20] Institutions can thus find themselves paralyzed and overburdened by such ambiguities,[21] causing further friction concerning their priorities and impacting upon how efficiency is assessed and realized.

The task of understanding what efficiency entails is aided by comprehending what it does not. Yuval Shany suggests inefficiencies occur when international courts generate negative externalities or unforeseen costs that offset any benefits they attain when pursuing their mandates in comparison to many national systems.[22] In this regard, ICCTs face unique systemic challenges that only further hinder their efficiency.[23] For example, they can be vulnerable to the occasional volatility of international cooperation. At the same time, their legitimacy can be dependent on the cooperation, recognition and support of the individual States they interact with. In contrast to domestic court systems, ICCTs are created by non-homogenous groups which can result in imperfect social agreement.[24] A lack of support from key States and the potential volatility and complexity of international relations can leave stakeholders with waning perceptions of an ICCT's legitimacy, which in turn can inhibit critical support and hinder ICCTs efforts to efficiently administer meaningful justice.[25]

This being said, all ICCTs are created for one core and defining purpose: facilitating the investigation and prosecution of alleged perpetrators of international(ized) crimes, through criminal proceedings conducted before a court of law. No matter how efficiency is conceptualized, the starting-point for any credible international criminal justice system is to deliver upon these aims (a) in the shortest time possible, (b) in accordance with procedures established by law, (c) giving due respect to the fairness of proceedings—taking into account the rights and/or interests of suspects, accused, defendants, witnesses, victims and wider society—and (d) in a manner that optimizes the use of the resources made available for that purpose. Different actors within each institution may have fundamentally different relationships to the various aims ascribed to international criminal justice, and therefore

[19]deGuzman (2012), p. 278; Sloan (2007), p. 41.

[20]Damaska (2008), p. 331.

[21]Shany (2012), p. 234.

[22]*Id.*

[23]*Id.*

[24]Danner and Martinez (2005), p. 96.

[25]Damaska (2008), p. 330.

different views as to what makes them effective and how to achieve their aims efficiently.

From the perspective of the judiciary, efficiency is rarely a clear-cut, categorical phenomenon that courts simply either do or do not possess in reference to some pre-defined combination of qualitative and quantitative factors striving towards one certain objective. Yet as our understanding of the role of international criminal justice matures and develops, our awareness of how judges can guarantee efficiency should follow suit. In spite of myriad broader objectives of international criminal law, at the core of any conversation about effectiveness and efficiency, from a judicial perspective, is the ability of a court to facilitate fair, timely, cost-effective proceedings in accordance with the law. In this context, there are certain expectations of any criminal justice system that are as fundamental as they are irrefutable: the rights of the accused and victims are to be respected, the interests of the community are to be served by bringing those responsible for crimes to justice in a timely fashion, and that laws will be applied fairly, equitably and consistently. Effectiveness can be thought of as the ability of a court or tribunal to achieve these outcomes within the context of its specific mandate; efficiency is concerned with the quality of the processes used to reach those aims.

In this context, the predictability, expeditiousness and quality of judicial proceedings are not merely relevant to the measurement of court performance: they are also the embodiment of the international human rights law that seeks to promote those core aims. It follows, therefore, that in order for ICCTs to truly be effective, they must ensure that their proceedings and processes are efficient. The Paris Declaration serves to further that aim. This article offers a brief commentary to the Paris Declaration, through the lens of its three interrelated foci: transparency and predictability, expeditiousness and governance. It explores how the thirty-one recommendations in the Paris Declaration can improve the efficiency of ICCTs and promote their long-term sustainability.

Despite all the challenges highlighted above, far from being held hostage by potential inefficiencies, ICCTs occupy space where there is room for progressive improvement while promoting international criminal justice as a sustainable, worthwhile and effective enterprise. The concrete lessons the Paris Declaration reflects are directed towards the roles of judges, judiciaries and judicial administrators in achieving that end. Aimed at improving the process deployed at ICCTs, they demonstrate that through enhanced efficiency, better quality justice outcomes and more effective ICCTs are an attainable reality.

3 Transparency and Predictability

Ensuring the transparency and predictability of proceedings before ICCTs is an obvious precursor to improving and maintaining their efficiency. Striving for transparent and predictable proceedings requires prioritization of processes by which the expectations—of litigants and stakeholders alike—are tempered. Conversely, when procedures are unpredictable or inaccessible, their quality, often viewed as the greatest indicator of their legitimacy,[26] is most difficult to assess. The frameworks that guide international criminal proceedings may be derived from provisions of statutes, court rules, and case-law or practice directions and guidelines. Guaranteeing that litigants are aware of discrete procedural steps and when to expect them requires accessible, coherent, decisive procedural frameworks, applied consistently across the proceedings. Such frameworks facilitate robust precedents that, in turn, can minimize the time and resources devoted to litigation that inevitably and necessarily arises where processes suffer from ambiguities, opacity or inconsistent application.

But rigidity in legal processes or their application can also exacerbate inefficiencies and detract from the ultimate objective of fair and expeditious proceedings. So ICCTs rely upon a degree of flexibility in their procedural frameworks both (a) as a means of facilitating compromise between drafters representing diverse legal backgrounds, and (b) to allow space for the judicial discretion that is inherent to ensuring proceedings are sufficiently adaptable and responsive to the needs of a given case.[27] The Paris Declaration's recommendations for improving transparency and predictability coexist alongside this legitimate judicial discretion.[28] Underpinning them is an understanding that efficiency does not occur by accident: only when elasticity in criminal procedure is intentionally deployed to facilitate efficiency, is efficiency likely to be attained.

In this tenor, Article 1 of the Paris Declaration recognizes that the constituent texts of the various ICCTs already strive towards clarity and expeditiousness. Article 1 thus endorses a culture whereby judges strictly adhere to the legal structures applicable to the institutions they serve, irrespective of the legal systems they may be familiar with as a result of their prior experience:

> Art. 1:
> Call upon each Judge, regardless of his or her legal system of origin, to apply the normative framework governing the court or tribunal of which he or she is a member;

Although international judges exercise substantial discretion, it is the mandates and governing legal frameworks of their respective institutions that should guide their decisions.[29] This is because the maintenance of a strict status quo in the normative framework applied can help to give consistency and credence to judicial

[26]Damaska (2008), p. 345, citing Tyler (1990).

[27]McLaughlin (2007), p. 345.

[28]These recommendations fall within the substantive portions of the Paris Declaration titled "Preliminaries" (Articles 1 to 3) and "Predictability" (Articles 4 to 6).

[29]*Cf.* Keenan (2016), p. 453.

decisions.[30] It also enhances the ability of litigants and stakeholders to understand every phase of every case at each tribunal as part of a cohesive whole.

The Paris Declaration thus implicitly acknowledges the challenges that can exist when Chambers are composed of judges from diverse legal backgrounds as is the case at all ICCTs. The ICC's international judges, for instance, are drawn from either so-called "List A" or "List B" categories of candidates. List A candidates must "[h] ave established competence in criminal law and procedure, and the necessary relevant experience, whether as judge, prosecutor, advocate or in other similar capacity, in criminal proceedings", whereas List B candidates are required to "[h] ave established competence in relevant areas of international law such as international humanitarian law and the law of human rights, and extensive experience in a professional legal capacity which is of relevance to the judicial work of the Court".[31] To the Chambers of the STL, by contrast, Lebanese Judges and International Judges are appointed by the UN Secretary-General, in accordance with the Tribunal's constituent texts.[32] Both examples result in Chambers boasting judges with an impressive array of expertise from diverse legal backgrounds.

In order to prioritize application of each institution's normative framework, the day-to-day challenge for judges is to embody a practice that treats their experience with particular legal systems prerequisite to their appointment as mere qualification criteria, not instructive of the perspective they are expected to bring to bear in interpreting legal texts and applying the law at ICCTs. There are nuances of course. Hybrid models can require judges to turn to domestic law. At the STL, which applies substantive Lebanese law and an interpretive framework that often requires deference to Lebanese criminal procedure,[33] the expertise of Lebanese Judges is irreplaceable. But in international criminal law and procedure generally, examples are exceptional and determined by law. The application of an institution's normative legal framework is therefore best achieved when judges resist temptations to revert to practices learned—over years if not decades of experience—in their legal system of origin, unless obliged by law to do so. As others have intimated, however, this can be easier said than done.[34]

When judges are perceived to address legal issues without conscious efforts to remain strictly within the lens of an institution's normative framework, both criticisms and complications can arise. No international court or tribunal is immune from these difficulties, which can be particularly conflated by the pressures of ambiguous

[30] See STL, Interlocutory Decision on the Applicable Law: Criminal Association and Review of the Indictment (Case No. 17-07-I/AC/R176*bis*), 18 October 2017, p. 2.

[31] Rome Statute, art. 36 (b).

[32] STL Statute, arts. 2, 8(1); Agreement between the UN and Lebanon, art. 9.

[33] STL Statute, art. 2. See STL, Interlocutory Decision on the Applicable Law: Criminal Association and Review of the Indictment (Case No. 17-07-I/AC/R176*bis*), 18 October 2017, para. 17; STL, *Prosecutor v. Ayyash et al.*, Interlocutory Decision on the Applicable Law: Terrorism, Conspiracy, Homicide, Perpetration, Cumulative Charging (Case No. STL-11-01/I/AC/R176*bis*), 16 February 2011, para. 22.

[34] See e.g., de Gurmendi (2018), p. 164.

and shifting goals of international criminal justice, as described above. For example, critics have singled out Regulation 55 of the ICC Regulations of the Court, adopted by the ICC Judges in 2004, as falling foul of that institution's normative framework. The Regulation—which permits the legal characterization of facts at the end of trial—has been described variously as *ultra vires* the ICC Judges' regulatory authority, and depriving the accused of certainty in legal process.[35] Another example is the practice of ICCTs using the trial process to create a factual record of historical importance that extends beyond what is strictly necessary for the adjudication of international crimes. This was exemplified in the trial of Slobodan Milošević, which was unable to be concluded prior to his death in March 2006. By that time, from Milošević's transfer to the ICTY in June 2001, the Trial Chamber had sat for 466 days and listened to 295 witnesses; the scale of the proceedings owing in part to the judges' attempts to produce an historical "record of events accompanying the disintegration of Yugoslavia".[36] The approach drew criticism as purposefully broadening the judicial directive outside of that tribunal's mandate, with the effect of unnecessarily complicating and delaying proceedings.[37] Whether or not these examples evidence judicial decisions extending beyond applicable normative frameworks is a matter for other commentators to decide. The point stressed by the Paris Declaration is that judges should be sensitive to the potential hazards associated with failing to prioritize strict adherence to normative frameworks.

The predictability of judicial proceedings also depends upon participants, including the parties, the judges and the registry, being able to understand and foresee the actions of other participants at different phases of the proceedings. Article 2 and 3 of the Paris Declaration embody this notion by recognizing that the opportunity exists to ensure participants better understand processes ahead of time and, importantly, can maximize on efficiencies by planning accordingly. These recommendations also emphasize the importance of continued dialogue, both between the judges within individual chambers and between chambers and other organs of each court. For example, Article 2 underscores the interrelationships between the different interlocutors within each institution, including between the different organs, and between judges, presiding judges, and presidents:

> Art. 2: Recall that, without prejudice to their respective responsibilities, there is a genuine interdependency between each organ of the court or tribunal, as well as between the Presidency and the Judges and Presiding Judges, which should be capitalized upon through dialogue in order to improve the expeditiousness and effectiveness of proceedings;

---

[35] ICC, *Prosecutor v. Katanga*, Decision on the Implementation of Regulation 55 of the Regulations of the Court and Severing the Charges Against Accused Persons (Case No. ICC-01/04-01/07), 21 November 2012, Dissenting Opinion of Judge Van den Wyngaert, para. 8; Dastugue (2015); Heller (2015), p. 981; Jacobs (2013).

[36] Damaska (2008), pp. 340–341.

[37] *Id.*

Article 3, meanwhile, underscores the importance of dialogue about professional practices between judges themselves:

> Art. 3:
> Ensure regular and ongoing communication between the Judges concerning professional practices, in a manner consistent with their independence;

In practice, these principles find their roots in existing provisions such as Rule 36 of the STL's Rules of Procedure and Evidence, which authorizes each presiding judge, in consultation with the other judges of their respective chambers, to appoint a judge rapporteur for the purpose of ensuring greater efficiency. A similar notion to that reflected in Article 3 has long been endorsed by the Security-Council, which incorporated amendments to the ICTR Statute regarding the composition of the common ICTY-ICTR Appeals Chamber, in an effort to give appellate judges greater insight into the specificities of the ICTR's experiences.[38] Those amendments required two ICTR Judges to be permanently assigned to the common Appeals Chamber.

These articles underscore both (a) the inherent value of acknowledging interdependencies between judges and, (b) how exploiting these interdependencies can help to pre-empt possible causes of inefficiency, while also ensuring that judges avoid becoming isolated or out of sync.

Not only does the Paris Declaration recommend that participants in ICCTs' proceedings should strive for deeper understanding about the activities of other participants; it underscores the value of introspective, hands-on approaches by judges as a means of enhancing the effectiveness of judicial processes. Article 4, for instance, emphasizes the importance of thorough preparation by judges:

> Art. 4: Call upon Judges, upon assignment to a case, to thoroughly prepare and maintain in-depth knowledge of the circumstances of the case, including by developing of common and pertinent methods of familiarization with and analysis of the alleged facts and issues in dispute;

Depending on the nature and stage of the proceedings, the character of the familiarization that can and should be undertaken by a judge can be malleable: from developing a thorough understanding of procedural steps ahead; to understanding the type, sources and potential relevance of evidence and possible challenges to its admissibility; to identifying areas of fact or law in contention between the parties. Advanced identification of potential issues empowers judges to intervene early in order to coordinate the parties, the proceedings and also the work of chambers.

Article 5, meanwhile, encourages introspection as to the application of criminal procedure. Echoing Article 1's emphasis on the application of each institution's

[38] Mundis (2001), p. 859.

normative framework, Article 5 recommends that, to the extent possible, distinct procedural steps are, unequivocally, treated as such:

> Art. 5: Ensure that each procedural phase of the proceedings serves its own purpose and avoids duplication to the extent possible;

In the world of hybrid or *sui generis* criminal courts and tribunals, it should not be taken for granted that constituent texts or rules of procedure and evidence are themselves sufficient to avoid unnecessary duplication. For instance, broad discretion provided for by statutes and rules of procedure and evidence can risk repetition between phases of a criminal case,[39] or the same issues being litigated repeatedly across the phases of multiple cases at the same tribunal. Minimizing the potential for repetition at one stage of proceedings thus requires a cautious, deliberate and measured approach with full consideration of the discrete role served at other stages of the proceedings.[40]

Article 6 calls upon courts and tribunals to devise specific, yet flexible work-plans for each phase of proceedings:

> Art. 6: Devise, at the earliest possible opportunity and in consultation with the Parties, a realistic work plan for the pre-trial, trial and appellate phases, taking into account the specific features of each case and which may be modified if necessary;

Judge-implemented work-plans are mandated by the procedural rules of many ICCTs as a means of indicating to the litigants, in advance, the obligations they are required to meet, and the dates by which they must do so.[41] Judges and participants should be entitled to sufficient flexibility in this planning process to enable work-plans to be tailored to respond to the idiosyncrasies of each case. Variables such as the scale, complexity, number of defendants, nature and volume of evidence, facts in dispute, legal issues in question, and even the dynamics between litigants can greatly impact upon how best to efficiently coordinate a case. But such flexibility should not be unfettered. Without clear guidance, unfettered flexibility for litigants and an absence of fixed deadlines greatly increases the risk of inefficiency and unpredictability creeping into proceedings. Article 6 recommends that work-plans are implemented as early as possible, and should be "realistic" and "take into

[39] *Cf.* ICC, *Prosecutor v. Gbagbo and Blé Goudé*, Reasons for Oral Decision of 15 January 2019 on the *Requête de la Défense de Laurent Gbagbo afin qu'un jugement d'acquittement portant sur toutes les charges soit prononcé en faveur de Laurent Gbagbo et que sa mise en liberté immédiate soit ordonnée* (Case No. ICC-02/11-01/15-12630), 16 July 2019, Reasons of Judge Geoffrey Henderson, para. 6.

[40] ICC, *Prosecutor v. Ruto and Sang*, Decision on the Defence Applications for Judgements of Acquittal, Trial Chamber V(A) (Case No. ICC-01/09-01/11), 5 April 2016, Reasons of Judge Fremr, para.144; *Id.*, Reasons of Judge Eboe-Osuji, paras 105–125.

[41] See e.g., ICC RPE, r. 132, ICTY RPE, r. 65; IRMCT RPE, r. 70; STL RPE, r. 91.

account the specific features of each case". The Paris Declaration thus seeks a balance between firm and responsive scheduling practices, recognizing that work-plans may be modified where the specific features of the case necessitate doing so.

4 Expeditiousness

The relationship between international criminal law and expeditiousness has a fraught history. The late Antonio Cassese once described the lack of expeditiousness as a result "intrinsic problems common to all international criminal courts".[42] The concept of timeliness is not administrative: its stems from universally accepted minimum standards for the conduct of criminal proceedings. Article 9.3 of the International Covenant on Civil and Political Rights, for example, requires arrested persons or detainees to be brought "promptly" before a judge and guarantees that they are "entitled to trial within a reasonable time or release". This is echoed in Article 6.1 of the European Convention on Human Rights, which guarantees the right to a fair hearing "within a reasonable time".

Many factors that can increase the length of proceedings without causing the threshold of reasonableness to be crossed *per se* are common to ICCTs, such as large numbers of charges, voluminous evidence, numerous victims and multi-accused cases. But the assessment of reasonableness does not stop at the existence of these factors. The European Court of Human Rights, for example, has declined to consider lengthy periods of unexplained inactivity as "reasonable", irrespective of the existence of complex of the proceedings.[43]

As Schwarz argues, if justice (J) is a function of factors A, B, C, D, and E (expeditiousness), it is wildly improbable that J would equal E.[44] On the other hand, this analogy suggests that improvements in efficiency can lead to improved justice outcomes overall. So while it has been widely acknowledged that justice should not be equated with expeditiousness, the later cannot be overlooked. With this in mind, the Paris Declaration offers eighteen recommendations based on the collective experience of ICCTs, aimed at improving expeditiousness through a variety of measures.

Some of the recommendations need little introduction, such as Article 22, which calls for the promotion, in line with "the respective responsibilities of those involved in the trial, [of] a dignified and constructive atmosphere for the hearings". Article 24, meanwhile, endorses the practices of the *ad hocs*, the IRMCT and SCSL, by calling for the establishment and regular maintenance of databases of ICCTs jurisprudence to facilitate rapid access to existing jurisprudence. The remaining sixteen

[42]Cassese (2006), para. 69.

[43]ECtHR, *Adiletta and Others v. Italy*, Judgment (No. 20/1990/211/271-273), 24 January 1991, para. 17.

[44]Schwartz (1987), p. 143.

recommendations can be broadly grouped into three thematic areas: judicial case management, deliberation and drafting, and innovation.

4.1 Judicial Case Management

While the procedural rules of the different ICCTs provide for specific judicial functions of the presiding judges of various chambers, they tend not to be prescriptive of the managerial tasks of case-coordination and case-management inherent to that role.[45] But presiding judges are uniquely placed to assist in planning both (a) internally within an institution, in their chambers and in consultation with the litigants, registry and presidency, and (b) externally, by furnishing information to bodies responsible for their institutions' administration, funding and/or oversight. Doing so can help boost chances of delivering expeditious proceedings, for example, by ensuring that chambers can be resourced and supported to a level commensurate with its expected output. As such, Article 7 of the Paris Declaration focuses on the role presiding judges can play in oversight and coordination of the judicial process:

> Art. 7:
> Encourage Presiding Judges, in addition to their purely judicial activities, to fulfil their managerial role;

A clear example of this notion evidenced in practice is the initiative of former ICTY President, Judge Gabrielle Kirk McDonald and her successor, Judge Claude Jorda, to seek the creation of a third trial chamber supported by the use of *ad litem* judges, to allow the ICTY to accomplish its mission more efficiently.[46] The initiative was credited with saving the ICTY from feared perceptions of illegitimacy expected to stem from an inability to effectively handle its anticipated case-load, and with prompting wider changes to the ICTY's trial procedures to further boost efficiency.[47]

In a similar vein but with a more inward-looking focus, Article 8 recommends that ICCTs incorporate provisions into their legal frameworks to streamline case-management through a single, dedicated judge at each stage of the proceedings:

> Art. 8: Support the implementation of provisions entrusting the pre-trial and pre-appeal case management to a Single Judge, with the obligation for the latter to discuss with and report regularly to the other Judges composing the Chamber;

This preference for pre-trial and pre-appeal case management through one judge reflects the practice that evolved at the ICTY, where a single judge from a trial

[45]See e.g., ICC RPE, rr. 122, 133, 140, 141, 143, 170, 171.

[46]Bourgon (2004), p. 527.

[47]*Id.*, at 528 (2004).

chamber of three served as a pre-trial judge, in an effort to simplify pre-trial case-management and reduce the length of pre-trial proceedings generally. At the SCSL, the rules of procedure allowed for one judge to be designated to perform case-management functions prior to the commencement of trial and during status conferences, and for the appointment of a "Pre-Hearing Judge" designated for the purpose of "supervising all appeals arising from a particular trial chamber" by exercising other pre-appeal hearing functions that would otherwise be exercised by the Appeals Chamber.[48] The Pre-Hearing Judge was explicitly directed "to ensure that proceedings are not unduly delayed and [to] take any measures related to procedural matters, including the issuing of decisions, orders or directions, with a view to preparing the case for a fair and expeditious hearing".

If the goal of effective judicial case management is to streamline proceedings, avoid inefficiencies and ensure parties' litigious strategies do not compromize the core aims of delivering fair, equitable and transparent justice, that task is inextricably linked to the management of disclosure of evidentiary material, the management of witnesses and evidence, and limiting the number of issues in dispute. The Paris Declaration contains clusters of recommendations directed at each of these challenges.

4.1.1 Oversight of Disclosure and Submission of Documents

Disputes relating to the disclosure of evidence and supporting materials between litigants, and particularly from the prosecution to the defence, is a frequent source of contention and litigation. David Scheffer has described such disagreement as "one of the most reliable constants of criminal procedure—domestic or international".[49]

Efficiency demands that the disclosure process in international criminal trials is closely managed by judges who, in turn, are fully informed of the features of the case and the characteristics of the evidence, and intimately familiar with the applicable evidentiary procedures. On one hand, so-called fishing-expeditions implicating vast quantities of potentially irrelevant and inconsequential evidence are to be discouraged; on the other, sufficient time and facilities must be made available to the litigants to inspect, assess and analyse documents to ensure that all relevant material changes hands sufficiently in advance of trial such that proceedings are not interrupted as a result of late disclosure or litigants' unfamiliarity with the evidence.

Two Articles of the Paris Declaration are dedicated to the issue of the disclosure. Article 9 focusses on the form that material intended for disclosure or submission before the court should be presented:

[48] SCSL RPE, r. 109 (A), (E).

[49] Scheffer (2008).

Art. 9: Encourage the Parties, and particularly the Prosecutor, to ensure that documents and supporting materials are disclosed or submitted in a manner that facilitates their consideration and analysis;

The task of understanding the purported relevance, or lack thereof, to a party's case, or to the proceedings more broadly, is dramatically less complex when material is organized, categorized, and disclosed in a manner that is designed to facilitate that task. In this vein, the Article 9 recognizes the potential benefits of judicial involvement in managing and prescribing the form of disclosure, as a means for ensuring efficiency in the disclosure process and the proceedings as a whole. This principle was recognized expressly in the rules of procedure and evidence of the KSC, which include a provision on the "Procedure for Disclosure". That procedure requires parties to provide "clear and concise" descriptions of the document—or categories of documents disclosed—and perhaps more significantly, to "categorise the information in accordance with the charges in the indictment specific reference to the underlying crimes, contextual elements of the crimes, the alleged conduct of the Accused or, where applicable, evidence to be presented by the Specialist Prosecutor".

Article 10 meanwhile, recognizes the potential for undermanaged or mismanaged disclosure to dramatically lengthen and complicate proceedings:

Art. 10: Strive to reduce the duration of proceedings, in particular by setting deadlines for the disclosure of materials and the filing of written submissions;

The evidentiary rules of the ICCTs generally attempt to guard against disclosure of new evidentiary material after parties have filed their witness and exhibit lists. In practice, the exceptions to this principle, and violations of it, are regular;[50] whereas sanctions for noncompliance are not at all commonplace. At the same time, disputes surrounding disclosure that are likely to arise during the course of proceedings can often be predicted in advance, if litigants are given sufficient opportunity to prepare and review material provided to them. Without judicial intervention, it may be left to the litigants to identify the most suitable time for a particular intervention, while it is not incumbent upon the litigants to protect the expediency of judicial processes.

Effective case-management can also be used to set deadlines for the filing of written submissions on disputed issues in advance, to avoid disruption to the trial process during the course of proceedings. For example, if the rules of procedure and evidence of a particular ICCT allow, consideration may be given to scheduling the filing of submissions on the admissibility of particular sources of evidence prior to the commencement of trial, or to making use of provisions that allow for reduction of time-limits set in the rules of procedure and evidence in appropriate circumstances. Closely supervised disclosure processes can also help judges and litigants to anticipate areas of contention and rectify or litigate potential disclosure violations in a

[50] See e.g., Ambos (2012), pp. 124–125; Caianiello (2011), p. 318.

manner that avoids slowing the proceedings generally. Of course, none of the recommendations in the Paris Declaration should be read in isolation. Strong, judge-led case-management from the outset, built around effective and responsive work-plans, the implementation of systems for the efficient disclosure and submission of material by the parties, together with firm deadlines for disclosure and the filing of written submissions, collectively, can help to streamline proceedings and reduce time-pressures. Where any of these steps is weak or deficient, however, inefficiencies can emerge and flourish.

4.1.2 Management of Witnesses and the Presentation of Evidence

Article 12 of the Paris Declaration focuses on ensuring the economy of time and resources dedicated to the proceedings before each chamber. It encourages presiding judges to consider the task of managing the scope and presentation of witness testimony and other evidence, as an exercise which begins prior to the commencement of proceedings and requires ongoing reflection on a recurring basis throughout:

> Art. 12:
> Encourage Presiding Judges, Pre-Trial Judges and Pre-Appeal Judges to play an active role prior to the opening of the case and during the course of the proceedings, in close consultation with the Parties, to continuously determine the number of witnesses to be heard, the modalities of hearings, and the time required for the presentation of evidence;

Cassese considered that the general onus of accountability for the conduct of proceedings should be borne by the judiciary because it "falls to [them] to endeavour to steer the case along the most direct possible course to its orderly and fair completion."[51] The intrinsic value of judicial involvement in planning the presentation of evidence was also recognized in the *Gbagbo* case, in which the ICC Appeals Chamber noted the importance of the Pre-Trial Chamber's early role in "evaluat[ing] ambiguities, inconsistencies and contradictions in the evidence or doubts as to the credibility of witnesses."[52]

Moving from the general to the more specific, Articles 14 and 17 of the Paris Declaration relate to the presentation of witness evidence. In adversarial systems in particular, the presentation of evidence through the examination and cross-examination of witnesses forms the centre-piece of the trial process. Even within domestic systems, vastly different practices as to the nature and extent of permissible

[51] Cassese (2006), para. 86.

[52] *See* ICC, *The Prosecutor v. Laurent Gbagbo*, Decision Adjourning the Hearing on the Confirmation of Charges Pursuant to Article 61(7)(c)(i) of the Rome State (Case No. ICC-02/11-01/11), 3 June 2013.

cross-examination by counsel have developed.[53] In the context of international trials, witnesses potentially number in the tens to hundreds. The motivation for ensuring the hearing of witness testimony is streamlined, to the extent possible, is evident. For this reason, Article 14 expresses a preference, where appropriate, for presentation of witness evidence in written form:

> Art. 14: Encourage, where appropriate, the use of procedures which allow for the presentation of witness evidence or portions of such evidence in written form, with the opportunity to examine and cross-examine the witness if required;

This principle can be seen in practice in the ICTY's approach to determining the nature and scope of evidence presented at trial. Faced with the same witnesses being called to testify at length on the same topics in multiple cases, the ICTY judges developed a preference for admitting written witness statements and transcripts of testimony. This reduced the need for extensive examination in-chief, thus preventing unnecessarily repetition of the time-consuming processes of calling individual witnesses to elicit substantially the same evidence in multiple cases.[54]

A related consideration is addressed in Article 17, which concerns the cross-examination procedures used at trial. In this regard, the Paris Declaration expresses a preference for the development of more nuanced and tailored approaches to cross-examination that are more attuned to the evidence presented by individual witnesses:

> Art. 17: Consider more streamlined cross-examination procedures that are better suited to individual witnesses, consistent with the rights of the Parties;

In practice, this might involve greater intervention by judges to focus questions posed in cross-examination to particular topics in dispute, or to impose limits to cross-examination that proves fruitless, repetitive, or irrelevant, or to coordinate questions on a particular topic from more than one defendant in a multi-accused case. While recognizing that such streamlining of cross-examination should not prejudice the legitimate rights of the parties, Article 17 of the Paris Declaration nonetheless encourages dramatic re-thinking of cross-examination practices as a means of improving the pace of proceedings.

4.1.3 Minimizing Areas in Dispute

One of the greatest tools available to judges in terms of increasing the expeditiousness of proceedings is to reduce the number of issues of in dispute. In order to achieve this aim, effective oversight of litigation requires more than familiarity with the various stages of the proceedings as set out in the procedural rules or the setting

[53] See Carlson (1967), p. 722.

[54] Mundis (2001), p. 856.

of appropriate deadlines. Expeditiousness of the trial process demands that the objective of judges during the pre-trial phases and throughout should be to strive to shape proceedings to provide for an expeditious trial, to the extent possible. Article 13 recognizes that one way to do so is to attempt to determine all preliminary and interlocutory issues raised during the pre-trial phase:

> Art. 13: Encourage Pre-Trial Judges to determine all preliminary and interlocutory issues raised at that stage unless the issue is one which ought plainly to be left for determination by the Trial Chamber;

Another means of minimizing areas in dispute at trial is through the procedures that exist at many ICCTs: entering points of agreement on matters of fact or law into the trial record. In other instances, it might be possible to substantiate facts that could otherwise be in dispute through taking judicial notice, for instance, when alleged facts pertain to matters of common knowledge or public record. The individual circumstances of each case will dictate when this is appropriate. For instance, agreement may be more difficult to come by *in absentia* proceedings, such as those conducted before the STL, where Defence Counsel do not have the benefit of being able to consult with clients for instructions. In order to improve expeditiousness, judges should be encouraged to take a leading role in guiding the litigants and exploring possibilities for eliciting as much agreement on non-contentious matters as possible in any given case. Recognizing that agreement will not always be achievable, Article 20 of the Paris Declaration nonetheless encourages the full exploitation of procedures for recording agreement:

> Art. 20: Recommend to the Parties, wherever possible, to make use of procedures for recording points of agreements on matters of law, and fact and to favour the taking of judicial notice of facts of common knowledge;

4.2 *Deliberations and Drafting*

The task of balancing the timeliness and "quality" of justice is one that is common to courts of all types. At the domestic level, time limits and indicative timelines have been adopted because they provide general boundaries for case proceedings, by balancing these two potentially-competing concerns.[55] Indicative timelines are a common tool in many jurisdictions not only for indicating in advance to litigants when decisions can be expected or filings will become due, but also in improving transparency by helping stakeholders understand the procedural steps involved and the likely time expended at each stage of proceedings. As their name suggests,

[55] See e.g., Ostrom and Hanson (1999), p. 4.

indicative timelines are not binding on a court; they recognize that litigation can be unpredictable, while nonetheless helping participants in the judicial process to plan and even adapt to unexpected turns in the litigation. At the international level, meaningful indicative timelines can be prepared on basis of past-practice in similar cases and deadlines fixed by the rules of procedure evidence. At the STL, for example, such indicative timelines have formed the basis of assessment of staffing and resource requirements, and importantly, have assisted individual chambers in anticipating their workload and to plan accordingly. As such, the utilization of indicative timelines has proven fruitful as a means of identifying when and where resources can best be used to streamline and shorten proceedings while enhancing their quality. Accordingly, Article 11 of the Paris Declaration encourages proactivity and effectiveness in the planning of deliberations and drafting of decisions through the adoption of indicative timelines in an effort to reduce the time needed to conduct fair, quality criminal justice procedures in accordance with the law:

> Art. 11: Strive to reduce the time spent on the final deliberations as well as the time spent writing judgments by setting indicative deadlines;

Similar measures have already been deployed to an extent on the international plane. For example, the ICTY adopted a practice of setting global time-limits to encourage high-levels of organization amongst the parties prior to the trial's commencement to maximize their own efficiency with witness and evidence presentation.[56] This measure helped maximize predictability by facilitating detailed planning for the trial phase after the parties had filed witness and exhibit lists, so that work-plans could be tailored to accommodate information already known to the bench. Such approach minimizes the chances of work-plans being too vague or overly speculative to effectively guide the litigants, or being derailed by unexpected changes in circumstances, such as the unavailability of witnesses, for instance. There are concrete developments in this respect. For example, in 2019, the ICC Judges adopted guidance on timeframes for the issuance of key decisions at trial and on appeal, which are now incorporated into the ICC Chambers Pratice Manual.[57] Moreover, in a practice that could be reflected upon at other ICCTs, the KSC has gone further than indicative timelines, incorporating into its rules of procedure and evidence predetermined deadlines that bind Judges in the various Chambers and can only be extended by reasoned, public decision where absolutely necessary.[58]

It has long been recognized that requiring judges to issue detailed written decisions issued in relation to routine matters and circumstances not required by law can be an antithesis of efficiency in the criminal justice processes.[59] In domestic

---

[56] ICTY (2009), p. 78.

[57] ICC (2019).

[58] See e.g., KSC RPE, rr. 159(1), 164(1), 183(1), 186(3).

[59] See Council of Europe (1987), p. 5.

systems it may be possible for courts to dispose of detailed written judgments altogether. The constituent texts of the ICCTs recognize that, in the context of the complexity and gravity of the crimes prosecuted in international criminal law, fully-reasoned written judgments are essential. Nonetheless, practice demonstrates that efficiencies can be gained through the issuance of oral decisions, in court, to rule on applications, motions and requests filed during the proceedings. The Paris Declaration recognizes this by calling for the use of oral decisions, wherever possible, to rule on applications before the court:

> Art. 15: Encourage the use of oral decisions to rule on applications, as appropriate;

At the ICTY, the utility of this practice was explicitly recognized by amendments incorporated into that tribunal's rules of procedure and evidence, specifically, as they related to the procedure for challenging the evidence presented by the prosecution as insufficient to substantiate allegations in the indictment beyond reasonable doubt at the end of the Prosecution case: the so-called "no case to answer" phase. In 2004, the ICTY rules were amended to require the trial chambers to issue oral, rather than written decisions.[60] While written decisions will be necessitated in some circumstances, efficiencies gained by this practice can be lost if oral decisions are routinely followed, at a later point, by lengthy written reasons. Consideration should be given to the normative framework as to the detail of reasoning required in relation to each decision in order to ensure that the length of reasoning does not unreasonably impact upon the duration of proceedings.

Opportunity also exists to improve efficiency in the process of preparing detailed written judgments. In this respect, Article 16 focuses on the practices of the legal officers who assist Chambers, and how they can be utilized to expedite the drafting processes:

> Art. 16: Encourage the development of professional practices whereby Chambers Legal Officers start drafting, on a provisional basis and at the earliest opportunity, those parts of a draft judgment which are unlikely to undergo significant changes;

For example, the procedural history, glossaries of key terms, and sections of judgments setting out applicable provisions of a statute or rules of procedure, can often be prepared in advance and without the need to incorporate significant changes at a later stage. Such an approach was employed by the ICTY, for example, which adopted specific criteria for legal officers tasked with preparing early version of judgment outlines.[61] This model allowed judges to identify drafting priorities and

---

[60] ICTY (2009), p. 79.

[61] *Id.*, p. 110.

served to assist them in ascertaining weaknesses, possibilities for seeking further submissions, or directing further research.[62]

Another means of expediting the preparation of written judgments is through continuing, provisional deliberations, as reflected in Article 18 of the Paris Declaration:

> Art. 18: Promote the practice of provisional but continuing deliberations after the testimony of each witness, rather than postponing all deliberations until the final stage;

This recommendation is premised on the experience of judges that the exercise of reflecting upon the characteristics of a witness' presentation will be most efficient when memory of a witness' testimony is fresh, immediately after their evidence is received. The practice does not suggest that a decision on assessment of a witness or the weight to be attached to their testimony should immediately follow their presentation of evidence. But continual provisional deliberations can reduce the need for extensive review of witness testimony at a later stage, and serve to provide effective *aides memoire* to expedite the final assessment of witness testimony after all evidence has been received. Doing so can also reduce the amount of drafting required at a later stage in proceedings, with the potential to expedite the period from the end of the hearings to the issuance of a judgment.

Article 19 recognizes that the drafting of written decisions and judgments can also be expedited by avoiding the practice, which has developed in some ICCTs, of restating the arguments developed by the parties in their written and oral submissions:

> Art. 19: Simplify the drafting of written decisions by referring to the arguments developed by the Parties in their written submissions without necessarily summarizing them in the body of the decision;

The practice of setting out the parties' submissions in detail was particularly useful in the days prior to the accessibility of online public databases of filings. Doing so helps to make judicial reasoning more accessible by providing greater context to the written decision. But in an environment where interlocutory filings can number into the hundreds if not thousands, and with ready access to online public databases containing relevant findings, there is room to revisit the desirability of this practice. This is especially so in the context of routine interlocutory decisions that, by their very nature, are of significantly less interest to the general public. In this respect, the Paris Declaration leans towards the adoption of practices that support the established principle that the efficiency of criminal justice can be improved by reducing the length of written decisions.[63]

---

[62] *Id.*

[63] See Council of Europe (1987), p. 5.

Criminal trials are, in essence, concerned with the presentation and assessment of evidence against the framework of the criminal law. Efficiency of the process by which evidence is presented and assessed is therefore closely correlated to the efficiency of the criminal justice process as a whole. The Paris Declaration recognizes the need for closer study in this area:

> Art. 21: Continue reflecting upon the practice of totally or partially postponing to the deliberation stage the assessment of the admissibility of the evidence presented;

Article 21 alludes to the procedures by which evidence is presented and assessed in a trial. The methods available exist on a scale. On one end is the practice whereby parties litigate any challenges to the admissibility of evidence by attempting to exclude it before that evidence is admitted by the court and becomes part of the trial record. In this model, an assessment of the weight to be attached to the evidence, its persuasive value, and its reliability are finally determined during deliberations that follow the presentation of the entirety of the evidence, *i.e.*, at the close of the trial hearings. This is the task, for example, of a common law jury. On the other end of the scale is the practice of formally submitting evidentiary material before the court to become part of a case file, but where decisions pertaining on the assessment of that evidence are deferred until deliberations. This model negates the need for separate processes dedicated to the question of admissibility. Generally, in this model, stringent rules regulating the collection of evidence are applicable. All criminal justice systems operate somewhere on this scale. In broad terms, common law adversarial systems have traditionally favoured the former, while civil law inquisitorial systems tend to prefer the latter.[64] But a divide between the practices of common law jurisdictions and civil law jurisdictions should not be overstated. In reality, many common law trials allow for the admission of a broad scope of evidence that passes the filter of admissibility, while many civil law systems and attach little or no weight to evidence that might be otherwise be deemed inadmissible in a common law jury trial.[65]

ICCTs, meanwhile, are generally afforded very broad discretion to determine the evidentiary practices they adopt.[66] In practice, the traditional common law approach has been applied widely, though commentators have observed a recent shift in practice at the ICC, from the classic common law admissibility model to a formal submission model.[67] Both models have their merit, but in the context of hybrid and *sui generis* procedures of the ICCTs, it is worth noting that, because of other differences in investigative and evidentiary procedure mandated by these

[64] Guariglia (2018), pp. 315–339.

[65] *Id.*

[66] See e.g., ICC RPE, r. 163; ICTR RPE, r. 89; ICTY RPE, r. 89; IRMCT RPE, r. 105; SCSL RPE, r. 89; STL RPE, r. 89.

[67] Guariglia (2018).

institutions' statutes and rules, neither model can be transposed perfectly, as they reflect only one portion of a much broader criminal justice process. Most important is not the choice of evidentiary practice *per se*, but that the choice is made at the outset of trial proceedings and is compatible with investigative practices, pre-trial procedure and the efficiency of other phases of the trial, in the full context of effectively completing an institution's mandate.

4.3 Innovation

The above commentary suggests that many of the recommendations included in the Paris Declaration are drawn from lessons learned in practice. Other articles emphasize that in some instances efficiencies can be promoted through innovation. Article 23, for example, urges ICCTs to consider how technical tools can enhance the expediency of proceedings:

> Art. 23: Develop technical tools tailored to the mandate of each court or tribunal that can facilitate and optimize the conduct of proceedings;

A key achievement in this respect at the STL has been the in-house development of *Legal Workflow* software, which is used by the parties, victims' counsel, registry and chambers in a variety of different contexts including (a) for the disclosure of evidence, (b) the transmission of filings, (c) as a database of the court record, and (d) as a tool for presentation of material in court. But Article 23 has a broader focus than judicial work, recognizing that ICCTs should promote and support the use of tailored technical tools, wherever possible, to help the institutions better achieve their mandate. The ICC has put this ideal into practice in regards to processes used to collect information about victims. Data on victims is now recorded digitally, using mobile applications on hand-held devices. Staff and intermediaries are increasingly encouraged to do away with paper forms because of the added security features and faster transfer possible with electronic data.[68] Future innovations planned by the ICC include digitalizing victim statements so as to enable algorithms to automatically assess application forms for admission.[69] Such technical solutions have arisen in response to acute needs resulting from the size, scale and complexity of crimes prosecuted at the international level. Yet, where technologies can be transferred, they may equally benefit domestic judiciaries too, potentially making tangible contribution's to an institution's legacy. A flow of knowledge between domestic and international judiciaries is to be encouraged to promote innovation and the dissemination of technical tools capable of improving the quality of justice services.

[68]Delagrange (2018), p. 559.
[69]*Ibid.*

Methods of achieving expediency through innovation are not confined to the deployment of new technologies. In this light, as well as technical solutions, the Paris Declaration calls for innovation in relation to the collection of evidence. Article 25 focuses on the possible role for judges in the gathering of evidence:

> Art. 25: Consider the use of innovative measures to allow for the gathering of evidence under judicial supervision at the pre-trial stage, including expanded use of provisions such as the unique investigative opportunities regime

The ICC, for example, has specific provisions applicable when a "unique opportunity" presents itself for taking testimony or a statement from a witness, or for examining, collecting or testing evidence, in circumstances that may not subsequently be available.[70] A similar rule is also found in the rules of procedure and evidence of the STL and the KSC.[71] While the circumstances in which such innovation is appropriate are highly-contextual and will vary case-to-case, judges that possess in-depth knowledge of a case and issues potentially in dispute will be best placed to innovate responsive approaches to the collection of evidence, and deploy the unique investigative opportunity regimes.

5 Good Governance

The final six recommendations in the Paris Declaration are centered on the common theme of "governance". Broadly, this is a topic that refers to the highly-contextual, "inherently normative and programmatic exercise" of regulating judges.[72] It also refers to the use of internal and external administrative and oversight powers by those tasked with ensuring the efficacy of judicial services at international courts and tribunals. Just as the subject matter jurisdiction, applicable criminal law and procedural rules differ greatly between the various international courts and tribunals, so too does the nature and extent of judicial regulation, administrative and oversight structures, and the way in which administrative and oversight powers are exercised. Articles 26 through 31 of the Paris Declaration seek to identify minimum standards capable of adaptation to the context-specific needs of each ICCT to reflect best-practices in this area.

Article 26 calls for the adoption of codes of conduct for Judges:

> Art. 26:
> Adopt codes of conduct for Judges, in line with international standards and drawing inspiration from national practices in this area

[70] Rome Statute, art. 56(1)(a). See ICC RPE, r. 114(1).

[71] KSC RPE, rr. 99-100; STL RPE, r. 89(I).

[72] Devlin and Dodek (2016), pp. 4–5.

To an extent, the past three decades have already witnessed significant progress towards the achievement of this aim. Upon the creation of the ICTY, ICTR, ICC, SCSL, STL, ECCC and IRMCT, no professional standards for judges of international criminal courts and tribunals were prescribed, other than the broad provisions contained in their constituent texts requiring them to be persons of high moral characters, impartiality and integrity.[73] The ICC was the pioneer in this respect, their judges adopting a Code of Judicial Ethics in 2005, a move replicated a few months later at the ECCC.[74] Judges at the IRMCT and ICTY followed suit with codes of professional conduct in 2015 and 2016, respectively, as did the plenary of judges at the STL, also in 2016.[75] The Roster of Judges of the KSC meanwhile, adopted their Code of Judicial Ethics at their first plenary in 2018.[76] These initiatives should be recognized as a serious effort of the international criminal judiciary to align regulation of judicial conduct with practices in common in national judiciaries. But, as Article 26 concedes, there is scope for more to be done in this area.

For example, a contrast between domestic and international codes of conduct is exemplified in the *Bologna Milano Global Judicial Code of Ethics*, which was approved by delegates at the International Conference on Judicial Independence held at the University of Bologna and at Bocconi University of Milano in June 2015. The Global Code distinguishes between standards for national judges and international judges, providing significantly more detail and prescriptive guidance in relation to the conduct of judges falling within the former category than those in the latter. With national practices serving as a muse, it is possible to move away from this two-tiered conceptualization of judicial ethics and shift the international criminal judiciary's focus from implementation of minimum standards, to the development of best-practices.

One such area where international criminal courts and tribunals have lagged behind their domestic counterparts, despite admirable progress in their own right, is in relation to the enforcement of codes of conduct. Article 27 seeks to redress this lacuna:

> Art. 27:
> Establish suitable disciplinary mechanisms in order to ensure that adopted codes of conduct are respected and to guarantee impartiality, the appearance of impartiality and the dignity of the disciplinary process. As far as possible use investigative bodies which are external to the relevant court or tribunal and entrust decision making to a separate panel of the Assembly of the Judges of the court or tribunal. Consideration could be given to establishing an investigative and decision-making body common to all international criminal courts and tribunals

[73] See Hrdličková and Plevin (forthcoming), p. 7.

[74] *Id.* at p. 34.

[75] *Id.* at p. 35.

[76] *Id.* at pp. 35–36.

To some observers, the introspective approach of Article 27 in accentuating this aspect of judicial governance reform might seem counter-intuitive or off-focus. But normalizing this discussion is of itself noteworthy. International judges wield extraordinary powers resulting from their appointment to independent high office. As a result, they are expected to embody the highest standards of professional and moral conduct.[77] Ensuring that judges are held to account when they fall short is essential to guaranteeing that these standards are more than mere rhetoric. Perhaps more importantly, however, providing opportunities for complaints to be raised and resolved in accordance with due processes set in law is an essential part of ensuring that the judiciary's independence strengthens, rather than undermines, the justice process.

Generally speaking, best-practice in disciplinary procedures reflects a three-step process.[78] First is an initial complaints-handling phase where complaints are received, assessed for receivability, and potentially resolved through alternative dispute resolution techniques or dismissed on a summary basis.[79] Second, investigations of complaints allow for underlying facts to be ascertained and for the judge subject to a complaint to respond to the allegations against them.[80] The third and final stage is whereby a decision-making authority adjudicates the dispute to determine whether the factual inquiries demonstrate misconduct and, if so, the appropriate sanction.[81]

Lending some practical guidance as to best-practice, Article 27 expresses a preference for investigations of misconduct complaints by "investigative bodies which are external to the relevant court or tribunal". At the ICCTs, this concept was first implemented in practice by the KSC. Article 18(2) of that court's Code of Judicial Ethics for Judges establishes a disciplinary process whereby complaints not summarily dismissed are referred to a Disciplinary Board.[82] That Board is composed of three members appointed by the KSC President, at least two of whom must be "judges of international or internationalized courts or judges of domestic courts with extensive experience in ethics or in the investigation of professional misconduct", while a third-member "may be a senior appointee of the European Union".[83] A similar model is contained in the Judicial Accountability Mechanism annexed to the Conditions of Service and Compensation of the STL's judges.[84] In broad strokes, these processes replicate practices common to internal investigations at international organizations such those conducted by the Investigations Division of the United Nations Office of Internal Oversight and OLAF, the EU's Anti-Fraud Office.

[77] See Hrdličková and Plevin (forthcoming); Terris et al. (2007).

[78] See e.g. van Zyl Smit (2015); UNOIOS (2015); EU (2013).

[79] See e.g., Burgh House Principles, arts. 17.1–17.2; Mt Scopus Standards, arts 26.1–26.4.

[80] See e.g., Burgh House Principles, art. 17.2; Mt Scopus Standards, art. 26.2.

[81] *Cf.* Burgh House Principles, art. 17.3; Mt Scopus Standards, art. 26.3.

[82] KSCPO (2017), art. 18 (2).

[83] *Ibid.*

[84] STL (2018), annex 2, arts 3–4.

Article 27 also offers guidance as to the decision-making process, suggesting that such authority be entrusted to "a separate panel of the Assembly of the Judges of the court or tribunal". By expressing favour for decision-making processes not vested in the plenary of judges, the Paris Declaration proposes a shift in emphasis from majority rule based decision-making processes,[85] to a view that ensuring effective accountability is a specialized task requiring specialized expertise.

Finally, Article 27 introduces one of the boldest and most important contributions of the Paris Declaration, recommending that "[c]onsideration should be given to establishing a joint investigative and decision-making body common to all international courts and tribunals". The recommendation is ambitious. However, the institutions themselves could not conceivably create such a mechanism without the support of States to facilitate imposition of regulatory frameworks, inter-organizational cooperation, funding, and appointment of requisite personnel needed to allow such a common body to function.

The existence of robust disciplinary frameworks is as significant for the appearance of a transparent and accountable judiciary as it is in order to provide fair, consistent and predictable responses to allegations of misconduct. The empirical evidence in this respect can be seen in domestic jurisdictions. For instance, one study of United States federal courts in the 2018 fiscal year revealed that while more than 959 complaints against judges were terminated by final action, over ninety-seven percent were dismissed without the need to institute formal disciplinary proceedings.[86]

As important as disciplinary mechanisms are, judiciary accountability is a broader concept than discipline alone. It also entails the responsibility judges have to stakeholders for ensuring that judicial work is conducted professionally, and that public resources are managed in a manner consistent with the expectations of the communities they serve. Articles 28 and 29 of the Paris Declaration are best understood in this context and when read together. Article 28, on the one hand encourages the standardized collection of statistical data:

> Art. 28: Encourage standardized collection of statistical data between international criminal courts and tribunals to identify possible common challenges and foster the dissemination of best practices

The reason behind calling for the standardization of data collection is simply that meaningful comparisons require like data to be compared with like data.[87] Considering that many of the challenges to efficiency that ICCTs face are common, even if they manifest differently at each institution, there is strong impetus for administrations to seek to compare common datasets across different institutions. In this light, Article 29 calls for reflection on the identification of suitable performance indicators:

---

[85] See e.g., ICC RPE, r. 29 (1); IRMCT (2018) art. 14.

[86] Administrative Office of the United States Courts (2018).

[87] See Dakolias (1999), pp. 91–96.

Art. 29: Reflect on the identification of indicators aimed at optimizing the work of international criminal courts and tribunals and making it more transparent, in order to benefit from qualitative information capable of enhancing procedures and practices

This call follows a global trend in favour of the development of such indicators for the judiciary, in which institutions such as the World Bank and CEPEJ (European Commission for the Efficiency of Justice) have taken a leading role. It is work that has already begun in practice, even if there is room for greater development and collaboration. For example, in a response to a request made by the Assembly of States Parties of the ICC in 2014, that court undertook a project to develop performance indicators as part of continuing efforts to improve efficiency.[88] The performance indicators developed have since become a feature of the ICC's reporting to the ASP. Similarly, between 2016 and 2017, the STL developed a series of performance indicators for the management of proceedings, divided across three categories:

- *Resource use indicators*: to measure the extent to which resources allocated are appropriately used, identify common interruptions to trial proceedings, and measures of counteracting them;
- *Timeline certainty indicators*: intended to measure the extent to which Chambers achieve goals they establish for themselves, to help determine the accuracy of timeline predictions, and positively impact the management of proceedings as a whole; and
- *Comparative activity indicators*: designed for use between multiple tribunals in order to act as a comparative tool, and to provide an opportunity to open dialogue with other tribunals regarding efficiency and resource-conscious practices.

For performance indicators to be truly effective as a means of improving efficiency in the future, more knowledge is needed about the past performance of ICCTs against such metrics. Some of this data may exist in the records of individual ICCTs, even if not expressly collected for this purpose. Turning that raw data into a useful resource will require collaboration between ICCTs and their governing institutions, a process which will benefit from the support of states and civil society.

Building upon the recommendations in Articles 26 to 29, Article 30 is focused on the question of audits. It is not uncommon for ICCTs to conduct internal audits and engage external auditors to examine efficiencies and inefficiencies, or even to have audit teams assigned to them by their governance institutions.[89] However, in the highly-context specific work of ICCTs, standard auditing procedures do not necessarily provide a full picture of performance, risk and potential for making improvement. In this vein, the Paris Declaration recognizes the opportunity to enhance and expand upon existing audit practices:

---

[88] See ICC (2017), p. 2.

[89] See e.g., UNOIOS (2016).

Art. 30: Ensure that audit teams are staffed with professionals who possess in-depth knowledge and expertise relating to the operation of the organs of international courts and tribunals and their work, and reflect upon the creation of a common international audit body;

By incorporating, for example, judicial expertise in the audit of chambers, or investigative and prosecutorial expertise into audits of the prosecution, and exploring practices against existing knowledge about how efficiencies can be achieved, auditing teams can be better placed to independently communicate recommendations as to how evaluate the quality and effectiveness of the work these ICCTs perform.[90] The idea of expert audits is not new. An expert group was convened to review the effective operation and functioning of the ICTY in 1999; Cassese thoroughly reviewed the practices of the SCSL in 2006, and in 2014 a group of independent experts recommended to the States Parties of the ICC that they "should ensure that, in the future, they receive regular expert evaluation of the performance of the Court and that they do not depend solely on information provided by the report to measure its performance."[91]

The final recommendation in the Paris Declaration relates to continuing legal education. In many domestic jurisdictions, continuing professional development for lawyers is highly encouraged if not a mandatory condition of their licenses to practice law. While the systems of training judges vary from country to country, formalized and regular judicial training, through judicial training institutions, is also common. For example, since its first issue in 2013, the Journal of the International Organization for Judicial Training has featured articles addressing practices in Australia, Austria, Canada, China, Denmark, England & Wales, Finland, France, Germany, Israel, Italy, Kosovo, Mexico, Nepal, Nigeria, the Netherlands, Mongolia, Pakistan, Papua New Guinea, the Philippines, Romania, Singapore, Spain, and Trinidad & Tobago. Various models of providing training are used in different national systems. For example, in Cyprus, it is the Supreme Court that is responsible for providing training.[92] In Switzerland, the training is provided by private institutions or universities with support of a foundation established for that purpose.[93] Luxembourg meanwhile, having a small number of judges, has made agreement for training to be provided by institutions in neighboring States, taking part in activities coordinated by the French National School for the Judiciary (ENM) and the Academy of European Law (ERA) in Trier, Germany.[94] It is this last model that the Paris Declaration proposes as suitable for adoption at ICCTs:

---

[90]See Mettraux et al. (2014), p. 7.

[91]*Ibid.*

[92]CEPEJ (2018), p. 151.

[93]*Ibid.*

[94]*Ibid.*

Art. 31: Promote the continuous education of Judges and Legal Officers, including through partnerships with national academies for the training of Judges;

Training and education is not uncommon at ICCTs, through retreats, workshops, and professional conferences. But to date, these efforts are frequently *ad hoc*, decentralized, and are not necessarily specifically focused on enhancing the effectiveness, efficiency or quality of judicial work. Collaboration with national institutions provides an opportunity for established service providers, with specialized expertise in the area of judicial training to fill a lacuna that presently exists. For the ICCTs, this represents a method of strengthening judicial training, without having to create specialized infrastructure. It also creates the possibility to pool resources, to maximize the opportunities for access to judicial training at ICCTs within their limited budgets.

6 Conclusion

Better quality and more effective criminal justice institutions can be built on the back of improvements to efficiency. As much as the Paris Declaration provides a roadmap for what that reform might look like, it is also an acknowledgement of the significant steps yet to be taken to create a sustainable international criminal justice sector.

The thirty-one recommendations of the Paris Declaration were created by experts with insights into the workings of various criminal courts and tribunals, and based upon their experiences and observations working within international criminal justice. The Paris Declaration is distinctive for its procedural and technical focus. Instead of attempting to wrestle with the consequences of the complex, overlapping and ambiguous expectations sometimes placed on international criminal justice as a whole, the Paris Declaration looks to the core expectations of the judiciary in achieving efficient criminal justice. It does so without attempting to determine, shape or subvert progress broader objectives of international criminal justice, or the specific mandates of individual ICCTs. In so doing, this approach to reform views procedural efficiency as incidental to promoting the overarching goals rather than inherently constrained within them.[95]

The Paris Declaration serves to allow ICCTs to evaluate their progress against benchmarks of efficiency centered on functionality and quality of judicial processes, avoiding the potential distraction of incidental by-products of constantly fluctuating and ambiguous goals of international criminal justice. Each of the thirty-one recommendations are the product of lessons learned from the successes of and challenges faced by the various ICCTs. Created from real-world experience, the recommendations are well-suited to deliver substantial and tangible impact in the future of

[95] Vasiliev (2014).

international criminal justice. But they also serve as a starting point. Further discussion on the Paris Declaration's recommendations and the promotion of their implementation represents but one pathway for ICCTs to pursue of more efficient criminal procedures.

As Damaska has suggested, ICCTs are not fitting for comparison with Atlas. They lack the strength to shoulder all the demands and challenges facing international criminal justice. Perhaps understanding that ICCTs need not be condemned, like Atlas, to perpetually carry the crushing weight of the entire celestial heavens for all eternity, should be some reprieve. The Paris Declaration shows that the challenge for ICCTs in responding to critiques of efficiency need not be so vast. Focus on its recommendations offers a prospect of implementing concrete reform, largely within existing frameworks, to palpably contribute to improved efficiency and in turn, sustainability, of ICCTs and international criminal justice as a whole. With the methods the Paris Declaration proposes, ICCTs can leave the heavy lifting to Atlas and focus on striving for sustainability and efficiency instead.

Acknowledgements and Disclaimer The authors extend their sincere gratitude to Judge Nicolas Guillou for his comments and contributions to earlier iterations of this paper. Any errors or inaccuracies remain those of the authors alone. The authors held or hold positions in national judicial systems, the Special Tribunal for Lebanon (STL) and the International Criminal Tribunal for the former Yugoslavia (ICTY). The opinions, views, conclusions and recommendations contained in this Chapter are expressed by the authors in their private capacity and do not necessarily reflect those of any respective national judiciaries, the STL, or ICTY, nor can be attributed to those entities and institutions, nor the United Nations in general.

References

Journal Articles

Ambos K (2012) The first judgement of the international criminal court (Prosecutor v. Lubanga). Int Crim Law Rev 12(2):115–153

Barria L, Roper S (2005) Providing justice and reconciliation: the criminal tribunals for Sierra Leone and Cambodia. Hum Rights Rev 7(1):5–26

Bourgon S (2004) Procedural problems hindering expeditious and fair justice. J Int Crim Justice 2 (2):526–532

Brinkley J (2008) Justice squandered: Cambodia's Khmer Rouge Tribunal. World Aff 176 (3):41–48

Caianiello M (2011) Law of evidence at the international criminal court: blending accusatorial and inquisitorial models. N C J Int Law Commer Regul 36(2):287–318

Carlson R (1967) Cross-examination of the accused. Cornell Law Rev 52(5):705–722

Ciorciari J, Heinde A (2013) Experiments in international criminal justice: lessons from the Khmer Rouge Tribunal. Mich J Int Crim Law 35(2):369–442

Dakolias M (1999) Court performance around the world: a comparative perspective. Yale Hum Rights Dev J 2(1):87–142

Damaska M (2008) What is the point of international criminal justice? Chic Kent Law Rev 83 (1):329–365
Danner AM, Martinez JS (2005) Guilty associations: joint criminal enterprise, command responsibility, and the development of international criminal law. Calif Law Rev 93(1):75–170
Dastugue M (2015) The faults in fair trials: an evaluation of Regulation 55 at the international criminal court. Vand J Transnatl Law 48(1):273–306
Delagrange M (2018) The path towards greater efficiency and effectiveness in the victim application process of the international criminal court. Int Crim Law Rev 18(3):540–562
de Gurmendi SF (2018) Judges: selection, competence and collegiality. AJIL Unbound 112:163–167
deGuzman M (2012) Choosing to prosecute: expressive selection at the international criminal court. Mich J Int Law 33:265–320
Guariglia F (2018) 'Admission' v. 'Submission' of evidence at the international criminal court. J Int Crim Justice 16(2):315–340
Higgins G (2007) Fair and expeditious pre-trial proceedings: the future of international criminal trials. J Int Crim Justice 5(2):394–401
Hignonnet E (2005) Restructuring hybrid courts: local empowerment and national criminal justice reform. Ariz J Int Comp Law 23(2):347–436
Keenan P (2016) The problem of purpose in international criminal law. Mich J Int 37(3):421–474
Kendall S (2011) Donor's justice: recasting international criminal accountability. Leiden J Int Law 24(3):585–606
McLaughlin C (2007) The *sui generis* trial proceedings of the international criminal court. Law Pract Int Courts Tribs 6(2):343–354
Mundis D (2001) The election of Ad Litem Judges and other recent developments at international criminal tribunals. Leiden J Int Law 14(4):851–866
Scheffer D (2008) A review of the experience of the pre-trial and appeal chambers of the international criminal court regarding the disclosure of evidence. Leiden J Int Law 21 (1):151–163
Schwartz L (1987) Justice, expediency and beauty. Univ Pa Law Rev 136(1):141–182
Shany Y (2012) Assessing the effectiveness of international courts: a goal-based approach. Am J Int Law 106(2):225–270
Sloan R (2007) The expressive capacity of international punishment: the limits of the national law analogy and the potential of international criminal law. Stan J Int Law 43(1):35–95
Sperfeldt C (2013) From the margins of internationalized criminal justice: lessons learned at the extraordinary chambers in the Courts of Cambodia. J Int Crim Justice 11(5):1111–1138
Stahn C (2012) Between faith and facts: by what standards should we assess international criminal justice. Leiden J Int Crim Law 25(2):251–282
Tidwell A, Lerche C (2004) Globalization and conflict resolution. J Int Peace Stud 9(1):47–59
Zacklin R (2004) The failings of ad hoc international tribunals. J Int Crim Justice 2(2):541–545

Books and Book Chapters

Books

Hafetz J (2018) Punishing atrocities through a fair trial. Cambridge University Press, Cambridge
Sokolić I (2018) International courts and mass atrocity: narratives of war and justice in Croatia. Palgrave Macmillan, Basingstoke
Terris D et al (2007) The international judge: an introduction to the men and women who decide the word's cases. Brandies University Press, Waltham
Tyler T (1990) Why people obey the law. Yale University Press, New Haven

Chapters in Books

Devlin R, Dodek A (2016) Regulating judges: challenges, controversies and choices. In: Devlin R, Dodek A (eds) Regulating judges: beyond independence and accountability. Edward Elgar, Cheltenham, pp 1–34

Heller KJ (2015) A stick to hit the accused with: the legal recharacterization of facts under Regulation 55. In: Stahn C (ed) The law and practice of the international criminal court. Oxford University Press, Oxford, pp 981–1006

Hrldičková I, Plevin AM (forthcoming) Judicial independence and accountability at international criminal courts and tribunals. In: Bergsmo M (ed) Integrity in international justice, an anthology of papers from the conference, Integrity in International Justice, The Hague, 1–2 December 2018. CILRAP and the International Nuremberg Principles Academy. (A copy of this paper is on file with the authors)

Jacobs D (2013) A shifting scale of power: who is in charge of the charges at the international criminal court. In: Schabas W, McDermott Y, Hayes N (eds) The Ashgate research companion to international criminal law: critical perspectives. Routledge, Abingdon, ch. 9

Online Publications

Administrative Office of the United States Courts (2018) Complaints Against Judges – Judicial Business Federal Judiciary. Judicial Branch of the United States Government. Available via United States Courts. https://www.uscourts.gov/statistics-reports/complaints-against-judges-judicial-business-2018

ICC (2018) Preliminary Examinations (5 Dec 2018). Available Via ICC-CPI. https://www.icc-cpi.int/itemsDocuments/181205-rep-otp-PE-ENG.pdf

News Articles

Griffiths, 'UN calls for genocide tribunal over Rohingya crisis', CNN (18 Sep 2018), https://edition.cnn.com/2018/09/18/asia/myanmar-united-nations-report-intl/index.html

'UNITAD Submits Biannual Report to the UN Security Council; Reports Substantial Progress', UN Iraq (23 May 2019), http://www.uniraq.org/index.php?option=com_k2&view=item&id=11113:unitad-submits-biannual-report-to-the-un-security-council-reports-substantial-progress&Itemid=605&lang=en

Warrell, 'Sweden Proposes international tribunal to try Isis [sic] fighters, Financial Times (19 May 2019), https://www.ft.com/content/9086250e-7802-11e9-bbad-7c18c0ea0201

Reports, etc.

Cassese A (2006) Report on the Special Court for Sierra Leone (12 Dec 2006)

CEPEJ (2018) Report, European Judicial Systems: Efficiency and Equality of Justice, (CEPEJ Studies No. 26)

ICC (2017) Report, Third Court's Report on the Development of Performance Indicators for the International Criminal Court (15 Nov 2017)

ICTY (2009) ICTY Manual on Developed Practices. UNICRI, Turin. http://www.icty.org/x/file/About/Reports%20and%20Publications/ICTY_Manual_on_Developed_Practices.pdf

Mettraux G, Fisher SA, Groom D et al (2014) Report, Expert Initiative on Promoting Effectiveness at the International Criminal Court. https://www.icc-cpi.int/itemsDocuments/171115-Third-Report-performance-indicators-ENG.pdf

Ostrom BJ, Hanson A (1999) Efficiency, Timeliness, and Quality: A New Perspective from Nine State Criminal Courts, National Institute of Justice and the State Justice Institute. https://www.ncjrs.gov/pdffiles1/nij/178403-1.pdf

Van Zyl Smit J (2015) The Appointment, Tenure and Removal of Judges under Commonwealth Principles: A Compendium of Analysis and Best Practice, Report of Research undertaken by Bingham Centre for the Rule of Law

UN Documents

HRC (2018) Situation of human rights of Rohingya Muslims and other minorities in Myanmar (3 Oct 2018). UN Doc. A/HRC/RES/39/2

UNGA (2016) International, Impartial and Independent Mechanism to Assist in the Investigation and Prosecution of Persons Responsible for the Most Serious Crimes under International Law Committed in the Syrian Arab Republic since March 2011 (21 Dec 2016). UN Doc. A/RES/71/248)

UNOIOS (2016) Evaluation of the methods and work of the International Tribunal for the former Yugoslavia (12 May 2016). UN Doc. A/70/837-S/2016/441, 12 May 2016

UNOIOS (2015) Investigations Manual, Office of Internal, Oversight Investigations Division (Jan 2015)

Other International Documents

Council of Europe (1987) Recommendation No. R (87) 18 of the Committee of Ministers to Member States Concerning the Simplification of Criminal Justice. Adopted by the Committee of Ministers (17 September 1987)

EU (2013) Guidelines on Investigations Procedures for OLAF Staff (1 Oct 2013). Ref: Ares (2013) 3077837

KSCPO (2017) Code of Judicial Ethics for Judges Appointed to the Roster of International Judges of the Kosovo Specialist Chambers (14 Mar 2017). KSC-BD-01/COR2/1

ICC (2019) Chambers Practice Manual (29 Nov 2019)

International Law Association (2004) Burgh House Principles on the Independence of the International Judiciary. International Law Association Conference, Berlin (Aug 2004)

IRMCT (2018) Code of Professional Conduct for the Judges of the Mechanism (9 April 2018). MICT/14/Rev.1

Judicial Group on Strengthening Judicial Integrity (2008) Mt Scopus Standards on the Independence of Judges, as amended (10 Mar 2008)

Representatives of International Courts and Tribunals (2017) Paris Declaration on the Effectiveness of International Criminal Justice

STL (2018) Conditions of Service and Compensation of Judges of the Special Tribunal for Lebanon, as amended

Dissertations

Vasiliev SV (2014) International criminal trials: a normative theory. Dissertation, Amsterdam Center for International Law

Speeches

Murdoch (2018) UK Statement to ICC Assembly of States Parties 17th Session (5 Dec 2018), https://www.gov.uk/government/speeches/uk-statement-to-icc-assembly-of-states-parties-17th-session

Cases

ECtHR, *Adiletta and Others v. Italy*, Judgment (No. 20/1990/211/271-273), 24 January 1991

ICC, *Prosecutor v. Gbagbo*, Decision Adjourning the Hearing on the Confirmation of Charges Pursuant to Article 61(7)(c)(i) of the Rome State (Case No. ICC-02/11-01/11), 3 June 2013

ICC, *Prosecutor v. Gbagbo and Blé Goudé*, Reasons for Oral Decision of 15 January 2019 on the *Requête de la Défense de Laurent Gbagbo afin qu'un jugement d'acquittement portant sur toutes les charges soit prononcé en faveur de Laurent Gbagbo et que sa mise en liberté immédiate soit ordonnée* (Case No. ICC-02/11-01/15-12630), 16 July 2019, Reasons of Judge Geoffrey Henderson

ICC, *Prosecutor v. Katanga*, Decision on the Implementation of Regulation 55 of the Regulations of the Court and Severing the Charges Against Accused Persons (Case No. ICC-01/04-01/07), 21 November 2012, Dissenting Opinion of Judge Van den Wyngaert

ICC, *Prosecutor v. Ruto and Sang*, Decision on the Defence Applications for Judgements of Acquittal, Trial Chamber V(A) (Case No. ICC-01/09-01/11), 5 April 2016, Reasons of Judge Fremr, para.144; *Id.*, Reasons of Judge Eboe-Osuji

STL, Interlocutory Decision on the Applicable Law: Criminal Association and Review of the Indictment (Case No. 17-07-I/AC/R176*bis*), 18 October 2017

STL, *Prosecutor v. Ayyash et al.*, Interlocutory Decision on the Applicable Law: Terrorism, Conspiracy, Homicide, Perpetration, Cumulative Charging (Case No. STL-11-01/I/AC/R176*bis*), 16 February 2011

Ivana Hrdličková President and Appellate Judge of the Special Tribunal for Lebanon, Leidschendam, The Netherlands.

Adrian Plevin Legal Officer, Special Tribunal for Lebanon, Leidschendam, The Netherlands.

Amanda Fang J.D. Candidate, New York University, United States of America; Former NYU Fellow, Special Tribunal for Lebanon, Leidschendam, The Netherlands.

The International Criminal Court on the Rohingyas' Situation and the Early Scholarly Echo of the Decision

Péter Kovács

Contents

It is often said that a judicial decision should speak for itself and judges participating in the decision making should refrain from explaining it *ex post facto*.

While recognizing the merits of this rule, on the kind proposal of the editor in chief of the Nigerian Yearbook of International Law, I accepted to prepare a short presentation on the scholarly remarks, comments and analysis that I have collected since the date of issuing the decision.

1 The Decision[1]

The problem underlying the decision is certainly known to the reader: recently more than 700,000 people belonging to the musulman religion have left Myanmar and entered Bangladesh. They are alleged victims of different crimes suffered in Myanmar which however—contrary to Bangladesh—is not a state party to the Rome Statute. As we can see on the home page of the International Criminal Court "[o]n

The article was made in personal capacity, the thoughts expressed hereby cannot be attributed to the International Criminal Court.

[1]Decision on the "Prosecution's Request for a Ruling on Jurisdiction under Article 19-(3) of the Statute", ICC-RoC46(3)-01/18-37 06-09-2018, https://www.icc-cpi.int/CourtRecords/CR2018_04203.PDF (later in this article: "ICC PTC Rohingya decision").

P. Kovács (✉)
International Criminal Court, The Hague, The Netherlands
e-mail: peter.kovacs@icc-cpi.int

C. Eboe-Osuji et al. (eds.), *Nigerian Yearbook of International Law 2018/2019*,
Nigerian Yearbook of International Law 2018/2019,
https://doi.org/10.1007/978-3-030-69594-1_10

9 April 2018, the Office of the Prosecutor ("OTP" or "Office") of the ICC filed a Request for a Ruling on Jurisdiction under Article 19(3) of the Statute ("Prosecutor's Request") seeking a ruling on the question whether the Court may exercise jurisdiction pursuant to article 12(2)(a) of the Statute over the alleged deportation of members of the Rohingya people from Myanmar to Bangladesh."[2]

The Pre-Trial Chamber I (by majority, judge Brichambaut partially dissenting) considered that the Prosecutor's Request should be answered *in merito* even if "article 19(3)[3] of the Statute is quite controversial based on the different readings of the Court's statutory documents and the literature interpreting this provision."[4]

"The Chamber observes that, based on the material available in the record, the jurisdiction of the Court is clearly subject to dispute with Myanmar. According to article 119(1) of the Statute, "[a]ny dispute concerning the judicial functions of the Court shall be settled by the decision of the Court". This provision has been interpreted as including questions related to the Court's jurisdiction. It follows that the Chamber is empowered to rule on the question of jurisdiction set out in the Request in accordance with article 119(1) of the Statute. Consequently, the Chamber does not see the need to enter a definite ruling on whether article 19(3) of the Statute is applicable at this stage of the proceedings."[5] The majority referred mainly to complementary impact of the principle of *Kompetenz-Kompetenz*[6] and it evoked article 119(1)[7] in conjunction with some public statements of the Myanmarian government.

Having studied the impact and the applicability of some exceptions from the rule above of the relative effects of treaties (*pacta tertiis nec nocent, nec pro sunt*) as recognized in the 1969 Vienna Convention on the law of treaties and general international law, and then some questions linked with the law and practice of rule of law states concerning the *ne bis in idem rule* (double jeopardy) and through the presentation of positions expressed by states participating at the Rome Diplomatic

[2]https://www.icc-cpi.int/rohingya-myanmar.

[3]Article 19(3) "The Prosecutor may seek a ruling from the Court regarding a question of jurisdiction or admissibility. In proceedings with respect to jurisdiction or admissibility, those who have referred the situation under article 13, as well as victims, may also submit observations to the Court."

[4]ICC PTC Rohingya decision § 27.

The referred scholarly controversial interpretation was linked to the importance to attribute to the title of Article 19 "Challenges to the jurisdiction of the Court or the admissibility of a case". If the second sentence of § 1 of this article seems to recognize a *proprio motu* action. ("The Court shall satisfy itself that it has jurisdiction in any case brought before it. The Court may, on its own motion, determine the admissibility of a case in accordance with article 17.") should it be considered that § 3 is forcibly linked to a "challenge"?

[5]ICC PTC Rohingya decision § 28.

[6]ICC PTC Rohingya decision §§ 30–33.

[7]Article 119 Settlement of disputes

1. Any dispute concerning the judicial functions of the Court shall be settled by the decision of the Court.

conference but who nevertheless did not become later states parties as well as some statements reflecting their effective cooperation in one or other given case and the position of main doctrinal schools and eminent scholars, the complex relationship of the ICC with the United Nations as well as the adaptability of ICJ *dictum* pronounced in the Bernadotte case,[8] the Chamber concluded that the ICC enjoys objective legal personality.

"In the light of the foregoing, it is the view of the Chamber that more than 120 States, representing the vast majority of the members of the international community, had the power, in conformity with international law, to bring into being an entity called the "International Criminal Court", possessing objective international personality, and not merely personality recognized by them alone, together with the capacity to act against impunity for the most serious crimes of concern to the international community as a whole and which is complementary to national criminal jurisdictions. Thus, the existence of the ICC is an objective fact. In other words, it is a legal-judicial-institutional entity which has engaged and cooperated not only with States Parties, but with a large number of States not Party to the Statute as well, whether signatories or not."[9] "Having said that, the objective legal personality of the Court does not imply either automatic or unconditional *erga omnes* jurisdiction. The conditions for the exercise of the Court's jurisdiction are set out, first and foremost, in articles 11, 12, 13, 14 and 15 of the Statute."[10]

Turning back to the Prosecutor's question the Chamber expressed its "view that acts of deportation initiated in a State not Party to the Statute (through expulsion or other coercive acts) and completed in a State Party to the Statute (by virtue of victims crossing the border to a State) fall within the parameters of article 12(2)(a) of the Statute. It follows that, in the circumstances identified in the Request, the Court has jurisdiction over the alleged deportation of members of the Rohingya people from Myanmar to Bangladesh, provided that such allegations are established to the required threshold. This conclusion is without prejudice to subsequent findings on jurisdiction at a later stage of the proceedings."[11]

Following this approach, the Chamber considered "it appropriate to emphasise that the rationale of its determination as to the Court's jurisdiction in relation to the crime of deportation may apply to other crimes within the jurisdiction of the Court as well. If it were established that at least an element of another crime within the jurisdiction of the Court or part of such a crime is committed on the territory of a State Party, the Court might assert jurisdiction pursuant to article 12(2)(a) of the Statute."[12]

---

[8]ICJ, Reparation for injuries suffered in the service of the United Nations, Advisory Opinion, [1949] ICJ Rep. 174, p. 185.

[9]ICC PTC Rohingya decision § 48.

[10]ICC PTC Rohingya decision § 49.

[11]ICC PTC Rohingya decision § 73.

[12]ICC PTC Rohingya decision § 74.

The Chamber gave as an example the persecution[13] [article 7(1)(h)] and the so called other inhuman acts[14] [article 7(1)(k)] thereto.

It pointed out that "(. . .) the Prosecutor is mandated to respect the internationally recognized human rights of victims with regard to the conduct and result of her preliminary examination, especially the rights of victims to know the truth, to have access to justice and to request reparations, as already established in the jurisprudence of this Court."[15]

What has happened since then? As one can see on the homepage of the ICC, "[o]n 18 September 2018, the Prosecutor announced the opening of a preliminary examination concerning the alleged deportation of the Rohingya people from Myanmar to Bangladesh. The Office received a number of Article 15 communications and reports concerning the alleged crimes. The preliminary examination focusses over the alleged deportation of the Rohingya people from Myanmar to Bangladesh, as well as potentially other crimes under article 7 of the Rome Statute."[16] Some basic information for potential victims has also been appended on that site.[17]

2 The Echo of the Decision

Far from being exhaustive and their selection being naturally dependent on a number of factors, the scholarly articles brought to my attention can be found online and mostly on legal blogs. They were written by Dov Jacobs,[18] Bennedikt Pirker and

---

[13]"Therefore, if it were established to the applicable threshold that members of the Rohingya people were deported from Myanmar to Bangladesh on any of the grounds enumerated in article 7(1)(h) of the Statute, the Court might also have jurisdiction pursuant to article 12(2)(a) of the Statute over the crime against humanity of persecution, considering that an element or part of this crime (i.e. the cross-border transfer) takes place on the territory of a State Party." ICC PTC Rohingya decision § 76.

[14]"Second, article 7(1)(k) of the Statute stipulates that "[o]ther inhumane acts of a similar character intentionally causing great suffering, or serious injury to body or to mental or physical health", amount to a crime against humanity within the jurisdiction of the Court. The Chamber notes that, following their deportation, members of the Rohingya people allegedly live in appalling conditions in Bangladesh and that the authorities of Myanmar supposedly impede their return to Myanmar." ICC Rohingya decision § 77.

[15]ICC PTC Rohingya decision § 88.

[16]https://www.icc-cpi.int/rohingya-myanmar.

[17]Information for communities affected by the alleged deportation of the Rohingya People from Myanmar to Bangladesh, https://www.icc-cpi.int/rohingya-myanmar.

[18]Dov Jacobs: ICC PTC issues advisory opinion (yes, yes) on ICC jurisdiction over Rohingya deportation, https://dovjacobs.com/2018/09/06/icc-ptc-issues-advisory-opinion-yes-yes-on-icc-jurisdiction-over-rohingya-deportation/.

Jennifer Smolka,[19] Michael A. Becker,[20] Michail G. Karnavas,[21] Raghav Bhargava,[22] Rasmi Raman,[23] James Hendry,[24] Michael Plachta,[25] Kevin Jon Heller,[26] Viren Mascarenhas, Brian Jacobi, Claire O'Connell, and Isabel San Martin.[27] The Harris Institute of the Washington University gave a very comprehensive overview,[28] and recently the American Journal of International Law published a

---

[19]Bennedikt Pirker and Jennifer Smolka: The ICC Pre-Trial Chamber's Reading of "or" in the Myanmar Jurisdiction Ruling: On the Relevance of Linguistics to Interpretation, https://www.ejiltalk.org/the-icc-pre-trial-chambers-reading-of-or-in-the-myanmar-jurisdiction-ruling-on-the-relevance-of-linguistics-to-interpretation/.

[20]Michael A. Becker: The Situation of the Rohingya: Is there a role for the International Court of Justice? https://www.ejiltalk.org/the-situation-of-the-rohingya-is-there-a-role-for-the-international-court-of-justice/.

[21]Michael G. Karnavas: The ICC's Ruling on the OTP's Rohingya Request over Jurisdiction: well-reasoned or a judicial overreach? http://michaelgkarnavas.net/blog/2018/09/10/icc-rohingya-jurisdiction/; Revisiting the ICC's Ruling on the OTP's Rohingya Request over Jurisdiction: a more critical look. Part 1 – The Majority's Decision, http://michaelgkarnavas.net/blog/2018/10/09/icc-rohingya-ruling-pt1/; Revisiting the ICC's Ruling on the OTP's Rohingya Request over Jurisdiction: a more critical look. Part 2 – The Dissent. http://michaelgkarnavas.net/blog/2018/10/11/icc-rohingya-ruling-pt2/.

[22]Raghav Bhargava: The Cost of Preventing Impunity: The ICC's Misplaced Understanding of the Rome Statute http://cilj.co.uk/2018/11/14/the-cost-of-preventing-impunity-the-iccs-misplaced-understanding-of-the-rome-statute/.

[23]Rashmi Raman: Where do the Rohingya go? http://www.jgls.edu.in/article/where-do-rohingya-go.

[24]James Hendry: Analysis: The International Criminal Court Decides that It Has Jurisdiction Over the Alleged Deportation of the Rohingya, http://www.kirschinstitute.ca/analysis-international-criminal-court-decides-jurisdiction-alleged-deportation-rohingya/.

[25]Michael Plachta: International Criminal Court Confirms Its Jurisdiction over Crimes Against the Rohingya, https://ielrblog.com/index.php/article/international-criminal-court-confirms-its-jurisdiction-over-crimes-against-the-rohingya/.

[26]Kevin Jon Heller: The ICC Has Jurisdiction over One Form of Genocide in the Rohingya Situation, http://opiniojuris.org/2018/09/07/33644/.

[27]Viren Mascarenhas, Brian Jacobi, Claire O'Connell, and Isabel San Martin: The Rohingyas' Plight: What Options Under International Law? What role can the ICC and ICJ play in bringing justice for the Rohingyas' suffering? https://thediplomat.com/2019/01/the-plight-of-the-rohingya-what-options-under-international-law/.

[28]Carolina Battistella and Jade Tyson: Part 1: Pre-Trial Chamber Grant Jurisdiction over Rohingya Deportation: One Step Closer to Accountability for these Atrocities http://sites.law.wustl.edu/WashULaw/harris-lexlata/part-1-pre-trial-chamber-grant-jurisdiction-over-rohingya-deportation-one-step-closer-to-accountability-for-these-atrocities/.

Claudia Magloire and Derek Van Becelaere: Part 2: Did the ICC Get it Right? A Look at the Decision to Establish ICC Jurisdiction in Myanmar. http://sites.law.wustl.edu/WashULaw/harris-lexlata/part-2-did-the-icc-get-it-right-a-look-at-the-decision-to-establish-icc-jurisdiction-in-myanmar/.

Matteo Colorio and Feyga Saksonov: Part 3: Justice for the Rohingya: Issues and Possible Solutions. http://sites.law.wustl.edu/WashULaw/harris-lexlata/part-3-justice-for-the-rohingya-issues-and-possible-solutions/.

Josh Handelman and Christian Rose: Part 4: Claiming Jurisdiction: Comparing the ICC Pre-Trial Chamber Decision Regarding Myanmar with Other Approaches. http://sites.law.wustl.edu/

rather lengthy commentary prepared by Michail Vagias.[29] Moreover, a short comment and a genuine scholarly article were also devoted to the analysis in Spanish by Nicolás Carillo Santarelli.[30]

I am satisfied with the positive comments and studied with great interest the remarks on deficiencies, imprecisions, missing or allegedly inappropriate legal arguments. Hereby, I try to make a short summary of these later remarks[31] but I refrain from reacting to them for two reasons: (1) As mentioned *supra*, an adopted judicial decision should speak for itself. (2) As the given situation may come back on the table, caution is legitimate.

Jacobs, Karnavas and Bhargava criticise the delivery of the decision and they find judge Brichambaut's partial dissent more convincing. According to their position, the decision as a *quasi* advisory opinion lacks a real statutory background and they consider that the OTP's request should have been rejected. They also dispute the main points of the decision and they contest the parallel with the Bernadotte-approach.

Pirker and Smolka put under scrutiny the linguistic meaning of the "*or*" (i.e. in the wording of article 7(1)(d) on "deportation or transfer") and conclude that in the ordinary meaning, it should have been understood in the given context rather as "*and*". Consequently, they do not find appropriate the conclusions of the Chamber on the existence of jurisdiction.

Apparently, several authors consider that the real issue is the question of the alleged genocide which was not mentioned in the Prosecutor's request and the Chamber did not treat it either.

Becker considers that genocide is the real question and follows a totally different path when as a result of his analysis of the ICC decision he concludes that the case should rather be brought before the International Court of Justice. Heller opines however that the Chamber's approach vis-à-vis the other crimes could also help in the appreciation of genocide.

WashULaw/harris-lexlata/part-4-claiming-jurisdiction-comparing-the-icc-pre-trial-chamber-decision-regarding-myanmar-with-other-approaches/.

[29] Vagias (2019), pp. 368–375.

[30] Nicolás Carillo Santarelli: SCP de la CPI toma decisión sobre jurisdicción, diciendo que la deportación y el traslado forzoso de población son delitos separados, y que tiene jurisdicción frente a casos sobre conductas cometidas, al menos en parte, en Estados parte al Estatuto, https://jusorbis.wordpress.com/author/nicolascs/;

La decisión "humanizadora" de la Sala de Cuestiones Preliminares de la Corte Penal Internacional sobre competencia y jurisdicción frente a algunos crímenes cometidos de forma transnacional: : el caso de los Rohingya expulsados hacia Bangladesh, Revista electrónica de estudios internacionales (REEI), ISSN-e 1697-5197, N°. 36, 2018, http://www.reei.org/index.php/revista/num36/notas/decision-humanizadora-sala-cuestiones-preliminares-corte-penal-internacional-sobre-competencia-jurisdiccion-frente-algunos-crimenes-cometidos-forma-transnacional-caso-rohingya-expulsados-hacia-bangladesh.

[31] Because of the particular nature of the legal blogs and on-line papers, I will not refer to respective page numbers.

Mascarenhas, Jacobi, O'Connell and San Martin emphasize that the OTP's request and the Chamber's reply cannot be separated from the repeated failures of the Security Council to tackle with the issue and to benefit from its rights to refer the situation before the ICC according to article 13(b) of the Rome Statute. They are of the view that the different aspects of the situation should be examined by the ICC, ICJ and the UN Human Rights Council, each of them according to their respective mandate.

Hendry concluded his reasoned analysis by stating that "[t]he Pre-Trial Chamber took a brave step to move justice in the Rohingya situation forward. The Chamber did what it thought necessary to advance the course of justice quickly, coming to a progressive interpretation of the Rome Statute. Its decision will allow the matter to proceed. The dissenting judge articulated the traditional judicial reasons about the dangers of advisory opinions and clearly expressed his preference for careful construction of a concrete case to properly ground a judicial decision. His reasons would have resulted in the affirming of traditional procedure, but set back the clock for the Prosecutor's office, the inevitable price for the Prosecutor's taking a chance on getting an answer to her Request."

Within the comprehensive analysis of the Harris Institute, Battistella and Tyson present the decision concerning which Magloire and Becelaere write that "the Pre-Trial Chamber appears to be finding the proper balance between respecting Myanmar's sovereignty and seeking a just solution to the crisis." Handelman and Rose back also the decision by pointing out the well known practice of extraterritorial criminal jurisdiction of a huge number of states. For the continuation, Colorio and Saksonov advocate for a more resolute action on behalf of states parties (namely Bangladesh) and of states of the United Nations and especially in the Security Council.

This also seems to be Plachta's concern, who, having presented the main parts of the decision apparently without any critic, adds that "[i]t remains to be seen whether the present decision delivered by the Pre-Trial Chamber I and followed by the opening of investigation by the ICC Prosecutor will be a real step towards achieving justice for the Rohingya, or whether these actions only create an illusion of an outcome which is hard to deliver."

Santarelli writes that a "humanizing decision" was adopted and he qualifies this fact as extremely positive. Vagias is of a similar opinion.[32] While sharing some concerns of the partial dissent on the premature character of the request and the decision, he highlights that "the Court could have chosen to shield itself from accusations of encroachment upon state sovereignty by postponing or avoiding a decision altogether. Instead, it tackled the issue head-on and quickly. In a rare constructive alignment of facts, prosecutorial initiative, and judicial courage, the

[32] "This ruling stands as a rare, yet significant reaffirmation that human rights inform the entire ICC system and the function of all its organs." Vagias: *op. cit* p. 374.

Court dared go with this advisory opinion—or perhaps because of it—where no binding judgment has gone before it."[33]

"Regardless of the merit of these critiques, however, this ruling has many positive aspects that make it stand out in the Court's jurisprudence. To begin with, even if only advisory, this decision is not doomed to collect dust in the Court's bookshelves. It has already had a significant impact on the plight of the Rohingya. (...) The greatest impact of this decision, however, is on the Court's relationship with non-party states. The Court's affirmation of its objective international legal personality appears designed to address a wider audience than just Myanmar's authorities."[34]

3 Conclusions

As mentioned *supra*, the aim of this short contribution is neither to enter into discussion with the critics, nor to furnish additional arguments for a decision already delivered.

Nothing is perfect, not even the ICC, nor its decisions.

The functioning of the United Nations or states' geopolitics are equally and continuously criticized all over the world. What really matters is that the referred articles should be read in full, whether they contain critics or appreciation and together with the decision itself. The decision will certainly be analysed in depth also in the future, in itself and in the mirror of subsequent steps of states and institutions.

Reference

Vagias M (2019) International Criminal Court – Pre-Trial Chamber – territorial jurisdiction over a crime committed in part on state-party territory – the ICC's objective international legal personality. Am J Int Law 113(2):368–375

Péter Kovács Professor of international law, Péter Pázmány Catholic University, Budapest and Judge of the International Criminal Court, The Hague, The Netherlands.

[33]Vagias: *op. cit* p. 375.

[34]Vagias: *op. cit* p. 374.

The Law's Response to the Plight of Victims of Trauma in the Context of International Criminal Justice

Daniel D. Ntanda Nsereko

Contents

1 Introduction

Trauma is a very personal experience, yet the linkages it has with the law are innumerable. This essay discusses the topic of trauma and resilience from a legal point of view, and more particularly, how the law responds to victims of trauma in an international context.

According to the Oxford English Dictionary, trauma is 'a psychic injury, especially one caused by either emotional shock the memory of which may be either

Based on a paper that the author presented at a Conference on Trauma and Resilience organized by Loma Linda University, ADRA Germany, Waldfriede Hospital, and Friedensau Adventist University in Berlin, Germany, 2–4 July 2014. The author acknowledges with thanks the valuable assistance of Ms. Wafa Ben Hassine and Mr. Joel Joseph in preparing this article. Nevertheless the author alone remains responsible for the views expressed in it. Equally, the views expressed in the article are solely the views of the author and not of the STL.

D. D. N. Nsereko (✉)
Special Tribunal for Lebanon, Leidschendam, The Netherlands
e-mail: nserekod@un.org

C. Eboe-Osuji et al. (eds.), *Nigerian Yearbook of International Law 2018/2019*,
Nigerian Yearbook of International Law 2018/2019,
https://doi.org/10.1007/978-3-030-69594-1_11

repressed and unresolved, or disturbingly persistent.'[1] The key term here is *shock*—the individual experiences an impact on his or her psychology that is strong, acute and threatens his or her very existence. Stress is a secondary stage of trauma, wherein a slow process of building tensions might result in a crisis or, if adequately managed, might resolve itself. A disaster, war, criminal episode, accident, or any stressful event will typically have this traumatic impact—which is a normal reaction to an abnormal situation.[2] The psychological and long-term consequences of trauma are numerous and challenge the well-being of those involved on a very intimate level. How, then, does international criminal justice connect with all of this?

The last (twentieth) century was the bloodiest of all centuries in human history so far. As the Preamble to the Rome Statute notes, during that century, 'millions of children, women and men have been victims of unimaginable atrocities that deeply shock the conscience of humanity.' The Holocaust and other horrors of the Nazis during World War II; the pogroms of Stalinist Russia and of other Communist regimes; the horrors of Pol Pot's Khmer Rouge in Cambodia; the enforced disappearances in Latin America and Africa; and more recently, the extermination, genocide and ethnic cleansing in Rwanda and in the territories of the former Yugoslavia, all left indelible scars on the people in the countries concerned. Also not to be forgotten was the Lebanese civil war which, between 1975 and 1990, pitted the various religious communities in Lebanon—Maronites, Druze, Shi'a and Sunnis—against each other. By the end of that conflict, 150,000 people were killed; 100,000 people were maimed or permanently disabled; cities and towns were destroyed; and 900,000 Lebanese people were forced to migrate to other countries. The civil war was followed by the current phenomenon of terrorism and its equally horrific consequences. The effects of one such terrorist attack recently prompted counsel for the victims during the trial in the *Ayyash et al.* case[3] to sardonically remark that a 'natural cause of death has become a privilege in my country [of Lebanon].'[4] The trial, aimed at combating impunity in Lebanon, was being conducted by the Special Tribunal for Lebanon (STL), established by the United Nations in 2009, to deal with the effects of that attack and others like it.[5]

The wars and other episodes mentioned above might have ended, but their effects on the survivors usually persist. Persons whose families were wiped out or whose loved ones disappeared, and others who were maimed, brutalized or reduced to paupers, continue to suffer mentally. Talking of the effects of war on a soldier, one writer has said:

---

[1] *Shorter Oxford English Dictionary – Volume 2 (N-Z)* (6th edn, Oxford University Press 2007), p. 3330.

[2] Revel (1996), p. 289.

[3] The *Prosecutor v. Ayyash et al.* trial (STL-11-01) deals with individuals charged with the attack of 14 February 2005, which resulted in the death of former Lebanese Prime Minister Rafik Hariri and in the death or injury of other persons.

[4] STL, *Prosecutor v. Ayyash et al.*, STL-11-01-T, Trial Hearing Transcript, 17 January 2014, 69, line 7.

[5] See generally Batchelor (2012).

> Wars are not over when the shooting stops. They live on in the lives of those who fight them. That is the curse of a soldier [. . .] War is haunting. Death. Pain. Blood. Dismemberment. A buddy dying in your arms. Imagine trying to get over the memory of a bomb splitting a Humvee apart beneath your feet and taking your leg with it.[6]

Judges at international criminal tribunals deal with cases of mass atrocities that arise out of the kind of events referred to above. The cases involve thousands of victims who suffer not only from physical and mental harm and, in particular, from trauma.

In the past, traditional criminal justice systems, particularly those of the western common law tradition, have tended to focus on the accused and his rights—fair trial, free legal representation and humane treatment during detention. Whilst such considerations are certainly important, little or no attention was paid to the victims, i.e. those to whom the accused caused pain and suffering as a result of their alleged criminal conduct. Victims are often relegated to the status of information providers, witnesses to the crime or as mere spectators. Yet, in my view, victims should be the focal point of the criminal justice system; they are the ones who have been wronged and whose rights have been violated; they need justice; they need restoration. Initially, the modern international criminal justice system also followed the trend of sidelining victims. For example, the International Criminal Tribunals for the Former Yugoslavia and Rwanda (ICTY and ICTR) do not have an explicit place for victims during judicial proceedings, except in so far as they are brought to the attention of the relevant court by the Prosecution, Defense or, on occasion, by the Chamber itself. However, the international criminal justice system has attempted to remedy this situation in recent years by including victim participation in judicial proceedings. In this article, I discuss the international legal framework that the international community has crafted for the purpose of preventing or minimizing the suffering caused to victims of unsavory episodes, particularly those related to war and to other manmade catastrophes of a criminal nature. I then highlight some of the measures that are currently in place on behalf of victims, to ameliorate their plight or to enable them to recover from traumatization. These measures include participation in legal proceedings, provision of services to victims and payment of reparations.

2 Humanitarian Law and Human Rights

With the exception of crimes connected to terrorist attacks, such as those that are tried by the Special Tribunal for Lebanon, the kind of crimes that result in traumatic suffering and are tried by international criminal tribunals have tended to be committed in the course of war or armed conflicts, the most violent of all human activities

[6] Max Cleland, 'The Forever War of the Mind' *The New York Times* (New York, 6 November 2009) A23, <http://www.nytimes.com/2009/11/07/opinion/07cleland.html>.

and the most traumatizing. These crimes include genocide, crimes against humanity, war crimes and, historically, crimes against peace or aggression.[7] As the International Military (Nuremberg) Tribunal put it, 'war is essentially an evil thing. Its consequences are not confined to the belligerent states alone, but affect the whole world.'[8] The Tribunal was dealing with the effects of World War II. But, in my submission, all wars, whether international or internal, are evil. As former UN Secretary-General Kofi Annan put it:

> There is no such thing as a war in which only the guilty are killed, or wounded, or see their homes destroyed and their loved ones perish. Even in the best of causes, young men are sacrificed. Even those who are clearly fighting on the side of right inflict terrible pain and injury on others.[9]

War tends to bring out the worst in the people of all races. Once war breaks out, it unleashes evil forces that can often result in the commission of genocide, crimes against humanity, war crimes and other outrages such as torture, rape, child abuse, pillage and plunder, and destruction of property. As the UN Human Rights Committee has also had occasion to lament, '[w]ar and other acts of mass violence continue to be a scourge of humanity and take the lives of thousands of innocent human beings every year.'[10] It is axiomatic, then, that the most effective way of addressing the issue of the trauma associated with war, is not to wage war or to engage in any armed conflict in the first place. As is often said, prevention is better than cure.

Nevertheless, as we all know, war among peoples and nations has existed for as long as the human race itself. Theologians such as St. Thomas Aquinas and St. Augustine attempted to sanitize or to provide a moral veneer for war by drawing a distinction between a just war (*bellum iustum*) and an unjust war (*bellum iniustum*). However, with the decline of the Catholic Church's influence and the attendant difficulty of defining what makes a war just or unjust, the theory fell into desuetude. Instead, the *jus ad bellum* theory—that every sovereign state has an inherent right to wage war—gained ascendency, with calamitous consequences. Following the disastrous effects of World War I, the international community attempted to limit the right to resort to war via the Kellogg-Briand Pact (or the Treaty for the Renunciation of War) of 1928. Unfortunately, these efforts were not effective enough to stop the outbreak of World War II and its attendant horrors. After that war, the Allied Powers

[7]Under Article 5(2) of the Rome Statute of the International Criminal Court, and following the adoption of Article 8*bis* at the Kampala Conference in 2010, the crime of 'aggression' may soon be added to the list of crimes tried by international tribunals. However, this amendment to the Rome Statute has not yet come into force.

[8]*United States of America et al. v. Göring et al.*, Judgment, in *Trial of the Major War Criminals before the International Military Tribunal – Volume 1: Official Documents* (Nuremberg International Military Tribunal 1947), p. 186.

[9]Annan (2004).

[10]UN Human Rights Committee, 'General Comment 14, Article 6: Right to Life' (23rd session, 1984), *Compilation of General Comments and General Recommendations Adopted by Human Rights Treaty Bodies*, UN Doc. HRI/GEN/1/Rev.1 (1994), 18, para. 2.

set up the United Nations 'to save succeeding generations from the scourge of war, which twice in our lifetime has brought untold sorrow to mankind.'[11] Most importantly, its Charter forbade Member States to resort to war as a means of resolving disputes between them, save in the case of self-defense or when the UN Security Council authorizes them pursuant to its Chapter VII powers.[12] But, alas, wars continue to plague planet Earth. It is true, though, that today the wars tend to have more of a civil war character rather than being fought between States.

Given this state of affairs, the additional and parallel response of the jurists was to develop rules and customs of war, *jus in bello* (the law of war or international humanitarian law), which apply in wars between States and in civil conflicts. The aim of these rules is to ameliorate the effects of war once it breaks out. Under the principles of humanity, proportionality, military necessity and distinction, the rules and customs of war attempt to regulate how war should be fought; what type of weapons should be used; what objects are legitimate or otherwise for attack; how to treat prisoners of war, the wounded or *hors de combat,* civilians and humanitarian workers (such as members of the Red Cross, doctors and nurses); and the responsibilities of an occupying power.[13]

It is noteworthy, though, that in regulating the conduct of war, international humanitarian law does not pass judgment on the underlying causes of the war or on the correctness of the positions of the warring parties—the waters of *jus ad bellum* and *jus in bello* do not mix. Instead, international humanitarian law seeks to ensure that, even in the midst of combat, the inherent dignity of the human person is respected, the sanctity of human life is protected, the infliction of unnecessary pain and suffering is avoided or minimized, and wanton destruction of property and of places of civilian sanctuary and of educational and cultural value is eschewed. This body of law is today codified by the four 1949 Geneva Conventions and the subsequent Protocols thereto, as well as under the Statutes of the various international criminal tribunals. Sadly, rules of international humanitarian law continue to be breached during armed conflicts. To address this situation, and following the Nuremberg precedent, the international community established international criminal tribunals to enforce that law. For instance, the ICTY was established in 1993 and vested with 'the power to prosecute persons responsible for serious violations of international humanitarian law committed in the territory of the former Yugoslavia since 1991.'[14] Furthermore, the International Criminal Court (ICC) was established in 1998 as a permanent and international institution to ensure that 'the most serious crimes of concern to the international community as a whole must not go

[11]Charter of the United Nations (adopted 26 June 1945, entered into force 24 October 1945), 1 UNTS XVI, Preamble, para. 1.

[12]*ibid.,* Art. 42 (UN Security Council authorization) and Art. 51 (self-defense).

[13]See generally, Thürer (2011).

[14]Statute of the International Criminal Tribunal for the Former Yugoslavia (adopted and entered into force 25 May 1993, as amended 17 May 2002), attached to UN Security Council Res. 827 (1993), S/RES/827 (1993), Art. 1.

unpunished.'[15] Importantly, the Rome Statute of the ICC and the Statutes of all the other international criminal tribunals, not only elaborate on the crimes that they have the jurisdiction to try, but they also embody the Principles of International Law Recognized in the Charter of the Nuremberg Tribunal and in the Judgment of the Tribunal, 1950 (or the Nuremberg Principles).[16] According to these Principles:

> 1. Any person who commits an act which constitutes a crime under international law is responsible therefor and liable to punishment;
> 2. The fact that internal law does not impose a penalty for an act which constitutes a crime under international law does not relieve the person who commits the act from responsibility under international law;
> 3. The fact that the person who committed an act which constitutes a crime under international law acted as Head of State or responsible Government official does not relieve him from responsibility under international law; [and]
> 4. The fact that a person acted pursuant to order of his Government or of a superior does not relieve him from responsibility under international law, provided a moral choice was in fact possible to him.[17]

These Principles are extremely important for the effective enforcement of international humanitarian law. The principle repudiating immunity for serving Heads of States and other high-ranking state officials has been particularly significant in reinforcing the deterrent effect of international criminal law and of combating impunity, despite it being recently questioned by the African Union.[18] Deterrence, which accompanies punishment, particularly punishment that is proportionate to the seriousness of the offences committed, serves the ultimate aim of criminal law: preventing the commission of trauma-causing acts, in a prophylactic sense. The ICTY underscored this point when it stated thus:

> [T]he purpose [of punishment] is to deter the specific accused as well as others, which means not only the citizens of Bosnia and Herzegovina but persons worldwide from committing crimes in similar circumstances against international humanitarian law. The Trial Chamber is further of the view that another relevant sentencing purpose is to show the people of not only the former Yugoslavia, but of the world in general, that there is no impunity for these types of crimes. This should be done in order to strengthen the resolve of all involved not to

---

[15] Rome Statute of the International Criminal Court (adopted 17 July 1998, entered into force 1 July 2002) 2187 UNTS 90 (ICC Statute) Preamble, para. 4.

[16] Principles of International Law Recognized in the Charter of the Nuremberg Tribunal and in the Judgment of the Tribunal [1950] (II) *Yearbook of the International Law Commission* 374.

[17] *ibid.*

[18] See AU Assembly Decision on Africa's Relationship with the International Criminal Court (12 October 2013) Ext/Assembly/AU/Dec.1(Oct.13). The AU Assembly affirmed 'the principles deriving from national laws and international customary law by which sitting Heads of State and other senior state officials are granted immunities during their tenure of office.' The Assembly then decided that 'no charges shall be commenced or continued before any International Court or Tribunal against any serving AU Head of State or Government or anybody acting or entitled to act in such capacity during their term of office;' and that 'the trials of President Uhuru Kenyatta and Deputy President William Samoei Ruto, who are the current serving leaders of the Republic of Kenya, should be suspended until they complete their terms of office.'

> allow crimes against international humanitarian law to be committed as well as to create trust in and respect for the developing system of international criminal justice.[19]

It is also instructive to note that international humanitarian law places heavy responsibility on military commanders to ensure that, through proper training and the exercise of control and discipline, the soldiers under their command observe its requirements. The rationale for such responsibility was lucidly articulated by the United States Supreme Court in a celebrated case involving General Yamashita of Japan, for his actions in the Philippines during World War II:

> It is evident that the conduct of military operations by troops whose excesses are unrestrained by orders or efforts of their commander would almost certainly result in violations which it is the purpose of the law of war to prevent. Its purpose to protect civilian populations and prisoners of war from brutality would largely be defeated if the commander of an invading army could, with impunity, neglect to take reasonable measures for their protection. Hence, the law of war presupposes that its violation is to be avoided through the control of the operations of war by commanders who are to some extent responsible for their subordinates.[20]

All in all then, for international humanitarian law to be effective, it is imperative that national armies, and even rebel or resistance groups, be properly trained and taught to observe its provisions. In this respect, one has to pay tribute to the International Committee of the Red Cross (ICRC) for its tireless efforts to disseminate the principles of international humanitarian law worldwide, not only from their offices in Geneva, but often in the very places where these wars are waged.

International human rights law, too, has rules and principles that aim at mitigating the trauma experienced by victims of man-made disasters, such as wars, terrorist attacks and political and religious persecution. Here one has in mind the principle of asylum, contained in Article 14 of the Universal Declaration of Human Rights which states that: 'Everyone has the right to seek and to enjoy in other countries asylum from persecution.' Even though the state of asylum has the ultimate right to decide who to admit or not to admit on its territory, other principles of refugee law work to temper the state's apparently absolute power in matters relating to the admission of foreigners.[21] For example, the principle of *non-refoulement* found in Article 33(1) of the 1951 Convention on the Status of Refugees, along with other international instruments on the subject, prohibits the expulsion or return (*refoulement*) of a refugee 'in any manner whatsoever to frontiers of territories where his life or freedom would be threatened.' The principle of *non-refoulement* has served to protect the thousands of Africa's refugees fleeing from armed conflicts in their home countries from almost sure death until the cessation of the hostilities. Nevertheless, besides the heavy financial, social and security burden that the refugee

---

[19] ICTY, *Prosecutor v. Kupreškić*, Case No. IT-95-16-T, Judgment, 14 January 2000, para. 848.

[20] *In re Yamashita*, 327 U.S. 1 (1946), 15. In this case, General Yamashita was tried and convicted by a United States Military Commission for his failure to prevent atrocities by forces under his command during the Japanese occupation of the Philippines. The Supreme Court confirmed the conviction.

[21] See generally, Gammeltoft-Hansen (2011).

influxes thrust on the state of asylum, it does also often sours its relations with the refugees' country of origin. Refugees are by definition invariably hostile to their home government and some may have been combatants. Their government may therefore consider their being granted asylum on the territory of another state as an unfriendly or hostile act on the part of the country granting them. Luckily, international law has addressed that issue. The 1967 Declaration on Territorial Asylum recognizes that 'the grant of asylum by a State to persons entitled to invoke Article 14 of the Universal Declaration of Human Rights is a peaceful and humanitarian act and that, as such, it cannot be regarded as unfriendly by any other State.'[22] Accordingly, international law imposes a duty on the state of origin to respect other states' right to grant asylum to the people seeking it on their territory. States of origin must therefore refrain from such acts as abduction and secret assassinations that render that right nugatory. In the same way, international law prohibits states of asylum from abusing the right of asylum. That is why the 1967 Declaration on Territorial Asylum explicitly further enunciates that 'States granting asylum shall not permit persons who have received asylum to engage in activities contrary to the purposes and principles of the United Nations.'[23] Such activities often include permitting refugees on their territory, directly or indirectly, to use their territory as launching pads against their country of origin. To guard against such activities, refugee law requires the state of asylum to settle the refugees 'at a reasonable distance from the frontier of their country of origin.'[24] In this respect it is interesting to note that the provisions of both the UN Declaration on Territorial Asylum and of refugee law are in accord with the general principle of law, expressed in the maxim that, *sic utere tuo ut alianum non laedas*, so use your own as not to injure others.

Generally speaking, refugee law also prescribes modes of treatment that ensure that the life of a refugee in the country of asylum is not like jumping from the frying pan into the fire; or as Shakespeare put it in *As You Like It*, 'from the smoke into the smother; from a tyrant Duke unto a tyrant brother.'[25] It prescribes treatment that helps lessen the refugee's trauma. The Office of the UN High Commissioner for Refugees also plays a huge role here. Under its mandate, it is able to provide both material and psychological care of refugees in their countries of sojourn.[26]

Another international instrument that protects victims is the UN Convention against Torture and Other Cruel, Inhuman and Degrading Treatment or Punishment of 1984 and its Optional Protocol of 2002. That Convention defines and makes freedom from torture a non-derogable human right. Its Optional Protocol also sets up international mechanisms that include inspections of places of detention by

[22]UN GA Res. 2312 (XXII), 22 UN GAOR Supp. (No. 16) at 81, UN Doc A/6716 (1967), preambular para.

[23]*ibid.*, Article 4.

[24]OAU, Convention Governing the Specific Aspects of Refugee Problems in Africa (adopted 10 September 1969, entered into force 20 June 1974) 1001 UNTS 45, Art. 2(6).

[25]William Shakespeare, *As You Like It* (1599) Act I, Scene 2, line 280.

[26]See Betts et al. (2008).

international bodies, such as the ICRC; these mechanisms aim to ensure that states treat inmates humanely and that they do not torture them, and can also intercede on behalf of the victims of torture.[27] Where acts of torture are committed as part of a widespread or systematic attack against a civilian population, it may amount to a crime against humanity or, if committed in the context of an armed conflict, a war crime. As some writers have commented, torture is indeed 'one of the most traumatizing types of human rights violations.'[28]

3 Victim Participation in Criminal Proceedings

A crime, as we know, is notionally committed against the state. It is equally true that mass atrocities or international crimes are committed not only against the affected victims but also the state on whose territory they take place *and* against the international community as a whole. This is so because, by their nature, gravity and extent, international crimes affect the entire international community. They violate internationally cherished values. For instance, crimes such as genocide threaten the continued existence of the human race. Others, such as crimes against humanity and war crimes, are an affront to the inherent dignity of the human person and shock the conscience of humankind. Yet others, such as aggression, interfere with the peaceful co-existence of states and imperil the peace and security of humankind. That is why the international community is and must be at the forefront of repressing these crimes. Ultimately, however, all crimes are committed against individual human beings. This is also why the Statutes of both the ICC[29] and the STL,[30] for instance, specifically refer to the rights of victims to participate in criminal proceedings and grant them rights pertaining to access to information, take part in proceedings and generally to be paid reparation.

---

[27]See Murray et al. (2011).

[28]See Introduction in Danieli and others (n 2) 11.

[29]See ICC Statute (n 15) Art. 68(3). See also Rules of Procedure and Evidence of the International Criminal Court, (adopted and entered into force 9 September 2002, as amended) available at <http://www.icc-cpi.int/iccdocs/PIDS/legal-texts/RulesProcedureEvidenceEng.pdf> (ICC Rules) Rules 85 and 89.

[30]See Statute of the Special Tribunal for Lebanon (adopted 30 May 2007), attached to UN Security Council Res. 1757 (2007), S/RES/1757 (2007) (STL Statute) Art. 17. See also Rules of Procedure and Evidence of the Special Tribunal for Lebanon (adopted 20 March 2009, as amended 12 February 2015) available at <http://www.stl-tsl.org/images/RPE/RPE_EN_February_2015.pdf> (STL Rules) Rules 86 and 87.

3.1 Who Is Entitled to Participate?

Who is a victim? The Basic Principles and Guidelines on the Right to a Remedy and Reparation (Basic Principles)[31] provide that the term 'victim' includes those who have suffered harm, whether individually or collectively, as a result of a crime. They may include the direct victim and his or her immediate family or dependents and persons who have suffered harm in intervening to assist the victims while in distress or to prevent the victimization from happening in the first place.[32] It is interesting to note in this respect a broader approach of the Extraordinary Chambers in the Courts of Cambodia (the ECCC), which extended the orbit of secondary victims to potentially the entire Cambodian society.[33] Thus in determining who was entitled to participate in the proceedings as "victims", the ECCC Pre-Trial Chamber based itself on the notion of Cambodian societal organization under which the concept of "family" is wider than in many other cultures.[34] Apparently, the alleged crimes that the ECCC was dealing with involved the implementation of policies which brought about the restructuring of the whole social structure and affected whole groups and communities and thus resulting in other forms of relationships—non-familial—to develop.[35] As the Pre-Trial Chamber summarized:

> [M]ere knowledge of the fate of another human who is a direct victim of crimes committed resulting from the implementation of policies to that effect must be more than not likely to be psychologically disturbing to any person of ordinary sensibility. Such disturbance flows not just from seeing such crimes being committed but also from the implied and constant threat generated by such occurrences that can reasonably be expected to instill fear on the others that this could also be their fate due to them belonging to the same targeted group or community as the direct victim of a crime committed as part of the implementation of the [Communist Party of Kampuchea] policies.[36]

As to the harm suffered and which would entitle a victim to participate in the proceedings, the Basic Principles provides that it includes:

> [P]hysical or mental injury, emotional suffering, economic loss or substantial impairment of their fundamental rights, through acts or omissions that constitute gross violations of international human rights law, or serious violations of international humanitarian law.[37]

---

[31]Basic Principles and Guidelines on the Right to a Remedy and Reparation for Victims of Gross Violations of International Human Rights Law and Serious Violations of International Humanitarian Law, annexed to UN General Assembly Res. 60/147 (2005), A/RES/60/147 (2005) (Basic Principles).

[32]*ibid.*, para. 8.

[33]ECCC, *Prosecutor v. Nuon Chea, Ieng Sary, Ieng Thirith and Khieu Samphan*, Decision on Appeals against Orders of the Co-Investigating Judges on the Admissibility of Civil Party Applications, Case No. 002/19-09-2007-ECCC/OCIJ (PTC76, PTC112, PTC113, PTC114, PTC115, PTC142, PTC157, PTC164, PTC165 and PTC172, 24 June 2011, paras. 49 and 86.

[34]*ibid.*, paras. 84–85.

[35]*ibid.*, paras. 85–86.

[36]*ibid.*, para. 86.

[37]Basic Principles (n 31) para. 8.

This is not too dissimilar to the definition of a 'victim' provided for under the Rule 85 of the ICC's Rules of Procedure and Evidence and ICC case-law[38] as well as the jurisprudence of the STL[39] and of the ECCC Internal Rules.[40]

However, with respect to the ICC and the STL, it is important to note that the harm suffered must be the result of one of the crimes under their respective Statutes, and committed by a person who has been convicted by either body. It is further instructive to note that under the STL Rules, the harm suffered must occur 'as a *direct result* of an attack within the Tribunal's jurisdiction.'[41] According to the STL Pre-Trial Judge, the adjective "direct" refers to the requirement of causation, and not to the harm itself.[42] All that is needed is a causal link between the harm suffered, physical or mental, and the attack. This interpretation would thus cover secondary victims as noted above. However, this requirement of a causal link between the harm and the original attack may be problematic with respect to traumatic stress, because of its long-term and sometimes inter-generational effects, as well as the fact that it could be intermittently triggered. So, is the causal link indefinite, at least for certain purposes such as claiming compensation? Here one can recall the demand for reparation by Americans of African origins, who assert that they continue to suffer from Post-traumatic Slave Syndrome as a result of the enslavement of their ancestors centuries ago.[43]

3.2 Modes of Participation

Victim participation in proceedings is an important component of healing for the victims, who suffer immense pain. It recognizes them as important participants and not just spectators in a case that concerns them; they are stakeholders. It gives them a chance to tell their story, not only as witnesses for the prosecution but in their own right as affected persons. Thus, the STL Statue provides that:

---

[38]See ICC, *Prosecutor v. Lubanga,* Case No. ICC-01/04-01/06 OA9 OA10 Judgement on the Appeals of the Prosecutor and the Defence against Trial Chamber I's Decision on Victims' Participation of 18 January 2008, Appeals Chamber 11 July 2008. For a more thorough review of ICC case law relating to the definition of a victim at the ICC, see Baumgartner (2008), pp. 409, 417–423. See also Ntanda Nsereko (2010), p. 399.

[39]See in particular, STL, *Prosecutor v. Ayyash et al.*, Case No. STL-11-01/PT/PTJ, Decision on Victims' Participation in the Proceedings, 8 May 2012 (STL, Ayyash, 8 May 2012).

[40]See ECCC, Internal Rules as revised on 16 January 2015, available at <https://www.eccc.gov.kh/en/document/legal/internal-rules-rev9>, Rule 23*bis*. See also ECCC, *Prosecutor v. Kaing Guek Eav (alias Duch)* Case No. 001/18-07-2007-ECCC/SC, Appeals Judgement, 3 February 2012, paras. 416–417.

[41]STL Rules (n 30) Rule 2(A) (emphasis added). In contrast, Rule 85(a) of the ICC Rules (n 29) defines 'victims' as 'natural persons who have suffered harm as a result of the commission of any crime within the jurisdiction of the Court.'

[42]*ibid*. See also STL, Ayyash, 8 May 2012 (n 39) paras. 38–46.

[43]See generally Leary (2005).

> Where the personal interests of the victims are affected, the Special Tribunal shall permit their views and concerns to be presented and considered at stages of the proceedings determined to be appropriate.[44]

Accordingly, victims are entitled to receive copies of documents filed by the parties; they may be present in the courtroom throughout the trial; and they may present opening and closing statements. Additionally, with the permission of the Trial Chamber, they may cross-examine witnesses called by either the prosecution or the accused, may call and examine their own witnesses, and may file motions and briefs. Furthermore, at the sentencing stage and with the authorization of the Trial Chamber, victims may make oral or written submissions relating to the personal impact of the crimes on them.[45] All in all, participation enables victims to contribute to the establishment of the truth and to ensuring that justice is done. It also acts as a catharsis and release to injured feelings. It is a form of effective remedy and reparation, to which they are entitled as an 'equal and effective right to justice.'[46] In this respect, it is instructive to note that the ICC has explicitly rejected the notion that the victims' interest in participation is solely linked to obtaining an award for reparations at the end of the proceedings. According to the ICC, victim interests 'should encompass their personal interests in an appropriately broad sense',[47] including the need to see that 'justice is done'[48] onto the perpetrators.

However, victim participation is subject to the rights of the accused. As the STL Appeals Chamber has stated, '[w]hile the Statute mandates us to protect the rights of the victims, in particular their entitlement to participate in the proceedings, it places paramount importance on the right of the accused to a fair trial.'[49] For this reason the Chamber rejected the demands of participating victims to remain totally anonymous throughout the proceedings. According to the Chamber, to allow anonymity would have resulted in the accused not knowing who was testifying against them and, as a result, not being able to defend themselves effectively, say, by properly cross-examining the witnesses. The Chamber confirmed the Pre-Trial Judge's order that the identity of the victims participating in the proceedings must be disclosed sufficiently in advance, so as to give the Defense adequate time to prepare.[50]

[44]STL Statute (n 30) Art. 17. See also ICC Statute (n 15) Art. 68(3).

[45]See STL Rules (n 30) Rule 87. See also ICC Rules (n 29) Rules 89–93.

[46]Basic Principles (n 31) para. 11(a).

[47]ICC, *Prosecutor v. Lubanga*, Case No. ICC-01/04-01/06-1119, Decision on Victims' Participation, 18 January 2008, para. 98.

[48]ICC, *Prosecutor v. Lubanga*, Case No. ICC-01/04-01/06-925, Decision of the Appeals Chamber on the Joint Application of Victims a/0001/06 to a/0003/06 and a/0105/06 concerning the 'Directions and Decision of the Appeals Chamber' of 2 February 2007 – Separate Opinion of Judge Sang-Hyun Song, 13 June 2007, para. 10.

[49]STL, *Prosecutor v. Ayyash et al.*, Case No. STL-11-01/PT/AC/AR126.3, Decision on Appeal by Legal Representative of Victims against Pre-Trial Judge's Decision on Protective Measures, 10 April 2013, para. 38.

[50]*ibid.* para. 39.

Again, subject to the rights of the accused, where victims are allowed to participate either as witnesses or as such, the Court must conduct the proceedings in such a manner so as to minimize the trauma and hardship that participation might occasion them. The process of giving evidence in court is almost invariably traumatic in itself. Therefore when victims appear in court as witnesses, they must not be required to give evidence in a manner that re-traumatizes them. To avoid this possibility, the STL Trial Chamber decided to merge the two cases of *Ayyash et al.* and of *Merhi*, so that the witnesses would not have to be called on multiple times to repeat the same potentially traumatic evidence before the Chamber.[51]

Again, to ensure their effective participation in the proceedings, the Statutes of both the ICC and STL put in place 'protective measures' to guard against reprisals and further victimization and traumatization. The measures include applying image or voice-altering devices; giving testimony through closed circuit television or video-conference link; assignment of a pseudonym; and hearing testimony in closed sessions.[52] Other measures include 'assistance services.' These services encompass support for victims, such as logistical support and counseling or psychological services. Victims are often far from home and are often unfamiliar with the court environment. To this, add the fact that they testify on horrendous crimes. To assist them cope with these factors, both the STL and the ICC have established specialized units, the Victims and Witnesses Unit (VWU) for the ICC, and the Victim Participation Unit for the STL, to provide the needed assistance. For instance, the STL's Victim Participation Unit is responsible for 'protecting witnesses, victims who participate in the proceedings and, where appropriate, others at risk on account of their interaction with the Tribunal.'[53] As for the ICC, the Rome Statute specifically mandates that its Unit 'shall include staff with expertise in trauma, including trauma related to crimes of sexual violence.'[54] Unlike protection services, the VWU does not need court authorization to counsel or provide logistical support to victims/witnesses or to render such assistance. This is particularly important when support may be needed on a more urgent timeline.

4 Reparation

We must remember that when all is said and done, justice does not mean merely punishing those who perpetrate crimes, but also remedying a wrong. Assistance, support, and reparation for victims go to the very heart of justice and to the very *raison d'être* for the existence of international institutions established to combat

[51] STL, *Prosecutor. Ayyash et al.*, Case No. STL-11-01/T/TC, Decision on Trial Management and Reasons for Decision on Joinder, 25 February 2014, para. 31.

[52] See ICC Statute (n 15) Art. 68(2); STL Rules (n 30) Rule 133.

[53] STL Rules (n 30) Rule 50.

[54] ICC Statute (n 15) Art. 43(6).

injustice. For this reason, both the ICC and STL confer on victims, including victims of trauma, the right to claim reparation against convicted persons.[55] The ICC Statute vests in the court itself the power to award the reparation,[56] whilst the STL Statute entitles victims, identified as such by the Tribunal, to file claims before the competent national courts for compensation.[57] Victims are able to base their claims on the judgments of the Tribunal that convict the persons named therein.[58] According to the STL Statute, for the purposes of reparations, a judgment is 'final and binding as to the criminal responsibility of the convicted person.'[59]

Payment of reparation is based on the general principle of law: *ubi jus ibi remedium*, which states that every legal right or prohibition of wrong is accompanied by a right to a remedy in the event that the legal right or the prohibition is breached.[60] In applying this principle as between states, the Permanent Court of International Justice stated that it is a principle of international law, and even a general conception of law, that any 'breach of an engagement involves an obligation to make reparation.'[61] At the ICC, reparations 'are concerned with redressing the harm—in principle, the full harm, both material and moral—suffered by victims of crimes within the jurisdiction of the Court.'[62] The same can be said of the STL. In this respect, the Basic Principles enumerate five specific types of reparations that are in turn defined in the document. They are, respectively: restitution, compensation, rehabilitation, satisfaction and guarantees of non-repetition. The form of reparation depends on the content of the substantive right that was infringed upon,[63] and on the circumstances of each case.

Specifically, restitution refers to the effort to restore the victim to their original situation before the relevant crimes, of which they are victims, occurred. This includes the restoration of liberty, enjoyment of human rights, identity, family life and citizenship, return to one's place of residence, restoration of employment and return of property.[64] Compensation, on the other hand, constitutes the quantifiable

---

[55] ICC Statute (n 15) Art. 75; STL Statute (n 30) Art. 25.

[56] *ibid.*

[57] STL Statute (n 30) Art. 25(3).

[58] See for example, ICC, *Prosecutor v. Lubanga*, Case No. ICC-01/04-01/06-2904, Decision Establishing the Principles and Procedures to be Applied to Reparations, 7 August 2012; ICC, *Prosecutor v. Lubanga*, Case No. ICC-01/04-01/06-3129, Judgment on the Appeals Against the 'Decision Establishing the Principles and Procedures to be Applied to Reparations' of 7 August 2012, 3 March 2015 (ICC, *Lubanga*, 3 March 2015); STL Statute (n 30) Art. 25(1).

[59] STL Statute (n 30) Art. 25(4).

[60] See Oxford Index: A Search and Discovery Gateway, 'Ubi Jus Ibi Remedium', available at <http://oxfordindex.oup.com/view/10.1093/oi/authority.20110803110448446>.

[61] PCIJ, *Case Concerning the Factory at Chorzów (Claim for Indemnity) (Merits) (Germany v. Poland)*, Series A, No. 17, 13 September 1928, 21.

[62] McCarthy (2012), p. 84.

[63] See generally ECtHR, *Aksoy v. Turkey*, Application No. 21987/93, Judgment, 18 December 1996, para. 95.

[64] Basic Principles (n 31) para. 19.

damages that can be paid to the victim in the form of money or other material goods. The damages do not only cover the economically assessed material damages (such as loss of earnings and the value of the victim's destroyed home), but also cover 'lost opportunities' in areas such as employment, education, and social benefits.[65] Rehabilitation is arguably the form of reparation than impacts the victim and his or her family most directly. According to the Basic Principles, rehabilitation includes mental and psychological care as well as social and legal services.[66] Satisfaction, on the other hand, covers a wide range of non-monetary compensation that aims to fulfill the long-term needs of victims through the course of reparation. Satisfaction includes effective measures aimed at the cessation of continuing violations, as well as commemoration and the establishment of truth-finding commissions to investigate the crimes that led to the victimization. This is because incorporating the truth about past violations into a nation's official history is another important method of positively highlighting the violations committed against victims and/or the families and descendants of those who suffered, as well as the society at large.[67] By exposing the truth of what happened to the victims, the affected society can integrate educational measures that help prevent the crimes from happening again. Apologies by the perpetrators, and the judgment which attributes criminal responsibility to individuals themselves, are also acknowledged to be included within satisfaction. Lastly, guarantees of non-repetition further assist in the future prevention of the crimes that have affected the victims. Measures under this category include the promotion of mechanisms that monitor and prevent social conflicts, reforming laws that may have facilitated the commission of the violations, strengthening the independence of the judiciary and ensuring responsible civilian control over police and military forces.[68]

At the ICC, Article 75(2) of the Rome Statute specifies that the Court can make 'an order directly against a convicted person specifying appropriate reparations to, or in respect of, victims, including restitution, compensation and rehabilitation.' Thus, legally speaking, the responsibility to provide reparations to the victims lies squarely on the shoulders of the convicted criminal.[69] In reality, however, he or she often cannot discharge that responsibility on his or her own. This is because, in the case of mass crimes which international criminal tribunals are mandated to prosecute and try, the number of victims entitled to reparations is simply too enormous. The general principle of *ubi jus ibi remedium* therefore requires that the community, both national and international, has an obligation to step in and to ensure that the victims receive justice. For the national community, the obligation is based on the

---

[65] *ibid.*, para. 20(b).

[66] *ibid.*, para. 21.

[67] See REDRESS, *Implementing Victims' Rights: A Handbook on the Basic Principles and Guidelines on the Right to a Remedy and Reparation*, March 2006, available at <http://www.redress.org/downloads/publications/Reparation%20Principles.pdf>, 38–39.

[68] See Basic Principles (n 31) para. 23.

[69] ICC, *Lubanga*, 3 March 2015 (n 58) para. 99: 'The Appeals Chamber agrees with the Trial Chamber's principle that it is the obligation of the convicted person to remedy the harm caused by the crimes for which he or she was convicted.'

duty of its government to protect its citizens. Here one has in mind the compensation scheme, the *Wiedergutmachung*, instituted by the German Government soon after World War II, under which Germany paid and continues to pay compensation to the victims of Nazi crimes. As for the international community, the duty to assist is related to its obligation to protect and ensure respect for human rights worldwide. That violations take place at such a massive scale betokens a failure to discharge that obligation; hence the duty to assist national governments to make right the wrongs done to victims of mass crimes. An alternative basis for the international community's action on behalf of victims is the principle of social solidarity.

The ICC Trust Fund for Victims (the Fund), which is funded through voluntary contributions, is one recent and veritable way by which the international community meets its responsibility to ensure reparations.[70] The Fund has a dual mandate: first, to provide beneficial support to victims and their families—independent of any reparations orders emanating from the Court—that simply cannot await the Court's verdict; and second, to implement reparation orders that the Court issues, when it so instructs.[71]

In respect of the above discussion, the Appeals Chamber of the ICC recently issued, in the *Lubanga* case, the first appeal judgment on the principles and procedures to be applied to reparations after the conclusion of the first trial and conviction of an accused before the ICC. This decision, among other things, outlined five essential elements that an order for reparation under Article 75 of the Rome Statute must contain. First, such an order must be directed against the person convicted of committing crimes by the Court; second, the order must outline the convicted person's liability with respect to the reparations awarded; third, the order must specify the type of reparations awarded and the reasons for doing so; fourth, the order must determine the harm that was caused to the victims, resulting from the crimes of the convicted person, as well as the modalities for the reparations ordered depending on the circumstances of the case; and finally, the order must determine the victims that are eligible to benefit from the ordered reparations or detail the criteria for victim eligibility.[72] In light of these principles, the original reparations order was amended and the ICC Trust Fund was ordered to submit a draft implementation plan for collective reparations within six months. It remains to be seen how effective the Fund will be in ensuring that reparations reach the victims of Lubanga's crimes in the Democratic Republic of the Congo.

---

[70] ICC Statute (n 15) Art. 79.

[71] See Peschke (2013).

[72] See ICC, *Lubanga*, 3 March 2015 (n 58).

5 Conclusion

The realities of our times are that trauma-causing events are ever on the increase. Every morning, media houses report on the occurrence of these distressing events: wars and rumors of wars, terror attacks, natural disasters such as tsunamis, earthquakes, floods, extreme weather conditions, pestilences, and accidents in the air, on land and at sea. These echo the words of the Holy Bible: 'On earth, nations will be in anguish and perplexity at the roaring and tossing of the sea. Men will faint from terror, apprehensive of what is coming on the world.'[73] Therefore, the international community must continue to brace for these calamities and be prepared to deal with their consequences.

This article has concentrated on the response of the international community, through law, to the plight of victims of trauma, particularly trauma caused by man-made disasters that constitute international crimes. The end of the Cold War and its concomitant cut-throat rivalry clearly necessitated this response. We have witnessed the elaboration and conclusion of various international instruments that set standards and prohibit trauma-causing conduct; the setting up of international criminal tribunals and human rights courts; the recent development of concepts like the responsibility to protect, which makes it easier today, than ever before, for states to take action to avert disasters or to minimize their horrendous effects; the deployment of peace-keeping forces in troubled areas of the world; and the more readily available funding to facilitate the humanitarian work of both governmental, inter-governmental, non-governmental, and international agencies on behalf of victims. Here, one has to commend organizations such as the UN Department of Humanitarian Affairs, UN High Commissioner for Refugees, UN Children's Fund (UNICEF), the ICRC, Caritas International and the Adventist Development and Relief Agency (ADRA), for their invaluable work on behalf of victims of both man-made and natural disasters.[74] Their work exemplifies the true Good-Samaritan spirit.

Nevertheless, even with these favorable conditions and the existence of beneficial provisions in the law, there are factors that continue to impede action on behalf of victims. These factors include the undue adherence to the principle of non-interference in the internal affairs of states, lack of political will, and the notion of national interest. For instance, the grievous genocide in Rwanda could have been averted had the necessary political will on the part of some states existed to take action in a timely manner. Without the appropriate political will to truly create a better world, the law can only do so much. Political leaders must remember that we are all each other's keeper, and must take heed to John Donne's words, who once said that:

[73]Bible, Luke 21:25–26.

[74]See Boullé (1996), p. 284.

No man is an island,

Entire of itself,

Every man is a piece of the continent,

A part of the main.

[...]

Any man's death diminishes me,

Because I am involved in mankind[.][75]

We are involved in the human race, and none of us is an island. Unless we begin acknowledging our responsibilities as such, we will do little to avert future suffering and pain.

References

Annan K (2004) Secretary General's Lecture. In: 35th National Conference of the Trinity Institute, New York, 2 May 2004. <http://www.un.org/sg/STATEMENTS/index.asp?nid=905>

Batchelor D (2012) "Lebanon of dignity, a people that perseveres": a psychological perspective on collective amnesia in Lebanon and its implications for transitional justice. In: Palmer N, Beaton R (eds) Critical perspectives in transitional justice. Intersentia

Baumgartner E (2008) Aspects of victim participation in the proceedings of the International Criminal Court. Int Rev Red Cross 90(870):409, 417–423

Betts A et al (2008) The United Nations High Commissioner for Refugees (UNHCR): the politics and practice of refugee protection into the twenty-first century. Routledge

Boullé PL (1996) Natural disasters and complex emergencies: prompt international response – the contribution of the United Nations Department of Humanitarian Affairs. In: Danieli Y et al (eds) International responses to traumatic stress. Baywood Publishing Company, Inc., p 284

Donne J (1959) Devotions upon emergent occasions together with death's duel. University of Michigan Press. Meditation XVII, pp 108–109

Gammeltoft-Hansen T (2011) Access to asylum: international refugee law and the globalization of migration control. Cambridge University Press

Leary JD (2005) Post traumatic slave syndrome: America's legacy of endurance and healing. Uptone Press

McCarthy C (2012) Reparations and victim support in the International Criminal Court. Cambridge University Press, p 84

Murray R et al (2011) The optional protocol to the UN Convention against torture. Oxford University Press

Ntanda Nsereko DD (2010) The role of victims in criminal proceedings – lessons national jurisdictions can learn from the ICC. Crim Law Forum 21:399

Peschke K (2013) The role and mandates of the ICC trust fund for victims. In: Bonacker T, Safferling C (eds) Victims of international crimes: an interdisciplinary discourse. Asser Press/ Springer

Revel JP (1996) Natural disasters and other accidents: provisions of psychological support – the contribution of non-governmental organizations. In: Danieli Y et al (eds) International responses to traumatic stress. Baywood Publishing Company, Inc., p 289

Thürer D (2011) International humanitarian law: theory, practice, context. Brill

[75] Donne (1959), pp. 108–109.

Daniel D. Ntanda Nsereko Judge, Appeals Chamber, Special Tribunal for Lebanon (Leidschendam, The Netherlands); formerly Judge, Appeals Chamber, International Criminal Court (The Hague, The Netherlands); formerly Professor of Law, University of Botswana, Gaborone, Botswana LL.B., University of East Africa, (Dar Es Salaam, Tanzania); M.C.J, Howard University, (Washington D.C., USA); LL.M., J.S.D., New York University, (New York, USA), Certificate in International Law, Hague Academy of International Law, (The Hague, The Netherlands). Advocate, High Court of Uganda.

Part V
International Human Rights and Humanitarian Law

TWAILing the Minimum Core Concept: Re-thinking the Minimum Core of Economic and Social Rights in the Third World

Caroline Omari Lichuma

Contents

I would like to thank Stanford University's IJFF (2017) where a first draft of this paper was presented, King's College TLSI (2017) for critiquing earlier versions and Prof. Obiora Okafor of the Osgoode Hall Law School for allowing me to present this paper as part of the International Law in the Global South Lecture Series (2018).

C. O. Lichuma (✉)
Georg-August Universität Göttingen, Göttingen, Germany
e-mail: caroline.lichuma@stud.uni-goettingen.de

C. Eboe-Osuji et al. (eds.), *Nigerian Yearbook of International Law 2018/2019*, Nigerian Yearbook of International Law 2018/2019,
https://doi.org/10.1007/978-3-030-69594-1_12

1 Introduction

Third World Approaches to International Law (hereinafter, TWAIL) is a broad dialectic opposition to certain features and aspects of international law.[1] TWAIL scholarship has addressed multiple issues related to various factors such society, politics, identity and economics.[2] However, in all these disparate instances TWAIL is unified at a certain level of abstraction—the underlying commitment to democratic values and concerns in relations within and between the third world and developed countries.[3] TWAIL scholars (hereinafter, TWAILers) are united by a shared mutual devotion in their concern for the so called global south.

One of the focal tasks undertaken by TWAIL is to identify areas of difference along numerous axes such as race, class, gender, economics etc., and in this way confront the hegemony of the dominant narratives of international law.[4] In challenging hegemony, TWAILers are solidly united by their shared ethical commitment to the intellectual and practical struggle to expose, reform, or even retrench those features of the intellectual legal system that help create or maintain the generally unequal, unfair, or unjust global order. This is a commitment to centre the rest by taking the lives and experiences of those who have self-identified as third world much more seriously than has generally been the case.[5] On the one hand TWAILers often ask how to transform international law to be more sensitive to the concerns of third world states but on the other hand, they do not have a false notion of third world innocence and first world guilt or dominance. There is room within TWAIL to be critical of third world governments whenever the circumstances warrant such critique.[6]

The present paper will undertake an ambitious TWAIL critique of the minimum core concept in the field of Economic and Social Rights (hereinafter, ESRs). The concept of the minimum core seeks to establish a minimum legal content for the arguably "notoriously indeterminate"[7] claims of ESRs by recognizing the minimum essential levels of the rights to food, health, housing, water, and education among others.[8] A long-standing criticism faults the minimum core for directing our attention only to the performance of developing states, leaving the legal discourse of ESRs beyond the reach of those facing material deprivation in the middle or high income countries.[9] It is precisely this kind of disparity that the present article intends to interrogate.

---

[1]Mutua (2000b), pp. 31–39.

[2]Gathii (2011), p. 26.

[3]Ibid.

[4]Ibid.

[5]Okafor (2005).

[6]Mutua (2000a), p. 841.

[7]Young (2008), pp. 113–175.

[8]Ibid.

[9]Ibid.

While guarding myself against legal nihilism, I posit that despite the continuing importance of the minimum core concept in requiring states to meet certain immediate obligations even as they progressively realize the more substantive aspects of the various ESRs, it is paramount to rethink the operation of the concept in order to ensure that the various differences between countries in the global north and global south are not only acknowledged, but if possible adequately provided for in the implementation of the doctrine. I am not advocating for a complete and total condemnation of the minimum core concept. Furthermore, no attempt will be made in this paper to justify on-going failures by third world governments to meet their obligations under the International Covenant on Economic, Social and Cultural Rights (hereinafter, the ICESCR), specifically as they relate to the current operation of the minimum core doctrine. Instead, I opine that adoption of a context blind minimum core as opposed to a more context specific and nuanced one will deprive the concept of legitimacy in the third world milieu. The analysis will be restricted to the minimum core concept as articulated and used by the Committee on Economic and Social Cultural Rights (hereinafter, the CESCR). Deployment of the concept in the various national and regional contexts is beyond the scope of the paper.

2 TWAIL and Human Rights: Unearthing the Core Precepts of TWAIL Ideology in the Human Rights Sphere

The nature of TWAIL scholarship has been comprehensively elaborated upon and explained in the existing literature.[10] As such, there is no need to embark upon a detailed treatment of that definitional question in the present research.[11] Instead, departing from the existing TWAIL scholarship, I will herein analyze the prospective use of TWAIL theory in interpreting and applying the minimum core concept in the field of ESRs. The idea of TWAIL is old and yet, new.[12] TWAIL has been argued to be an old idea that has been given new momentum by current international realities.[13] One such reality is the now pervasive acceptance of ESRs. It is unassailable that there is a hitherto unprecedented increase in the widespread affirmation of the indivisibility and equal worth of all human rights, ESRs included.[14] In the span of two decades these rights have emerged from the shadows of human rights jurisprudence to claim their rightful place next to Civil and Political rights (hereinafter, CPRs).[15] Now that the initial hesitance to classify ESRs as real human rights

[10]See the bibliography given in Gathii (2011).

[11]Okafor (2014), pp. 9–105.

[12]Mutua (2000a).

[13]Ibid.

[14]UN General Assembly, *Vienna Declaration and Programme of Action*, 12 July 1993, A/CONF.157/23, available online: https://www.refworld.org/docid/3ae6b39ec.html.

[15]Langford (2008).

when compared to civil and political rights is a thing of the past, attention has shifted from what Philip Alston has termed the name calling phase, in which opponents contented themselves with proclaiming that social rights were simply not susceptible to judicial review and implementation to a more mature and diverse phase with a wide range of national courts adopting positions in relation to social rights and an increasingly expansive array of international instances generating social rights jurisprudence.[16] I argue that the time is ripe to rethink the standard of review relied upon in assessing realization of ESRs at the international level. This is so especially because of the criticisms that have already been levied upon the minimum core concept.[17]

The actuality of international law is that there exist hierarchical relationships between the so called first and third world. These hierarchies may be scrutinized through disparate planes of difference. Despite the illusion of sovereign equality amongst the countries of the world, there are power, resource, political, economic and other imbalances between peoples and states. Notwithstanding the universalist claims of international law, one of the key contentions of this paper is that doctrines such as that of the minimum core which are alleged to be of universal application cannot, and should not be universally applied in light of the existing variations between states. This is because universality may very well be the sweet nothing that has drawn the third world into the sometimes oppressive embrace of international law.

It has been stated that the most fundamental characteristic of TWAIL scholarship is that it is fundamentally oppositional to an important question in international law.[18] At a minimum, the TWAILer in question should expose, attack, or unpack a particular phenomenon that is inimical to the Third World.[19] Several issues have framed TWAIL scholarship in the area of international human rights both historically and in contemporary times. For instance, one of the foremost issues was the call by the so called TWAIL I[20] scholars for the recognition of a right to development.[21] On the other hand, a key concern that arguably permeates the concern of TWAIL II[22] scholars is giving a voice to the marginalized people within third world states.[23] This emphasis on giving a voice to the suffering and critiquing human rights now seems to be a primary focus of TWAIL with regards to international human rights law.[24]

Is there room for this TWAIL II critique to be extended to the specific sphere of ESRs in order to assess the viability or otherwise of the minimum core doctrine as it

[16]Alston (2008).

[17]Young (2008).

[18]Mutua and Anghie (2000), pp. 31–40.

[19]Ibid.

[20]Anghie and Chimni (2003), pp. 77–103.

[21]Mickelson (1998), p. 375.

[22]Anghie and Chimni (2003).

[23]Badaru (2008), pp. 379–387.

[24]Ibid.

currently exists? Badaru points out that in examining ESRs in Africa it is paramount that the effects of international economic law and international trade law in particular be interrogated.[25] One would then ask questions such as, 'what are the effects of international trade law on the right to health, especially with regards to the availability of generic drugs?' or 'how does international economic law impact on the right to food?'[26]

The present paper departs from this line of inquiry and instead restricts itself to a TWAIL analysis of the minimum core doctrine that is widely accepted to be one of the *raison d'êtres* of the ICESCR.[27] As Sect. 3 will show, this doctrine that was first transposed to the field of ESRs in 1990 by the CESCR has been widely touted as being of universal appeal and application despite its limitations.[28] Universality however, as has already been mentioned, may sometimes have an oppressive potential. A TWAIL perspective seeks to scrutinize which aspects of human rights may be made universal and which aspects need to be re-examined.[29] Despite the purportedly universal application of the minimum core concept by the CESCR this article calls for the adoption of a more cautious stance in deploying this doctrine in order to ensure that in its utilization injustice is not perpetuated. The emphasis will be on the fact that existing resource differences between states makes it impossible for an absolute minimum core to be applied uniformly and fairly to state parties of the ICESCR.

3 Maximum Dissemination and Minimum Clarity? Existing CESCR Discourse on the Minimum Core Concept

The CESCR first articulated the minimum core concept in one of its earlier general comments.[30] Specifically, they advanced the view that a minimum core obligation should be imposed on State parties to the ICESCR in order to ensure the satisfaction of, at the very least, minimum essential levels of each of the rights. The CESCR went further and elaborated that a State party in which any significant number of individuals is deprived of essential foodstuffs, of essential primary health care, of basic

[25] Ibid.

[26] Ibid.

[27] UN Committee on Economic, Social and Cultural Rights (CESCR), General Comment No. 3: The Nature of States Parties' Obligations (Art. 2, Para. 1, of the Covenant), 14 December 1990, para. 10.

[28] Chowdhury (2009).

[29] Badaru (2008).

[30] UN Committee on Economic, Social and Cultural Rights (CESCR), General Comment No. 3: The Nature of States Parties' Obligations (Art. 2, Para. 1, of the Covenant), 14 December 1990 paragraph 10.

shelter and housing, or of the most basic forms of education is, prima facie, failing to discharge its obligations under the Covenant.[31] Acknowledging the direct proportionality that exists between availability of resources and the capacity to realize ESRs, the CESCR stipulated that resource constraints applying within the country concerned would be factored into the analysis of whether the minimum core had been achieved or not. This would have been the ideal point to expound upon the scope of a minimum core concept that would vary from country to country depending on availability of resources. Unfortunately, the CESCR deliberately failed to venture further and explain exactly how the minimum core concept would be applied in practice. A lingering question therefore remains. How will existing resource differentials be factored into the analysis as to whether a country has discharged its minimum core obligations? As Young points out the primary conceptual questions remained unanswered.[32] The concept has been criticized as being plagued by paradox from its very inception.[33]

Subsequently the CESCR began to outline the application of the minimum core doctrine to specific rights in the ICESCR. For instance, the right to food has been said to include a core obligation to take the necessary action to mitigate and alleviate hunger as provided for in paragraph 2 of article 11 of the ICESCR, even in times of natural or other disasters.[34]Additionally, this implies that there should be availability of food in a quantity and quality sufficient to satisfy the dietary needs of individuals, free from adverse substances, and acceptable within a given culture and the accessibility of such food in ways that are sustainable and that do not interfere with the enjoyment of other human rights.[35]

In the context of the right to education, the CESCR confirmed that the core of this right includes a duty to ensure the right of access to public educational institutions and programmes on a non-discriminatory basis; to ensure that education conforms to the objectives set out in article 13 (1); to provide primary education for all in accordance with article 13 (2) (a); to adopt and implement a national educational strategy which includes provision for secondary, higher and fundamental education; and to ensure free choice of education without interference from the State or third parties, subject to conformity with "minimum educational standards" (art. 13 (3) and (4)).[36]

[31]Ibid.

[32]Young (2008).

[33]Chowdhury (2009).

[34]UN Committee on Economic, Social and Cultural Rights (CESCR), General Comment No. 12: The Right to Adequate Food (Art. 11 of the Covenant), 12 May 1999, paragraph 6.

[35]UN Committee on Economic, Social and Cultural Rights (CESCR), General Comment No. 12: The Right to Adequate Food (Art. 11 of the Covenant), 12 May 1999, paragraph 8.

[36]UN Committee on Economic, Social and Cultural Rights (CESCR), General Comment No. 13: The Right to Education (Art. 13 of the Covenant), 8 December 1999 paragraph 13.

A minimum core has also been communicated for the right to the highest attainable standard of health[37] and for the right to water.[38] It is however worthwhile to note that despite this emphasis on the importance of the minimum core content of the various rights in the ICESCR, the CESCR has failed to go further and outline if and how the minimum core of a right varies from country to country and what this in turn means for the corresponding obligations imposed upon respective governments. It is precisely this silence that can be interpreted as suggesting that the minimum core doctrine applies universally and uniformly to all state parties of the ICESCR, at least according to the CESCR.

One of the most important functions of the CESCR is to receive state party reports and to issue a response on whether the State in question is meeting its obligations under the ICESCR. States must report initially within 2 years of accepting the ICESCR and thereafter every 5 years. The CESCR then examines each report and addresses its concerns and recommendations to the State party in the form of concluding observations. In discharging this mandate the CESCR has time and again made reference to the minimum core concept in assessing whether or not the state is realizing the rights under the ICESCR.

For instance, in its 41st session held in Geneva in 2008 the CESCR advised the Government of Kenya to effectively implement and allocate sufficient resources to relevant programmes and funds, such as the Child Survival and Development Strategy and the Constituencies Development Fund, to ensure physical and economic access for everyone, including children in rural and deprived urban areas, to the *minimum essential food*, which is sufficient, nutritionally adequate and safe, to ensure freedom from hunger, in line with the Committee's General Comment No. 12 on the right to adequate food.[39]

In its 2010 session the CESCR urged the Government of the Kingdom of Netherlands to ensure that they meet their core obligations under the ICESCR, and specifically to guarantee that the *minimum essential level* relating to the right to housing, health and education is respected, protected and fulfilled in relation to undocumented migrants.[40]

---

[37]UN Committee on Economic, Social and Cultural Rights (CESCR), General Comment No. 14: The Right to the Highest Attainable Standard of Health (Art. 12 of the Covenant), 11 August 2000 paragraph 43 and 44.

[38]UN Committee on Economic, Social and Cultural Rights (CESCR), General Comment No. 15: The Right to Water (Arts. 11 and 12 of the Covenant), 20 January 2003 paragraph 37.

[39]UN Committee on Economic, Social and Cultural Rights (CESCR), Consideration of reports submitted by States parties under articles 16 and 17 of the Covenant: concluding observations of the Committee on Economic, Social and Cultural Rights: Kenya, 19 November 2008, E/C.12/KEN/CO/1.

[40]UN Committee on Economic, Social and Cultural Rights (CESCR), Consideration of reports submitted by States parties under articles 16 and 17 of the Covenant: concluding observations of the Committee on Economic, Social and Cultural Rights: the Kingdom of Netherlands, 9 December 2010, E/C.12/NLD/CO/4-5.

Similarly in its 2012 session the CESCR urged the Government of Iceland to ensure that any proposed policy change or adjustment in times of economic crisis should identify a social protection floor and the *minimum core content* of rights, ensuring the protection of this core content of rights at all times.[41]

Finally, in its 2014 concluding observations to Ukraine, the CESCR urged the Government of Ukraine to ensure that any measures taken to stabilize the economic condition in light of the country's fragile political and economic situation would not result in a disproportionate effect on the most disadvantaged and vulnerable individuals and groups, especially if this would result into a lowering of enjoyment of various rights below their *minimum core content.*[42]

In an open letter to states published in May 2012, the chairperson of the CESCR urged states to ensure that any proposed policy change or adjustment in times of economic and financial crises should identify the *minimum core content* of rights or a social protection floor as developed by the International Labour Organization, and should ensure that this core content is met at all times.[43]

As these brief examples show the CESCR has continually made strides to use the minimum core concept as a marker of state achievement in realization of ESRs. There is thus no question about the widespread dissemination of the doctrine. It is apparent however, that in utilizing the concept the CESCR makes no distinction between developed/high income and developing/low income countries. Whether a country lies in the global north or in the global south they will be held to the same standard in as far as delivering on the promise of the minimum core is concerned. Thus, while it is unassailable that the minimum core concept is widely recognized as one of the most important doctrines in ESRs, the question that remains to date is the ambiguity surrounding how the doctrine should be, and is actually, implemented in reality, and whether this passes muster when subjected to a TWAIL gaze.

Because of the lack of clarification on the operation of the minimum core concept as articulated by the CESCR recourse has to be had to research done by academics in the area in order to bolster any understanding of the concept. While the dissemination of this concept at the international, regional and even national levels is beyond refute, disagreements abound about how the doctrine should be understood, applied and even whether or not the doctrine should continue in use. For example, Max argues that the concept of the minimum core should be abandoned.[44] Of interest to this article's TWAIL argument is his reasoning that the minimum core concept can

[41]UN Committee on Economic, Social and Cultural Rights (CESCR), Concluding observations on the 4th report of Iceland, adopted by the Committee at its 49th session, 12–30 November 2012: Committee on Economic, Social and Cultural Rights, 11 December 2012, E/C.12/ISL/CO/4.

[42]UN Committee on Economic, Social and Cultural Rights (CESCR), Concluding observations on the sixth periodic report of Ukraine, 13 June 2014, E/C.12/UKR/CO/6.

[43]Chairperson of the CESCR, Letter Dated 16 May 2012 Addressed by the Chairperson of the Committee on Economic, Social and Cultural Rights to States Parties to the International Covenant on Economic, Social and Cultural Rights (2012) UN Doc HRC/NONE/2012/76, UN reference CESCR/48th/SP/MAB/SW.

[44]Max (2013), p. 10.

only be deployed against those in developing countries, deflecting attention away from injustices in developed countries.[45] Wesson echoes this sentiment by arguing that in the developed world one might say that the minimum core has generally already been realized through the welfare state.[46] Implicit in this thinking is the assertion that the minimum core must therefore be the preserve of less developed countries in the third world, therefore defeating the universalist argument in favor of applying the minimum core.

Some courts have also been quick to reject the doctrine. For instance, in South Africa, the Constitutional Court has out rightly spurned the minimum core approach. One of the reasons given by the court is the lack of extensive information resources available to the CESCR that makes it possible for the latter to assess whether the minimum core of specific rights have been met.[47] In another case the court refused to rely on the minimum core on the ground that it is impossible to give everyone access to a core service immediately. The Court went on to enunciate that courts are not institutionally equipped to make the wide-ranging factual and political enquiries necessary for determining what the minimum-core standards should be.[48]

Academics such as Young on the other hand argue that despite the controversies surrounding it, the minimum core concept has not outlived its usefulness.[49] She argues that instead of jettisoning the concept, a better alternative would be to reverse the inquiry, by searching not for content to the minimum core concept, but rather for new concepts to facilitate the rights' content operating as law.[50]

Much has been said about the minimum core. I do not intend to rehash these debates here. However, despite the criticisms levied against the concept it is near impossible to achieve consensus on its abandonment. The third section of this paper will add on to the already existing discontent surrounding the operation of the minimum core concept by censuring it from a TWAIL perspective.

4 Something Old and Something New: The Minimum Core Through a TWAIL Gaze

Is there room for a TWAIL critique of the minimum core concept?

Both TWAIL and the minimum core concept are old ideas. The novelty of the present paper lies in its attempt to marry these two old ideas in order to birth a new one. That is, the argument that the minimum core as espoused by the CESCR fails to acknowledge that universality in the claims of differentially situated people is an

---

[45]Ibid.

[46]Wesson (2012), p. 221 at 242.

[47]Government of Republic of South Africa v Grootboom, 2001 (1) SA 46 (CC) para. 24.

[48]Minister of Health v Treatment Action Campaign (No. 2) 2002 (5) SA 721 (CC) para 26.

[49]Young (2008).

[50]Ibid.

impossible (and unfair) goal, and as such, that the current application of the minimum core is unjust from a TWAIL perspective.

In assessing the realization of ESRs by third world governments it is paramount to acknowledge that there are historical root causes of the current dismal state of ESRs in the Third World. With regards to the right to food, for example, a TWAIL perspective helps one to ask questions such as, 'what effects did colonialism have on the politics of food production in Africa?' or 'how did the cash crop economy evolve and how did or does it perpetuate hunger and malnutrition in many Third World countries?'[51]

TWAIL scholars have long critiqued the tendency of international human rights praxis and discourse to foster and reproduce a binary dichotomy that ruptures the globe into two conceptual communities, the one "heavenly" and the other "hellish"; a dichotomy that draws fairly neat and bright lines between "the Good West" and "the Bad Third World."[52] Thus, in utilizing a minimum core concept that appears to be context blind, it may very well be that the west is good because by virtue of the existing welfare state they have satisfied the minimum core, while the third world is bad because they are unable to deliver the most basic content of the ESRs to their often disenchanted populations. The problem therefore lies in the fact that if the minimum core concept is uniformly applied across the board, then it may be fairly easy for the former countries to appear as though they are meeting their obligations under the ICESCR while the latter group of countries will be forever demonized for failing to meet the core content of the myriad rights.

It is incontrovertible that resource and power asymmetries are deeply etched in and characterize the relationships between the global north and the global south. However, it has been convincingly argued that today, international law prescribes rules that deliberately ignore the phenomena of uneven development in favor of prescribing uniform global standards. It has more or less cast to flames the principal of special and differential treatment.[53] International law tends to transcend differences in order to impose uniform global legal regimes.[54] As Chimni has pointed out there seems to be a refusal to affirmatively differentiate between States at different stages of the development process. Equality rather than difference seems to be the prescribed norm.[55] It has been posited that there would be no point in having a minimum core of state responsibility if it was not universal.[56] This may explain why the CESCR opted for what appears to be a universal minimum core concept that applies evenly to all states rather than a more nuanced one when it first outlined the operation of the minimum core in the field of ESRs.

[51]Badaru (2008).

[52]Okafor (2014).

[53]Chimni (2006), p. 5.

[54]Ibid.

[55]Ibid.

[56]Brand and Russel (2008).

Certain proponents of the minimum core concept advocate for its utilization on the basis that it provides an objective standard across different state systems of political economy. The concept purports to advance a baseline of socioeconomic protection across varied economic policies and vastly different levels of available resources. States parties are obligated regardless of the level of economic development, to ensure respect for minimum subsistence rights for all.[57] Such minimum core obligations have been said to apply irrespective of the availability of resources of the country concerned or any other factors and difficulties.[58] The CESCR has reiterated time and time again that resource scarcity does not relieve states of certain minimum obligations in respect of ESRs. If this is the case then shouldn't the resource abundance that characterizes the so called global north be factored into the analysis of what the minimum core is in these states? A minimum core that boasts of equal application to unequal states does not merit the acceptance of the international community. There is a very real fear that affluent states may take advantage of escapist interpretations of the minimum core doctrine. Once these states comply with the minimum standards, which may be fairly easy to do given the incidence of resource abundance, their governments are likely to assert that they have met their core obligations and nothing more remains to be done in this regard.

For instance, as outlined previously in this article, the right to food has been said to include a core obligation to take the necessary measures to mitigate and alleviate hunger.[59] Now imagine two countries such as Kenya (in the global south) and France (in the global north). Both of these countries are state parties to the ICESCR having ratified the covenant in 1972 and in 1980 respectively. The governments of both Kenya as well as France are therefore expected to ensure that they take all necessary measures to alleviate hunger, failing which the CESCR would likely assert that there has been a failure to meet core obligations of the covenant in as far as the right to food is concerned. Is this a level playing field? I think not. France is classified as a developed/high income country while Kenya is classified as a developing/low income country.[60] It is clear that relying upon a context blind minimum core would undoubtedly result into Kenya being ranked as a poor performer in juxtaposition to its more developed counterpart.

To date, Young's article on the minimum core concept remains one of the most seminal academic works in the field of ESRs.[61] She argues that there are three rival approaches to defining the minimum core doctrine. Borrowing heavily from her

[57]Limburg Principles on the Implementation of the International Covenant on Economic, Social and Cultural Rights, Annex, U.N. Doc. E/CN.4/1987/17 (June 2–6, 1986).

[58]Maastricht Guidelines on Violations of Economic, Social and Cultural Rights, U.N. Doc. E/C.12/2000/13.

[59]UN Committee on Economic, Social and Cultural Rights (CESCR), General Comment No. 12: The Right to Adequate Food (Art. 11 of the Covenant), 12 May 1999, paragraph 6.

[60]Development Policy and Analysis Division (DPAD) of the Department of Economic and Social Affairs of the United Nations Secretariat (UN/DESA), World Economic Situation and Prospects, 2012.

[61]Young (2008).

work I will posit that only certain conceptions of the minimum core will satisfy a TWAIL analysis, and as such these are the conceptions that should be favored by the CESCR.

4.1 The Minimum Core as Normative Essence

This so called essence approach is distinguished by its search for the essential minimum of each right. This can be done in two ways. In the first formulation the minimum core is identified as a needs based core. Thus, satisfaction of the basic needs of the rights holders takes precedence over more ambitious levels of interests.[62] This is because basic needs are required as a minimum condition for a bearable life[63] or for a decent chance at a reasonably healthy and active life of more or less normal length.[64]

The problem with conceptualizing the minimum core as a needs based core lies in the fact that the requirements for survival are not as straightforward as they might appear to be at first blush.[65] From a TWAIL perspective, a needs based core would immediately mean that in developed countries typically characterized by a welfare state the minimum core will be seen as having been satisfied with most of the population enjoying the basic needs necessary to survive while in the developing and least developed countries often characterized by scarcity of resources the minimum core may very well remain aspirational and not a tangible goal.

The second approach, touted as a value based core, goes further than the basic needs inquiry by emphasizing not what is strictly required for life, but rather what it means to be human.[66] The emphasis here is on values such as human dignity, equality and freedom. While it is indomitable that values such as human dignity have universal appeal and application, I would opine that despite the fact that every human being deserves to live a life with dignity, this idea of what living with dignity actually is must necessarily vary from one society to another. The type of clothing and shelter required to allow a rights holder in Kenya to live in dignity may very well vary from that required for a right holder in the United States. As convincingly explained by Amartya Sen, the baseline of goods required for appearing in public without shame will be variable between different societies. The content of ESRs, and thus the minimum core, will be similarly inconsistent, not only because of varied resources, but also because of the different cultural expectations that may run parallel to this influence.[67] As such, in conceptualizing a minimum core as normative

[62]Ibid.

[63]Waldron (2009).

[64]Shue (1996).

[65]Sen (1981).

[66]Young (2008).

[67]Sen (1992).

essence a value based core would be a more viable option to a needs based core, at least from a TWAIL perspective, but only if there is acknowledgment of the fact that values like human dignity may not be homogenous but may actually vary depending on the society in question.

4.2 The Minimum Core as Minimum Consensus

In the consensus approach the minimum core content is the right's agreed upon nucleus.[68] This means that instead of asking what normative minimum should be given priority in each right, the emphasis should instead be on uncovering whether consensus has been reached on content. The subscribers to the consensus approach attest to a wider agreement,[69] an accumulation of state practice[70] and a synthesis of jurisprudence as founding a core content of each right.[71] Young argues that the consensus approach is likely to render politically legitimate, and valid, the universal application of the minimum core.

Consensus may be gleaned as a result of what Young calls a positivist inquiry. This is the same approach taken by the CESCR, which has relied explicitly on the reports of state parties to elucidate the developing content of the minimum core.[72] For example, in 1991, its then chairperson, Philip Alston, suggested that clarification of the normative content of the rights to food, health, housing and education should be achieved through the examination of state parties' reports.[73] While this kind of consensus is undoubtedly important, the hurdle that immediately becomes apparent from a TWAIL perspective is whose consensus is to count. If the consensus emanates from countries in the global north and is imposed on countries on the global south there is a likelihood that the consensus on what the core is may be an unfair articulation beneficial to the former countries but detrimental to the latter.

As Young further questions, should this consensus be judicial consensus, governmental and intergovernmental declarations or the consensus established between social experts in policy areas influencing economic and social rights.[74] The difficulty lies in the fact that for instance, if judges from a more developed welfare state identify a core of the various rights which will be used as a yardstick to assess the actions of their respective government it is likely that this so called consensus may not be agreeable to the judiciary of a less developed state struggling to assess its own government which is not similarly placed in terms of resources. Alternatively, what

[68]Young (2008).

[69]Id.

[70]Leckie (1989), pp. 522–560.

[71]Bolivar and Gonzalez (2000).

[72]Young (2008).

[73]Alston (1992).

[74]Young (2008).

if the consensus is garnered from the work of social experts? Are social experts equally drawn from the developed and less developing countries? Probably not. Consensus as a way of articulating the minimum core may therefore be argued to be inimical to the TWAIL agenda because in deriving the consensus there is a high likelihood of unequal representation in the voices clamoring to be heard.

Young also asserts that consensus may alternatively be interrogated as a normative concept, tied to ideas of sovereignty and self-government. The importance of consensus here lies in its ability to deliver legitimacy to the operation of both international and constitutional law. Basically consensus becomes a proxy for the more stringent requirement of state consent and to the ideal of democratic self-rule in constitutional law.[75] Viewed in this way consensus may fail to equip the minimum core with adequate content precisely because no single state will concede to a minimum core that places more strain on the government, than the powers that be are willing to bear. In this sense then, the problem becomes achievement of consensus on what exactly the minimum core ought to be. This magnifies the universality problem previously mentioned, that it is impossible to have a universal minimum core that is agreed upon by all the parties to the ICESCR regardless of their unique backgrounds as either well to do countries in the global north or ne'er do well countries in the global south.

Many commentators argue that consensus should not count for human rights as it does for other obligations, because human rights treaties have been established to protect minorities.[76] As such, from a TWAIL stance there ought to be a more principled way of identifying the applicable minimum core that does not leave this determination to the vagaries of consensus. As Young points out, if we take a more realist view of how and where consensus is achieved in international and national policy debates, we become even more uneasy. Official agreements are heavily influenced by compromise rather than reason. Sometimes, the compromise tends towards coercion.[77] The consensus in this case may therefore not be truly given. Focusing on consensus alone may ultimately thwart the definition and operation of a universal minimum core.[78]

4.3 The Minimum Core as Minimum Obligation

Because of the limitations inherent in the first two conceptions of the minimum core, Young offers a third, somewhat different, approach. The question to be answered here is whether there is a minimum set of obligations that can correlate to the minimum core. The advantages here are twofold. The first is that a focus on the

[75]Ibid.

[76]Benvenisti (1999), p. 843.

[77]Young (2008).

[78]Ibid.

duties required to implement the rights rather than the elements of the rights themselves enables the analysis of realistic, institutionally informed strategies of rights protection. That is, it becomes possible to come up with solutions for what it actually takes to enable people to be secure against the standard predictable threats to their rights.[79] The second is that an analysis of the duties that correlate to each right confronts the erroneous dichotomy of positive and negative rights making it clear that all rights, whether CPRs or ESRs, contain correlative duties of the state to both refrain from and perform certain acts in certain circumstances. Thus, core obligations are both negative and positive obligations and are actively addressed to both judicial and other legal institutional settings.[80] Arguably, it is this kind of thinking that has in recent times influenced the CESCR's recent attempts to circumvent the difficult questions of form and content of legal entitlement and instead led them to focus their efforts on producing a template of core obligations that straddle different rights, duties of positive provision and wider institutional strategies.[81]

There are many different categorizations of duties under the ICESCR. For instance, one may speak of the tripartite classifications of duty to protect, duty to respect and duty to fulfill.[82] Another possible classification could be between obligations of conduct and those of result.[83] Using the latter category of obligations for illustration purposes, it is clear that there is a difference between obligations of conduct and obligations of result. The obligation of conduct requires action reasonably calculated to realize the enjoyment of a particular right. In the case of the right to health for example, the obligation of conduct could involve the adoption and implementation of a plan of action to reduce maternal mortality. The obligation of result on the other hand requires states to achieve targets to satisfy a detailed substantive standard. With respect to the right to health for instance, the obligation of result could require the reduction of maternal mortality to levels agreed at the 1994 Cairo International Conference on Population and Development and the 1995 Beijing Fourth World Conference on Women.[84]

Some commentators have suggested that the minimum core concept relates only to obligations of result because it is able to signal only the extent to which individuals are enjoying their rights rather than assess the policies and procedures

---

79 Ibid.

80 Ibid.

81 Ibid.

82 International Commission of Jurists (ICJ), *Maastricht Guidelines on Violations of Economic, Social and Cultural Rights*, para. 6 (Jan. 1997).

83 Ibid. para 7.

84 Ibid.

that bring about that result.[85] However, the CESCR has been quick to recognize both types of obligations and includes both within its assessment of core obligations.[86]

Young critiques attempts by the CESCR to enumerate core obligations as being far from coherent. She argues that the CESCR has followed a meandering course of logic as to what amounts to such obligations, delivered by recourse to the work of United Nations specialized agencies, the declarations of international gatherings of particular expertise and a consensus of the committee members themselves.[87]

From a TWAIL standpoint there is an inescapable tension in attempting to identify and use minimum obligations as a way to substantiate the minimum core. For instance if the minimum core is assessed only on the basis of obligations of result, it may very well be that states in the global south would find themselves harshly judged for failing to achieve the identified targets and standards. If however, the emphasis is on obligations of conduct then there would be room to analyze state behavior taking into consideration the unique circumstances of each state in question in order to determine whether the conduct of the government in question is reasonable given factors such as resource availability, and geared towards fulfilment of the specific right in question. This latter conceptualization of the minimum core from the obligations of conduct vantage point is therefore more compatible with the TWAIL thinking because it leaves room for variations among states to be factored into the analysis of whether a state is meeting its duties as opposed to imposing a lesser burden on more developed states which could easily happen if the former approach is favored.

The enumeration of the core as an expression of core obligations or justiciable complaints is ultimately unsatisfactory. Despite collecting a set of important institutional duties and challenges together, the project is prone to unravel. This is because the insurmountable problem for the notion of core obligations is that the particular forms of duties are intrinsically polycentric and cannot be subject to a definitive ranking.[88]

5 What Next: A Context Specific Minimum Core and Its Potential Ambit

Young concludes her seminal work by arguing that instead of demarcating different rights and obligations as core and non-core the CESCR and other relevant bodies are better equipped to supervise and enforce the predominantly positive obligations

[85] Melish (2006), p. 171.

[86] UN Committee on Economic, Social and Cultural Rights (CESCR), General Comment No. 3: The Nature of States Parties' Obligations (Art. 2, Para. 1, of the Covenant), 14 December 1990, E/1991/23.

[87] Young (2008).

[88] Waldron (1985).

attached to ESRs by using benchmarks and indicators and the predominantly negative obligations by an assessment of state responsibility and causality.[89] Which is to say that instead of abandoning the minimum core concept, we should focus on beginning to prescribe content using benchmarks and indicators, rather than get bogged down by attempts to satisfactorily conclude the search for the content of the minimum core using the essence, consensus or obligations approach.

I agree with Young, at least to the extent that she argues for the continuing importance of the minimum core concept. However, I will herein propose an alternative conception of the minimum core that may potentially alleviate some of the TWAIL concerns identified in the preceding sections of this paper.

TWAIL has been critiqued for being critical, and not pragmatic. It has been advanced that TWAIL needs to move beyond intellectual critique to the level where it proposes or develops concrete means by which its critiques can be addressed—either in knowledge production or pragmatic institutional development. What alternatives to the perceived wrongs of international human rights can TWAIL proffer? More specifically, how would TWAIL posit that some of the failings that have been observed with international human rights law be remedied?[90] As Chimni has remarked TWAIL critique of international human rights has to further develop and make use of the language of human rights to pragmatically defend the interests of the poor and marginal groups.[91]

Undoubtedly, the CESCR had valid reasons to propound the minimum core concept and extol its importance in ESR jurisprudence, without delving into the exact details of how the minimum core would operate in practice, especially in light of the very real differences that exist among the various states that have ratified the ICESCR. Indeterminacy in law does exist, and it is not always a bad thing. Hans Kelsen divides legal norms into two categories, higher level norms and lower level norms. He then goes on to make a distinction between two kinds of indeterminacy in law; intended and unintended, asserting that these exist as a result of the hierarchical structure of the legal system.[92] According to him, intended indeterminacy can be part of the intention of the authority issuing the higher-level norm while the unintended indeterminacy can transcend the intention of the authority issuing the higher-level norm. However, as Kelsen acknowledges,

> This determination, however, is never complete. The higher-level norm cannot be binding with respect to every detail of the act putting it into practice. There must always remain a range of discretion, sometimes wider, sometimes narrower, so that the higher-level norm, in relation to the act of applying it has simply the character of a frame to be filled in by way of the act. Even a meticulously detailed command must leave a number of determinations to those carrying it out. If official A orders official B to arrest subject C, B must use his own discretion to decide when, where, and how he will carry out the warrant to arrest C; and these

[89] Young (2008).
[90] Badaru (2008).
[91] Chimni (2006).
[92] Kelsen (1997).

decisions depend upon external circumstances that A has not foreseen and, for the most part, cannot foresee.[93]

Akin to Kelsen, Hart also arrives at the conclusion that some degree of indeterminacy is inevitable in Law. However unlike Kelsen, Hart argues that the systemic indeterminacy of law stems from the open texture of language.[94] His analytical argument runs as follows,

If all language (considered as a whole is open textured or has open texture and law is expressed in terms of language; thus, it logically follows that law is open textured or has open texture, and as such is indeterminate or has indeterminacy...[95]

Hart goes further and posits that determinacy is a question of degree. Law is determinate in some areas but indeterminate in others. I.e. law is determinate in the core and indeterminate in the penumbra.[96] There must be a core of settled meaning, but there will be, as well, a penumbra of debatable cases in which words are neither obviously applicable nor obviously ruled out.[97] Nothing can eliminate this duality of a core of certainty and a penumbra of doubt when we are engaged in bringing particular situations under general rules. This imparts to all rules a fringe of vagueness or 'open texture.'[98]

Extending this thinking to the operation of the minimum core I would argue that a certain level of intended indeterminacy was and is still necessary in order to generate consensus on the (continuing) importance of the minimum core concept as one of the *raison d'êtres* of the ICESCR. This possibly explains the very deliberate vagueness of the CESCR's first articulation of the concept in its General Comment No. 3.[99] However, it is the unintended indeterminacy that merits censure from a TWAIL perspective. This is because the potentially unanticipated effect of this kind of indeterminacy lies in the fact that there lies a loophole in the operation of the doctrine that seems to impose an easier minimum core obligation on countries in the global north than that imposed on countries in the global south when it comes to the respective governments' responsibility to deliver on ESRs in their various jurisdictions.

Rather than thinking of the minimum core concept as an absolute and universal measure of state performance, why not think of it as a sliding scale that will impose varying obligations on states depending on factors such as resource availability? A country with more resources should have a higher level of core content or immediate

[93]Ibid.

[94]Flores (2011).

[95]Hart (2012).

[96]Ibid.

[97]Hart (1957), pp. 593–629.

[98]Hart (2012).

[99]UN Committee on Economic, Social and Cultural Rights (CESCR), General Comment No. 3: The Nature of States Parties' Obligations (Art. 2, Para. 1, of the Covenant), 14 December 1990.

duties than that with more limited resources. I will hereinafter refer to this scale as a *sliding scale of core obligations*. The scale could hypothetically function as follows.

In the first instance there could be an absolute and non-derogable core (a first-tier obligation) that applies to the governments of all states equally regardless of resource differentials. This is analogous to the core of certainty identified by Hart. In outlining what exactly this absolute core can be said to encompass, the CESCR could have recourse to certain pre-identified indicators as suggested by Young. Indicators usually refer to a set of statistics which indicate phenomena that are not directly measurable and may be based on either quantitative or qualitative information as long as it can be consistently measured over time.[100]

After this initial appraisal, a subsequent level of obligations (a second tier of obligations) may be imposed on the state party in question depending on availability of resources. In the words of Hart this second tier of obligations could be said to be shrouded in a penumbra of doubt. As an example, the Gross Domestic Product (hereinafter, the "GDP") of the country concerned could be a useful tool for assessing the resources at the state's disposal for fulfilment of their ICESCR commitments. The higher the GDP the higher the level of obligations that the country in question will be expected to satisfy as part of the second tier of the sliding scale of core obligations. (The use of GDP here is mainly for illustrative purposes. A more suitable indicator of state's resource capabilities can be utilized with the same end goal).

The difference between this penumbra of doubt (doubt in the sense that the level of additional obligations owed by a government depends on the resources available as measured by GDP which is a variable measure) and the core of certainty previously mentioned (which is a fixed level of obligation identified by the CESCR and applying evenly to all governments regardless of the GDP) lies in the fact that instead of the CESCR bearing the responsibility of articulating the exact nature of the second tier obligations the onus will be on the state in question to justify in its communication to the CESCR that given its level of resource abundance they have taken certain measures to deliver on ESRs that go beyond the absolute core. In some ways this is an argument for obligations of conduct (as opposed to those of result) being utilized as a gauge to assess the level at which second tier core obligations are enjoyed in a particular country.

This could be graphically represented as shown in Fig. 1.

The immense appeal that is apparent from reconceptualizing the minimum core in this way lies in the fact that the aforementioned TWAIL critiques of a single and universal minimum core are somewhat diminished. The double pronged assessment that all states will be subjected to as part of the sliding scale of core obligations implies that the minimum core concept can and will be deployed in a way that effectively acknowledges differences between countries in the global north and in the global south and among countries in the global south itself.

[100] Young (2008).

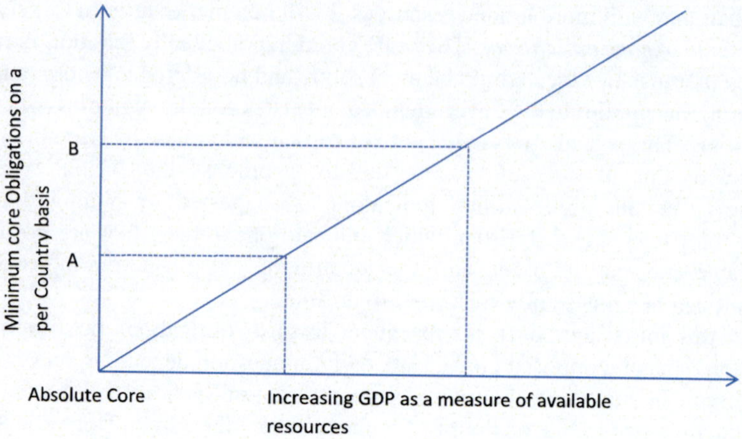

Fig. 1 Sliding scale of core obligations

For example, consider two countries A and B represented on the graph above. Assume that country A lies in the global south while country B lies in the global north as measured by the availability of resources in each country, as a factor of their respective GDPs. In utilizing the sliding scale of core obligations to assess whether these countries are meeting their minimum core obligations the CESCR will undertake the following analysis. First, both country A and B will have to prove that they have each met the absolute core of obligations. As previously mentioned the exact measure of the absolute core will have been identified by the CESCR and will not vary as between the two countries. Assuming that both countries have met their first-tier absolute core obligations, the analysis will then shift to the question of resources available to both as measured by their respective GDPs. As inelegantly depicted by the rudimentary graph above country B has a higher GDP than country A. The CESCR will therefore require both countries to adumbrate upon the steps that they have taken (or the obligations of conduct that they have fulfilled) in order to fulfil their second-tier core obligations, holding country B to a higher standard than country A.

The dialogue anticipated by the sliding scale analysis of core obligations could easily occur as part of the CESCR duty to audit state reports and issue concluding observations on the basis of their findings. That is to say that this reconceptualized minimum core can easily function within the already existing framework, and will ensure that there is a certain measure of fairness in the deployment of the minimum core doctrine that has arguably been hitherto lacking, at least from a TWAIL perspective.

Finally, to be clear, the intention of this paper has been to provoke a debate on the potential tension between the current conceptualization of the minimum core doctrine and TWAIL theory. The paper does not attempt to offer any conclusive answers to what are undoubtedly very difficult and complex questions.

References

Alston P (ed) (1992) The Committee on Economic, Social and Cultural Rights, in the United Nations and human rights: a critical appraisal. Oxford University Press

Alston P (2008) Foreword. In: Langford M (ed) Social rights jurisprudence: emerging trends in international and comparative law. Cambridge University Press, Cambridge

Anghie A, Chimni BS (2003) Third world approaches to international law and individual responsibility in internal conflicts. Chinese J Int Law 2(1):77–103

Badaru OA (2008) Examining the utility of third world approaches to international law for international human rights law. Int Commun Law Rev 10:379–387

Benvenisti E (1999) Margin of appreciation, consensus and universal standards. N Y Univ J Int Law Policy 31(843)

Bolivar L, Gonzalez E (2000) Defining the content of economic, social and cultural rights – problems and prospects. In: Circle of rights: economic, social and cultural rights activism: a training resource (International Human Rights Internship Program, October)

Brand D, Russel S (eds) (2008) Exploring the core content of socio-economic rights: South African and international perspective. University of Michigan Press

Chimni BS (2006) Third world approaches to international law: a manifesto. Int Commun Law Rev 8:5

Chowdhury J (2009) Judicial adherence to a minimum core approach to socio-economic rights – a comparative perspective. Paper presented at the Cornell Law School Inter-University Graduate Student Conference, March 2009

Flores IB (2011) H.L.A. Hart's "The Concept of Law" and the moderate indeterminacy thesis reconsidered. In: 25th IVR World Congress: Law, Science and Technology, Frankfurt am Main

Gathii J (2011) TWAIL. A brief history of its origins, its decentralized network, and a tentative bibliography. Trade Law Dev 3(26)

Hart HLA (1957) Positivism and the separation of law and morals. Harv Law Rev 71(4):593–629

Hart HLA (2012) The concept of law, 3rd edn. Oxford University Press

Kelsen H (1997) Introduction to the problems of legal theory: a translation of the first edition of the Reine Rechtslehre or pure theory of law. Clarendon Press

Langford M (2008) Social rights jurisprudence: emerging trends in international and comparative law. Cambridge University Press, Cambridge

Leckie S (1989) The UN Committee on Economic, Social and Cultural Rights and the right to adequate housing: towards an appropriate approach. Hum Rights Q 11(4):522–560

Max H (2013) Downsizing rights: why the minimum core concept in International Human Rights Law should be abandoned. New Zealand Public Int Law J 10

Melish T (2006) Rethinking the "Less as More" thesis: supranational litigation of the economic, social and cultural rights in the Americas. N Y Univ J Int Law Policy 39(171)

Mickelson K (1998) Rhetoric and Rage: third world voices in international legal discourse. Wisconsin Int Law J 16:375

Mutua M (2000a) Critical race theory and international law: the view of an insider-outsider. Villanova Law Rev 45:841

Mutua M (2000b) What is TWAIL? ASIL proceedings of the 94th annual meeting, pp 31–39

Mutua M, Anghie A (2000) What is TWAIL? Proc Annu Meeting (ASIL) 94:31–40

Okafor O (2005) Newness, imperialism, and international legal reform in our time: a TWAIL perspective. Osgoode Hall Law J 43(1/2)

Okafor O (2014) International human rights fact-finding praxis in its living forms: a TWAIL perspective. Trans Hum Rights Rev 1(1):9–105

Pieterse M (2007) Eating socio-economic rights: the usefulness of rights talk in alleviating social hardship revisited. Hum Rights Q 796

Sen A (1981) Poverty and famine: an essay on entitlement and deprivation. Clarendon Press, Oxford

Sen A (1992) Inequality reexamined. Oxford University Press

Shue H (1996) Basic rights: subsistence, affluence and U.S. foreign policy, 2nd end. Princeton University Press

Waldron J (ed) (1985) Introduction to theories of rights. Oxford University Press

Waldron J (2009) Rights and needs: the myth of disjunction. In: Sarat A, Kearns R (eds) Legal rights: historical and philosophical perspectives. University of Michigan Press

Wesson M (2012) Disagreement and the constitutionalization of social rights. Hum Rights Law Rev 12:221 at 242

Young K (2008) The minimum core of economic and social rights: a concept in search of content. Yale Int Law J 33:113–175

Caroline Omari Lichuma Law Faculty at Riara University in Nairobi, Kenya (currently on study leave); PhD Candidate, Georg-August Universität Göttingen; LLM in Public International Law, New York University; LLB, University of Nairobi.

Health and Development in Africa: How Far Can the Human Rights Jurisprudence Go?

Olasupo Owoeye

Contents

1 Introduction

The gross inequalities between richer and poorer nations and the economic inequalities between people in poorer countries are believed to account for 20 million deaths every year in the past two decades.[1] Health disparities, excluding those relating to inequalities in high income countries, are estimated to be responsible for about one-third of reported deaths globally.[2] While several international law regimes could play a significant role in combating health inequities, human rights law is the major international legal regime that significantly addresses this problem.[3] The unfulfillment of economic, social and cultural rights has also been shown to have adverse health consequences. For instance, 5.9 million children under the age of 5 died in 2015 mostly from preventable diseases with the figures indicating that

[1] Gostin and Friedman (2013), p. 4.

[2] Ibid.

[3] Ibid 5.

O. Owoeye (✉)
School of Business and Law, CQUniversity, Brisbane, QLD, Australia

C. Eboe-Osuji et al. (eds.), *Nigerian Yearbook of International Law 2018/2019*,
Nigerian Yearbook of International Law 2018/2019,
https://doi.org/10.1007/978-3-030-69594-1_13

children from sub Saharan Africa are 14 times more likely to die before attaining the age of 5 than their counterparts in developed regions.[4] In a similar vein, more than three hundred thousand women died in pregnancy and childbirth in 2015, with an overwhelming preponderance of such deaths occurring in Sub Saharan Africa.[5] It is therefore right to view respect for human rights in the struggle to alleviate the suffering caused by HIV/AIDS as both a moral and legal imperative.[6]

Infectious diseases remain a major cause of death in developing countries; they also constitute a major threat to public health in every part of the world.[7] While it is correct that the global incidence of HIV is declining with more than eight million people receiving HIV treatment in developing countries in 2011, approximately seven million people in need of anti-retroviral medication were still unable to get it.[8] The 2015 World Health Organisation Malaria report indicates a 48% decline in the number of malaria related deaths globally between 2000 and 2015.[9] Thus while malaria is no longer the leading cause of death for children in sub Saharan Africa, it is still, unacceptably, the fourth highest cause of death for children in the region.[10] It has been shown that poor health can have adverse impact on economic growth and development and the link between health and development has been well accentuated.

This paper explores the connection between the right to health and the development. It discusses the international framework for the protection of health rights and the significance of development as a right in international law. It notes that while there has been some improvement in the actualisation of some health rights, especially those related to the Millennium Developmental Goals, there is still much to do in the campaign for obliterating global health inequities and this is particularly so in Africa. It argues that safeguarding health rights is very important to the pursuit of development in Africa. The paper concludes that beyond the health and development rhetoric, there is a compelling need for African states to devise pragmatic strategies for ensuring the progressive actualisation of health rights and the right to development. It notes that doing this will require transcending the realm of legislative articulation of human rights in legal texts to the adoption of administrative and judicial measures for the efficacious realisation of health and development rights.

The paper begins with a background discussion of the development objectives of developing countries and how this is pursued under the United Nations and World Trade Organisation systems. It then examines the right to health and its connection to

---

[4]WHO, Children: Reducing Mortality, WHO Media Centre Fact Sheet January 2016 available at http://www.who.int/mediacentre/factsheets/fs178/en/.

[5]WHO, Global Health Observatory (GHO) data: Maternal mortality available at http://www.who.int/gho/maternal_health/mortality/maternal_mortality_text/en/.

[6]Iacopino et al. (2011), pp. 149 and 175.

[7]Gostin and Friedman (2013), p. 11.

[8]Ibid.

[9]WHO (2015), p. x.

[10]Ibid.

the pursuit of human development. The paper then proceeds to highlight how health and development are recognised and well established human rights in Africa while accentuating the need to put in place stronger mechanisms for the enforcement and implementation of the rights.

1.1 Development and Developing Countries

The concept of development has been receiving significant attention in international relations for decades and it currently plays a particularly important role in international law.[11] While development has traditionally been an important part of the objectives of the United Nations and the World Bank, it is a more recent phenomenon in organisations such as the World Trade Organisation (WTO) and the World Intellectual Property Organization (WIPO).[12] Development is also becoming a major issue in international trade and international intellectual property negotiations. Thus, WIPO adopted a Development Agenda at its 2004 annual meeting[13] and pursuant to this agenda, the WIPO General Assembly adopted 45 recommendations with a view to incorporating development concerns in all of WIPO's activities.[14] Development is a prominent part of the WTO's objectives. The WTO Doha round of trade negotiations has been popularly tagged the 'Doha development round' as a result of its main aim of integrating development concerns into the WTO multilateral trading system.[15] Indeed, with the launching of the Doha Development Round, the WTO has clearly positioned development issues and the concerns of developing countries 'at the heart of WTO's work'.[16] The 2005 WTO Hong Kong Ministerial Declaration further reiterates the significance of development by emphasising 'the central importance of the development dimension in every aspect of the Doha Work Programme' and the commitment of the WTO members to making it a reality.[17] It is pertinent to add that the term 'developing countries' is not a clearly defined concept in international law even though the term continues to be used by international organisations such as the United Nations and its agencies, the International Monetary Fund, the World Bank, the Organization for Economic Cooperation and Development (OECD) and the WTO. The United Nations however maintains a clearly defined

---

[11]Kwakwa (2012), pp. 221 and 222.

[12]Ibid 224.

[13]World Intellectual Property Organization, Proposal by Argentina and Brazil for the Establishment of a Development Agenda for WIPO, WIPO Doc. WO/GA/31/11 (Aug. 27, 2004); WIPO Development Agenda: Background (2004–2007).

[14]Kwakwa (2009), p. 1.

[15]Qureshi (2009), p. 173.

[16]See WTO, Trade and Development, available at https://www.wto.org/english/tratop_e/devel_e/devel_e.htm.

[17]WTO, Hong Kong Ministerial Declaration, WT/MIN(05)/DEC adopted 18 December 2015 https://www.wto.org/english/thewto_e/minist_e/min05_e/final_text_e.htm.

list of least developed countries[18] which is recognised for transitional arrangements purposes under the WTO Agreement on Trade Related Aspects of Intellectual Property Rights.[19] Developing countries often receive special concessions and foreign assistance under the WTO and United Nations' systems. To this end developing countries, for the purposes of the present discourse, may be considered to include all the countries recognised by the OECD as eligible to receive official development assistance (ODA).[20]

Given the fact that the WTO provides for a decision making by consensus mechanism, each WTO country has a veto power and this puts developing countries in a more powerful position in the WTO[21] than they are in the World Bank or even the United Nations given the latter's Security Council's veto powers. It has thus been suggested that developing countries would benefit more by promoting their interest through the WTO.[22] It is also argued that it is more advantageous for developing countries to negotiate in a multilateral setting like the WTO than to proceed on a bilateral basis.[23] Although it is generally believed that developing countries did not benefit much from the Uruguay round of trade negotiations, it is right to say that the Doha Development round was designed to address many of their concerns.[24] Indeed, the only amendment to any WTO Agreement ever made since the establishment of the organisation in 1994 was the Decision of the WTO to amend Article 31(f) of the Agreement on Trade Related Aspects of Intellectual Property Rights (TRIPS Agreement) to enable developing countries without significant manufacturing capacity in the pharmaceutical sector to benefit from the TRIPS compulsory licensing regime by importing drugs from other countries under a compulsory licensing scheme.[25] There are also a number of provisions in WTO Agreement that are specifically for the benefit of developing countries.[26]

Developed nations have made significant progress in reducing infant and maternal mortality as well as in curtailing the spread of HIV and the risk of malaria as the

[18]See UN-OHRLLS, 'About LDC's' available at http://unohrlls.org/about-ldcs/.

[19]See Marrakesh Agreement Establishing the World Trade Organisation, opened for signature April 15, 1994, 1867 U.N.T.S. 3 (entered into force January 1, 1995), Annex 1C (Agreement on Trade Related Aspects of Intellectual Property Rights) (TRIPS) Art. 66.

[20]See OECD, DAC List of ODA Recipients, available at http://www.oecd.org/dac/financing-sustainable-development/development-finance-standards/daclist.htm.

[21]See Kwakwa (2012), p. 228.

[22]Amorim (2000), p. 95.

[23]Kwakwa (2012), p. 228.

[24]See Matsushita et al. (2006), pp. 782–784.

[25]Implementation of Paragraph 6 of the Doha Declaration on the TRIPS Agreement and Public Health, WTO Doc WT/L/540 (September 2) (Decision of August 30, 2003).

[26]See WTO, Work on Special and Differential Provisions, World Trade Org., http://www.wto.org/english/tratop_e/devel_e/dev_special_differential_provisions_e.htm.

vast majority of these cases occur in developing countries.[27] Various efforts both at national and international levels have also led to significant reduction in maternal mortality rates[28] and have equally facilitated access to medicines for millions of HIV positive people.[29] Experience has thus shown that societal action can reduce diseases and pain and international law can play a pivotal role in extending the benefits of good health to people living in the world's most disadvantaged regions.[30]

1.2 *Health and Human Rights*

The right to health is well recognised in several international human rights declarations and legal instruments. A human rights framework will not only help in identifying the varying social factors that have impacts on health, it will also facilitate the identification of policies and interventions capable of maximising health and human rights benefits.[31] Thus, by resolution 2002/31 The UN Special Rapporteur on the right of everyone to the enjoyment of the highest attainable standard of physical and mental health was given a mandate by the Commission on Human Rights (now Human Rights Council) in 2002 to amongst other things:

> [G]ather, request, receive and exchange information from all relevant sources, including Governments, intergovernmental and non-governmental organizations, on the realization of the right of everyone to the enjoyment of the highest attainable standard of physical and mental health, as well as policies designed to achieve the health-related Millennium Development Goals.

The Special Rapporteur on the right to health also has a mandate to make recommendations on the appropriate measures that may be taken to promote the actualisation of the right to health while supporting States' efforts to promote public health. The human rights system may thus be a strong tool for the identification of policies that could be implemented at national levels for the actualisation of public health objectives.

The preamble to the Constitution of the World Health Organization notes that 'the enjoyment of the highest attainable standard of health' is a fundamental right of every human being.[32] According to Article 25 of the Universal Declaration of Human Rights (UNDHR):

---

[27] See WHO, Newborns: Reducing mortality, Media Centre Fact Sheet, January 2016 available at http://www.who.int/mediacentre/factsheets/fs333/en/; WHO, HIV/AIDS, available at http://www.who.int/immunization/topics/hiv/en/index1.html; WHO, World Malaria Report 2015, p. x.

[28] See Gostin and Friedman (2013), p. 10.

[29] George (2011), pp. 167 and 171.

[30] George (2011), p. 171; Novogrodsky (2014), pp. 643 and 646–651.

[31] Iacopino et al. (2011), p. 150.

[32] Constitution of the World Health Organization, adopted 22 July 1946, entered into force 7 April 1948 available at http://apps.who.int/gb/bd/PDF/bd47/EN/constitution-en.pdf?ua=1.

(1) Everyone has the right to a standard of living adequate for the health and well-being of himself and of his family, including food, clothing, housing and medical care and necessary social services, and the right to security in the event of unemployment, sickness, disability, widowhood, old age or other lack of livelihood in circumstances beyond his control.

(2) Motherhood and childhood are entitled to special care and assistance. All children, whether born in or out of wedlock, shall enjoy the same social protection.[33]

Although the UNDHR is not a legally binding document but an aspirational one, it is nevertheless generally regarded as reflecting the principles of customary international law.[34] According to legal positivism as propounded by Jeremy Bentham and John Austin, '*law is the command of the uncommanded commanders of society - the creation of the legally untrammelled will of the sovereign who is by definition outside the law*'.[35] Thus, given the positivist theory of law which conceives of law as the immutable decree of an "uncommanded commander", for the right to health to be a legal right in international law, its principles would have to be legally binding on all nations and judicially enforceable against states that derogate from the right.

The principles enunciated in the UNDHR have been fully incorporated into the two major international charters of rights; International Covenant on Civil and Political Rights (ICCPR)[36] and the International Covenant on Economic, Social and Cultural Rights (ICESCR).[37] While the ICCPR and ICESCR may not be directly enforceable at national levels without the domestic incorporation of international obligations at national levels, the adoption of the Optional Protocol to the International Covenant on Economic, Social and Cultural Rights in 2008 has made it possible to explore enforcement options for the UNDHR rights that have become incorporated in the ICESCR, including the right to health.

Article 12.1 of the International Covenant on Economic, Social and Cultural Rights further reiterates the right of everyone to the highest attainable standard of physical and mental health. Under article 12.2 of the ICESCR, states have an obligation to reduce infant mortality and promote healthy development of children. States are also obliged to promote the improvement of the environment, industrial hygiene, prevention, treatment and control of diseases as well as the creation of conditions that would enable their nationals to have access to medical services and

---

[33]Universal Declaration of Human Rights, GA Res 217A (III), UN Doc A/810 (10 December 1948), Art 25.

[34]Castleberry (2015), p. 189.

[35]See Hart (1958), pp. 593 and 603 available at http://www.umiacs.umd.edu/~horty/courses/readings/hart-1958-positivism-separation.pdf.

[36]International Covenant on Civil and Political Rights (ICCPR), adopted 16 December 1966, 999 UNTS 171 (entered into force 23 March 1976).

[37]International Covenant on Economic, Social and Cultural Rights (ICESCR), opened for signature 16 December 1966, 993 UNTS 3 (entered into force 3 January 1976).

'medical attention in the event of sickness'.[38] Up to 164 countries have ratified the ICESCR.[39] Unlike the International Covenant on Civil and Political Rights which imposes obligations that are expected to be implemented without delay, states parties to the ICESCR are required to progressively work towards the realisation of the social, economic and cultural rights enshrined in the convention having regard to the resources available to them. To this end, article 2.1 of the ICESCR provides:

> *Each State Party to the present Covenant undertakes to take steps, individually and through international assistance and cooperation, especially economic and technical, to the maximum of its available resources, with a view to achieving progressively the full realization of the rights recognized in the present Covenant by all appropriate means, including particularly the adoption of legislative measures.*

The reason for the difference in the implementation expectations of the ICCPR and the ICESCR has been attributed to the fact that the ICCPR is a charter of negative rights which states parties to the convention are restrained from refusing to uphold, while the ICESCR encompasses positive rights that require states to expend significant financial and human resources to fulfil them.[40] Human rights violations, be they civil, political, social, cultural or economic, can have substantial impact on the health of individuals and the communities in which they live.[41] The fact that the right to health covered by the ICESCR is subject to progressive and not immediate realisation does not however mean that states have no obligation to ensure meaningful progress towards its realisation. As a matter of fact, states have a continuing obligation to take concrete measures towards the expeditious realisation of the rights.[42] Other international human rights treaties enshrining the right to health include:

- the International Convention on the Elimination of All Forms of Racial Discrimination (1965): art. 5 (e) (iv);
- the Convention on the Elimination of All Forms of Discrimination against Women (1979): arts. 11 (1) (f), 12 and 14 (2) (b);
- the Convention on the Rights of the Child (1989): art. 24;
- the International Convention on the Protection of the Rights of All Migrant Workers and Members of Their Families (1990): arts. 28, 43 (e) and 45 (c);
- and the Convention on the Rights of Persons with Disabilities (2006): art. 25.

---

[38] ICESCR, Art. 12.2.

[39] See Status of Ratification Interactive Dashboard: International Covenant on Economic, Social and Cultural Rights, OFFICE OF THE HIGH COMM'R ON HUMAN RIGHTS (OHCHR), http://indicators.ohchr.org/.

[40] See Borelli (2009), p. 1.

[41] Iacopino et al. (2011), p. 162.

[42] Office of the United Nations High Commissioner for Human Rights, The Right to Health, factsheet No. 31 (June 2008) p. 5 http://www.ohchr.org/Documents/Publications/Factsheet31.pdf.

There are also a number of regional instruments that recognise the right to health. These include:

- the European Social Charter (1961);
- the African Charter on Human and Peoples' Rights (1981);
- and the Additional Protocol to the American Convention on Human Rights in the Area of Economic, Social and Cultural Rights (popularly known as the Protocol of San Salvador) (1988).

The right to health is particularly recognised in the constitutions of a number of countries in Africa. A very good example is the 1996 Constitution of South Africa. Section 27 of the South African Constitution provides thus:

1) *Everyone has the right to have access to health-care services, including reproductive health care...*
2) *The State must take reasonable legislative and other measures, within its available resources, to achieve the progressive realization of each of these rights.*
3) *No one may be refused emergency medical treatment.*

In a similar vein, section 17(3) of the Nigerian Constitution provides thus:

(3) The State shall direct its policy towards ensuring that-

(a) all citizens, without discrimination on any group whatsoever, have the opportunity for securing adequate means of livelihood as well as adequate opportunity to secure suitable employment;

(b) .....

(c) the health, safety and welfare of all persons in employment are safeguarded and not endangered or abused;

(d) there are adequate medical and health facilities for all persons:...

The provisions of section 17(3) of the Nigerian Constitution quoted above clearly relate to ensuring the enjoyment of the highest attainable standard of health, availability of good healthcare facilities and access to medicines. However, given the fact that section 17(3) of the Nigerian Constitution is contained in Chapter II of the Constitution which deals with 'Fundamental Objectives and Directive Principles of State Policy', the provisions relating to health rights are not justiciable by virtue of section 6 of the Constitution which effectively excludes Chapter II of the constitution from the jurisdiction of the Nigerian courts. Nonetheless, Nigeria is a party to the African Charter on Human and Peoples' Rights and the country has incorporated the African Charter into the corpus of its local laws by virtue of its passage into law by the Nigerian legislature. The Supreme Court of Nigeria has held in *Abacha v*

Fawehinmi[43] that the African Charter is part of the laws of Nigeria and described it as a local law 'with international flavour'. Given the fact that the Nigerian apex court directly enforced the provisions of the African Charter as a local law in *Abacha v Fawehinmi,* it is submitted on the authority of that decision that the right to health guaranteed by the African Charter may be directly enforced in Nigeria as a right protected by Nigerian national laws.

According to the Office of the United Nations High Commissioner for Human Rights, the right to health is an inclusive right that covers safe food, water, adequate sanitation, gender equality, prevention, treatment and control of disease and functioning public healthcare facilities.[44] OHCHR has also emphasised the fact that while it is not the responsibility of states to ensure their populations are healthy (as the determinants of good health are not within the control of states), states do have a clear obligation to make all possible efforts, within available resources and without delay, to ensure the realisation of the right to health.[45] The OHCHR has also opined that a country's difficult financial situation does not absolve it from fulfilling its obligations under the right to health and even where the country is experiencing an economic decline, there is still a continuing obligation on the country to fulfil its health obligations to the maximum level of the resources at the country's disposal.[46]

States' obligations in relation to the right to health include the obligation to respect, protect and fulfil.[47] The obligation to respect entails refraining from acts that may hinder the enjoyment of the right to health.[48] The obligation to protect requires states to take steps to restrain third parties from hindering the enjoyment of the right to health.[49] The obligation to fulfil mandates states to adopt necessary legislative, administrative and judicial measures to ensure the realisation of the right to health.[50] The right to health is equally connected to the right to life. Article 6.1 of the ICCPR guarantees the right to life in the following terms:

> *Every human being has the inherent right to life. This right shall be protected by law. No one shall be arbitrarily deprived of his life.*[51]

The right to health has been interpreted to include a duty on states not only to protect life but to also take measures that enhance the quality of life and the

[43]*Abacha v Fawehinmi* [2000] Nigerian Weekly Law Report, part 660.

[44]Office of the United Nations High Commissioner for Human Rights, The Right to Health, factsheet No. 31 (June 2008) pp. 3–4 http://www.ohchr.org/Documents/Publications/Factsheet31.pdf.

[45]Ibid 5.

[46]Ibid.

[47]Ibid 25.

[48]Ibid.

[49]Ibid 26.

[50]Ibid 27.

[51]ICCPR Art 6.1.

jurisprudence of the Inter American Human Rights Court clearly supports the view that health rights are so intrinsically linked with the right to life such that the right to health may be enforced through the right to life.[52]

It has been opined that although the right to health, like many other human rights, is not legally enforceable in every part of the world, there is increasing public awareness of human rights and the more the society continues to accord human rights a normative status, the more likely it is that states will feel obligated to implement health protection even if they are not legally enforceable.[53]

The right to health has been described as the most significant health related international obligation for all nations.[54] The concept of international health aid thus seems to be indeed profoundly flawed[55] as it presupposes a divide between the donors and the nations in need.[56] Describing international health assistance as 'aid' seems to undermine the fact that safeguarding human health is a shared responsibility of the human race as global health entails common risks and common vulnerabilities for humankind.[57] The World Conference on Human Rights has in fact declared that human rights are the birth rights of every human being and their promotion is the first duty of states.[58] The view has been expressed that a state's refusal to recognise a human right does not in any way undermine the fact that the right exists and human rights may be violated by actions authorised by national laws.[59]

Regional human rights instruments can play a unique role in contributing to the realisation of human rights given the fact that they occupy the legal space between national and international levels and are therefore able to influence and draw from both.[60] This is particularly so in Africa through the operation of the Protocol to the African Charter on Human And Peoples' Rights on the Establishment of an African Court on Human and Peoples' Rights.[61] This point is explored further below. Peace and health can also be intricately interconnected.[62] The implementation of obligations emanating from the right to health can be relevant to the development of an

[52]See generally Keener and Vasquez (2009), p. 595 at 599; see also Owoeye (2014), pp. 900–919.

[53]Castleberry (2015), p. 232.

[54]Gostin and Friedman (2013), p. 35.

[55]Ooms and Van Damme (2008), p. 893; Ooms et al. (2010), p. 17 available at http://globalizationandhealth.biomedcentral.com/articles/10.1186/1744-8603-6-17.

[56]Gostin and Friedman (2013), p. 34.

[57]Ibid 35.

[58]World Conference on Human Rights, June 14–25, 1993, Vienna Declaration and Programme of Action, P 1, U.N. Doc. A/CONF.157/24 (June 19, 1993), available at http://www.ohchr.org/EN/ProfessionalInterest/Pages/Vienna.aspx.

[59]Castleberry (2015), p. 189.

[60]Mattar (2013), p. 91.

[61]Protocol to the African Charter on Human and Peoples' Rights on the Establishment of an African Court on Human and Peoples' Rights, adopted June 10, 1998, entered into force January 25, 2004.

[62]See Muller (2014), pp. 415 and 416.

effective and responsive health system.[63] Such a health system can be helpful in building a peaceful society and it may also contribute to the prevention of civil unrest and armed conflicts.[64]

The right to health imposes obligations on states to make available health care facilities such as hospitals, clinics and institutions offering counselling and mental health care.[65] Another essential component of the responsibility of states under the right to health is to ensure the availability of adequate qualified medical personnel including doctors and other medical professionals.[66] The availability of an effective transportation and referral system is also very germane to the efficiency of a public health system as this will facilitate the physical access of people to health services. The UN Special Rapporteur's reports on the right to health have identified inadequate transportation and expensive transportation systems as major factors unduly limiting patient's access to adequate healthcare in a number of countries.[67]

Flowing from the right to health is also an obligation to take decisive steps to build an all-inclusive health plan and strategy for the establishment of an effective and responsive healthcare system.[68] According to the UN Special Rapporteur on the right to the enjoyment of the highest attainable standard of health, a comprehensive health plan should include:

> clear objectives and how they are to be achieved, time frames, indicators and benchmarks to measure achievement, effective coordination mechanisms, reporting procedures, a detailed budget that is attached to the plan, financing arrangements, evaluation arrangements, and one or more accountability devices. In order to complete the plan, there will have to be a process for prioritizing competing health needs[69]

Reducing infant mortality and morbidity is also an important right to health issue. Thus the UN Convention on the Rights of the Child states that taking measures to reduce infant mortality is an essential part of states obligations with respect to the right of the child to health. A strong health system has been described as one that promotes equality, accountability, and accessibility. The right to health also entails a

---

[63]Ibid 431.

[64]Ibid.

[65]See CESCR, General Comment 14: The Right to the Highest Attainable Standard of Health, U.N. Doc. E/C.12/2000/4 (Aug. 11, 2000) PP 12(a), 36.

[66]CESCR, General Comment 14, ibid, P 36.

[67]The U.N. Special Rapporteur on the Right to Health, Report of the Special Rapporteur on the Right to Health on His Visit to Tajikistan, P 27, U.N. Doc. A/HRC/23/41/Add.1 (May 2, 2013); Report of the Special Rapporteur on the Right to Health on His Visit to India, PP 48, 52, U.N. Doc. A/HRC/14/20/Add.2 (April 15, 2010); Report of the Special Rapporteur on the Right to Health on His Visit to Ghana, PP 37, 39, 61(d), U.N. Doc. A/HRC/20/15/Add.1 (April 10, 2012); Report of the Special Rapporteur on the Right to Health on His Visit to Guatemala, P 88(f), U.N. Doc. A/HRC/17/25/Add.2 (March 16, 2011).

[68]CESCR, General Comment 14, PP 43(f) and 53–56.

[69]Paul Hunt, Report of the Special Rapporteur on the right of everyone to the enjoyment of the highest attainable standard of physical and mental health, (2008 UN Doc A/HRC/7/11) available at http://www.who.int/medicines/areas/human_rights/A_HRC_7_11.pdf.

commitment to international cooperation and assistance. Thus, Article 2.1 of the ICESCR provides

> *Each State Party to the present Covenant undertakes to take steps, individually and through international assistance and co-operation, especially economic and technical, to the maximum of its available resources, with a view to achieving progressively the full realization of the rights recognized in the present Covenant by all appropriate means, including particularly the adoption of legislative measures.*

There is therefore an obligation on high income states to provide cooperation and assistance to low income countries to facilitate the realisation of the right to health. Doing this will not only help in improving public health in the countries receiving the assistance, it will also help ensure global health security as frequency in travels and increased migration have all shown that the pathogens of diseases are no longer easily curtailed by territorial delineations.

1.3 Health and Intellectual Property

Since the adoption of the WTO Agreement on Trade Related Aspects of Intellectual Property Rights (TRIPS Agreement) in 1994, there have been many concerns in relation to the effect of the TRIPS patent regime on health standards in developing countries.[70] This is largely due to the fact that patents on pharmaceuticals inexorably inhibit generic competition thereby making pharmaceutical products far too expensive for populations in developing countries.[71] As a result of the serious concerns expressed by developing countries in relation to the public health consequences of the TRIPS Agreement, the WTO Doha Declaration on TRIPS and Public Health was adopted in 2001 to affirm the commitment of WTO members to the use of TRIPS flexibilities such as compulsory licensing and the exhaustion of intellectual property rights to address public health crises in developing countries.[72] The approach of the United States in incorporating TRIPS-plus standards in the various free trade agreements entered into by it with different nations across the globe may however significantly curtail effectiveness of the TRIPS flexibilities.[73] The US continues to exert significant pressure on developing countries that attempt to use the TRIPS compulsory licensing mechanism to enhance access to medicines to meet their

---

[70]Kapczynski et al. (2005), pp. 1031 and 1043–1044.

[71]Wisser (2012), pp. 261 and 262.

[72]See Doha Ministerial Declaration on the TRIPS Agreement and Public Health, WT/MIN(01)/Dec/2 (November 20, 2001) (Adopted November 14, 2001) PP.4-5 (Doha Declaration).

[73]Kapczynski et al. (2005), pp. 1059–1060.

public health needs.[74] For instance, the US brought an action against Brazil in 2001 under the WTO dispute settlement mechanism because Brazil's intellectual property law allowed compulsory licenses to be issued for the purposes of producing generic version of patented HIV drugs.[75] The action was later withdrawn due to significant international pressure. The US also placed Thailand on its special 301 watch list as a result of Thailand's issuance of a compulsory licence for Plavix, a drug used for heart related ailments.[76] The Special 301 report is an annual report from the Office of the United States Trade Representative prepared pursuant to section 182 of the US Trade Act 1974 and its aim is to identify countries that fail to comply with international intellectual property protection standards to the detriment of the US trade or commercial interest in such protection.[77] Although the US continues to affirm its full commitment to encouraging the use of TRIPS flexibilities and the Doha Declaration on TRIPS and Public Health in its special 301 report, it is pertinent to note that many countries with the ability to manufacture generic medicines for developing countries continue to be on the US Special 301 watch list for their national standard of patentability criteria, pharmaceutical test data protection or compulsory licensing practices that are considered detrimental to the commercial interest of American intellectual property (IP) rights holders.[78] Such countries include Canada, Brazil, China, India and Turkey.[79]

Countries on the US Special 301 priority watch list are the focus of bilateral relations aimed at addressing the identified problem areas.[80] The United States Trade Representative is empowered under section 306 of the Trade Act of 1974 to monitor a trading partner's compliance with measures required to ensure adequate protection of IP rights and may impose unilateral trade sanctions where such measures are not satisfactorily implemented.[81] The legality of such unilateral trade sanctions under WTO law is however suspect as the whole essence of the WTO dispute settlement framework is to dissuade nations from adopting unilateral trade sanctions.[82] In the 2017 Special 301 report, the USTR noted thus in relation to India:

> India has yet to take steps to address longstanding patent issues that are affecting innovative industries. These include the application of narrow patentability criteria, challenges faced by the pharmaceutical industry due to Section 3(d) of the India Patents Act, and the issuance of problematic guidelines that appear to restrict the patentability of computer implemented inventions. Innovative companies remain concerned about the potential threat posed to their

[74]Outterson (2005), pp. 193 and 225.

[75]See Brazil — Measures Affecting Patent Protection, DS 199 available at https://www.wto.org/english/tratop_e/dispu_e/cases_e/ds199_e.htm.

[76]Kevin Outterson, Disease-Based Limitations on Compulsory Licenses Under Articles 31 and 31bis 1-2 (Boston University School of Law Working Paper No. 09-26, 2009).

[77]USTR 2015 Special 301 Rep. 1 (2015).

[78]See generally USTR 2015 Special 301 Rep. 1 (2015).

[79]Ibid.

[80]Ibid p. 74.

[81]Ibid.

[82]See Article 23.1 of the WTO Dispute Settlement Understanding.

IP through the possible use of compulsory licensing and patent revocation, as well as overly broad criteria for issuing such licenses and revocations under the India Patents Act.[83]

It is beyond doubt that pharmaceutical companies generally have little incentives to invest in diseases ravaging populations in developing countries as most of the people in such countries are unable to afford the costs of novel pharmaceutical products.[84] It has been observed that the continuing harmonisation of patent laws worldwide is likely to continue for the foreseeable future and there is need for the international aid community to take measures to ensure international patent laws do not decrease global social welfare.[85] This leads to the health financing challenge which is also a major issue in many developing countries and one that is very crucial to their development agenda.

1.4 Health Financing and Development

While it would ordinarily be expected that governments in developing countries should provide incentives and funding for medical research, the reality is that government's expenditure on healthcare in many poor countries is too low to even cover the most basic public health needs.[86] The international community is providing an increasing amount of financial and health related support to promote public health in developing countries and international health aid continues to represent a substantial part of health expenditures in most developing nations.[87]

The WHO and the World Bank play significant roles in the distribution of health assistance to developing countries. The WHO has 194 member states[88] that are all members of the World Health Assembly which is the major decision-making organ of the organisation. Decisions are taken through majority voting and each member state has an equal vote.[89] The WHO has nonetheless been criticised for the cumbersome nature of its majority decision making process.[90] The WHO is funded partly from the compulsory dues paid by member states with the largest contributions coming from the developed countries.[91] For instance, the United States alone accounted for not less than 23% of the total invoiced contribution from member

[83]USTR 2017 Special 301 Rep. 42.

[84]Quick (2003), pp. 1 and 2.

[85]Wisser (2012), p. 288.

[86]See generally Collier (2008), pp. 9 and 11–14.

[87]Farag et al. (2009), pp. 1045 and 1049–1051.

[88]See WHO, Countries, available at http://www.who.int/countries/en/.

[89]See generally Burci and Vignes (2004), pp. 35–44.

[90]Sridhar and Gostin (2011), pp. 1585 and 1585–1586.

[91]WHO, Assessed Contribution Status Report as at 31 July 1983 available at http://www.who.int/about/finances-accountability/funding/AC_Status_Report_2017.pdf?ua=1.

states in 2017.[92] The WHO is also funded through voluntary contribution from member states and private organisations.[93]

With respect to the World Bank, the International Bank for Reconstruction and Development, which is the major World Bank organ has 188 member states.[94] Voting power is however determined in accordance with money given in dues.[95] As developed countries provide the substantial part of World Bank's funding, the bank is effectively under the control of the World Bank.[96] For instance, as of 27 July 2017, the United States alone controlled 16.30% voting power of the International Bank for Reconstruction and Development.[97] The World Bank has indeed been criticised as a result of the dominant role of the US in the World Bank Group and the Bank's somewhat undemocratic decision making process.[98] Thus, developing countries relying on foreign aid or assistance to meet their health related obligations will continue to be in a vulnerable position where their national interests are not in full alignment with the foreign policy expectations of the developed countries offering aid or assistance.

Continued reliance on international aid may thus not be the best strategy for sustainable health financing in developing countries as the funding from the WHO and World Bank come largely from countries with strong interests in trade in IP related products and economic interests that are not always in tandem with the national interests of the receiving countries. Developing countries especially in Africa must therefore develop a health financing plan that is largely self-sustaining and that is unlikely to trade away the health and development rights of their populations. This will most likely require cooperation and collaborations at regional levels to achieve the best possible outcomes and where necessary, resources at regional levels may be pooled together for the purpose of regional health financing.

92 Ibid.

93 WHO, About WHO: Voluntary Contributions, available at http://www.who.int/about/finances-accountability/funding/voluntary-contributions/en/.

94 See World Bank, International Bank for Reconstruction and Development, available at http://www.worldbank.org/en/about/what-we-do/brief/ibrd.

95 See World Bank, Voting Powers, available at http://www.worldbank.org/en/about/leadership/VotingPowers.

96 Paul Ladd, Options for Democratising the World Bank and the IMF (Southern African Regional Poverty Network May 2003) 4–6 available at http://www.sarpn.org/documents/d0000527/Ladd_WB_IMF.pdf.

97 See, World Bank, International Bank for Reconstruction and Development: Subscriptions and Voting Power of Member Countries available at http://siteresources.worldbank.org/BODINT/Resources/278027-1215524804501/IBRDCountryVotingTable.pdf.

98 Ladd, above n 96 at 4–6.

1.5 Development and the African Public Health Imbroglio

The devastating course of the recent Ebola Virus Disease in West Africa has been attributed to a conglomeration of factors such as the '*scarcity of qualified health workers, poor surveillance and information systems, unreliable access to medical supplies, and limited public health infrastructure*'.[99] It is estimated that over eight billion people suffer each year as a result of their inability to have access to adequate healthcare.[100]

The Millennium Declaration adopted by the United Nations General Assembly in 2000 emphasised the collective responsibility of states to foster the principles of human dignity, equity and egalitarianism at the global level. The Millennium Development Goals (MDGs) are thus enshrined in the Millennium Declaration and the deadline for the actualisation of the MDGs objectives was 2015. The MDGS sought to achieve the following objectives: the eradication of poverty and hunger; universal primary education; gender equality and women's empowerment; reduction in child mortality; improved maternal health; reduction in the spread of HIV and other diseases; environmental sustainability and a global partnership for development.[101] Of particular relevance to a discourse on health and development is paragraph 20 of the Millennium Declaration by which the United Nations resolves:

- *To encourage the pharmaceutical industry to make essential drugs more widely available and affordable by all who need them in developing countries.*
- *To develop strong partnerships with the private sector and with civil society organizations in pursuit of development and poverty eradication.*[102]

It would be pertinent to examine the extent to which the health related MDGs objectives were actualised as of December 2015. With respect to maternal health, maternal mortality ratio declined by 45% globally from the figure in 1990 with a substantial part of the decline occurring after 2000.[103] There was a 64% decline in maternal mortality in Southern Asia from 1990–2013.[104] In Sub Saharan Africa, the decline rate for the period 1990–2013 was 49%.[105] There was also a 12% global increase in the number of births assisted by skilled health professionals in 2014 compared with the 1990 figure.[106]

---

[99]Frey (2015), pp. 419 and 420.

[100]Kieny (2014) available at http://www.who.int/mediacentre/commentaries/health-systems-ebola/en/.

[101]Ibid.

[102]Ibid.

[103]UN, Millennium Development Goals Report 2015 p. 6 http://www.un.org/millenniumgoals/2015_MDG_Report/pdf/MDG%202015%20rev%20(July%201).pdf.

[104]Ibid.

[105]Ibid.

[106]Ibid.

With respect to the war against HIV/AIDS, globally, HIV infection rates declined by about 40% between 2000 and 2013.[107] As of June 2014, 13.6 million people infected with HIV were receiving treatment worldwide as against the 800,000 figure for people with access to HIV treatment in 2003.[108] In addition, tuberculosis mortality rate fell by 45% and the prevalence rate declined by 41% between 1990 and 2013.[109]

In 2013, about 6.3 million children under the age of five died mostly from preventable and treatable diseases.[110] While child morbidity and mortality have evidently reduced due to concerted efforts at national and international levels to ensure child's survival, the mortality rate nonetheless remains unnervingly high especially amongst children from disadvantaged populations and low income countries.[111] According to the UN Special Rapporteur on the right of everyone to the enjoyment of the highest attainable standard of physical and mental health 2015 report, 'Health, survival and development are not sequential but are intrinsically linked and simultaneous processes.'[112]

At the United Nations Conference on Sustainable Development ("Rio+20") held in Rio de Janeiro, Brazil in 2011, world leaders under the auspices of the United Nations, civil organisations and policy makers established an Open Working Group to develop a set of Sustainable Development Goals (SDGs) that would build on the UN Millennium Development Goals beyond the 2015 deadline. Prior to the adoption of the SDGs, there was a general consensus that the post 2015 development agenda should include universal health coverage to ensure the availability of health services to all without unnecessary financial burden.[113] The Sustainable Development Goals were adopted by the United Nations in September 2015 through the UN resolution entitled *Transforming our world: the 2030 Agenda for Sustainable Development.*[114]

Goal 3 of the Sustainable Development Goals is to '*ensure healthy lives and promote well-being for all at all ages.*' Goal 3 of the SDGs is wide enough to cover the right to health in all its ramifications. Ensuring healthy lives as well as the well-being of all at all ages is synonymous with safeguarding the enjoyment of the highest attainable standard of health. This will require the provision of adequate health-care

---

[107] Ibid.

[108] Ibid.

[109] Ibid.

[110] United Nations Children's Fund (UNICEF) and others, Levels and Trends in Child Mortality: Report 2014 (2014), p. 1.

[111] Report of the Special Rapporteur on the right of everyone to the enjoyment of the highest attainable standard of physical and mental health (2015) UN Doc A/70/213. P1 http://daccess-dds-ny.un.org/doc/UNDOC/GEN/N15/238/25/PDF/N1523825.pdf?OpenElement.

[112] Ibid P 3.

[113] World Health Org., The World Health Report 2013 (WHO, 2013) 22 available at http://apps.who.int/iris/bitstream/10665/85761/2/9789240690837_eng.pdf?ua=1.

[114] UN General Assembly, Transforming our world: the 2030 Agenda for Sustainable Development, UN Resolution No. A/RES/70/1 http://www.un.org/ga/search/view_doc.asp?symbol=A/RES/70/1&Lang=E.

facilities, access to affordable medicines, a well organised and effective public health system, and, to a very large extent, a universal health coverage system.

The history of universal health coverage system dates back to 1883 when Germany launched its Social Health Insurance (SHI) through the enactment of the German Health Insurance Act of 1883.[115] Although the eligibility criteria for the cover initially limited coverage to only about 10% of the population, subsequent expansions of the coverage over a period of about 100 years eventually saw the SHI transforming into a universal health coverage.[116] In 1948, the United Kingdom commenced its universal health coverage system with the creation of the National Health Service scheme in response to the agitation for a healthcare system that is accessible to all.[117] With the continuing increase in countries' gross domestic product since the end of World War II, the number of countries that have embraced health insurance coverage extension has grown exponentially.[118] Not less than seventy-five countries have enacted laws establishing universal access to healthcare.[119] In low income countries, the achievement of universal access coverage is made more daunting by the pervasive culture of corruption and weak management structures.[120]

Health is very germane to development. While significant progress has been made in combating major infectious diseases including malaria, tuberculosis and AIDs, much still has to be done beyond the MDGs 2015 target especially in lowest income nations, sub-Saharan Africa and South Asia.[121] There is an increasing unease worldwide at the failure of economic growth to offer equitable benefits and the dilemma caused by inequalities is one of the major causes of political unrest and reforms in many parts of the world.[122] The levels of investment in health in many countries is neither adequate nor efficient and with the increasing resource constrictions, there are concerns that the current dramatic gains such as the survival of HIV positive people and the reduction in infectious diseases like malaria and measles may not be sustainable.[123] It is therefore very important to maintain levels of investment both nationally and internationally, that would ensure substantial progress towards the realisation of health related goals.[124]

---

[115] Frey (2015), p. 429.

[116] Ibid.

[117] Light (2003), p. 25.

[118] Ibid 430.

[119] David Stuckler et al., Background Paper for the Global Symposium on Health Systems Research: The Political Economy of Universal Health Coverage 2 (Nov. 16–19, 2010).

[120] Marten et al. (2014), pp. 2164 and 2165.

[121] UN System Task Team on the Post-2015 UN Development Agenda, Health in the post-2015 UN development agenda (2012) p 4 available at http://www.un.org/millenniumgoals/pdf/Think%20Pieces/8_health.pdf.

[122] ibid 4–5.

[123] Ibid 5.

[124] Ibid 5.

1.6 Health and Development as Human Rights in Africa

The connection between health and development is well acknowledged.[125] It is indisputable that attaining sustainable good public health outcomes is germane to the economic development of any country.[126] In Africa, it was estimated that the HIV/AIDs scourge reduced economic development in the continent by about 2–4% in a report published by the Special Rapporteur on the right of everyone to the enjoyment of the highest attainable standard of physical and mental health in 2011.[127] The report further noted that the long term negative consequences of malaria was estimated to have reduced gross national product in some countries by 1.3%.[128] Earlier definitions of development largely focused on gross national product (GNP), increase in personal incomes, technological sophistication and modernisation without giving much attention to the human rights dimension to development.[129] Following the increasing dissatisfaction with the economic growth theory of development, Amartya Sen and Martha Nussbaum pioneered the human development approach to development.[130] In 1987, an epoch-making study commissioned by the United Nations Children's Fund (UNICEF) led to highly stimulating global debates on the adverse social impacts of the structural adjustments programmes recommended by international financial institutions as a strategy for attaining economic growth.[131] Three years later, the first Human Development Report was published by the United Nations Development Programme and the objective of the Human Development Report, which has since become an annual publication, is all about how development enlarges people's choices.[132]

The United Nations Declaration on the Right to Development (UNDRTD) was adopted three decades ago[133] and the UNDRTD was reaffirmed in the 1993 Vienna Declaration and Programme of Action.[134] The right to development is an all-encompassing right that seeks to enhance the realisation of all human rights. Thus, Article 6 of the Right to Development provides thus:

---

[125] Anand Grover, Report of the Special Rapporteur on the right of everyone to the enjoyment of the highest attainable standard of physical and mental health, (2011) UN Doc A/HRC/17/25 p. 3 http://www2.ohchr.org/english/bodies/hrcouncil/docs/17session/A-HRC-17-25.pdf.

[126] Jocelyn E. Finlay, The Role of Health in Economic Development, PGDA Working Papers 2107, Program on the Global Demography of Aging, 2007.

[127] Grover above n 125 at p. 4.

[128] Ibid.

[129] Sen (1999), p. 3.

[130] Grover, above n 125 at p. 4.

[131] Ibid 5.

[132] UNDP, Human Development Report 1990 (UNDP, 1990) p. 1 available at http://hdr.undp.org/sites/default/files/reports/219/hdr_1990_en_complete_nostats.pdf.

[133] UN Declaration on the Right to Development, GA Res 41/128, 97th plen mtg, UN Doc A/RES/.

[134] A/CONF.157/23.

1. All States should co-operate with a view to promoting, encouraging and strengthening universal respect for and observance of all human rights and fundamental freedoms for all without any distinction as to race, sex, language or religion.
2. All human rights and fundamental freedoms are indivisible and interdependent; equal attention and urgent consideration should be given to the implementation, promotion and protection of civil, political, economic, social and cultural rights.
3. States should take steps to eliminate obstacles to development resulting from failure to observe civil and political rights, as well as economic, social and cultural rights.

While the right to development is indisputably a distinct and 'stand-alone right', the tenor of Article 6 of the UN Declaration on the Right to Development unequivocally shows that the right to development does not only recognise all human rights, it is also a right that seeks to promote the realisation of civil, political, economic, social and cultural rights in the pursuit of human development. The UN Declaration on the Right to Development explicitly reinforces the link between health and development in Article 2.3 and Article 8.1. For clarity and emphasis, these provisions are reproduced below:

Article 2.3

States have the right and the duty to formulate appropriate national development policies that aim at the *constant improvement of the well-being of the entire population and of all individuals*, on the basis of their active, free and meaningful participation in development and in the fair distribution of the benefits resulting therefrom (italics mine).

Article 8.1

States should undertake, at the national level, all necessary measures for the realization of the right to development and shall ensure, inter alia, *equality of opportunity for all in their access to basic resources, education, health services, food, housing*, employment and the fair distribution of income (italics mine).

Thus, the right to development entails the right to health, the right to access to medicines and health services and the right to the enjoyment of the highest attainable standard of health. Although the declaration on right to development is a UN declaratory statement, there is support for the view that the right has become well established enough to constitute part of customary international law.[135] The

[135] Oduwole (2014), p. 6 available at http://www.iss.nl/fileadmin/ASSETS/iss/Documents/Academic_publications/PCC_Inaugural_Lecture_20May2014.pdf.

justiciability of the right is, however, yet to be tested.[136] Like the right to health, the right to development is subject to progressive realisation and states have a duty to formulate, adopt and implement policies as well as legislative and other measures that may be required for the actualisation of the right.[137]

It is pertinent to note that prior to the UN adoption of the UNDRTD in 1986, the right to development was already enshrined in Article 22 of the African Charter on Human and Peoples' Rights which was adopted by the defunct Organisation of African Unity (succeeded by the African Union) on 27 June 1981. While the justiciability of the right to development may be doubtful in international law, the same cannot be said of the Peoples' Right to Development enshrined in Article 22 of the African Charter on Human and People's Rights. Article 22 of the African Charter provides thus:

1. All peoples shall have the right to their economic, social and cultural development with due regard to their freedom and identity and in the equal enjoyment of the common heritage of mankind.
2. States shall have the duty, individually or collectively, to ensure the exercise of the right to development.

Article 30 of the African Charter on Human and Peoples' Rights establishes the African Commission on Human and Peoples' Rights with the mandate to ensure the protection of all the rights enshrined in the African Charter. The African Court of Human and Peoples' Rights was established in 2004 and the court is empowered to exercise jurisdiction over all the rights guaranteed in the African charter as well as all other human rights treaties to which the parties before it are signatories. The enjoyment of the highest attainable standard of health is very important to human and economic development. Protecting health rights is therefore an important part of the human development process. It cannot however be said that the human rights framework available under the African Charter is being fully utilised.

For the human rights framework to provide real succour to vulnerable populations across the African continent, it is exigent that African countries put in place strong legislative and judicial structures at national levels for the implementation and enforcement of human rights obligations. African nations should equally be willing to fully ratify the Protocol Establishing the African Court of Human and Peoples' Rights so that the court may assume jurisdiction over cases of human rights violations emanating from signatory countries. The decision of the Supreme Court of Nigeria in *Abacha v Fawehinmi* is a clear testament to the great promises of the human rights framework in delivering real outcomes for development and the continuing actualisation of human development.[138] It is however for the state to

136 Ibid.

137 UN Declaration on the Right to Development Article 10.

138 See above n 43.

create and maintain the requisite legal apparatuses and paraphernalia for the actualisation of those promises.

2 Conclusion

The right to health is a widely recognised right in international human rights law and it is also recognised in many regional and national legal instruments. In a similar vein, the right to development is well recognised in international human rights law although it is not a judicially enforceable right under the United Nations framework. Nonetheless, development is a fundamental objective of the international legal order and one that can be rightly considered as forming part of the principles of customary international law. The connection between health rights and human as well as economic development is widely acknowledged. Safeguarding health rights is very germane to the pursuit of development in Africa and populations in Africa are fully guaranteed the right to health and development under the African Charter. Although, both health and development rights are enforceable rights under the African Charter, Africa continues to have the highest global burden of disease and it is also the least developed continent of the world with 34 out of the 54 fully recognised sovereign nations in Africa currently ranked as least developed countries by the UN.[139]

It would seem the human rights framework has been largely under-utilised in Africa especially in relation to the judicial enforcement of human rights. While there seems to be sufficient legal basis for promoting health rights and the right to development in Africa, translating the rights enshrined in the legal texts from mere rhetoric into compelling realities will depend on whether African states are willing to summon the political will and doggedness required for the actualisation of these rights. The starting point will certainly require the development of a strategic plan for the protection of health rights and the right to development at national levels and regional levels. States must also be willing to adopt strong legislative, administrative and judicial measures for safeguarding human rights while strengthening the necessary structures for the implementation of the rights. Safeguarding health and adopting a pragmatic and holistic approach to the right to development are daunting hurdles Africa must be ready to surmount in promoting human development in the continent.

References

Amorim CLN (2000) The WTO from the perspective of a developing country. Fordham Int Law J 24:95

[139]See UN-OHRLLS, 'About LDC's' available at http://unohrlls.org/about-ldcs/.

Borelli S (2009) Positive obligations of states and the protection of human rights. Interights Bull 15:1
Burci GL, Vignes C-H (2004) World Health Organization. Kluwer Law International, pp 35–44
Castleberry C (2015) A human right to health: is there one and, if so, what does it mean? Intercult Hum Rights Law Rev 12:189
Collier P (2008) Laws and codes for the resource curse. Yale Hum Rights Dev Law J 11:9, 11–14
Farag M et al (2009) Does funding from donors displace government spending for health in developing countries? Health Aff 28:1045, 1049–1051
Frey AL (2015) Positioning universal health coverage in the post-2015 development agenda. Pacific Rim Law Policy J 24:419, 420
George E (2011) The human right to health and HIV/AIDS: South Africa and south-south cooperation to reframe global intellectual property principles and promote access to essential medicines. Indiana J Glob Leg Stud 18:167, 171
Gostin L, Friedman E (2013) Towards a framework convention on global health: a transformative agenda for global health justice. Yale J Health Policy Law Ethics 1, 4
Hart HLA (1958) Positivism and the separation of law and morals. Harv Law Rev 71(4):593, 603
Iacopino V et al (2011) HIV/AIDS and human rights in Botswana and Swaziland: a matter of dignity and health. Hastings Int Comp Law Rev 149, 175
Kapczynski A et al (2005) Addressing global health inequities: an open licensing approach for university innovations. Berkeley Technol Law J 20:1031, 1043–1044
Keener SR, Vasquez J (2009) A life worth living: enforcement of the right to health through the right to life in the Inter American Court of Human Right. Columbia Hum Rights Law Rev 40:595 at 599
Kieny M-P (2014) Ebola and health systems: now is the time for change. World Health Organization
Kwakwa E (2009) Mainstreaming "Development" in international organizations. Int Organ Law Rev 6:1
Kwakwa E (2012) Reflections on "Development," "Developing Countries" and the "Progressive Development" of International Trade and Intellectual Property Law. Denver J Int Law Policy 40:221, 222
Light DW (2003) Universal health care: lessons from the British experience. Am J Public Health 93:25
Marten R et al (2014) An assessment of progress towards universal health coverage in Brazil, Russia, India, China, and South Africa (BRICS). Lancet 384:2164, 2165
Matsushita M, Schoenbaum TJ, Mavroidis PC (2006) The World Trade Organization: law practice and policy. Oxford University Press, pp 782–784
Mattar MY (2013) Article 43 of the Arab Charter on human rights: reconciling national, regional, and international standards. Harv Hum Rights J 26:91
Muller A (2014) The right to health and international humanitarian law: parallel application for building peaceful societies and the prevention of armed conflict. Wisconsin Int Law J 32:415, 416
Novogrodsky NB (2014) After AIDS. Melbourne J Int Law 643, 646–651
Oduwole O (2014) International law and the right to development: a pragmatic approach for Africa. International Institute of Social Studies, Hague
Ooms G, Van Damme W (2008) Impossible to 'Wean' when more aid is needed. Bull World Health Organ 86:893
Ooms G et al (2010) Financing the millennium development goals for health and beyond: sustaining the 'Big Push'. Globalization Health 6:17
Outterson K (2005) Pharmaceutical arbitrage: balancing access and innovation in international prescription drug markets. Yale J Health Policy Law Ethics 5:193, 225
Owoeye O (2014) Patents and the obligation to protect health: examining the significance of human rights in the protection of pharmaceutical patents. J Law Med 21(4):900–919

Quick JD (2003) Essential medicines twenty-five years on: closing the access gap. Health Policy Plan 18:1, 2

Qureshi AH (2009) International trade for development: the WTO as a development institution? J World Trade 43:173

Sen A (1999) Development as freedom. Oxford University Press, Oxford. p. 3

Sridhar D, Gostin LO (2011) Reforming the World Health Organization. J Am Med Assoc 305:1585, 1585–1586

WHO (2015) World Malaria Report 2015. World Health Organization, p x

Wisser E (2012) Simulating pharmaceutical markets in the developing world: the problems with "Pull" funding mechanisms. Boston Univ Int Law J 30:261, 262

Determining the Termination of a Non-International Armed Conflict: An Analysis of the Boko Haram Insurgency in Northern Nigeria

Solomon Ukhuegbe and Alero I. Fenemigho

Contents

S. Ukhuegbe (✉)
Agbakwas LLP, Toronto, ON, Canada

A. I. Fenemigho
Faculty of Law, University of Benin, Benin, Nigeria

Centre for Human Rights, University of Pretoria, Pretoria, South Africa

C. Eboe-Osuji et al. (eds.), *Nigerian Yearbook of International Law 2018/2019*,
Nigerian Yearbook of International Law 2018/2019,
https://doi.org/10.1007/978-3-030-69594-1_14

1 Introduction

The capture of Camp Zero,[1] the headquarters of the *Boko Haram* group in Sambisa Forest,[2] North-eastern Nigeria, by the Nigerian Army on 22 December 2016,[3] was hailed as signifying an end to the insurgency that has plagued Nigeria since 2009, and which rose to the level of a non-international armed conflict (NIAC) in 2013.[4] The *Boko Haram* group, or "People Committed to the Propagation of the Prophet's Teachings and Jihad" (*Jama'atu Ahlis Sunna Lidda'awati Wal-Jihad*)[5] grew from a small Islamic sect into one of the deadliest terrorist groups in the world,[6] active in Nigeria and her neighbours Cameroon, Chad and Niger. The insurgency has spawned a grave humanitarian crisis in the Lake Chad region.[7]

The overrunning of the Camp in Sambisa Forest had largely been seen by the government as the last push that delivered the 'killing blow' to the insurgency.[8]

[1]Camp Zero (also spelled "Camp Zairo") is said to have comprised of a "cluster of dreaded camps and cells," chief among them being a former structure built for the training of the now disbanded National Guards, established in 1989 by the then military President, Ibrahim Babangida to combat crime and terrorism. The structure has underground cells and an armoury. Ironically, it became the "strongest and most fortified" camp of a criminal and terrorist group when the Boko Haram group seized and adopted it as its base. See 'The Rise and Final Fall of Boko Haram in Nigeria' NTA (2016).

[2]Sambisa Forest, which takes its name from the Sambisa village in Gwoza Local Government Area, Borno state in Northeastern Nigeria, close to the border with Cameroon, covers an area of about 60,000 km^2, cutting across six states in Northern Nigeria namely Borno, Yobe, Gombe, Bauchi, Jigawa and Kano. Originally created as a Game Reserve, the forest entered infamy when it became one of the strongholds of the Boko Haram group. It is particularly infamous for being the rumoured site where the Chibok Secondary School girls abducted in April 2014 were held. See generally, Kayode (2014).

[3]See 'The Rise and Fall of Boko Haram' NTA (2016).

[4]This will be discussed in detail in Sect. 3 below.

[5]This is the proper name of the group. However, it is widely known by 'Boko Haram,' which translates into "western education is forbidden" in the local Hausa language.

[6]See Dudley (2018).

[7]See UNHCR 'Nigeria Emergency.' No attempt is made here provide an exhaustive review of the Boko Harm insurgency or the burgeoning literature on it. The scope of the present article is limited to issues relating to legal determination of the end of the Boko Haram insurgency. Our review of the insurgency is accordingly only to the extent that is necessary for this objective. For some more details on the insurgency itself, see the following: Adesoji (2010), Onuoha (2011, 2014), Mantzikos (2014), de Montclos (2014a), International Crisis Group (2014), Pantucci and Jesperson (2015), Cold-Ravnkilde and Plambech (2015), Torbjörnsson and Jonsson (2017), Langer et al. (2017), Adelaja et al. (2018), Campbell and Harwood (2018), Brechenmacher (2019), and International Crisis Group (2019).

[8]President Muhammadu Buhari in a goodwill address to the troops on 24 December 2016, stated thus: "I am delighted at, and most proud of the gallant troops of the Nigerian Army, on receipt of the long-awaited and most gratifying news of the final crushing of Boko Haram terrorists in their last enclave in Sambisa Forest." See Adetayo (2016).

Thus, when the troops of Operation *Lafiya Dole*[9] accomplished the mission, the government considered it a consolidation of the technical defeat of the group which had been announced at the end of 2015.[10] However, neither the 'technical defeat' of Boko Haram in December 2015 nor even the subsequent capture of Camp Zero put an end to attacks by the group on the Nigerian forces and citizens. Though the group has been degraded, it retains a demonstrated capability to strike at military and non-military objectives.[11] The group is still alive and somewhat well enough to operate, diminished as its capacity may be. Although the government insists that Boko Haram today attacks mostly non-military objectives, civilians in particular, there are also widely reported lethal attacks on the military as well.

The situation with the declaration of defeat of Boko Haram in 2015 and its continued activities afterwards raises a key question: At what point is a NIAC such as the Boko Haram insurgency, considered over? What, indeed, conclusively determines that a NIAC has ended? The international law rule for the end of a NIAC is quite complicated.[12] This will be critically scrutinized in the legal perspective of the Boko Haram insurgency set out in the pages that follow.

To achieve the above stated aim, the discussion in this paper is divided into five parts. The first part is this introduction, while the second part provides a brief account of the Boko Haram insurgency. The third part ascertains the legal status of the insurgency as a NIAC under international law, while the fourth part delves into the crux of the paper, which is determining the endpoint for the insurgency as a NIAC. The fifth and final part concludes the paper.

---

[9] *Lafiya Dole* is a Hausa language phrase which translates into "peace by force." See 'Army Chief in Maiduguri; Changes Code to *Lafiya Dole*' Vanguard Nigeria (2015).

[10] The President of Nigeria, Muhammadu Buhari, declared, that the war with Boko Haram was "technically" won, as the group could no longer launch conventional attacks, but were now confined to Borno State. See 'Nigeria Boko Haram: Militants 'Technically Defeated'- Buhari' BBC News (2015).

[11] See Counter Extremism Project, 'Boko Haram,' pp. 32–34, for a list of some 38 attacks carried out by Boko Haram against both military and civilian targets, between December 25, 2015 to January 14, 2019.

[12] Bellal (2018), p. 26.

2 Understanding the Boko Haram Insurgency in Nigeria: An Account of the Crisis

Nigeria is no stranger to religious sectarianism.[13] Several sects, predominantly Islamic,[14] have existed, and currently exist, within the nation's borders, many of them in relatively peaceful coexistence.[15] Some others turned out be violent to the extent of challenging the authority and sovereignty of the Nigerian State. An earlier major incident of violent Islamic insurgency was the *Maitatsine* sect, whose clash with security forces caused the December 1980 riots in Kano State, Nigeria, and led to the death of at least 4179 persons and considerable loss of property.[16] The group was a precursor to Boko Haram but on a much-localised scale and was short-lived.[17]

The Boko Haram group has its origins in Maiduguri, Borno State, North-east Nigeria, where it was founded by an Islamic Scholar, Mohammed Yusuf. About 2002, Yusuf started a religious movement where he preached against the political institutions and other Islamic scholars.[18] Yusuf advocated rule by *Sharia* law in Nigeria as against constitutional secular rule,[19] proposing it as the panacea to the corruption prevalent in the political system that has resulted in social inequalities that

---

[13]Nigeria is deeply divided by religion, which is a very influential force in the socio-political stability of the country. The country is almost equally divided between a predominantly Muslim North, and a predominantly Christian South. As an author surmised, "hardly can the Nigerian State be talked about without reference to religion." See Danjibo (2009), p. 3.

[14]Islamic sects in Nigeria are said to include the *Derika*, the *Kaulu* (*Kablu*), the *Izala*, the *Tijjaniya* and the *Quaddiriya*, the Shiite, the Muslim Brotherhood, etc. See ibid, p. 5.

[15]de Montclos (2014b), p. 6.

[16]The *Maitatsine* sect was formed by an Islamic Scholar, Muhammed Marwa, who was concerned with purification of Islam which he believed had been corrupted through westernization and "the formation of the modern State." Marwa, based in Kano, attracted a large and faithful following among the poor with his fiery and provocative preaching against the established political institutions as well as the ruling emirate. His "abusive" style of preaching earned him the name '*maitatsine*' which means "one who curses." He consistently spoke against western influence and modernization. See Danjibo (2009), pp. 6 and 9.

[17]Parallels are often drawn between the Maitatsine sect and the Boko Haram group because of their ideological similarity. See de Montclos (2014b), p. 8; Cook (2011), p. 6; Bagaji et al. (2012), p. 33; Adesoji (2011), pp. 98–119.

[18]de Montclos (2014b), p. 7.

[19]Section 10 of the Constitution of the Federal Republic of Nigeria (as amended) states as follows: "The Government of the Federation or of a State shall not adopt any religion as State religion." Although there are possible competing interpretations, the provision is almost universally cited for the mandate that Nigeria is a constitutionally secular State. It can be argued, therefore, that this provision was violated when 12 Northern States (Kano, Kaduna, Katsina, Kebbi, Jigawa, Sokoto, Borno, Yobe, Bauchi, Gombe, Zamfara and Niger) adopted *Sharia* Law beginning in 2000. This would seem to have been a move designed to pacify and quell elements that were agitating against the secular nature of the Nigerian State. However, this limited application of *Sharia* within a democratic and "secular" country did not go far enough for sects like the Boko Haram group, who want full implementation of *Sharia* not only in Northern Nigeria, but in the entire country. See Adesoji (2011), p. 103.

were, and are still, very apparent in North-eastern Nigeria. He rejected elements of westernization, attributing the ills of the country to its embrace of western civilisation.[20] Yusuf's movement attracted a large following, which came mostly from the poor, as they saw in him some hope for social justice and an end to social inequalities.[21] Over the years leading up to 2009, Boko Haram expanded in followership and influence. Yusuf became established as a major political player, no longer a mere religious figure, with the Nigerian authorities starting to recognise him as a threat.[22]

In June 2009, some members of the group in a funeral procession were killed by law enforcement officers.[23] This led to an uprising by Boko Haram in July 2009, where the city of Maiduguri was held to siege for about a week.[24] The armed forces were called in to dislodge the sect, which it did with a heavy hand, resulting in the death of several members of Boko Haram and the destruction of the group's main mosque.[25] Yusuf was arrested, but was subsequently killed extrajudicially in police custody.[26]

After a brief period underground, Boko Haram resurfaced with Abubakar Shekau[27] as their new leader in July 2010.[28] The structure of the group is reported as decentralised and fluid. It has a Supreme Council (*Shura*) headed by the leader, with its various cells operating with "relative autonomy and control."[29] Shekau

---

[20]Boko Haram indeed rejects more than western education. They reject the entire western culture and way of life in preference for Islamic culture. This was clarified by Sani Mohammed, a temporary leader of the group on August 8, 2009 in a statement that reads in part thus:

> ...Boko Haram does not in any way mean "Western Education is a sin" as the infidel media continue to portray [sic] us. Boko Haram actually means "Western Civilization" is forbidden. The difference is that while the first gives the impression that we are opposed to formal education coming from the West, that is Europe, which is not true, the second affirms our believe [sic] in the supremacy of Islamic culture (not Education), for culture is broader, it includes education but is not determined by Western Education.

See Cook (2011), pp. 13–14.

[21]However, even educated youths fell for Yusuf's teachings largely because of his charisma to the extent that some reportedly tore up their degree diplomas to show full commitment to the cause. See Danjibo (2009), p. 7.

[22]See 'Boko Haram: Behind the Rise of Nigeria's Armed Group' Al Jazeera Special Series (2016).

[23]ibid.

[24]ibid.

[25]Arraf (2018), p. 102.

[26]ibid.

[27]Ironically, Shekau, who Yusuf had named as his right-hand man before his death (see Al Jazeera Special Series (Text), "Boko Haram," (n 32)) had been declared dead by the security operatives in 2009. This will not be the last time Shekau "miraculously" rises from the dead after been declared killed or mortally wounded by the Nigerian authorities. See Akinyelure (2016).

[28]Arraf (2018), p. 103.

[29]See Amnesty International (2015), p. 15. See also de Montclos (2014b), p. 11; Counter Extremism Project, 'Boko Haram' p. 3; Stratfor (2014).

pledged to exact vengeance for the killing of Yusuf and other members of the group.[30]

Boko Haram attacked a prison in September 2010, where it freed over 700 inmates, 150 of whom were suspected members of the group.[31] Between September 2010 to November 2011, Cook noted not less than 45 major operations by the group.[32] These attacks were not limited to the North-east, which had been the main base of the group but spread across to Kano, Plateau, Bauchi, Kaduna, and Abuja, the federal capital territory. The major modes of attack by the group included direct gun-fire, drive-by shootings, bombings, assassinations, and suicide attacks.[33]

Perhaps the most audacious of the Boko Haram's attacks during that period were the suicide attacks it carried out in Abuja, the nation's capital and seat of power, on the National Police Headquarters on 16 June 2011,[34] and the United Nations compound on 26 August 2011.[35] These attacks made President Goodluck Jonathan to send the army to North-east Nigeria in a bid to stamp out the insurgency.[36] However, the introduction of the army had the effect of intensifying the insurgency. They caused more harm than good by indiscriminate extra-judicial killings and repressive action, which drove more people to join Boko Haram for protection.[37] In May 2013, a state of emergency was declared in the North-Eastern states of Borno, Yobe and Adamawa states.[38]

In March 2014, the Boko Haram insurgency became a cross-border phenomenon when it began executing attacks in Cameroon, thus, introducing a 'regional dimension' to the conflict.[39] In April 2014, Boko Haram abducted 276 secondary school girls from Government Secondary School, a boarding school in Chibok, Borno State.[40] Shekau, in a video address, announced his intention to sell the girls.[41] This incident brought the group wider global attention and coverage. In mid-2014, Boko Haram also expanded its territory, seemingly having an upper hand against the Nigerian army.[42] It seized and held several towns in North-eastern Nigeria (Borno

[30]Amnesty International (2015), p. 10.

[31]'Boko Haram Attack' Frees Hundreds of Prisoners' BBC News (2010).

[32]Cook (2011), p. 16.

[33]ibid.

[34]Two persons were killed in this attack. See 'Blast Rocks Police Headquarters in Nigeria' Al Jazeera News (2011).

[35]18 persons were killed in this attack. See 'Abuja Attack: Car Bomb Hits Nigeria UN Building' BBC News (2011).

[36]See 'Boko Haram: Behind the Rise of Nigeria's Armed Group' Al Jazeera Special Series (2016).

[37]ibid.

[38]See ibid, and de Montclos (2014b), p. 10.

[39]Arraf (2018), p. 105.

[40]See 'The Rise and Final Fall of Boko Haram in Nigeria' NTA (2016).

[41]See 'Boko Haram 'to sell' Nigeria Girls Abducted from Chibok' BBC News (2014).

[42]See 'Boko Haram: Behind the Rise of Nigeria's Armed Group' Al Jazeera Special Series (2016).

and its environs), proclaiming an Islamic state of its own within the borders of Nigeria, a Caliphate under its sole rule.[43]

In January 2015, a Multinational Joint Task Force (MNJTF) formed by a coalition between Nigeria, Chad, Cameroon and Niger began a joint offensive against Boko Haram.[44] In response to this, Boko Haram spread its attacks to Niger and Chad.[45] Boko Haram, on 7 March 2015 pledged its allegiance to the Islamic State (IS), even renaming itself "Islamic State West Africa Province (ISWAP),"[46] a move that was regarded in some quarters as an attempted morale and image boost.[47] The tide of the battle had begun to turn against them, following the creation of the MNJTF and a reported delivery of new military hardware to the Nigerian Army, with many of their captured towns and districts reclaimed by the end of March 2015.[48]

With the inauguration of President Muhammadu Buhari in May 2015 came a renewed fight against Boko Haram, with shake-ups in the military command.[49] By the end of the year, Boko Haram had retreated into Sambisa forest, the Mandara mountains along the Nigerian-Cameroonian border and the islands of Lake Chad.[50] In December 2015, President Buhari declared a technical defeat of the Boko Haram group.[51]

In August 2016, a rift in Boko Haram's leadership was revealed with the declaration by IS of Abu Musab al-Barnawi[52] as leader of ISWAP, a move Shekau rejected. This led to two main factions within Boko Haram,[53] with Shekau reverting to his position as leader of *Jama'atu Ahlis Sunna Lidda'awati Wal-Jihad* (JAS)[54] and al-Barnwai operating as Islamic State in West Africa (ISWA).[55] By the end of December 2016, Boko Haram's base at Sambisa forest, Camp Zero was captured by the Nigeria army to much elation by President Buhari. This could be seen as a consolidation of the 'technical defeat' already achieved.[56]

---

[43]The area held by Boko Haram was estimated to be around 50,000 km^2 in January 2015. See 'The Rise and Final Fall of Boko Haram in Nigeria' NTA (2016).

[44]ibid.

[45]Arraf (2018), p. 107.

[46]ibid.

[47]See Adegoke (2015). See also Arraf (2018), p. 107.

[48]See 'The Rise and Final Fall of Boko Haram in Nigeria' NTA (2016) and Adegoke (2015).

[49]Arraf (2018), p. 108.

[50]See 'The Rise and Final Fall of Boko Haram in Nigeria' NTA (2016); Arraf (2018), p. 108.

[51]See 'Nigeria Boko Haram: Militants 'Technically Defeated'- Buhari' BBC News (2015).

[52]He is reported to be the son of the late Boko Haram leader, Mohammed Yusuf. See Arraf (2018), p. 108.

[53]ibid.

[54]See Institute of Security Studies (2018), pp. 3 and 14. However, Shekau has not revoked his pledge of allegiance to IS. See ibid, p. 14.

[55]ibid, 3. It is noted that ISWA is also referred to as ISWAP (Islamic State West Africa Province).

[56]Adetayo (2016).

Unfortunately, however, the capture of Camp Zero has not led to a cessation in attacks by Boko Haram. Though their capacity is diminished, both factions of the group have not relented in their attacks.[57] For example, in June 2017, Boko Haram attacked Maiduguri, although it was repelled by the Nigerian Army.[58] In July 2017, an ambush by the group on a Nigerian National Petroleum Corporation (NNPC) oil exploration team, near Maiduguri, resulted in the death of 67 persons.[59] On 19 February 2018, 110 school girls were abducted by Boko Haram from a school in Dapchi, Yobe state.[60] On 18 November 2018, Boko Haram attacked a military base in Melete, Borno state, resulting in the death of over 100 soldiers.[61] The attacks by Boko Haram have continued into 2019.[62]

The general trend in the attacks of the factions of Boko Haram i.e. JAS and ISWA, are different. JAS mainly employing suicide bombings by civilians, whereas ISWA concentrates mostly on attacking the military security forces.[63] ISWA is currently regarded as the bigger threat.[64] There have been reported clashes between both factions, although such were sporadic, with no evidence of further confrontations.[65] This split of Boko Haram into two main factions, though separated in organization and operation, has not necessarily altered the legal character of the armed conflict. The Rule of Law in Armed Conflicts (RULAC) Project notes that although it cannot be confirmed, with the information at hand, that the factions can still be regarded as forming a single armed group, "arguably the conflict remains a single non-international armed conflict in light of the absence of fighting between Boko Haram factions."[66]

[57]Counter Extremism Project's Report on Boko Haram contains a record of violent activities by the group from December 2003 to January 14, 2019. It lists over 35 attacks executed by the group (both factions) between 25 December 2015 (just after the alleged technical defeat) and January 14, 2019, with 27 of those attacks were carried out after December 2016 (after the capture of Camp Zero). See Counter Extremism Project 'Boko Haram' pp. 25–33.

[58]'Boko Haram Launches Major Attack on Northeast Nigerian City' Reuters (2017).

[59]Human Rights Watch 'Nigeria: Events of 2017.'

[60]101 girls have since been returned. See Maclean and Abrak (2018) and 'Nigeria Dapchi Abductions: Schoolgirls Finally Home' BBC News (2018). However, one girl, Leah Sharibu, remains in Boko Haram captivity.

[61]See Burke (2018) and Ogundipe (2018).

[62]See for example, Ogundipe (2019) and 'Police Reinforce Stations, Armouries After Boko Haram Attack in Borno' Channels TV (2019).

[63]See Institute of Security Studies (2018), pp. 3, 19–21.

[64]See ibid, pp. 36–37.

[65]RULAC 'Non-international Armed Conflict in Nigeria: Classification- Organization.' See also Institute of Security Studies (2018), pp. 3 and 15.

[66]RULAC 'Non-international Armed Conflict in Nigeria: Classification- Organization.'

3 Establishing the Status of the Boko Haram Insurgency Under International Law

The Boko Haram insurgency has run for over one decade (since 2009). In November 2013, the Office of the Prosecutor (OTP) of the International Criminal Court (ICC) determined that the insurgency had risen to the status of a non-international armed conflict (NIAC) since at least May of that year.[67] The goal of this section of the article is to assess whether the insurgency did indeed rise to such status, by an examination of the criteria for the existence of a NIAC under international law.

The initial question is, What is an armed conflict? The Appeals Chamber of the International Criminal Tribunal for the former Yugoslavia (ICTY), held in *Prosecutor v. Tadic*, Decision on Jurisdiction,[68] that, "an armed conflict exists whenever there is resort to armed force between States or protracted armed violence between governmental authorities and organized armed groups or between such groups within a State."[69] This definition reveals two types of armed conflicts—international armed conflicts (IAC) and NIACs. These conflicts are regulated by different sets of treaty rules under international law.

IACs are essentially inter-state conflicts.[70] These are mainly regulated by the Geneva Conventions of 12 August 1949[71] (save for the provisions of Article 3 which is common to all the Conventions (Common Article 3)) as well as the First Additional Protocol to the Geneva Conventions (Additional Protocol I).[72] NIACs on the other hand are, generally, internal conflicts within a State.[73] They are regulated by

---

[67]See Office of the Prosecutor, ICC (2013a), paragraph 218. It is also noted that in the International Committee of the Red Cross, in its Annual Report for 2013, referred to the situation in north-eastern Nigeria as an "armed conflict between military forces and armed groups." See ICRC (2014), p. 183.

[68]*Prosecutor v. Tadic,* IT-94-1-AR72, Decision on the Defence Motion for Interlocutory Appeal on Jurisdiction, October 2, 1995.

[69]ibid, paragraph 70.

[70]Situations of struggles against colonial domination and alien occupation and racist regimes, in the exercise of the right to self-determination, also qualify as IACs. This is as provided in Article 1(4), Protocol Additional to the Geneva Conventions of 12 August 1949, relating to the Protection of Victims of International Armed Conflicts, (Additional Protocol I), June 8, 1977, 1125 UNTS 3.

[71]Geneva Convention for the Amelioration of the Condition of the Wounded and Sick in Armed Forces in the Field, 75 UNTS 31 (Geneva Convention I); Geneva Convention for the Amelioration of the Condition of the Wounded, Sick and Shipwrecked Members of Armed Forces at Sea, 75 UNTS 85 (Geneva Convention II); Geneva Convention relative to the Treatment of Prisoners of War, 75 UNTS 135 (Geneva Convention III); and the Geneva Convention relative to the Protection of Civilian Persons in Time of War, 75 UNTS 287 (Geneva Convention IV).

[72]Protocol Additional to the Geneva Conventions of 12 August 1949, and relating to the Protection of Victims of International Armed Conflicts, (Protocol I), June 8, 1977, 1125 UNTS 3.

[73]While NIACs are generally internal conflicts within a state's territory, the category of NIACs also covers all armed conflicts wherein at least one of the involved parties is not a state. This is because, under extant international law, only two types/categories of armed conflicts are recognised—IACs and NIACs. IACs only cover conflicts where two or more states are in opposition as under Common Article 2 to the Geneva Conventions, save for the exception under Article 1(4) of Additional

the provisions of Article 3 common to the Geneva Conventions of 12 August 1949 and the Second Additional Protocol to the Geneva Conventions (Additional Protocol II).[74]

The body of laws regulating NIACs is not as robust as those regulating IACs. This is because, traditionally, they fell outside the scope of international humanitarian law (IHL) because they were held to be within the scope of the internal affairs of States wherein other States could not interfere. However, this way of thinking gradually eroded over time because of the spate of violence in NIACs which recommended them to international attention and concern. Thus, in 1949, Common Article 3 was included in the Geneva Conventions to regulate NIACs or "armed conflict not of an international character" as stated in the Article. This was to provide minimum guarantees of protection in such conflicts. In 1977, under Additional Protocol II, more detailed, but still limited, provisions dealing with NIACs were agreed upon.[75] Additional Protocol II is intended to develop and supplement "Article 3 common to the Geneva Conventions of 12 August 1949 without modifying its existing conditions of application."[76] Thus, the legal regimes of Common Article 3 and the provisions of Additional Protocol II coexist. Common Article 3 applies in all NIACs while Additional Protocol II applies only in NIACs that fulfil the specific requirements needed to trigger its application.[77]

Protocol I relating to wars of national liberation (against colonial domination, alien occupation, and racist regimes). The international element in IACs is the fact of sovereign states being on opposing sides. Every other conflict falls under the NIAC category—'an armed conflict not of an international character' as stated in Common Article 3 to the Geneva Conventions. It does not matter whether there is a transnational element to the conflict, i.e. whether the armed group is operational in more than one state or in a region. The conflict is assessed from the perspective of every state involved in a conflict with the armed group. Hence for example, Boko Haram may simultaneously be in a NIAC with Nigeria, and in a separate NIAC with Chad, depending on the factual circumstances within the states. See further, Vite (2009) and generally, Sassoli (2019), pp. 168–186.

[74]Protocol Additional to the Geneva Conventions of 12 August 1949, and relating to the Protection of Victims of Non-international Armed Conflicts, (Protocol II), June 8, 1977, 1125 UNTS 609.

[75]The provisions of Customary International Humanitarian Law (CIHL) are helping to bridge this gap. See the International Committee of the Red Cross' compilation of CIHL rules as it relates to NIACs in Henckaerts and Doswald-Beck (2005).

[76]See Article 1(1) of Additional Protocol II.

[77]The ICRC Commentary on the Article states in part:

> . . . in circumstances where the conditions of application of the Protocol are met, the Protocol and Common Article 3 will apply simultaneously, as the Protocol's field of application is included in the broader one of Common Article 3. On the other hand, in a conflict where the level of strife is low and which does not contain the characteristic features required by the Protocol, only Common Article 3 will apply. In fact, Common Article 3 retains an autonomous existence, i.e., its applicability is neither limited nor affected by the material field of application of the Protocol. This formula, though legally rather complicated, has the advantage of furnishing a guarantee against any reduction of the level of protection long since provided by Common Article 3.

Sandoz et al. (1987), p. 1350, paragraph 4457.

3.1 *Identification of a Non-International Armed Conflict*

As to the definition and identification of a NIAC, the provisions in Common Article 3 and that of Additional Protocol II are not very helpful. On its part, Common Article 3 only mentions the phrase "armed conflict not of an international character" and leaves it unexplained.[78] Article 1 of Additional Protocol II also does not define what a NIAC is. However, the article does one better by excluding in its paragraph (2), "situations of internal disturbances and tensions, such as riots, isolated and sporadic acts of violence and other acts of a similar nature," from situations that qualify as armed conflicts.[79] While this is undoubtedly useful, it still left the gap for a positive definition of a NIAC.[80]

In 1995, the ICTY Appeals Chamber in *Tadic,* Decision on Jurisdiction[81] set out a definition of a NIAC which is widely regarded as authoritative.[82] The Appeals Chamber defined it as "protracted armed violence between governmental authorities and organized armed groups or between such groups within a State."[83] The Trial Chamber of the ICTY in applying the definition stated out by the Appeals Chamber noted indeed, that:

> The test applied by the Appeals Chamber to the existence of an armed conflict for the purposes of the rule contained in Common Article 3 focuses on two aspects of a conflict: the intensity of the conflict and the organization of the parties.[84]

By this, the Trial Chamber thus clarifies 'protracted' in the test, to mean 'intensity' and not a reference to length or duration of the conflict.[85] To the mind of the Trial Chamber, the two criteria i.e. intensity of the conflict and the organization of the parties, were the distinguishing factor between NIACs and other forms of internal violence within a state.[86] However, whether these two criteria i.e. the necessary levels of intensity of violence and organization of the armed group, are

---

[78]See the text of Common Article 3 to the Geneva Conventions.

[79]See Article 1(2) of Additional Protocol II.

[80]See Casey-Maslen and Haines (2018), pp. 52–53.

[81]*Prosecutor v. Tadic,* IT-94-1-AR72, Decision on the Defence Motion for Interlocutory Appeal on Jurisdiction, October 2, 1995.

[82]Sivakumaran (2012), pp. 157 and 166. See also Cullen (2010), pp. 120–122; Casey-Maslen and Haines (2018), pp. 57–61.

[83]*Prosecutor v. Tadic* IT-94-1-AR72, Decision on the Defence Motion for Interlocutory Appeal on Jurisdiction, October 2, 1995, paragraph 70.

[84]*Prosecutor v. Tadic* IT-94-1-T, Opinion and Judgement, 7 May 1997, paragraph 562.

[85]See Casey-Maslen and Haines (2018), p. 57.

[86]*Prosecutor v. Tadic* IT-94-1-T, Opinion and Judgement, 7 May 1997, paragraph 562.

present in a situation to make it a 'NIAC *simpliciter*'[87] must be determined on a case-by-case basis.[88] The two criteria will now be examined.

3.1.1 Intensity of Violence

Several factors are used to show that the requisite intensity of violence has been reached to elevate an internal crisis/disturbance to the status of a NIAC. They include: the duration of such violence;[89] its geographical spread over the territory of the State;[90] the resultant casualties and destruction;[91] the types of weapons used;[92] involvement in the situation of external bodies such as the United Nations Security Council;[93] the choice by the State to use its armed forces to quell the violence;[94] etc.[95]

It should be noted that none of these factors is compelling and can only assist in making the determination as to whether the requisite threshold of intensity of

[87] The term *simpliciter* is used to refer to NIAC as under Common Article 3. It has already been explained above that Article 1(1) of Additional Protocol II adopts the notion of NIAC under Common Article 3 but attaches additional requirements for the application of Additional Protocol II in any given situation. This term is adopted from Sivakumaran's usage of it, to distinguish between "the 'ordinary' non-international armed conflict" and "the non-international armed conflict that is required to satisfy certain additional elements in order for particular rules to apply." See Sivakumaran (2012), p. 164, footnote 66.

[88] See *Prosecutor v. Rutaganda*, Trial Chamber Judgment, 6 December 1999, I-96-3, paragraph 93.

[89] See *Prosecutor v. Tadic* IT-94-1-T, Opinion and Judgement, 7 May 1997, paragraphs 565–566 and *Prosecutor v. Haradinaj, Balaj and Brahimaj,* IT-04-08-T, Judgment, 3 April 2008, paragraph 49.

[90] *Prosecutor v. Milosevic,* IT-02-54-T, Decision on Motion for Judgment of Acquittal,16 June 2004, paragraph 29 and *Prosecutor v. Boskoski and Tarculovski,* IT-04-82-A, Judgment, 19 May 2010, paragraph 22.

[91] See *Prosecutor v. Tadic* IT-94-1-T, Opinion and Judgement, 7 May 1997, paragraphs 565–566 and *Prosecutor v. Limaj, Bala and Musliu,* IT-03-66-T, Judgement, 30 November 2005, paragraphs 135–167.

[92] See *Prosecutor v. Boskoski and Tarculovski,* IT-04-82-A, Judgment, 19 May 2010, paragraph 22 and *Prosecutor v. Haradinaj, Balaj and Brahimaj,* IT-04-08-T, Judgment, 3 April 2008, paragraph 49.

[93] See *Prosecutor v. Haradinaj, Balaj and Brahimaj,* IT-04-08-T, Judgment, 3 April 2008, paragraph 49 and *Prosecutor v. Boskoski and Tarculovski,* IT-04-82-A, Judgment, 19 May 2010, paragraph 22.

[94] See *Prosecutor v. Boskoski and Tarculovski,* IT-04-82-A, Judgment, 19 May 2010, paragraph 22 and *Jean Carlos Abella v. Argentina,* Case 11.137, 18 November 1997, OEA/Ser.L/V/II.98, Doc.6 rev, 13 April 1998, paragraphs 154–156.

[95] See *Boskoski and Tarculovski,* IT-04-82-T, Judgment, 10 July 2008, paragraphs 177–178; and Sivakumaran (2012), pp. 167–170. See also Cullen (2010), pp. 128–129; Bartels (2014), p. 307.

violence to qualify a security situation as a NIAC has been reached.[96] They must be assessed within the context of the peculiarities of the situation at hand.[97]

3.1.2 Organization of the Armed Group

The requirement for organization in determining a NIAC is relevant only to the armed group or groups in question, as the armed forces of a State are presumed to meet the requirement.[98] The necessary degree of organization for an armed group in this regard is quite unclear as a result of somewhat conflicting statements by judicial bodies, such as: they are groups "organized to a greater or lesser extent,"[99] or that, "some degree of organization by the parties will suffice."[100] It has been suggested that this shows that "the threshold is not all that high."[101]

Just as in the case of 'intensity of violence,' several indicative factors can be used to determine whether the requirement of organization has been met. These factors[102] include: the presence of an official chain of command within the group;[103] existence of group headquarters;[104] use of uniforms by group members;[105] ability to recruit

[96]Sivakumaran (2012), p. 168.

[97]ibid, 169–170.

[98]See ibid, 170; Bartels (2014), p. 306.

[99]*Prosecutor v. Jean Paul Akayesu,* ICTR-96-4-T, Judgment, 2 September 1998, paragraph 620.

[100]See *Prosecutor v. Limaj, Bala and Musliu,* IT-03-66-T, Judgement, 30 November 2005, paragraph 89.

[101]Sivakumaran (2012), p. 170.

[102]In *Boskoski and Tarculovski,* IT-04-82-T, Judgment, 10 July 2008, paragraphs 199–203, the ICTY categorises the factors that prove the organization of an armed group in five: "factors signalling the presence of a command structure;" "factors indicating that the group could carry out operations in an organized manner;" "factors indicating a level of logistics;" "factors relevant to determining whether an armed group possessed a level of discipline and the ability to implement the basic obligations of Common Article 3;" and "factors indicating that the armed group [is] able to speak with one voice." See ibid.

[103]See *Prosecutor v. Milosevic,* IT-02-54-T, Decision on Motion for Judgment of Acquittal, 16 June 2004, paragraph 23; *Boskoski and Tarculovski,* IT-04-82-T, Judgment, 10 July 2008, paragraph 271; *Prosecutor v. Boskoski and Tarculovski,* IT-04-82-A, Judgment, 19 May 2010, paragraph 23 and *Prosecutor v. Limaj, Bala and Musliu,* IT-03-66-T, Judgement, 30 November 2005, paragraphs 97 and 110.

[104]See *Prosecutor v. Haradinaj, Balaj and Brahimaj,* IT-04-08-T, Judgment, 3 April 2008, paragraphs 60 and 65–68 and *Prosecutor v. Milosevic,* IT-02-54-T, Decision on Motion for Judgment of Acquittal, 16 June 2004, paragraph 23.

[105]See *Prosecutor v. Limaj, Bala and Musliu,* IT-03-66-T, Judgement, 30 November 2005, paragraph 123 and *Prosecutor v. Boskoski and Tarculovski,* IT-04-82-T, Judgment, 10 July 2008, paragraph 285.

and train members;[106] the ability to acquire, transport and supply/distribute arms;[107] issuance of communications by the group such as political statements;[108] territorial control;[109] existence of designated zones of operations;[110] existence of regulations and disciplinary measures within the group;[111] delegation of tasks and responsibilities within the group;[112] etc.[113]

An important factor is the notion of 'responsible command.' This is said to be "inherent in the idea of organization."[114] The ICTY Appeals Chamber in *Prosecutor v. Hadzihasanovic, Alagic and Kubara*[115] stated that "military organization implies responsible command,"[116] and that "there cannot be military force save on the basis of responsible command."[117] This also holds true for organized armed groups.[118]

Where a number of these factors showing organization of an armed group which is involved in a situation of internal tension or disturbance are found to be present, along with the necessary indicative factors to show that the requisite intensity of violence has been met, the existence of a NIAC *simpliciter* can be determined.

---

[106]See *Prosecutor v. Limaj, Bala and Musliu,* IT-03-66-T, Judgement, 30 November 2005, paragraph 118 and *Prosecutor v. Haradinaj, Balaj and Brahimaj,* IT-04-08-T, Judgment, 3 April 2008, paragraph 60.

[107]See *Prosecutor v. Boskoski and Tarculovski,* IT-04-82-T, Judgment, 10 July 2008, paragraph 281 and 286; and *Prosecutor v. Haradinaj, Balaj and Brahimaj,* IT-04-08-T, Judgment, 3 April 2008, paragraph 60.

[108]See *Prosecutor v. Limaj, Bala and Musliu,* IT-03-66-T, Judgement, 30 November 2005, paragraph 101.

[109]*Prosecutor v. Haradinaj, Balaj and Brahimaj,* IT-04-08-T, Judgment, 3 April 2008, paragraphs 60, 70–75; and *Prosecutor v. Thomas Lubanga Dyilo,* ICC-01/04-01/06, Decision on the Confirmation of Charges, 29 January 2007, paragraph 236.

[110]See *Prosecutor v. Limaj, Bala and Musliu,* IT-03-66-T, Judgement, 30 November 2005, paragraph 95; and *Prosecutor v. Milosevic,* IT-02-54-T, Decision on Motion for Judgment of Acquittal, 16 June 2004, paragraph 23.

[111]See *Prosecutor v. Haradinaj, Balaj and Brahimaj,* IT-04-08-T, Judgment, 3 April 2008, paragraph 60; *Prosecutor v. Limaj, Bala and Musliu,* IT-03-66-T, Judgement, 30 November 2005, paragraphs 110, 113–117; *Prosecutor v. Boskoski and Tarculovski,* IT-04-82-T, Judgment, 10 July 2008, paragraph 274–275; and *Prosecutor v. Boskoski and Tarculovski,* IT-04-82-A, Judgment, 19 May 2010, paragraph 23.

[112]See *Prosecutor v. Limaj, Bala and Musliu,* IT-03-66-T, Judgement, 30 November 2005, paragraphs 100–101.

[113]See generally, Sivakumaran (2012), pp. 170–171. See also Cullen (2010), pp. 123–127.

[114]Sivakumaran (2012), p. 174.

[115]IT-01-47-AR72, Decision on Interlocutory Appeal Challenging Jurisdiction in Relation to Command Responsibility, 16 July 2003.

[116]ibid, paragraph 17.

[117]ibid, paragraph 16. See generally Sivakumaran (2012), pp. 174–175.

[118]It is should be noted that responsible command is not the same as command responsibility. See Sivakumaran (2012), p. 175.

3.2 *Non-International Armed Conflict for the Purpose of Additional Protocol II*

Attention is turned now to the scope of Article 1(1) of Additional Protocol II, which prescribes its own requirements for NIAC. Article 1(1) provides as follows:

> This Protocol... shall apply to all armed conflicts which are not covered by Article 1 of the Protocol Additional to the Geneva Conventions of 12 August 1949, and relating to the Protection of Victims of International Armed Conflicts (Protocol I) and which take place in the territory of a High Contracting Party *between its armed forces and dissident armed forces or other organized armed groups which, under responsible command, exercise such control over a part of its territory as to enable them to carry out sustained and concerted military operations and to implement this Protocol.*[119]

The requirements of the Article are examined in turn.

3.2.1 Armed Forces of a State as a Party to the Conflict

Additional Protocol II specifically requires that government armed forces be a party to a NIAC before it can fall within its purview. Thus, where the conflict is merely between two armed groups, however the intensity of the conflict or the organization of the armed groups, Additional Protocol II is inapplicable.

3.2.2 Organized Armed Groups Under Responsible Command

As seen above, the organization of an armed group and with it, responsible command within the group is already a requirement for a NIAC *simpliciter*. However, to fall within the scope of Additional Protocol II, a higher degree of organization on the part of the armed group in the conflict is required.[120]

The ICRC Commentary on the Additional Protocols describes the notion of responsible command under Article 1(1) thus:

> The existence of a responsible command implies some degree of organization of the insurgent armed group or dissident armed forces but this does not necessarily mean that there is a hierarchical system of military organization similar to that of regular armed forces. It means an organization capable, on the one hand, of planning and carrying out sustained and concerted military operations, and on the other hand imposing discipline in the name of a defacto authority.[121]

---

[119]Emphasis ours.

[120]Sivakumaran (2012), p. 185. See further *Prosecutor v. Boskoski and Tarculovski,* IT-04-82-T, Judgment, 10 July 2008, paragraph 197.

[121]Sandoz et al. (1987), p. 1352, paragraph 4463.

3.2.3 Control of Territory for Sustained and Concerted Military Operations, and Implementation of the Protocol

Under this requirement, the control of territory by the armed group refers to such degree of control as gives it the capacity for sustained and concerted military operations and the implementation of the provisions of Additional Protocol II.[122]

As for 'sustained and concerted military operations,' there are two viewpoints as to the meaning. On one hand, it is believed that the level of intensity of violence required to meet the standard of 'sustained and concerted violence' is higher than needed to meet the standard of 'protracted violence' under a NIAC *simpliciter*.[123] Cullen in line with this, states that this requirement is "[p]erhaps the most significant of the criteria contained in Article 1(1)."[124] This is because it "sets a particularly high threshold for the application of the Protocol"[125] and "rules out all situations of low-intensity armed conflict."[126] Also in line with this view, the ICRC Commentary on the Additional Protocol II stated thus:

> 'Sustained'... means that the operations are kept going or kept up continuously. The emphasis is therefore on continuity and persistence. 'Concerted'... means agreed upon, planned and contrived, done in agreement according to plan. Thus, we are talking about military operations conceived and planned by organized armed groups... At the beginning of a conflict military operations rarely have such a character; thus it is likely that only common Article 3 will apply to the first stage of hostilities.[127]

On the other hand, 'sustained and concerted military operations' is not seen as substantially different from 'protracted violence' and thus requires the same level of violence to meet both requirements.[128]

Lastly, the armed group needs only to have the ability to implement the Protocol. Actual implementation of it is irrelevant.[129]

When the above requirements are present in a NIAC situation, the application of Additional Protocol II is triggered.

---

[122] See ibid, paragraphs 4464–4467. See further, Sivakumaran (2012), p. 186.

[123] See *Prosecutor v. Boskoski and Tarculovski,* IT-04-82-T, Judgment, 10 July 2008, paragraph 197. See also Sivakumaran (2012), p. 188.

[124] Cullen (2010), p. 103.

[125] ibid.

[126] ibid, 105.

[127] Sandoz et al. (1987), p. 1353, paragraph 4469.

[128] Sivakumaran (2012), p. 188.

[129] See ibid.

3.3 *Establishing the Boko Haram Insurgency as a Non-International Armed Conflict*

As noted above, in November 2013, the OTP of the ICC determined that the Boko Haram insurgency had attained the status of a NIAC since at least May 2013.[130] This came at the backdrop of two previous reports of the OTP, in November 2012[131] and in August 2013[132] respectively, which concluded that the insurgency had not attained the status of a NIAC. The OTP did this in a bid to determine whether there was present, a situation covered by Article 8(2)(c) and (e) of the Rome Statute of the International Criminal Court (Rome Statute)[133]—in order to determine whether war crimes could be said to have been committed in Nigeria. The first step towards this is the determination of the existence of a NIAC.[134]

The OTP, in accordance with existing IHL rules, considered whether there was the requisite level of intensity of violence and organization of the Boko Haram group respectively. It is apt to note here that the OTP did not consider the existence of the additional requirements of Additional Protocol II, as those requirements are not found in the Rome Statute.[135] Regarding the level of intensity of the Boko Haram crisis in Nigeria, the OTP stated as follows:

> 216. With respect to the level of intensity of the armed confrontations between Boko Haram and Nigerian security forces, the Office has analysed over 200 incidents occurring between July 2009 and May 2013. In particular, the Office has assessed the extent and sustained nature of such incidents, as well as their seriousness; the frequency and intensity of armed confrontations; their geographical and temporal spread; the number and composition of personnel involved on both sides; the mobilization and the distribution of weapons; and the extent to which the situation has attracted the attention of the UN Security Council.
>
> 217. The Office observes that there appears to be some correlation between the deployment of the Nigerian Government Joint Task Force in June 2011 and an increase in frequency and intensity of the incidents between Boko Haram and security forces. Two declarations of a state of emergency in the north-eastern parts of Nigeria in December 2011 and May 2013 were followed by a surge of troops, increased security operations and renewed armed confrontations. The Offices [sic] notes that the latter declaration defined Boko Haram's activities as an "insurgency."[136]

[130]See Office of the Prosecutor, ICC (2013a), paragraph 218.

[131]Office of the Prosecutor, ICC (2012), paragraph 90.

[132]Office of the Prosecutor, ICC (2013b), paragraph 130.

[133]Rome Statute of the International Criminal Court, July 17, 1998, 2187 UNTS 90. Article 8(2)(f) of the Rome Statute explains that the preceding sub-paragraph (e) is applicable "... when there is *protracted armed conflict* between governmental authorities and organized armed groups or between such groups." (Emphasis ours.) While this is seemingly a new category of a NIAC, it is however only relevant for the purpose of establishing the jurisdiction of the ICC over specific war crimes. See Vite (2009), pp. 80–83.

[134]See Office of the Prosecutor, ICC (2013a), paragraphs 214–218.

[135]See the provisions of Article 8(2)(c) and (e) of the Rome Statute.

[136]See Office of the Prosecutor, ICC (2013a), paragraphs 216–217.

With regard to the level of organization of Boko Haram as an armed group, the OTP stated thus:

> 215. In terms of organization, the Office has considered the hierarchical structure of Boko Haram; its command rules and ability to impose discipline among its members; the weapons used by the group; its ability to plan and carry out coordinated attacks; and the number of Boko Haram forces under command. The Office has concluded that Boko Haram fulfils a sufficient number of relevant criteria to be considered an organized armed group capable of planning and carrying out military activities.[137]

In summary, the OTP stated as follows:

> 218. In view of the above, the required level of intensity and the level of organization of parties to the conflict necessary for the violence to be qualified as an armed conflict of non-international character appear to have been met. The Office has therefore determined that since at least May 2013 allegations of crimes occurring in the context of the armed violence between Boko Haram and Nigerian security forces should be considered within the scope of article 8(2)(c) and (e) of the Statute.[138]

Thus, factors such as the geographical spread of the violence, involvement of third parties, declaration of a state of emergency and the deployment of State armed forces are considered relevant to assessing the level of intensity of violence. In the same vein, factors such as the chain of command or hierarchy of Boko Haram, the number of forces under its control, and its rules and its ability to discipline its members, are indicative of the requisite level of organization of the armed group. The OTP assessment therefore rightly found to be in existence a NIAC *simpliciter* between the Nigerian armed forces and the Boko Haram armed group. The two previous reports mentioned above wherein the OTP concluded that the violence hitherto had not risen to the status of a NIAC also reflected the facts on ground.[139]

Did the situation ever exceed NIAC *simpliciter*, as to trigger application Additional Protocol II in the armed conflict between the Nigerian armed forces and the Boko Haram armed group, even during the period in mid-2014 when Boko Haram seized and held towns in Borno State and declared a Caliphate? The first requirement in Additional Protocol II, of the state armed forces being a party to the conflict ticks off easily, as the Nigerian Army has been involved in the fight against Boko Haram from July 2009 onward. The requirement, of the armed group being organized and under responsible command, is trickier. The determination of the existence of a NIAC *simpliciter* (above) means that there is some degree of organization drawing from the finding of a hierarchical structure within the group, and thus a responsible command, in the Boko Haram armed group. For Additional Protocol II however, a higher degree of organization than for an armed conflict under Common Article 3 is required. This higher degree of organization and responsible command should be such as to enable the group, according to the text, "implement th[e] Protocol." For

[137]ibid, paragraph 215.

[138]ibid, paragraph 218.

[139]See Office of the Prosecutor, ICC (2012), paragraph 90; Office of the Prosecutor, ICC (2013b), paragraph 130.

this purpose, "the existence of disciplinary procedures and internal rules" takes priority.[140]

Can it be said that Boko Haram possessed the requisite higher degree of organization and responsible command capable of imposing the discipline needed to ensure compliance with Additional Protocol II? The present writers think not. Though the level of organization of the group as described above may be sufficient to justify a NIAC *simpliciter*, the same cannot be readily said for a NIAC governed by Additional Protocol II. The best that can be said for now is that the matter is inconclusive, as there is insufficient information on the subject. However, our inclination is that the decentralised nature of the sect suggests that Boko Haram lacks the requisite organization.

As regards the requirement of territorial control such that would enable the armed group to carry out sustained and concerted attacks and implement the provisions of Additional Protocol II, it is submitted that this requirement was indeed satisfied. Boko Haram did physically hold some towns and villages that gave it the ability to carry out sustained and concerted military operations and to implement the Protocol. Although, as for the requirement of implementation of the Protocol, Boko Haram never at any time pretended to obey any provisions of IHL let alone Additional Protocol II, as discussed above, it is the ability to implement the Protocol that counts and not the actual implementation of the Protocol. Lastly, on the requirement of carrying out sustained and concerted military operations, the answer will depend on the view taken as to the meaning of the phrase. If the view that it means the same as protracted violence is adopted, then that requirement has been met. If the view is taken that it means the operations must be ongoing and planned, the requirement was also met as there were indeed persistent, ongoing and planned attacks by the group around that period.

The inability of the present writers to accept that the Boko Haram NIAC ever reached the threshold in Additional Protocol II to trigger its application thus turns on the absence, seemingly, of a sufficient level of organization and responsible command to ensure compliance with the provisions of Additional Protocol II. Although the other requirements are possibly met, the absence of the level of organization and responsible command therefore kept this NIAC within the scope of Common Article 3 only.

[140]Just as important as the indicia of organization are the reasons why organization is a prerequisite for the existence of a party to a non-international armed conflict. An armed group may be organized for one purpose, such as conducting large-scale violence, but not for another, such as being able to comply with the law. The reason why a certain level of organization is a prerequisite will thus affect the weight to be afforded to the various indicia. . . . For example, if organization is required in order to demonstrate that the group has the ability to carry out intense hostilities, factors such as the ability to procure, distribute, and use weaponry should be the crucial indicia. However, if organization is required in order that the group be able to enforce international humanitarian law, factors such as the existence of disciplinary procedures and internal regulations should take priority.

Sivakumaran (2012), p. 176. See also ibid, pp. 66–68.

4 Determining the End Point for the Boko Haram Insurgency as a Non-International Armed Conflict

Having determined the commencement, the question here is, What marks the end, or termination, of a NIAC, considering the claim of the Nigerian government to have achieved the 'final crushing' of Boko Haram, and then a seeming resurgence of the group? When can we say for certain that, a NIAC has ceased to exist?

Under international law, there is a lack of clarity on the matter of the end of armed conflicts,[141] especially with regard to NIACs. For IACs, it is quite settled that they could end in a number of ways such as the conclusion of peace agreements (followed by actual cessation of hostilities between the parties), surrender by one of the parties, *debellatio* i.e. a total defeat of one of the parties to the conflict, implied mutual consent or a unilateral declaration accepted by the other party.[142] Less clear however, is the current effect of armistices in IACs, i.e. whether they still only result in a suspension of hostilities, which was their traditional role, or can now definitively terminate an armed conflict, this view resulting from some state practice since the end of World War II.[143]

For NIACs, the situation is more complicated. Compared to those of IACs, the markers for the end point of NIACs are quite unclear, with no real direction in this regard in the relevant IHL treaties. For guidance on this matter, we may turn to case law and literature. The existing views on the end point of a NIAC resulting from these sources can be grouped into two broad categories: the "peaceful settlement" standard and the "threshold of a NIAC" standard.[144] These two categories are discussed in turn.

4.1 *Peaceful Settlement Standard*

This standard mainly originates from the seminal decision of the Appeals Chamber of the ICTY in *Tadic* Decision on Jurisdiction.[145] While discussing the temporal application of IHL (which is directly linked with the existence of an armed conflict)

[141] Lewis et al. (2017), p. 1.

[142] Dinstein (2011), pp. 48–51.

[143] Lewis et al. (2017), pp. 31–32.

[144] Lewis et al categories the views into four: (1) The "two-way-ratchet" theory; (2) The "no-more-combat-measures" theory; (3) The "no-reasonable-risk-of-resumption" theory; and (4) The "state-of-war-throwback" theory. See ibid, p. 96.

[145] *Prosecutor v. Tadic,* IT-94-1-AR72, Decision on the Defence Motion for Interlocutory Appeal on Jurisdiction, 2 October 1995.

in the case of the NIAC, the Court held that IHL applied, "until a peaceful settlement is achieved."[146] Terming this viewpoint the "state-of-war-throwback" theory, Lewis *et al* trace the root of this viewpoint to the traditional state-of-war doctrine whereby a state of war generally existed between belligerent states until a peace agreement was reached between them.[147] According to them, the theory "presumes that the parties to a NIAC are capable in principle of agreeing to end the conflict and in practice of exercising sufficient control over their relevant components in order to effectively implement that agreement."[148]

The "peaceful settlement" standard has the advantage of presenting quite a clear benchmark for the end of a NIAC, promoting legal certainty,[149] and also a 'continuous war crime jurisdiction' for the courts.[150] A recent example of a peaceful settlement ending a non-international armed conflict is the peace accord between the government of Colombia and the Revolutionary Armed Forces of Columbia (FARC) signed in 2016, which ended over 50 years of conflict between both parties.

However, this 'peaceful settlement' standard is much disputed,[151] having been labelled by Bartels as "too strict,"[152] and "not supported by IHL."[153] The ICRC, on its own part, adopts a flexible interpretation to *Tadic's* 'peaceful settlement' standard, stating thus in the 2016 Commentary on the First Geneva Convention:

> It is necessary to rely on the facts when assessing whether a non-international armed conflict has come to an end, or, in other words, a 'peaceful settlement' has been reached. This approach not only reflects the purely fact-based assessment of the beginning of a non-international armed conflict but is also in line with modern humanitarian law more generally, for whose applicability formal requirements are not decisive.[154]

---

[146] See ibid, paragraph 70. This has been cited in cases such as *Prosecutor v. Haradinaj, Balaj and Brahimaj,* IT-04-08-T, Judgment, 3 April 2008, paragraph 100; and *Prosecutor v. Lubanga,* ICC-01/04-01/06 Judgment, 14 March 2012, paragraphs 533 and 548. In *Haradinaj,* the Court in its judgment noted that: "... since according to the *Tadic* test an internal armed conflict continues until a peaceful settlement is achieved, and since there is no evidence of such a settlement during the indictment period, there is no need for the Trial Chamber to explore the oscillating intensity of the armed conflict in the remainder of the indictment period". See *Prosecutor v. Haradinaj, Balaj and Brahimai,* ibid, paragraph 100.

[147] Lewis et al. (2017), p. 103.

[148] ibid, 103.

[149] See *Prosecutor v. Ante Gotovina et al.* (Judgment) IT-06-90-T, Judgment, 15 April 2011, paragraph 1694, where the court held thus:

> Once the law of armed conflict has become applicable, one should not lightly conclude that its applicability ceases. Otherwise, the participants in an armed conflict may find themselves in a revolving door between applicability and non-applicability, leading to a considerable degree of legal uncertainty and confusion.

[150] Lewis et al. (2017), p. 104. See also Milanovic (2014), pp. 179–180.

[151] See for example Bartels (2014), p. 301; Milanovic (2014), pp. 179–180; Kleffner (2014), p. 291; Casey-Maslen and Haines (2018), pp. 70–71.

[152] Bartels (2014), p. 301.

[153] Ibid.

[154] ICRC (2016), paragraph 487.

This is in line with Kleffner's stance on the matter, having said that the 'peaceful settlement' standard, "only holds true as a matter of law to the extent that the "peaceful settlement" is also an accurate description of the factual situation on the ground."[155]

Discussing further, the ICRC noted that:

> ... armed confrontations sometimes continue well beyond the conclusion or unilateral pronouncement of a formal act such as a ceasefire, armistice or peace agreement. Relying solely on the existence of such agreements to determine the end of a non-international armed conflict could therefore lead to a premature end of the applicability of humanitarian law in situations when in fact a conflict continues. Conversely, armed confrontations may also dissipate without any ceasefire, armistice or peace agreement ever being concluded, or before the conclusion of such an agreement. Thus, while the existence of such agreements may be taken into account when assessing all of the facts, they are neither necessary nor sufficient on their own to bring about the termination of the application of humanitarian law.[156]

The above highlights some of the drawbacks of the 'peaceful settlement standard.' A peace agreement may not be observed by the belligerent parties, or may fall apart as was the case with the 2015 South Sudan Peace Agreement made with a view to ending the South Sudanese Civil War. A revitalised agreement had to be reached in 2018. On the other hand, hostilities may cease without any such settlement or agreement reached, or have ceased for a while before an agreement is actually concluded. Also, as Lewis *et al* point out, it is unclear whether a surrender by one of the parties, without more, counts as a 'peaceful settlement' in view of this standard.[157]

Applying this "peaceful settlement" standard to the Boko Haram insurgency, it would mean that the NIAC would only end when there is a peace agreement reached between the Nigerian government and the Boko Haram group. While this would mark a clear and objective end to the conflict, subject to the agreement actually being observed, this is quite an unlikely scenario, at least currently, because the group is highly radicalized. Hence, if the "peaceful settlement" standard is indeed the accepted benchmark for determining the endpoint or termination of a NIAC, the Boko Haram insurgency may end up becoming an indefinite NIAC barring a complete military defeat of the armed group (as was the case in Sri Lanka with the Liberation Tigers of Tamil Eelam (LTTE) in 2009) or a dissolution of the group. The current factionalization of the group further complicates matters. Whatever agreement that may be reached now needs to encompass both JAS and ISWA. Also, if there comes a time when the Boko Haram insurgency is determined to involve two separate non-international armed conflicts (i.e. between the Nigerian government

[155]Kleffner (2014), p. 291.

[156]ICRC (2016), paragraph 490.

[157]Lewis et al. (2017), p. 103.

and JAS on one hand, and then the government and ISWA on the other hand), then peaceful settlements would again need to be reached on both fronts.

4.2 *Threshold of a NIAC Standard*

As against the "peaceful settlement" standard, another viewpoint which has gained traction in the literature, termed here the "threshold of a NIAC" standard. This argues that a NIAC ceases to exist when the conditions necessary for its existence, i.e. the requisite intensity of violence and organization of parties, are no longer present.[158] Simply put, the armed conflict has lost its qualifications to be a NIAC because either the armed group or the intensity of the conflict has degraded to a level below the lower threshold of NIAC. In this vein, Bartels contends that "if a NIAC only starts when organized groups are engaged in fighting of a certain intensity, then logically, the armed conflict ends when these two criteria are no longer present."[159] This he refers to as the use of the "lower threshold criteria," meaning the use of the threshold for determining the existence of a NIAC to also determine its termination.[160]

Similarly, with regard to the end of a NIAC, Milanovic states that "what would matter is whether the intensity of the hostilities or the organization of the non-State actor factually eroded to such an extent that the threshold is no longer met."[161] While noting that a NIAC could be said to end through a peace agreement, complete defeat or a surrender by a party to the conflict, Milanovic remarks that regardless, "the only legally relevant question would be whether the threshold continues to be satisfied."[162]

While this "threshold of a NIAC" standard seemingly takes the facts-on-the-ground reality into consideration by determining the termination of a NIAC with reference to the absence of the twin criteria for the existence of a NIAC, assessing the absence or not of the criteria is a difficult task. The difficulty of this task was recognised by Bartels,[163] and in light of the consequences that may result from a hasty assessment i.e. a "revolving door between applicability and non-applicability

[158]The content of the "threshold for a NIAC" standard as discussed here, is split in two theories i.e. the "two-way-ratchet" theory, and the "no-reasonable-risk-of-resumption" theory, by Lewis et al. The former as categorised by the authors, turns quite strictly on the absence of the criteria for the existence of a NIAC, while the latter imposes a lower standard, giving allowance for a determination to be made that there is no real risk that hostilities would be resumed between the parties. See Lewis et al. (2017), pp. 97–99 and 100–102.

[159]Bartels (2014), p. 303.

[160]See ibid.

[161]Milanovic (2014), p. 180.

[162]ibid.

[163]See Bartels (2014), pp. 309–310.

[of IHL],"[164] he notes that: "when considering the proposed lower threshold with regard to the end of a NIAC, it makes sense that this end-threshold would probably have to be set at a lower level than the threshold that would bring about the start of the conflict."[165]

Given the quite usual oscillation in intensity of an armed conflict, the ICRC cautions that a "temporary lull" in intensity of violence should not be regarded as determinative of the end of a NIAC.[166] Instead, the situation on ground must attain a degree of stabilization which "equates to a peaceful settlement."[167] Milanovic, similarly, notes that the intensity of violence needs to drop below the requisite threshold "with a certain degree of permanence and stability" so as to enable a positive determination of the end of a NIAC.[168] The ICRC notes that the length of time without "armed confrontations" by the parties—not minding "minor isolated or sporadic acts of violence"—which would determine an attainment of the necessary degree of stabilization, is heavily dependent on the circumstances of each conflict.[169] There can be no generalization in this regard. Such careful analysis would help to prevent the consequences of a hasty assessment.[170]

The above analysis is still relevant to a NIAC that qualifies under Additional Protocol II. For such a NIAC, Additional Protocol II would cease to apply when the situation on ground no longer fulfils the requirements stated in Article 2(1): a State being one of the parties to the conflict; the armed groups are organised and under responsible command; and territorial control for the purpose of carrying out sustained and concerted operations, and the implementation of the Protocol.[171] In such a case, if the factual circumstances meet the requirements of a NIAC simpliciter, then Common Article 3 becomes the applicable regime.[172]

Applying the "threshold of a NIAC" standard to the Boko Haram insurgency, it is now quite clear that although the government was quick to declare a technical defeat

---

[164] *Prosecutor v. Ante Gotovina et al.* (Judgment) IT-06-90-T, Judgment, 15 April 2011, paragraph 1694.

[165] Bartels (2014), p. 310.

[166] ICRC (2016), paragraphs 492 and 494.

[167] ICRC (2016), paragraph 492.

[168] Milanovic (2014), p. 180.

[169] ICRC (2016), paragraph 492.

[170] ICRC (2016), paragraph 493 and 496. Lewis *et al* also note a fourth theory, the "no-combat-measures" theory, which is to the effect that a NIAC ends "upon the general close of military operations as characterized by the cessation of actions of the armed forces with a view to combat." This concept is borrowed from IHL rules relating to IACs. Here, cessation of military actions towards combat and not actual hostilities is key. See Lewis et al. (2017), p. 100. In a sense, this theory could be brought under the "threshold for a NIAC" standard, seeing that if actual hostilities have ceased but still, some sort of military action towards combat such as deploying of troops or continued building up of military capacity remain, this signifies that the intensity of violence of the NIAC have obviously fallen below the threshold for the existence of a NIAC, although not to a degree of stabilization that would not be seen as a hasty assessment in that regard.

[171] See Milanovic (2014) p. 180; Bartels (2014), p. 304.

[172] Milanovic (2014), p. 180; Bartels (2014), p. 304.

over Boko Haram, the NIAC between Nigeria and the armed group never came to an end. This is because, despite the substantial military gains recorded against the group in 2015 and 2016, there has remained quite a consistently high intensity of violence between both parties (and between the government and both factions i.e. JAS and ISWA, although more with ISWA), and the organizational structure has remained quite firm, enough to meet the threshold for an armed conflict under Common article 3. For the insurgency to be deemed over as a NIAC, in line with this standard, the intensity of violence of the conflict must drop below the threshold required to bring a NIAC into existence, or the organisation of the Boko Haram group must erode to the extent that it fails to meet the criteria necessary for a NIAC. This must be so for such a period of time that would enable an objective determination of stabilization of the situation, and thus an end of the NIAC, despite remnants of isolated and sporadic attacks.

As with the "peaceful settlement" standard, the factionalization of Boko Haram also complicates matters with regard to the "threshold of a NIAC" standard. Even where the armed conflict continues to be seen as a single one, any determination to be done with regard to the "threshold of a NIAC" standard must of necessity take both JAS and ISWA into consideration. It may be that in future, the current single NIAC, becomes concretised as two separate ones, and then it would take both conflicts meeting the standard, for the insurgency as a NIAC to be deemed ended.

5 Conclusion

The future of the Boko Haram insurgency as a long-term or prolonged NIAC is very likely, especially given its factionalization into *Jama'atu Ahlis Sunna Lidda'awati Wal-Jihad* (JAS) and the Islamic State in West Africa (ISWA). Although the splinter groups currently operate in a diminished capacity, they (JAS and ISWA) still retain their ability to strike at military and civilian targets, and they continue to do so, despite the efforts of the Nigerian military forces.

This paper set out to analyze the rules regarding the termination of a NIAC from the perspective of the Boko Haram insurgency. The analysis above in relation to the insurgency clearly reveals how problematic definitively determining the end of a NIAC is. This is further compounded by the current factionalization of the armed group. The two broad viewpoints on the end of a NIAC i.e. the "peaceful settlement" standard and the "threshold of a NIAC" standard both have their advantages, but they also have their drawbacks. Given that the beginning and the end of a NIAC together mark the scope of the temporal application of IHL, it is imperative that more attention should be paid to agreeing on bright markers for the end of a NIAC under international law. This is even more so in this age of counterterrorism with the current prevalence of non-state armed groups engaged in conflicts with states.

References

Journal Articles

Adelaja AO et al (2018) Public opinion on the root causes of terrorism and objectives of terrorists: a Boko Haram case study. Perspect Terrorism 12(3):35

Adesoji A (2010) The Boko Haram uprising and Islamic revivalism in Nigeria. Afr Spectr 45 (2):95–108

Adesoji A (2011) Between Maitatsine and Boko Haram: Islamic fundamentalism and the response of the Nigerian State. Afr Today 57(4):98–119. https://doi.org/10.1353/at.2011/0016

Bagaji AY et al (2012) Boko Haram and the recurring bomb attacks in Nigeria: attempt to impose religious ideology through terrorism? Cross-Cult Commun 8(1):33–41. https://doi.org/10.3968/j.ccc.1923670020120801.1370.

Danjibo ND (2009) Islamic fundamentalism and sectarian violence: the "Maitatsine" and "Boko Haram" crises in Northern Nigeria. Peace and Conflict Studies Paper Series, Institute of African Studies, University of Ibadan, pp 1–21

Langer A et al (2017) Killing people, dividing a nation? Analyzing student perceptions of the Boko Haram crisis in Nigeria. Stud Confl Terrorism 40(5):419–438. https://doi.org/10.1080/1057610X.2016.1214434

Mantzikos I (2014) Boko Haram attacks in Nigeria and neighbouring countries: a chronology of attacks. Perspect Terrorism 8(6) II:63

Milanovic M (2014) The end of application of international humanitarian law. Int Rev Red Cross 96 (893):163–188. https://doi.org/10.1017/S181638311500003X

Onuoha FC (2011) The audacity of the Boko Haram: background, analysis and emerging trend. Secur J:1–18. https://doi.org/10.1057/sj.2011.15

Vite S (March 2009) Typology of armed conflicts in international humanitarian law: legal concepts and actual situations. Int Rev Red Cross 91(873):69

Book

Casey-Maslen S, Haines S (2018) Hague law interpreted: the conduct of hostilities under the law of armed conflict. Hart Publishing, Oxford

Cullen A (2010) The concept of non-international armed conflict in international humanitarian law. Cambridge University Press, Cambridge

de Montclos M-AP (2014a) Boko Haram: Islamism, politics, security and the state in Nigeria. African Studies Centre, Leiden

Dinstein Y (2011) War, aggression and self-defence, 5th edn. Cambridge University Press, Cambridge

Henckaerts J-M, Doswald-Beck L (eds) (2005) Customary international humanitarian law: volume I – Rules. International Committee of the Red Cross (ICRC)/Cambridge University Press, Cambridge

Sandoz Y et al (eds) (1987) Commentary on the additional protocols of 8 June 1977 to the Geneva Conventions of 12 August 1949. International Committee of the Red Cross (ICRC)/Martins Njihoff, Geneva

Sassoli M (2019) International humanitarian law: rules, controversies, and solutions to problems arising in warfare. Edward Elgar Publishing, Cheltenham

Sivakumaran S (2012) The law of non-international armed conflict. Oxford University Press, Oxford

Chapter in a Book

Bartels R (2014) From jus in bello to jus post bellum: when do non-international armed conflicts end? In: Stahn C et al (eds) Jus post bellum: mapping the normative foundations. Oxford University Press, Oxford, pp 297–314

Kleffner JK (2014) Towards a functional conceptualization of the temporal scope of jus post bellum. In: Stahn C et al (eds) Jus post bellum: mapping the normative foundations. Oxford University Press, Oxford, pp 287–296

Online Publications

Brechenmacher S (2019) 'Stabilizing Northeast Nigeria After Boko Haram' 3 May 2019. Carnegie Endowment for International Peace. https://carnegieendowment.org/2019/05/03/stabilizing-northeast-nigeria-after-boko-haram-pub-79042

Campbell J, Harwood A (2018) 'Boko Haram's deadly impact' 20 August 2018. Council on Foreign Relations. https://www.cfr.org/article/boko-harams-deadly-impact. Accessed 30 Jan 2020

Cook D (2011) Boko Haram: a prognosis. James A. Baker III Institute for Public Policy Rice University Research Paper, 16 December 2011

de Montclos M-AP (2014b) Nigeria's interminable insurgency? addressing the Boko Haram crisis. Research Paper, African Programme, Chatham House, the Royal Institute of International Affairs, September 2014

Human Rights Watch, 'Nigeria: Events of 2017'. https://www.hrw.org/world-report/2018/country-chapters/nigeria

ICRC (2016) 2016 Commentary on the Convention (I) for the Amelioration of the Condition of the Wounded and Sick in Armed Forces in the Field. Geneva, 12 August 1949. https://ihl-databases.icrc.org/applic/ihl/ihl.nsf/Comment.xsp?action=openDocument&documentId=59F6CDFA490736C1C1257F7D004BA0EC

Onuoha FC (2014) A danger not to Nigeria alone- Boko Haram's transnational reach and regional responses. Friedrich-Ebert-Stiftung (FES) Peace and Security Series No 17. https://library.fes.de/pdf-files/bueros/nigeria/11066.pdf

Pantucci R, Jesperson S (2015) From Boko Haram to Ansaru: the evolution of Nigerian Jihad. Royal United Services Institute (RUSI) Occasional Paper, April 2015. https://rusi.org/sites/default/files/201504_op_from_boko_haram_to_ansaru.pdf

RULAC. 'Non-international armed conflict in Nigeria: Classification- Organization.' http://www.rulac.org/browse/conflicts/non-international-armed-conflict-in-nigeria#collapse2accord

Stratfor (2014) 'Nigeria: Examining Boko Haram' 15 July 2014. www.stratfor.com/analysis/nigeria-examining-boko-haram

Torbjörnsson D, Jonsson M (2017) Boko Haram: On the verge of defeat or a long term threat? FOI-R--4488--SE. https://www.foi.se/rest-api/report/FOI-R%2D%2D4488%2D%2DSE

UNHCR. 'Nigeria emergency' https://www.unhcr.org/nigeria-emergency.html

News Articles

'Abuja attack: Car bomb hits Nigeria UN building' BBC News (27 August 2011), www.bbc.com/news/world-africa-14677957

'Army chief in Maiduguri; changes code to *Lafiya Dole*' Vanguard Nigeria (21 July 2015), http://www.vanguardngr.com/2015/07/army-chief-in-maiduguri-changes-code-to-operation-lafiya-dole/

'Blast rocks Police headquarters in Nigeria' Al Jazeera News (16 June 2011), www.aljazeera.com/news/africa/2011/06/201161611451344807.html

'Boko Haram Attack' frees hundreds of Prisoners' BBC News (8 September 2010), www.bbc.com/news/world-africa-11229740

'Boko Haram: behind the rise of Nigeria's armed group' Al Jazeera Special Series (22 December 2016), http://www.aljazeera.com/programmes/specialseries/2016/11/boko-haram-rise-nigeria-armed-group-161101145500150.html

'Boko Haram launches major attack on northeast Nigerian city,' Reuters (7 June 2017), https://www.reuters.com/article/us-nigeria-security/boko-haram-launches-major-attack-on-northeast-nigerian-city-idUSKBN18Y2Q3

'Boko Haram 'to sell' Nigeria girls abducted from Chibok' BBC News (5 May 2014), https://www.bbc.com/news/world-africa-27283383

'Nigeria Boko Haram: militants 'technically defeated'- Buhari' BBC News (24 December 2015), http://www.bbc.com/news/world-africa-35173618

'Nigeria Dapchi abductions: schoolgirls finally home,' BBC News (25 March 2018), https://www.bbc.com/news/world-africa-43535872

'Police reinforce stations, armouries after Boko Haram attack in Borno,' Channels TV, (28 March 2019), https://www.channelstv.com/2019/03/28/police-reinforce-stations-armouries-after-boko-haram-attack-in-borno/

'The rise and final fall of Boko Haram in Nigeria' NTA (25 December 2016). http://www.nta.ng/news/security-news/20161225-videos-rise-final-fall-boko-haram/

Adegoke Y, 'Boko Haram's pledge of allegiance to ISIL is a symptom of weakness, not strength' Quartz (9 March 2015), https://qz.com/358264/why-boko-harams-pledge-of-allegiance-to-isil-is-a-symptom-ofweakness-not-strength

Adetayo O 'Buhari hails troops over capture of Boko Haram's Camp Zero' Punch Nigeria (24 December 2016), http://punchng.com/buhari-excited-troops-capture-sambisa-forest/

Akinyelure D, 'The six lives of Boko Haram's Abubakar Shekau' BBC news (27 September 2016), www.bbc.com/news/world-africa-37476453

Burke J 'Nigerian Islamists kill scores of soldiers in military base attack,' The Guardian (23 November 2018), https://www.theguardian.com/world/2018/nov/23/nigerian-islamists-kill-scores-of-soldiers-in-military-base-attack

Dudley D (2018) 'The deadliest terrorist groups in the world today' Forbes (5 December 2018), https://www.forbes.com/sites/dominicdudley/2018/12/05/deadliest-terrorist-groups-in-the-world/#45c889852b3e

Kayode B (2014) Inside Nigeria's Sambisa forest, Boko Haram hideout where kidnapped school girls are believed to be kept. The Guardian (29 April 2014), https://www.theguardian.com/world/2014/apr/29/nigeria-sambisa-forest-boko-haram-hideout-kidnapped-school-girls-believed-to-be-held

Maclean R, Abrak I 'Boko Haram returns some of the girls it kidnapped last month,' The Guardian (21 March 2018), https://www.theguardian.com/world/2018/mar/21/boko-haram-returns-some-of-the-girls-it-kidnapped-last-month

Ogundipe S, 'Melete Boko Haram attack: Soldiers' death toll rises to 118; Over 150 Missing,' Premium Times (24 November 2018), https://www.premiumtimesng.com/news/headlines/297343-metele-boko-haram-attack-soldiers-death-toll-rises-to-118-over-150-missing.html

Ogundipe S, 'Premium Times- Nigeria: Eight soldiers killed in fresh Boko Haram attack,' AllAfrica (25 January 2019), https://allafrica.com/stories/201901250378.html

Reports

Amnesty International (2015) 'Our job is to shoot, slaughter and kill': Boko Haram's reign of terror in north-east Nigeria

Arraf S (2018) Nigeria: a focus on the Boko Haram insurgency. In: Bellal A (ed) (2018) The war report: armed conflicts in 2017. Geneva Academy of International Humanitarian Law and Human Rights, pp 100–113

Bellal A (ed) (2018) The war report: armed conflicts in 2017. Geneva Academy of International Humanitarian Law and Human Rights

Cold-Ravnkilde S, Plambech S (2015) Boko Haram: from local grievances to violent insurgency. Danish Institute for International Studies (DIIS) Report, p 21

Counter Extremism Project., 'Boko Haram' https://www.counterextremism.com/sites/default/files/threat_pdf/Boko%20Haram-08222019.pdf

ICRC (2014) Annual report 2013

International Crisis Group (2014) Curbing violence in Nigeria (II): The Boko Haram insurgency. Africa Report No 216, 3 April 2014

International Crisis Group (2019) Facing the challenge of the Islamic State in West Africa Province. Africa Report No 273, 16 May 2019

ISS (2018) Research report (Mahmood OS, Ani NC), 'Factional dynamics within Boko Haram' July 2018. https://issafrica.s3.amazonaws.com/site/uploads/2018-07-06-research-report-2.pdf

Lewis DA et al (2017) Indefinite war: unsettled international law on the end of armed conflict. Harvard Law School Programme of International Law and Armed Conflict. Legal Briefing

Office of the Prosecutor, ICC (2012) Report on preliminary examinations activities. November 2012

Office of the Prosecutor, ICC (2013a) Report on preliminary examinations activities. November 2013

Office of the Prosecutor, ICC (2013b) Situation in Nigeria: article 5 report. 5 August 2013

Solomon Ukhuegbe, LL.M., PhD, Agbakwas LLP, Toronto, Canada

Alero I. Fenemigho, LL.M, Faculty of Law, University of Benin, Nigeria; LLD Candidate, Centre for Human Rights, University of Pretoria, South Africa

The United Nations Human Rights Machinery: Too Big to Fail? An Examination of the Flaws of the Machinery and Proposals from a Third World Scholar's Perspective

Thamil Venthan Ananthavinayagan

Contents

1 Introduction

With the beginning of the United Nations in 1945 human rights became a central piece in the international agenda of this prime international organisation. The outgoing United Nations High Commissioner for Human Rights, Prince Zeid bin Ra'ad Zeid al-Hussein ascertained in an interview with the *Le Monde* that: "[L]a pression sur les droits universels est une évidence. Les mécanismes et les lois sur les droits de l'homme doivent être défendus et promus en permanence."[1]

[1]Le Monde, 'Les violations des droits de l'homme d'aujourd'hui sont les conflits de demain', (Le Monde, 1 August 2018), <https://www.lemonde.fr/international/article/2018/08/01/zeid-ra-ad-

T. V. Ananthavinayagan (✉)
Maastricht University, Maastricht, Netherlands

NUI Galway, Galway, Ireland

Griffith College, Dublin, Ireland

School of Law, University of Nottingham, Nottingham, UK
e-mail: ilangayan@googlemail.com; Thamil.Ananthavinayagan@nottingham.ac.uk

C. Eboe-Osuji et al. (eds.), *Nigerian Yearbook of International Law 2018/2019*,
Nigerian Yearbook of International Law 2018/2019,
https://doi.org/10.1007/978-3-030-69594-1_15

According to the High Commissioner, the violations of universal human rights are a reality and only the resort to human rights laws and mechanisms can be the bulwark and remedy for and against the violations. However, isn't it the existence of the Western power dominance at the United Nations and its paternalistic view on the dissemination of universal goals such as on human rights that is impeding equal human rights dialogue between the developed and developing world? Hasn't power politics and colonial history contaminated the effective human rights protection and promotion?

To this end, the article will, firstly, focus on the historical evolution of the United Nations human rights machinery. In this part, the article will discuss the development of the machinery and its early contribution to formerly colonial countries as a, truly, international project for liberation from colonial subjugation. Secondly, the article will examine the colonial/postcolonial infiltration of the machinery. In this part, the article aims to elaborate more on the postcolonial policy and neo-imperial entrenchment within the United Nations. Against this background, the article will, thirdly, examine the actual impact of international human rights engagement on postcolonial countries, and fourthly, by using the example of Sri Lanka, decipher the limited impact the United Nations human rights engagement had and has on postcolonial countries due to a variety of reasons. But, in particular, the Sri Lankan example will enunciate that the engagement with Sri Lanka has changed the United Nations more than it has changed Sri Lanka. Fifthly and finally, the article will provide a concluding observation of the United Nations' failure to effectuate international human rights law and serve in the interest of majority of the world, while providing suggestions from a Third World view to enhance the current system.

1.1 Historical Development of the Human Rights Machinery at the United Nations

When the League of Nations was replaced by the United Nations, there was a prevailing expectation that the new international body must address grave human rights violations and the infringement upon of state sovereignty that were causes for the Second World War.[2] Already during the Second World War, certain plans and ideas were devised, so as to ensure, -*inter alia*- the inclusion of

> [h]uman rights provisions in treaties with former enemies, human rights conferences, human rights commissions with investigatory and quasi-judicial authority, and, of particular importance, an international declaration of human rights and the inclusion of human rights articles in the charter of a post-war international organization.[3]

---

al-hussein-les-violations-des-droits-de-l-homme-d-aujourd-hui-sont-les-conflits-de-demain_5338061_3210.html> accessed 1 August 2018.

[2]Smith (2018), p. 27.

[3]Lauren (1983), pp. 1, 7.

One of the first proposals to draft an international human rights document came from the United States Department of State. For this reason, a special legal subcommittee was created in 1942 to deal with work in the field of post-war international organisation.[4] It was asserted by one participant that "[t]he Legal Subcommittee assumed that the recognition and guarantee of basic human rights would be conducive to the development of conditions favourable to the maintenance of international peace."[5]

Ushering in direct results, the preambular paragraphs of the United Nations Charter stressed the emphasis on the equality and inherent dignity of every human being. While it is true that the main goal of the United Nations is the maintenance of peace and security, it became a dominant opinion during the drafting process of the United Nations Charter human rights must take a crucial role.[6] However, human rights provisions of the United Nations Charter have been, as Steiner, Alston and Goodman put it, "[s]cattered, terse, even cryptic.'[7] There was neither a comprehensive human rights protection enshrined in the Charter, nor a definition nor articulation of human rights in the Charter.[8] Also it is unlikely that the drafters of the Charter had the wise foresight to see the development of international human rights law.[9] The end of the Second World War witnessed the constant proliferation of human rights treaties and the "[a]dvancement of the concept of human rights as a diplomatic and political currency, largely due to its function as a legitimizing device."[10] It began with the unenforceable, but noble Universal Declaration for Human Rights (UDHR).[11]

By 1966, however, many of the substantive provisions of the UDHR migrated into two binding treaties: the International Covenant on Civil and Political Rights (ICCPR) and the International Covenant on Economic, Social and Cultural Rights (ICESCR).[12] The rights entailed substantive and far-reaching aspects, such as right to speech and fair trial, the right to life, to the right to good and the right to education and so on. As Samuel Moyns holds, it was "[t]he finalization of the human rights covenants finally occurred in 1966, thanks to the transformative role of the new states."[13]

And yet, the human rights regime remained largely ineffective, as there were sparse enforcement mechanisms—the United Human Rights Commission, on the one hand, was a human rights charter-based body in the making and remained

---

4 *Ibid.*

5 Alice McDiarmid, "The Legal Subcommittee," Secret, 22 September 1944, RG 59, Alger Hiss Files, Box 2, National Archives, Washington, D.C.

6 *Supra* note 2, Smith.

7 Steiner et al. (2008), p. 135.

8 *Supra* note 2, Smith, 28.

9 *Supra* note 2, Smith, 28.

10 Kabasakal Arat (2013), p. 389.

11 Hannum (2006), pp. 287, 288.

12 *Supra* note 2, Smith, 44, 45.

13 Moyn (2012), p. 100.

largely inactive due to considerations by the powerful states at the point of its creation[14] and the human rights treaty bodies were yet to be created. The United Nations Human Rights Commission, hoped to be bestowed upon with a wide mandate to comprehensively promote human rights and formulate specific recommendations that were intended to create a basis for a body more receptive to addressing human rights violations. Its parent body, the Economic and Social Council, however, deemed these proposals as too far-reaching.[15] Instead, the Council implemented a governmental membership to the Commission and made it a politicised organ, the battlefield of political and competing worldviews. Any actions that were undertaken by the United Nations Human Rights Commission were the inevitable consequences of the political agenda of the respective members of the Commission. Moreover, following the Resolution 9 (II) of 1946, the Commission was only reduced to the role of submitting and assisting the Council to ensure respect for human rights.[16] Two phases must be ascertained for the timeline of the Commission's existence: the phase of abstention from the day of its inception up to 1967, and then the phase of interventionism from 1967 until its dissolution in 2005.[17] At this crucial juncture for international human rights law, the Commission suffered from the birth defects of its creation: firstly, politicisation and, secondly, inaction to remedy postcolonial ills.

Nearly every United Nations body is involved in the protection and promotion of human rights, with the responsibility the human rights monitoring being placed in the aforementioned bodies.[18] The replacement of the Commission by the Council must be contributed to a postcolonial battle between the developing world against the developed world, with the Cold War as an important element in the human rights discourse. Or, as the former United Nations Secretary General put it in his Report, *In Larger Freedom*:

> [T]he Commission on Human Rights has been discredited in the eyes of many. Too often states seek membership to insulate themselves from criticism or to criticize others, rather than to assist in the body's true task, which is to monitor and encourage the compliance of all states with their human rights obligations. The time has come for real reform. The commission should be transformed into a new Human Rights Council.[19]

The treaty-based bodies, on the other hand, try to defuse politicisation by incorporation of human rights experts and professionalisation of human rights monitoring. They situate themselves between the "[o]pen-ended approach of the

[14]Forsythe (2018), p. 100.

[15]Alston (1995), p. 2.

[16]United Nations, Resolution: Commission on Human Rights, adopted 21 June 1946, E/RES/9 (II).

[17]Marie (1980), pp. 355, 355.

[18]*Supra* note 2, Smith, 52, 53.

[19]United Nations: "In Larger Freedom": Decision Time at the UN, by Kofi Annan, From Foreign Affairs, May/June 2005, <http://www.unis.unvienna.org/pdf/freedom_annan.pdf>, accessed 6 August 2018.

charter-based bodies and the relatively structured approach of the judicial institutions."[20] The treaty bodies' work offers certain room for interpretation along with legal consistency according to which a "[c]redible standard for the reconciliation of tensions between the diversity of cultural practices on the one hand and the universal respect for human rights on the other" can be achieved.[21] The reporting process at the treaty bodies is, however, unable to exert political pressure and, once politicisation becomes evident, produces negative consequences on the credibility of the treaty bodies.[22]

On the one hand, scholarship suggests that international human rights treaties are inefficient, while pointing out to the adverse effects of treaty membership, namely that human rights violations increased after the ratification, calling this phenomenon "[r]adical decoupling."[23] States parties showed a lack of commitment and a selective human rights approach, paired with a strong emphasis on the notion of state sovereignty.[24] On the other hand, Sikkink and Risse write that: 'In sum, we argue that the diffusion of international norms in the human rights area crucially depends on the establishment and sustainability of networks among domestic and transnational acts who manage to link up with international regimes to alter Western public opinion and Western governments.'[25]

It is true, however, that the international development after the 1950s in the phase of decolonisation made international law truly international. As a process, it had impact on the definition of international and regional human rights standards.[26]

Noteworthy is the United Nations General Assembly Resolution 616B[27] which marked a milestone in the decolonisation period and the liberation of international law from colonial debris: it compelled member states for "[r]espect for human rights and fundamental freedoms for all, without distinction to race, sex, language or religion"[28] and moved on to hold that any member to the United Nations who allowed discrimination violates article 56 of the United Nations Charter (which specifies that member states pledged to further the purposes of the United Nations, as enunciated in Article 55 and which included the promotion of "fundamental human rights").

To this end, Antony Anghie asserts that

> [T]he conceptualization of the problem in this way suggested again that the non-European world was completely peripheral to the discipline proper; and it was only the disconcerting

[20] Addo (2010), pp. 601, 615.

[21] *Ibid.*

[22] Carraro (2017), pp. 943, 969.

[23] Cole (2012), pp. 1131, 1132.

[24] *Supra* note 10, Kabaskal Arat.

[25] Sikkink and Risse (2009), p. 5.

[26] Barreto (2013a), p. 160.

[27] United Nations General Assembly, Resolution 616B, <https://documents-dds-ny.un.org/doc/RESOLUTION/GEN/NR0/079/59/IMG/NR007959.pdf?OpenElement>, accessed 6 August 2018.

[28] *Ibid.*

prospect of Africans and Asians acquiring sovereignty in the 1950s and 1960s that alerted international lawyers to the existence of a multicultural world.[29]

International lawyers understood that the actual access to the emerging Third World would increase the presence and true internationalisation of the law. International human rights law, for this reason, must be examined in manifold manners: as a branch of international law and it allowed different institutions to penetrate the body politic, enter beyond the sovereign boundaries while addressing those unaware of human rights and regulate the civilising mission within the sovereign state.[30]

The Bandung Conference, a conference sponsored by five countries, India, Pakistan, Ceylon, Burma and Indonesia (collectively known as the Conference of South-East Asian Prime Ministers or Colombo Powers) marked the beginning of restoration of national sovereignty and enunciated the growing self-esteem of the developing word.[31] The Bandung conference took place from in April 1955 and it was attended by 29 independent countries.[32] While the conference contested Western dominance, it also contributed towards a post-war narrative and provided impetus for a global normative framework which more adequately reflects the views and also grievances of the newly independent nations.[33] The Bandung participants, in particular, offered their normative contribution to the idea of universal human rights, often overlooked by Western governments, as well as human rights scholars and activists.[34] The assumption and prevailing view was that the Bandung countries where, if not opposed to human rights, were at the very least cultural relativists. But there was no hint of cultural relativism in the discussions about human rights at Bandung. The very first of the Ten Principles called for 'respect for fundamental human rights and for the purposes and principles of the Charter of the United Nations' (Indonesian Ministry of Foreign Affairs 1955).[35] Finally, the conference affirmed support for the United Nations.

While countries from the Western hemisphere feared that the conference might undermine the United Nations and the principle of universalism by creating an alternative Afro-Asian bloc (nine of the 29 participants at Bandung were not yet United Nations members), the Bandung Declaration stated that "[m]embership in the United Nations should be universal", and demanded that the United Nations Security

[29] Anghie (1999), p. 1, 3.

[30] Anghie (2001–2002), pp. 541, 547.

[31] Chimni (2017), p. 40; Acharya (2016), pp. 342, 343.

[32] The other countries were Afghanistan, Burma, Cambodia, Ceylon, China, Egypt, Ethiopia, Gold Coast, India, Indonesia, Iran, Iraq, Japan, Jordan, Laos, Lebanon, Liberia, Libya, Nepal, Pakistan, the Philippines, Saudi Arabia, Syria, Sudan, Thailand, Turkey, the Democratic Republic of Vietnam, the State of Vietnam and the Kingdom of Yemen. Cyprus, though not yet independent, also attended at the invitation of the sponsors.

[33] *Supra* note 31, Acharya, 350.

[34] *Supra* note 31, Acharya.

[35] Ministry of Foreign Affairs, Indonesia. 24 April 1955. "Final Communiqué of the Asian-African Conference of Bandung", <http://franke.uchicago.edu/Final_Communique_Bandung_1955.pdf> accessed 6 August 2018.

Council admit those Bandung participants that were not yet members of the United Nations. In short, the conference defended universalism and sought its expansion, rather than suggesting any alternative to it.[36] The developing world, for this purpose, laid the provided a momentum to make not only the international human rights law international, but also create favourable conditions to make the United Nations a global organisation with far-reaching impact.

1.2 *Colonial and Postcolonial Traces of the Human Rights Machinery*

The idea of rights, to begin with, was heralded in with the birth of colonialism and the gradual expansion of the imperial project, the spread of 'the civilising idea', the creation of the ideal man, the perpetuation of the ideal Christian imbued with values of citizenship and democracy.[37] Samuel Moyn makes an interesting statement in his book "The Last Utopia: Human Rights in History". He explains how human rights are the gaining moral authority for asserting international idealism and the management of world affairs—the standard of civilisation.[38]

Although colonial governments tried to avert international intervention, the colonial powers had to accept the fact that at the signing of the United Nations Charter there was such a strong international public force which sought to create an environment in which colonial peoples were able to reclaim international space and pursue their rights in a mode of emancipation.[39] Human rights vision, however, without a clear and inclusive view on economic and social rights is, even with a limited view, not practically able to encounter the neoliberal policy expansion.[40] The failed attempt by the Third World to emphasise on economic and social rights by highlighting a "right to development" will not achieve legal or policy credibility, regardless issues grounded in their validity.[41]

However, according to Antony Anghie, human rights and neoliberalism seem to find a peaceful biosystem where they can exist together, "[i]f not complement each other."[42] The author here goes further: human rights law as it stands now, provides the fertile ground for neoliberalism to flourish with international trade agreement requiring Third World States to accept agreements which foresee human rights treaties to be part of the neoliberal parcel. By way of example, the GSP and GSP (+) Scheme by the European Union exploits international human rights law as an

[36]*Supra* note 31, Acharya, 350.

[37]Mignolo (2013), p. 48.

[38]*Supra* note 13, Moyn, 14.

[39]Pearson (2017), pp. 525, 541.

[40]Anghie (2015), pp. 145, 154.

[41]*Ibid.*

[42]Ibid; see also: Slaughter (2018), p. 735.

incentive to trade.[43] As one scholar has argued: "[T]he EU's GSP Regulation is a reflection of the gross abuse of the limited bargaining power of the developing world. This can eventually lead to a rather dangerous situation. The EU seeks to advocate globally values that inspired its own creation."[44] To this end, the international human rights machinery lends its support, inadvertently to Western powers to pursue their international trade goals. According to one scholar holds, it is not

> [a]bstract entities such as countries which suffer: it is the people living in these regimes who suffer. And unfortunately, it is not the elites who have typically benefited from the abuses who suffer; rather it is the bulk of the population at the other end of the economic spectrum who typically suffer the consequences of these programmes.[45]

The ultimate beneficiaries are the strong Western institutions and the elite of the Third World who devise and agree to such programmes reap the benefits for their ends. In fact, human rights law has attempted to contest neoliberal versions of globalisation and the hardships they seem to generate.[46] It is a global environment where the humanitarian project seems to take pace and generates more humanitarian policies, actors and instruments. This effort, though, mobilises a range of practices to "[e]stablish and sustain global relations of domination."[47] The manipulation of human rights law serves and legitimises a wide ambit of dubious practices, like the justification of the use of force, in other violent interventions and wars, and the "[a]melioration of painful local conditions engendered by globalization through a neo-liberal political and economic package whose objective is to restore and extend the reign of transnational capital."[48]

Neocolonialism with domestic agents, i.e. weak leaders from the Third World, are part of this force. While it is true that the United Nations promoted the cause of decolonisation, neo-colonialism steadily grew within the United Nations.[49] And more so in the sphere of economic relations that have been of vital nature to the

---

[43]The GSP allows vulnerable developing countries to pay fewer or no duties on exports to the EU, giving them allegedly vital access to the market of the European Union, while contributing to the growth of their respective economic infrastructure. The Scheme postulates to pursue three goals: 1. contribute to poverty eradication by expanding exports from countries most in need, 2. promote sustainable development and good governance, 3. ensure that the EU's financial and economic interests are safeguarded. According to the Scheme, it aims to support EU businesses' competiveness by lowering the costs of imports from these countries and value fair, multilateral and rules-based order in trade arrangements. This means that beneficiary countries are expected to put into practice key UN human rights and International Labour Organization conventions. The Scheme was created following recommendations by the United Nations Conference on Trade and Development (UNCTAD). It is also based on the WTO's enabling clause, which permits developed countries to create trading preferences for developing countries. For more information: Yap (2013), pp. 283–301; Jayasinghe (2015), pp. 555–575.

[44]Jayasinghe (2015), pp. 555, 575.

[45]Wardhaugh (2013), pp. 827, 846.

[46]*Supra* note 29, Anghie.

[47]Chimni (2000), pp. 243, 244.

[48]*Ibid.*; read also Baxi (2017), pp. 163–177.

[49]Anghie (2017), pp. 540, 541.

emerging developing countries with the power movement towards the World Bank and the International Monetary Fund. Newly independent states were not members when these Western-dominated organisations were created. In this context, the good governance agenda of these institutions served a rhetorical-political function, an attempt to depoliticise ideas of democracy and human rights (and by avoiding any allegation of infringing upon state sovereignty).[50]

Certainly, it was not the idea of the drafters of the UDHR, ICCPR and the ICESCR to envisage "[shoring up banking reserve requirements, improving accounting standards, or liberalizing current accounts when they constructed the original human rights edifice."[51] Rather, the United Nations contained, fostered and reinforced (its own) inequalities.[52] It is true that the United Nations was formed after the Second World War by dominant Western powers to achieve a global order based on peace, security and cooperation among states.[53] The new global order, according to Mutua, entailed two distinct features, First, "[n]on-European powers were now recognized as having the right to self-determination which was the direct repudiation of direct colonialism", and, second, "[s]tates were be governed by human rights."[54] The international human rights machinery, originally initiated as a mechanism to serve the world, is now an assisting instrument to give force to aspiration of global monetary institutions. Universalising European principles and norms is the offspring of Western liberalism and jurisprudence. These principles and norms were now imposed, cemented and furthered for their self-executing purpose, the Western hegemony through the fallacy of an international organisation, the United Nations.[55]

1.3 International Human Rights Engagement and Its Impact on Postcolonial Countries

Starting with the UDHR, human rights have been always treated as what they seem from what they seem to be, i.e. universal.[56] The path of the expansion of the human rights concept is indeed delayed progress, especially in the Third World. Human rights is often seen as a "[m]eans for the powerless to fight back and try to wrestle dignity from institutions of social power."[57] But, by vernacularising rights, powerful and the powerless create systems of specifics of rights that are separate.[58] However,

[50] Uvin (2002) pp. 1, 4–5.

[51] *Ibid.*

[52] *Ibid.*

[53] Mutua (2000), pp. 31, 34.

[54] *Ibid.*

[55] Ramina (2018), pp. 261,267.

[56] Tagliarina (2015), pp. 1191, 1193.

[57] *Ibid.*

[58] *Ibid.*

the initial focus of human rights law was to underpin, validate and export the liberal-democratic state to the non-Western world.[59] Many countries from this region, though, wish to eradicate poverty and unemployment in their domestic systems. Development, to this end, is the main concern for the countries from the Third World.[60] However, to explain it with Rajagopal,

> [M]any scholars and practitioners believe that, in the light of our experience with development and globalization, human rights violations are often essential for the production and reproduction of wealth and productivity in the economic sense. In this view, the violation of human rights is often part and parcel of what we call successful development or globalization. Such a view maintains that in fact it is not the denial of development or the exclusion from globalization that causes human rights violations and economic and social deprivation in general, but rather that the misery of the poor is in fact a "planned misery" (. . .).[61]

Third World countries have often displayed certain restraint in engaging with the international human rights bodies. The fundamental problem is that, given structural differences, rigid international human rights engagement might hamper the development progress.[62] Moreover, this rigid engagement, it is feared, leads to internal tension.[63] Finally, reluctance in engaging with the United Nations goes along with a postcolonial reflex, invoking the fear that newly won sovereignty, international openness and economic weakness might invite to imperial intrusion as

> [i]t is the weaker countries that have the highest propensity of falling prey to the human rights vigilantes. In the case of the later category of states, the relative ease of access (including the safety factor and the availability of a sycophantic or pliant officialdom in the host country) also appears to be a principle covariant of the intensity of intervention. (. . .) In short, it is the economically weak, dependent, conflict-ridden countries with a tradition of subservience to the West that bear the brunt of the challenge to sovereignty from supposedly "humanitarian" external intervention.[64]

At the end of history, the TWAIL vision must pursue equality, going beyond formal equality while including the rejection of international norms or decisions that ignore the equal problems of different parts of the society: marginalisation, low incomes, lack of accommodation, exposure to poor environment. As TWAIL is informed and contextualised in "universality" and "common humanity" claims, TWAIL has to encounter long facilitated and justified Europe's colonial subjugation and continuing exploitation of much of the Third World.[65] Current efforts of universality through human rights engagement are ongoing to attempts to, not

[59]Mutua (2001), pp. 201, 215.

[60]Patnaik (2004), pp. 499, 511.

[61]Rajagopal (2013), pp. 893, 895.

[62]*Supra* note 60, Patnaik, 509.

[63]*Supra* note 60, Patnaik, 509.

[64]Peiris (2010), p. 252.

[65]Okafor (2005), pp. 171, 179.

only facilitate, but further entrench the underlying politics of domination. As Sornarajah notes, "a lesson to be learnt [from third-world history] ... is that one must beware of self-proclaimed universalists whose ... reasons for taking universalist stances must be constantly scrutinized."[66] The reality of human rights of being universal is far from universal in the sense that everyone is equally understanding human rights as rights. Political and cultural differences are creating an abyss and, in consequence, differences need to be translated into human rights norms and laws that contribute to ideas in consistence with the group's word view.[67] More poignantly, Laura Nader sums up

> [A] quel tempo l'attivismo in tema di diritti umani era largamente un progetto egemonico, principalmente euro-americano. È corretto notare che oggi il linguaggio dei diritti dell'uomo ha perduto la sua forza iniziale, soprattutto perché, come sottolineano i critici, la prospettata universalità si è dimostrata irraggiungibile. Dopo la guerra fredda, gli Stati Uniti hanno cominciato a perseguire scopi imperiali per mezzo di un marcato discorso umanitario.[68]

Scholars from Critical Legal Studies have long argued that the law can function as a means of social oppression, and thus is not inherently a tool of the oppressed.[69] There is an urgent need to deparochialise Western legal and human rights theory from processes of globalisation through a true human rights engagement, a dialogue between the West and the Third World which ushers in: a cosmopolitan approach to human rights.[70]

1.4 Case Study: Sri Lanka: The United Nations' Nemesis

The failure of the United Nations to address the catastrophic Sri Lankan civil war which lasted for 26 years and which came to an end in May of 2009 when it ended caused the death of more than 20,000, perhaps 40,000 civilians, but also more than 10,000–15,000 disappearances.[71] The poor reflection upon the international human rights engagement to create favourable conditions for peace, the weak resistance of the United Nations to oppose constant intimidation by the Sri Lankan government and the subsequent expulsion of the United Nations personnel towards the end of the

[66]Sornarajah (2001), pp. 284, 285.

[67]*Supra* note 56, Tagliarina, 1193.

[68]Nader (2013), pp. 106, 116–117: Translation: 'At that time, human rights activism was largely a hegemonic project, mainly Euro-American. It is correct to note that today the language of human rights has lost its initial strength, above all because, as critics point out, the proposed universality has proved unattainable. After the Cold War, the United States began pursuing imperial purposes by means of a particular humanitarian language'.

[69]see: Balbus (1977), pp. 571–588; Crenshaw (2011), pp. 247–284; Hunt (1982), pp. 148–150.

[70]Barreto (2013b), p. 15.

[71]Kingsbury (2012), p. 80.

war ushered into three remarkable responses within the United Nations system at large.

First and foremost, though, it is vital to acknowledge that Sri Lanka has a long history of international human rights engagement. With a letter dated 25th of May 1948 the first Prime Minister of Sri Lanka, Dudley S. Senanayake, requested admission to the United Nations. Dudley S. Senanayake affirmed the country's will to accept the obligations laid out in the United Nations Charter and considered the country to be "[p]repared to demonstrate the ability and willingness (. . .) to carry out these obligations."[72] Reflecting this willingness, Sri Lanka has ratified twelve human rights treaties accepted two individual complaints procedures and two inquiry procedures.[73] Moreover, Sri Lanka was a member of the United Nations Human Rights Commission in 1957 and for three other terms, namely 1985–1990, 1992–2000, 2003–2005 and member to the United Nations Human Rights Council from 2006 to 2008.[74] The country appeared before numerous human rights treaty bodies,[75] opened itself to different special procedures under both, the United Nations Human Rights Commission and the United Nations Human Rights Council.[76] Finally, the country was subjected to three times to the new human rights mechanism of the United Nations Human Rights Council, the Universal Periodic Review.[77]

And yet, it seems that international human rights engagement had barely impacted the Sri Lanka human rights infrastructure in the decades since it joined the United Nations. On the contrary, Sri Lanka was subjected to an inter-ethnic civil war which lasted 26 years, two intra-ethnic clashes and numerous other human rights violations.[78] The United Nations human rights machinery has, first, failed as an early

[72]United Nations, 'Letter dated from the 25th of May 1948 from the Prime Minister and Minister for External Affairs of Ceylon to the Secretary-General', Document: S/820.

[73]Office of the High Commissioner for Human Rights, 'Ratification Status for Sri Lanka', <http://tbinternet.ohchr.org/_layouts/TreatyBodyExternal/Treaty.aspx?CountryID=164&Lang=EN> accessed 6 August 2018.

[74]see also: Office of the High Commissioner for Human Rights, 'United Nations Commission on Human Rights, Members from 1947 to 2006', <http://www.ohchr.org/EN/HRBodies/CHR/Pages/Membership.aspx>, accessed 6 August 2018; Office of the High Commissioner for Human Rights, 'List of past members of the Human Rights Council, 19th of June 2006 until 31st of December 2017', <https://www.ohchr.org/EN/HRBodies/HRC/Pages/Group20062007.aspx>, accessed 6 August 2018.

[75]For more information: Office of the High Commissioner for Human Rights, <https://tbinternet.ohchr.org/_layouts/treatybodyexternal/TBSearch.aspx?Lang=En&CountryID=164>, accessed 6 August 2018.

[76]For more information: Office of the High Commissioner for Human Rights, 'Country visits of Special Procedures of the Human Rights Council since 1998', <https://spinternet.ohchr.org/_Layouts/SpecialProceduresInternet/ViewCountryVisits.aspx?Lang=en&country=LKA>, accessed 6 August 2018.

[77]Universal Periodic Review—Sri Lanka, <https://www.ohchr.org/EN/HRBodies/UPR/Pages/LKindex.aspx>, accessed 6 August 2018.

[78]BBC News: Sri Lanka profile—Timeline <https://www.bbc.com/news/world-south-asia-12004081>, accessed 6 August 2018.

warning mechanism and, second, acted as a wilful tool for Western hegemony. This can be illustrated with two examples.

First, the first Universal Periodic Review of Sri Lanka took place in 2008, a year before the end of the close of hostilities in 2009. And while the war was ongoing, this new mechanism failed completely to trigger other mechanisms within the human rights machinery and the United Nations system at large to halt the human rights violations, initiate an intervention to the catastrophic outcome of that vicious war. Solely the state delegation of Germany mentioned concerns with view to the end of the ceasefire and the eruption of hostilities.[79]

Second, decision of the Sri Lankan Supreme Court in the case of *Singarasa v. Attorney General* the Supreme Court held that, while the accession of Sri Lanka to the ICCPR was legal, valid, and bound the State at international law, it created no additional rights as recognised in the ICCPR for individuals within the jurisdiction of Sri Lanka in the absence of domestic legislation.[80] This highly controversial decision, was problematic on different levels (but the scope of this article does warrant further elaboration). However, the decision urged policymakers to draft and adopt the domestic ICCPR Act.[81]

To this end Wijewardana writes in light of the renewal in 2017:

> [O]ne may wonder how GSP Plus which is a special tariff concession could become an aid flow. The aid flows to poor countries could be classified into two categories. One is the direct aid in the form of grants, concessionary loans and assistance in physical form like technical support and food supplies. The other is the indirect aid given in the form of preferential tariff concessions extended to developing countries through bilateral trade agreements to have larger market access in developed countries. Both have added to poor country woes, because they are linked to political affiliations, loyalty shown in international fora and in recent times, the commitment to good behaviour by aid recipient countries. The last string encompasses a wide spectrum of national behaviour traits as explained above.[82]

In the end, the ICCPR has never made a real impact on the human rights infrastructure, it was just a springboard for international investment and trade. More interestingly, however, is the response of the United Nations human rights machinery to the Sri Lankan human rights situation after 2009.[83] A series of sessions

[79]United Nations Human Rights Council, Universal Periodic Review, Report of the Working Group on the Universal Periodic Review Sri Lanka, A/HRC/8/46, fn. 54.

[80]Singarasa v. Attorney General, (S.C. Spl. (LA) No. 182/99; SCM 15th September 2006).

[81]ICCPR Act, No. 56. 2007,<http://srilankalaw.lk/Volume-IV/international-covenant-on-civil-and-political-rights-iccpr-act.html>, accessed 6 August 2018.

[82]W.J. Wijewardana, GSP + May Be Restored But Sri Lanka Has To Act Fast To Harness Its Full Benefits, online at: https://www.colombotelegraph.com/index.php/gsp-may-be-restored-but-sri-lanka-has-to-act-fast-to-harness-its-full-benefits/, last visited 14.03.2020.

[83]The scope of this article does not warrant for a detailed discussion. However, noteworthy are these resolutions: A/HRC/S-11/2: Assistance to Sri Lanka in the promotion and protection of human rights; A/HRC/19/L.2: Promoting reconciliation and accountability in Sri Lanka; A/HRC/22/L.1/Rev.1: Promoting reconciliation, accountability and human rights in Sri Lanka; A/HRC/RES/25/1: Promoting reconciliation, accountability and human rights in Sri Lanka; A/HRC/30/61: Promoting reconciliation, accountability and human rights in Sri Lanka—Report of the Office of the United Nations High Commissioner for Human Rights; A/HRC/RES/30/1: Promoting reconciliation,

at the United Nations Human Rights Council dealt with Sri Lanka. Crucial in this regard was the involvement and leadership of the United States.

However, it is interesting to assess the impact that Sri Lanka made on the United Nations than the United Nations made vice versa. The United Nations Secretary General requested a Panel to advise him on the implementation of the joint commitment included in the statement issued by the President of Sri Lanka and the Secretary-General at the conclusion of the Secretary-General's visit to Sri Lanka on 23 March 2009.[84] At first, the Sri Lankan government showed willingness to cooperate, only then to move to a hostile environment and refusal to cooperate with this Panel to look into alleged war crimes. The Panel, nevertheless, issued its report and found several war crimes allegation credible and called for an accountability mechanism.[85]

Following the recommendations of the Panel of Experts, the Secretary-General set up an Internal Review Panel on United Nations actions in Sri Lanka. The Panel began work in late April 2012 and submitted its report to the Secretary-General in early November 2012.[86]

To this end, the Petri Report stated that

> [S]een together, the failure of the UN to adequately counter the government's underestimation of population numbers in the Wanni [warzone], the failure to adequately confront the government on its obstructions to humanitarian assistance, the unwillingness of the UN in UNHQ and Colombo to address government responsibility for attacks that were killing civilians, and the tone and content of UN communications with the government on these issues, collectively amounted to a failure by the UN to act within the scope of institutional mandates to meet protection responsibilities (. . .) The UN's failure to adequately respond to events like those that occurred in Sri Lanka should not happen again. When confronted by similar situations, the UN must be able to meet a much higher standard in fulfilling its protection and humanitarian responsibilities.[87]

This report was of far-reaching impact. In response, to this Petri Report, the United Nations Secretary-General Ban Ki-Moon adopted the Human Rights Up Front (HRUF).[88] The HRUF changed the internal structure and action plan due to Sri Lanka. Sri Lanka, eventually, introduced a cultural change within the United Nations, an operational change to bring the three pillars of the United Nations

---

accountability and human rights in Sri Lanka; A/HRC/32/CRP.4: Promoting reconciliation, accountability and human rights in Sri Lanka.

[84] Joint Statement by United Nations Secretary-General, Government of Sri Lanka, SG/2151 26 May 2009, <https://www.un.org/press/en/2009/sg2151.doc.htm>, accessed 6 August 2018; Report of the Secretary-General's Panel of Experts on Accountability in Sri Lanka, <http://www.un.org/News/dh/infocus/Sri_Lanka/POE_Report_Full.pdf>, accessed 6 August 2018.

[85] *Ibid*, Panel of Experts, pp. i–ix.

[86] United Nations, 'The Secretary-General's Internal Review Panel', November 2012, p. 7. <http://www.un.org/News/dh/infocus/Sri_Lanka/The_Internal_Review_Panel_report_on_Sri_Lanka.pdf>, accessed 6 August 2018.

[87] *Ibid*, pp.27 and 35.

[88] United Nations, Human Rights up Front: A summary for staff, <https://www.un.org/News/dh/pdf/english/2016/Human-Rights-up-Front.pdf>, accessed 6 August 2018.

Charter, i.e. development, peace and security, and human rights closer together, and a change to United Nations engagement with Member States.[89] In effect, the Sri Lankan experience has changed the United Nations human rights response mechanism more than the United Nations did vice versa. The feasible examples are the Panel of Experts, the Special Sessions at the Human Rights Council and the revived response of the Office of the High Commissioner for Human Rights to human rights crises within the human rights level, along with the Petri Report and the HRUF at the organisational level.

As it was illustrated, human rights engagement with Sri Lanka changed United Nations machinery at large. International human rights engagement, eventually, serves to renew international legitimacy on Sri Lankan governments, achieve favourable international trade conditions and attract international investors from greater powers. One of the consequences of being one of the greater powers is that there is the inevitable extension from the domestic sphere that outreaches into the global sphere.[90] Last but not least, the impact of human rights engagement is limited to what policy-makers allow to suit their power goals. International human rights language is, for that reason, solely the pretext for neoliberal policy dissemination, whereas Third World leaders become the unreluctant *Erfuellungsgehilfen* for neoliberal economic policies. B.S. Chmini correctly asserts that

> [T]he fact that the omnipresence of the discourse of human rights in international law has coincided with increasing pressure on third world States to implement neo-liberal policies is no accident; the right to private property, and all that goes along with it, is central to the discourse of human rights. While the language of human rights can be effectively deployed to denounce and struggle against the predator and the national security state, its promise of emancipation is constrained by the very factor that facilitates its pervasive presence viz., the internationalisation of property rights. This contradiction is in turn the ground on which intrusive intervention into third world sovereign spaces is justified. For the implementation of neo-liberal policies is at least one significant cause of growing internal conflicts in the third world.[91]

2 Conclusion

It is the predominant power imbalance in international law and international institutions that creates a schism between the developed and the developing world, propounded by wealth distribution that serves solely the elites of the developed and developing world. International human rights praxis has been subject to dominant elements of the West. Certain particular violations of human rights are

[89] Strauss (2018), pp. 48, 51; for more information: Gerrit Kurz, GPPi: With Courage and Coherence The Human Rights up Front Initiative of the United Nations, Policy Paper, July 2015 Policy Paper, <http://www.gppi.net/fileadmin/user_upload/media/pub/2015/Kurtz_2015_Courage_and_Coherence_UN_Human_Rights.pdf>, accessed 6 August 2018.

[90] Weiss (2012), p. 263.

[91] Chimni (2006), pp. 3, 11.

considered as such, emphasised as human rights violations in the dominant discourse, embedded in Western dialogue.

Even though certain dialogue has been led by Third World countries (for example apartheid), the "[i]mprimatur of the strongest Western states" was needed to succeed in the human rights cause as such at the United Nations.[92] This remains true with regards to the case study that was conducted with Sri Lanka. United States' leadership was required to bring about change and constant vigilance on the—indeed—urgent situation in the country. But this raises questions about the dominance and imbalance at the United Nations human rights machinery. Western states become the self-proclaimed custodians of human rights and invigilators of human rights protection when it suits their dominant power discourse and geopolitical incentives. Or, as Uvin formulates: "[M]uch of it is about the quest for moral high ground: draping oneself in the mantle of human rights to cover the fat belly of the development community while avoiding challenging the status quo too much, cross-examining oneself, or questioning the international system."[93] Makau Mutua, holds that the human rights corpus is slowly disposing its Western antecedents and slowly towards the construction of a truly inclusive, international project.[94] With the end of the Cold War, more impetus is generated for the "[e]conomic powerlessness and the effect of globalization on people."[95] Mutua thinks that "[a] truly legitimate human rights movement cannot be cabined by powerful states and elites. It must be material for battle in the hands of the powerless. This, however, will not be possible unless the movement is purged of its Eurocentric, racist, free-market biases."[96] Against this background, Pooja Parmar, wishes academic research to imagine the realities of Third World peoples with all their problems and complexities, "[i]n order to examine how the modern human rights discourse relates and responds, or as is the case more often, fails to respond to them."[97]

Uneven application of human rights entrenches the hostility and the reluctance to engage with the human rights machinery that is considered to be infiltrated by the Western hemisphere. However, a genuine partnership that values justice over power is afforded. Looking at Sri Lanka, a postcolonial country is captured by political opportunism which has defeated justice and individual dignity. Human rights engagement on the international plane is only about showcasing half-promises to receive international legitimacy as a precondition for international trade. The United Nations human rights machinery, in this respect, is just the venue for human rights marketplace.

Gathii is correct in his view that to state that TWAIL scholars easily highlight the dichotomy of Third World innocence or First World guilt. He furthers that it is

---

[92]*Ibid.*

[93]*Supra* note 50, Uvin, 10.

[94]Mutua (2007), pp. 3,3.

[95]*Ibid.*

[96]*Supra* note 94, Mutua.

[97]Parmar (2008), pp. 363, 366.

necessary to transform International law by including the lived circumstances of some oppressed people. He speaks that the change of international law is difficult against the background of the 'imperial legacy as well as its post-imperial promises, including self-determination and human rights.'[98]

Echoing this message of Gathii, the United Nations human rights machinery must not be understood as static, as passive, as subjected to Western fiat. Early Third World scholars such as Malik and Romulo tried to interpret the United Nations human rights regime as dynamic and forceful enough to take into considerations the grievances existing in the Third World.[99] The human rights framework operates in a fluid state of aggregation in the Third World, not because of Western hegemony, but because it is conducive to new forms of articulations, imaginations and interpretations.[100] This, in effect, means that the human rights machinery is hospitable enough to a wide range of rearrangements in social justice and create a new relationship between the developed and developing world. The Third World buttressed by its theory can be, to this end, "[a] valid interlocutor in any conversation about rights – not simply listener without a voice, or a ventriloquist dummy."[101] It is affirmation of the exigency to exchange ideas, engage in dialogue and where the whole geography of knowledge is transformed, imbalance addressed and hegemony is redressed.

References

Acharya A (2016) Studying the Bandung conference from a global IR perspective. AJIA 70(4):342, 343

Addo MK (2010) Practice of United Nations human rights treaty bodies in the reconciliation of cultural diversity with universal respect for human rights. Human Rights Q 32(601):615

Alston P (1995) Appraising the United Nations Human Right Regime. In: Alston P (ed) The United Nations and human rights, a critical appraisal. Clarendon Press, p 2

Anghie A (1999) Finding the peripheries: sovereignty and colonialism in nineteenth-century international law. Harv Int Law J 40(1):3

Anghie A (2001–2002) Colonialism and the birth of international institutions: sovereignty, economy, and the mandate system of the league of nations. N Y Univ J Int Law Policy 34(541):547

Anghie A (2015) Legal aspects of the new international economic order. Humanity 6(1):145, 154

Anghie A (2017) Bandung and the origins of the third world sovereignty. In: Eslava L, Fakhri M, Nesiah V (eds) Bandung, global history, and international law: critical pasts and pending futures. Cambridge University Press, p 540, 541

Balbus I (1977) Commodity form and legal form: an essay on the "relative autonomy" of the law'. Law Soc Rev 11(3):571–588

Barreto J-M (2013a) Imperialism and decolonization as scenarios of human rights history. In: Bareto J-M (ed) Human rights from a third world perspective, history and international law. Cambridge University Press, p 160

[98] Gathii (2013), pp. 494, 500.

[99] Mitoma (2013), p. 436.

[100] *Ibid.*

[101] Barreto (2013b), p. 32.

Barreto M (2013b) Decolonial strategies and dialogue in the human rights field. In: Bareto J-M (ed) Human rights from a third world perspective, history and international law (First published 2013). Cambridge University Press, p 15

Baxi U (2017) Towards socially sustainable globalization: reflections on responsible contracting and the UN guiding principles on business and human rights. Indian J Int Law 57(1–2):163–177

Carraro V (2017) The United Nations treaty bodies and universal periodic review: advancing human rights by preventing politicization. Human Rights Q 39(943):969

Chimni BS (2000) Globalization, humanitarianism and the erosion of refugee protection. J Refugee Stud 13(243):244

Chimni BS (2006) Third world approaches to international law: a Manifesto. Int Commun Law Rev 8(3):11

Chimni BS (2017) Anti-imperialism: then and now. In: Eslava L, Fakhri M, Nesiah V (eds) Bandung, global history, and international law: critical pasts and pending futures. Cambridge University Press, p 40

Cole WM (2012) Human rights as myth and ceremony? Reevaluating the effectiveness of human rights treaties. Am J Sociol 117(4):1131, 1132

Crenshaw KW (2011) Race, reform, and retrenchment: transformation and legitimation in antidiscrimination law. German Law J 12(1):247–284

Forsythe DP (2018) Human Rights in International Relations, (first published 2000). Cambridge University Press, p 100

Gathii JT (2013) Book review: decolonising international law: development, economic growth and the politics of universality by Sundhya Pahuja. Am J Int Law 107(2):494, 500

Hannum H (2006) The status of the universal declaration of human rights in national and international law. Georgia J Int Comp Law 25(287):288

Hunt A (1982) Law, society and political action: towards a strategy under late capitalism (book review). J Law Soc 9(1):148–150

Jayasinghe V (2015) The legality of the European Union's special incentive arrangement. J Int Econ Law 18(3):555–575

Kabasakal Arat ZF (2013) Forging a global culture of human rights: origins and prospects of the international bill of rights. In: Jose-Manuel B (ed) Human rights from a third world perspective, history and international law. Cambridge University Press, 389

Kingsbury D (2012) Sri Lanka and the responsibility to protect (first published 2012). Routledge, p 80

Lauren PG (1983) First principles of racial equality: history and the politics and diplomacy of human rights provisions in the United Nations Charter. Human Rights Q 5(1):7

Marie J-B (1980) La Pratique de la Commission des Droits de l'Homme de L'ONU en matiere de violation des droits de l'homme. RBDI 2(355):355

Mignolo W (2013) Who speaks for the "Human" in human rights? In: Bareto J-M (ed) Human rights from a third world perspective, history and international law. Cambridge University Press, p 48

Mitoma G (2013) Mode d'assujetissement: Charles Malik, Carlos Romulo and the Emergence of the United Nations Human Rights Regime. In: Bareto J-M (ed) Human rights from a third world perspective, history and international law (first published 2013). Cambridge University Press, p 436

Moyn S (2012) The last Utopia: human rights in history (first published 2010). Harvard University Press, p 100

Mutua M (2000) What is TWAIL? ASIL Proceedings Washington 94(31):34

Mutua M (2001) 'Savages, victims and saviors, the metaphor of human rights. Harv Int J Law 42 (1):201, 215

Mutua M (2007) Change in the human rights universe. Harv Human Rights J 20:3

Nader L (2013) Giustizia, diritti umani e sentimento d'ingiustizia. Antropologia 8(11):106, 116–117

Okafor OC (2005) Newness, imperialism, and international legal reform in our time: a Twail perspective. Osgoode Hall Law J 43(171):179

Parmar P (2008) TWAIL: an epistemological inquiry. Int Commun Law Rev 10(4):363, 366

Patnaik JK (2004) The human rights: the concept and perspectives: a third world view. LXV:4, 499, 511

Pearson JL (2017) Defending empire at the United Nations: the politics of international colonial oversight in the era of decolonisation. J Imperial Commonw Hist 45(3):525, 541

Peiris GH (2010) Twilight of the tigers (first published 2009). Oxford University Press, p 252

Rajagopal B (2013) Right to development and global governance: old and new challenges twenty-five years on. Human Rights Q 35(4):893, 895

Ramina L (2018) Third world approaches to international law" and human rights: some considerations. Revista de Investigações Constitucionais, Curitiba 5(1):261, 267

Sikkink K, Risse T (2009) The socialization of international human rights norms into domestic practices: introduction. In: Sikkink K, Ropp SC, Risse T (eds) The power of human rights. Cambridge University Press

Slaughter JR (2018) Hijacking human rights: neoliberalism, the new historiography, and the end of the third world. Human Rights Q 40:735

Smith RKM (2018) International human rights law (first published 2018). Oxford University Press, p 27

Sornarajah M (2001) The Asian perspective to international law in the age of globalization. SJCL 5 (284):285

Steiner HJ, Alston P, Goodmann R (2008) International human rights in context: law, politics, morals : text and materials, (first published 1996). Oxford University Press, p 135

Strauss E (2018) The UN Secretary-General's human rights up front initiative and the prevention of genocide: impact, potential, limitations. Genocide Stud Prev Int J 11(3):48, 51

Tagliarina D (2015) Power, privilege and rights: how the powerful; and powerless create a vernacular of rights. Third World Q 36(6):1191, 1193

Uvin P (2002) On high moral ground: the incorporation of human rights by the development enterprise', Praxis. Fletcher J Dev Stud XVII:1, 4–5

Wardhaugh B (2013) GSP+ and human rights: is the EU's approach the right one? J Int Eur Law 16 (827):846

Weiss G (2012) The cage (first published 2011). Vintage, p 263

Yap J (2013) 'Beyond 'Don't Be Evil': the European Union GSP+ trade preference scheme and the incentivisation of the Sri Lankan garment industry to foster human rights. Eur Law J 19 (2):283–301

Part VI
International Economic Law/International Investment Law

African Investment Agreement Reform and Its Contribution to Sustainable Foreign Investment

Gudrun Monika Zagel

Contents

G. M. Zagel (✉)
University of Salzburg, School of Law, Department of Public, International and European Law, Salzburg, Austria
e-mail: gudrun.zagel@sbg.ac.at

C. Eboe-Osuji et al. (eds.), *Nigerian Yearbook of International Law 2018/2019*, Nigerian Yearbook of International Law 2018/2019,
https://doi.org/10.1007/978-3-030-69594-1_16

1 Introduction

Sustainable foreign investment, that is foreign investment that is not only financially viable but also complies with the sustainability policies of its host states,[1] can substantially contribute to achieving the sustainable development objectives established in the AU Agenda 2063[2] and the UN 2030 Agenda.[3] African states have concluded several hundred International Investment Agreements (IIAs) with home states of foreign investors to attract foreign investment from within and outside the continent.[4] IIAs grant foreign investors certain standards of treatment with a view to protecting their property against expropriation and unfair, arbitrary, or discriminatory treatment in the host state.[5] These guarantees apply to all host state conduct affecting foreign investors and can be enforced through investor-state dispute settlement (ISDS) mechanisms provided for in IIAs, typically without resorting to the national court system.[6]

In recent years, it has been increasingly controversial whether IIAs facilitate sustainable foreign investment.[7] Opponents argue that IIAs prevent rather than promote sustainable foreign investment as they impede host states from adopting environmental, social, and other sustainability policies necessary to realize sustainable development.[8] IIAs presumably create the infamous "regulatory chill effect" because national sustainability measures may conflict with substantive IIA obligations, and breaches of these obligations require the host state to compensate foreign investors for their losses. As the ISDS mechanism permits foreign investors to enforce IIA obligations against the host state, the mere existence of an IIA purportedly constitutes an enormous burden to host states generally and the tight budgets of most African states in particular.

The public critique prompted a veritable IIA crisis followed by extensive reform efforts. Well-established instruments such as the North American Free Trade Agreement (NAFTA)[9] were renegotiated, the Trans-Atlantic Trade and Investment Partnership (TTIP) negotiations have been abandoned,[10] and the implementation of the

---

[1]See Sauvant and Mann (2017), p. 2.

[2]African Union Commission, Agenda 2063: The Africa We Want (April 2015), <http://www.un.org/en/africa/osaa/pdf/au/agenda2063.pdf> (AU Agenda 2063 (2015)).

[3]UN General Assembley, Transforming our World, The 2030 Agenda for Sustainable Development (2015) UNGA Res A/Res/70/1, 25 September 2015 (UN 2030 Agenda (2015)).

[4]See UNECA (2016), p. 16 and p. 28; see for details UNCTAD, Investment Policy Hub, <http://investmentpolicyhub.unctad.org/IIA> (The database contains all IIAs cited in this article unless otherwise specified) and infra text accompanying n25ff.

[5]For an overview see Dolzer and Stevens (1995), Salacuse (2015) and UNCTC (1988).

[6]See Dolzer and Schreuer (2012), p. 232.

[7]See Traidcraft (2015) and Mann (2013).

[8]Ibid.

[9]North American Free Trade Agreement, 17 December 1992, 32 ILM 289 (1993) (NAFTA 1992).

[10]See Council of the European Union, Council Decision Authorizing the Opening of Negotiations with the United States of America for an Agreement on the Elimination of Tariffs for Industrial Goods, 6052/19, 9 April 2019, art. 3.

already signed Comprehensive Economic and Trade Agreement (CETA)[11] has been delayed. Yet, despite comprehensive IIA reforms opposition in the Global North continues. In contrast, the African continent has pursued its own way to handle the IIA crisis: Notwithstanding the deficiencies of IIAs, Africa continues to rely intensely on IIAs to attract foreign investment as a means to promote economic development.[12] To ensure that IIAs contribute to sustainable development, African states have started a reform process about 15 years ago,[13] and today there are a number of African investment instruments with innovative approaches to remedy the shortcomings of traditional IIAs. These instruments include the Draft Pan-African Investment Code (2017),[14] the SADC Protocol on Finance and Investment Amendment (2016),[15] the SADC Model BIT Template (2012),[16] and several recent BITs.[17] These instruments have in common that they strongly focus on sustainable development and on balancing the investors' interests in property protection and the host states' interests in preserving their regulatory sovereignty to implement sustainability policies.[18]

The reformed African IIAs reflect the spirit of the AU Agenda 2063,[19] whose first "aspiration" is "a prosperous Africa based on inclusive growth and sustainable development".[20] The AU Agenda 2063 promotes sustainable economic development that considers the environmental and social aspects of development with a view to enabling long-term progress.[21] To accomplish sustainable development, the AU Agenda 2063 recommends Pan-African cross-border projects, but also investment from outside the continent,[22] which constitutes a cost-effective alternative to economic development through foreign debt. The AU Agenda 2063 suggests creating a climate conducive to foreign investment,[23] an intention that many of the currently

[11]Comprehensive Trade and Economic Agreement between Canada and the European Union, 30 October 2016, OJ L11/23 of 14 January 2017 (CETA 2016).

[12]E.g. SADC Investment Protocol Amendment (2017), preamble, 2nd and 6th recital.

[13]An early example is the ECOWAS Supplementary Act (2008).

[14]PAIC (2017).

[15]SADC Investment Protocol Amendment (2017).

[16]SADC Model BIT Template (2012).

[17]E.g. China-Tanzania BIT (2013); Morocco–Nigeria BIT (2016).

[18]Cf for many UN Addis Ababa Action Agenda (2015), para. 91; PAIC (2017), preamble, 11th recital; Morocco-Nigeria BIT (2016), preamble, 6th recital; SADC Investment Protocol Amendment (2017), preamble, 8th recital; AfSIL Principles (2016), principles 1 and 4.

[19]Cf e.g. PAIC (2017), preamble, first recital.

[20]AU Agenda 2063 (2015), p. 2, paras. 9ff.

[21]AU Agenda 2063 (2015), paras. 72ff.

[22]AU Agenda 2063 (2015), paras. 11, 24, 72a, 72d; African Union Commission, Agenda 2063, First Ten-Year Implementation Plan 2014–2023, p. 28 and Plan Framework at p. 47; see also AfSIL Principles (2016), preamble, 4th recital; ECOWAS Supplementary Act (2008), preamble, 3rd recital.

[23]Cf AU Agenda 2063 (2015), para. 72d.

negotiated and recently concluded IIAs reflect.[24] To ensure that investment promotion and protection and sustainable development policies mutually reinforce each other, African states have refined critical IIA provisions and introduced new provisions in the light of the AU Agenda 2063. The reformed African IIAs contain a number of innovative elements that are rarely used in reformed IIAs outside Africa.

The purpose of this article is to identify the challenges of traditional IIAs for the sustainable development policies of African host states and to examine the viability of the African reform approaches to achieve sustainable foreign investment. The first part provides an overview of the African experience with traditional IIAs and shows how IIAs affect the host states' regulatory sovereignty. The second part explains the requirements of sustainable foreign investment and shows the conceivable conflicts between the traditional substantive IIA provisions on expropriation, fair and equitable treatment (FET) and indemnification and the sustainability policies of African host states. A critical question is how to distinguish a non-compensable general regulatory measure from a regulatory measure that amounts to a compensable interference with a foreign investor's property. The third part discusses the African IIA reform approaches to prevent that substantive IIA provisions unduly limit the regulatory sovereignty of host states to implement their sustainable development goals. Innovative elements embrace reformulating the rules on expropriation and the FET standard, refining of the rules on compensation, specifying the requirements of sustainable development in IIAs, and including investor obligations. The elements are examined on their feasibility to create IIAs with a fair balance of the investors' interests in protecting their property and the host states' interests in achieving sustainable development.

2 The Impact of IIAs on the Regulatory Sovereignty of Host States

African states have relied on IIAs to foster foreign investment since their independence in the 1960ies.[25] The first IIA on the African continent was concluded between Togo and Germany.[26] From the few thousand IIAs existing worldwide today, around 900 involve one or two African parties.[27] Originally, African states concluded IIAs as Bilateral Investment Treaties (BITs) with industrialized states. Such North-South IIAs were generated as instruments to promote and protect investments from industrialized countries in the newly independent developing

[24]Cf e.g. PAIC, preamble, 4th and 8th recital; SADC Investment Protocol Amendment (2017), preamble, 2nd and 6th recital.

[25]UNECA (2016), p. 20; Mbengue and Schacherer (2018), p. 548.

[26]Germany-Togo BIT (1961).

[27]For an overview see UNCTAD, Investment Policy Hub, <https://investmentpolicy.unctad.org/international-investment-agreements>; UNECA (2016), p. 16.

countries.[28] Starting in the 1990ies, African states increasingly have concluded BITs as South-South treaties with states within and outside Africa.[29] In addition, African regional organizations have adopted multilateral IIAs, comprehensive multilateral economic instruments including IIA chapters, and model IIAs.[30] The ultimate aim of the African Union today is to create a continent-wide IIA on the basis of the Draft Pan-African Investment Code.[31]

IIAs constitute the international legal framework on the treatment of foreign investors and their investments. Primarily, the national law of the host state governs the admission and conduct of business of foreign investors.[32] As part of their regulatory sovereignty, host states have the power to decide on their economic, social, and environmental policies that also apply to foreign investors and their investments. The national legal framework and any host state conduct affecting foreign investors must comply with the host state's IIA obligations. A breach of IIA obligations not only triggers the responsibility of the host state towards the home state of the investor[33] but also entitles the foreign investor to directly settle the dispute with the host state through international arbitration.[34]

The structure and style of African IIAs follow the world-wide IIA pattern.[35] African IIAs with European partners typically encompass the lean European-style IIA provisions,[36] whereas IIAs concluded with the US or Canada follow the detailed NAFTA-style manner.[37] Furthermore, the focus of traditional and modern IIAs is different.[38] The traditional African IIAs up to the mid-2000s mainly aim at the protection of foreign investors and are largely silent on the regulatory sovereignty of host states. The slim rules of these early IIAs give broad discretion to arbitrators to further define the substantive standards of treatment guaranteed to foreign investors. In contrast, modern IIAs concluded since the mid-2000s have a more balanced content. They incorporate the interests of host states to regulate foreign investment

[28]Dolzer and Stevens (1995), p. 1; Salacuse (2015), p. 100; UNCTAD (2015), p. 121.

[29]See UNECA (2016), pp. 16, 20, 51 and 82; very active within Africa are e.g. Egypt, South Africa, Mauritius and Morocco; the main partner state outside Africa is China; for relevant treaties see UNCTAD Investment Policy Hub; for South-South BITs generally see Salacuse (2015), p. 105.

[30]In addition to the instruments mentioned in n13, n14, n12, and n16, the most important regional IIAs are the EAC Model Investment Treaty (2016); the COMESA Investment Agreement (2007), and the SADC Investment Protocol (2006); for details see UNECA (2016), p. 28 and p. 72; Mbengue and Schacherer (2018), p. 548.

[31]PAIC (2017); for details see Mbengue and Schacherer (2018), p. 550; Kane (2018).

[32]Salacuse (2013), p. 51.

[33]Cf Crawford (2012), p. 540 with further references.

[34]Cf for details Salacuse (2015), p. 411.

[35]Salacuse (2015), p. 126; for a general overview see also Dolzer and Stevens (1995) and UNCTC (1988).

[36]Examples are the Denmark-Tanzania BIT (1999) or the China-Ethiopia BIT (1998).

[37]Examples are the Canada-Tanzania BIT (2013) or the Mozambique-USA BIT (1998).

[38]Salacuse (2015), p. 104.

with a view to promoting national policy goals[39] and contain more detailed provisions to provide clearer interpretive guidance for arbitral tribunals.

All IIAs contain three areas of regulation, although their content varies when it comes to the details of the provisions: First, IIAs contain definitions to determine whether a foreign investor and its investment come under the scope of application of an IIA and enjoy protection.[40] As the aim of IIAs is to attract foreign investment, the definitions are generally formulated in an all-encompassing manner. The definition of 'investor' typically includes all natural persons with the nationality of the other contracting party and judicial persons incorporated under the law of a contracting party.[41] Similarly, the definition of 'investment' is usually broadly formulated and comprises anything of monetary value.[42] The sector of business is typically irrelevant unless the IIA contains exceptions on specific sectors.[43] To limit the potentially overly-broad scope of application, many IIAs specify that only investment admitted in accordance with national law is covered by the scope of protection.[44] This element is essential because it reinforces the regulatory sovereignty of host states to determine the conditions for admission and conduct of business of foreign investment in the light of their sustainable development objectives. Moreover, investors violating the national law of the host state, for instance, investors engaged in corrupt practices, may be excluded from the protection of the IIA or the access to international arbitration.[45]

The second area of IIA regulation establishes substantive standards of treatment that host states must grant to legally admitted foreign investors and their investments. The most important guarantee for foreign investors is the rules on expropriation, which protect against host state interferences with the property of investors that either take or severely restrict the use of the investors' property.[46] Other substantive standards of treatment include FET, non-discrimination, national treat-

[39]E.g. Canada-Tanzania BIT (2013); Morocco-Nigeria BIT (2016); for further reference see Chapter 4.2.

[40]Cf Salacuse (2015), p. 174.

[41]Cf e.g. Tanzania-United Kingdom BIT (1994), art. 1(c) and (d); China-Ethiopia BIT (1998), art. 1 (2); for further examples Dolzer and Stevens (1995), p. 31; Salacuse (2015), p. 206.

[42]E.g. Tanzania-United Kingdom BIT (1994), art. 1(a); China-Ethiopia BIT (1998), art. 1(1); Salacuse (2015), p. 176; Dolzer and Schreuer (2012), p. 62; Dolzer and Stevens (1995), p. 26; Bischoff and Happ (2015).

[43]This approach exists in US BITs, which contain a right to admission and therefore have limitations in specific sectors. Another treaty with an express limitation is the Energy Charter Treaty (1994), art. I(6), which is limited to investment in the energy sector; for further reference see Salacuse (2015), p. 194.

[44]Cf e.g. China-Ethiopia BIT (1998), art. 2(1).

[45]See e.g. *Unión Fenosa Gas, S.A. v Arab Republic of Egypt* (Award, 2018) ICSID Case No. ARB/14/4 [7.46–7.48] (UFG); *Cortec Mining Kenya Limited, Cortec (Pty) Limited and Stirling Capital Limited v Republic of Kenya* (Award, 2018) ICSID Case No ARB/15/29 [333] (Cortec).

[46]Cf e.g. China-Ethiopia BIT (1998), art. 4(1); Tanzania-United Kingdom BIT (1994), art. 5(1); for details Dolzer and Schreuer (2012), p. 98; Salacuse (2015), p. 313; Chapter 3.2.

ment, or most-favored-nation treatment.[47] The substantive standards of treatment apply to any host state conduct affecting foreign investors and their investments, i.e. legislative acts, administrative acts, court decisions and factual conduct attributable to the host state. All host state conduct to implement sustainability policies must comply with these substantive standards, and violations trigger the responsibility of the host state and entitle the foreign investor to indemnification.

The third area of IIA regulation is the rules on ISDS. They entitle foreign investors to bring claims against host state conduct in breach of substantive IIA obligations before an international arbitral tribunal.[48] The aim of ISDS is to replace the time-consuming and highly political dispute settlement between home state and host state under the rules of international law by direct dispute settlement between host state and investor. Most traditional African IIAs have relied on the International Center for the Settlement of Investment Disputes (ICSID).[49] The possibility to settle disputes outside the national court system has been strongly criticized not only for discriminating national investors that are excluded from access to this system but also for its major systemic deficiencies.[50] A problem that contributes to the "regulatory chill effect" of IIAs is that the outcome of arbitral decisions is hardly predictable for a number of reasons: First, all IIAs vary, when it comes to the details of their provisions; second, traditional IIAs with lean provisions give wide discretion to arbitral tribunals; third, arbitral tribunals are composed differently in each case and are not bound by interpretations of other tribunals.[51] As a result, the case-law is frequently inconsistent,[52] and critics argue that host states become reluctant to implement sustainability measures at all as the legality and indemnification criteria in IIAs are uncertain.[53]

The experience of African states with international arbitration has been mixed. Most African states became ICSID members right after their independence.[54] Until today, African states have been represented in roughly 25% of all investment

[47]E.g. Tanzania-United Kingdom BIT (1994), arts. 2 and 3; China-Ethiopia BIT (1998), art. 3; for further details see Salacuse (2015), p. 131ff; Dolzer and Schreuer (2012), p. 130; Chapter 3.3.

[48]Dolzer and Schreuer (2012), p. 235; Salacuse (2015), p. 411.

[49]Convention on the Settlement of Investment Disputes between States and Nationals of other States (signed 18 March 1965, entered into force 14 October 1966) 575 UNTS 159 (ICSID Convention 1965); most African states have relied on ICSID since its inception; out of 54 African states only Angola, Djibuti, Eritrea, Equatorial Guinea, and Libya do not participate in ICSID, and Ethiopia, Guinea-Bisseau, Namibia, and Sao Tome and Principe have only signed but not ratified the ICSID Convention; for ICSID membership see <https://icsid.worldbank.org/en/Pages/about/Database-of-Member-States.aspx>; see also Agyemang (1988), p. 177 and p. 187; Le Cannu (2018), p. 462.

[50]Zagel (2020), p. 41; for the debate in the context of TTIP and CETA see for many Traidcraft (2015), p. 13; for a detailed analysis of these issues see e.g. CJEU Opinion 1/17, Opinion of Advocate General Bot, 29 January 2019, ECLI:EU:C:2019:72, paras. 185ff.

[51]Cf for instance *Biwater* [313].

[52]See for instance *UFG* [9.108–9.112].

[53]Cf Mann (2013), p. 532; for details see Chapter 3.

[54]See Agyemang (1988), p. 177; Le Cannu (2018), p. 462.

disputes,[55] which stands in sharp contrast to the worldwide share of foreign investment going into Africa—amounting to merely 3.5% of foreign investment worldwide.[56] The majority of the ICSID disputes up to the mid-nineties involved African states.[57] Frequently, arbitral tribunals decided the disputes in favor of the investor.[58] Only in recent years, the outcome of investment awards involving African host states has been more balanced.[59] Yet, the damages awarded pose an enormous challenge to the tight budgets of African states.[60] But even if a host state wins the case, the costs for the proceedings and legal services may be huge.[61] Moreover, publicly known investment disputes—irrespective of their outcome—affect the reputation and therefore the investment climate of a host state and may deter foreign investors.

To conclude, IIAs provide the international legal framework that host states must observe when adopting sustainability measures affecting foreign investors. While traditional IIAs permit host states to determine the conditions of admission, which allows pursuing sustainability policies vis-à-vis foreign investors without restriction, any host state conduct after admission must comply with the IIA's substantive standards of treatment. As foreign investors operate under the law of the host state, all sustainability measures of host states affect the business conduct of foreign investors and are therefore potentially subject to ISDS claims. Although substantive IIA obligations contain standards generally conducive to the investment climate of host states, the systemic shortcomings of traditional IIAs are perceived as prompting a regulatory chill effect for sustainability measures of host states that are required to achieve the sustainable development objectives formulated in the AU Agenda 2063 and the UN 2030 Agenda.

[55]Cf ICSID (2019), p. 11 and p. 26; for details see Le Cannu (2018), p. 469ff and case-law until 31 December 2017 at 495ff; UNECA (2016), p. 24, for case-law until 2014 see id Annex 4.

[56]See UNCTAD (2019), p. 34.

[57]Cf UNECA (2016), Annex 4; ICSID, Concluded Cases with Details, <https://icsid.worldbank.org/en/Pages/cases/ConcludedCases.aspx?status=c>.

[58]See UNECA (2016), Annex 4; see also Agyemang (1988), p. 178.

[59]See ICSID (ed), The ICSID Caseload – Statistics Special Focus Africa (May 2017), <https://icsid.worldbank.org/en/Documents/resources/ICSID%20Web%20Stats%20Africa%20(English)%20June%202017.pdf>, p. 17.

[60]Cf e.g. UNECA (2016), p. 25 (Table 5).

[61]Mann (2013), p. 532; for instance, in *Cortec*, Kenya had to bear 3.2mio US$ in costs and legal fees although the tribunal rejected Cortec's claim, see *Cortec* [405].

3 Substantive Rules in Traditional African IIAs Affecting the Sustainable Development Policies of Host States

3.1 The Sustainable Development Paradigm

Sustainable development is the currently prevailing paradigm of international economic governance.[62] Sustainable development stands for economic development that also accomplishes social inclusion and environmental sustainability.[63] The term "sustainable development" has been constantly evolving since it was first conceptualized in the 1987 "Brundtland Report" as "development that meets the needs of the present without comprising the ability of future generations to meet their own needs".[64] On the global level, the UN 2030 Agenda on Sustainable Development and the enshrined 17 Sustainable Development Goals (SDGs)[65] are the latest step in the efforts to realize sustainable development.[66] The AU Agenda 2063 establishes a comprehensive development plan for the African continent that reflects the SDGs[67] and adapts them for the 50-year life span of the AU Agenda 2063.[68]

Sustainable development requires economic development that focuses on the wellbeing of the peoples while at the same time not jeopardizing the interests of future generations.[69] Whereas sustainable development initially mainly aimed at converging economic development and environmental protection,[70] sustainable development today consists of three dimensions, namely economic growth, social inclusion and environmental protection with a view to eradicating poverty in all its forms.[71] To promote environmental protection, states shall pursue a wide range of environmental policies and measures to ensure that economic development does not lead to the degradation of the environment.[72] Similarly, states must adopt

---

[62]Cf for many AU Agenda 2063 (2015), aspiration 1; UN 2030 Agenda (2015), Declaration, paras. 2 and 9.

[63]UN 2030 Agenda (2015), preamble, 3rd recital; UN 2030 Agenda (2015), Declaration, para. 2.

[64]World Commission on Environment and Development, Our Common Future (1987), UNGA Doc A/42/427, para. 27; for the further development of the notion "sustainable development" Gehring and Newcombe (2011), p. 6; Cordonier Segger and Khalfan (2004), p. 15; Zagel (2020), p. 4.

[65]UN 2030 Agenda (2015), paras. 54ff; for details see UN, 17 Goals to Transform Our World, <https://www.un.org/sustainabledevelopment/>.

[66]See UN 2030 Agenda (2015), para. 16.

[67]See African Union, Linking the Agenda 2063 and the SGDs <https://au.int/agenda2063/sdgs>.

[68]African Union Commission (ed) (2015) Agenda 2063. The Africa We Want. Background Note 01 <https://au.int/sites/default/files/documents/33126-doc-01_background_note.pdf>, p. 19.

[69]Cordonier Segger and Khalfan (2004), p. 15; see also UN 2030 Agenda (2015), para. 9.

[70]Cf UN General Assembly, Rio Declaration on Environment and Development (1992) A/CONF.151/26 (Vol. I).

[71]UN 2030 Agenda (2015), preamble, 3rd recital; UN 2030 Agenda, Declaration, paras. 2 and 9; see also UN General Assembly, Rio+20 Declaration "The Future We Want" (2012) A/RES/66/288, paras. 3 and 4; see also AU Agenda 2063 (2015), aspiration 1, paras. 10–18.

[72]E.g. UN 2030 Agenda (2015), SDGs 13, 14, 15; AU Agenda 2063 (2015), paras. 72f and 72g.

comprehensive health, educational and other social policies to facilitate social well-being for all peoples.[73] Implementing measures include the creation of new and the adaptation of existing infrastructure in a sustainable manner, such as energy projects, water and sewerage systems, transportation networks, medical facilities, schools, public transportation systems, and the creation of jobs.[74] Moreover, sustainable development includes the sustainable exploitation of natural resources.[75] To facilitate sustainable development, states must adapt the regulatory framework on the national, regional, and international levels.[76]

The sustainable development paradigm also informs the regulation of foreign investment. Both the AU Agenda 2063 and the UN 2030 Agenda acknowledge the role of foreign investment in realizing sustainable development objectives.[77] But only sustainable foreign investment, that is foreign investment that is not only economically feasible but also respects the sustainability policies of the host state,[78] can make a positive contribution. General international law recognizes the regulatory sovereignty of states to adopt national measures to implement the sustainable development goals set in the UN 2030 Agenda and the AU Agenda 2063.[79] These "police powers"[80] constitute an essential element of the capability of states to perform their functions.[81] They include the right of states to decide on the adoption and the scope of environmental, social, and other measures to achieve sustainable development. For instance, states may adopt and raise emission standards, establish protected areas,[82] regulate water prices,[83] or raise minimum wages.[84] Moreover, they may impose sanctions against negative environmental and social impacts of businesses and industries.[85] However, if such sustainability measures affect foreign investors, they must comply with the substantive IIA standards to prevent

[73]E.g. UN 2030 Agenda (2015), SDGs 2, 3, 4, 6; AU Agenda 2063 (2015), aspiration 6, paras. 47–58 and paras. 72b, 72c, and 72i.

[74]See e.g. AU Agenda 2063 (2015), paras. 72c and 72g.

[75]AU Agenda 2063 (2015), paras. 72d.

[76]UN 2030 Agenda (2015), para. 63 and SDG 1, para. 1b; AU Agenda 2063 (2015), para. 72d.

[77]See n22, and UN 2030 Agenda (2015), Declaration, paras 28 and 67 and SDGs, paras 1b, 2a, 7a, and 10b.

[78]Sauvant and Mann (2017), p. 2.

[79]Cf Gazzini (2010), p. 38; see also *Técnicas Medioambientales Tecmed v United Mexican States* (Award, 2003) ICSID Case No ARB(AF)/00/2, [119] (Tecmed); *ADC Affiliate Limited and ADC & ADMC Management Limited v Republic of Hungary* (Award, 2006) ICSID Case No ARB/03/16, [423] (ADC).

[80]*Tecmed* [119]; for further details see UNCTAD (2012a), p. 79.

[81]Cf *Marvin Roy Feldman Karpa v United Mexican States* (Award, 2002) ICSID Case No ARB (AF)/99/1 (Feldman), [83].

[82]This question was at issue in e.g. *Compañia del Desarrollo de Santa Elena SA v Republic of Costa Rica* (Award, 2000) ICSID Case No ARB/96/1 (Sta Elena) or in *Cortec*.

[83]E.g. *Biwater*.

[84]*Veolia Propreté v Arab Republic of Egypt* (Award, 2018) ICSID Case No ARB/12/15) (Veolia).

[85]E.g. *Cortec*.

responsibility.[86] Particular challenges for sustainability measures are the IIA rules on expropriation, FET, and indemnification.

3.2 *Expropriation and Sustainable Development*

Sustainability measures may interfere with the property of foreign investors either directly or indirectly. A direct expropriation involves taking of the investor's property,[87] for instance for environmental protection reasons.[88] Indirect expropriations are measures that leave the property title of an investor untouched but restrict the use of the property in a manner that prevents the investor from using it entirely or using it in an economically viable manner.[89] Examples of sustainability measures that substantially constrain the use of a foreign investment include the denial of a license[90] or the termination of a lease[91] necessary for the operation of a business, or the limitation of water prices that reduces the profits of the investment to the extent that it puts the investor out of business.[92] As the expropriatory nature of sustainability measures is frequently not apparent at first sight, such measures generally go uncompensated on the national level. However, if they affect the business of a foreign investor disproportionally, the investor may be entitled to compensation under the rules on expropriation.

The rules on expropriation constitute a core element of IIAs that enshrine virtually all African IIAs.[93] They codify the customary right of host states to regulate property, which includes the right to expropriate property for political, economic or social reasons.[94] Typically IIAs permit expropriations, nationalizations, and measures amounting to an expropriation for a public purpose, in a non-discriminatory

[86]Cf *ADC* [423f]; *Tecmed* [120f].

[87]See UNCTAD Expropriation (2012a), p. 5; Dolzer and Schreuer (2012), p. 101.

[88]Cf e.g. *Sta Elena*; see also Newcombe and Paradell (2009), p. 324.

[89]Cf *Suez, Sociedad General de Aguas de Barcelona, SA and Interagua Servicios Integrales de Agua, SA v Argentine Republic* (Decision on liability, 2010) ICSID Case No ARB/03/17 [121] (Suez); *Urbaser SA and Consorcio de Aguas Bilbao Biskaia, Bilbao Biskaia Ur Partzuergoa v Argentine Republic* (Award, 2016) ICSID Case No. ARB/07/26 [1000] (Urbaser); for the distinction between a direct and an indirect expropriation see *Tecmed* [113f]; see also Dolzer and Stevens (1995), p. 98; Newcombe and Paradell (2009), p. 325.

[90]E.g. *Tecmed.*

[91]E.g. *Biwater.*

[92]*Compañía de Aguas del Aconquija SA and Vivendi Universal SA (formerly Compañía de Aguas del Aconquija, SA and Compagnie Générale des Eaux) v Argentine Republic (I)* (Award II, 2007) ICSID Case No ARB/97/3 (Vivendi I).

[93]Cf for many China-Ethiopia BIT (1998), art. 4; Sweden-Tanzania BIT (1999), art. 4; Morocco-Rwanda BIT (2016), art. 4; Morocco-Nigeria BIT (2016), art. 8; PAIC (2017), art. 11; ECOWAS Supplementary Act (2008), art. 8.

[94]Jennings and Watts (1992), p. 911, in particular p. 918; Crawford (2012), p. 620.

manner, following the rule of law, and against compensation.[95] While host states have the right to adopt sustainability measures, it is controversially discussed if and at what level of interference with a foreign investor's property they constitute an expropriation that requires compensating the foreign investor.

The level of interference, which foreign investors must accept without being entitled to compensation, is hotly debated. Arbitral tribunals choose several different approaches to determine whether measures affecting foreign investment amount to a compensable indirect expropriation. The sole effects doctrine only considers the impact on the investor's use of its property but does not take into account the nature, purpose, and character of a measure.[96] Consequently, if a sustainability measure interferes substantially with the use of the investor's property, compensation is required irrespectively of the purpose of the measure.[97] Accordingly, the aim to implement sustainable development policies is irrelevant and the host state must pay compensation in any case. In contrast, the police powers doctrine focuses on the intent of the measure, which implies that the protection of sustainable development interests becomes relevant for determining whether a regulatory measure amounts to an expropriation.[98] Following the police powers doctrine, sustainability measures are not indirect expropriations if they meet the conditions of a legitimate expropriation, namely if they pursue a public purpose, are non-discriminatory and respect the principles of due process.[99] Finally, some tribunals have applied a mix of both approaches. They consider both the intent of the measure and the effect on the investor's property and have applied the proportionality principle to determine whether and to what extent foreign investors must accept measures without compensation.[100]

As traditional IIAs do not guide arbitral tribunals on how to determine the threshold between an expropriation and a general regulatory measure, the case-law on the level of interference that investors must accept is inconsistent.[101] In practice,

[95] E.g. Denmark-Tanzania BIT (1999), art. 5(1); Morocco-Rwanda BIT (2016), art. 4(1); for further IIA provisions see Dolzer and Stevens (1995), p. 97; details on the criteria for lawful expropriation see Dolzer and Schreuer (2012), p. 99ff; UNCTAD (2012a), p. 27ff; Newcombe and Paradell (2009), p. 369; Jennings and Watts (1992), p. 918.

[96] E.g. *Metalclad* [103]; *Biloune and Marine Drive Complex Ltd v Ghana Investments Centre and the Government of Ghana* (Ad-hoc Award on Jurisdiction and Liability of October 27, 1989 and Ad-hoc Award on Damages and Costs of June 30, 1990) (Biloune); *Vivendi I*; for further reference see Dolzer and Schreuer (2012), p. 114 with case-law.

[97] See e.g. *Metalclad* [111]; *Sta Elena* [72].

[98] E.g. *SD Myers, Inc v Government of Canada* (1st Partial Award (merits), 13 November 2000) [285] (Myers).

[99] See e.g. *Methanex Corporation v United States of America* (Final Award on jurisdiction and merits, 3 August 2005), Part IV, Chapter D [7] (Methanex); *Saluka Investments BV v The Czech Republic* (Partial Award, 17 March 2006), [255] (Saluka); *ADC* [423ff]; see also Dolzer and Schreuer (2012), p. 122; Schreuer (2010), p. 133.

[100] Cf *Tecmed* [122]; for further reference see UNCTAD (2012a), p. 98; Gazzini (2010), p. 42.

[101] See for an overview Dolzer and Schreuer (2012), p. 104.

arbitral tribunals have become increasingly reluctant to qualify regulatory measures as indirect expropriations.[102] As a state's police powers include the right to adopt rules that "cause economic damages to those subject to its powers [...] without entitling them to any compensation whatsoever",[103] possibly only a severe interference with the investor's property that results in a permanent or near-total deprivation of the investment will amount to an unacceptable interference that entitles the investor to compensation.[104] However, lacking a generally recognized threshold or constant practice on acceptable interference[105] host states hardly can assess whether or not their sustainability measures constitute an indirect expropriation that requires compensating foreign investors.[106] This uncertainty has possibly far-reaching impacts on a host state's inclination to implement sustainability measures.

3.3 *Fair and Equitable Treatment and Sustainable Development*

Another controversial IIA provision that potentially affects a host state's willingness to implement sustainability policies is the FET clause.[107] This standard IIA clause, which exists in all traditional African IIAs,[108] addresses the manner in which a host state must treat foreign investors and their investments. It expresses the principle of good faith[109] and requires host states to act vis-à-vis foreign investors fairly, which entails reasonable and proportionate state conduct.[110] The FET clause complements the rules on expropriation[111] and is particularly relevant if the host state conduct affects a foreign investor's legitimate expectations, but is not sufficiently substantial to constitute an indirect expropriation.[112] If foreign investors challenge host state regulatory measures, they typically bring forward the FET standard together with the

---

[102]Newcombe and Paradell (2009), p. 357.

[103]See *Tecmed* [119]; see also Newcombe (2005), p. 23.

[104]E.g. *Metalclad Corporation v The United Mexican States* (Award, 2000) ICSID Case No ARB (AF)/97/1, [103] (Metalclad); for further case-law see Dolzer and Schreuer (2012), p. 112, n80; UNCTAD (2012a), p. 63.

[105]Cf only *Myers* [281]; *Methanex* Part IV, Chapter D [7].

[106]On the controversies regarding the valuation of compensation see Chapter 3.4.

[107]For a general discussion see Kläger (2011a), Schreuer (2010) and Jacob and Schill (2015).

[108]Cf e.g. Morocco-Gabon BIT (2004), art. 2(2); Sweden-Tanzania BIT (1999), art. 2(3); China-Tanzania BIT (2013), art. 5(1).

[109]See *Tecmed* [153]; *Myers* [134].

[110]*Tecmed* [153]; see also *El Paso* [373].

[111]Schreuer (2010), p. 133; e.g. *Sempra* [300ff].

[112]Cf e.g. *PSEG Global Inc and Konya Ilgin Elektrik Üretim ve Ticaret Limited Sirketi v Republic of Turkey* (Award, 2007) ICSID Case No ARB/02/5, [238] (PSEG); *Continental Casualty Company v Argentine Republic* (Award, 2008) ICSID Case No ARB/03/9, [254] (Continental Casualty).

provision on expropriation.[113] In fact, it is the most invoked IIA standard in investment disputes, and arbitral tribunals frequently find a breach of the FET standard rather than an illegal expropriation.[114]

The FET standard determines the mode in which host states must treat foreign investors. Host states must comply with this standard when adopting sustainability measures affecting foreign investors. The FET standard has triggered considerable criticism for being vague[115] and giving too much discretion to arbitral tribunals to determine its content. The problem originates in the lean wording of traditional FET provisions, which mention the term without further reference to its actual meaning.[116] While arbitral tribunals have developed an extensive and mixed interpretation of the FET clause,[117] they repeatedly resort to specific FET obligations,[118] including the obligation of due process, transparency in decision-making, compliance with contractual obligations, freedom from coercion and harassment of the investors, and a stable and predictable legal framework.[119] But as the interpretation of one arbitral tribunal does not bind other arbitral tribunals, it is uncertain, which FET elements an arbitral tribunal will utilize when deciding on sustainability measures.

For sustainability policies, the most controversial FET element is the protection of the legitimate expectations of foreign investors in a stable legal and business environment.[120] The FET standard protects legitimate expectations in the stability of the host state's legal framework at the time the investment was admitted[121] and specific assurances host state made towards the investor at that point in time.[122] While the protection of the investor's legitimate expectation is a key aspect of the FET standard,[123] it is subject to debate to what extent host states can change the legal

---

[113]E.g. *Tecmed*; *Biwater*; *Metalclad*; see also UNCTAD (2012b), p. 10.

[114]Mbengue and Schacherer (2017), p. 429; Schreuer (2010), p. 133; Dolzer and Schreuer (2012), p. 130; Newcombe and Paradell (2009), p. 255.

[115]De Brabandere (2017), p. 4; UNCTAD (2012b), p. 11; Jacob and Schill (2015), p. 713; see e.g. *Sempra* [296]; *Suez* [296]; *Total SA v Argentine Republic* (Decision on liability, 2010) ICSID Case No ARB/04/1, [106ff] (Total).

[116]E.g. Denmark-Tanzania BIT (1999), art. 3(1).

[117]For an overview see Newcombe and Paradell (2009), p. 263.

[118]Cf Schreuer (2010), p. 125 with reference to case-law; Jacob and Schill (2015), p. 717; Kläger (2011b), p. 246; Newcombe and Paradell (2009), p. 275.

[119]For details and related case-law see Dolzer and Schreuer (2012), p. 145; Newcombe and Paradell (2009), p. 279; Schreuer (2010), p. 126; UNCTAD (2012b), p. 61; Jacob and Schill (2015), p. 719.

[120]Cf e.g. *CMS Gas Transmission Company v The Argentine Republic* (Award, 2005) ICSID Case No ARB/01/8, [274ff] (CMS); *Sempra* [298] and [303]; Jacob and Schill (2015), p. 724, n125 with further references.

[121]Schreuer (2010), p. 126; see also Dolzer and Schreuer (2012), p. 145 for relevant case-law.

[122]*Sempra* [298f]; *Total* [119f]; *Metalclad* [74ff].

[123]See e.g. *Saluka* [302] with further reference to earlier case-law; see also *El Paso* [348]; for details see UNCTAD (2012b), p. 63 with further references; Jacob and Schill (2015), p. 724 with further references; Kläger (2011b), p. 247.

framework to implement sustainable development policies without conflicting with this FET element.[124]

Interpretations of the permitted legislative change vary.[125] In some cases arbitral tribunals have chosen investor-friendly approaches and merely looked at the impact of the regulatory measure;[126] in other cases, they have considered qualifying elements, such as specific representations made to the investor,[127] or the legitimacy and reasonableness of the investor's expectations in the light of the circumstances.[128] Similar to the rules on expropriation, traditional FET clauses lack guidance on which criteria apply for balancing the legitimate expectations of investors against the host states' interests to implement sustainable development measures.[129] In practice, arbitral tribunals increasingly accept reasonable changes of legislation to pursue public policy goals and only find unexpected and arbitrary changes of the legal framework a breach of the FET standard.[130] Yet, it is hardly predictable for host states, which standard of legitimate expectations arbitral tribunal will apply when they decide on the legality of sustainability measures under the FET standard.[131] This legal uncertainty may prevent host states from adopting sustainability measures.

3.4 Indemnification and Sustainable Development

The IIA rules on indemnification severely impact the implementation of sustainable development policies. When arbitral tribunals find that sustainability measures constitute an expropriation or violate the FET standard, the rules on indemnification provide guidance for the payments due to foreign investors. Host states must either pay compensation as an element of a lawful expropriation, or they must pay reparation for an unlawful expropriation or a breach of the FET standard.[132] Both forms of indemnification have different standards and modes of valuation that result in different amounts to be paid by the host state.[133] As traditional IIAs fail to

[124] Cf *El Paso* [402].

[125] For details see Jacob and Schill (2015), p. 726; UNCTAD (2012b), p. 64.

[126] Cf *Occidental Exploration and Production Company v Republic of Ecuador (I)* (Award, 2004) LCIA Case No UN3467, [196] (Occidental); *Tecmed* [154]; *CMS* [274]; see for further case-law UNCTAD (2012b), p. 66.

[127] *Methanex* Part IV, Chapter D [7ff].

[128] *Saluka* [304]; *El Paso* [368ff].

[129] See e.g. *El Paso* [402]; *Saluka* [306]; *Vivendi I* [7.4.18–7.4.24].

[130] For an overview of case-law see Newcombe and Paradell (2009), p. 279.

[131] Cf also UNCTAD (2012b), p. 11 with further references.

[132] Cf *The Factory at Chorzów* (Claim for Indemnity) (The Merits), Germany v Poland (Judgment, 1929) 1928 PCIJ (Ser A) No 17 [47] (*Chorzów Factory*); see also for many *ADC* [484ff].

[133] *Chorzów Factory* [47] for details see Marboe (2017), p. 80.

sufficiently address the complexities of determining indemnification under international law, they prevent host states from assessing the possible costs for sustainability measures if they conflict with the equally uncertain substantive IIA standards.

Under general international law, lawful expropriations require the payment of compensation.[134] The standard of compensation, namely whether compensation must be full or less than full, has long been disputed between capital-exporting and capital-importing states.[135] Today, most IIAs contain the standard of adequate, prompt, and effective compensation or compensation of the fair market value.[136] Both standards require replacing the value of the investment at the time of the expropriation and the interests until the day of payment.[137] The standard of compensation for lawful expropriations is an objective standard and does not consider causation or mitigating effects, such as the sustainability goal of regulatory measures.[138] In contrast to the standard of compensation, the standard of reparation requires states not only to replace the value of the investment but also any financially assessable damage including lost profits and incidental expenses.[139] Reparation "must, as far as possible, wipe out all consequences of the illegal act and re-establish the situation which would, in all probability, have existed if the act had not been committed".[140] The reparation standard is a subjective standard that permits to mitigate or offset the amount by considering the causation of the host state,[141] the condition of the property, and the conduct of the investor.[142] Yet, sums for reparation typically surmount sums for compensation as they consider increases in the value of the investment between the date of the IIA violation and the date of the arbitral decision.[143]

Although both standards of indemnification differ in their replacement requirements, and therefore theoretically result in different amounts of monetary damages,[144] IIAs typically do not differentiate between the indemnification standards and use the terms "indemnification", "compensation" and "damages"

[134]Cf Marboe (2017), p. 44.

[135]See UN General Assembly, Declaration on Permanent Sovereignty over Natural Resources (1962), UNGA Res 1803 (XVII); for details see Dolzer and Stevens (1995), p. 108.

[136]E.g. China-Ethiopia BIT (1998), art. 4(1); Tanzania-United Kingdom BIT (1994), art. 5(1); for further reference see also Dolzer and Stevens (1995), p. 109.

[137]See *Chorzów Factory* [47]; UNCTAD (2012), p. 111.

[138]Cf UNCTAD (2012a), p. 111; Marboe (2006), p. 729; Marboe (2015), p. 1033; Dolzer and Schreuer (2012), p. 287.

[139]See Marboe (2017), p. 88; Dolzer and Schreuer (2012), p. 294.

[140]*Chorzów Factory* [47]; *ADC* [484ff]; *Biwater* [773]; see also Articles on Responsibility of States for Internationally Wrongful Acts (2001), UNGA Res A/RES/56/83, Annex (ASR), arts. 34ff; UNCTAD (2012a), p. 111ff; Marboe (2015), p. 1034.

[141]See e.g. *Biwater* [778].

[142]Marboe (2006), p. 733; see also art. 39 ASR.

[143]Marboe (2006), p. 728; see also UNCTAD (2012a), p. 114.

[144]See for many *CMS* [400ff]; *ADC* [481]; *Metalclad* [118]; for details see Marboe (2006), p. 725; Marboe (2015), p. 1033.

indistinctively.[145] Usually, IIAs only regulate compensation for expropriation but lack rules on reparation for breaches of IIA obligations.[146] But even the rules on compensation for lawful expropriation are scarce and rarely specify valuation methods for investments.[147] This lack of clear rules gives wide discretion to arbitral tribunals to determine the amount to be paid by host states for regulatory measures.[148] While arbitral tribunals usually acknowledge the difference between compensation and reparation,[149] the application of both standards is typically blurred,[150] and the resulting case-law is inconsistent.[151]

The problems arising from the imprecise application of these different standards of indemnification for sustainability measures are manifold. For instance, arbitral tribunals have used the discounted-cash-flow-method,[152] which includes expected future profits, to determine the value of an investment irrespective of whether the standard of compensation for expropriation or the standard of full reparation is applicable.[153] However, this method is not appropriate for determining compensation for lawful expropriation, which does not include lost profits.[154] Consequently, the sum of indemnification awarded for a sustainability measure amounting to an expropriation may be higher than the sum required under the rules of compensation for lawful expropriation.[155] Problematic is also the role of offsetting or mitigation reasons. Whereas the standard of compensation does not provide for mitigating or offsetting reasons such as investor behavior or purpose of the regulatory measure,[156] mitigation is allowed under the subjective standard of full reparation. As a result, a host state's intent to implement sustainable development policies can be taken into account as a mitigating reason, when a host state unlawfully expropriates an investment for environmental reasons, but not if it *lawfully* expropriates the investment for environmental reasons. In addition to these legal inconsistencies, arbitral awards occasionally do not explain the choice of method or how the figures were calculated.[157] At times, arbitral tribunals simply take the middle between the

---

[145]Cf also Marboe (2006), p. 723; Marboe (2015), p. 1032.

[146]See for many *Feldman* [194]; *ADC* [481]; *CMS* [409]; see also Salacuse (2015), p. 254.

[147]Cf Dolzer and Stevens (1995), p. 110.

[148]E.g. *Azurix Corp v The Argentine Republic (I)* (Award, 2006) ICSID Case No ARB/01/12, [421ff] (Azurix) with further references; see also UNCTAD (2012a), p. 122.

[149]Cf for many *ADC* [480ff].

[150]Cf e.g. *CMS* [410]; *Metalclad* [113]; *Biwater* [777]; see also Ratner (2017), p. 16; UNCTAD (2012a), p. 120.

[151]Cf e.g. *Azurix* [421ff] with further reference.

[152]World Bank Guidelines (1992), art. IV.6; for further reference see General Council of the World Bank (1992), para. 42; UNCTAD (2012a), p. 120.

[153]E.g. *ADC* [501ff]; *CMS* [411ff].

[154]See Marboe (2006), p. 727ff.

[155]For a discussion and examples see Marboe (2006), p. 735.

[156]Cf e.g. *Sta Elena* [72f].

[157]E.g. *Sta Elena* [93ff]: the tribunal gave no explanation on how the figure was calculated; see also Marboe (2006), p. 723.

investor's claims and the host state's offer for compensation.[158] In fact, some case-law suggests that the amounts due for indemnification rather reflect the result of a horse-trade than being based on traceable legal principles.[159]

To conclude, traditional IIAs lack a clear legal framework for determining the amount of indemnification for sustainability measures amounting to an expropriation or constituting an unlawful expropriation or a breach of the FET standard. The scarce rules on compensation for expropriation and the lack of rules on reparation in traditional IIAs prevent host states to foresee the amount of indemnification to be paid for sustainability measures. Likewise, it is uncertain whether arbitral tribunals will consider the host state's sustainable development intent of the measures in question as a reason for mitigating indemnification. As arbitral awards on damages are largely unpredictable, host states may be reluctant to adopt sustainability measures because the possibly arising costs are unclear. This lack of detailed rules on indemnification aggravates the uncertainty about the equally unclear rules on expropriation and FET.

4 African Approaches to Reconcile the Regulatory Sovereignty of Host States and Investment Protection

4.1 General Remarks

African states have undertaken major reform efforts to address the adverse impacts of traditional IIAs on the sustainable development policies of host states. They have replaced many traditional IIAs by modern versions, and have negotiated new BITs, multilateral IIAs and model IIAs in the framework of African regional organizations.[160] The IIA reforms aim to shift the focus of IIAs on promoting sustainable foreign investment and better balancing the interests of host states and foreign investors.[161] They clarify the ambiguous IIA provisions and strengthen the regulatory authority of host states with regard to sustainability policies. To achieve this goal, African IIA negotiators have developed their own specific methods that are only rarely used outside the African continent.

Modern African IIAs typically retain the traditional pattern of IIAs, but amend, refine, or delete controversial provisions and include entirely new provisions. Clarifications exist on the rules of expropriation and the host states' right to implement sustainable development policies, the FET standard, and the rules on compensation. New features include express provisions on sustainable development and on investor

[158]E.g. *Sta Elena* [95].

[159]For an overview on the inconsistent practice see UNCTAD (2012a), p. 120; Ratner (2017), p. 16.

[160]For details see text and references accompanying n29ff.

[161]Cf e.g. Morocco-Nigeria BIT (2016), preamble; SADC Investment Protocol Amendment (2017), preamble, 8th recital; PAIC (2017), preamble, 10th and 11th recital.

obligations. The reformed IIAs aim to guide arbitral tribunals on how to take into account sustainable development objectives when applying and interpreting the substantive IIA provisions. However, not all approaches are equally viable to facilitate sustainable foreign investment and to achieve a satisfactory balance between the regulatory sovereignty of host states and the protection of foreign investors.

4.2 *Expropriation and Host State Regulatory Powers to Adopt Sustainability Measures*

An essential reform element of modern African IIAs is to clarify the rules on expropriation with a view to creating certainty for host states as to whether sustainability measures must be compensated or not. Reformed African IIAs typically regulate the scope of a host state's regulatory powers by expressly establishing the difference between non-compensable regulatory measures and compensable indirect expropriations. African IIAs show different approaches to address this question.

First, some IIAs expressly include carve-outs for general regulatory measures in the provisions on expropriation. An example is art. 5(7) SADC Protocol Amendment which provides that measures of general application that are "designed and applied to protect or enhance legitimate public welfare objects," including public health or the environment, do not constitute indirect expropriations.[162] Art. 11(3) PAIC and art. 20(8) COMESA Investment Agreement include similar provisions but establish qualifications the measure must meet to be exempted, namely that the measure must be non-discriminatory[163] or a *bona fide* regulatory measure.[164] An even more moderate approach pursue, for instance, the China-Tanzania BIT or the Canada-Tanzania BIT: They provide for a proportionality test and establish that good-faith, non-discriminatory regulatory measures including measures to protect health or the environment do not constitute indirect expropriations unless they substantially exceed what is necessary for maintaining reasonable public welfare; for determining whether a measure is proportionate the provisions list several factors, including the economic impact of the regulatory measure, the extent to which the measure interferes with distinct, reasonable investment-backed expectations, and the character of the measure.[165] A similar weighting and balancing test is provided for in art. 8 (2)(b) Morocco-Nigeria BIT. Common to this first approach is that regulatory measures meeting these requirements are exempted from the rules on expropriation and therefore do not require compensation.

[162] Cf also SADC Model BIT Template (2012), art. 6.7.

[163] PAIC (2017), art. 11(3).

[164] COMESA Investment Agreement (2007), art. 20(8).

[165] Canada-Tanzania BIT (2013), art. 5(5); China-Tanzania BIT (2013), art. 6(3); this approach follows the US and the Canadian Model BITs, cf Spears (2010), p. 1051.

A second approach inserts general exception clauses in IIAs. In traditional IIAs, such exception clauses are common for taxation or essential security measures.[166] An increasing number of reformed IIAs expand these exception clauses to environmental or social measures. Examples are art. 14(1) PAIC, art. 22(1) COMESA Investment Agreement, or art. 10(2) China-Tanzania BIT. These clauses permit for public health or environmental measures and enshrine the criteria of art. XX GATT, which implies a proportionality test for regulatory measures.[167] The purpose of general exception clauses is to excuse the host state from breaching IIA provisions, such as the expropriation standard: a regulatory measure that qualifies as an indirect expropriation does not require compensation if it is an environmental or social measure that complies with the criteria stated in the general exception clause.[168] Although general exception clauses on the right to regulate typically lack a direct reference to the rules on expropriation, they serve a similar function as the carve-outs in the provisions of expropriation.

Third, some IIAs enshrine provisions that expressly establish the host state's right to regulate.[169] For instance, arts. 13(4) and 23 Morocco-Nigeria BIT explicitly permit states to adopt regulatory measures to ensure that development is consistent with the principles of sustainable development and to adopt measures to protect the environment or labor standards. Art. 14 SADC Investment Protocol stresses the right of host states to regulate in the public interest and adopt any measures they consider appropriate to ensure that an investment is undertaken in a manner sensitive to health, safety or environmental concerns. A similar provision exists in art. 22 (2) COMESA Investment Agreement. Although the provisions on the right to regulate do not directly refer to the rules on expropriation, they constitute relevant context in the sense of art. 31(1) Vienna Convention on the Law of Treaties (VCLT)[170] that arbitral tribunals must take into account when interpreting the rules on expropriation and determining the threshold of acceptable regulatory measures.[171] However, the details of the definitions of regulatory measures vary. Some clauses merely state the right to adopt regulatory measures,[172] whereas others mention further specifications of regulatory measures, such as their non-discriminatory nature.[173]

---

[166] Dolzer and Stevens (1995), p. 71; Spears (2010), p. 1059; see e.g. SADC Investment Protocol (2006), art. 7.

[167] See Spears (2010), p. 1060.

[168] See Spears (2010), p. 1059.

[169] For a detailed discussion on the right to regulate see Titi (2014).

[170] Vienna Convention on the Law of Treaties (signed 23 May 1969, entered into force 27 January 1980) 1155 UNTS 331 (VCLT).

[171] See Dörr (2018), p. 582, paras. 43ff.

[172] E.g. art. 14 SADC Investment Protocol (2006).

[173] E.g. Morocco-Nigeria BIT (2016), arts. 13(4) and 23; art. 22 COMESA Investment Agreement (2007).

Fourth, many reformed African IIAs contain clauses establishing the general IIA objective of achieving sustainable development[174] or clauses on investor obligations.[175] These clauses shift the treaty purpose from mere investment protection to sustainable foreign investment and influence the interpretation of the expropriation provisions in line with Art 31(1) VCLT, which requires interpreting treaties taking into account their context and their object and purpose.[176] Interpreting the expropriation clauses in the light of the IIA's sustainable development objective may raise the acceptable level of interference with the investor's property in case of sustainability measures of the host state. Likewise, as following the UN 2030 Agenda investors must contribute to sustainable development,[177] the provisions on investor obligations suggest that the provisions on expropriation may be interpreted as requiring investors to accept a higher level of host state interferences with their property. Moreover, a severe breach of investor obligations may be interpreted as justifying regulatory measures of host states or as reasons for mitigating or offsetting compensation.[178]

Clarifying the regulatory powers of host states contributes substantially to guiding the discretion of arbitral tribunals when deciding whether regulatory measures constitute a compensable indirect expropriation. The various reform approaches prevent that arbitral tribunals apply the sole-effects doctrine[179] and ensure that the host states' regulatory powers are taken into account when tribunals interpret the IIA rules. Yet, not all approaches are equally feasible to balance the investors' interests in protecting their investments and host states' interests in pursuing sustainability policies. Problematic are provisions that exempt regulatory measures from the rules on expropriation or establish the host state's right to regulate without further qualifications.[180] Although such provisions codify the police powers of host states under customary international law,[181] they shift the full risk of policy changes to the investor. A better approach is to introduce some qualifications that regulatory measures must meet to be exempted, for instance, that they must constitute bona fide regulatory measures[182] or that they must be non-discriminatory.[183] Similarly, a proportionality test examining whether the measure is necessary to achieve the

[174]See Chapter 4.5.

[175]See Chapter 4.6.

[176]Dörr (2018), p. 584, paras. 52ff.

[177]UN 2030 Agenda, Declaration, para. 67.

[178]For specific rules on investor obligations in modern African IIAs see text accompanying n255ff.

[179]Cf text accompanying n96ff.

[180]E.g. SADC Investment Protocol (2006), art. 14; SADC Investment Protocol Amendment (2017), art. 5(7).

[181]See Spears (2010), p. 1051f; see also Chapter 3.2.

[182]E.g. COMESA Investment Agreement (2007), art. 20(8); Canada-Tanzania BIT (2013), art. 5(5); China-Tanzania BIT (2013), art. 6(3).

[183]E.g. PAIC (2017), art. 11(3) and 14(1).

sustainability aim serves this purpose.[184] Such qualifications, which also exist in arbitral case-law,[185] ensure that host states meet certain fairness standards when adopting sustainability measures and that foreign investors do not bear the full risk of regulatory measures affecting their property. As a result, the rules on expropriation permit for a fair balance between host states' and investors' interests that is necessary to ensure that IIAs continue to attract foreign investment.

A problem that could limit the effectiveness of the reforms is that it is frequently unclear how the exception clauses on host state regulatory powers relate to the rules on expropriation. Whereas the express inclusion of such exemptions in the expropriation provision leaves little discretion to arbitral tribunals, a general exception clause is less clear. Even more problematic are IIAs that merely establish the host states' regulatory powers or merely include the goal of sustainable development in the preamble of an IIA without linking these elements to the rules of expropriation. Although arbitral tribunals must interpret IIAs according to the methods of interpretation codified in art. 31 VCLT and both the context of a provision as well as the object and purpose of a treaty constitute relevant elements, choosing the interpretation method is discretionary rather than obligatory.[186] For that reason, tribunals may interpret the rules on expropriation in the context of the host state's right to regulate, but it is not mandatory if a tribunal considers other methods of interpretation more appropriate. A clear reference in the provisions on expropriation is advisable to limit the discretion of arbitral tribunals.

A related problem is that the conditions for adopting regulatory measures in the relevant IIA provisions frequently are not evident and at times inconsistent. For instance, the Morocco-Nigeria BIT requires in art. 8(2)(b) a proportionality test for regulatory measures, in art. 13(4) that environmental and social regulatory measures must be non-discriminatory, and in art. 23 that regulatory measures must balance the rights and obligations of investors and host states. Similarly, the PAIC establishes in art. 11(3) that non-discriminatory measures are not considered indirect expropriations, whereas art. 14(1) prohibits only arbitrary and unjustifiably discriminatory measures between investors in like circumstances and requires a proportionality test. Another example is art. 5(7) and art. 12 SADC Investment Protocol Amendment. To provide clear guidance to arbitral tribunals as to what criteria apply and limit their discretion, it is advisable to streamline such provisions or at least include cross-reference between these provisions if appropriate to make the conditions for a non-compensable regulatory measure clear.

Another question is whether an IIA that entirely exempts regulatory measures from the protection against indirect expropriation can also exclude protection against such measures under customary international law. If a regulatory measure results in

---

[184]See e.g. China-Tanzania BIT (2013), art. 6(3); see also art. 14 PAIC (2017); Morocco-Nigeria BIT (2016), art. 8(2)(b).

[185]Cf references in n100.

[186]Cf Jennings and Watts (1992), p. 1270 with further reference; Dörr (2018), p. 560, para. 2.

the complete deprivation of the investor's property,[187] even if this is for environmental or social reasons, it amounts to an expropriation that requires compensation under general international law. Although IIA rules constitute *leges speciales* that precede over the rules of general international law,[188] IIAs frequently establish that the applicable law not only comprises the IIA provisions, but also the rules of general international law.[189] For that reason, an investor may be entitled to protection under customary international law against flagrant breaches of the customary rules of expropriation or the minimum standard of treatment of aliens despite an exemption of regulatory measures from the rules on expropriation. As it is unclear whether arbitral tribunals will accept the total exclusion of this protection standard, the qualification of measures to ensure that they prevent abuses of powers from the host state, as done in most IIAs, is advisable.

To conclude, not all African IIA reform approaches are equally suitable to clarify the line between the police powers of host states and compensable expropriations. Whereas some IIAs generally exempt regulatory measures from the rules of expropriation, which shifts the entire risk to investors, other IIAs establish criteria for exempted regulatory measures. The best approach is to clearly determine the conditions for permissible regulatory measures, such as their sustainable development objective, their non-discriminatory nature, or the principles of fair administrative conduct. It is also useful to introduce a proportionality requirement that obliges arbitral tribunals to balance the host state's and the investor's interests. These criteria ensure a fair and predictable legal framework that reconciles the aim of investment protection and regulatory sovereignty of host states. Whether the criteria established in the reformed African IIAs are sufficiently clear to discern measures amounting to an indirect expropriation from general regulatory measures remains to be seen from arbitral practice.

4.3 *Fair and Equitable Treatment Standard: Deletion or Redrafting*

The FET standard has been perceived as an impediment to implementing sustainable development policies even more than the rules on expropriation.[190] It applies to all sustainability measures affecting foreign investors and ensures fair host state behavior, including protection against changes in the national legal system affecting the "legitimate expectations" of foreign investors. The FET standard is also relevant if an expropriation process is not complying with rule of law standards, and even if general regulatory measures are exempted from the scope of application of the rules

[187] For relevant cases see Newcombe and Paradell (2009), p. 347.

[188] Cf e.g. *ADC* [480ff].

[189] Cf e.g. Morocco-Rwanda BIT (2016), art. 8; PAIC (2017), art. 44.

[190] For details see Chapter 3.3.

on expropriation, they must comply with the FET standard. Due to the broad scope of the FET standard, the interpretations of arbitral tribunals are hardly predictable. African IIAs pursue different models to cope with the uncertainties of the FET standard.[191]

Some IIAs delete the FET standard. Examples include the PAIC and other modern IIAs.[192] The SADC Model BIT Template also recommends the deletion of this clause.[193] However, although the content of the FET standard is unclear, its deletion is not the best option to address the problem. First, the guarantees of fair administrative conduct, good governance, rule of law, transparency and stability are not only important for foreign investors but beneficial for the economy and all citizens of a host state generally. Second, these elements contribute to achieving sustainable development[194] and are even enshrined in the UN 2030 Agenda.[195] Third, deleting the FET clause form an IIA does not necessarily exclude the application of the FET standard if the very IIA includes a most-favored-nation clause, which makes FET clauses from other IIAs concluded by the host state applicable.[196] For instance, the Morocco-Rwanda BIT does not provide for FET, but a most-favored-nation clause[197] that permits a Moroccan investor to rely on the unqualified FET clause enshrined in art. 4(1) Mauritius-Rwanda BIT.[198] Fourth, IIAs do not exclude the application of general international law,[199] but at times even expressly refer to the rules of general international law.[200] As a result, the customary international law standard of the treatment of aliens, which includes international minimum standards of treatment similar and even vaguer than the FET standard, may apply.[201]

Another approach is the replacement of the FET standard with other general standards of treatment. For instance, the SADC Investment Protocol Amendment has replaced that standard with the national treatment standard.[202] The aim is to create equal competitive opportunities for domestic and foreign investors and to prevent preferential treatment of foreign investors compared to national businesses.[203] However, this approach also raises legal problems. If the national

[191]Cf also De Brabandere (2017), p. 9.

[192]E.g. Brazil-Malawi BIT (2015); Morocco-Rwanda BIT (2016); see also Mbengue and Schacherer (2017), p. 431.

[193]SADC Model BIT Template (2012), art. 5, commentary, at 22.

[194]See also Gazzini (2014), p. 949.

[195]UN 2030 Agenda, SDG 16.

[196]See for further reference UNCTAD (2012b), p. 19.

[197]Morocco-Rwanda BIT (2016), art. 3.

[198]Mauritius-Rwanda BIT (2001).

[199]Cf for many *ADC* [288ff]; for further references see Dolzer and Schreuer (2012), p. 291.

[200]E.g. PAIC (2017), art. 44.

[201]Cf also UNCTAD (2012b), p. 18.

[202]SADC Investment Treaty Protocol Amendment (2016), art. 6.

[203]De Brabandere (2017), p. 17.

treatment standard in a host state is below the international minimum standard under international law,[204] the same problem as in case of the complete exclusion of the FET standard occurs: The investor may either invoke the rules of general international law or may be able to invoke the FET standard included in other IIAs if the applicable IIA contains a most-favored-nation clause.

A better alternative is to redraft the FET clause and specify the meaning of FET to provide better guidance to future arbitrators. The SADC Model BIT includes two options: One option suggests replacing the general FET clause with a definition of fair administrative treatment, which includes principles of the rule of law, transparency, and fair administration.[205] For instance, the SADC Investment Protocol Amendment and the ECOWAS Supplementary Act contain similar provisions.[206] Also, the Morocco-Nigeria BIT adopts this approach in art. 7(2)(a) and art. 10. The elements reflect the principles of fairness and good governance, standards that are not only important for the business of foreign investors but for the sustainable development of the host state in general.[207] The other option suggested by the SADC Model BIT Template defines the quality of an act that constitutes a breach of FET: Only acts of government that "are an outrage, in bad faith, a willful neglect of duty or an insufficiency so far short of international standards that every reasonable and impartial person would readily recognize its insufficiency"[208] violate the FET standard. Both approaches define an express threshold for host state conduct that is not acceptable for foreign investors and therefore constitutes a breach of the FET standard. They guide arbitrators on how to assess sustainability measures as they make clear that host state regulatory measures are generally permitted and do not affect an investor's legitimate expectations unless there is a certain mode or level of interference.

Another approach to qualifying the FET standard is to refer to the principles of general international law or to the international minimum standard for the treatment of aliens. For instance, arts. 7(1) and (4) Morocco-Nigeria BIT or art. 7(2) ECOWAS Supplementary Act pursue this approach. Yet, this reference is hardly useful to clarify the meaning of FET because these standards are equally uncertain and provide the same wide margin of discretion to arbitral tribunals as the term FET itself.[209]

Strikingly, none of the reformed IIAs directly addresses the relationship between the legitimate expectations of investors in a stable legal framework and host states' right to regulate. While some reformed African IIAs contain clauses on the host

[204]See Jennings and Watts (1992), p. 904.

[205]SADC Model BIT Template (2012), art. 5, option 2.

[206]SADC Investment Protocol Amendment (2017) art. 7; ECOWAS Supplementary Act (2008), art. 19.

[207]See UN 2030 Agenda, SDG 16.

[208]SADC Model BIT Template (2012), art. 5, option 1, para. 5.2.

[209]See for a general discussion UNCTAD (2012b), p. 22 and p. 28.

state's right to adopt environmental and social standards,[210] or on investor obligations to contribute to sustainable development,[211] their FET clauses lack references to these provisions. If an explicit link were included in the FET provisions, arbitral tribunals would have clear guidance on how to assess the investor's legitimate expectations in case of a host state sustainability measure. Likewise, the substantive standards for sustainability measures established in some IIAs by reference to international environmental or labor agreements[212] could provide guidance on host state measures an investor must legitimately expect. Not addressing these questions at all is definitely a critical gap in the reformed African IIAs.

As a result, the best alternative to reform the FET rules is to keep the FET standard in a modified form. The FET standard contains elements that are not only beneficial for foreign investors but also for the sustainable development of host states and their citizens as a whole. These elements include the principles of the rule of law, fair administration, transparency, and good faith conduct of host states. In addition, it is advisable to expressly regulate whether and under what conditions the FET standard protects the legitimate expectations of foreign investors to ensure that the FET standard does not impede the sustainability policies of host states. Moreover, it is important that host states harmonize all their IIAs because otherwise regulatory differences in the IIAs may nullify IIA reform efforts, as a most-favored-nation clause in a reformed IIA can make the plain FET clauses from a traditional IIA applicable to an investment dispute under the reformed IIA.

4.4 Indemnification

A major drawback for sustainable development is the rules on indemnification in traditional IIAs. As traditional IIAs lack clear rules on determining the amount of compensation or reparation to be paid for sustainability measures amounting to a compensable expropriation, unlawful expropriation, or breach of the FET standard, host states can hardly assess the possible costs for sustainability policies.[213] Traditional IIAs typically give arbitral tribunals a wide margin of discretion to determine indemnification and do not require to take into account the purpose of regulatory measures, namely the implementation of sustainability policies, when determining the amount of indemnification. Although these shortcomings impact the adoption of sustainability measures, many reformed African IIAs still contain the traditional scarce rules on indemnification.[214] A notable example to the contrary is the China-Tanzania BIT, which contains separate provisions on compensation for

[210] Cf text accompanying n169.

[211] Cf Chapter 4.3.

[212] Cf Chapter 4.5.

[213] Cf for details Chapter 3.4.

[214] Cf e.g. Morocco-Rwanda BIT (2016), art. 4; Tanzania-United Kingdom BIT (1994), art. 5.

expropriation and on damages for breaches of IIA obligations.[215] Some reformed African IIAs, however, include specifications on the standard of indemnification, the choice of valuation methods, and reasons for mitigating or offsetting indemnification that apply to both forms of indemnification and limit the uncertainties on conceivable costs of sustainability measures.

A number of reformed African IIAs regulate the standard of compensation for expropriation in a more detailed manner than traditional IIAs. For instance, some reformed IIAs refer to adequate or appropriate compensation and equal it to the fair market value of the investment.[216] In the light of the debate on "appropriate" v "adequate" compensation in the context of the claims on permanent sovereignty over national resources in the 1960s and 1970s[217] this development is remarkable as it reflects the traditional capital-exporting state approach. Some IIAs contain further specifications for determining the fair market value that aim at limiting the amount of compensation. For instance, art. 12(1) PAIC establishes that the fair market value of the property shall exclude consequential or exemplary losses or speculative and windfall profits[218] and moral damages or loss of goodwill. Other IIAs also provide guidance on the valuation method. For instance, art. 8(2) ECOWAS Supplementary Act specifies valuation criteria to determine the fair market value that include the going concern value, the asset value including the declared tax value of tangible property, and "other criteria" as appropriate.[219] A similar provision contains art. 10 (2) Canada-Tanzania BIT. Although these rules on the standard of compensation and valuation still leave ample discretion to arbitral tribunals to determine the value of the investment, they are at least a start to address the problem of ambiguous standards.

A novel feature of many reformed African IIAs is to specify elements that mitigate or offset compensation. For instance, art. 12(2) PAIC introduces an element of proportionality and requires balancing public interest and interests of the investor affected when determining the amount of compensation. Art. 5(2) SADC Investment Protocol Amendment contains a similar provision and specifies the elements to be considered in more detail. The elements include, in addition to the fair market value, the current and past use of the property, the extent of the previous profits, the duration of the investment, or the purpose of the expropriation. As the purpose of the expropriation permits to take into account the realization of sustainable development, these provisions permit to mitigate the amount of compensation for sustainability measures. Some IIAs also contain express provisions on the mitigating

---

[215]China-Tanzania BIT (2013), arts. 6(4) and 13(7).

[216]Appropriate compensation: ECOWAS Supplementary Act (2008), art. 8(2), COMESA Investment Agreement (2007), art. 20(2); adequate compensation: PAIC (2017), art. 12(1), Morocco-Nigeria BIT (2016), art. 8(1)(c); SADC Investment Protocol Amendment (2017), art. 5(2).

[217]Cf for details on the debate Jennings and Watts (1992), p. 920; Vervey and Schrijver (1994); see also text accompanying n225.

[218]Cf *Metalclad* [122].

[219]ECOWAS Supplementary Act (2008), art. 8(2).

and offsetting effects of investor conduct. The most comprehensive rules are arts. 18 (2) and (4) ECOWAS Supplementary Act that provide the mitigating or offsetting effects of breaches of specific investor obligations; similar but less extensive rules contain art 19 SADC Model BIT Template or art 43 PAIC.[220] All these mitigation and offsetting elements constitute express door-openers for arbitral tribunals to weigh the host states' interests in the adoption of sustainability measures against the investors' interests in the protection of their property when determining the amount of compensation. In contrast to the carve-outs for regulatory measures in the rules of expropriation,[221] they avoid imposing the entire risk of regulatory measures without compensation to the investor and facilitate instead that arbitral tribunals distribute the costs of sustainability measures fairly between host states and investors.

From a doctrinal point of view, it is noteworthy that the mitigation and offsetting elements established in the ECOWAS Supplementary Act and the PAIC apply to both standards of indemnification,[222] namely the standard of compensation for lawful expropriation and the standard of reparation for breaches of the IIA.[223] Whereas it is suitable to clarify the mitigating and offsetting causes in detail for the subjective standard of reparation for breaches of IIAs, it is a new feature to include such subjective elements in the objective standard of compensation for lawful expropriation, which generally does not provide for mitigating or offsetting the value of compensation.[224] Providing for mitigating and offsetting elements and the requirement to balance host state and investor interests when calculating compensation also reminds of the debate on the standard of compensation in the 1960s and 1970s.[225] At that time, capital-exporting states strongly opposed the claims of capital-importing states to accept 'appropriate' compensation, namely a standard of less than full compensation, which would allow host states to mitigate damages in the interest of facilitating their economic development.[226] Whether this new element will be accepted by home states of foreign investors outside Africa remains to be seen. So far, IIAs with non-African states do not contain these elements. However—in the light of the criticism of IIAs worldwide—they may be a feasible option to give IIAs a more balanced content and increase their acceptability.

To conclude, reformed African IIAs pursue various approaches to provide improved interpretative guidance for arbitral tribunals on the standards of indemnification, methods of valuation and the mitigation and offsetting of indemnification.

---

[220]For details on the ECOWAS Supplementary Act and the PAIC rules see text accompanying n258ff.

[221]Cf Chapter 4.2., text accompanying n162.

[222]Cf ECOWAS Supplementary Act (2008), art. 18 (2) and (4); PAIC (2017), art. 43(1).

[223]Cf text accompanying n133ff.

[224]Cf text accompanying n138.

[225]Cf Charter on Economic Rights and Duties of States (1974) UNGA Res 3281(XXIX) art. 2(c) 1st sentence; see also Dolzer and Stevens (1995), p. 108 with further references.

[226]Cf Marboe (2017), p. 46.

Yet, most reformed IIAs still do not clearly differentiate between compensation for lawful expropriation and compensation for breaches of IIA obligations, and also the rules on valuation remain scarce. A novel feature is that some reformed IIAs require arbitral tribunals to mitigate or offset damages for sustainability measures of host states or for adverse conduct of foreign investors. These provisions improve the balance of host state rights and obligations and investor rights and obligations in IIAs. So far, however, African IIAs refining the rules on indemnification still are scarce and quite heterogeneous and do not show a systematic approach. Whether the current reforms suffice to ensure that arbitral tribunals take into account a host state's sustainable development objectives when determining compensation for sustainability measures amounting to an expropriation or in breach with IIA obligations remains to be seen.

4.5 *Novel Element: Sustainable Development*

A novel approach of reformed African IIAs is to shift the focus of the IIA from mere investment promotion and protection to reconciling investment protection and sustainable development. Many modern African IIAs include the promotion of sustainable development as an objective of IIAs. Most IIAs enshrine such language in the preamble[227] or contain an express provision that sustainable development is a treaty objective.[228] Others also integrate sustainable development in substantive provisions: For instance, art 1 Morocco-Nigeria BIT requires that investments contribute to the sustainable development of the host state to fall under the scope of application of the BIT; art 24 (1) provides that "investors and their investments should strive to make the maximum feasible contribution to the sustainable development of the host state...". Similarly, art. 22 PAIC contains an obligation of investors to contribute to sustainable development. Shifting the treaty objective to sustainable development provides guidance to arbitral tribunals to interpret IIA provisions in the light of this purpose.[229] In *Siemens v Argentina* the arbitral tribunal confirmed that the treaty had to be interpreted in the light of the object and purpose of its preamble, in this case the promotion and protection of investors.[230] If IIAs establish sustainable development as an additional goal, arbitral tribunals must take into account both objectives when interpreting IIA provisions, which induces a more balanced application of the IIAs.

[227]E.g. COMESA Investment Agreement (2007), preamble, 1st and 7th recital; Morocco-Nigeria BIT (2016), preamble; SADC Investment Protocol (2006), preamble.

[228]PAIC (2017), art. 1; SADC Model BIT Template (2012), art. 1; ECOWAS Supplementary Act (2008), art. 3.

[229]Art. 31(1) VCLT.

[230]See *Siemens AG v The Argentine Republic* (Decision on jurisdiction, 2004) ICSID Case No ARB/02/8, [81]; see also *Myers* [220f].

Thoroughly integrating sustainable development in IIAs is a fundamental element to guide arbitral tribunals to apply and interpret the IIA provisions in a sustainable development-friendly manner. However, a number of problems may limit the effectiveness of sustainable development clauses. A challenge is that the content of "sustainable development" as a concept is unclear. As the notion of sustainable development has constantly developed since its first use in 1987,[231] the details of sustainable development and the extent to which it includes environmental, social, and human rights obligations remain disputed.[232] While today many universal international environmental, labor, and human rights treaties are perceived to constitute relevant substantive standards for the achievement of sustainable development,[233] the reference to sustainable development alone without further specifications may not prove sufficient to encourage but rather prevent arbitrators from engaging with this uncertain concept. The option chosen in the Morocco-Nigeria BIT is a more effective approach: it defines environmental, social, labor and human rights obligations of investors and host states and identifies relevant treaties.[234] As the content of these treaties is more tangible than the principle of sustainable development, such reference provides clearer guidance to arbitrators and makes the application of the sustainable development standard more predictable.

Due to the vagueness of the term sustainable development, the application and interpretation of IIA rules referring to sustainable development are hard to predict. For example, art. 1 Morocco-Nigeria BIT or art. 4(4) PAIC state that investment must contribute to the sustainable development of the host state. This definition reminds of the *Salini*-test,[235] namely the requirement that an investment must contribute to the economic development of the host state to fall under the scope of application of an IIA. In practice, tribunals are, however, reluctant to assess the contribution of an investment to the economic development in a host state.[236] For instance, in *SGS v Paraguay*[237] the tribunal stated that it would be inappropriate for tribunals to assess the 'contribution to economic development' criterion of an investment ex-post. *A fortiori* tribunals may find it inappropriate to assess whether an investment contributes to the *sustainable* development of a host state. Consequently, it is unclear how the term sustainable development will impact arbitral practice. Again, to refer to international environmental, labor or human rights

[231] Cf text accompanying n64ff.

[232] For a discussion and further reference see Gehring and Newcombe (2011), p. 6; Cordonier Segger and Newcombe (2011), p. 104; Gazzini (2014), p. 930.

[233] Cf Gazzini (2014), p. 932ff.

[234] Cf Morocco-Nigeria BIT (2016), arts. 13–15, 18, 19 and 24.

[235] Cf *Salini Costruttori SpA and Italstrade SpA. v Kingdom of Morocco* (Decision on jurisdiction, 2001) ICSID Case No ARB/00/4 [52] (Salini); for details see Bischoff and Happ (2015), p. 510; see also Mbengue and Schacherer (2017), p. 434.

[236] Cf Bischoff and Happ (2015), p. 513.

[237] *SGS Société Générale de Surveillance SA v Republic of Paraguay* (Award, 2012) ICSID Case No ARB/07/29, [107] (SGS).

conventions may be the better approach to provide guidance for interpretation to arbitral tribunals.

Another concern is that reformed IIAs do not clearly establish the legal effect of a sustainable development clause on other IIA provisions, such as the clauses on expropriation, FET, or compensation. For instance, would—lacking more detailed provisions[238]—a regulatory measure pursuing a sustainable development policy *not* constitute a compensable expropriation?[239] Or, would the sustainable development objective of a regulatory measure amounting to an expropriation or breach of IIA standards rather constitute a reason to mitigate indemnification?[240] An example of an effective regulation of the impact of a sustainable development clause provides the PAIC: Following art. 43 PAIC, arbitral tribunals must take into account breaches of investor obligations, including their sustainable development obligations enshrined in art. 22 PAIC, as reasons to mitigate or offset the merits of the claim or the damages awarded. Similar rules are contained in ECOWAS Supplementary Act arts. 11ff and art. 18.[241] But if IIAs only establish the purpose of sustainable development in the preamble or a general clause without determining the legal effects of such clauses on specific IIA provisions, the application of sustainable development clauses will remain ambiguous and weak.

To conclude, sustainable development clauses in IIAs are an important step to ensure that arbitral tribunals consider sustainable development objectives of host states when applying and interpreting IIAs. However, not all sustainable development clauses in African IIAs are feasible to make the outcome of arbitral case-law relating to sustainable development better predictable for host states. To make sustainable development clauses operative and effective, IIAs must define express substantive legal obligations derived from the concept of sustainable development and specify the legal effects of these sustainable development obligations on the substantive IIA provisions. Reformed IIAs that only contain a sweeping reference to sustainable development leave ample discretion to the arbitrators to interpret the scope and effects of sustainable development and are hardly suitable to provide adequate guidance to arbitral tribunals on how to take into account sustainable development in the application and interpretation of substantive IIA provisions.

4.6 Novel Element: Investor Obligations

A unique new element in reformed African IIAs is the inclusion of investor obligations.[242] It reflects the UN 2030 Agenda's demand that private investors must

[238] Cf Chapter 4.2. text accompanying n162ff.

[239] Cf Chapter 4.2.

[240] Cf Chapter 4.3.

[241] Cf also text accompanying n257ff.

[242] Cf Mbengue and Schacherer (2017), p. 434; on investor obligations generally see Nowrot (2015).

contribute to sustainable development.[243] The aim of including investor obligations in IIAs is to address the unbalanced content of traditional IIAs, which typically contain obligations for host states and rights for investors but no corresponding host state rights or investor obligations.[244] The scope of investor obligations in African IIAs varies. For instance, the SADC Investment Protocol Amendment merely contains a basic obligation of investors to abide by the laws of the host state.[245] In contrast, the ECOWAS Supplementary Act, the Morocco-Nigeria BIT, or the PAIC enshrine a comprehensive chapter on investor obligations comprising substantive and procedural obligations for foreign investors.[246] Some instruments even provide for remedies to enforce these investor obligations.

The most inclusive set of substantive and procedural investor obligations contains the Morocco-Nigeria BIT.[247] It codifies obligations on environmental protection, labor and social standards, human rights protection, anti-corruption, and corporate governance and refers to international treaties where appropriate. To implement environmental and social standards, the BIT specifies wide-ranging pre- and post-establishment impact assessment obligations[248] and corporate governance obligations for foreign investors.[249] The provisions appear to be inspired by the ECOWAS Supplementary Act, which contains similar rules, but in a more streamlined manner than the Morocco-Nigeria BIT.[250] Slightly less comprehensive are the rules of the PAIC.[251] The detailed obligations in these IIAs provide clear guidance to foreign investors on their obligations in the host state. Moreover, they reinforce the sustainable development focus of reformed IIAs because the investor obligations complement and correspond to the host state's obligations to contribute to sustainable development.[252]

To make investor obligations effective, many African IIAs include remedies for breaches of these obligations. Some IIAs provide that breaches of investor obligations may be brought before the national courts of the host states or the home states of investors.[253] However, the provisions facilitating enforcement of investor obligations in national courts do not regulate all relevant legal questions sufficiently and

[243] UN 2030 Agenda, para 67.

[244] Cf e.g. SADC Investment Protocol Amendment (2017) preamble, 8th recital, Morocco-Nigeria BIT (2016), preamble, 6th recital; PAIC (2017), preamble, 11th recital.

[245] SADC Investment Protocol (2006), art. 10; also SADC Investment Protocol Amendment (2017) art. 8.

[246] ECOWAS Supplementary Act (2008), arts. 11ff; PAIC (2017), arts. 19ff; Morocco-Nigeria BIT (2016), arts. 13ff.

[247] Morocco-Nigeria BIT (2016), arts. 13ff.

[248] Morocco-Nigeria BIT (2016), arts. 14 and 18.

[249] Morocco-Nigeria BIT (2016), arts. 19 and 24.

[250] ECOWAS Supplementary Act (2008), arts. 11ff.

[251] PAIC (2017), arts. 19ff.

[252] Cf text accompanying n233ff.

[253] ECOWAS Supplementary Act (2008), art. 17 (host state court, civil liability for damages) and art. 29 (home state court, civil liability for damages); Morocco-Nigeria BIT (2016), art. 18.

contain some pitfalls. For instance, it is questionable, whether the home states' obligation to prosecute investors constitutes an effective remedy as it only includes an obligation to bring a case against the investor before a national court, but does not guarantee effective proceedings or an actual conviction of the investor for breaches of its IIA obligations in its home state. A problem for court proceedings in the host state may be the FET and due process obligations of an IIA that also apply to proceedings to enforce investor obligations. Therefore, shortcomings in the national court systems may induce additional ISDS claims of foreign investors against the host states and thus entail more harm than benefits for host states. In addition, the lack of fair trial in national court proceedings may entitle the home state to bring a claim against the host state under the state-to-state dispute settlement rules of IIAs.[254] To make the enforcement of investor obligations in national courts more effective, it is advisable to address these issues in more detail.

The role of investor obligations in arbitral proceedings is rarely addressed in IIAs. For instance, neither the SADC Finance and Investment Protocol nor its Amendment provide any legal consequences of breaches of investor obligations[255] in arbitration proceedings. Similarly, the Morocco-Nigeria BIT does not regulate the legal effects of such breaches in arbitral proceedings. Lacking rules on the impact of investor obligations, the consequences of violating investor obligations in investment disputes remain uncertain,[256] which severely diminishes the effect of the substantive provisions on investor obligations. To improve the effectiveness of investor obligations, it is advisable to specify the legal effects of breaches of investor obligations: Possible approaches are that the breach of investor obligations excludes protection under the IIA entirely, affects the level of acceptable interference with the investor's property or the legitimate expectations of investors,[257] mitigates claims of compensation, or entitles host states to bring counterclaims in arbitral proceedings.[258]

An example of a comprehensive regulation addressing most of these aspects is art. 18 ECOWAS Supplementary Act (2008), which establishes the relation of the investor's liability to dispute settlement: It provides how an investor's failure to comply with its obligations, if proven, shall be considered by arbitral tribunals with regard to its mitigating or offsetting effects on the merits of the claim or on the amount of compensation.[259] Moreover, host state and home state may initiate arbitral proceedings against investors to remedy such breaches.[260] Host states are also

[254]See e.g. Morocco-Nigeria BIT (2016), art. 28; for state-to-state dispute settlement in IIAs see generally Dolzer and Schreuer (2012), p. 234; Dolzer and Stevens (1995), p. 122.

[255]SADC Investment Protocol (2006), art. 8; SADC Investment Protocol Amendment (2017), art. 10.

[256]On the assessment of investor conduct in arbitral practice see Nowrot (2015), p. 1174.

[257]See also Muchlinski (2006).

[258]For a further discussion of the consequences of breaches of investor obligations see Nowrot (2015), p. 1173.

[259]ECOWAS Supplementary Act (2008), art. 18(2) and (4).

[260]ECOWAS Supplementary Act (2008), art. 18(3).

entitled to bring counterclaims in arbitral proceedings.[261] Similar but slightly less comprehensive rules are enshrined in the PAIC: Art. 43(1) requires arbitral tribunals to examine allegations of host states on breaches of investor obligations and consider their mitigating effects on the substantive claims or the amount of compensation awarded. Art. 43(2) entitles host states to bring counterclaims for damages or other relief resulting from such breaches. Both of these comprehensive regulations could serve as a viable model for other African IIAs.

To conclude, investor obligations in IIAs are a feasible approach to ensure that foreign investment contributes to the sustainable development of a host state and that the rights and obligations of investors and host states in this regard are equally balanced. Yet, so far only few modern African IIAs include such provisions. To make investor obligations effective, it is necessary to specify in detail the substantive and procedural obligations of foreign investors to ensure that their conduct complies with the needs of host states and their sustainable development policies. Moreover, it is advisable to provide for remedies to enforce investor obligations to ensure their implementation. A viable option is an enforcement in national courts, but the existing provisions require clarification to make these remedies effective. Furthermore, it is essential to clarify the legal impact of investor obligations on substantive IIA provision and indemnification to guide arbitral tribunals on how to take into account investor obligations in ISDS proceedings to ensure a predictable outcome of cases involving sustainable development questions. Art. 18 ECOWAS Supplementary Act constitutes a feasible model in this respect. Binding rules on how breaches of investor obligations relating to sustainable development mitigate or offset host state obligations on investment protection substantially contribute to promoting sustainable foreign investment.

5 Conclusion

Traditional African IIAs are a mixed blessing for the promotion of sustainable foreign investment in African host states. On the one hand, IIAs create a favorable investment climate necessary to attract foreign capital to foster sustainable development, and many of the substantive IIA standards are beneficial not only for foreign investors but for the business climate in a host state generally. On the other hand, the scarce substantive provisions in traditional IIAs do not permit host states to assess whether their sustainability measures comply with the IIA obligations or rather require to compensate foreign investors. Problematic are the rules on expropriation that do not clearly establish the difference between compensable acts of expropriation and non-compensable regulatory measures. Likewise, the FET rules do not clarify to what extent investors are protected against changes in the host state legal framework. These uncertainties are reinforced by the scarce rules on

[261] ECOWAS Supplementary Act (2008), art. 18(5).

indemnification, which do not permit to assess the potential costs of sustainability measures. As a result, traditional African IIAs do not enable African host states to foresee the legal and financial consequences of sustainability measures necessary to attain sustainable foreign investment.

The reform efforts of the African IIA landscape have resulted in several remarkable approaches to modify controversial IIA provisions and better balance the interests of investors and host states. Although the traditional pattern of IIAs remains largely unchanged, a number of critical rules have been refined to give better guidance to arbitral tribunals to duly take into account the host states' sustainable development policies in the application and interpretation of IIAs. Reform elements include a clear distinction between non-compensable regulatory measures and compensable indirect expropriation, more detailed specifications of the FET standard, or more specific rules on compensation. In addition, African reformed IIAs also use novel approaches. They redirect the purpose of IIAs from mere investment protection to the reconciliation of investment protection and sustainable development and introduce investor obligations to ensure that foreign investors contribute to the sustainable development policies of host states. These reform approaches shift the focus of IIAs to sustainable foreign investment and create a more balanced content of IIAs.

Although modern African IIAs show a number of unique features to reconcile investment protection and sustainable development, the reform process will have to continue. Many reformed IIAs do not address all controversial legal questions or do not adequately refine unclear provisions to sufficiently limit the discretion of arbitral tribunals. For instance, most reformed FET clauses do not expressly address the question of legitimate expectations of foreign investors, which leaves uncertainty to what extent host states may adopt sustainability measures without conflicting with the FET standard. Or, many IIAs still contain rules on indemnification that do not establish how arbitral tribunals must take into account the sustainable development purpose of a host state measure when determining the amount of indemnification. Another problem poses the insertion of plain sustainable development clauses in IIAs that neither specify their meaning nor their effect on other IIA provisions. Likewise, investor obligations frequently lack the specification of their impact on the substantive IIA obligations of host states or on determining indemnification. In addition, while the reform process is ongoing, refined provisions of reformed IIAs limiting the scope of discretion of arbitral tribunals may be trumped by most-favored-nation clauses that require arbitral tribunals to apply still existing traditional IIA standards. These problems may again cause unexpected interpretations in arbitral case-law that adversely affect the sustainability policies of host states.

In sum, the African way to reform IIAs is a promising answer to the criticism of the adverse impacts of IIAs on sustainable development. The reformed African IIAs contain a number of novel approaches to refine the content of IIAs and integrate host state interests in achieving sustainable development. They guide arbitral tribunals to consider sustainable development aspects in the application and interpretation of substantive IIA provisions and include at the same time elements to ensure that arbitral tribunals balance the interests of investors and host states. Overall, the reforms strengthen the regulatory authority of host states to adopt the sustainability policies necessary to achieve sustainable foreign investment. Whether and to what extent these reforms will influence the arbitral practice remains to be seen.

References

African Union, Linking the Agenda 2063 and the SGDs <https://au.int/agenda2063/sdgs>

African Union Commission (ed) (2015) Agenda 2063. The Africa We Want. Background Note 01 <https://au.int/sites/default/files/documents/33126-doc-01_background_note.pdf>

Agyemang AA (1988) African States and ICSID arbitration. Comp Int Law J South Afr 21:177–189

Bischoff JA, Happ R (2015) The notion of investment. In: Bungenberg M, Griebel J, Hobe S, Reinisch A (eds) International investment law. Beck, Hart, Nomos, Baden-Baden, München, Oxford, pp 495–544

Cordonier Segger M-C, Khalfan A (2004) Sustainable development law. Principles, practices & prospects. Oxford University Press, Oxford

Cordonier Segger M-C, Newcombe A (2011) An integrated agenda for sustainable development in international investment law. In: Cordonier Segger M-C, Gehring MW, Newcombe A (eds) Sustainable development in world investment law. Wolters Kluwer, Alphen an den Rijn, pp 101–142

Crawford J (2012) Brownlie's principles of public international law. Oxford University Press, Oxford

De Brabandere E (2017) Fair and equitable treatment and (full) protection and security in African investment treaties. Grotius Centre Working Paper 2017/063-IEL, Leiden

Dörr O (2018) Article 31. In: Dörr O, Schmalenbach K (eds) Vienna Convention on the Law of Treaties, 2nd edn. Springer, Heidelberg, pp 559–616

Dolzer R, Schreuer C (2012) Principles of international investment law, 2nd edn. Oxford University Press, Oxford

Dolzer R, Stevens M (1995) Bilateral investment treaties. Martinus Nijhoff Publishers, The Hague, Boston, London

Gazzini T (2010) Drawing the line between non-compensable regulatory powers and indirect expropriation of foreign investment – an economic analysis of law perspective. Manchester J Int Econ Law 7:36–51

Gazzini T (2014) Bilateral investment treaties and sustainable development. J World Invest Trade 15:929–963

Gehring M, Newcombe A (2011) An introduction to sustainable development in world investment law. In: Cordonier Segger M-C, Gehring MW, Newcombe A (eds) Sustainable development in world investment law. Wolters Kluwer, Alphen an den Rijn, pp 3–11

General Council of the World Bank, the International Finance Corporation, and the Multilateral Investment Guarantee Agency (1992) Report to the development committee on the legal framework for the treatment of foreign investment. In: World Bank Group (ed) Legal framework for the treatment of foreign investment, vol 2. The World Bank, Washington, p 7

ICSID (ed) (2017) The ICSID Caseload – Statistics Special Focus Africa (May 2017), <https://icsid.worldbank.org/en/Documents/resources/ICSID%20Web%20Stats%20Africa%20(English)%20June%202017.pdf>

ICSID (ed) (2019) The ICSID Caseload – Statistics (Issue 2019-1), <https://icsid.worldbank.org/en/Documents/resources/ICSID%20Web%20Stats%202019-1(English).pdf>

ICSID, Concluded Cases with Details, <https://icsid.worldbank.org/en/Pages/cases/ConcludedCases.aspx?status=c>

Jacob M, Schill S (2015) Fair and equitable treatment: content, practice, method. In: Bungenberg M, Griebel J, Hobe S, Reinisch A (eds) International investment law. Beck, Hart, Nomos, Baden-Baden, München, Oxford, pp 700–763

Jennings R, Watts A (1992) Oppenheim's international law, volume I peace. Longman, Harlow

Kane MM (2018) The Pan-African Investment Code: a good first step, but more is needed. Columbia FDI Perspectives No 217 <http://ccsi.columbia.edu/files/2016/10/No-217-Kane-FINAL.pdf>

Kläger R (2011a) Fair and equitable treatment in international investment law. Cambridge University Press, Cambridge

Kläger R (2011b) Fair and equitable treatment and sustainable development. In: Cordonier Segger M-C, Gehring MW, Newcombe A (eds) Sustainable development in world investment law. Wolters Kluwer, Alphen an den Rijn, pp 241–263

Le Cannu P-J (2018) Foundation and innovation: the participation of African states in the ICSID dispute resolution system. ICSID Rev – Foreign Invest Law J 33:456–500

Mann H (2013) Reconceptualizing international investment law: its role in sustainable development. Lewis Clark Law Rev 17:521–544

Marboe I (2006) Compensation and damages in international law. The limits of "fair market value". J World Invest Trade 7:723–759

Marboe I (2015) The system of reparation and questions of terminology. In: Bungenberg M, Griebel J, Hobe S, Reinisch A (eds) International investment law. Beck, Hart, Nomos, Baden-Baden, München, Oxford, pp 1031–1044

Marboe I (2017) Calculation of compensation and damages in international investment law, 2nd edn. Oxford University Press, Oxford

Mbengue MM, Schacherer S (2017) The "Africanization" of international investment law: the Pan-African Investment Code and the reform of the international investment regime. J World Invest Trade 18:414–448

Mbengue MM, Schacherer S (2018) Africa and the rethinking of international investment law. About the elaboration of the Pan-African Investment Code. In: Roberts A, Stephan PB, Verdies PH, Versteeg M (eds) Comparative international law. Oxford Universtity Press, Oxford

Muchlinski P (2006) Caveat investor? The relevance of investor conduct under the fair and equitable treatment standard. Int Comp Law Q 55:527–557

Newcombe A (2005) The boundaries of regulatory expropriation in international law. ICSID Rev - Foreign Invest Law J 20:1–57

Newcombe A, Paradell L (2009) Law and practice of investment treaties: standards of treatment. Wolters Kluwer, Austin, Boston, Chicago, New York, The Netherlands

Nowrot K (2015) Obligations of investors. In: Bungenberg M, Griebel J, Hobe S, Reinisch A (eds) International investment law. Beck, Hart, Nomos, Baden-Baden, München, Oxford, pp 1154–1185

Ratner SR (2017) Compensation for expropriations in a world of investment treaties: beyond the lawful/unlawful distinction. Am J Int Law 111:7–56

Salacuse JW (2013) The three laws of international investment. Oxford University Press, Oxford

Salacuse JW (2015) The law of investment treaties, 2nd edn. Oxford University Press, Oxford

Sauvant KP, Mann H (2017) Towards an indicative list of FDI sustainability characteristics. International Center for Trade and Development, World Economic Forum, Geneva

Schreuer C (2010) Fair and equitable treatment. In: Hoffmann AK (ed) Protection of foreign investment through modern treaty arbitration: diversity and harmonization. Association Suisse de l'Arbitrage, Geneva, pp 125–135

Spears SA (2010) The quest for policy space in a new generation of international investment agreements. J Int Econ Law 13:1037–1075

Titi A (2014) The right to regulate in international investment law. Nomos, Baden-Baden

Traidcraft (ed) (2015) International investment agreements under scrutiny: bilateral investment treaties, EU investment policy and international development. Traidcraft, Gateshead

UN Economic Commission for Africa (UNECA) (2016) Investment policies and bilateral investment treaties in Africa: implications for regional integration. Economic Commission for Africa, Addis Ababa

UNCTAD (2015) World Investment Report 2015. UNCTAD/WIR/2015. UNCTAD, New York, Geneva

UNCTAD (2019) World Investment Report 2019. UNCTAD/WIR/2019. UNCTAD, New York, Geneva

UNCTAD (ed) (2012a) Expropriation, UNCTAD Series on Issues in International Investment Agreements II. United Nations, New York, Geneva

UNCTAD (ed) (2012b) Fair and equitable treatment, UNCTAD Series on Issues in International Investment Agreements II. United Nations, New York, Geneva

UNCTAD, Investment Policy Hub, <https://investmentpolicy.unctad.org/international-investment-agreements>

UNCTC (ed) (1988) Bilateral investment treaties. Graham and Trotman, London, Dordrecht, Boston

Vervey WD, Schrijver NJ (1994) The taking of foreign property under international law: a new legal perspective? Neth Yearb Int Law 15:3–96

Zagel GM (2020) Achieving sustainable development objectives in international investment law. In: Chaisse J, Choukroune L, Jusoh S (eds) Handbook of international investment law and policy. Springer, Singapore

International Investment Agreements

Accord entre le Gouvernement du Royaume du Maroc et le Gouvernement de la République Gabonaise portant sur la promotion et la protection réciproques des investissements (signed 21 June 2004, entered into force 27 July 2009) (Morocco-Gabon BIT (2004))

African Union Draft Pan-African Investment Code (adopted in Addis Ababa 31 March- 2 April 2016, revised December 2016) ECOSOC Doc E/ECA/CM/50/1/AU/STC/FMEPI/MIN/1(III) (8 February 2017) (PAIC (2017))

Agreement between the Government of Canada and the Government of the United Republic of Tanzania for the promotion and reciprocal protection of investments (signed 17 May 2013, entered into force 9 December 2013) (Canada-Tanzania BIT (2013))

Agreement between the Government of the Federal Democratic Republic of Ethiopia and the Government of the People's Republic of China concerning the encouragement and reciprocal protection of investments (signed 11 May 1998, entered into force 1 May 2000) (China-Ethiopia BIT (1998))

Agreement between the Government of the People's Republic of China and the Government of the United Republic of Tanzania governing the promotion and reciprocal protection of investments (signed 24 March 2013, entered into force 17 April 2014) (China-Tanzania BIT (2013))

Agreement between the Government of the Republic of Rwanda and the Government Kingdom of Morocco on the reciprocal promotion and protection of investments (signed 19 October 2016, not in force) art. 4(1) (Morocco-Rwanda BIT (2016))

Agreement between the Government of the United Kingdom of Great Britain and Northern Ireland and the Government of the United Republic of Tanzania for the promotion and protection of investments (signed 7 January 1994, entered into force 2 August 1996) (Tanzania-United Kingdom BIT (1994))

Agreement between the Government of the United Republic of Tanzania and the Government of the Kingdom of Denmark concerning the promotion of reciprocal protection of investments (signed 22 April 1999, entered into force 21 October 2005) (Denmark-Tanzania BIT (1999))

Agreement between the Government of the United Republic of Tanzania and the Government of the Kingdom of Sweden on the promotion and reciprocal protection of investments (signed 1 September 1999, entered into force 1 March 2002) (Sweden-Tanzania BIT (1999))

Agreement for the promotion and reciprocal protection of investments between the Government of the Republic of Mauritius and the Government of the Republic of Rwanda (signed 30 July 2001, not in force)

East African Community Model Investment Treaty (February 2016) <https://www.eac.int/documents/category/investment-promotion-private-sector-development> (EAC Model Investment Treaty 2016)

ECOWAS Supplementary Act A/SA.3/12/08 adopting community rules on investment and the modalities for their implementation with Economic Community of West African States (ECOWAS) (signed 12 December 2008, entered into force 19 January 2009) (ECOWAS Supplementary Act (2008))

Investment Agreement for the Common Market for Eastern and Southern Africa (COMESA) Common Investment Area (signed 23 May 2007, not in force) <https://investmentpolicy.unctad.org/international-investment-agreements/treaty-files/3092/download> (COMESA Investment Agreement)

Investment Cooperation and Facilitation Agreement between the Federative Republic of Brazil and the Republic of Malawi (signed 24 June 2015, not in force) (Brazil-Malawi BIT 2015)

Reciprocal Investment Promotion and Protection Agreement between the Government of the Kingdom of Morocco and the Government of the Federal Republic of Nigeria (signed 3 December 2016, not in force) (Morocco-Nigeria BIT (2016))

SADC Model Bilateral Investment Treaty Template (SADC 2012) <http://www.iisd.org/itn/wp-content/uploads/2012/10/SADC-Model-BIT-Template-Final.pdf> (SADC Model BIT Template (2012))

SADC Protocol on Finance and Investment (signed 18 August 2006, entered into force 16 April 2010) <https://www.sadc.int/documents-publications/show/Protocol_on_Finance__Investment2006.pdf> (SADC Investment Protocol)

South African Development Community (SADC) Amendment 2016 to the SADC Protocol on Finance and Investment (2006) (signed 17 May 2017, not in force) <https://www.sadc.int/documents-publications/show/4999> (SACD Investment Protocol Amendment (2017))

Traité entre la République fédérale d'Allemagne et le République Togolaise relative àl'encouragement des investissements de capitaux (signed 16 May 1961, in force 21 December 1964) <https://investmentpolicy.unctad.org/international-investment-agreements/treaty-files/1432/download> (Germany-Togo BIT (1961))

Treaty between the United States of America and the Argentine Republic concerning the reciprocal encouragement and protection of investment (signed 14 November 1991, entered into force 20 October 1994) (Argentina-US BIT (1991))

Treaty between the United States of America and the Republic of Mozambique concerning the encouragement and reciprocal protection of investment (signed 1 December 1998, in force 3 March 2005) (Mozambique-USA BIT (1998))

Case-Law

ADC Affiliate Limited and ADC & ADMC Management Limited v Republic of Hungary (Award, 2006) ICSID Case No ARB/03/16 (ADC)

Azurix Corp v The Argentine Republic (I) (Award, 2006) ICSID Case No ARB/01/12 (Azurix)

Biloune and Marine Drive Complex Ltd v Ghana Investments Centre and the Government of Ghana (Ad-hoc Award on jurisdiction and liability of October 27, 1989 and Ad-hoc Award on Damages and Costs of June 30, 1990) ILR 95:183-232 (Biloune)

Biwater Gauff (Tanzania) Limited v United Republic of Tanzania (Award, 2008) ICSID Case No ARB/05/22 (Biwater)

CMS Gas Transmission Company v The Argentine Republic (Award, 2005) ICSID Case No ARB/01/8 (CMS)

Compañía de Aguas del Aconquija SA and Vivendi Universal SA (formerly Compañía de Aguas del Aconquija, SA and Compagnie Générale des Eaux) v Argentine Republic (I) (Award II, 2007) ICSID Case No ARB/97/3 (Vivendi I)

Compañia del Desarrollo de Santa Elena SA v Republic of Costa Rica (Award, 2000) ICSID Case No ARB/96/1 (Sta Elena)

Continental Casualty Company v Argentine Republic (Award, 2008) ICSID Case No ARB/03/9 (Continental Casualty)

Cortec Mining Kenya Limited, Cortec (Pty) Limited and Stirling Capital Limited v Republic of Kenya (Award, 2018) ICSID Case No ARB/15/29 (Cortec)

El Paso Energy International Company v Argentine Republic (Award, 2011) ICSID Case No ARB/03/15) (El Paso)

Marvin Roy Feldman Karpa v United Mexican States (Award, 2002) ICSID Case No ARB(AF)/99/1 (Feldman)

Metalclad Corporation v The United Mexican States (Award, 2000) ICSID Case No ARB(AF)/97/1 (Metalclad)

Methanex Corporation v United States of America (Final Award on jurisdiction and merits, 3 August 2005) UNCITRAL <https://www.italaw.com/cases/683> (Methanex)

Occidental Exploration and Production Company v Republic of Ecuador (I) (Award, 2004) LCIA Case No UN3467 (Occidental)

PSEG Global Inc and Konya Ilgin Elektrik Üretim ve Ticaret Limited Sirketi v Republic of Turkey (Award, 2007) ICSID Case No ARB/02/5 (PSEG)

S D Myers, Inc v Government of Canada (1st Partial Award (merits), 13 November 2000) UNCITRAL <https://www.italaw.com/cases/969> (Myers)

Salini Costruttori SpA and Italstrade SpA. v Kingdom of Morocco (Decision on jurisdiction, 2001) ICSID Case No ARB/00/4 (Salini)

Saluka Investments BV v The Czech Republic (Partial Award, 17 March 2006) UNCITRAL, <https://www.italaw.com/cases/961> (Saluka)

Sempra Energy International v Argentine Republic (Award, 2007) ICSID Case No ARB/02/16 (Sempra)

SGS Société Générale de Surveillance SA v Republic of Paraguay (Award, 2012) ICSID Case No ARB/07/29 (SGS)

Siemens AG v The Argentine Republic (Decision on jurisdiction, 2004) ICSID Case No ARB/02/8 (Siemens)

Suez, Sociedad General de Aguas de Barcelona, SA and Interagua Servicios Integrales de Agua, SA v Argentine Republic (Decision on liability, 2010) ICSID Case No ARB/03/17 (Suez)

Técnicas Medioambientales Tecmed v United Mexican States (Award, 2003) ICSID Case No ARB (AF)/00/2 (Tecmed)

Total SA v Argentine Republic (Decision on liability, 2010) ICSID Case No ARB/04/1 (Total)

Unión Fenosa Gas, S.A. v Arab Republic of Egypt (Award, 2018) ICSID Case No. ARB/14/4 (UFG)

Urbaser SA and Consorcio de Aguas Bilbao Biskaia, Bilbao Biskaia Ur Partzuergoa v Argentine Republic (Award, 2016) ICSID Case No. ARB/07/26 (Urbaser)

Veolia Propreté v Arab Republic of Egypt (Award, 2018) ICSID Case No ARB/12/15 (Veolia)

Other Documents

African Society of International Law, AfSIL Principles on Foreign Investment (adopted on 28-28 October 2016 at the 5th Annual Conference of the AfSIL in Accra, Ghana) <https://www.unil.ch/investmentafrica/files/live/sites/investmentafrica/files/Events/AfSIL%2028-29.10.2016/2016%20AFSIL%20Principles%20Investment.pdf> (AfSIL Principles (2016))

African Union Commission, Agenda 2063: The Africa We Want (April 2015), <http://www.un.org/en/africa/osaa/pdf/au/agenda2063.pdf> (AU Agenda 2063 (2015))

African Union Commission, Agenda 2063, First Ten-Year Implementation Plan 2014-2023 (September 2015) <https://au.int/sites/default/files/documents/33126-doc-ten_year_implementation_book.pdf>

African Union, Common African Position on the Post-2015 Development Agenda, March 2014, <https://www.un.org/en/africa/osaa/pdf/pubs/2014cappost2015.pdf> (AU Common African Position (2014))

Articles on Responsibility of States for Internationally Wrongful Acts (2001), UNGA Res A/RES/56/83, Annex (ASR)

Charter on Economic Rights and Duties of States (1974) UNGA Res 3281(XXIX) (CERDS 1974)

Comprehensive Trade and Economic Agreement between Canada and the European Union, 30 October 2016, OJ L11/23 of 14 January 2017 (CETA 2016)

Convention on the Settlement of Investment Disputes between States and Nationals of Other States (signed 18 March 1965, entered into force 14 October 1966) 575 UNTS 159 (ICSID Convention 1965)

Council of the European Union, Council Decision Authorizing the Opening of Negotiations with the United States of America for an Agreement on the Elimination of Tariffs for Industrial Goods, 6052/19, 9 April 2019

Declaration on Permanent Sovereignty over Natural Resources (1962), UNGA Res 1803 (XVII) (PSNR 1962)

Energy Charter Treaty (concluded 17 December 1994, entered into force 16 April 1998) 2080 UNTS 95 (Energy Charter Treaty 1994)

North American Free Trade Agreement, 17 December 1992, 32 ILM 289 (1993) (NAFTA 1992)

Opinion 1/17, Opinion of Advocate General Bot, 29 January 2019, ECLI:EU:C:2019:72

Report of the World Commission on Environment and Development, Our Common Future (1987) UNGA Doc A/42/427

The Factory at Chorzów (Claim for Indemnity) (The Merits), Germany v Poland (Judgment, 1929) 1928 PCIJ (Ser A) No 17 (Chorzów Factory)

UN, Addis Ababa Action Agenda of the Third International Conference on Financing for Development (13-16 July 2015), <http://www.un.org/esa/ffd/wp-content/uploads/2015/08/AAAA_Outcome.pdf> (UN Addis Ababa Action Agenda (2015))

UN General Assembly, Rio Declaration on Environment and Development (1992) A/CONF.151/26 (Vol. I)

UN General Assembly, Transforming our World, The 2030 Agenda for Sustainable Development (2015) UNGA Res A/Res/70/1 (UN 2030 Agenda (2015))

UN General Assembly, Rio+20 Declaration "The Future We Want" (2012) A/RES/66/288

Vienna Convention on the Law of Treaties (signed 23 May 1969, entered into force 27 January 1980) 1155 UNTS 331 (VCLT)

World Bank (1992) Guidelines on the Treatment of Foreign Investment. In: World Bank Group, Legal Framework for the Treatment of Foreign Investment, Volume 2. The World Bank, Washington, p 33

The African Continental Free Trade Area (AfCFTA) and the Imperative of Democratic Legitimacy: An Analysis

Babatunde Fagbayibo

Contents

1 Introduction

The adoption of the Agreement Establishing the African Continental Free Trade Area (AfCFTA) on 21 March 2018 at the extraordinary African Union (AU) summit in Kigali, Rwanda continue to receive overwhelming support across the continent. If properly implemented, the projection is that the AfCFTA will be the largest free trade arrangement in the world, increase intra-African trade by 52% by 2022, thereby stimulating Africa's economic development and global positioning.[1] The number of countries that have thus far adopted the agreement further match this positive outlook. The AfCFTA Agreement has entered into force. As at the time of writing,

This article is an expanded version of an op-ed that first appeared on the AfronomicsLaw Blog: Fagbayibo B (2019) A case for democratic legitimacy of the AfCFTA process. AfronomicsLaw Blog. Available via http://www.afronomicslaw.org/2019/01/16/a-case-for-democratic-legitimacy-of-the-afcfta-process/.

[1]UNECA and AUC (2018).

B. Fagbayibo (✉)
College of Law, University of South Africa, Pretoria, South Africa
e-mail: fagbabo@unisa.ac.za

C. Eboe-Osuji et al. (eds.), *Nigerian Yearbook of International Law 2018/2019*,
Nigerian Yearbook of International Law 2018/2019,
https://doi.org/10.1007/978-3-030-69594-1_17

the Agreement has been ratified by 36 member states (54 countries have already signed the Agreement, with Eritrea been the only African country that is yet to sign) and became operational in January 2021.[2]

While the economic benefits of implementing the AfCFTA remain a key discursive focus, there exists very little consideration of the role of democracy within its operational context. Put differently, the question that has not been fully conceptualised is how democratic elements such as inclusivity, openness and genuine participation of civil society should shape member states' engagement in AfCFTA activities at both the national and transnational levels. As the United Nations Economic Commission for Africa (UNECA) rightly noted, the AfCFTA process should 'recognise the importance of . . . democracy, human rights, and the rule of law'.[3] While Article 3(e) of the 'Agreement Establishing the AfCFTA',[4] makes reference to 'sustainable and inclusive socio-economic development, gender equality' little has been done in terms of providing further articulation regarding the institutional and normative framings for achieving this. In other words, the Agreement, including its annexes, makes no further attempt to provide institutional and normative expression of how to organise its objectives around democratic principles.

Although some may argue that the Agreement be interpreted within the context of existing AU normative frameworks on democracy and human rights, such exclusion still speaks to the prevalent breach of such principles in practise. This is, however, not to say the mere inclusion of the principles of democracy will automatically amount to its practise. Rather, the idea of stipulating such principles provide both symbolic and practical imperatives for setting realisable parameters for application. In other words, it provides clear and objective standards for assessing the actions of member states in implementing AfCFTA.

The importance of centering democratic norms in the implementation of the AfCFTA cannot be under-emphasised. As shown in the Nigerian case, lack of consultation with broader civil society can prove to be an obstacle. Despite Nigeria's active involvement in the negotiations and drafting of the AfCFTA Agreement, the government made a last minute decision not to sign the Agreement as a result of pressure from stakeholders such as the Nigerian Labour Congress (NLC) and the Manufacturing Association of Nigeria (MAN).[5] The Nigerian president, Muhammadu Buhari, later released a statement citing the need to engage in more domestic sensitisation and consultation before signing the Agreement.[6] Had such process preceded the plan to sign the Agreement, the Nigerian government would not have been entangled in an avoidable embarrassing diplomatic situation. Another factor that points to the imperative of democratic norms in the AfCFTA operational

[2]AU (2019).

[3]UNECA (2017), p. 32. See also, Arts 3 and 4 of the AU Constitutive Act (AU 2000).

[4]AfCFTA Agreement (2018a).

[5]Aremu (2018).

[6]Ibid. Nigeria finally signed the AfCFTA Agreement on the 7th of July 2019. The Nigerian parliament has ratified the document.

matrix is that the independence and quality of national institutions such as the judiciary, parliamentary and technocratic agencies are central to ensuring that citizens meaningfully benefit from the AfCFTA arrangement. In the same vein, the choices regarding tariff and non-tariff barriers are bound to affect citizens in multi-dimensional ways, and as such accord them the right to engage.

This article aims to make a case for enhancing the democratic legitimacy of the AfCFTA. Using existing AU normative frameworks as a guideline, this article argues for a policy mechanism that binds member states to measures that provide for a meaningful participatory, agenda-setting environment. The article is organised as follows. It starts with an overview of the Agreement Establishing the AfCFTA. It then engages in a normative discussion of the nexus between the AfCFTA and the principles of democracy. It concludes with the consideration of specific measures necessary for centralising democratic practise in the operationalisation of the AfCFTA.

2 An Overview of the Agreement Establishing the AfCFTA

The politico-legal journey towards the adoption of the Agreement Establishing the AfCFTA started in 2012, when the 18th Ordinary Session of the Assembly of Heads of State and Government of the AU adopted the decision to create a Continental Free Trade Area by 2017.[7] In pursuant of this decision, the summit further adopted the 'Action Plan on Boosting Intra-African Trade (BIAT)', which identified seven policy clusters for achieving meaningful trade integration.[8] These include: trade facilitation, trade policy, productive capacities, trade related infrastructure, trade finance, trade information and factor market integration.[9]

Negotiations around the details to be included in the final agreement commenced at the 25th Ordinary Summit of Head of States and Governments in Johannesburg, South Africa in June 2015.[10] Between 2015 and early March 2018, just before the Agreement was adopted, the negotiating forum had met 10 times to discuss the technical details of AfCFTA.[11] The negotiations are divided into phases. The first phase, which is now largely completed, was devoted to addressing issues such dispute settlement mechanism, rules of origin, phasing out 90% tariffs on goods, and the elimination of non-tariff barriers.[12] The second phase of the negotiations, which commenced in late 2018 and was expected to be finalised by January 2020,

---

[7]AU (2012a), pp. 1–2.

[8]AU (2012b).

[9]Ibid.

[10]AU (2015).

[11]UNECA and AUC (2018), p. 5.

[12]Ibid. However, there are still some outstanding issues from the first phase. This includes rules of origin and the regulation of services.

focuses on investment, competition and intellectual property rights, and a possible inclusion of e-commerce facilities.[13]

The Agreement Establishing the AfCFTA was adopted on the 21st of March 2018 at the extraordinary African Union (AU) summit in Kigali, Rwanda, alongside the Protocol to the Treaty Establishing the African Economic Community relating to the Free Movement of Persons, Right to Residence and Right to Establishment, which further reinforced the understanding that free movement is an indispensable component of free trade. The AfCFTA Agreement stipulated the objectives, principles, and the institutional framework.

Articles 3 and 4 of the Agreement deals with the general and specific objectives of AfCFTA. The general objectives of the AfCFTA include the creation of a single market for goods, services and free movement of persons; the establishment of a Continental Customs Union; inclusive socio-economic development that encompasses gender equality and structural transformation; enhanced competitiveness and industrial development of African economies.[14] The specific objectives speak to issues such as the progressive elimination of tariffs and non-tariff barriers; cooperation on trade and services related matters; establishment of dispute settlement mechanisms; cooperation on custom matters, investment, intellectual property rights and competition policy; and establishment and sustainability of the institutional and implementation structures of the AfCFTA.[15] The Agreement identifies the following as the governing principles of the AfCFTA: central driving role of member states, Regional Economic Communities' (RECs) FTA as building blocs, differentiated integration approach, consensus decision-making process,[16] transparency measures, and Most-Favoured-Nation (MFN) treatment.[17] It is important to emphasise that civil society is excluded from the list of drivers of AfCFTA, thereby reinforcing the state-centric conception of the idea.

In terms of the institutional and implementation framework, the Agreement identified the following structures as drivers of the AfCFTA: the AU Assembly, Council of Ministers, Committee of Senior Trade officials and the Secretariat.[18] In addition to these are other bodies that are expected to assist in ensuring the effective implementation of specific AfCFTA issues. These include: Committee for Trade in Services, Committee for Trade in Goods, AU Sub-Committee of the Directors

---

[13]Ibid. See also AfCFTA Agreement, Article 7. In February 2020, the AU Assembly adopted the decision to commence the negotiations of the third phase of AfCFTA Agreement.

[14]AfCFTA Agreement, Article 3.

[15]Ibid., Article 4.

[16]According to Article 14, decisions on substantive issues shall be taken by consensus while decisions on procedural issues will be decided based on a simple majority vote by eligible member states. In terms of Article 15, a decision of waiver of obligations of a state party concerning the Agreement can be taken three-fourths of member states. The rule of consensus strictly locates the AfCFTA within an intergovernmental framework, instead of a supranational process that would have allowed for a majority voting system on substantive issues.

[17]AfCFTA Agreement, Article 5.

[18]Ibid., Article 9.

General of Customs, Sub-Committee on Trade Facilitation, Committee on Rules of Origin, Committee for Technical Barriers to Trade, Committee for Non-Tariff Barriers, Committee on Trade Remedies, Committee on Sanitary and Phytosanitary Measures, and Dispute Settlement Body.[19] According to Article 20 of the AfCFTA Agreement, the envisaged Dispute Settlement Body shall only have jurisdiction to hear matters between state parties.

The AU Assembly is the highest decision-making body of AfCFTA, and is expected to provide strategic guidance and oversight of the AfCFTA.[20] The Council of Ministers (responsible for trade or any other designated ministries in member states) reports to the Assembly and is responsible for providing strategic policy directions relating implementation and enforcement of the AfCFTA.[21] The Committee of Senior Trade officials is responsible for implementing the decisions of the Council of Ministers and the monitoring and evaluation of the functioning of the AfCFTA.[22] The Secretariat is an autonomous body with an independent legal personality that will be established by the Assembly and allocated specific functions by the Council of Ministers.[23] The Secretariat will operate separately from the AU Commission.[24]

At the core of the institutional and implementation structure of the AfCFTA is the intergovernmental approach. In this respect, three key intergovernmental organs, the Assembly, the Council of Ministers and the Committee of Senior Trade Officials, hold the supreme political and legislative decision-making powers. These organs are politically interlocked entities, with the Assembly having the final say on all matters.[25] Furthermore, the Agreement explicitly stipulates that the decisions on substantive issues relating to the AfCFTA will be taken by consensus.[26] This is in tandem with the overall institutional philosophy of the AU, one which prioritises the role of member states over supranational bodies and decision-making mechanisms.[27] Ansong, however, argues that the provision for variable geometry under Article 5 (c) of the Agreement could serve as a window of opportunity for member states to experiment with supranational decision-making mechanisms.[28] The idea behind this is that member states that wish to deepen AfCFTA process at a much faster pace can proceed as a collective.[29] Fasan notes that variable geometry could hamper the

---

[19] See Compiled AfCFTA Annexes (2018b).

[20] AfCFTA Agreement, Article 10.

[21] Ibid., Article 11.

[22] Ibid., Article 12.

[23] Ibid., Article 13.

[24] Ibid., Article 13(4). Ghana hosts the AfCFTA Secretariat. In February 2020, Wamkele Mene was elected as the first secretary-general of the AfCFTA Secretariat.

[25] According to Article 6(2) of the AU Constitutive Act (2000), the AU Assembly is the supreme decision-making organ of the AU. It can, however, delegate its functions to other organs of the AU.

[26] AfCFTA Agreement, Article 14.

[27] See e.g. Fagbayibo (2013), pp. 414–415.

[28] Ansong (2018), p. 5.

[29] Ibid. See also, Fagbayibo (2016), pp. 166–167.

creation of an African single market as its application conflicts with the aim of member states operating at the same levels of obligation and implementation of objectives.[30]

Furthermore, the Agreement limits the scope of civil society involvement through a number of mechanisms. One is the stipulation regarding the limitation of the jurisdiction of the dispute settlement body to state parties.[31] This position curtails civil society participation in a number of ways. Firstly, states are likely to prioritise a diplomatic route or adopt self-help measures in resolving trade disputes rather than dragging it before a transnational dispute settlement body.[32] In addition, the politics of regionalism in Africa, which tends to bend towards regime boosting and solidarity among leaders, would most likely ensure that member states view the body as antithetical to standard state-centric practises.

Another way in which this limits the participation of civil society is that the Agreement makes no provision for the involvement of domestic courts in the juridical operational context of AfCFTA. By elaborating the subsidiarity or complementary role of domestic courts in relation to the dispute settlement body, or even the creation of an 'ad-hoc trade chamber' within the African Court of Justice and Human Rights (ACJ&HR),[33] individuals and civil society would be given the space to shape the legal discourse of the AfCFTA. The idea of individual access to regional courts in Africa is not a new one. Regional courts such as the East African Court of Justice (EACJ), the Common Market for Eastern and Southern Africa (COMESA) Court of Justice, and the Economic Community of West African States (ECOWAS) Community Court of Justice all provide for varying degrees of individual access.[34] Both EACJ and ECOWAS CCJ allow for individual access without the need for the exhaustion of local remedies.[35] As Oppong rightly noted, individual access to regional courts enhances its legitimacy by ensuring consistency of support from national courts.[36]

It remains to be seen whether AU member states will still maintain a state-to-state dispute settlement system upon the adoption of the envisaged AfCFTA investment protocol, as investment disputes mostly involve individuals. While the AfCFTA investment protocol is yet to be finalised, the Pan African Investment Code (PAIC), although it is not a binding instrument, provides some indication regarding AU's approach to investor-state dispute.[37] Article 42(1) of the PAIC stipulates that the resolution of investor-state dispute will be governed by applicable domestic laws.

---

[30] Fasan (2019).

[31] AfCFTA Agreement, Article 20.

[32] Ansong (2018), p. 6; Gathii (2019); Akinkugbe (2019).

[33] Coefelice (2018), p. 34.

[34] Art. 30 of the EAC Treaty, Article 26 of the COMESA Treaty, ECOWAS Supplementary Protocol A/SP.1/01/05, Art. 4 (ECOWAS 2005).

[35] Oppong (2014), p. 73.

[36] Ibid.

[37] AU (2016).

According to Ngobeni, this reflects the lack of agreement among AU member state on the issue of investor-state dispute, and this is likely going to be the position the envisaged AfCFTA investment protocol will take.[38] This attitude is in line with recent trend in African countries to move away from investor-state dispute settlement to state-state arbitration.[39]

Lastly, the exclusion of the Pan-African Parliament (PAP) from the institutional structure of the AfCFTA, and the unwillingness to endow it with binding legislative powers, largely reduces the participation of civil society and the democratic oversight over its activities. A PAP with full legislative powers, and directly elected parliamentarians, could serve as a platform for civil society actors to influence the monitoring and evaluation processes of the AfCFTA. In this regard, civil society can be involved in influencing the law-making activities around the regulation of institutional and normative measures, particularly the need for an accountable AfCFTA process. In this context, a powerful PAP will be operating outside the curtailing influence of national executive dominance and rather be accountable to the AU Constitutive Act and a continental configuration that spreads political action and accountability beyond the national milieu.

3 The AfCFTA-Democracy Nexus

3.1 The State of Democracy in Africa

Any discussion on AfCFTA's democracy deficit has to start from a much broader consideration of the general state of democracy on the continent. This analytical viewpoint derives from the simple understanding that AfCFTA's democratic, or lack thereof, DNA cannot exist outside of the variables shaping democratisation across the continent. This position is further reinforced by the understanding that national institutions will have to play a significant part in the implementation of many of AfCFTA's obligation. It thus goes without saying that the strength of these institutions, be it in their legal and political forms, corresponds with the effectiveness to carry out such obligations. As such, it is pertinent to understand how the state of democracy in member states enhances or impedes institutional effectiveness.

In surveys, and through demonstrated actions, majority of Africans continue to show their preference for multi-party democracy and the rule of law.[40] In recent years, the continent has witnessed mass movement, mainly with the help of the military, in places like Burkina Faso, Zimbabwe, Tunisia, Egypt, Algeria and Sudan to force out autocratic leaders.[41] In The Gambia, the regional body, the Economic

---

[38]Ngobeni (2019), pp. 8–9.

[39]Ibid., p. 8.

[40]Pelz (2018); Mattes and Bratton (2016), pp. 3–4.

[41]Pelz (2018) and Cheeseman (2019).

Community of West African States (ECOWAS), was able to push out Yahaya Jammeh when he refused to step down after losing elections to the opposition.[42] These developments have, however, not halted the growing tendency to curtail and/or manipulate democratic advancement in many African countries.[43] For example, in places like Egypt and Zimbabwe, the old order remain in charge in spite of change of power, and continue to use repressive tactics to suppress opposition voices.[44] The language of the old politico-military guards in Algeria and Sudan, after the removals of Abdelaziz Bouteflika and Omar al-Bashir respectively, is one that is still against the wishes of the masses regarding the enthronement of genuine and sustainable democracy.[45] Tunisia has, however, been able to consolidate a relatively stable democracy since the ousting of the former dicatator, Ben Ali, in 2011.[46]

Cheeseman paints a worrying picture of the state of Africa's democracy:

> Half of all African states are autocracies (36% hardline, 14% moderate), while the other half are democracies (5% consolidating, 34% defective, 11% highly defective. Between 2015 and 2017, this situation became even more stark: on the whole, the continent's autocratic countries become more repressive, while its more democratic states have seen relatively little change.[47]

Similarly, the Freedom House 2019 report shows that while there have been some reform efforts in former autocracies such as The Gambia, Ethiopia and Angola, there remains significant resistance to democratic advancement.[48] According to the report, out of 54 African countries (which included Somaliland and Western Sahara) surveyed, only 10 are considered as 'Free', 23 are 'partly free', and 21 are 'not free'.[49] A breakdown of this statistics show that in the 'Free' category, West Africa leads with 5 countries, followed by Southern Africa with 4 and North Africa with only one.[50] In the 'not free' category, East, Central and North Africa have the highest number of countries (19), followed by Southern Africa with just two countries.[51] In the 'partly free' category, West Africa leads with 10 countries, followed by Southern African (8), East Africa (3), and North and Central Africa with one country each.[52] This statistics prove that both West and Southern Africa have the most democratic nations in Africa, while North, East and Central Africa remain problematic.

---

[42]See e.g. Kaaba and Fagbayibo (2019), pp. 39–41.

[43]Cheeseman (2019), p. 5; Pelz (2018); Ibrahim Index of African Governance (2018), pp. 36–44.

[44]Ndawana (2018), pp. 133–148.

[45]Daragahi (2019) and BBC (2019).

[46]Cheeseman (2019), p. 10.

[47]Cheeseman (2019), p. 5.

[48]Freedom House (2019).

[49]Ibid.

[50]Ibid.

[51]Ibid.

[52]Ibid.

Similarly, the AU paints a worrying picture of the state of adherence to democratic values in member states:

> The continent fell significantly short of realising its targets on ensuring that democratic values and practices are the norm, realising 27% of her 2019 target. The only significant progress that was recorded was on operationalising the African Charter on Democracy – with a score based on countries that have signed and ratified the Charter achieving 98% and 87% of the 2019 target respectively. However, progress on integrating the Charter into national planning and development instruments has been slow – exhibited by the weak performance of 22% against the 2019 target. Similarly, the percentage of the African population who believe that elections are free, fair and transparent; and the proportion of the population on the continent that perceives that there is press freedom and associated freedom of speech – pitched at 26% and 13% respectively of the 2019 targets. This reflects a weak performance of the continent. Furthermore, the continent fell short by 86% of its 2019 target regarding the proportion of people who believe that there are effective mechanisms and oversight institutions to hold their leaders accountable.[53]

This negative trend in democratic development manifests itself in a number of disturbing ways. One is the increasing use of national institutions such as the parliament, judiciary and electoral management bodies to manipulate the rules governing terms of office. In countries such as Djibouti, Congo, Zambia, Rwanda, Uganda, Egypt, and Burundi, national institutions have been used to remove age restrictions, reinterpret the meaning of 'two terms', and the outright elimination of term limits so as to entrench the incumbent in office.[54] The second is the trend by a number of African countries to make laws aimed at clamping down on civil society organisations (CSOs), curtailing internet services, and the jailing of opposition voices.[55] Countries such as Ethiopia, Cameroon, Uganda, Zimbabwe, Congo, Gabon, and Burundi have at different times shut down internet services either during elections or protests by citizens.[56] Uganda, Tanzania and Egypt have passed laws that either place tax on social media usage or make online criticism of the authorities a criminal offence.[57] The third point is the extent to which continuing repression of the opposition and the manipulation of elections increases the levels and/or possibility of political instability. Post-election violence in Kenya (2008), Zimbabwe (2010 and 2018), Burundi (2015), and Gabon (2016) all exposed the fragility of these countries and the potential for large scale disruption.[58] Similarly, the unwillingness of the incumbent to step aside has in a number of cases enhanced underlining issues and pushed violent conflicts to the fore in places such as Burundi, Democratic Republic of Congo (DRC), Sudan and Cameroon.[59] Lastly is the tepid position of the

[53] AU (2020), p. 16.

[54] See e.g. Cheeseman (2019), p. 9.

[55] Ibid, p. 12.

[56] Ibid., Anna (2019).

[57] Ibid.

[58] See e.g. Kanyinga (2018), pp. 147–168.

[59] Cheeseman (2019), pp. 20–21.

AU towards the strengthening of democracy on the continent.[60] While the AU has been consistent in condemning military coups, and even suspended member states for engaging in such acts, it remains fundamentally uncritical towards deeply flawed elections and repressive tactics of incumbents in holding on to power. It rarely acts against human rights violations and large scale violence perpetuated by incumbents against civilians, and only adopts a wait-and-see approach to escalating political tensions. In addition, the AU has no policy to prevent leaders with questionable human rights records, such as Teodero Obiang Nguema, Paul Biya, Abdel Fattah el-Sisi, and Paul Kagame, from holding leadership positions and/or driving the AU integration process.[61]

3.2 *AfCFTA and the Question of Democratic Legitimacy*

The above analysis on the state of democracy in Africa largely explains the little or no attention paid to situating AfCFTA within the stated AU principles of democratic norms and values. A regime that is rooted in autocracy and repression of all national institutions and civil society cannot be expected to create a democratic window of opportunity for the same citizens to openly express their views about the ratification or non-ratification of AfCFTA. In the same vein, it cannot be expected to export democratic practises to the sub-regional and/or continental levels. As Reinold rightly puts it, member states 'tend to replicate domestic practises at the regional level'.[62]

The AU integration process is typically state-centric and elitist, allowing very little or no space for meaningful civil society participation. As such, the lack of enthusiasm regarding mandating member states to provide qualitative platform for broader civil society involvement in the AfCFTA process is not out of character. The thinking that national legislative and executive ratification of the AfCFTA equals civil society participation as they are elected representatives of the people is one that misses the point and ignores the growing tendency of 'democratic backsliding'[63] in member states.

As the Nigerian case mentioned in the foregoing shows, it is not so much about the acceptance of AfCFTA by governmental elites as it is the concerns of organised and broader civil society regarding its impact on their existential concerns. The question of how AfCFTA will impact Micro, Small and Medium Enterprises (MSMEs), free movement of persons, women informal cross border traders,

[60] Ibid., p. 13; Fagbayibo (2017).

[61] Fagbayibo (2017), pp. 166–167.

[62] Reinold (2019), p. 62.

[63] Cheeseman (2019, p. 4) describe 'democratic backsliding' as the growing tendencies by many governments in Africa to deploy legal and security measures repress the spread of social media and the increasing assertiveness of civil society and opposition parties. Regarding the weaknesses of national legislature in Africa, particularly as it relates to the overbearing influence and bullying tactics of national executives, see the following sources: Opalo (2019); Barkan (2009), pp. 1–31.

compensatory measures for losses arising from adherence to AfCFTA rules, and meaningful jobs for Africa's bulging youth population are matters that require genuine and robust participatory measures.[64] Similarly, the important role the private sector can play in providing jobs, skills, and other entrepreneurial activities makes consultation an imperative point. This point is further reinforced by the active role played by the AfroChampions Initiative, a public-private partnership jointly chaired by former president Thabo Mbeki and Aliko Dangote, in raising funds for operationalisation of the AfCFTA. In 2019, it proposed a US$1 trillion investment framework for projects such as the Djibouti to Dakar railway and the Democratic Republic of Congo's Inga Dam.[65]

Situating the AfCFTA processes within democratic norms and values fundamentally points to legitimacy. Legitimacy in this context rests on awareness of issues by the citizenry, rigorous deliberation of pros and cons, and the ownership and support from such citizens as a result of careful understanding. It is suffice to add that this requires existence of quality national institutions that are able to support and coordinate people-driven initiatives. AfCFTA's legitimacy cannot rest on the assumption that it is sufficient that elected national executive and legislature engage in binding activities without meaningful consultations. Neither can it rely on a binary conception of trade and democracy, one which prioritises derived economic gains over genuine expression of fundamental rights and values. It is this assumption of economic benefits that has become the main discursive point around the AfCFTA, with more efforts channelled towards numbers and technocratic issues. However, statistics show that democracy variables, such as the respect for the rule of law (property rights, respect of contracts and the guarantee of political freedoms), usually have positive impact on inter-regional trade.[66] Conversely, political instability negatively affects trade and investment environment.[67] According to Muhammad et al., the 2007–2008 post-election violence in Kenya resulted in negative import growth, where 'prior to the conflict, imports from Kenya were increasing by 3% per year on average, but after the conflict, imports were decreasing by 1.9% per year'.[68]

As Ebobrah rightly argued, the relationship between human rights and economic integration in Africa has become entrenched through the jurisprudence of sub-regional courts, sub-regional treaties, human rights related activities by civil society.[69] In ECOWAS, there is a relatively developed process of civil society involvement in regional integration measures. For example, the West African Civil Society Forum (WACSOF) is the umbrella network for CSOs from ECOWAS member states, and it actively participates in activities such as election monitoring,

[64]For a detailed analysis of the challenges and opportunities of AfCFTA for informal cross-border trade in Africa, see e.g. Sommer and Nshimbi (2018).

[65]Collins (2019).

[66]According to Durmaz and Kagochi (2018), p. 12.

[67]Guillaumont et al. (1999) and Muhammad et al. (2011).

[68]Muhammad et al. (2011), p. 15.

[69]Ebobrah (2013), pp. 178–179.

peace and security issues, gender, development and trade related activities.[70] As Iheduru observed, the active engagement of civil society in ECOWAS on regional trade and investment policy design and implementation can be assessed through the following prisms: contributions to industrial and investment policies and public–private partnerships in infrastructure development; the exercise of private authority in deepening financial sector integration; the framing of the norms of legal and regulatory reforms; and complication of the inter-regional relations between ECOWAS and the EU.[71] Through these processes, CSOs in ECOWAS have collaborated with the organisation in developing and implementing projects such as regional payment system, develop a common agriculture programme, establish the Ecobank Group, harmonise laws governing motor insurance, establish the West African Bar Association (WABA) as a pressure group for monitoring and advancing the implementation of regional norms, and the involvement in the European Union Economic Partnership Agreement (EPA) negotiations.[72] Unlike ECOWAS, civil society in other regional economic communities such as the East African Community (EAC) and the Southern African Development Community (SADC) remain marginalised due to the unwillingness of member states to allow them play active roles.[73] This attitude continues to play itself out at the continental level, and has resulted in the negligible consideration of the role of civil society or meaningful consultation in the AfCFTA process.

Democracy deficit is an albatross around AfCFTA's neck and could potentially detract from the expectation of mass support from African citizens. With little or no awareness around its complex operational mechanisms, its association with repressive regimes who use it as a regime boosting badge, and the short-to-medium term losses or disruptions that may arise from its initial implementation, there could be some resistance from citizens. Although the AU failed to stipulate meaningful consultation as an integral part of the negotiation process, there is still an opportunity to ensure that after it comes into force, member states are mandated to implement the AfCFTA within a more democratic context. This is the subject of the next section.

4 Concluding Observation: Towards a More Inclusive and Democratic AfCFTA

The AfCFTA is an idea that is central to building a truly integrated Africa. However, its sustainability will depend on the extent to which policy-makers are able to centre democratic values of openness, respect for fundamental rights and good governance

---

[70]Reinold (2019), p. 57. For a detailed analysis on how organised business has played a substantial role in the regional integration process in West Africa, see e.g. Iheduru (2015), pp. 910–940.

[71]Iheduru (2015), p. 917.

[72]Ibid., pp. 917–932.

[73]Reinold (2019), pp. 58–60.

within its operational context. As shown in the foregoing, the economic benefits to be realised from this initiative is prioritised over and above the democratic content. Little or no consideration is given to how democracy deficit in member states can negatively impact its momentum. Similarly, there is no serious attention given to clothing transnational institutions at the heart of its implementation with the necessary democratic legitimacy. As the requisite 22 ratifications needed for its operationalisation has been met, the task now is to invest in activities that enhances its democratic legitimacy. This will require serious commitment on the part of national and regional officials involved in negotiating the process.

The first step in this respect is the express inclusion of respect for democratic values in the Agreement. In this regard, Articles 3 (General Objectives), 4 (Specific Objectives), 5 (Principles), and 16 (Transparency) should make explicit references to the following imperatives:

(a) The stipulation in the Agreement, and other constitutive documents, that the AfCFTA derives its legitimacy from Articles 3 and 4 of the AU Constitutive Act.[74] This should be underlined by the indication of the specific AU human rights and democratic governance instruments that will guide both institutional and normative AfCFTA processes. These should include the African Charter of Human and Peoples' Rights (ACHPR), the African Charter of Democracy, Elections and Governance (ACDEG), the African Youth Charter (AYC), and the Protocol to the African Charter on Human and Peoples' Rights on the Rights of Women in Africa (the Maputo Protocol).
(b) There is the need to highlight the roles of the African Commission on Human and Peoples' Rights (African Commission), the African Peer Review Mechanism (APRM) and PAP in assessing the democratic and human rights commitment of member states to the AfCFTA process. The advantage of going this route is based on a number of factors. One is that all African countries, except for Morocco, has ratified the ACHPR. This thus gives it a continent-wide reach to influence and advance human rights elements of the AfCFTA. As such, it makes it an important continental instrument for 'gather[ing] evidence of potential human rights impacts, to influence negotiations as well as to provide a platform to civil society groups to advocate for equitable, poverty-reducing and human rights-consistent outcomes'.[75]

[74]This includes principles such as promotion of democratic principles, institutions and popular participation and governance (Article 3(g)); promotion and protection of human rights (Article 3 (h)); participation of African peoples in the activities of the AU (Article 4(c)); promotion of gender equality (Article 4(l)); and the promotion of social justice (Article 4(n)) (AU 2000).

[75]UNECA (2017), p. 37.

Although the APRM is yet to become a legal instrument,[76] it already has 38 member countries, and has done governance reviews of 17 member states.[77] In addition, the AU Assembly has extended its mandate to include the monitoring and implementation of the AU Agenda 2063, United Nations Sustainable Development Goals (SDGs) and Agenda 2030.[78] This development makes the extension of its mandate to the monitoring of the governance and democratic process of the AfCFTA in member states is a logical step. In the context of AfCFTA, the APRM should assess the quality of public institutions charged with implementing AfCFTA obligations, the availability of participatory structures at the national level, and the socio-economic impact of AfCFTA obligations on citizens and institutions.

Although it remains an advisory body with limited powers, the PAP is an important structure for civil society participation in AfCFTA. Its effectiveness in the AfCFTA matrix will require some innovative institutional adjustments and actions. One is to exploit the PAP's limited powers to make model laws[79] as a tool for providing some guidelines on citizens' involvement in AfCFTA processes at both regional and national levels. Such guidelines could then be adopted by both APRM and African Commission in its assessment of the participatory dimensions of AfCFTA at the national level. Another measure is to use differentiated integration, as stipulated under the AfCFTA Agreement,[80] as a mechanism for encouraging willing member states to establish arrangements with PAP on the modalities of allowing the latter to collaborate with national legislatures and make binding legislative rules on participatory mechanisms around AfCFTA.[81]

The AU Assembly should also put in place coordinating mechanisms that ensure that African Commission, PAP and the APRM work in tandem in assessing the democratic content of the AfCFTA process.

(c) Finally, Article 16 of the AfCFTA Agreement should elaborate on the context and nature of transparency of the process. This should include the stipulation of the publication and dissemination laws and regulations on AfCFTA in local languages, encouraging traditional African methods of consultation, and ensuring that there is a robust feedback from organised and broader civil society on such matters. These should also form part of the assessing roles of the African Commission, APRM and PAP.

---

[76]In August 2016, the African Peer Review (APR) Forum adopted the Statute of the African Peer Review Mechanism in Nairobi, Kenya. The aim is to make the voluntary APRM process binding on member states.

[77]Turianskyi (2019).

[78]Ibid.

[79]PAP Protocol (2014), article 8(1).

[80]AfCFTA Agreement, Article 5(c).

[81]Fagbayibo (2018), p. 638.

The second measure in this regard is the need to incentivise member states' compliance with democratic norms and values in the implementation of AfCFTA. In this respect, member states should be assessed against identifiable standards such as:

- the quality of national institutions, transparent electoral process;
- innovative methods of disseminating information on AfCFTA to the wider community (which should include training activities and stakeholders' sensitisation campaigns);
- timely and robust response to civil society concerns;
- focus on skilling and including marginalised groups such as women, youth, disabled and small scale farmers in all AfCFTA activities; and
- demonstrated genuineness of commitment to AfCTA agreements.

Where a member state has a favourable score, such member state should then be given access to a range of options that may include technical assistance, grants for infrastructure development, and rebates on financial contributions to the AfCFTA funds. The AfCFTA Secretariat should collaborate with the African Commission and APRM in determining the extent to which member states qualify for such opportunities. In addition, the activities of institutions such as the United Nations Economic Commission for Africa (UNECA) and the African Development Bank (ADB) around AfCFTA should be mainstreamed into AU processes. This will require that they are brought on board to assist with technical issues relating to financial assistance, capacity building programmes and investment strategies that could enhance compliance and reward mechanisms of the AfCFTA process. The idea is not to permanently lock out any country or group of countries but mainly to emphasise the importance of democratic compliance and the benefits that flow from such compliance.

In conclusion, the importance of rooting the AfCFTA process in democratic values and principles cannot be overstated. By committing to democratic norms and values, member states will not only have laid the fertile ground for the robust actualisation of AfCFTA goals but also emphasise the centrality of the choice of Africans in determining how best to move the continent forward. The idea that AfCFTA will contribute positively to the socio-economic wellbeing of Africans is one that logically requires that such citizens be placed at the heart of its articulation and implementation strategies. The steps recommended in the foregoing are part of such inclusive process.

References

African Union (2000) Constitutive Act. African Union

African Union (2012a) Assembly of the Union: eighteen ordinary session 29–30 January 2012 Addis Ababa, Ethiopia. African Union. Available via https://au.int/sites/default/files/decisions/9649-assembly_au_dec_391_-_415_xviii_e.pdf

African Union (2012b) BIAT – Boosting Intra-African Trade. African Union. Available via https://au.int/en/ti/biat/about

African Union (2014) Protocol to the Constitutive Act of the African Union relating to the Pan African Parliament. African Union

African Union (2015) The African Union Assembly launches the Continental Free Trade Area (CFTA) negotiations. African Union. Available via https://au.int/fr/newsevents/29332/african-unionassembly-launches-continental-free-trade-area-cfta-negotiations

African Union (2016) Pan African Investment Code. Available via https://au.int/sites/default/files/documents/32844-doc-draft_pan-african_investment_code_december_2016_en.pdf

African Union (2018a) Agreement Establishing the African Continental Free Trade Agreement. African Union. Available via https://au.int/sites/default/files/treaties/34248-treaty-consolidated_text_on_cfta_-_en.pdf

African Union (2018b) Compiled Annexes to the Establishment of the Continental Free Trade Area. Trade and Law Centre (TRALAC). Available via https://www.tralac.org/documents/resources/african-union/2163-compiled-annexes-to-the-afcfta-agreement-legally-scrubbed-version-signed-16-may-2018/file.html

African Union (2019) AfCFTA Agreement secures minimum threshold of 22 ratification as Sierra Leone and the Saharawi Republic deposit instruments. African Union. Available via https://au.int/en/pressreleases/20190429/afcfta-agreement-secures-minimum-threshold-22ratification-sierra-leone-and

African Union (2020) First continental report on the implementation of Agenda 2063. Available via https://au.int/sites/default/files/documents/38060docagenda_2063_implementation_report_e_web_version.pdf

Akinkugbe O (2019) What the African Continental Free Trade Agreement protocol on dispute settlement says about the culture of African States to dispute resolution. AfronomicsLaw Blog. Available via http://www.afronomicslaw.org/2019/04/09/what-the-african-continental-free-trade-agreement-protocol-on-dispute-settlement-says-about-the-culture-of-african-states-to-dispute-resolution/

Anna C (2019) AP Explains: 2019 a busy year for African internet shutdowns. Associated Press. Available via https://www.apnews.com/b0b4612e401241bab01c5bb4be81904e

Ansong A (2018) International economic law in Africa: is the African Continental Free Trade Area a viable project? Available via https://papers.ssrn.com/sol3/papers.cfm?abstract_id=3285290

Aremu I (2018) AfCFTA and Nigexit. Daily Trust. Available via https://www.dailytrust.com.ng/afcfta-and-nigexit.html

Barkan J (2009) African legislatures and the "third wave" of democratization. In: Legislative power in emerging African democracies. Lynne Reiner Publishers, Boulder, pp 1–31

BBC (2019) Sudan army rejects civilian majority in ruling council. BBC. Available via https://www.bbc.com/news/world-africa-48146256

Cheeseman N (2019) A divided continent – BTI 2018 regional report Africa. Bertelsmann Stiftung. Available via https://www.bertelsmannstiftung.de/fileadmin/files/BSt/Bibliothek/Doi_Publikatioen/Regional-Report_NW_BTI-2018_Africa-A-Divided-Continent_2019.pdf

Coefelice A (2018) African Continental Free Trade Area: opportunities and challenges. The Federalist Debate XXXI:32–35

Collins T (2019) AfroChampions Initiative presents $1trn AfCFTA investment framework. Available via https://africanbusinessmagazine.com/sectors/finance/afrochampions-initiative-presents-1trn-afcfta-investment-framework/

Daragahi B (2019) Sudan and Algeria are part of a new wave of peaceful regime change – other dictators should be worried. Independent. Available via https://www.independent.co.uk/voices/omar-albashir-sudan-protests-arrest-abdelaziz-bouteflika-algeria-a8865406.html

Durmaz N, Kagochi J (2018) Democracy and inter-regional trade enhancement in sub-Saharan Africa: gravity model. Economies 6:1–17. Available via https://ideas.repec.org/a/gam/jecomi/v6y2018i3p45-d162215.html

Ebobrah S (2013) Human rights developments in African sub-regional economic communities during 2012. Afr Hum Rights Law J 13:178–213

Economic Community of West African States (ECOWAS) (2005), Supplementary Protocol A/SP.1/01/05. Available via http://prod.courtecowas.org/wp-content/uploads/2018/11/Supplementary_Protocol_ASP.10105_ENG.pdf

Fagbayibo B (2013) Looking back, thinking forward: understanding the feasibility of normative supranationalism in the African Union. S Afr J Int Aff 20:411–426

Fagbayibo B (2016) Flexibility arrangements in the African Union: a way out of the integration conundrum? Afr Rev 8:156–170

Fagbayibo B (2017) A normative appraisal of the African Union's membership admission rules. Verfassung und Recht in Ubersee 2:156–174

Fagbayibo B (2018) Nkrumahism, Agenda 2063, and the role of intergovernmental institutions in fast tracking continental unity. J Asian Afr Stud 53:629–642

Fasan O (2019) Why AfCFTA may not be a credible forerunner of single African market. AfronomicsLaw Blog. http://www.afronomicslaw.org/2019/02/06/why-afcfta-may-not-be-a-credible-forerunner-of-single-african-market/

Freedom House (2019) Democracy in retreat: freedom in the world 2019. Freedom House website: https://freedomhouse.org/sites/default/files/Feb2019_FH_FITW_2019_Report_ForWeb-compressed.pdf

Gathii J (2019) Evaluating the dispute settlement mechanism of the African Continental Free Trade Agreement. AfronomicsLaw Blog. Available via http://www.afronomicslaw.org/2019/04/10/evaluating-the-dispute-settlement-mechanism-of-the-african-continental-free-trade-agreement/

Guillaumont P, Guillaumont-Jeanneney S, Brun J (1999) How instability lowers African growth. J Afr Econ 8:87–107

Ibrahim Index of African Governance (2018) Index report. Mo Ibrahim Foundation. http://s.mo.ibrahim.foundation/u/2018/11/27173840/2018-Index.Report.pdf?_ga=2.45239076.1481371308.1556440682-46253753.1556440682

Iheduru O (2015) Organised business and regional integration in Africa. Rev Int Polit Econ 22:910–940

Kaaba O, Fagbayibo B (2019) Promoting the rule of law through the principle of subsidiarity in the African Union: a critical perspective. Global J Comp Law 8:27–51

Kanyinga K (2018) Elections without constitutionalism: votes, violence, and democracy gaps in Africa. Afr J Democr Gov 5:147–168

Mattes R, Bratton M (2016) Do Africans still want democracy? Afrobarometer Policy Paper No. 36. Available via http://afrobarometer.org/sites/default/files/publications/Policy%20papers/ab_r6_policypaper_o36_do_africans_want_democracy.pdf

Muhammad A, D'Souza A, Amponsah W (2011) Violence, political instability, and international trade: evidence from Kenya's cut flower sector. Paper prepared for presentation at the Agricultural & Applied Economics Association's 2011 AAEA & NAREA Joint Annual Meeting, Pittsburgh, Pennsylvania, July 24–26, 2011. Available via https://ageconsearch.umn.edu/record/118374/files/muhammad_dsouza_amponsah_oct2011_20_AAEA_.pdf

Ndawana E (2018) The military and democratization: a comparison of the Egyptian and Zimbabwean experiences. Afr Secur 11:127–159

Ngobeni L (2019) The African justice scoreboard: a proposal to address rule of law challenges in the resolution of investor-state disputes in the Southern African Development Community. Comp Int Law J South Afr 52:1–21

Opalo K (2019) Legislative development in Africa: politics and postcolonial legacies. Cambridge University Press, Cambridge

Oppong R (2014) Legitimacy of regional economic integration courts in Africa. Afr J Leg Stud 7:61–85

Pelz D (2018) Is Africa's democracy dying? Deutsche Welle website. Available via https://www.dw.com/en/is-africas-democracy-dying/a-46455550

Reinold T (2019) Civil society participation in regional integration in Africa: a comparative analysis of ECOWAS, SADC, and the EAC. S Afr J Int Aff 26:53–71

Sommer L, Nshimbi C (2018) The African Continental Free Trade Area: an opportunity for informal cross-border trade. Bridges Africa 7:7–10. Available via https://www.ictsd.org/sites/default/files/bridges_africa_june2018.pdf

Treaty Establishing the Common Market for Eastern and Southern Africa (COMESA) (2009)

Treaty Establishing the East African Community (1999)

Turianskyi Y (2019) African peer review: progress is being made, but there are problems. The Conversation Africa. Available via https://theconversation.com/african-peer-review-progress-is-being-made-but-there-are-problems-113048

United Nations Economic Commission for Africa and Friedrich Ebert Stiftung (2017) The Continental Free Trade Area (CFTA) in Africa – a human rights perspective. United Nations Economic Commission for Africa and Friedrich Ebert Stiftung. Available via https://www.uneca.org/sites/default/files/PublicationFiles/2017_07_cfta_hria_publication_e.g.pdf

United Nations Economic Commission for Africa and the African Union Commission (2018) African Continental Free Trade Area Questions & answers. African Union. Available via https://au.int/sites/default/files/documents/33984-doc-qa_cfta_en_rev15march.pdf

Part VII
Contemporary Challenges/Emerging Issues

Technology and the Law: The Impact of Artificial Intelligence (AI) on Litigation and Dispute Resolution in Africa

Izuoma Egeruoh Egeruoh-Adindu

Contents

I. E. Egeruoh-Adindu (✉)
Nigerian Institute of Advanced Legal Studies, Abuja, Nigeria

University of Jos, Jos, Nigeria

C. Eboe-Osuji et al. (eds.), *Nigerian Yearbook of International Law 2018/2019*,
Nigerian Yearbook of International Law 2018/2019,
https://doi.org/10.1007/978-3-030-69594-1_18

1 Introduction

Artificial intelligence technology is deeply integrated into business, politics, leisure, travel and other spheres of our life. This integration process also affects legal practice and the justice system.[1] Many homes and motor vehicles are equipped with voice recognition devices that learn our speech patterns and habits turn on the TV and provide us with road directions.[2] Self-Driving cars are also on the rise and very soon legal actions to ascertain liability in accident or death involving self-driving cars will flood the courts.[3] It is therefore noteworthy, that the emergence of technology has brought forth transformation in both law practice and the adjudicatory process. The use of AI legal technologies, such as 'Luminance' and LexisNexis 'Ravel law' are just some of the major technological advancements that have in recent times transformed law practice and most justice delivery system.[4]

Nevertheless, the various methods of using Technology and Artificial intelligence (AI) in adjudication of cases in Africa are not quick. They require research, planning, resource building, trial and error, a continuous approach and cultural shift before any benefit is realized. AI should not be seen as a replacement for lawyers and judges, but rather an augmentation tool to improve efficiency and accuracy in dispute resolution especially litigation.[5] For successful application of AI in Africa, the "technology" is only a part of the process. Thus, a foundation founded on clean, relevant and structured data; a defined, accurate and optimal processes, procedures, policies and laws; flexible culture that is open to change and risk and the ability to interact, understand and develop the AI system are fundamental.[6]

Technology and AI are useful tools to investigators, prosecutors, lawyers and judges, especially during investigation, analysis of facts, filling of processes, record of proceedings, conducting a case, writing of verdicts and preservation of precedents. The use of technology and AI in dispute resolution will also reduce manual

---

[1]Alina Pastukhova, Artificial Intelligence as a Judge can we rely on a Machine? <https://lib.ugent.be/fulltxt/RUG01/002/376/194/RUG01-002376194_2017_0001_AC.pdf>.

[2]Andrew C Hall, The Impact of Artificial Intelligence on commercial Litigation <http://www.hlhlawfirm.com/wp-content/uploads/2018/01/The-Impact-of-AI-on-Commercial-Litigation.pdf>.

[3]Raja Jurdak, Salil S Kanhere, Who is to Blame when Driverless cars have an Accident? <https://theconversation.com/whos-to-blame-when-driverless-cars-have-an-accident-93132>, see the recent reported case involving Uber driverless car that killed a woman in Tempe Arizona USA, *Robert L Rabin*, 'Uber Self driving Cars Liability, and Regulation' <https://law.stanford.edu/2018/03/20/uber-self-driving-cars-liability-regulation/>.

[4]Abby Cessna, Future of AI and The Law, Cornell University Law School <https://scholarship.law.cornell.edu/cgi/viewcontent.cgi?referer=https://www.google.com/&httpsredir=1&article=1051&context=lps_papers>.

[5]Erin Hichman, 'Law Firms Need Artificial Intelligence to stay in the game' <https://www.alm.com/intelligence/solutions-we-provide/business-of-law-solutions/analyst-reports/law-firms-need-artificial-intelligence-to-stay-in-the-game>.

[6]Ibid (n.1).

and intensive tasks, bring forth accurate decisions, minimise cost and increase revenue opportunities in Africa.

The use of these emerging trends in litigation and dispute resolution are not without roadblocks such as lack of regulatory frameworks on AI application and the fact that AI will disrupt the traditional practice of law and adjudication process.[7] While the onset of roadblocks can be overwhelming, there are quite a number of identified steps that will help focus and improve manageability of the application of AI technology in litigation and dispute resolution in Africa. The steps begin with trainings on the use of AI legal application, define the goal, assess maturity and closing any gap inform of regulatory and cultural barriers, identify and deploy quick wins for continuous development of technology and AI in litigation and dispute resolution in the continent.

For proper interrogation of issues, the research will be divided into five sections. Conceptualisation of key terms used in this research will be next after this introductory section; section three will address the emergence of litigation and dispute resolution process in Africa while in section four, the research will attempt to find out if Africa is lagging in the use of AI legal technology, by examining the role of technology and AI in litigation and dispute resolution from a comparative perspective. The work will be concluded in part five with recommendations on the necessity of AI legal technology in litigation and other dispute resolution mechanisms in Africa.

2 Conceptualization of Terms

2.1 Technology

Technology in its literal meaning is the body of knowledge devoted to creating tools, processing actions and the extracting of materials.[8] The concept can also be defined as the 'theoretical and practical knowledge, skills, and artefacts that can be used to develop products and services as well as their production and delivery systems.'[9] According to Kumar, technology consists of two primary components: (1) a physical component which comprises of items such as products, tooling, equipment, blueprints, techniques, and processes; and (2) the informational component which consists of know-how in management, marketing, production, quality control, reliability, skilled labour and functional areas.[10] According to Lovell, the concept

[7]Steven Richman, Legal Profession Facing Challenges from all Sides <https://www.alliottgroup.net/practice-management-resources-for-owner-managed-firms/future-of-legal-profession/>.

[8]Karehka Ramey, What is Technology-Meaning of Technology and Its Use <https://www.useoftechnology.com/what-is-technology/.

[9]Burgelman et al. (1996).

[10]Kumar et al. (1999).

of technology does not only relate to the innovation in the product but it is also associated with the knowledge or information of it use, application and the process in developing the product.[11] Rosenberg and Frischtak, also considered technology as 'firm-specific information concerning the characteristics and performance properties of production processes and product designs', therefore technology is tacit and cumulative in nature.[12]

Apart from defining the concept, understanding the various classification of technology is also crucial. Technology is used to accomplish different tasks so it comes in different forms.[13] These forms are simply identified as communication technology, information technology, education technology, legal technology, business technology, medical technology and entertainment technology. This study will however focus on legal technology which is the center of this research.

Legal Technology also known as 'Legal Tech' is the process of using technology to solve legal problems.[14] Though, legal tech is emerging, there are quite a large number of them in existence. Technologies such as Cloud Based applications, Cyber security/block chain, litigation management software, Courtroom Audio Visual Technology and Artificial Intelligence are experiencing significant growth in law practice and adjudication process.

The advantages of these technologies abound. Some identified advantages are; speedy trials, excellent record keeping, reduced costs, increased productivity, improves access to justice, flexibility and increased security.[15] When it comes to dispute resolution, some of these technologies are slowly being adopted by court systems, this is as a result of roadblocks, such as lack of funds and skilled personnel to make significant changes. Outside the courtroom setting, however, lawyers can use these technologies to improve other dispute resolution process.[16]

---

[11]Sazali Abdul Wahab, Suzana Idayu, and Wati Osman, Defining the Concepts of Technology and Technology Transfer: A Literature Analysis <https://www.researchgate.net/publication/318015152/download>.

[12]Rosenberg and Frischtak (1985).

[13]Karehka Ramey, What is Technology-Meaning of Technology and Its Use <https://www.useoftechnology.com/what-is-technology/>.

[14]Tom Martin, What does Legal Tech mean and Why should you care? <https://glsaonline.org/blog/what-does-legal-tech-mean-and-why-should-you-care/>.

[15]Synkomtech, How Audio Vedio Conference benefits courtroom and Legal <proceedings http://synkomtech.com/Audio-Video-Conference-benefits-Courtroom-and-Legal-Proceedings>.

[16]Arbitration Resolution Services, Legal Technology Trends Impacting Dispute Resolution <https://www.arbresolutions.com/legal-technology-trends-dispute-resolution/>.

2.2 *Artificial Intelligence (AI)*

AI was first defined as "the science and engineering of making intelligent machines."[17] The term refers to the intelligence of machines and the branch of computer science that aims to create it. AI also means the science and engineering of making intelligent machines, especially intelligent computer programs.[18] It is related to the task of using computers to understand human intelligence, but AI does not confine itself to methods that are biologically observable.[19] The term Artificial intelligence (AI) was coined by John McCarthy in 1956. Although, the journey to understand if machines can truly think began much before that as Vannevar Bush, proposed a system which amplifies people's own knowledge and understanding much earlier. Five years later Alan Turing wrote a paper on the notion of machines being able to simulate human beings and the ability to do intelligent things.[20]

AI technology uses tools and insights from many fields, including computer science, psychology, philosophy, neuroscience, cognitive science, linguistics, operations research, Law, economics, control theory, probability, optimization and logic. AI technology also overlaps with tasks such as robotics, control systems, scheduling, data mining, logistics, speech recognition, facial recognition and many others.

Globally, the intersection of AI and the Law has captured the attention of both the bar and bench. There are a number of potential applications for the utilization of AI systems in the legal industry especially as they relate to the automation of repetitive and routine tasks to help lawyers and judges in law practice and adjudication. The quick wins in application of AI in litigation and other dispute resolution processes include; investigation, analysing evidence, reviewing documents during litigation, due diligence, analysing contracts to determine whether they meet pre-determined criteria, performing legal research, and predicting case outcomes and assisting in easy access of Judicial precedents. However, the barriers in application of AI in dispute settlement was identified by Yuen Thio, who is of the opinion that AI is yet to replicate advocacy, negotiation, or structuring of complex deals.[21] Thus, AI is making waves in other fields and the legal profession should not be left out.

---

[17]Chris Smith, and others, 'The History of Artificial Intelligence', https://courses.cs.washington.edu/courses/csep590/06au/projects/history-ai.pdf.

[18]Swaru (2012), p. 4.

[19]Chris Smith, and others, 'The History of Artificial Intelligence', https://courses.cs.washington.edu/courses/csep590/06au/projects/history-ai.pdf.

[20]Ibid.

[21]Donahue (2018).

2.3 Dispute Resolution

Dispute resolution is a term that refers to a number of processes that can be used to resolve a conflict, dispute or claim.[22] It is the process of resolving a dispute or a conflict by meeting at least some of each side's needs and addressing their interests.[23] It also refers to one of several different processes used to resolve disputes between parties, including negotiation, mediation, arbitration, collaborative law, and litigation.[24] Dispute resolution processes are mainly categorized into two; Litigation and Alternative Dispute Resolution mechanisms.

Litigation in its simplest meaning is the process of carrying on a lawsuit.[25] It also means the process of taking legal action by a party who is known as a litigant.[26] Litigation means an action brought in court to enforce a particular right. The act or process of bringing a lawsuit in and of itself.[27] It refers to an action brought by a person (plaintiff or claimant) against another person (defendant) based on legal principles by which the former asserts some right or legal entitlements from the later.[28] Litigation most time is a cumbersome process. The features of litigation include; adversarial, binding decisions, not voluntary, publicly conducted, state conducted, win/lose situation, and expensive. Cases Suited for this mode of dispute resolution include; criminal cases, interpretation of legal documents, where the law mandates and where there is need for precedents.[29]

The search for alternative means of dispute settlement led to the emergence of Alternative Dispute Resolution (ADR) mechanisms.[30] These mechanisms are recognised and practiced in most jurisdiction. It also serve as alternative to litigation which was the traditional practice. Today parties are enjoined to use all reasonable means to settle their dispute before coming to court and even when they are in court they can be referred to ADR centers for amicable settlement of the dispute. Furthermore, some jurisdictions have made it mandatory for practicing lawyers to inform their client about ADR processes.[31] ADR therefore refers to a range of procedures

---

[22]American Bar Association, 'What is Dispute Resolution?' <https://www.americanbar.org/groups/dispute_resolution/resources/DisputeResolutionProcesses.html>.

[23]Ibid.

[24]Pon Staff, Dispute Resolution, Harvard law School <https://www.pon.harvard.edu/daily/dispute-resolution/what-are-the-three-basic-types-of-dispute-resolution-what-to-know-about-mediation-arbitration-and-litigation/>.

[25]Garner (2009), p. 1017.

[26]John Bouvier, 'Litigation' Legal Dictionary <https://legal-dictionary.thefreedictionary.com/litigation>.

[27]Curzon and Richards, p 356.

[28]Stanley-Idum and Agaba (2015).

[29]Ibid.

[30]Stanley-Idum and Agaba (2015), *see also* Muhammad (2010).

[31]Rules of Professional Conduct for Legal Practitioners 2007, Rules 15 (3) (d) makes it mandatory for lawyers in Nigeria to inform their clients of the option of alternative dispute resolution mechanisms before resorting to or continuing with litigation on behalf of the client. Also C

that serve as alternatives to litigation through the courts for the resolution of disputes, generally involving the intercession and assistance of a neutral and impartial third party.[32] It includes the various processes of resolving disputes between parties other than the formal court system.[33] It also means a procedure for settling dispute by means other than litigation, such as arbitration or mediation.[34] ADR also refers to modes of resolving an issue without resort to the normally applicable court trial process.[35]

The term ADR is an umbrella term which houses other dispute resolution mechanism such as arbitration, negotiation, mediation, conciliation etc.[36] The common features of these ADR mechanisms include; privacy and party autonomy, informal, speedy disposition of cases, flexibility, ability to choose members of the tribunal and cost efficient. In this research dispute resolution will be the umbrella term for both litigation and ADR mechanisms.

3 The Emergence of Litigation and Dispute Resolution Mechanisms in Africa

Historically, disputes in Africa were predominantly resolved by kings, community heads, elders and the oldest male in the community.[37] In exceptional circumstances, the first daughter of the family or in a community was called upon to resolve disputes. Due to the patriarchal nature of most African society, the men were vested with the responsibility of the maintenance of peace, and a conflict-free communities regardless of the challenges that confronts them.[38] This method of dispute resolution was effective and existed as the foremost method of dispute resolution.

Consequently, this informal method of dispute resolution became a part of the African culture and was largely in used, right before colonialism which brought forth a formal method of dispute resolution or what we know today as litigation. Over the years, litigation has been the conventional method of resolving disputes across the continent. It virtually replaced the informal method of dispute resolution which was

Ngo-Pondi, Alternative Dispute resolution (ADR) in Ghana: Tools and Mechanisms for Resolving Commercial and Corporate Disputes in Muhammad (2010).

[32]Idornigie (2004).

[33]Stanley-Idum and Agaba (2015).

[34]Garner (2009), p. 91.

[35]Curzon and Richards, p. 26.

[36]Abubakar (2010).

[37]Idornigie (2004). Role of the emergence of Online Dispute Resolution in African <www.kenyalaw.org/LVI2014/docs/RoleoftheemergenceofODRontheAfricancontinent.pdf>.

[38]Ibid.

a part of the African culture. The courts were seen as a sanctuary, and a refuge of hope in times of disputes.[39]

However, as the society became more complex, human activities increased, the demand for judicial services also increased and people became more aware of their rights as well as desirous of protecting those rights.[40] Disputes however became prevalent in most societies. Nwaneri, was of the view that despite the increased number of courts in most African States, the demand for justice could not be met.[41] Delays, formalities, technicalities crept into the system and the volume of cases before the courts increased at a proportion higher than the courts can handle.[42] According to Justice M D Abubakar, these factors slowed down the justice dispensation process and there became a need for alternatives to litigation. The search for other alternative means of resolving dispute and also reducing the volume of cases before the courts led to the emergence and application of ADR mechanisms in use across the continent till date.[43] Thus, when it comes to dispute resolution across African, litigation and ADR mechanisms are the frequently used methods.

4 The Role of Technology and Artificial Intelligence in Dispute Resolution

4.1 Applying Technology and AI in Litigation and ADR Mechanisms vis-a-vis Natural Intelligence

In 1965, Herb Simon predicted that by 1985 "machines will be capable of doing any work that a man can do."[44] The prediction was based on the Church-Turing thesis which was used to ascertain whether or not a computer can think intelligently like human.[45] Though the prediction, failed to materialize within the estimated time, however, AI is the game changer of our time and is here to stay. Human intelligence on the other hand, is a biological phenomenon, rather than a logical or mathematical phenomenon.[46] It is also said to be a mental activity that we, as human beings, are uniquely qualified to exercise.[47]

[39]Abubakar (2010).

[40]Nwaneri (2010).

[41]Ibid (n 40).

[42]Ibid (n 40).

[43]Ibid (n 40).

[44]Smith (1998), p. 277.

[45]GreeksforGreeks, 'Turing Test in Artificial Intelligence' <https://www.geeksforgeeks.org/turing-test-artificial-intelligence/>.

[46]Ibid (n 43).

[47]De Spiegeleire et al. 'Artificial Intelligence and the Future Of Defense: Strategic Implications For Small- And Medium-Sized Force Providers' Hague Center for Strategic Studies, <https://hcss.nl/

The application of AI technology in dispute resolution will not make the professional judgment and expertise of lawyers obsolete as argued by some lawyers. It will rather facilitate growth and productivity by increasing accuracy and driving efficiency in the legal profession. Cleverly integrated AI algorithms are already transforming outcomes in dispute resolution, corporate compliance, due diligence, contract management, and e-discovery. Other legal routine jobs such as legal research, and predicting case outcomes, are becoming faster, better, and cheaper with the assistance of intelligent software.[48]

Application of AI technology in dispute resolution should not deter lawyers and judges in Africa from exercising their independent professional judgment, which is a higher-order cognitive skill involving human intelligence.[49] Though, AI legal technology may have the nature of the human mind or even be way smarter than you and I, they can never replace human minds.[50] This is because AI legal technology is a product of human mind created to increase productivity. It also lacks emotional intelligence which is inherent in every member of the legal profession and essential in dispute resolution.[51] The researcher is of the opinion that AI and human intelligent should be applied jointly in the law practice and justice delivery in Africa as none is more important than the other. A combination of the duo, (AI and human intelligence) will also end delays surrounding the justice system and assist in the speedy resolution of disputes. Therefore, Judicial Institutions, firms, Judges and Lawyers who embrace AI legal technology today will have a competitive advantage over those who do not.[52]

4.1.1 Patterns/Practices of AI in Dispute Resolution in Africa: Comparative perspective

4.1.1.1 Forms of AI Technology Application in Dispute Resolution in Africa

The Application of AI in litigation and ADR in Africa is emerging. This is not to say that lawyers in Africa have not embraced or applied AI both in law practice and dispute resolution. A research of this nature will not be complete without examining some of the patterns of application of AI in dispute resolution in Africa.

---

sites/default/files/files/reports/Artificial%20Intelligence%20and%20the%20Future%20of%20Defense.pdf>.

[48]Law Technology Today, 'Artificial Intelligence Wont Replace Lawyers-It will free them' <https://www.lawtechnologytoday.org/2018/02/artificial-intelligence-wont-replace-lawyers-it-will-free-them/>.

[49]Ibid (n 47).

[50]Ibid (n 47).

[51]Dennis Garcia, Preparing for Artificial Intelligence in the Legal Profession Lexis Practice Advisor Journal <https://www.lexisnexis.com/lexis-practice-advisor/the-journal/b/lpa/archive/2017/06/07/preparing-for-artificial-intelligence-in-the-legal-profession.aspx>.

[52]Ibid (n 50).

Currently, South Africa is doing well in this area as AI application in the South African legal space has been promising. Linklaters LLP which is one of the leading law firm launch of ‘Nakhoda’ is an evidence of the above assertion. However, Nakhoda is an AI backed data analysis and extraction tool.[53] Further Webber Wentzel law firm’s investment and adoption of ‘Luminance’ from University of Cambridge is another prove. Luminance is the world’s most advanced artificial intelligence platform for the legal profession. Luminance’s groundbreaking AI technology reads, understands and learns from the interaction between lawyers and documents, offering a faster and more comprehensive platform for review.[54] Further, Bowmans another South African law firm which is in operation in Kenya, Uganda, Tanzania and with affiliations in other African countries, recently invested in an AI start-up called “Kira Systems.” Kira and a similar AI tool called ‘RAVN’ assist lawyers in processing high volumes of documents in an efficient, effective and cost-appropriate manner.[55]

Consequently, the South Africa’s LexisNexis offers an AI enhanced legal research datasets with machine learning, cognitive computing/natural language processing technologies and streamlines legal research. In addition, the company’s ‘Lex Machina’ mines litigation data from millions of pages to provide litigation predictive models based on the area of law, presiding judge and representative counsel.[56]

AI application in law practice and dispute litigation in Africa is not limited to South Africa, as Grace InfoTech Limited, a Nigerian based company and the publisher of electronic law report known as Law Pavilion has introduced an artificial intelligence legal assistance technology named ‘TIMI’, which provides legal analytics and will help legal practitioners to do their work more efficiently.[57] Timi was coded to assist lawyers in reviewing their case files, inform them on how to file processes in court and also serve as case managers. Although the AI legal technologies currently applicable in Africa are limited, however, ‘Law Pavilion Timi’ is a step in the right direction for the legal profession and dispute resolution in Africa.

[53]Patel, ‘The Legal Aspects Behind Artifical Intelligence’ <http://www.itnewsafrica.com/2017/06/the-legal-aspects-behind-artificial-intelligence/>.

[54]Webber Wentzel, Webber Wentzel deploys Luminance’s artificial intelligence platform in South Africa http://www.webberwentzel.com/wwb/content/en/ww-press releases?oid=62761&sn=Detail-2011&pid=32711.

[55]Digest Africa, This is the AI company that South African law-firm, Bowmans, recently invested in <http://digestafrica.com/ai-south-africa-bowmans/#.W6enl_ZFzIU>.

[56]Ibid (n 50).

[57]Vanguard online, Law Pavellion Set to realease Nigeria’s first Artificial Intelligence Legal Assistant, <https://www.vanguardngr.com/2018/08/lawpavilion-set-to-release-nigerias-first-artificial-intelligence-legal-assistant/>.

4.1.1.2 AI Patterns and Practices in Other Climes

AI patterns and application in litigation and dispute resolution in advanced climes[58] exist in the following form;

i. **Legalmation:** Legalmation is a California based AI technology developed by lawyers for lawyers. It is a litigator's trusted assistant. *LegalMation's Complaint Analyzer* produces high quality first drafts of answers and initial written discovery in about 2 min. These are tasks that normally take attorneys or paralegals hours to complete in the early stages of litigation. LegalMation combines the artificial intelligence and cognitive computing abilities of leading AI solutions with its own proprietary system.[59]

ii. **Lex machina**: Lexisnexis Lex Machina's legal analytics software is used to find out "who is the plaintiff, who is their counsel, who have they represented, and who else have they sued.[60] Lex Machina is also domiciled in California.

iii. **Premonition:** Premonition which claims to be the world's largest litigation database. The data bases uses AI tools to predict lawyer's success by analyzing his win rate, case duration, case type, and his pairing with a judge at an accuracy of 30.7% average case outcome. According to the company, the product can also aid in looking at different cases and how long they're going to take for each attorney. The company is a USA based company.[61]

iv. **Ravel Law:** LexisNexis ravel law is a software that can be used in pitching a law firm's services to potential clients by providing intelligence on the opposing counsel, generating values on probability of winning the case and identifying litigation trends to use in their marketing campaigns. Apart from prediction technology, the software also claims to provide lawyers with judges' data on cases, circuits and ruling on their dashboard, which can be used in landing new clients. The software can aid in litigation strategy by providing information on how judges make decisions. Ravel law is also based in California, USA.[62]

v. **ANAQUA Studio:** The cloud-based ANAQUA Studio designed by patent lawyers for patent lawyer's. It is specifically designed for drafting patents and prosecution of cases on patent. Anaqua Studio is also a USA based company with branches in Japan, Germany, UK, France, Italy and India.[63]

vi. **Intraspexion:** Intraspexion has patented software systems that claim to present early warning signs to lawyers when the AI tool detects threats of litigation. The system works by searching for high-risk documents and displays them

---

[58] Advanced Climes such as Germany, Canada, US.

[59] Legalmation, 'What is Legalmation' <https://www.legalmation.com/faq/>.

[60] Lex Machina, 'What is Legal Analytics?' <https://lexmachina.com/>.

[61] Premonition, 'Premonition makes the News' <https://premonition.ai/tag/litigation-database/>.

[62] Ravel Law, 'Court Analytics', <https://home.ravellaw.com/products>.

[63] Anaqua, 'Anaqua Studio Data Sheet' <https://www.anaqua.com/info/anaqua-studio-data-sheet>.

according to the level of risk that the AI has determined. When a user clicks on a document, risk terms as identified by subject matter experts through the algorithm are highlighted. According to the company, users can determine which documents put them at risk for litigation when they use the software. Intraspexion is based in Washington USA.[64]

vii. **Ross Intelligence:** Ross intelligence software provides natural language search capability by asking questions, and receiving information such as recommended readings, related case law and secondary resources. Ross Intelligence has its headquarter in San Francisco, California, United State[65]

viii. **Cara AI:** Casetext's CARA claims to allow lawyers to forecast an opposing counsel's arguments by finding opinions that were previously used by lawyers. Lawyers can also detect cases that have been negatively treated and flagged as something that lawyers may deem unreliable. Cara AI is also USA based.[66]

ix. **Loom:** Loom features win/loss rates and judge ruling information but only for civil cases in select Canadian provinces.[67] It is a Canadian based firm.

x. **Judicata:** The Judicata Clerk technology only serves California state law as of this writing. Its software, Clerk, is said to be capable of reading and analyzing legal briefs. It also evaluates their pros and cons and then assigns a score for each brief based on arguments, drafting and context. The recommendations intended to reduce content mistakes are listed as part of the action items for the user.[68]

xi. **Luminance**: Luminance's advanced machine learning technology claims to be the only legal tool that searches and ranks unusual and anomalous documents and clauses, including points of risk that a user may not have been looking for. It is also a UK based Software developed for lawyers by lawyers.[69]

xii. **LitIQ**: Lit IQ is an Add-In for MS Word to help spot errors in drafting contracts and other legal documents. It which capitalizes on computational linguistics technology to reduce contract-related disputes. Lit IQ is at the forefront of machine learning[70]

There are also other AI legal technologies that exist, though not directly applicable in litigation and ADR but relevant to law practice. Some of them are; LegalSifter, Seal, Perfect NDA, M&A Due Diligence Robot, Brainspace Discovery, Exterro's WhatSun, Denver-based Catalyst, DISCO, Everlaw's Prediction Technology, Legal Robot, LawGeex, ThoughtRiver, J P Morgans COIN, eBrevia and LEVERTON.[71]

---

[64]Intraspexion, 'Prevent Litigation' <https://intraspexion.com/>.

[65]Ross, 'AI meets Legal Research', <https://rossintelligence.com/>.

[66]CaseTest, 'Cara Search' <https://casetext.com/>.

[67]Loom, 'Loom Analytic' <https://www.loomanalytics.com/careers/>.

[68]Judicata, 'Introducing Clerk', <https://www.judicata.com/>.

[69]Luminance, Cutting Edge Machine Learning Technology <https://www.luminance.com/>.

[70]Law Made, 'Lit IQ' <https://lawmade.com/advisory/lit-iq/>.

[71]Edgar Alan Rayo, 'AI in Law and Legal Practice – A Comprehensive View of 35 Current Applications' <https://www.techemergence.com/ai-in-law-legal-practice-current-applications/>.

However the researcher will highlight the positive impact of some of the above mentioned AI legal technology (Luminance and Ravel Law) in dispute resolution and legal practice.

Luminance: Luminance uses advanced machine learning technology to cater for the specific challenges and workflows and preparation of briefs of both law firms and in-house legal teams. Luminance Discovery brings a fresh approach to litigation, with a focus on speed, stability and simplicity. Advanced machine learning means it is incredibly cost effective, delivering powerful visualisation during Early Case Assessment and deeper insights during the review.[72] Luminance offers legal advisory services as Luminance technology identifies similarities, differences and anomalies at all levels of the review, meaning legal teams have more confidence than ever in their recommendations to client and can compete in a changing market.

Luminance also impacts positively on in-house counsel as it assists in-house teams with the growing demands of digitalisation, sweeping global regulatory and compliance, change and stretched resources. Lawyers can identify exposure, focus their outsourcing and save significant time and resources for their organisation. Other positive impacts of Luminance to dispute litigation are finding hidden risk from a missing page or clause to a minor difference in wording, Luminance empowers lawyers with a comprehensive understanding of a project. It also helps in accelerating review as it understands language in volumes and at speeds beyond human capacity, cutting down reviews by up to 75% if they review was to be done by human being, it has therefore reduced the workload of lawyers and also cut down on expensive bills that would have been paid by clients. It has also reduced delays associated with reviewing contracts as contracts can now be reviewed in the shortest possible time. Luminance is not without a negative impact as it will lead to loss of jobs as most law firms will not hire young lawyers that will assist with this review but rather use Luminance to achieve effective resolute.[73] In dispute resolution, Luminance will help put an end to long hours used by lawyers to prepare briefs and therefore put an end to unnecessary adjournments which stalls trials.

Ravel Law: LexisNexis Ravel Law is a new legal search analytics and collaboration platform for lawyers. Through an intuitive interface lawyers doing research can find the most relevant cases understand them in context and access knowledge about how they should be interpreted. Ravel Law applies visualization to the search process helping lawyers quickly understand legal landscapes and provides advanced citation-based analytics to inform litigators about cases and judges. One of their highlights called Judge Analytics enables a legal advisor to see if a judge is thoughtful towards his/her contentions by breaking down his past decisions. This is a reasonable evolution in the field of law. Ravel Law's Machine learning and innovation have saved law firms a lot of time by easing the workload of lawyers.[74]

---

[72]Luminance Advisory, <https://www.luminance.com/advisory.html>.

[73]Ibid (n 72).

[74]Priya Dialani, "Impact of Big Data in the Legal Industry" <https://www.analyticsinsight.net/impact-of-big-data-in-the-legal-industry/>.

Ravel Law will therefore help facilitate brief writing and also help in achieving speedy trial.[75] It is therefore important to state that these AI technology are impacting positively in dispute resolution processes as they assist the law firms in brief writing while helping them avoid unnecessary delays associated by human efforts and errors. They are also useful tools for Judicial Officers when writing their judgments. AI legal technology is therefore valuable in speedy trials, contract drafting and quick review of legal documents which are usually in large volumes. Above all they have help to reduce the bills paid by clients.

4.1.1.3 Comparative Perspective

AI application in dispute resolution in other climes is huge and is impacting positively in their law practice and justice delivery system.[76] The essence of the comparative study is to ascertain the pattern and practice of application of AI legal technology in dispute resolution in other climes with the aim of discovering if Africa is lagging behind.

A statistical survey of top 386 law firms in the USA conducted by Altman Weil and updated in April 2018 indicates that over half (54.6%) of firms with over 1000 lawyers on their payroll are already using tools involving AI and 0% of them identified themselves as being unaware of legal technology developments. In stark contrast, only 5.7% of the smallest firm size surveyed (50–99 lawyers) said that they were already using tools involved with AI and 38.3% were unaware of developments in legal technology.[77] The firms however, acknowledged that AI legal technology was mostly used for contract review and comparison, case analysis and precedent analysis, data management and retrieval and legal discussions as they are yet to apply it fully in litigation.[78]

In Canada, the Montreal based EXEO, a law firm that specializes in immigration and international mobility, has launched its Immigration Virtual Assistant (IVA). IVA is a free virtual assistant that aims to help people looking to immigrate to

[75]Definition of Ravel Law <https://www.definitions.net/definition/ravel+law>.

[76]AI applications are mostly used for contract review and comparison, case analysis and precedent analysis, data management and retrieval and audio visual trials. It has also reduce billing to their client and boosted clients confidence in their lawyers. AI applications have reduced human workforce of law firms while increasing most firms output. For Judicial systems, the adoption of audio visual trials, and hosting of websites that has help for access to justice has increased access to justice in most developed climes.

[77]Nadaline Webster, How Many Law Firms are using Artificial Intelligence Right Now? <https://Www.Trademarknow.Com/Blog/Lawyers-Artificial-Intelligence>.

[78]Ibid (n 70).

Canada. While in India law firms such as Cyril Amarch and Mangaldas, are about the only firm that have deployed the services of AI in their legal services.[79]

Comparing these climes with Africa reveals that Africa is obviously lagging behind in application of AI legal technology in litigation and other dispute resolution mechanisms. This may be due to the fact that African legal environment is not yet prepared for it, judging from expensive cost of internet facilities, lack of skilled personnel's, absence of a legal framework on the use of AI legal technology and inadequate infrastructure for Virtual Courts[80] and ODR to thrive. An examination of the court systems in Africa reveals that the courts are yet to be fully digitalised as judges still take note via long hand and many are in dilapidated state.[81] Also, a look at most AI legal technology hugely subscribed to in Africa is from the advanced climes. These may be due to absence of data bank in most African country, considering that AI technology feeds on huge data. The absence of data bank in most judicial system in Africa may stall the application of AI legal technology in Africa. Absence of data bank is enough prove that African legal environment and judicial systems are not yet AI ready. From the brief analysis above we can comfortably state that Africa is lagging behind and we need to innovate by developing our data bank and getting AI ready as other climes are fast embracing AI legal technology and Africa must not be left behind.

4.2 The Impact of Technology and Artificial Intelligence on Litigation and Dispute Resolution in Africa

The capability of using AI in litigation and other dispute resolution mechanisms, is poised to taking machines beyond simple search tools, to partners with whom members of the profession will team up to deliver better, faster, and cheaper legal services. Accordingly, AI applications will transform the justice system in Africa and also have positive effects on litigation and other dispute resolution mechanism via the following:[82]

[79]D O Odumosu, Innovate or Die: The Unseen Benefits Of Artificial Intelligence In The Legal Profession In Nigeria <https://www.lawyard.ng/innovate-or-die-the-unseen-benefits-of-artificial-intelligence-in-the-legal-profession-in-nigeria/>.

[80]Virtual Court is a concept aimed at eliminating presence of litigant or lawyer in the court and adjudication of the case online, Virtual Courts, 'About Virtual Courts' <https://vcourts.gov.in/virtualcourt/index.php>.

[81]Although some African countries e.g. Nigeria has embarked on court digitalisation process and also made e-filling mandatory. Kingsley Obiejesi, Email your case to Supreme Court –Manual Filling of cases <Terminated https://www.icirnigeria.org/e-mail-your-case-to-supreme-court-manual-filing-of-charges-terminated/>.

[82]Larry Kamener, 'Courting Change: The Verdict on AI and The Courts' <https://www.centreforpublicimpact.org/courting-change-verdict-ai-courts/>. See Also D O Odumosu (n 79).

a. Lawyers: AI technology will assist lawyers in automating creative processes (including some writing) in legal work; it will also be a useful tool for electronic billing as Lawyers' billable hours are computed automatically. It will also assist lawyers in document automation as most law firms use software templates to create filled out documents based on data input; lawyers can use data points from past case law, win/loss rates and a judge's history to be used for trends and patterns, AI technology can also serve as a Prediction technology by generating results that forecast litigation outcome. It is also a useful tool to carry out due diligence as Litigators perform due diligence with the help of AI tools to uncover background information. We've decided to include contract review, legal research and electronic discovery in this section, AI will assist in proofreading, error correction, and document organization. AI will increase clients relation and reduce stress and physical meeting time as the client –lawyer meeting can be conducted via conference calls. AI technology is also useful in training of lawyers.
b. Judges: AI will assist the Judge in the following ways; personal legal research, carry out case reviews within a short time, increase speedy disposition of cases, help digitalise the court and also assist the judge in electronic recording and analysis of proceedings, serve as administrative legal support to the judges, AI software could diagnose the situation and produce a draft judgment for the judge to review, assist in proofreading, error correction, and document organization and a useful tool in the training of judges
c. Litigants: AI is very valuable to the litigants in the following ways; Speedy resolution of dispute, reduce time of trial, reduce cost of legal services, make legal services available to low income earners, increase lawyer- client relationship, makes dispute resolution flexible especially via the use of virtual courts and Online dispute Resolution (ODR) mechanisms, and also restore confidence in the justice delivery system.

4.3 Revisiting the Existing Legal, Policy and Regulatory Framework on Information and Communication Technology (ICT) in Africa

Most African Countries currently have domestic laws and policies regulating the use of ICT.[83] However, the suitability of these current laws/policies on application of

[83]Susan Schorr, 'ICT policy visionaries leading African revolution' International Telecommunication Union, <https://www.itu.int/itunews/manager/display.asp?lang=en&year=2004&issue=03&ipage=ICT-policy&ext=html>, see also Mark D J Williams, Rebecca Mayer, and Michael Minges, 'African's ICT Infrastructure Building on the Mobile Revolution', WorldBank, <http://siteresources.worldbank.org/INFORMATIONANDCOMMUNICATIONANDTECHNOLOGIES/Resources/AfricasICTInfrastructure_Building_on_MobileRevolution_2011.pdf>, see Ghana ICT for

artificial intelligence is an issue that cannot be ignored, considering the fact that AI is a disruptive technology that brings new economic and societal change. Accordingly, it is important to state that the existing domestic ICT laws in some Africa countries as at date may not adequately address issues on AI, especially with the creation of humanoids that are expected to interact with the world. The unsuitability of the current laws will therefore create legal gaps which require urgent attention.[84] A close look at the Nigerian ICT legal framework[85] reveals that AI technologies are not adequately captured. This is because the National ICT Policy which was developed to support Nigeria's Vision 2020 developmental goals is yet to fully achieve its purpose, which include digitalising Nigeria by the year 2020. Here we are in the year 2020 and still far behind developed climes like United States of America in digitalisation and adoption of Artificial Intelligence technology. This obviously reveals that Africa is below expectation in embracing AI. There is an urgent need for African Countries especially Nigeria to review their ICT legal framework to integrate AI technology so as to address AI related ICT issues. This will help Nigeria achieve her developmental goals in all sectors of the economy.

Although, the justice system in some African countries have embraced technology especially in litigation and other dispute resolution mechanisms,[86] however, for AI technology evolution to happen in Africa, the onus is on policy makers in all African countries to review existing domestic laws and policies on ICT.[87] This will enable them bring in new laws that will accommodate AI legal technology, close existing gaps on the pace of technological change and also develop ethical codes for application of this new trend in Africa.[88]

Accelerated Development Policy of 2003 <https://cdn.modernghana.com/images/content/report_content/ICTAD.pdf>, National Information and Communication Technology Policy 2012 <http://nitda.gov.ng/wp-content/uploads/2016/06/National-ICT-Policy.pdf>, National information and Communication Technology (ICT) Policy of Kenya, 2016 <http://icta.go.ke/pdf/National-ICT-Policy-20June2016.pdf, National Integrated ICT Policy White paper of South Africa 2016 <https://www.dtps.gov.za/images/phocagallery/Popular_Topic_Pictures/National_Integrated_ICT_Policy_White.pdf>.

[84]Microsoft, 'How Africa Can Embrace AI Enabled Future' <https://www.itweb.co.za/content/WnpNgq2AgZAMVrGd>.

[85]The National Information and Communication Technology (ICT) Policy of 2012 <https://nitda.gov.ng/wp-content/uploads/2018/07/National-ICT-Policy1.pdf>.

[86]Ibid (n.83).

[87]Ibid (n 84).

[88]Ibid (n 84). The need for legal reform to accommodate AI technology in Africa cannot be over emphasized as there are needs to enact laws that will expressly cover liability in use of AI legal technology, jurisdiction of courts and enforcement of Judgement arising from judicial decisions on application of AI technology. See Idornigie (2004).

4.4 The Future of Technology and Artificial Intelligence on Dispute Resolution in Africa

AI legal technology as an emerging trend and the face of the 'New Law[89]' poses a lot of threat to the old method of legal practice in Africa. Yet, we cannot ignore the fact that AI legal technology is the future of dispute resolution as virtual court rooms and online dispute resolution (ODR) mechanisms are here to stay.[90] An example of the fact that Virtual courts are here to stay is the "mobile court" offered on popular Chinese social media platform "WeChat" which has already handled more than three million legal cases and other judicial procedures since it was launched in March 2017. In a demonstration, Chinese authorities have showed how the Hangzhou Internet Court operates, featuring an online interface with litigants appearing by video chat as an AI judge complete with on-screen avatar prompts them to present their cases. The majority of cases handled at the Hangzhou court include online trade disputes, copyright cases, and e-commerce product liability claims. Litigants can register their civil complaints online and later log on for their court hearing. Putting simple functions like that in the hands of the virtual judge helps ease the burden on human justices, who also monitor the proceedings and make the major rulings in each case.[91] This is definitely a great innovation on application of AI legal technology.

While many lawyers argue that AI will disrupt the law, we however cannot close our eyes to globalisation and benefits of AI, which are key in achieving speedy resolution of disputes in Africa.[92] Thus, in the words of former UN Secretary – General Kofi Annan, "arguing against globalisation is like arguing against the laws of gravity."[93]

[89]Ilina Rejeva, 'What Is NewLaw and How It Is Changing the Legal Industry Forever' <https://legaltrek.com/blog/2016/04/what-is-newlaw-and-how-it-is-changing-the-legal-industry-forever/>, Apart from the flexible work and billing arrangements, disruptive technology and business practices are the main features of the NewLaw.

[90]Jeremy Barnett, The Virtual Courtroom and Online Dispute Resolution https://www.mediate.com/Integrating/docs/Barnett(1).pdf. A virtual court is a court that has no physical presence but still provides the same justice services that are available in physical courtrooms. Access to virtual courts would, however, be limited to online access, videoconferencing and teleconferencing. See Kaplan (2013), p. 32. Idornigie (2004).

[91]AI judges and verdicts via chat app: the brave new world of China's digital courts <https://www.france24.com/en/20191206-ai-judges-and-verdicts-via-chat-app-the-brave-new-world-of-china-s-digital-courts>.

[92]VR Ferose, and Lorien Pratt, How AI is Disrupting the Law <https://www.digitalistmag.com/digital-economy/2018/04/03/ai-is-disrupting-law-06030693>.

[93]United Nations, Secretary-General Kofi Annan's opening address to the fifty-third annual DPI/NGO Conference <http://www.un.org/dpi/ngosection/annualconfs/53/sg-address.html>.

4.4.1 Roadblocks

Though, the benefits of AI legal technology on dispute resolution has been stated in this research and the need for transition to AI legal technology has been advised, application of AI legal technology in Africa now and in the near future will not be without barriers. Hence, the need to examine the possible roadblocks.

a. Ethical Standards: As lawyers and judges use AI systems in dispute resolution, issues of ethics will definitely arise. There will be a need to ensure that judges and lawyers in Africa comply with ethical rules and standards of the legal profession. In Nigeria for example ethical issues such as aiding the unauthorised practice of Law which is against Rule 3 of the Rules of Professional Conduct (RPC)[94] may arise since application of AI legal technology has not been embraced and also covered under the RPC the use of AI applications may run contrary to the provisions of the RPC. Also, what amounts to professional misconduct (Rule 55 of RPC)[95] in a Virtual court has to be defined and lawyers' duty to the virtual courts[96] has to be made clear. The current Rules of Professional Conduct applicable to Lawyers in Nigeria needs to be reviewed to be in line with globalisation and technological innovations.
b. Lack of Regulatory Frameworks: With rapid development of AI technology in legal practice and justice delivery system, several issues are likely to arise on the regulatory front. The first is the question of bias. While algorithms are usually coded to be neutral, the programmers who code them may not be, or are likely to operate with some assumptions that may lead to bias. This is why it is important for African countries to have a data bank. This is to ensure that the data used to code the AI algorithm comes from the African region or country where the technology is sought to be deployed. However, lack of an AI regulatory framework is definitely a gap that must be filled.[97]
c. Intellectual Property Protection: Elements of an AI system may be subject to intellectual property protection. AI service providers are seeking patents where applicable. As AI becomes more popular and advanced, AI patent litigation may arise.
d. Loss of Jobs: Among the key reasons holding back the use of AI legal technology in Africa, is the fear the technology will result in loss of jobs for young lawyers and also disrupt law practice.
e. Financial challenges for young law firms: inadequate Funds to acquire AI technology will pose a barrier to young firms in Africa.

[94]Rules of Professional Conduct 2007, Rule 3.

[95]Rules of Professional Conduct 2007, Rule 55.

[96]Rules of Professional Conduct 2007, Rule 30 and 31.

[97]de Souza, Transforming the Legal Profession: The impact and Challenges of Artificial Intelligence <http://www.digitalpolicy.org/transforming-legal-profession-impact-challenges-artificial-intelligence/>.

f. Data privacy: It is essential that, as consumers of large volumes of data, service providers may have unrestricted access to data and confidential information which are the subject of litigation or the verdict of the judge.
g. Issues of liability: As lawyers and judges adopt AI systems in analysing evidence in litigation and other dispute resolution mechanisms, it is inevitable that such systems will make mistakes that may result in damages. How will liability be determined in such situations? How do lawyers and judges mitigate these risks and other potential liability issues associated with AI?
h. Issues of governing laws, jurisdiction, place of business, service of processes, are also roadblocks that a legal framework will address.

4.4.2 Way Forward

Having examined the roadblocks in application of AI legal technology, it is important to also project the prospects for application of AI legal technology in Africa.

a. The need for all lawyers, judges and every judicial institution in Africa to embrace the new trend and reskill.
b. The need for a data bank and fully digitalised court systems for African countries yet to embrace legal technology in their justice delivery system
c. Continuous legal Training and retraining of members of the lawyers and judges on the need to embrace the new trend
d. AI and technology skill and training should be made a condition precedent in any appointment to the bench in every Africa country.
e. AI and the law should be made part of the curriculum in training of lawyers both at the university and professional training (Law schools) to prepare the next generation of lawyers in Africa.
f. The need to strengthen the existing ethical codes of conduct for legal practitioners and Judges to regulate the use of AI technology in dispute resolution by members of the legal profession.
g. Lawyers and various law societies/associations in Africa should champion the course to strengthen existing ICT laws so as to regulate AI technologies and issues of liability that may arise from the application of AI legal technology.

5 Conclusion

The research has revealed that, while the application of AI technology in dispute resolution is emerging, it will however expedite dispute resolution in Africa. The paper discovered that Africa is lagging behind in the application of this emerging trend and therefore needs to innovate. Thus, in Simon Dingle's view, "if you know anyone studying law, tell them to get a side-project in computer science".[98] Drawing insights from the above statement, lawyers, judges and the various justice delivery systems in Africa are hereby advised to fully embrace the 'New law' or risk losing their legal space to foreign law firms who now double as AI service providers.

Finally, this research will conclude with the words of Professor Richard Susskind in *The End of Lawyers*, where he said lawyers must "reskill or die".[99]

References

Journals Articles

Online Journals

Dennis Garcia, Preparing for Artificial Intelligence in the Legal Profession Lexis Practice Advisor Journal <https://www.lexisnexis.com/lexis-practice-advisor/the-journal/b/lpa/archive/2017/06/07/preparing-for-artificial-intelligence-in-the-legal-profession.aspx>

Donahue L (2018) A primer on using artificial intelligence in the legal profession. Harv J Law Technol. <https://jolt.law.harvard.edu/digest/a-primer-on-using-artificial-intelligence-in-the-legal-profession>

Kaplan K (2013) Will virtual courts create courthouse relics? Judges' J 52(2):32

Kumar V, Kumar U, Persaud A (1999) Building technological capability through importing technology: the case of Indonesian Manufacturing Industry. J Technol Transfer. https://doi.org/10.1023/A:1007728921126

Smith JC (1998) Machine intelligence and legal reasoning - the Charles Green Lecture in law and technology. Chic-Kent Law Rev 73:277. <https://scholarship.kentlaw.iit.edu/cgi/viewcontent.cgi?referer=https://www.google.com/&httpsredir=1&article=3115&context=cklawreview>

Susskind R (2010) The end of lawyers. OUP, <http://www.oupcanada.com/catalog/9780199593613.html>

Swaru P (2012) Artificial intelligence. JCCR (2) 4. <https://www.ijccr.com/july2012/4.pdf>

Books and Chapters

Abubakar MD (2010) Alternative dispute resolution and restorative justice: challenges and prospects in Nigerian Courts. In: Muhammad IT (ed) Alternative dispute resolution and some contemporary issues. MO Press & Publishers Ltd, see also Jide Olakanmi, Alternative dispute resolution cases and materials (Panaf Press 2013)

Burgelman RA, Maidique MA, Wheelwright SC (1996) Strategic management of technology and innovation, 2nd edn. I. L, Irwin, Chicago

Curzon LB, Richards PH, 'Litigation' The Longman Dictionary of Law, p 356

[98]Wilson, Young Lawyers Should not Fear technology, Whipping the Cat <https://whippingthecat.com/in-the-news/>. Simon Dingle made this statement at Whipping the cat's Heavy Chef's seminal Block chain event 2017.

[99]Susskind (2010).

de Souza SP, Transforming the Legal Profession: The impact and Challenges of Artificial Intelligence <http://www.digitalpolicy.org/transforming-legal-profession-impact-challenges-artificial-intelligence/>

De Spiegeleire S, Maas M, Sweijs T, Artificial intelligence and the future of defense: strategic implications for small- and medium-sized force providers. Hague Center for Strategic Studies, <https://hcss.nl/sites/default/files/files/reports/Artificial%20Intelligence%20and%20the%20Future%20of%20Defense.pdf>

Garner BA (2009) 'Litigation' Black's Law Dictionary, 9th edn. West Publishing Co, p 1017

Idornigie PO (2004) From Alternative Dispute Resolution (ADR) to online dispute resolution: evidential issues. In: Ojo B (ed) Nigerian Journal of Arbitration and Mediation 1(1)

Law Technology Today, 'Artificial Intelligence Wont Replace Lawyers-It will free them' <https://www.lawtechnologytoday.org/2018/02/artificial-intelligence-wont-replace-lawyers-it-will-free-them/>

Muhammad IT (2010) Alternative dispute resolution and some contemporary issues. MO Press & Publishers Ltd

Nwaneri AC (2010) An appraisal of the ADR process in Nigeria. In: Muhammad IT (ed) Alternative dispute resolution and some contemporary issues. MO Press & Publishers Ltd, see also Jide Olakanmi, Alternative dispute resolution cases and materials (Panaf Press 2013)

Patel S, 'The Legal Aspects Behind Artifical Intelligence' <http://www.itnewsafrica.com/2017/06/the-legal-aspects-behind-artificial-intelligence/>

Rosenberg N, Frischtak C (1985) International technology transfer: concepts, measures and comparisons. Praeger, New York

Stanley-Idum MM, Agaba JA (2015) Litigation, civil litigation in Nigeria. Nelag and Company Limited

Webber Wentzel, 'Webber Wentzel deploys Luminance's artificial intelligence platform in South Africa' <http://www.webberwentzel.com/wwb/content/en/ww-press-releases?oid=62761&sn=Detail-2011&pid=32711>

Wilson G, Young Lawyers Should not Fear technology, Whipping the Cat <https://whippingthecat.com/in-the-news/>

Online Articles

D O Odumosu, Innovate or Die: The Unseen Benefits Of Artificial Intelligence In The Legal Profession In Nigeria <https://www.lawyard.ng/innovate-or-die-the-unseen-benefits-of-artificial-intelligence-in-the-legal-profession-in-nigeria/>

GreeksforGreeks, 'Turing Test in Artificial Intelligence' <https://www.geeksforgeeks.org/turing-test-artificial-intelligence/>

Jeremy Barnett, The Virtual Courtroom and Online Dispute Resolution <https://www.mediate.com/Integrating/docs/Barnett(1).pdf>

John Bouvier, 'Litigation' Legal Dictionary <https://legal-dictionary.thefreedictionary.com/litigation>

Kingsley Obiejesi, Email your case to Supreme Court –Manual Filling of cases <Terminated https://www.icirnigeria.org/e-mail-your-case-to-supreme-court-manual-filing-of-charges-terminated/>

Larry Kamener, 'Courting Change: The Verdict on AI and The Courts' <https://www.centreforpublicimpact.org/courting-change-verdict-ai-courts/>

Mark D J Williams, Rebecca Mayer, and Michael Minges, 'African's ICT Infrastructure Building on the Mobile Revolution', WorldBank, <http://siteresources.worldbank.org/INFORMATIONANDCOMMUNICATIONANDTECHNOLOGIES/Resources/AfricasICTInfrastructure_Building_on_MobileRevolution_2011.pdf>

Pon Staff, Dispute Resolution, Harvard law School <https://www.pon.harvard.edu/daily/dispute-resolution/what-are-the-three-basic-types-of-dispute-resolution-what-to-know-about-mediation-arbitration-and-litigation/>

Role of the emergence of Online Dispute Resolution in African. <www.kenyalaw.org/LVI2014/docs/RoleoftheemergenceofODRontheAfricancontinent.pdf>

Susan Schorr, 'ICT policy visionaries leading African revolution' International Telecommunication Union, <https://www.itu.int/itunews/manager/display.asp?lang=en&year=2004&issue=03&ipage=ICT-policy&ext=html>

VR Ferose, and Lorien Pratt, How AI is Disrupting the Law <https://www.digitalistmag.com/digital-economy/2018/04/03/ai-is-disrupting-law-06030693>

News Articles

Abby Cessna, Future of AI and The Law, Cornell University Law School <https://scholarship.law.cornell.edu/cgi/viewcontent.cgi?referer=https://www.google.com/&httpsredir=1&article=1051&context=lps_papers>

Alina Pastukhova, Artificial Intelligence as a Judge can we rely on a Machine? <https://lib.ugent.be/fulltxt/RUG01/002/376/194/RUG01-002376194_2017_0001_AC.pdf>

American Bar Association, 'What is Dispute Resolution?' <https://www.americanbar.org/groups/dispute_resolution/resources/DisputeResolutionProcesses.html>

Anaqua, 'Anaqua Studio Data Sheet' <https://www.anaqua.com/info/anaqua-studio-data-sheet> Intraspexion, 'Prevent Litigation' <https://intraspexion.com/>

Andrew C Hall, The Impact of Artificial Intelligence on commercial Litigation <http://www.hlhlawfirm.com/wp-content/uploads/2018/01/The-Impact-of-AI-on-Commercial-Litigation.pdf>

Arbitration Resolution Services, Legal Technology Trends Impacting Dispute Resolution <https://www.arbresolutions.com/legal-technology-trends-dispute-resolution/>

CaseTest, 'Cara Search' <https://casetext.com/>

Chris Smith, and others, 'The History of Artificial Intelligence', <https://courses.cs.washington.edu/courses/csep590/06au/projects/history-ai.pdf>

Digest Africa, This is the AI company that South African law-firm, Bowmans, recently invested in <http://digestafrica.com/ai-south-africa-bowmans/#.W6enl_ZFzIU>

Erin Hichman, 'Law Firms Need Artificial Intelligence to stay in the game' <https://www.alm.com/intelligence/solutions-we-provide/business-of-law-solutions/analyst-reports/law-firms-need-artificial-intelligence-to-stay-in-the-game>

Ilina Rejeva, 'What Is NewLaw and How It Is Changing the Legal Industry Forever' <https://legaltrek.com/blog/2016/04/what-is-newlaw-and-how-it-is-changing-the-legal-industry-forever/>

Judicata, 'Introducing Clerk', <https://www.judicata.com/> Luminance, Cutting Edge Machine Learning Technology <https://www.luminance.com/>

Karehka Ramey, What is Technology-Meaning of Technology and Its Use <https://www.useoftechnology.com/what-is-technology/>

Law Made, 'Lit IQ' <https://lawmade.com/advisory/lit-iq/>

Edgar Alan Rayo, 'AI in Law and Legal Practice – A Comprehensive View of 35 Current Applications' <https://www.techemergence.com/ai-in-law-legal-practice-current-applications/>

Legalmation, 'What is Legalmation' <https://www.legalmation.com/faq/>

Lex Machina, 'What is Legal Analytics?' <https://lexmachina.com/>

Loom, 'Loom Analytic' <https://www.loomanalytics.com/careers/>

Microsoft, 'How Africa Can Embrace AI Enabled Future' <https://www.itweb.co.za/content/WnpNgq2AgZAMVrGd>

Nadaline Webster, How Many Law Firms are using Artificial Intelligence Right Now? <https://Www.Trademarknow.Com/Blog/Lawyers-Artificial-Intelligence>

Premonition, 'Premonition makes the News' <https://premonition.ai/tag/litigation-database/>

Raja Jurdak, Salil S Kanhere, Who is to Blame when Driverless cars have an Accident? <https://theconversation.com/whos-to-blame-when-driverless-cars-have-an-accident-93132>, see the recent reported case involving Uber driverless car that killed a woman in Tempe Arizona USA, *Robert L Rabin*, 'Uber Self driving Cars Liability, and Regulation' <https://law.stanford.edu/2018/03/20/uber-self-driving-cars-liability-regulation/>

Ravel Law, 'Court Analytics', <https://home.ravellaw.com/products>

Ross, 'AI meets Legal Research', <https://rossintelligence.com/>

Sazali Abdul Wahab, Suzana Idayu, and Wati Osman, Defining the Concepts of Technology and Technology Transfer: A Literature Analysis <https://www.researchgate.net/publication/318015152/download>

Steven Richman, Legal Profession Facing Challenges from all Sides <https://www.alliottgroup.net/practice-management-resources-for-owner-managed-firms/future-of-legal-profession/>

Synkomtech, How Audio Vedio Conference benefits courtroom and Legal <proceedings http://synkomtech.com/Audio-Video-Conference-benefits-Courtroom-and-Legal-Proceedings>

Tom Martin, What does Legal Tech mean and Why should you care? <https://glsaonline.org/blog/what-does-legal-tech-mean-and-why-should-you-care/>

United Nations, Secretary-General Kofi Annan's opening address to the fifty-third annual DPI/NGO Conference <http://www.un.org/dpi/ngosection/annualconfs/53/sg-address.html>

Vanguard online, Law Pavilion Set to release Nigeria's first Artificial Intelligence Legal Assistant, <https://www.vanguardngr.com/2018/08/lawpavilion-set-to-release-nigerias-first-artificial-intelligence-legal-assistant/>

Izuoma Egeruoh Egeruoh-Adindu LLB, BL, LLM, is a Research Fellow at the Nigerian Institute of Advanced Legal Studies, Abuja, Nigeria and Phd Candidate at the University of Jos, Nigeria.

Child Rights Protection, Nigerian Federalism and Culture: Irreconcilable Goals?

Fife Ogunde

Contents

A prevalent dilemma in human rights discourse is the development of universal standards of rights protection in an international community comprising of states with diverse customs and cultural practices. In federal states comprising of a central government with different constituent governments having a certain degree of autonomy, the prospects of developing universal standards of rights protection may be further undermined by such existent autonomy. Aside from this, there is in addition a notable suggestion, especially in non-Western countries that the concept of rights (in its contemporary form) is antithetical to well-established customary practices that are regarded as fundamental to the preservation of societal order. Nigeria, by virtue of its constitutional arrangement and societal outlook, is an epicentre of the dilemma created by these realities.

Nigeria, theoretically speaking, operates a federal system of government. The protection of federalist ideals through its constitutional arrangement has hitherto sustained its deep religious and ethnic divisions. These divisions remain entrenched in the constitution and inadvertently serve as a stumbling block to developing a universal child rights protection framework. The aim of this paper is to examine the federalist and cultural challenge to a universal child rights protection framework in

F. Ogunde (✉)
Ministry of Justice, Government of Saskatchewan, Regina, SK, Canada

C. Eboe-Osuji et al. (eds.), *Nigerian Yearbook of International Law 2018/2019*,
Nigerian Yearbook of International Law 2018/2019,
https://doi.org/10.1007/978-3-030-69594-1_19

Nigeria. The first aspect of this paper will briefly examine federalism from a Nigerian standpoint and outline the manner of its impact on child rights protection in Nigeria. The second aspect of this articles examines the intricacies created by the concept of culture in Nigeria. It will be argued that the existing structure of Nigerian federalism inadvertently inhibits the effectual protection of children's right, a problem which can only be resolved by proper constitutional restructuring in line with contemporary child rights standards. A further argument of this paper will be that securing an effective balance between the preservation of culture and protection of the rights of the child requires a multi-dimensional approach to rights protection.

1 What Is Federalism?

Federalism is the form of government where the component units of a political organization participate in sharing powers and functions in a cooperative manner in spite of existent divisions created by ethnic pluralism and cultural diversity.[1] It is also described as a 'compromise solution in a multinational state between self-determination provided by a national government and that of component states.[2] It emphasizes decentralization of powers and constitutional guarantees of the powers of each component unit of a federal system.[3] In a federal system, the participating political communities agree to pursue some objectives together and other objectives on their own.[4] More specifically, they agree to establish a central government and to empower it to make and administer laws in some areas; and they agree to retain the power to make and administer laws themselves in other areas.[5]

Nigeria operates a federal system of government, recognizing the legitimacy and autonomy of different levels of government. As stated in Attorney-General of Lagos State vs. Attorney General of the Federation[6]

> ...Nigeria operates a federal system of government. This ensures the autonomy of each government. None of the governments is subordinate to the other...under this system, each tier of government has its legislative competence or functions[7]

As stated above, federalism as a concept decentralizes power and in the process enables citizens to participate more effectively in political life and confers greater influence on a smaller section of people.[8] This by implication enables states to enjoy

[1]Tamuno (1998), p. 13.

[2]Elaigwu (2007), p. 6.

[3]Nwabueze (1983b), p. 377.

[4]Ibid.

[5]Ibid.

[6](2003) 6 S.C.

[7]Ibid.

[8]Woehrling, Federalism and Human Rights in Breitenmoser, Ehrenzeller and Sassoli (eds) Human Rights, Democracy and the Rule of Law (2007), p. 897.

discretion in terms of enforcing certain legislation and as a result, a dissenting state is not obliged to apply the provisions of the Act. Furthermore, it also prevents the federal legislature from exercising authoritarian control over state legislature which, had it been exercisable, could lead to abuse of power.

1.1 Federalism and Child Rights in Nigeria: The Nigerian Constitution in Focus

In Nigeria, legislative powers are divided between the federal and state governments. Section 4 of the Constitution of the Federal Republic of Nigeria 1999 provides exclusive law-making powers to the National Assembly[9] on matters contained in the Exclusive legislative list.[10] National Assembly Law-making powers are shared with the state Houses of Assembly[11] in matters under the concurrent legislative list.[12] Matters not contained in the exclusive or concurrent legislative list are considered to be residual matters, in which case federal legislation on such matters ae only applicable in states in so far as such legislation is incorporated into state legislation.

There is no explicit reference to child rights protection or indeed human rights as a specific subject under either of the legislative lists in the Constitution. This does not however imply a complete lack of reference to any matter that has an effect on child rights protection. For instance, Item 61 of the exclusive legislative list vests exclusive lawmakers in the National Assembly for the 'formation, annulment and dissolution of marriages, save for marriages under Islamic and Customary Law'. This implies for instance that the provisions of the Child Rights Act prohibiting child marriage[13] would be applicable to the exclusion of all other legislation except in instances where such a marriage is contracted under Islamic or Customary law. From a child rights protection perspective, such powers are largely ineffectual as the majority of child marriages are contracted under Islamic or customary law.[14] Schedule I also lists the promotion and the observance of the fundamental objectives of the constitution as a matter within the exclusive legislative jurisdiction of the federal government.[15] Among others, one of the fundamental objectives of state policy is the

---

[9]Section 4(3).

[10]The Exclusive Legislative List is contained in Schedule II of the Constitution of the Federal Republic of Nigeria 1999.

[11]Section 4(7).

[12]The Concurrent Legislative List is contained in Schedule II of the Constitution of the Federal Republic of Nigeria.

[13]Section 21.

[14]Available evidence indicates that almost 80% of the number of child marriages are in North-West and North-East Nigeria, where civil, personal and criminal conduct is regulated by Islamic law. See "Every last child; Changing the story of the girl child" available at https://resourcecentre.savethechildren.net/node/10043/pdf/nigeria.pdf.

[15]Item 60.

protection of children and young persons from exploitation as well as moral and material neglect.[16] However, such exclusive powers are limited to the 'establishment and regulation of authorities'[17] for the promotion of such objectives. Applying this to the Child Rights Act for example, this arrangement suggests that the establishment of the National Child Rights implementation committee is a matter for the National Assembly under the exclusive list but legislative protection of the child from exploitation remains a residual matter. Notwithstanding, the exclusive list also considers 'any matter incidental or supplementary' to any item on the list as being under the jurisdiction of the National Assembly.[18] A conclusion that the National Assembly can establish a committee to protect children without being able to determine the nature of protection afforded to children renders ineffective the exclusive powers granted under Item 60. The concurrent legislative list also makes little explicit reference to issues discussed under the Child Rights Act except in empowering the state House of Assembly to make laws with respect to university or post-primary education 'including the establishment of institutions for the pursuit of such education'.[19]

The above discussion of the nature of legislative powers under the constitution to an extent highlights the intricacies created by a federal system of government with division of powers between each legislative house. However, the major matter of contention for the purpose of this article is with respect to the exact position of child rights as a legislative subject. As noted earlier, child rights is not a matter listed under any of the legislative lists. This therefore implies as is the case with all residual matters, child rights as a legislative subject is not under the exclusive control of any of the houses with each state retaining discretion as to enactment of laws guaranteeing and protecting the rights of the child. About two-third of Nigerian states have incorporated the CRA into domestic law.[20] The remaining states, all of which are in Northern Nigeria have refused to incorporate the Child Rights Act on grounds of cultural incompatibility.[21] However, Section 12 (2) of the Constitution explicitly vests in the National Assembly powers to 'make laws for the Federation or any part thereof with respect to matters not included in the exclusive legislative list for the purpose of implementing a treaty'. Some scholars have argued that this provision renders the CRA universally applicable. According to Egede, the CRA can be deemed legislation applicable to any part of the federation given the status of the

[16] Section 17(3).

[17] Ibid.

[18] Item 68.

[19] Items 27–29.

[20] See 'Child Rights Manual: Nigeria' available at http://www.barhumanrights.org.uk/wp-content/uploads/2013/12/The-Child-Rights-Manual_Nigeria-29.10.13.pdf.

[21] Daniel Ogunniyi, 'There are still huge gaps in Nigeria's efforts to protect children' (2019) available at https://theconversation.com/there-are-still-huge-gaps-in-nigerias-efforts-to-protect-children-127031.

CRA as being an implementation of an international treaty.[22] A key question in this regard is the appropriateness of such a description in view of the nature of the Act itself. According to UNICEF, the CRA 'aimed at principally enacting into law in Nigeria the principles enshrined in the Convention on the Rights of the Child (CRC) and the AU charter on the Rights and Welfare of the Child'.[23] In the first state report submitted by Nigeria to the Committee on the Rights of the Child, the government considered the Act (then a draft bill) as 'taking into consideration the provisions of the Convention' with the rights being contained in the Act being 'well articulated in the draft bill'.[24] The third report submitted in 2008 regarded the substantive Act as 'domesticating the provisions of the CRC'.[25] This corroborates the view of Egede with regard to the status of the Act. This in his view implies that the Act would be applicable even in the territory of a dissenting state in so far as it has been validly enacted.[26] Crucially however, the CRA is not described in the manner unlike the African Charter on Human and People's Rights (Ratification and Enforcement Act)[27] which is expressly described as an Act giving effect to the African Charter on Human and People's Rights. In any case, this is however not the case in Nigeria as the CRA is currently deemed inapplicable in states that have failed to domesticate the Act.

A reason for this outcome, it is submitted is linked to the nature of the federalist system of government. It must be noted that the CRA itself was only enacted in 2003, ten years after it was proposed as a draft bill. It was opposed at the time for various considerations, including religious and cultural considerations, considerations key to the development of a federalist concept.[28] The subsequent challenges to the universal applicability of the CRA domestic legislation also revolve around these considerations.

The discussion above to a large extent highlights a complicated system of ratification of the CRC in the Nigerian federation, which is regarded by Woehrling the most important disadvantage of federalism.[29] On the one hand, there is the protection of the legislative autonomy of states and prevention of 'legislative encroachment' by the federal legislative body.[30] On the other hand, there is the need for a cross-carpeted guarantee of individual rights and freedoms not only in line

[22]Egede (2007), p. 249.

[23]UNICEF Factsheet: Nigeria available at http://www.unicef.org/wcaro/WCARO_Nigeria_Factsheets_CRA.pdf.

[24]State Report to the Committee on the Rights of the Child (1995) CRC/C/8/Add 26.

[25]Third and Fourth State Report to Committee on Rights of the Child (2009) CRC/C/NGA/3-4.

[26]Egede (2007).

[27]Chapter 10 Laws of the Federation of Nigeria 1990.

[28]Alemika, E.E.O, Chukwuma, I, Laffrata, D, Messerli, D and Suckova, J, 'Report on the Implementation on the Convention of the Rights of the Child by Nigeria (2005) available at https://www.omct.org/files/2005/09/3074/report_children_nigeria_eng.pdf.

[29]Woerhling, n.7.

[30]Ibid.

with existing international standards, but also in tenor with constitutional guarantees of rights and freedoms to 'every person'.[31]

1.2 What Hope for Universal Child Rights Protection in a Federalist System?

The intricacies of the federal system of government and its effect on child rights protection in Nigeria have been discussed in preceding sections.

For the purpose of this discussion, one major method of reconciling federalism and child rights is rooted in the recognition of the nature of rights and child rights as a specific subject. A major aspect of the concept of rights is its universal application.[32] Various human rights instruments affirm the universal nature of rights[33] and while this concept has been challenged by certain scholars,[34] such challenges have been more concerned with the universality of a particular conception of rights as opposed to the universality of the underlying tenets grounding the conception of rights.[35] This is particularly more pronounced with respect to the CRC, which has been described for instance as being 'more intrusive into areas of traditional state control' than previous human rights instruments.[36]

A possible approach could be the incorporation of specific provisions guaranteeing the rights of children in the constitution. Some African countries such as South Africa[37] and Ethiopia[38] as well as a significant number of European countries[39] include specific provisions in the constitutions guaranteeing children's rights. Under the Nigeria constitution, the fundamental rights provisions are regarded as being applicable to 'every person', which according to Egede, should also be interpreted as including children.[40] Such an interpretation is highly plausible from a child rights protection perspective, particularly in view of the supremacy of the

---

[31]Ibid.

[32]https://www.un.org/en/chronicle/article/are-human-rights-universal.

[33]Ibid.

[34]Donnelly (1984), p. 400.

[35]Van den Vyver (1998).

[36]Kilbourne (1998), p. 330.

[37]Constitution of the Republic of South Africa available at https://www.gov.za/documents/constitution/chapter-2-bill-rights#28Section 28.

[38]Constitution of the Federal Democratic Republic of Ethiopia, available at https://www.wipo.int/edocs/lexdocs/laws/en/et/et007en.pdf.

[39]See 'Report on the protection of children's rights: international standards and domestic institutions' available at https://www.venice.coe.int/webforms/documents/default.aspx?pdffile=CDL-AD(2014)005-e.

[40]Egede (2007).

constitution.[41] However, this would imply that the only universally applicable rights would be as provided under the Constitution. Another alternative is an interpretation of the CRA as an express incorporation of the CRC, which would make the CRA universally applicable pursuant to Section 12(2). However, such interpretation can only apply if the CRA was ratified by a majority of the state Houses of Assembly. While Egede presumes this to be the case,[42] there is no evidence that this was the case and there is no constitutional requirement for such majority assent However, it must be noted that there is no other domestic legislation specifically related to groups of people in Nigeria in the manner of the CRA. For such a legislation to be universally accepted, there is a need to reconcile differing ethnic and religious notions regarding the child, which are constitutionally guaranteed.[43] The United Nations Committee on the Rights of the Child has also recommended the inclusion of child rights as a legislative subject under the concurrent legislative list, by which method the CRA may be applied in states that have not domesticated the Act in view of section 4(4) of the Constitution.[44] A further implication of such a step is the supremacy of the CRA over existing legislation with the CRA prevailing over state legislation in cases of inconsistency.[45] This is plausible for several reasons, chief of which is the fact that it ensures children are protected as right-holders where no such protection existed without necessarily undermining the power of states to implement legislation specifically suited to meet the needs of children in each state further to the CRA. This is not to imply that such an approach is without its challenges. States dissenting to the adoption of the CRA may not necessarily be satisfied with having legislative powers in that respect, especially in view of the fact that the CRA remains supreme in the event of conflict between the CRA and other legislation.[46] This may lead to certain compromises and adjustments being tolerated in the interest of preserving federalism which may be inimical to the interests of the child. An example of this is seen in the Child Rights Law of Akwa-Ibom State, which domesticates the CRA but outlines the age of majority as sixteen years.[47]

---

[41] Section 1(1) expressly states that the constitution is supreme and its provisions shall have binding force on the authorities and persons throughout the Federal Republic of Nigeria. Under Section 1(3), any law that is inconsistent with the provisions of the constitution is void to the extent of its inconsistency.

[42] Egede (2007), p. 272.

[43] Section 315 of the Nigerian constitution contains saving clauses for Islamic and customary law. Item 61 of the Second Schedule to the Nigerian constitution also provides that marriages contracted under Islamic and customary law are excluded from family law powers vested exclusively in the federal legislature.

[44] UN Committee on the Rights of the Child (CRC), *Consideration of Reports Submitted by States Parties under Article 44 of the Convention: Concluding observations - Nigeria*, 21 June 2010, CRC/C/NGA/CO/3-4, available at: http://www.refworld.org/docid/4efb2c612.html, para 8.

[45] Section 4(5).

[46] Section 274.

[47] Alemika, E.E.O, Chukwuma, I, Laffrata, D, Messerli, D and Suckova, J, 'Report on the Implementation on the Convention of the Rights of the Child by Nigeria (2005) available at https://www.omct.org/files/2005/09/3074/report_children_nigeria_eng.pdf.

The problem of compelling states to adopt the domesticated provisions of a treaty is not peculiar to the Nigerian federation and in Canada, the federal government concludes a 'federal-provincial treaty agreement' where provinces agree to fulfil their responsibility at the implementation stage in return for involvement in the ratification process.[48] To an extent, this may have been adopted with respect to the CRA with opposition from representatives of various states being responsible for the delay in its implementation. However, there is no evidence of such express state undertaking with states only being urged to implement the CRA on other grounds different from a matter of obligation.

There is also the possibility of reviewing the legislative lists under Schedule II of the constitution in order to ensure that the protection of children is regarded as a specific subject involving interaction between state and federal legislative houses. It is noteworthy that the current legislative lists in the Nigerian constitution to a large extent reflect the position under the 1979 constitution, which was enacted in a political era where international human rights law was in a relatively infant stage of development. This is not the case today and as a result there is a greater need for legislative responsibility to be defined explicitly in this area. For as rightly noted by Tran, human rights constitute too vast and diffuse a legislative subject to be assigned exclusively to either one of the governmental levels.[49]

2 Child Rights Protection in Nigeria: The Cultural Diversity Perspective

2.1 What Is Culture?

The concept of culture is a highly ambiguous one. Various definitions of culture have been postulated in the past and others may arise in the future.[50] There is a view of culture as 'the set of shared characteristics of a particular community or nation'.[51] It may also refer to 'everything enabling man to be successful and active in his universality and more freely to turn to good account all forms of expression in the interest of human contacts'.[52] Alternatively, it is 'a sum of human activities, the totality of values, knowledge and practices'.[53] Culture is considered to be 'closely connected with the diverse ways in which social groups construct their lives

[48]Ibid. 905.

[49]Tran (2000), p. 205.

[50]*CESCR General Comment No 21: Right of everyone to take part in Cultural Life* (2009) E/C.12/GC/21, Paragraph 10.

[51]Hotlmaat and Naber (2011), p. 52.

[52]Szabo (1974).

[53]Symonides (1998), p. 559.

ideologically, economically, socially, legally and politically'.[54] The various approaches to culture according to Szabo reveal culture as a constituent of 'social man'.[55]

In previous times, the notion of culture was considered self-reproducing and unchanging.[56] However, contemporary notions of culture suggest an element of dynamism and evolution to which end culture is viewed in a political context as principles established by the consensus of the individuals of a society[57] rather than a pre-existent, static ideology. Thus, culture is 'far more effectively characterized as an ongoing adaptation to a changing environment rather than as a static supraorganic entity'.[58] The United Nations Committee on Economic, Social and Cultural Rights describes culture as encompassing 'ways of life.....religion or belief systems, rites and ceremonies....customs and traditions through which individuals, groups of individuals and communities express their humanity and meaning they give to their existence.[59] According to the United Nations Educational, Scientific and Cultural Organization (UNESCO), culture should be regarded as the set of distinctive spiritual, material, intellectual and emotional features of society or a social group which encompasses, in addition to art and literature, lifestyles, ways of living together, value systems, traditions and beliefs.[60] The foregoing definitions establish culture as a comprehensive and multi-faceted concept which unsurprisingly makes the task of providing a precise definition of culture difficult. While there may be conceptual differences as to the precise definition of culture, culture is clearly a great influence on societal behaviour.

2.2 *Child Rights Law and Culture*

The Convention on the Rights of the Child (CRC) 'takes due account of the importance of the traditions and cultural values of each people for the protection'.[61] In addition Article 1 of the CRC defines a child as every human being below the age of 18 years 'unless under the law applicable to the child, majority is attained earlier'. Under the African Charter on the Rights and Welfare of the Child, a child is regarded

[54] Hotlmaat and Naber (2011), p. 53.

[55] Szabo (1974).

[56] Wright (1998), p. 8.

[57] Ibid,10.

[58] Zechenter (1997), pp. 332–333.

[59] See CESCR General Comment no 21, n.45.

[60] UNESCO Universal Declaration on Cultural Diversity (2001) available at http://portal.unesco.org/en/ev.php-URL_ID=13179&URL_DO=DO_TOPIC&URL_SECTION=201.html.

[61] UN General Assembly, *Convention on the Rights of the Child*, 20 November 1989, United Nations, Treaty Series, vol. 1577, p. 3, available at: http://www.refworld.org/docid/3ae6b38f0.html, Preamble.

as an individual under the age of 18 years.[62] Unlike the CRC, the definition of a child is not subject to the laws of a member state under the ACRWC. Under Article 30, children belonging to ethnic minorities have the right to enjoy their culture, practise their religion and use their own language. Article 31 recognizes the right of the child to participate freely in cultural life and the arts with states required to respect and promote this right. The cultural rights of the child are also restated in Article 12 of the African Charter on the Rights and Welfare of the Child. Unlike the CRC, the African Charter also considers the effect of harmful cultural practices with Article 21 in particular imposing an obligation on states to take appropriate measures to eliminate 'customs and practices' prejudicial to the health of the child as well as discriminatory customs and practices. To this end, the practice of child marriage and betrothal is specifically prohibited under the ACRWC.[63] The CRA defines a child in the same manner as the ACRWC; as "a person under the age of eighteen years" with no exceptions. Under the Nigerian Child Rights Act, every child has the right to participate in the cultural and artistic life of the Nigerian, African and world communities.[64]

2.3 *Engagement of Child Rights with Culture Under the Nigerian Federal System*

As indicated by the constitutional preservation of existing customary law in Nigeria under section 315 of the constitution, there is a certain degree of legal protection ascribed to cultural norms which cannot be disregarded, even in favour of incorporating contemporary child rights protection standards. Bearing this in mind, it is important to consider the possibility of establishing a child rights protection framework consistent with the concept of cultural diversity, particularly for the purpose of encouraging the adoption of the CRA in dissenting states. It is submitted that such a possibility exists. Doing so would however necessitate a shift from an undue reference to the "rights concept" which in itself can be counterproductive. According to Osiatynski,

> An excessive rhetoric of rights can be counterproductive and harmful to interpersonal relationships. Nevertheless, in cases of abuse, violence or drastic neglect, children should be protected even within their own family. But such protection should be assured by family law and penal law alone, without the need to invoke the concept of rights[65]

This should not be taken to imply that the concept of rights cannot be directly invoked in certain circumstances. For as he rightly observes,

---

[62]Article 2.

[63]Article 21 (2).

[64]Section 12 (2).

[65]Osiatynski (2009), p. 203.

> However, when the law does not offer such protection-or when the law exists but is neglected-the assertion of rights can protect victims and compel state authorities to issue and enforce proper laws[66]

A contextual approach to societal practices does not preclude legislative prohibitions. It is noted that an increased awareness of the negative effects of certain harmful practices such as female genital mutilation (FGM) created by increased sociological engagement with these practices has not necessarily resulted in its eradication.[67] Thus in certain instances, legal prohibitions may be necessary for legitimizing growing societal intolerance with respect to certain behaviour evidenced as inimical to the development of its members. However, it remains the case that such legal prohibitions would be most effective where an 'enabling environment' has been created through effective education and establishment of social conventions which serve in themselves as an opposition to those practices sought to be prohibited under the CRA.

A notorious criticism of children's rights documents is the fact that such documents are based on Western perspectives and fail to reflect other cultures.[68] In an ethnically diverse country such as Nigeria, a universalist perspective of rights in the manner espoused by the CRA or CRC may give rise to such criticisms especially where cultural values clash with rights protection standards. Building an effective rights framework must therefore entail some form of interaction between rights and culture as opposed to an outright imposition of rights on culture. Having said this, culture may be used as an instrument to protect selfish political interests.[69] It is hardly inconceivable that the main proponents of the 'cultural defence' to the influence of human rights are the political elite who are by no means directly involved in the 'cultural practices' serving as the basis for their justification.[70] In Nigeria for instance, there is a tangible disconnect between the political elite and the individuals whose interests they claim to protect particularly as is related to children. It is therefore difficult to argue that the 'culture' defence which serves as a hindrance in the universal applicability of the CRA is specifically directed towards protection of children. This is especially given the fact that as shown by empirical research, children are relatively unaware of their status as rights holders.[71] In a sense, one could therefore argue that the cultural defence in the Nigerian context is more symbolic of a paternalistic and elitist view of the best interests of children.

Having said this, progress in child rights protection in Nigeria necessitates an interaction with Nigeria's cultural diversity. Can this be done under Nigeria's federalist system? This question is a difficult one to answer. Federalism in itself, is not a panacea to all diversity related problems and with respect to Nigeria, has been

[66]Ibid.

[67]Ibekwe et al. (2012), pp. 117–122.

[68]Harris-Short (2003), pp. 130–181.

[69]Kaime (2005), pp. 221–238.

[70]Ibid.

[71]See Ejeih and Akinola (2009), pp. 176–182.

unable to solve all the problems the architects of the system intended that it solve.[72] Nevertheless, experience has also shown that federalism remains adaptable and can be tailored to satisfy contemporary needs, in this case, the development of a universalist child protection framework. In doing so, certain significant steps must be taken.[73] First, as was the strategy of the original architects of federalism, points of convergence must be identified. With respect to child rights, one would argue that this has to be centred around the four foundational principles: the best interests of the child, the right to participation, right to survival and development, and non-discrimination.[74] These principles are promoted in both the CRC and ACRWC. Unfortunately, the CRA might be deficient in this respect. Significant sections of the Act share greater similarities with the English Children's Act[75] and other means of child protection enforcement symbolic of the colonial era. However, major provisions of the Act, particularly those related to substantive rights, have been considered to be generally acceptable and to a certain extent legally enforceable even in states that have outrightly refused to incorporate the CRA. The Children and Young Persons Act 1943 applicable in Northern States already outlines certain provisions consonant with best interests and the child's right to survival and development. While participatory rights may prove to be a bone of contention, it is worth arguing that perhaps the main problem is not necessarily the concept of child rights, but the manner in which it is presented under the CRA. Perhaps therefore, there is a place for compromise in the development of a universal child rights framework, in that pursuant to federalist structures, states that have failed to domesticate the CRA can be encouraged to do so in a manner that upholds the cardinal principles enshrined in the CRC and ACRWC and provides allowance for modification in accordance with existing cultural norms. Such a compromise is not without its challenges. Significant portions of the CRA challenge culturally acceptable practices for instance child labour and child marriage, particularly in Northern Nigeria, and this is unlikely to change in the nearest future. Furthermore, there is a notable lack of consensus as to what exactly is regarded as "culture" in the states that reject the CRA on grounds of incompatibility with culture. There is therefore every possibility that compromising on the universal standards espoused in the CRA may be manipulated in favour of a majority notion which is antithetical to child rights protection.

[72]Babalola (2015).

[73]Ibid.

[74]https://www.acyp.nsw.gov.au/about/the-convention-on-the-rights-of-the-child.

[75](1989) Chapter 41 available at http://www.legislation.gov.uk/ukpga/1989/41/contents.

3 Concluding Thoughts

In conclusion, one notes the relationship between human rights and federalism as a highly complex one, both in a political and socio-cultural context. Federalism in itself harnesses the concept of diversity in population in various context and in a sense attempts to 'satisfy all comers' in the hope that such an approach fosters national integration and development. Human rights on the other hand considers as fundamental to its existence a 'transcendental notion' of rights based on a set of shared characteristics considered fundamental to the notion of a common humanity.[76] As is the case with federalism, there is recognition of the concept of diversity among groups, which is nevertheless subject to the need to protect individual rights and freedoms. In the context of child rights in Nigeria, it is important to understand that child rights protection as symbolized by the CRA is not necessarily at odds with the notion of federalism. In order to ensure such an outcome, the philosophies grounding both concepts must be effectively harmonized. For instance, child rights in its universalistic sense regards the submission of competing cultural beliefs and value systems to the protection of the welfare of the child. Similarly, federalism aims at reconciling different cultures and submitting it to the protection of the overall interest of the federation albeit through a different approach of granting limited autonomy to groups comprising the federation. Notwithstanding the distinction in method, a useful starting point in reconciling child rights and federalism as far as the Nigerian state is concerned is by recognising the similarity in their objective, which is the protection of an overall interest that transcends existing divisions in groups of people. This view is corroborated by Kilbourne who concludes thus on federalism and the CRC in the United States:

> The United States system of federalism should not be a barrier to ratification and implementation of the Convention. It may be true that it would be bad policy or bad politics for the federal government to "interfere" in traditional state functions such as family law, education, and juvenile justice. As a matter of constitutional doctrine, however, ratification of the Convention, and enactment of federal legislation pursuant to the Convention, would not necessarily offend or imperil federalism values.[77]

Another useful mechanism, especially as an interim measure is the enforcement of the provisions of the CRA on the basis of its fundamental nature not only to the interest of the child, but also to the Nigerian state. For instance, Section 17 of the Constitution regards as a fundamental objective of government policy 'the protection of the child from exploitation and neglect'.[78] The exclusive legislative list regards matters incidental to fundamental objectives a matter for exclusive federal legislation. Thus, it may be argued that to the extent as the CRA applies to protect the child from exploitation and neglect, dissenting states are bound by its provisions. Although such states could argue in the context of legislative autonomy that existing

---

[76] Hughes (2011), pp. 1–24.

[77] Kilbourne (1998), p. 334.

[78] Section 17(3).

laws already protect such interests, the CRA may retain legislative supremacy in such areas. This is not incompatible with federalism for federalism does not entail equality in division of powers, neither does it by definition aim at transferring powers from a central authority to regional authorities[79] as appears to currently be the case with respect to child rights protection in Nigeria. Such a position is untenable, given its inconsistency with constitutional provisions on division of legislative powers. It is therefore encouraged that for the purpose of protecting the rights of the child, the CRA should be universally applicable at the very least to the extent provided by the provisions of the constitution. This would by implication answer, though not completely, a charge against federalism of crystallizing differences and making it impossible for people to rise above their loyalties to a higher order.[80]

4 Conclusion

This paper has examined the relationship between federalism, child rights and culture with particular emphasis on the Nigerian legal system. While the relationship is a highly complex one, it has been argued that these notions can be effectively harmonized in a federal legal system. It has been particularly suggested that federalism should work to serve the interests of rights protection for which purpose certain elements of it may require revision. It is also the view of the author that interaction and engagement with culture is highly essential for developing an effective child rights framework.

References

Alemika EEO, Chukwuma I, Laffrata D, Messerli D, Suckova J (2005) Report on the Implementation on the Convention of the Rights of the Child by Nigeria. Available at https://www.omct.org/files/2005/09/3074/report_children_nigeria_eng.pdf

Attorney-General of Lagos State vs. Attorney-General of the Federation (2003) 6 S.C

Babalola A (2015) The efficacy of federalism in a multi-ethnic state: the Nigerian experience. J Pan Afr Stud 8(2):86

Breitenmoser S, Ehrenzeller B, Sassoli M (eds) (2007) Human Rights, democracy and the rule of law. Dike Verlag

CESCR General Comment No 21: Right of everyone to take part in Cultural Life (2009) E/C.12/GC/21

Constitution of the Federal Democratic Republic of Ethiopia

[79]Nwabueze (1983a), p. 147.

[80]Ibid.

Constitution of the Federal Republic of Nigeria 1999 (as amended)

Constitution of the Republic of South Africa 1996

Donnelly J (1984) Cultural universalism and universal human rights. Human Rights Q 6(4):400

Egede E (2007) Bringing human rights home: an examination of the domestication of human rights treaties in Nigeria. J Afr Law 51(2):249

Ejeih MUC, Akinola OB (2009) 'Children's rights and participation in schools: exploring the awareness level and views of Nigerian Primary School Children. Elem Educ Online 8 (1):176–182

Elaigwu JI (2007) The politics of federalism in Nigeria. Adonis and Abbey, p 6

Harris-Short S (2003) International human rights law: imperialist, inept and ineffective? Cultural relativism and the UN Convention on the rights of the child. Human Rights Q 25(1):130–181

Hotlmaat HMT, Naber J (2011) Women's human rights and culture: from deadlock to dialogue. Intersentia Publishing

Hughes G (2011) The concept of dignity in the universal declaration of human rights. J Relig Ethics 39(1):1–24

Ibekwe PC, Onoh RC, Onyebuchi AK, Ezeonu PO, Ibekwe RO (2012) Female genital mutilation in Southeast Nigeria: a survey on the current knowledge and practice. J Public Health Epidemiol 4 (5):117–122

Ikpe UB. 'Public Culture and National Integration in multicultural states: Comparative observations from the United States and Nigeria' available at http://www.tandfonline.com/doi/pdf/10.1177/1477570004041687

Kaime T (2005) The Convention on the rights of the child and the cultural legitimacy of children's rights in Africa: some reflections. Afr Human Rights Law J 2:221–238

Kilbourne S (1998) The Convention on the rights of the child: federalism issues for the United States. Geograph J Fighting Poverty 5(2):327–334

Nwabueze BO (1983a) A constitutional history of Nigeria. C. Hurst & CO

Nwabueze BO (1983b) Federalism in Nigeria under the presidential constitution. Sweet and Maxwell

Osiatynski W (2009) Human rights and their limits. CUP

Symonides J (1998) Cultural Rights, a neglected category of human rights. Int Sci J 50 (158):559–572

Szabo I (1974) Cultural rights. AW Sijthoff-Leiden

Tamuno T (1998) Nigerian federalism in historical perspective. In: Amuwo K, Agbaje A, Suberu R, Herault G (eds) Federalism and political restructuring in Nigeria. Spectrum Books, p 13

Tran L-VN (2000) Human rights and federalism: a comparative study on freedom, democracy and cultural diversity. Martinus Nijhoff, p 205

UN Committee on the Rights of the Child (CRC), *Consideration of Reports Submitted by States Parties under Article 44 of the Convention: Concluding observations - Nigeria*, 21 June 2010, CRC/C/NGA/CO/3-4, available at: http://www.refworld.org/docid/4efb2c612.html

UN General Assembly, *Convention on the Rights of the Child*, 20 November 1989, United Nations, Treaty Series, vol. 1577, p. 3, available at: http://www.refworld.org/docid/3ae6b38f0.html

UNESCO Universal Declaration on Cultural Diversity (2001). available at http://portal.unesco.org/en/ev.php-URL_ID=13179&URL_DO=DO_TOPIC&URL_SECTION=201.html

UNICEF Factsheet: Nigeria available at http://www.unicef.org/wcaro/WCARO_Nigeria_Factsheets_CRA.pdf

Van den Vyver J (1998) Universality and relativity of human rights: American relativism. Buffalo Human Rights Rev 4(1)

Wright S (1998) The politicization of culture. Anthropol Today 14(1):7–15

Zechenter EM (1997) In the name of culture: cultural relativism and the abuse of the individual. J Anthropol Res 53(3):319–347

Fife Ogunde is a Legal Scholar and Researcher.

Part VIII
Case Comment

Decolonising the Chagos Islands?

John Reynolds

Content

Portuguese 'discovery', French colonisation and British treaty dealings. Plantation and extraction. Racial capitalism and slave labour. Coercion and partition. Imperial alliance and militarisation. Displacement and exile. The story of the Chagos archipelago is a familiar one in the history of international law and relations between peoples. It is indicative of international law's complicity in European oppression and dispossession of colonised peoples and places. Yet while much of the machinations of colonial rule were spannered—at least nominally in the form of sovereignty-as-independence—by the national liberation movements of the twentieth century, the Chagos travesty persists into our twenty-first century colonial present. Britain's refusal to let go of the small group of faraway islands serves as a contradictory symbol of both its self-deluding pretensions of empire on one hand, and its self-abasing servitude to United States imperialism on the other. It reminds us that colonialism is still very much with us, and that self-determination remains contingent. International law's ode to sovereign equality and territorial integrity is as much about concealing its own colonial foundations as it is about delivering on a promise of liberation.

In February 2019, the International Court of Justice (ICJ) issued an advisory opinion to confirm in law what we knew already as a matter of social and political and material reality: the British state had wrongfully kept control of the Chagos islands after Mauritius asserted its independence, and the process of decolonisation there is not yet complete. The core finding of the Court was that that Britain 'has an obligation to bring to an end its administration of the Chagos Archipelago as rapidly

J. Reynolds (✉)
Department of Law, National University of Ireland, Maynooth, Ireland
e-mail: John.Reynolds@mu.ie

C. Eboe-Osuji et al. (eds.), *Nigerian Yearbook of International Law 2018/2019*,
Nigerian Yearbook of International Law 2018/2019,
https://doi.org/10.1007/978-3-030-69594-1_20

as possible'.[1] On the face of it, this is a solid confirmation of international law's belated but definitive prohibition of colonialism. And yet we can also read the judgment as ringing somewhat hollow.

1960 was the high-water mark of formal decolonisation, before the swift tightening of 'the grip of neo-colonialism'[2] and the restructured economic subjugation of the Third World. That year, 468 long years after Columbus claimed the island of Guanahani for the Spanish royals and set in chain a sequence of events whereby the veins of multiple continents were cut open and 'transmuted into European capital',[3] the UN General Assembly passed Resolution 1514. Colonialism 'in all its forms and manifestations' (bar the small matter of settler colonies that had reconstituted themselves as sovereign states) was prohibited. Any attempt at the partial or total disruption of the national unity and the territorial integrity of any country was deemed incompatible with the purposes and principles of the UN Charter. Seventeen newly independent states joined the UN in 1960 and the Third World bloc became the majority in the General Assembly.

'Existing colonies may linger on', Nkrumah wrote in 1965, 'but no new colonies will be created'.[4] Fading empires like Britain—and newer imperial powers like the US—were all too conscious of this. That same year, the British government orchestrated a way to carve a lingering colony out of the existing-but-not-for-too-much-longer colony of Mauritius. By this time, the idea of territorial and military bases in relatively unpopulated areas was particularly appealing to Western powers. The "strategic island concept" being pursued by the US in particular sought to locate uninhabited island bases as a way to bypass rising anti-imperial sentiment around the globe. The potential of Chagos was clear: military planners would be 'thrilled at the idea of a base with no civilian population within almost 500 miles', and indeed 'planning between the British and U.S. governments had been underway since at least 1964'.[5] Britain's task was, so to speak, to make Chagos terra nullius again. This would involve removing the Chagossians—Creole-speaking people descended from African slaves and indentured labourers—who had been inhabiting the islands for 200 years.

Through coercive means, the British government imposed the Lancaster House "agreement" on leaders of the Mauritius Council of Ministers to partition the colony and excise the Chagos archipelago as part of a newly constructed 'British Indian Ocean Territory' in 1965. No more than four days later, the Colonial Office sent instructions to the administration of this new territory stating that 'contingency

[1]ICJ, *Legal Consequences of the Separation of the Chagos Archipelago from Mauritius in 1965*, Advisory Opinion (25 February 2019) para. 182.

[2]Nkrumah (1965), p. x.

[3]Galeano (1973), p. 2.

[4]Nkrumah (1965), p. ix.

[5]Vine (2009), p. 90.

planning for evacuation of existing population. . .should begin at once'.[6] In the lead-up to Mauritian independence in 1968, Britain began displacing the Chagossians from their archipelago: preventing those who travelled from returning, and forcibly removing others. Archive documentation has shown that the Foreign Office consistently lied about this during these years. For fear of being called out by the Committee of Twenty-Four (the UN Special Committee on Decolonisation), legal advisor Anthony Aust recommended that British officials 'maintain the fiction that the inhabitants of Chagos are not a permanent or semi-permanent population' but rather itinerant workers with no connection to the islands.[7] Diplomatic correspondence from August 1966 is revealing of the attitudes prevalent in the colonial view of Chagos and its people. Paul Gore-Booth, Permanent Under-Secretary of State in the Foreign Office wrote: 'We must surely be very tough about this. The object of the exercise was to get some rocks which will remain ours; there will be no indigenous population except seagulls who have not yet got a Committee (the Status of Women does not cover the rights of Birds).' His colleague Denis Greenhill added: 'Unfortunately along with the birds go some few Tarzans or Men Fridays whose origins are obscure, and who are being hopefully wished on to Mauritius etc. When this has been done I agree we must be very tough'.[8]

In December 1966, Britain leased the largest of the Chagos islands, Diego Garcia, to the US for the establishment of a naval and military base. International law facilitated this in an international treaty between the two,[9] under which sovereignty over the territory was retained by Britain but competence for its administration was transferred to the US. There was no direct payment for the lease; instead the US contributed to the administrative costs of establishing the new colonial territory ('diplomatic legalese for the costs of deporting the Chagossians, buying out the plantation owners, and paying off Mauritius and the Seychelles'[10]) and gave Britain a discount on the Polaris nuclear submarine ballistic missile system. The Chagossians were entirely absent from these arrangements, and the assumption underlying the agreement was that they would be entirely absent from the archipelago. Construction of the military base began in 1971, at which time forced expulsions ramped up, and between 1971 and 1973 the remaining inhabitants were put onto cargo ships and deported to Mauritius and the Seychelles. Just before the final deportations, 'British agents and U.S. troops on Diego Garcia herded the

[6]U.K. Trial Bundle (litigation documents) 4–132, Sheridans Solicitors, London, cited in Vine (2009), *ibid*.

[7]Anthony Aust, 'Immigration Legislation for BIOT', Memorandum, 16 January 1970, quoted in Vine (2009), p. 92.

[8]Foreign Office confidential memo ZD4/56, 'British Indian Ocean Territory', 24 August 1966, cited in *R (on the application of Bancoult) v. Secretary of State for Foreign & Commonwealth Affairs Rev 1* [2006] EWHC 1038 (Admin), Judgment, 11 May 2006, para. 27.

[9]Agreement Concerning the Availability for Defence Purposes of the British Indian Ocean Territory, 30 December 1966.

[10]Vine (2009), p. 87.

Chagossians' pet dogs into sealed sheds and gassed and burned them in front of their traumatized owners'.[11]

Since then, all human and economic activity in the Chagos archipelago has been concentrated in the military facilities on Diego Garcia. There has been no functioning agriculture on the islands. The Chagossians remain exiled but have continued a campaign to return. They plan to re-establish their lives and livelihoods there through fishing and coconut copra production. In recent years, much of the energy of this struggle has been supported by litigation—for return of the Chagossians, and for the archipelago to be reunified with Mauritius. In 2000, the High Court in Britain ruled that the 1965 colonial ordinance used as the basis to deport the islanders was unlawful. Instead of complying with the judgement and allowing them to return, Tony Blair's government issued an Order-in-Council to explicitly bar the Chagossians from re-inhabiting the archipelago. This was again challenged in the courts, but this time ultimately approved in 2008 by the House of Lords.[12] In 2012, the European Court of Human Rights also rejected a case brought by 1786 Chagossians against Britain as inadmissible; the Court felt it did not have jurisdiction over a colonial territory to which Britain had not actively extended its European human rights law obligations.[13] So the Chagossians and Mauritius looked to international courts beyond the national and regional domain of the colonial power.

In 2015, an arbitral tribunal of the Permanent Court of Arbitration ruled that the Chagos 'Marine Protected Area' which Britain had created in 2010 (publicly for conservation purposes but actually, in confidence, 'to assure that U.S. interests were safeguarded', 'to get through the various Chagossian lobbies', to 'put paid to resettlement claims' and make it 'difficult, if not impossible' for the Chagossians to return[14]) violates international law.[15] It also ruled that Britain does have

[11] Vine (2009), p. 1.

[12] *R (on the application of Bancoult) v. Secretary of State for Foreign & Commonwealth* [2008] UKHL 61, Judgment, 22 October 2008. See further Allen (2014), Chapter 1.

[13] *Chagos Islanders v. UK*, European Court of Human Rights, Application No. 35622/04, Fourth Section Decision, 11 December 2012. See further Allen (2014), Chapter 2.

[14] 'HMG Floats Proposal for Marin Reserve Covering the Chagos Archipelago (British Indian Ocean Reserve)', Confidential Cable from US Embassy in London, REF: 08LONDON2667, 5 May 2009, published by *Wikileaks* and *The Guardian*, 2 December 2010. Colin Roberts, the British Foreign and Commonwealth Office Director for Overseas Territories is quoted in the cable: '"We do not regret the removal of the population," since removal was necessary for the BIOT to fulfill its strategic purpose'. The US State Department author of the cable concludes that: 'Establishing a marine reserve might, indeed, as the FCO's Roberts stated, be the most effective long-term way to prevent any of the Chagos Islands' former inhabitants or their descendants from resettling in the BIOT.'

[15] Permanent Court of Arbitration, Arbitral Tribunal Constituted under Annex VII of the United Nations Convention on the Law of the Sea, *In the Matter of the Chagos Marine Protected Area: Mauritius v. the United Kingdom*, Award of 18 March 2015. While finding in favour of Mauritius on this point of the incompatibility of the Marine Protected Area with British obligations under the UN Convention on the Law of the Sea (UNCLOS), the Arbitral Tribunal at the same ruled that Mauritius's claim to sovereignty over the Chagos archipelago was not something for the Tribunal to consider under UNCLOS.

obligations towards Mauritius over the return of the archipelago, but only when it is no longer needed for defence purposes. This left enough space for the British Foreign Office to announce in 2016 that 'the government has decided against resettlement of the Chagossian people'—on grounds that it would be expensive and impractical—and that, with the initial 50-year lease period expiring in December 2016, the agreement with the US would be extended: 'In an increasingly dangerous world, the defence facility is used by us and our allies to combat some of the most difficult problems of the twenty-first century including terrorism, international criminality, instability and piracy. I can today confirm that the UK continues to welcome the US presence, and that the agreements will continue as they stand until 30 December 2036.'[16] Within a month of this extension kicking in, the African Union resolved to work to ensure 'the completion of the decolonization of the Republic of Mauritius'.[17]

And so, to the ICJ. In June 2017, after many iterations over the years of UN General Assembly, African Union and Non-Aligned Movement condemnation of British policy on Chagos, the General Assembly requested the Court's advisory opinion on the questions of: (i) whether the process of decolonisation of Mauritius was lawfully completed when Mauritius gained independence in 1968 following the separation of the Chagos Archipelago from Mauritius; and (ii) what the consequences are under international law arising from the continued administration of the Chagos Archipelago by Britain, including with respect to the resettlement of the Chagossians.[18] The resolution was carried by the global South, with many European countries opting to abstain and a smallish collection of states voting with Britain against the move.

***

The history of international law is a history of unequal relations. In the Chagos proceedings at the ICJ, a number of Third World states made representations about the unequal nature of treaties imposed by colonial powers on representatives of the colony prior to independence. They noted the structural biases in favour of colonial states as a persistent feature of international treaties. While this was hardwired into international law historically, the argument is that this was no longer valid by the time of the Vienna Convention on the Law of Treaties in the late 1960s: 'one could hardly deny that treaties dictated by the stronger to the weaker party would qualify as unequal treaties. This idea of inequality has been recognized and has played a crucial role in the development of international law.'[19]

In 1964, the Committee of Twenty-Four made clear its opinion that the constitutional arrangements in Mauritius 'do not allow the representatives of the people to

[16]Foreign and Commonwealth Office, 'Update on the British Indian Ocean Territory: Written statement - HCWS260', 16 November 2016. The statement was delivered in parliament by Alan Duncan, Minister of State for Foreign and Commonwealth Affairs.

[17]African Union, 'Resolution on Chagos Archipelago', Assembly/AU/Res.1 (XXVIII), 30 January 2017.

[18]General Assembly Resolution 71/292, UN Doc. A/RES/71/292, 22 June 2017.

[19]*Legal Consequences of the Separation of the Chagos Archipelago from Mauritius in 1965*, Statement by Thailand, *Verbatim Record*, 6 September 2018, para. 10.

exercise real legislative or executive powers, and that authority is nearly all concentrated in the hands of the United Kingdom Government and its representatives.'[20] The advisory opinion narrates the story of the Lancaster House agreement from there. The Colonial Office and the Governor of Mauritius informed the native Council of Ministers and the Premier of their proposal to constitutionally sever the Chagos archipelago from the rest of Mauritius. The Council of Ministers opposed this. Britain's Foreign Secretary and Defence Secretary said that if Mauritius would not agree, they would have to implement a 'forcible detachment'. The counter-offer made by the Premier of Mauritius was that Britain should first concede independence to Mauritius, including sovereignty over Chagos, and then the Mauritian Government could negotiate with the Britain and the US on the question of Diego Garcia. The Brits were not open to this. In planning a meeting with the Premier of Mauritius, the aim of the British Prime Minister was to: 'frighten him with hope: hope that he might get independence; Fright lest he might not unless he is sensible about the detachment of the Chagos Archipelago.'[21] Judge Robinson cites a subsequent comment from the Premier: 'There was a noose around my neck. I could not say no. I had to say yes, otherwise the [noose] could have tightened.'[22]

And so it was. Amputating Chagos was the price of Mauritian independence. The ICJ, while not casting it explicitly in terms of coercion or duress, concluded that this was illegitimate: 'heightened scrutiny should be given to the issue of consent in a situation where a part of a non-self-governing territory is separated to create a new colony'—and in this specific situation 'detachment was not based on the free and genuine expression of the will of the people concerned.'[23]

On that foundation, the Court makes a series of short, snappy steps from the applicable law to its main findings: the right of peoples to self-determination was established as a normative principle of customary international law by 1965; state practice and opinio juris at the time confirmed that respect for the territorial integrity of a non self-self-governing territory was a key element of self-determination; the General Assembly has important functions in overseeing the implementation of self-determination in the context of decolonisation; because the Chagos archipelago was an integral part of the non-self-governing territory of Mauritius and was illegitimately separated in 1965, the process of decolonisation of Mauritius was not lawfully complete when the rest of the territory became independent in 1968; Britain's continuing administration of the territory is an internationally wrongful

[20]'Report of the Special Committee on the Situation with regard to the Implementation of the Declaration on the Granting of Independence to Colonial Countries and Peoples', UN Doc. A/5800/Rev.1, 1964–1965, p. 352, para. 154.

[21]*Legal Consequences of the Separation of the Chagos Archipelago*, para. 105, quoting note from Private Secretary to Prime Minister Harold Wilson, 22 September 1965.

[22]ICJ, *Legal Consequences of the Separation of the Chagos Archipelago from Mauritius in 1965*, Separate Opinion of Judge Robinson (25 February 2019) para. 93, citing Mauritius Legislative Assembly, Reply to PQ No. B/1141 (25 November 1980) p. 4223.

[23]*Legal Consequences of the Separation of the Chagos Archipelago*, para. 172.

act which must be ended as quickly as possible, and all members states must cooperate with the UN to complete the decolonisation of Mauritius.[24]

This is all well and good in terms of the Court's baseline commitment to self-determination and the upshot that the colonial protagonist here 'totally lost the case. There's no silver lining'.[25] The brevity of the opinion's reasoning on the substance and its lack of engagement with some of the arguments made in state submissions, however, leaves a sense of hollowness. It exposes the opinion to both doctrinal objections and deeper critique. On the question of whether self-determination was already a rule of customary international law by the period between 1965 and 1968, for example, it has been suggested that 'the Court completely fudges it' by making a 'plain assertion' unsupported by sufficient evidence of state practice or opinio juris.[26] From a more critical perspective, the weight given in the first place to a traditional conception of customary international law highlights the very 'nature and politics of "custom" as a continuing source of international law', which, with its twin requirements of attesting "state practice" and "opinio juris" has facilitated and advanced the imperial order.'[27] B.S. Chimni has illustrated that the historic role of customary international law 'has been to facilitate the functioning of global capitalist system by filling crucial gaps in the international legal system'—gaps relating to either short term interests of capitalist states or the systemic interests of the global capitalist system.[28] While very definitively linking (or, some argue, 'shrinking'[29]) self-determination to decolonisation, the advisory opinion does little to advance the more radical, humane, "postmodern" conceptualisation of customary international law that Chimni suggests.[30] The African Union submissions also gave the court the opportunity to (re)develop in the interests of the Third World the doctrine of specially-affected states ("concerned states") as an essential component of determining customary international law: 'There is no doubt that those who are the concerned States in the present proceeding are, first and foremost, the African States and then those states that have been victims of colonialism (most of whom are part of the Non-Aligned Movement)'.[31] But again the Court sidesteps this opportunity.

Ultimately, the advisory opinion pushes up against the limitations imposed by international law's state-centricity. The Chagossians themselves remain somewhat

---

[24]*Legal Consequences of the Separation of the Chagos Archipelago*, paras. 139–182.

[25]Milanovic (2019).

[26]Milanovic (2019), *ibid.*

[27]Kanad Bagchi, 'Imperialism, International Law and the Chagos Islands: Reflections on Legal Consequences of the Separation of the Chagos Archipelago', *Völkerrechtsblog*, 1 March 2019.

[28]Chimni (2018), pp. 1–46.

[29]Klabbers (2019).

[30]For explication, see Chimni (2018), pp. 36–43. In a passage on opinio juris in this analysis, Chimni draws on (and critiques) Judge Cançado Trindade, who (characteristically) makes clear in his Separate Opinion that he wanted to go further than the Court on this aspect of the *Chagos* case.

[31]*Legal Consequences of the Separation of the Chagos Archipelago from Mauritius in 1965*, Written Comments of the African Union on other Written Statements, 15 May 2018. See also Jon Heller (2018), pp. 191–243.

peripheral. A few of the separate opinions do make the point that the Court does not do enough to account for their human and material experience. And Judges Robinson and Cançado Trindade both write the testimony of Liseby Elysé into their opinions, giving voice to her personal experience as illustrative of the voice of the colonised and the plight of the Chagossians.[32] This is necessarily an individual testimony, however, not the type of 'powerful collective representations' which have solicited powerful support for the Chagossian cause but which do not fit the 'more positivistic understanding of history imposed by formal concepts of legal evidence.'[33]

Beyond this, the core focus of the advisory opinion, by virtue of international law's traditions and structures, is overwhelmingly on Mauritius's territorial sovereignty rather than the Chagossians' right to return. Even with the restoration of Mauritian sovereignty over the archipelago and the completion of the process of decolonisation from the perspective of international law as the Court sees it, the fate of the people and ecology of Chagos remains contingent on the priorities of (and pressures on) the state of Mauritius. The substantive findings section of the Court's advisory opinion devotes just a single sentence to the uprooted Chagossians.[34] It casts their situation as a human rights issue which should be considered in the General Assembly's work subsequent to the advisory opinion, but which is beyond the scope of the ICJ itself. Cançado Trindade's discussion of the 1955 Bandung conference[35]—and his reference to the collection of essays that a substantial number of TWAIL-oriented scholars contributed to[36]—is a welcome acknowledgment of the role that the Third World played in influencing international law and the UN at the time. But it is also emblematic of the deficiencies of international law—even that shaped by Bandung—in being able to adequately address the Chagos situation. The pluralism of Bandung and the Non-Aligned Movement ultimately meant that in the distillation of the "spirit of Bandung" into doctrinal positions, the more radical strands of Third Wordlist thought and praxis were filtered out, and the core focus was a statist one preoccupied with national political independence and territorial sovereignty.

***

In April 2019, the British Foreign Office responded to the ICJ's findings with a confident, if unsubstantiated, rebuttal: 'The Government has considered the content of the Opinion carefully, however we do not share the Court's approach. . .we have no doubt about our sovereignty over the Chagos Archipelago'.[37] A former empire

---

[32]ICJ, *Legal Consequences of the Separation of the Chagos Archipelago from Mauritius in 1965*, Separate Opinion of Judge Robinson (25 February 2019), para. 104; Separate Opinion of Judge Cançado Trindade, para. 219.

[33]Jeffery (2007), pp. 951–968.

[34]*Legal Consequences of the Separation of the Chagos Archipelago*, para. 181.

[35]ICJ, *Legal Consequences of the Separation of the Chagos Archipelago from Mauritius in 1965*, Separate Opinion of Judge Cançado Trindade (25 February 2019) paras. 43–49.

[36]Eslava et al. (2017).

[37]Foreign and Commonwealth Office, 'British Indian Ocean Territory: Written statement – HCWS1528', 30 April 2019.

remains happily ensconced in its global board-game activities, with real-world consequences. Its statement to the UN General Assembly in May 2019 reveals a continuing belief in the validity of its own self-appointment as global police force: 'In this important part of the world, the joint United Kingdom and United States defence facility on the British Indian Ocean Territory plays a vital role in our efforts to keep our allies and friends, including Mauritius, in the region, and beyond, safe and secure.'[38] The General Assembly voted that day to welcome the ICJ advisory opinion and demand that Britain 'withdraw its colonial administration unconditionally within a period of no more than six months'.[39] 116 member states voted in favour of the resolution, with just six voting against. Five of them—Britain, the US, Israel, Australia and Hungary—form a type of settler-colonial/white-nationalist alliance that is reminiscent of the 'unholy alliance between Portuguese colonialism, South African racism and Israeli imperialism' which the General Assembly used to condemn in the 1970s.[40] (The sixth, the Maldives, defends its vote as seeking to protect itself against a potential reduction in its Exclusive Economic Zone in the Indian Ocean, which could occur if sovereignty over Chagos was returned to Mauritius before pending claims over the maritime boundaries between the two states are resolved). Six months later, in November 2019, Britain had not withdrawn its colonial administration, and was described by commentators as 'a rogue state'.[41]

There has been much talk in recent years of the imperatives of decolonising—"decolonising the university", "decolonising dialectics", "decolonising international law", and so on. This work of 'decolonising' as reimagining or restructuring is vital—if not always rooted in material struggles in the colonised world, and perhaps sometimes better not labelled as decolonisation. In sites where colonial rule and occupation continues, or where Indigenous peoples struggle against settler-colonial structures and suffocation, decolonisation is not a metaphor.[42] In 1965, while the fate of the Chagos archipelago and its people was being altered by imperial coercion, across the continent Amílcar Cabral was appealing to his revolutionary party (under Portuguese rule in Guinea and Cape Verde) to be wary of seeing decolonisation as simply the liberation of the mind: 'Always bear in mind that the people are not fighting for ideas, for the things in anyone's head. They are fighting to win material benefits, to live better and in peace, to see their lives go forward, to guarantee the future of their children.'[43] For the Chagossians, these material benefits and these futures are wrapped up in their bond with the lands and waters of the archipelago. Decolonisation is inseparable from their right to return. The ICJ advisory opinion's

---

[38]Foreign and Commonwealth Office, 'Statement and explanation of vote on the resolution on the British Indian Ocean Territories by Ambassador Karen Pierce, UK Permanent Representative to the UN', 22 May 2019.

[39]UN General Assembly Resolution 73/295, UN Doc. A/RES/73/295, 22 May 2019, para. 3.

[40]UN General Assembly Resolution 3151 (XXVIII), 14 December 1973, para. (G)5.

[41]Kennedy (2019).

[42]Tuck and Wayne Yang (2012), pp. 1–40.

[43]Cabral (1969), p. 70.

deflection of the question of their return is telling. The opinion fails to acknowledge that—just as their removal was essential to the latest stage of imperialism in the archipelago—their return is intrinsic to the process of decolonisation, not an ancillary element to be negotiated.

The scale and significance of the US war base operation on Diego Garcia since its establishment cannot be underestimated: billions invested in the largest build-up of any location after the Vietnam War; lucrative contracts for private military contractors; nuclear-capable bombers and likely nuclear weapons storage; NASA facilities and electro-optical deep space surveillance systems; pivotal wartime functions in the first Gulf War, the war on Afghanistan and the 2003 invasion of Iraq; site of rendition flight stop-offs, clandestine "black site" detentions and possibly 'secret prison ships' in the waters of the archipelago.[44] It is 'the single most important military facility we've got. . .the base from which we control half of Africa and the southern side of Asia', according to US military specialists.[45] Since the ICJ advisory opinion came down, the realpolitik pragmatism espoused in establishment circles has returned to the fore. Channelling the logic of "there is no alternative", this position assumes that the Diego Garcia base will remain and that Mauritius will acquiesce. As one former diplomat puts it: 'Eventually, the issue of sovereignty will have to be finessed by agreements that allow continuation of the military base at Diego Garcia with guarantees that Mauritius will retain sovereignty over the Chagos archipelago. Mauritius will agree to lease out the island for a long period to the U.S. for maintaining the military base.'[46] As it stands, the US position remains that, for security reasons, the Chagos archipelago must not be inhabited. The structures of the international economic order ensure that unequal relations continue, and that global North powers can get much of what they want by incentive and coercion.

Cabral's warnings of the dangers of neo-colonialism are prescient here. He conceptualises the liberation of a people in terms of 'the regaining of the historical personality of that people, its return to history through the destruction of the imperialist domination to which it was subjected. . .for us the basis of national liberation, *whatever the formulas adopted on the level of international law*, is the inalienable right of every people to have its own history'. Given 'the essential characteristics of the present world economy' and the 'experiences already gained in the field of anti-imperialist struggle', the principal struggle is against neo-colonialism.[47] For Cabral, anti-colonialism must be an interruption of the colonial practices and structures that have been imposed. A process of decolonisation that leaves an imperial military base intact will remain incomplete, even if sovereignty is transferred from one state to another. In this sense, the struggle for the abolition of the Diego Garcia base and for the people's return to Chagos is part of a broader

[44]Vine (2009), pp. 8–10.

[45]Vine (2009), p. 10.

[46]Ranjan Chakravarty (2019).

[47]Amílcar Cabral, 'The Weapon of Theory', Address delivered to the first Tricontinental Conference of the Peoples of Asia, Africa and Latin America, Havana, January 1966. Emphasis added.

struggle to (re)make the world anew—a struggle to claim the future, to restore local economies and ecologies in place of global war-game capitalism. This will be a constant struggle. Decolonisation and social emancipation, as Galeano reminds us, must be built with convincing strategy and clenched teeth: 'after all, if the future came on a platter, it would not be of this world.'[48]

References

Allen S (2014) The Chagos Islanders and international law. Hart

Cabral A (1969) Extracts from Party directive 1965. In: Cabral A (ed) Revolution in Guinea: an African People's Struggle (Stage 1)

Chakravarty PR (2019) Decolonising the Chagos Archipelago. The Hindu, 4 June 2019

Chimni BS (2018) Customary international law: a third world perspective. Am J Int Law 112 (1):1–46

Eslava L, Fakhri M, Nesiah V (eds) (2017) Bandung, global history, and international law - critical pasts and pending futures. Cambridge University Press

Galeano E (1973) The open veins of Latin America: five centuries of the pillage of a continent. Monthly Review Press

Jeffery L (2007) How a plantation became paradise: changing representations of the homeland among displaced Chagos Islanders. J R Anthropol Inst 13(4):951–968

Heller KJ (2018) Specially-affected states and the formation of custom. Am J Int Law 112 (2):191–243

Kennedy R (2019) UK labelled 'rogue state' after missing UN deadline to hand Chagos Islands back to Mauritius. EuroNews, 22 November 2019

Klabbers J (2019) Shrinking self-determination: the Chagos opinion of the International Court of Justice. ESIL Reflection 8:2

Milanovic M (2019) ICJ Delivers Chagos Opinion, UK Loses Badly. EJIL: Talk!, 25 February 2019

Nkrumah K (1965) Neo-colonialism: the last stage of imperialism. Thomas Nelson & Sons

Tuck E, Wayne Yang K (2012) Decolonization is not a Metaphor. Decolonization Indigeneity Educ Soc 1(1):1–40

Vine D (2009) Island of shame: the secret history of the U.S. Military Base on Diego Garcia. Princeton University Press, p 90

[48]Galeano (1973), p. 77.